D0713517

Parent Education and Intervention Handbook

Parent Education and Intervention Handbook

Edited by

RICHARD R. ABIDIN, Ed.D.

Director, Combined School/Clinical Child Psychology Program
Department of Foundations of Education
Parent Research Project
University of Virginia
Charlottesville, Virginia

CHARLES C THOMAS • PUBLISHER
Springfield • Illinois • U.S.A.

HQ
755.8
P37

Published and Distributed Throughout the World by

CHARLES C THOMAS ● PUBLISHER

Bannerstone House

301-327 East Lawrence Avenue, Springfield, Illinois, U.S.A.

This book is protected by copyright. No part of it
may be reproduced in any manner without
written permission from the publisher.

© *1980, by* CHARLES C THOMAS ● PUBLISHER

ISBN 0-398-03937-2

Library of Congress Catalog Card Number: 79-18113

With THOMAS BOOKS *careful attention is given to all details of
manufacturing and design. It is the Publisher's desire to present books that
are satisfactory as to their physical qualities and artistic possibilities and
appropriate for their particular use.* THOMAS BOOKS *will be true to those
laws of quality that assure a good name and good will.*

Printed in the United States of America
V-OO-2

Library of Congress Cataloging in Publication Data

Main entry under title:

Parent education and intervention handbook.

   Includes bibliographical references and index.
   1. Parenting--Addresses, essays, lectures.
2. Parent and child--Addresses, essays, lectures.
3. Child development--Addresses, essays, lectures.
I. Abidin, Richard R. [DNLM: 1. Child development--
Handbooks 2. Parent-child relations--Handbooks.
3. Parents--Education--Handbooks. WS105.5.F2 P228]
HQ755.8.P37   301.42'7   79-18113
ISBN 0-398-03937-2

CONTRIBUTORS

RICHARD R. ABIDIN, Ed.D.
Professor of Education
Director, Combined School/Clinical Child Psychology Program
Department of Foundations of Education
Director of Parent Research Project
University of Virginia
Charlottesville, Virginia

WILLIAM T. BURKE, Ph.D.
Staff Child Psychologist
Blue Ridge Comprehensive Community Mental Health Center
Charlottesville, Virginia
Project Consultant, Parent Research Project
University of Virginia
Charlottesville, Virginia

FRANK J. CANINO, M.S.
Staff Psychologist
Blue Ridge Comprehensive Community Mental Health Center
Charlottesville, Virginia
Doctoral Candidate
Combined School/Clinical Child Psychology Program
Department of Foundations of Education
University of Virginia
Charlottesville, Virginia

BRYAN D. CARTER, Ph.D.
Clinical Psychologist
Wilford Hall USAF Medical Center
San Antonio, Texas

LINDSAY CHASE-LANSDALE, M.S.
Fellow, Center for Child Development and Social Policy
University of Michigan
Ann Arbor, Michigan

2-21-81 B&T APRS

51191

JAMES P. COMER, M.D.
Professor of Psychiatry
Child Study Center
Department of Psychiatry and Institute of Social Services
Yale University
New Haven, Connecticut

A. MARGARET EASTMAN, M.S.
Resident in Pediatric Psychology
University of Oregon-Health Services Center
Department of Medical Psychology
Portland, Oregon

ANN M. FRODI, Ph.D.
Assistant Professor of Psychology
University of Northern Iowa
Cedar Falls, Iowa

BERNARD G. GUERNEY, Jr., Ph.D.
Professor of Human Development
Director, Individual and Family Consultation Center
Pennsylvania State University
University Park, Pennsylvania

LOUIS J. HEIFETZ, Ph.D.
Associate Professor of Special Education
Director, Psycho-Educational Laboratory/Clinic
Syracuse University
Syracuse, New York

ALICE STERLING HONIG, Ph.D.
Associate Professor of Child and Family Studies
Syracuse University
Syracuse, New York

JOHN B. HOPKINS, Ph.D.
Lecturer
Department of Psychology
University of South Carolina
Beaufort, South Carolina

ARTHUR M. HORNE, Ph.D.
Professor and Acting Director
Division of Counseling
Department of Graduate Studies
Indiana State University
Terre Haute, Indiana

BARBARA D. INGERSOLL, Ph.D.
Assistant Professor of Behavioral Medicine and Community Dentistry
Department of Behavioral Medicine
West Virginia University Medical Center
Morgantown, West Virginia

JOAN B. KELLY, Ph.D.
Co-Principal Investigator
Children of Divorce Project
Community Mental Health Center
Marin County, California
Instructor — Extension Division
University of California
Berkeley, California

SHERRY P. KRAFT, Ph.D.
Assistant Professor
Combined School/Clinical Child Psychology Program
Department of Foundations of Education
Adjunct Assistant Professor
University Counseling Center
Director, Center for Youth and Family Studies
University of Virginia
Charlottesville, Virginia

MICHAEL E. LAMB, Ph.D.
Professor of Psychology
Center for Human Growth and Development
University of Michigan
Ann Arbor, Michigan

HAROLD P. MARTIN, M.D.
Associate Professor of Pediatrics and Psychiatry
Associate Director, John F. Kennedy Child Development Center
University of Colorado Medical Center
Boulder, Colorado

J. JEFFRIES McWHIRTER, Ph.D.
Professor of Counselor Education
Arizona State University
Tempe, Arizona

MARGARET TRESCH OWEN, M.S.
Staff Psychologist
Center for Human Growth and Development
University of Michigan
Ann Arbor, Michigan

GERALD R. PATTERSON, Ph.D.
Oregon Social Learning Center
The Wright Institute
Professor of Education
University of Oregon
Eugene, Oregon
Past President, Association for the
Advancement of Behavior Therapy

RONALD E. REEVE, Ph.D.
Assistant Professor of Education
Department of Foundations of Education
Assessment Coordinator
Learning Disabilities Research Institute
Associate Director for Clinical Services
Child Development Center
University of Virginia
Charlottesville, Virginia

MICHAEL R. ROSMANN, Ph.D.
Assistant Professor of Psychology
University of Virginia
Charlottesville, Virginia
Director, Family Counseling Program
Charlottesville, Virginia
Principal Investigator and Director
Division of Justice and Crime Prevention Family
Counseling Program
State of Virginia
University of Virginia
Charlottesville, Virginia

CAROL M. SCHRAFT, M.S.
Doctoral Candidate, Columbia University Teachers College
New York, New York
Clinical Instructor, Child Study Center
Department of Psychiatry and Institute of Social Sciences
Yale University
New Haven, Connecticut

JOSEPH B. TAVORMINA, Ph.D.
Associate Professor of Psychology
Assistant Professor of Psychiatry
University of Virginia
Charlottesville, Virginia

PETER M. VIETZE, Ph.D.
Senior Staff Fellow
Social and Behavioral Sciences Branch
National Institute of Child Health and Human Development
Bethesda, Maryland

EDWARD L. VOGELSONG, Ph.D.
Assistant Professor of Human Development
Pennsylvania State University
Executive Director, Institute for the Development
of Emotional and Life Skills, Inc.
University Park, Pennsylvania

JUDITH S. WALLERSTEIN, M.S.W.
Principal Investigator
Children of Divorce Project
Community Mental Health Center
Marin County, California
Professor of Social Welfare
University of California
Berkeley, California

ROBERT H. WILLOUGHBY, Ph.D.
Associate Professor of Pediatrics and Psychiatry
Supervisor of Psychological Services
Children's Rehabilitation Center
University of Virginia Medical Center
Charlottesville, Virginia

INTRODUCTION

THIS volume is a direct outgrowth of the growing professional recognition of the importance of parents in nearly all psychological and educational interventions with children. Professionals engaged in a wide range of interactions with children find themselves increasingly involved in the training of various groups of parents or parent surrogates. In the mental health area, the traditional model of professional service delivery that focuses on "therapy sessions for the child and/or parents" has increasingly been questioned as to its effectiveness and the high cost associated with such an approach. The individual contributors to this volume, while focusing on different specific aspects of the parent-child interaction and relationship, share a deep respect for the central role parents and other child care providers can and do play in the psychological development of children. This respect has led the authors to develop alternative and innovative interventions in which parents are viewed as the central figure in educational and therapeutic interventions with children. By holding this view, the professional becomes committed to working through parents for the benefit of their child. The professional no longer is the child's therapist or teacher, but rather becomes a consultant to the parent or more generically a "parent educator."

While there exists a wide array of research, information, and training materials available and applicable to working with parents, what does not exist is a major primary resource or handbook that professionals can consult concerning scientific, professional, and practical issues. The *Parent Education and Intervention Handbook* is aimed at filling the role of interface between the existing scientific and professional knowledge base and the professional practice of psychologists, special educators, counselors, and others who work with parents. Hopefully, this handbook will serve both as a professional resource volume and as a textbook through which the various authors can share the research, convictions, and the professional expertise they have gained in their experiences in working with parents. In the early stages of assembling the Handbook, the editor was overwhelmed by the enthusiasm and interest of the contributors to participate in this project. Their interest in the opportunity to share their methods and insights was only surpassed by their desire to read the other chapters. The material contained in the Handbook represents the information, insights, and methods that have proven productive for the authors and that should assist others in their efforts to function as parent educators and consultants.

Structure of the Handbook

The Handbook is divided into three sections, each of which attempts to meet a different aspect of the interface issue. Section I covers some basic information that forms part of the necessary background for the professional who works with parents. These chapters present information designed to influence the attitudes and belief systems of professionals concerning the interaction between parents and children. The authors, who for the most part are primarily researchers, conclude each chapter by leaving the role of pure scientist to fill the interface role between research and professional practice. The final section of each chapter, therefore, represents a mixture of professional judgment and reasoned extrapolations.

In Chapter 1, Vietze and Hopkins explore the increasing data base that recognizes that the mother-infant interaction is reciprocal in nature. The traditional naive view of the infant as *tabula rasa* is replaced by a scientifically developed understanding that early infant-mother interaction is essential to all aspects of the child's development and that this interaction is complex in terms of the direction of interaction effects and the channels of communication. Vietze and Hopkins conclude their chapter with the suggestion that the style of mother-infant interaction as well as the content of the interaction is of major importance. They supply some helpful suggestions on the process by which mothers can learn to understand the interactive style of their infant.

Lamb and Frodi in Chapter 2 raise a number of issues concerning traditional views of the father's role in a family related to a child's development. Through a combination of logical analysis and research data, they present a more central role for the father in a child's psychological and social development. The research they review suggests that the father's influence extends to areas such as moral development, cognitive development, and sex role identity for children of both sexes.

While the issue of the effects on children of a mother going to work has been debated at great length over the past 50 years, there have until recently been few research studies on the issue. Lamb, Owen, and Chase-Lansdale provide in Chapter 3 a review of the current state of research information on the subject. They conclude that there are no consistent outcomes suggesting adverse effects upon the adjustment, achievement, and sex role functioning of children of working mothers in intact families. While this review provides a helpful understanding to the parent educator, the authors go further and present a heuristic model that is helpful in understanding the conditions under which negative outcomes may occur in the development of children of working mothers.

"General Issues in Working with Parents of Handicapped Children" (Chap. 4) by Canino and Reeve provides the parent educator with a sensitive understanding of the impact of the birth of a handicapped child and the subsequent care demands placed upon the parents. While some delineation of the adjustment and coping process is present, the chapter is not sentimental in nature, but informative and directive. The final section of the chapter reviews the needs of the parents of handicapped children and the roles that professionals must play if they are to be of assistance to these parents.

"Workshops and Parent Groups" (Chap. 5) by Abidin and Carter represents an attempt to share many of the practical issues that must be considered in setting up workshops and parent groups. The authors present a number of guidelines for establishing and conducting the parent group. This chapter should prove most useful to the individual who is just beginning to work with parents in a didactic/consultative format.

Tavormina's Chapter 6 represents an update of an article published in 1974 in the *Psychological Bulletin*. The current chapter considers the relative outcomes of behaviorally oriented parent training groups versus social communication approaches. He indicates that while both approaches appear to produce positive outcomes, the nature of these outcomes is quite different, and the parent educator will need to consider these findings in relation to the targeted parent population. Tavormina suggests on the basis of some recent research that an integration of both approaches may capture the benefits of both.

The chapters in Section II are designed to deal with the practical issues, special knowledge, and skills required to function as a parent educator with special populations of parents and parent surrogates. In general, each chapter contains three parts: (1) a review of research and program descriptions relative to a special population; (2) a description of a particular program for working with the special population with which the author is associated; and (3) suggestions and practical issues involved in working with the special population.

Particular attention is given to common parental reactions, problems, defenses, etc. Guidelines for actions that should be taken and those that should be avoided are presented. The information provided should help the prospective parent educator to avoid common problems and pitfalls. The authors of the chapters in Section II are practitioners as well as scientists; therefore, they provide a special clinical orientation gained through the experience of working with a particular special population.

Horne and Patterson, in their chapter "Working With Parents of Aggressive Children," trace the 14-year history of the Oregon Social Learning Project. The project's development suggests a shift from radical behaviorism to an integration of humanistic social communication approaches into what is basically a behavioral approach. The training format of the current program is described in some detail. Horne and Patterson conclude their chapter with some very valuable information concerning factors associated with therapeutic failures in their program. The issues they raise are appropriate for consideration by all parent educators when considering client selection.

In the chapter "Working With Parents of Hyperactive Children," Willoughby provides the reader with an excellent working definition of hyperactivity in children. He not only considers the various causative factors, but also issues such as "will he grow out of it?" He describes the diagnostic procedures and intervention strategies developed and used by him at the Children's Rehabilitation Center of the University of Virginia. The value of this information is enhanced by the concluding section of the chapter, which provides clear direction on important issues concerning working with the parents of hyperactive children. The topics covered include such areas as "enlisting parental involvement," "troubleshooting the intervention plan," and "confronting failure."

Learning disabilities are the one cluster of handicapping conditions in which the appropriate methods of diagnosis and intervention are least clear. This lack of clarity in the area according to McWhirter is but one of the problems faced by the parents of children with these conditions. McWhirter considers a number of the issues professionals need to be aware of when working with parents of learning disabled children. McWhirter concludes his chapter with a number of helpful suggestions about ways parents can become part of the intervention program.

In discussing the topic of "Working with Parents of Abused and Neglected Children," Martin draws upon his many years of work in the area as part of the National Center for Prevention and Treatment of Child Abuse and Neglect in Denver. Martin urges the reader not to see child-abusing parents as a type of individual, but rather to seek an understanding of each individual's uniqueness. He provides a number of guiding principles for potential helpers and concludes his chapter with a set of criteria that can be used by the helper in making decisions regarding the termination of intervention.

The Wallerstein and Kelly chapter, "Divorce Counseling: A Community Service for Families in the Midst of Divorce," is the only previously published portion of the handbook. This chapter was selected for inclusion because it presents a very practical model for the delivery of service to families in the midst of divorce. Wallerstein and Kelly confront many of the issues that form both the content and process of divorce counseling, e.g. visitation conflicts and disengaging the marital relationship from the parental relationship.

The need to improve the relationship between disturbed adolescents and their parents is presented by Vogelsong and Guerney as a major element in any intervention program with such a population. In their chapter, "Working With Parents of Disturbed Adolescents," Vogelsong and Guerney describe the educational program they have developed for parents of troubled adolescents. The program of Relationship Enhancement is designed to serve as either a therapeutic or a preventive intervention system. The basic skills taught in the program are verbal communication skills that center around the reciprocal roles of Expressor and Empathic Responder. The interactive nature of the Relationship Enhancement Program represents an improvement and extension of other similar programs such as Parent Effectiveness Training.

Comer and Schraft, in their chapter "Working With Black Parents," provide the prospective parent educator with insights and understandings of the experience of black parents as they relate to their attempts to assist their children's development. While it is necessary to describe some of the realities of prejudice, discrimination, and socioeconomic circumstances, Comer and Schraft go beyond that point and describe the impact upon the parents. By examining the experience of the Yale Child Study Schools Program, they are able to generate recommendations about needed features of programs that involve black parents. Genuine opportunity for parental participation is seen as the key element of any program that hopes to have a successful long-term outcome.

The recent enactment of P.L. 94-142 and the changing community responsibilities and attitudes towards the handicapped child provide the context for the chapter by Heifetz. Heifetz's thesis requires professionals who work with parents of handicapped children to rethink and recast their roles in relation to the parents of a handicapped child. The professional can no longer simply do "a treatment on the child" or "prescribe an expert intervention plan"; rather, the posture for the delivery of professional services must be a collaboration between two different experts with different kinds of expertise. The parents possess the knowledge of the family situation, the knowledge of the child gained from day-to-day contact, and an awareness of their own strengths and weaknesses. In many ways, Heifetz's chapter represents the theme of the entire *Parent Education and Intervention Handbook* since he places parents in a central role in the treatment of their children and the professionals in a collaborative or consultative role.

In the chapter "Working With Parents of Preschool Children," Honig presents an overview of the early childhood education area in terms of those features that have and have not proven successful as interventions. She presents a model that emphasizes home visits as the central element of a child development program. The prospective parent educator will find the many practical suggestions made at the end of the chapter particularly useful in conducting parent workshops.

The use of paraprofessionals in education and in some mental health areas is reviewed by Ingersoll and Eastman. They suggest that by using a structured training program for paraprofessionals, it is possible to bring such individuals to a level of competence that they can be effective parent educators when using structured program materials. Ingersoll and Eastman briefly describe the materials, Exercises in Successful Parenting, developed by them for use by paraprofessionals.

Rosmann, in his chapter on "Working With Foster Parents," provides an overview of both the current state of affairs in foster care and some of the specific problems in the area. The shift away from institutional foster care to family placement requires the development of relevant new educational models and approaches for the professional parents who provide foster care. Rosmann's experience with foster care parents through the Family Counseling Program enables him to make a number of specific suggestions concerning the operation of foster care programs. His suggestions concerning selection of foster care parents, child-home matching, and guidelines for placement are particularly valuable.

Kraft provides the readers with a vivid account of the nature of rural life and some of the factors of culture and previous life experiences that have the effect of causing rural inhabitants to resist professional interventions aimed at changing parent-child interactions. Her review of programs designed to reach high-risk children yields the conclusion that home visitor approaches to intervention are likely to be maximally effective. This approach requires maximal attention to and awareness of the local social and economic environment. The intervention approach suggested includes such elements as an ecological focus, "natural helpers," and "consultant" orientation versus "expert helper."

Burke and Abidin, in the chapter "Parenting Stress Index: A Family System Assessment Approach," present a questionnaire that is designed to provide a mechanism for the early identification of parent-child systems under stress. The questionnaire can be used in a variety of pediatric health care settings. The instrument is a broad-spectrum device aimed at assessing the total stress, from many sources, that is present in a given parent-child system. It is anticipated that in many cases, early identification of systems under high stress will allow brief interventions to achieve positive short-term and long-term effects.

Section III provides the reader with a representative overview of materials and prestructured programs that may be used in parent education efforts. The materials are presented through a brief critical review. Each review includes (1) a description of the material; (2) an evaluation of the materials in terms of limitations and appropriate uses of the material; (3) research references; and (4) ordering information.

Many professionals currently involved in parent education work began their work by initially employing materials and ideas developed by others. Section III therefore should prove to be a valuable resource to beginning parent educators or to individuals seeking to change the focus of their present parent work.

This volume will provide prospective parent educators with a wide overview on the various approaches used in the area of parent education and intervention. It should also increase the chances that any parent educator or intervention program developed by the reader will be successful in reaching its objectives. Finally, it is hoped that the *Parent Education and Intervention Handbook* will serve as one additional stimulus for professionals to develop approaches to working through parents for the benefit of children and families.

R.R.A.

CONTENTS

SECTION III
REVIEWS OF PARENT EDUCATION MATERIALS
AND PACKAGED PROGRAMS

Parent Education and Intervention Handbook

SECTION I

GENERAL ISSUES

Chapter 1

MOTHER-INFANT INTERACTION: THE ARENA OF EARLY LEARNING

PETER M. VIETZE AND JOHN B. HOPKINS

IN trying to understand the relationship between parents and children, many writers and researchers have chosen the relationship between infant and mother as their starting point. There are some obvious reasons for this choice, and these are worthy of a brief discussion. It appears obvious that since the infant issues forth from the mother at birth, there is likely to be an irrevocable bond between the two based on this biological fact. This bond is further reinforced by the act of nursing the infant. Thus, there is a compelling biological argument for focusing on the mother as the initial parental figure in trying to understand the growth of the parent-child relationship. In addition, it is not uncommon to study a process such as the parent-child relationship by adopting a developmental stance and beginning one's study at the commencement of the process. A number of assumptions might also be made that would further enhance the value of attempting to understand mother-child relationships as they occur in infancy. One of these is that the relationship between mother and infant forms the basis for the relationship between mother and child at older ages. A second possible assumption is that the mother-infant relationship lays the foundation for child development in general. And finally, one might assume that since the mother-infant relationship is the child's first social relationship, it forms the basis for other social interactions that the child will have. In fact, all three of these assumptions have been made by theorists writing in the area of child development and child psychology.

Freud (1938) assumed that the mother-infant relationship, as a formative influence on the infant's personality, provided the basis for all subsequent social experiences. Dollard and Miller (1950) explicated this relationship in behavioral terms using the mechanism of secondary reinforcement. This mechanism was based on the success of the caretaker in satisfying the infant's primary needs.

The infant came to associate its mother's physical characteristics with the fact that she provided warmth and sustenance. Through this association, the mother acquired reinforcement value herself. The infant, in associating the mother with relief from the discomfort of hunger, responded with positive signals to her. Thus, through the secondary reinforcement value conferred on the mother, the initially asocial infant developed humanly social behaviors. Through generalization to other people who shared the characteristics of the mother, the infant's network of social relationships became expanded.

However, there existed evidence that suggested that the secondary reinforcement mechanism might not be the only way in which infants came to respond socially. Studies with infrahuman organisms such as Sluckin's (1965) investigation of the imprinting of presocial birds and Harlow's (1961) studies of rhesus monkeys fed by wire mesh surrogate "mothers" demonstrated that interaction between infants and mothers was important even if the mother was not providing satisfaction of basic biological needs. Consequently, the secondary reinforcement hypothesis as an explanation for the development of sociability became less tenable (cf. Walters & Parke, 1965).

As one alternative, research and theoretical presentations based on Skinnerian reinforcement principles were proposed. The main proponents of this view about the emergence of the infant as a social being were Gewirtz (1968) and Bijou and Baer (1965). The behavioral position stated that infant social responses came under the control of reinforcing stimuli produced by the caretaker and that the nature of these stimuli could be established by empirical investigation. For example, when the infant makes a cooing vocal sound, the mother might approach the infant and talk to it. This might increase the tendency for the infant to vocalize again. This orientation suggested that the caretaker's behavior also fell under stimulus control as a function of infant stimuli that were reinforcing to the caretaker. Though parents had the capacity, by virtue of their extended response repertoires, to exert considerable control over the behavior of their infants, it was also evident that the infants exerted a great deal of influence over the behavior of their parents.

In the past several years, the focus of understanding infant development in the context of interaction between infant and caretaker has shifted from an emphasis on the parent's role in shaping the infant to concern for the infant's contribution to transactions between itself and its environment. Some attempts to illustrate this have centered on demonstrations that the arousal state, sex, and age of the infant have differential effects on the kinds of behavior in which the mother engages with her infant (Korner, 1974). Moss (1967), in one such study, concluded that the infant initially controlled maternal behavior and, if the mother responded contingently to the infant, the mother later acquired value as a reinforcing agent, a process that enhanced her ability to control the infant's behavior. Bell (1971) and others have termed this interactive process *the effect of the infant on the caretaker,* and it has been documented by many studies, as in the volume edited by Lewis and Rosenblum (1974), which presented several perspectives that illustrate the infant effects phenomenon.

There are many ways to study the effect of the infant on the caregiver and the effect of the infant on caregiver-infant interactions. A number of studies have focused on differential responses of care givers to atypical infants (e.g., Vietze, Abernathy, Ashe, & Faulstich, 1978). However, the immediate effect of the infant's behavior on that of the parent has been neglected as a topic of study. This has been true in both the experimental setting and the naturalistic context. Although we have experimental evidence of some ways in which adults can have direct effects on the level of infant responding (e.g., Bloom & Esposito, 1975; Weisberg, 1963), there is not much direct evidence of the immediate effect of the infant's behavior on that of the parent. Recent experiments carried out by Gewirtz and Boyd (1976) have demonstrated that infant head turns and vocalizations were effective in conditioning mothers' communicative responses; however, there is little empirical evidence for infant (or parent) effects that can be construed as enduring longitudinal attributes.

Despite the fact that data appear to be sparse and at times conflicting with respect to these developmental issues, there is a widely accepted view that the parent-child interaction system is the arena of early learning. The view of the infant's behavioral contribution to its own development has evolved in the present century from discoveries that stimulation, especially that originating with the human caregiving environment, is essential for normal healthy development (e.g., Hunt, 1961; Yarrow, 1968). There were substantial theoretical reasons for believing that the mother-infant relationship is extremely important in the science and practice of child psychology. From some of these theoretical convictions regarding the importance of the early mother-infant relationship came studies to substantiate them (Spitz, 1945). The earliest research focused on natural experiments in which infants and their mothers were separated for long periods of time due to the illness of one of them or for some other reason. These studies brought to light the important impact of mother-infant separation on the child's behavior and development. Spitz and his colleagues (Spitz, 1945) found that infants raised in institutions without consistent caretakers showed retarded intellectual and inadequate personality development. This and other early research on the effects of maternal privation and deprivation served to focus attention on the psychological role of the mother or substitute care giver in influencing the infant's development. These findings contributed to the great interest already shown by many psychologists in the role of the mother-infant relationship on later development.

Experimental studies with infrahuman organisms revealed a plethora of effects that could be attributed to varying amounts and varieties of early stimulation. In applying these results to research on early experience in human infants, the emphasis was placed on whether or not there was sufficient stimulation. Casler (1968) and Yarrow (1961, 1963), however, pointed out the need to differentiate the kinds of early stimulation that might account for varying developmental outcomes in infants. These views have led some investigators to examine various aspects of care-giving environments in order to better understand how the developing organism interacts with its surroundings.

At least one formulation of the environment's influence on development has been concerned with a number of dimensions, each of which has been derived from theoretical writings. Yarrow, Rubenstein, and Pederson (1975) reported the results of an extensive investigation in which they attempted to characterize environmental variables in terms of the variety, complexity, and responsiveness of the inanimate as well as the social environment. Yarrow et al. have emphasized the importance of developing methodologies to define more precisely the responsiveness of the animate environment. In their position they have found commonality between psychoanalytic and behavioral persuasions in the emphasis of each of the salience of a responsive environment for early development. The psychoanalytic school has portrayed responsiveness of the caretaker as a reflection of sensitivity to the infant's needs. For behaviorists, the salient feature of the environment is regarded as its responsiveness or contingency. The issue of responsiveness has served as a basis for agreement between learning-oriented researchers and psychoanalytic-based investigators studying mother-infant relationships. As a result of the interest in documenting how maternal responsiveness or sensitivity is related to infant development, focus has shifted from global aspects of the mother-infant relationship to more fine-grain behaviors.

During the last 20 years, there has been an accumulation of research results documenting the actual interactions that ensue between infants and mothers. These interaction observations have come to serve as the evidence from which inferences about the relationship between infants and mothers could be made. In another chapter in this volume, the infant's attachment to the father is explored. In the remainder of this chapter, several issues will be discussed concerning the course and function of mother-infant interaction. In order to provide a developmental perspective, the first section will focus on mother-newborn interaction, with subsequent portions discussing mother-infant interaction with older infants. Finally, we will suggest how the research literature can be utilized in the design of education programs aimed at mothers and their infants.

EARLY CONTACT BETWEEN INFANTS AND MOTHERS

Most mothers experience intensely positive feelings for their children; however, there has not been extensive research investigating developmental aspects of these affectional relationships. The following questions might be suitable for study: When do mothers first show that they are strongly attached to their infants? How can we measure mother-to-infant attachment? What are the consequences of separation of mother from infant on the maternal bond to the infant? Recently, several investigators have been asking these questions and others in a systematic way and have arrived at some very interesting conclusions.

In the forefront of this area are two pediatricians, Marshall Klaus and John Kennell (1976). They are concerned with the effect of the forced separation of infant and mother immediately after birth, which occurs in most hospital deliveries. They believe that the earliest interaction between mother and infant serves to establish the bond of the mother to the infant and that there is a biological basis for early and continuing contact for the mother. It is their contention that the infant acts as a stimulus for the mother and elicits her mothering and caretaking behaviors. Interruption of the process of mother-to-infant bonding might, in extreme cases, lead to such severe syndromes as failure to thrive, child abuse, and various kinds of emotional disturbances in the child. Usually only minimal effects are seen. However, Klaus and Kennell feel that any threat to the integrity of the mother-infant bond increases the likelihood of problems in the later emotional well-being of the child.

Another phenomenon of modern medical practice is the separation of infant and mother in cases where the infant is premature or of low birth weight. In such cases, the infant is placed in an incubator and given special medical attention. To avoid infections or other medical complications, the infant has less contact with caregivers and parents and usually remains in the "high-risk" nursery beyond the time the mother goes home from the hospital. These infants have a greater chance for suffering a variety of problems, such as delayed development, emotional disturbances, learning disabilities, and other childhood disturbances (Pasamanick & Knobloch, 1966). While it is probably not the case that the early separation solely accounts for these problems, it is quite likely that it contributes to them. Many parents of premature or low-birth-weight infants report that they feel distant from their babies when the babies finally do come home. This is true even in cases where the parents have visited the baby in the hospital often. (At this point, the failure of "early contact" between parents and their premature infant to counteract the effects of the infant's remaining in the hospital after the mother goes home is not fully understood. It may relate to the parents' active avoidance of attachment to an infant that they fear they may lose. Klaus has seen such avoidance with parents of handicapped or very ill infants.) (O'Connor, Altemeier, Sherrod, Sandler, & Vietze, 1978)..

Studies with premature infants have shown consistent findings that opportunities for contact between mothers and premature infants increased mothers' frequencies of looking at, smiling at, closely holding, and caressing their infants (Barnett, Leiderman, Grobstein, & Klaus, 1970; Klaus & Kennell, 1970; Leiderman, Leifer, Seashore, Barnett, & Grobstein, 1973). These findings, in light of ethological data (Bowlby, 1967; Robson & Moss, 1970), further demonstrated evidence for a relationship between extended contact and attachment behaviors operating in the mother-infant dyad.

Beginning with an ethologically-oriented observation of mothers with their newborns, Klaus, Kennell, Plumb, and Zuelhke (1970) documented strong similarity in the behavior patterns of mothers of normal, full-term infants and mothers of premature infants. However, the timing of the occurrence of these similar behavior patterns was not at all alike; mothers of prematures were much slower in manifesting these patterns. Noting that prematurity results in an extended period of mother-infant separation from birth to first contact, Klaus et al. hypothesized that the amount of contact between mother and infant during the postpartum period influenced the behavioral processes related to bonding and subsequent attachment in the dyad.

Several experimental studies have been conducted in which the mother was permitted to have early and extended contact with her full-term newborn infant in order to investigate the effect this procedure might have on attachment. In the first of these studies, 28 low-income women were selected at random, and half of them were given 1 hour of contact with their newborns in the first 2 hours after birth.

In addition, this extended-contact group was allowed 5 hours additional time with their infants on each of the first 3 days of life. The other half of the sample saw their babies only on a routine basis at feeding times. When the infants reached 1 month of age, the mothers and their infants were given a number of evaluations to test the effects of the early contact (Klaus, Kreger, McAlpine, Steffa, & Kennell, 1972). Interviews were conducted with all the mothers; filmed observations were made of them feeding their babies; and observations of mother and infant were made during a physical examination of the baby.

Several differences between the extended-contact group and the control group were found. The interviews indicated that the extended-contact mothers were much more attached to their infants than were the control mothers. This was shown by generally higher concern and attentiveness expressed for the infant. Observations of the physical examination revealed that the extended-contact group tended to be more involved in the examination, showing more soothing behaviors. Finally, ratings of the filmed feeding revealed that the control mothers engaged in much less fondling behavior and less *en face* behavior (where the infant is held close and the mother aligns her face with that of the infant). The results of this research suggest that the extra time the mothers in the extended-contact group had with their babies had a major effect on their caretaking behavior, an effect that lasted at least as long as 1 month.

These two groups of infants and mothers were seen again when the infants were 1 and 2 years of age. At 1 year, it was found that the mothers who had experienced extended contact with their infants still showed some differences when compared with the control group (Kennell, Jerauld, Wolfe, Chesler, Kreger, McAlpine, Steffa, & Klaus, 1974). Some of the mothers in each group had returned to school or to work. When these mothers were interviewed, it was found that the extended-contact mothers showed considerably more evidence of missing their babies than did the control mothers. In addition, observations of the physical examination again indicated that the extended-contact group continued to display more concern and attentiveness toward their babies than did the control group. Finally, a slight but statistically significant difference was found between the babies in the two groups. The infants who had had the extended-contact experience with their mothers showed higher scores on the Bayley Scales of Infant Development than did the infants in the control group.

At 2 years of age, a subsample of each of the two groups described above was studied to evaluate whether the mothers showed any differences in language interaction with their infants (Ringler, Kennell, Jarvella, Navojosky, & Klaus, 1975). The mothers in the extended-contact group displayed language patterns that were more conducive to learning than did the control mothers; extended-contact mothers more often encouraged the child to talk and also provided opportunities for the child to understand more. On the other hand, control mothers used more commands, more words with simple content, and less variety and elaboration. These results suggest that the initial contact served to set up a closer reciprocal relationship between mother and infant, the effects of which endured for a long time. Results of other early-contact studies in a variety of cultural settings (Kennell, Trause, & Klaus, 1975) indicate that outcomes can also include superior weight gain, greater success in breast-feeding, higher rates of maternal visual attention directed at infants, and higher 42-month IQ scores.

The implications of these investigations are many. It may be said that standard hospital practice inhibits the chances for optimal mother attachment by separating mother and infant immediately after the baby is born. This may have far-reaching effects on the infant's life, especially in low-income families such as the ones studied by Kennell and Klaus. Children born into families of limited financial resources are more vulnerable and at greater risk to develop problems later in childhood (Birch & Gussow, 1970). By providing the mothers with the opportunity for early and extended contact with their infants, some of the developmental casualties expected for this segment of society might be avoided.

Despite the compelling nature of these results, one should be careful to remember that providing opportunities for mother and infant to be together may not be sufficient for insuring optimal mother-infant relationships. The quality of the experience they provide for one another must also be considered. It is clear that mothers and infants are not always mutually satisfying. If a mother has an infant whose temperament is such that it cries a good deal of the time, the mother-child relationship might be enhanced by their not often being in each other's company. From another point of view, the mother may not be very sensitive to the baby's needs, in which case extended time with the infant may not be advantageous unless the mother is given some sort of training. Although it is possible to specify extremes of interaction style that are surely detrimental to children, we have not been able to come to any agreement regarding what is optimal mother-infant interaction style. Nevertheless, a number of investigators have been able to demonstrate that certain procedures or strategies on the part of the mother may have specific effects that may be shown to be desirable.

MOTHER-INFANT INTERACTION — THE FIRST FEW MONTHS

In the previous section, we have presented discussion and evidence suggesting that the initial opportunity for contact between infant and mother immediately after birth may be extremely important for the early adjustment of the two to each other. A number of studies suggest that the infant is tuned to accept certain kinds of stimulation from its environment and that such stimulation is typically provided by the mother. As we have pointed out earlier, it may not be useful to think of this stimulation as important because the infant associates it with being comforted. However, it should be pointed out that the young infant does seem to be sensitive to a variety of sensory modalities, especially where another person provides the stimulation. Thus, there exists evidence that the infant is responsive to socially produced olfactory, auditory, visual, tactile, and vestibular information provided by adults in its environment.

Olfactory Stimulation

Perhaps olfactory stimulation has been the most difficult type of stimulation with which to demonstrate infant social awareness. Olfactory imprinting had been demonstrated in a number of organisms other than human infants when a British pediatrician, Aidan Macfarlane (1975), undertook a series of experiments to show that human infants could recognize maternally produced olfactory cues. Although these experiments were not conducted using the naturalistic research techniques more typically used to study mother-infant interaction, they are relevant to the present discussion. In order to determine whether newborn infants can use their sense of smell to locate food, Macfarlane presented them with two breast pads, one saturated with breast milk and the other saturated with sterile water. Observations were made to determine the direction to which the infants turned their heads. The results showed that, for the most part, these breast-fed infants seemed to turn their heads to the milk-laden pad more often than to the pad with no milk.

However, Macfarlane wanted to know whether the infants could differentiate their own mother's milk from that of another mother. In a second experiment, infants were given a choice between a breast pad containing milk from their own mother and one with milk from another mother. These infants were tested when they were 2, 6, and 8 to 10 days of age. The results showed that although the 2-day-old infants did not seem to show a preference to their own mother's breast pad, when they were 6 days or older, they turned to their mother's pad significantly more often than to the other pad. The results of the second experiment show that not only do infants show some differential sensitivity to the odor of their own mother's milk on the breast pad, but this discrimination ability also seems to improve with age.

Findings such as these have implications for the feeding practices of mothers in the modern world. Substitution of bottles and formulas for breast milk may decrease the possibility of the infant and mother adjusting to one another. This does not mean that bottle-fed infants are necessarily at risk for less adequate relationships with their mothers. As we shall see, the mother-infant relationship has a variety of other possible modalities through which contact can be established. Furthermore, such experimental findings fail to provide any answers regarding the other possible olfactory cues that the mother gives off. Finally, we are also left with the question of the mother's olfactory sensitivity to her own infant. We are unaware of any research regarding these issues.

Vocal and Auditory Stimulation

In the realm of auditory stimulation, however, are studies suggesting that mothers are sensitive to their own infants' auditory cues as well as research demonstrating infant sensitivity to maternal vocalizations. Condon and Sander (1974) have reported results of filmed sequences of infant behavior and maternal vocalization. Microanalysis of these films shows that the infant's motor behavior seems to be coordinated with the rhythm of the adult's behavior. These results have been found with infants under 2 weeks of age. During these experimental sessions, the adult's face was out of the infant's visual field.

The Brazelton Neonatal Assessment Scale (Brazelton, 1973) contains a procedure during which the infant's ability to localize the human voice is examined. Newborns can easily be shown to turn in the direction of a voice in the absence of visual cues. Other evidence of the infant's unique sensitivity to human voices as compared to other auditory cues has been presented by a number of investigators (Eimas, in press; Eisenberg, 1976). Considering the maternal half of the mother-infant dyad, several investigators have studied the effects of infant cry vocalizations on maternal behavior. The detailed studies of

Peter Wolff (1969) concerning the cries of young infants and the behavior those cries elicited from the mothers suggest that mothers recognize different cries early in the infant's lives and respond in nonrandom fashion. Lind and his associates (1973) showed that the characteristic hunger cry causes a physiological reaction in nursing mothers that makes nursing the most likely response.

These experimental studies suggest that mothers as well as infants may be set to respond to the auditory stimulation produced by the other quite early. However, naturalistic observations of the effects of such stimulation on each dyad member must be considered in order to provide a complete view of the way in which the auditory environment of the mother-infant dyad progresses. There exists an extensive literature describing the vocal interaction of mothers and infants in both experimental and naturalistic settings. Some of these will be considered in the following discussion.

The significance of vocal behavior in the mother-infant interactional system has been emphasized by several writers. Bowlby (1969), in his presentation of attachment theory, has pointed out that infant vocalizations serve to elicit and maintain proximity with the care giver, which is important for the development of infant attachment. Maternal vocal behavior in turn stimulates additional infant vocalization, which may enhance the value of both interaction and mother-infant proximity. Other investigators have suggested the importance of the reciprocal nature of mother-infant vocal interaction (Bateson, 1975; Brazelton, Koslowski, & Main, 1974; Anderson & Vietze, 1977; Anderson, Vietze, & Dokecki, 1977; Stern, Jaffe, Beebe, & Bennett, 1975). These investigators have emphasized the fact that the vocal interchange, as opposed to the content of the transaction, solidifies the bond between the infant and adult.

Several different methods for studying vocal interchange in the context of mother-infant interaction have been reported. Some have used time sampling (Lewis, 1972; Yarrow, Rubenstein, & Pedersen, 1975); others have videotaped or filmed interactions (Brazelton, Kozlowski, & Main, 1974; Condon & Sander, 1974; Stern, 1974); whereas still other investigators have coded mother and infant behaviors continuously (Jones & Moss, 1971; Strain, 1975; Vietze, Strain, & Falsey, 1975). Results of these investigations have suggested that for infants between the ages of 3 and 6 months, maternal vocalization contingent on the vocal responding of the infant was positively related to the overall infant vocalization, although measures of total maternal vocal responding were not related to infant vocalization (Jones & Moss, 1971; Yarrow, Rubenstein, & Pedersen, 1975).

Most recently, investigators have begun to look more closely at the structure of vocal interaction between mothers and infants. Anderson, Vietze, and Dokecki (1977) and Stern, Jaffe, Beebe, and Bennett (1975) have reported that 3-month-old infants show signs of approximating dialogue interactions with their mothers, alternating vocal responding with them. (Both of these reports are based on a model suggested by Jaffe and Feldstein, 1970). Furthermore, Vietze, Strain, and Falsey (1975), in a longitudinal study of 51 mother-infant pairs, found that from 2 to 6 months of age, the infant seems to become a more active participant in the reciprocal "conversations" with the mother. The low variability across different mother-infant dyads reported in these investigations suggests that the conversational model might be one of the characteristics of social interaction between mother and infant that is relatively unaffected by individual differences. In a study comparing the vocal interaction of dyads with retarded infants and those with normal infants, Vietze, Abernathy, Ashe, and Faulstich (1978) further examined the question of individual differences. By following the dyadic interactions of normal infants from 2 to 12 months of age, they found that the infants become more active participants and that the dyad seemed to show greater evidence of reciprocity with the infants' increasing age. This could be explained in terms of both the mothers' increasing awareness of the infants' vocal capability and the infants' greater tendency to vocalize. In the analysis of retarded infants and their mothers according to the developmental level of the infants, Vietze, Abernathy, Ashe, and Faulstich (1978) reported that lower-functioning infants showed less awareness of the mother's vocalization, so they may have stimulated lower levels of vocal reciprocity than did higher-functioning infants.

The analyses of contingency in vocal behavior between infants and mothers carried out by a number of investigators suggest several points. Whereas typically contingent interaction refers to onset of behaviors, Anderson, Vietze, and Dokecki (1977) point out that both *onset* and *offset* of behavior can and should be evaluated for interpersonal contingencies. The implications of these two parameters are different when one considers vocal behavior. As the evidence suggests, infants as young as 2 months approximate an adult model of vocal interchange or dialogue. This means that when one person is vocalizing, the other typically stops. Initiation of vocalization contingent on the vocalization of another person tends to "interrupt" the speaker. Therefore, the important relationship with regard to contingency of vocal behavior seems to be the onset of one person's vocalization contingent on the cessation of vocalization of the other person. Both infant and mother must be sensitive to these parameters for the normal development of vocal interaction.

The implications of the research on mother-infant vocal interaction for the understanding of language development have become evident only recently. A number of theorists in the area of language development (Bateson, 1975; Bruner, 1975) have begun to recognize the dependence of the ontogeny of communicative behavior on the preverbal behavior of infants in interaction with their care givers. It has become evident that the structure of expressive language is built on the foundation of structural interchange between infant and parent that occurs as early as 2 months, when regular vocal production begins to appear.

Mother-Infant Visual Interaction

It has been quite firmly accepted by now that the young infant's visual system is functional at the level of being selective almost at birth. This establishes the possibility that the visual modality is one that can be utilized for making and maintaining contact with the social environment. In a review of the then-available evidence on the role of the distance receptors in infancy, Walters and Parke (1965) concluded that the visual as well as the auditory modality served to facilitate the development of social responsiveness. Since then a number of investigators have suggested that visual regard of infant and caregiver for one another serves a number of functions. In the Walters and Parke study of early contact between mothers and their newborn infants, the importance of the *en face* position or face-to-face orientation was stressed. In their discussion of mother-to-infant bonding, Klaus and Kennell (1976) suggest that the mutual visual regard engendered by the *en face* position is one of the most powerful mechanisms that stimulate maternal attachment. Robson (1967) emphasizes that eye-to-eye contact may act as an innate releasing mechanism for maternal caretaking responses. In a study of 54 firstborns and their mothers, Moss and Robson (1968) evaluated the visual behavior of the dyads in relation to maternal attitudes. They found that the amount of time that infant and mother spent looking at each other's faces was correlated with positive prenatal attitudes toward infants. However, the importance of visual interaction between mother and infant has not been firmly established by relating it to subsequent infant behavior. It is believed that the infant regulates social behavior with the other people in its environment through selective visual attention.

Daniel Stern, a child psychiatrist, has studied the detailed visual interactional behavior of mothers and infants. Borrowing the paradigm of adult verbal interaction from Jaffe and Feldstein (1970), Stern (1974) recorded the filmed visual behavior of 8 infants and mothers. These behaviors were recorded during play and feeding episodes videotaped in the infants' homes. Using a highly refined interactional analysis, Stern was able to establish that although the mother seems to maintain her visual attention on her 3- to 4-month old infant, the infant alternates looking toward and looking away from the mother's face in cycles. Stern sees these cycles serving to regulate the mother-infant stimulation so that during play an optimal level of arousal is maintained. The significance of mutual visual regard seems to be to provide a context or background in which other play activities such as vocalization or smiling can occur. However, Stern maintains that it is the infant who regulates the activity through its visual gaze alternation with the mother. A major contribution to the study of mother-infant visual interaction lies in Stern's discussion of the infant's role in the regulation of stimulation by the mother. However, by focusing on infants under 6 months, we do not have a complete picture of how mother-infant visual behavior might change as the infant matures.

Friedman and his colleagues (Friedman, Thompson, Crawley, Criticos, Drake, Iacobbo, Rogers, & Richardson, 1976) have compared infants 4, 6, and 8 months of age in order to better understand how mutual visual regard changes and how such behavior is related to other affectional signals. Their analyses revealed that although the number of instances of mutual regard did not differ for the dyads with different age infants, the duration of mutual visual regard did differ for the three groups. The differences indicated that as the infant's age increased, the mothers and infants were less likely to spend time gazing at each other. The authors also found a great deal of variability within each age group, indicating that the style of communication might be different for different dyads. In addition, moderately high correlations were found at each age between mutual visual regard and smiling. This suggests that, as Stern has noted (1974), mutual regard is one of the hallmarks of affective mother-infant play.

It is of interest to note that other investigators have reported the relationship between visual regard and facial expressions. In one of their reports, Tronick and his colleagues (Tronick, Als, Adamson, Wise, & Brazelton, 1978) describe what occurs when a mother violates the infant's expectation of positive facial expressiveness. If the mother approaches the infant and, although making eye contact with it, fails to smile or move her face, the infant eventually turns its head away and avoids looking at the mother completely. This finding means that the correlations from the Friedman et al. study reported earlier may indicate that mutual eye contact is a signal that positive interaction and facial expression are going to take place. When the expected behavior fails to happen, the infant withdraws from the interaction. This reflects the younger infant's inexperience with a variety of social interaction styles. As the child gets older, greater understanding will come for situations in which the typical interaction does not take place. The child will develop alternative ways of adapting to such situations in order to maintain the interaction. For instance, a more experienced child might laugh when its mother enters the visual field with a "deadpan" expression. Or the child might try to get her to laugh by poking her in the ribs. Nevertheless, the younger infant is not yet adept in such social tricks and can only look away or turn away. The young infant uses its visual system as a signaling mechanism to indicate when it is ending an interaction and expects the mother to do so also.

The combined research that has been carried out on visual communication between mother and infant suggests that the mother's visual attention functions as a setting or context within which the infant may or may not establish and maintain contact. The infant seems to use its visual regard of the mother to signal the beginning of a communication. In addition, the visual modality also seems to serve as a signal of positive affect for mother and infant; most of the smiling within the social context occurs when the two dyad members are looking at one another. The research points out, however, that merely focusing on mutual visual regard is not sufficient for understanding the mother-infant interaction system.

Tactile and Vestibular Stimulation

When an infant cries, the most likely maternal response is to approach and pick up the child. It has been suggested (Bowlby, 1969) that crying is one of the infant's most powerful signaling behaviors to establish or maintain contact with its mother. However, once the infant has been picked up, a variety of possible events can occur. The mother can talk to her baby or she can rock it. She might merely pat or caress the baby to soothe it. Infant researchers have included such behaviors as touching, rocking, jiggling, caressing, and tactile/playing among the categories observed in their studies (Lewis, 1972; Moss, 1967). Despite the fact that several investigators have pointed out the importance of tactile and vestibular stimulation of healthy development in infrahuman organisms, e.g., Harlow (1961) with rhesus monkeys and Denenberg with rats (Denenberg, 1964) and rabbits (Denenberg, DeSantis, Waite, & Thoman, 1977), there are few studies of the effects of these kinds of stimulation on human infants. There is even some controversy in the animal literature as to whether tactile and vestibular stimulation per se has beneficial effects or whether other kinds of stimulation can produce the same beneficial outcomes for the treated individuals. Among the benefits that have been reported with human infants who received extra tactile or vestibular stimulation are increased weight gain for prematures (e.g., Hasselmeyer, 1964; Solkoff, Yaffee, Weintraub, & Blase, 1969); enhanced visual alertness (Korner, 1972); higher developmental scores on the Gesell Developmental Schedule (Casler, 1965); and lower levels of crying (Ambrose, 1969). Nevertheless, there has been little focus on such behavior in the study of human infants in interaction with their mothers.

One study has treated tactile and vestibular stimulation as separate variables. Yarrow, Rubenstein, and Pedersen (1975), in a study of mother-infant interaction, observed mothers and their 5-month-old infants at home. A focus of this research was the relationship between maternal stimulation of the infant and the infant's performance on a commonly used developmental test, the Bayley Scales. The findings of the study revealed that mother's tactile stimulation of the infant — such things as patting, stroking, or caressing the baby — was modestly related to two measures of cognitive-motivational behavior derived from the Bayley Scales — goal-directed behavior and secondary circular reactions. Furthermore, these authors reported that kinesthetic stimulation, which included any maternal behavior in which the infant's whole body was moved, was related to both summary scores derived from the Bayley Scales as well as five other measures constructed from individual items on the Bayley — social responsiveness, goal-directed behavior, secondary circular reactions, fine motor behavior, and object permanence. The authors interpret their results to indicate that kinesthetic stimulation by the mother may serve to arouse the infant and make it more likely to focus on the external environment. However, there are other possible ways to explain the results. Those infants who experienced greater kinesthetic stimulation may have been the ones who were carried around extensively by their mothers. This would allow them to have a great deal of visual contact with a variety of objects in their environment and might enhance their motivation to interact with objects. These results have been partially replicated in Yarrow's lab with a second sample of infants at 12 months of age (Yarrow, Morgan, Jennings, Harmon, Gaiter, &

Vietze, 1977). This research continues to be conducted in Yarrow's lab in order to elucidate further the functions and consequences of tactile and vestibular stimulation in the context of mother-infant interaction.

Goldberg has reported (1977) that in Zambia, as in other African countries, infants are carried about by their mothers for many months. She suggests that the fact that the infants are carried provides them with both vestibular stimulation and access to many visual experiences. Her data suggest that being carried may facilitate development in the early months but may interfere with development later when the infant would be moving around on its own. As yet there have been no tests of this interesting possibility. Although it is clear that cross-cultural evidence of this sort would serve to clarify some of the findings based on families living in Euro-American cultures, the particular functions of different sorts of stimulation in various modalities may not be easily clarified.

In much of the research on mother-infant interaction (e.g., Moss, 1967; Lewis, 1972; Clarke-Stewart, 1973), a behavioral approach was taken in which individual behaviors were observed and tabulated. However, in some of these cases, the results were reported according to these behaviors rather than by aggregating the behaviors into naturally occurring clusters or even superordinate categories. Other researchers have taken the latter approach (e.g., Yarrow, Rubenstein, & Pedersen, 1975; Brazelton, Tronick, Adamson, Wise, & Als, 1975) and tried to give meaning to behaviors that are emitted by either mother or infant. In this approach, the focus has been on dyadic interaction measures such as *reciprocity* and *contingency*. However, in order to understand the importance of reciprocity or mutual interdependency, it seems that we must know how such measures relate to the infant's development. In the following section, we review several studies that have examined the relationships of mother-infant interaction to infant developmental behavior.

MOTHER-INFANT INTERACTION AND INFANT DEVELOPMENT

While there has been an explosion in recent years in research on parent-infant interaction, few investigations report taking independent measures of child development, either at the age they studied the interaction behavior or later, as criteria for prediction from the interactional variables. The few studies that have related independent measures of development to variability in parent-child interaction will be reviewed here.

Rubenstein (1967) observed 44 families in a study investigating the hypothesis that attentive mothers have infants who show more exploratory behavior at 5 months than inattentive mothers. Results indicated support for the hypothesis on four of the six measures of exploration. Rubenstein suggests that it is the variety of maternal attentiveness that may be critical in influencing the infant's exploratory behavior. A more extensive investigation, based in part on Rubenstein's earlier study, lends further support to the notion that the variety of stimulation by mothers may have profound effects on infant exploratory behavior (Yarrow, Rubenstein, Pedersen, & Jankowski, 1972; Yarrow, Rubenstein, & Pedersen, 1975). In this research 41 lower-income infants and mothers were observed in interaction, and the infants were tested using the Bayley Scales as well as Rubenstein's test of exploratory behavior. Results of this study showed that level, variety, affect, and responsiveness of the primary caregiver's interactions were related to a variety of cognitive-motivational variables when the children were 5 months of age. Unfortunately, because both of these studies were cross-sectional, it is difficult to infer the direction of effect between the interactional variables and the measures of infant functioning.

Using different measures of infant functioning, Lewis and Goldberg (1969) studied relationships between decrement in infant attentional responses and measures of maternal responsiveness. Their results show that infant response decrement was related to maternal looking at the infant and maternal touching of the infant. Based on these findings, they propose a "generalized expectancy model," which suggests that infant expectation of control or helplessness with respect to environmental stimulation results from the quality of care giver/infant interaction and has an effect on the infant's cognitive development. This research was also cross-sectional and therefore provides no information about the developmental outcomes of different patterns of mother-infant interaction. However, the authors make a strong point of emphasizing the importance of maternal responsiveness for the development of cognitive and motivational competence in the infant.

In another cross-sectional study, Beckwith (1972) found that middle-class, adopted 8-month-old-infants' scores on the Cattell Infant Test were influenced by social experience with the mother and other people. In addition, she found that restricted exploration of the house also affected Cattell performance, although the direction of influence is not clear from the report. Beckwith summarizes her study by stating, "If the infant was spoken to less, touched less, and had less opportunity to explore the house, then he tended to score lower on the infant scale" (p. 1083). It is not clear from the data presented that this was the case. However, if we assume that it is, Beckwith's findings further suggest the importance of maternal interactional behavior for infant development.

One of the most extensive studies of the relationship between mother-infant interaction and child outcome was carried out by Clarke-Stewart (1973). Her sample of 36 lower-income infants and their mothers was observed and tested when the infants were 11 and 17 months of age. Included in her observational measures were variables assessing the responsiveness of the mother to the infant as well as many other measures of maternal attentiveness. As this was a longitudinal study, Clarke-Stewart was able to investigate the causal relationship between maternal behavior and infant performance on the Bayley Scales. Using cross-lag correlations, she found that the mother's level of responsiveness and the quality of her stimulation predicted the child's level of cognitive functioning. Clarke-Stewart's longitudinal results provide a necessary validation of those reported earlier from cross-sectional investigations.

Most recently, Beckwith, Cohen, Kopp, Parmelee, and Marcy (1976) have reported the results of a longitudinal investigation of care giver/infant interaction and cognitive development in preterm infants. Observing the infants and their mothers at 1, 3, and 8 months, these investigators reported relationships between interactional variables and infant test data collected when the infants were 9 months old. Results suggested that the infants with higher scores on sensorimotor tests had been exposed to mutual gaze with the mother at 1 month, more contingent response to fretful behavior at 3 months, and greater maternal attentiveness and contingent reaction to nonfussy vocalization at 8 months. In addition, infants with higher DQs on the Gesell scales had been given greater "floor freedom" by their mothers. These results provide added support for the view that maternal responsiveness, sensitivity, and attentive behavior are important in the infant's cognitive and motivational development. These may be reflections of reciprocity or mutual mother-infant behavior.

The research cited in this section, taken together with findings showing few noteworthy differences between middle- and lower-income mothers in their interactional behavior with their infants (e.g., Lewis & Wilson, 1972; Tulkin & Kagan, 1972), warrant a number of conclusions. These conclusions are in agreement with those of several other reviews (Clarke-Stewart, 1977; Goldberg, 1977; Streissguth & Bee, 1972; Wandersman, 1973). On the one hand we might be cautious, since much of the research reported relating parent-child interaction to child developmental behavior suffers from methodological problems that affect interpretation of the results. On the other hand, we might accept the suggestive nature of the results reported and proceed to develop further the concept of individual differences in parent-child development. The studies reviewed do suggest that among the variables that can be studied in parent-child interaction, the ones that seem to influence early development are parental responsiveness, sensitivity, and the variety of parental behavior. Before applying these ideas to intervention, however, perhaps a brief look at the intervention literature is necessary to facilitate the development of a model of parent-child interaction style.

INTERVENTION RESEARCH FOCUSING ON PARENT-CHILD DYAD

Bronfenbrenner (1974) has reviewed American early intervention programs in great detail and formulated several summary statements based on his review. It is useful to recapitulate his conclusions here. Although he focused on child- and classroom-based intervention programs as well as home-based, parent-focused ones, we will mainly draw on his conclusions from the latter. He concluded from the findings reported by various investigators (Levenstein, 1970; Karnes, 1969; Klaus & Gray, 1968; Weikart, 1967; Gordon, 1971) that programs or components of programs that involved both or one of the parents as the primary targets of the intervention were the most effective in showing enduring change in the developmental competence of the children as measured by IQ tests. Bronfenbrenner also reviewed several examples of what has come to be called *ecological intervention*. These include the Milwaukee project (Heber & Garber, 1975) and the famous experiments carried out by Harold Skeels and his colleagues (Skeels & Dye, 1939; Skodak & Skeels, 1949). He concluded from these studies that ecological intervention is a viable strategy only when parents have given up parental rights. However, when the child still resides in the home with one or both parents, such a strategy may not be justifiable ethically.

The major conclusions from Bronfenbrenner's review of significance for the present are that the intervention, when warranted, should begin as early as possible and, at these early stages, should focus on the mother as the agent of change until the child is ready for a group experience. However, Bronfenbrenner points out that the child must be included in the intervention focus. The mother cannot be given intervention experiences in isolation from the child in the same way that the infant tutoring studies (Schaefer, 1968, 1970, 1972; Schaefer and Aaronson, 1972; Kirk,. 1969) showed that the infant living at home could not be given intervention experience in isolation from the mother.

Among the most important principles that Bronfenbrenner derived from the research he reviewed is the following:

> The psychological development of the young child is enhanced through his involvement in progressively more complex, enduring patterns of reciprocal contingent interaction with persons with whom he has established a mutual and enduring emotional attachment. (p. 31)

This speaks eloquently for the importance of the parent-child dyad as the target of intervention in the early years. However, there has not been an effort to implement Bronfenbrenner's sequence of intervention strategies in one comprehensive, well-controlled, and well-evaluated study.

Though the foregoing review was neither extensive nor exhaustive, it has shown that several features of parent-child interaction are important for predicting cognitive-motivational outcomes in the children and for success in parent-child intervention programs. The inclusion of strategies to foster reciprocal mother-child interaction as a mechanism for strengthening the relationship, and hence the teaching milieu, between mother and child is most essential. In addition, it would appear that inclusion of increasing interactional complexity and variety is also vital for the mother's effect on the child and, if we believe that relationships are bidirectional, for the child's effect on the mother.

Our review of selected research in the area of mother-infant interaction has shown that the earliest moments of contact between mother and infant may have far-reaching implications for the mother-child relationship. A recent study (O'Connor, Altemeier, Sherrod, Sandler, & Vietze, 1978) showed that provision of an opportunity for the newborn infant to "room-in" with its mother soon after birth reduced the chances of child abuse and neglect later. A simple intervention such as rooming-in or early mother-infant contact may have a variety of enhancing effects for disadvantaged families. (This is not to say that lack of such early contact is detrimental to families living in more affluent environments.) Other studies have shown that the young infant seems to be sensitive to stimulation provided in all sense modalities by adult care givers. Some of this research demonstrates the importance of patterning of stimulation in relation to the infant's behavior. Although there still remains much to be studied in this area, a number of implications may presently be drawn from the foregoing review. Furthermore, the pressure from practitioners in need of information to design intervention programs places further demands for a different sort of research than has been carried out heretofore. The following section will present a number of suggestions for interventionists working in the area of mother-infant interaction.

IMPLICATIONS FOR INTERVENTION

The foregoing review has included research undertaken to describe the mother-infant interaction observed in behavioral terms. The field in general has emphasized observation schemes in which discrete behaviors were observed with a minimum of inferences made by the observers. Such observation schemes lend themselves well to application, since it is easier to describe discrete behaviors than it is to teach more abstract concepts. This is especially true when one deals with infants, since they are seen as having somewhat limited capabilities. However, as some of the studies reviewed have suggested, the way in which behaviors are aggregated may have common meaning to parents. Also, the particular behaviors that a mother uses in interaction with her baby may be less important than the timing of her behavior in relation to that of the infant.

Recently it has been suggested (Vietze and Anderson, 1979) that the "style" of interaction may be especially important for the development of infant competence. A model of parent-infant interaction style was presented that emphasized three interactional components in evaluating a particular parent-infant dyad. These three components are (1) the form of behaviors used — whether they occur as aggregates, sequences, or single modality behaviors; (2) timing of parent behaviors in relation to the infant — simultaneous, contingent, or noncontingent behaviors; (3) sensitivity to the infant — taking into account the state of the infant as well as the situational context. In addition, the model considers that the parent may utilize a wide variety of methods for interacting with the infant and that this also must be considered. The model was proposed as a method for evaluating the style of parent-infant interaction and as a tool to facilitate intervention. Such a model serves to focus on dimensions identified in the literature as important for understanding the development of the infant early in life.

Having proposed a model for describing and analyzing styles of mother-infant interaction, Vietze and Anderson (1979) suggest that their model might also be used as an intervention tool. The goal of intervention in the sphere of mother-infant interaction might be to provide the mother with conditional strategies for fostering the child's optimal development. The term *conditional* as it is used here means that the selection of interactional strategy would be based on the mother's increased attention to and understanding of the child's unique characteristics. The mother must first become attuned to certain prerequisites for interaction. The prerequisites are individual difference factors such as gender, temperament, and developmental level. In addition, the mother must be cognizant of the fact that infants also have different interactional styles and that she must discover her own child's style of interacting with her. It is expected that the styles of interaction most conducive to the enhancement of the child's motivation to explore and learn from its environment are those that allow for extensive variety of behavior on the part of both dyad members. Styles having maximal flexibility are expected to optimize the child's developmental potential. Perhaps this is the aspect of the care-giving environment that Sameroff and Chandler (1974) refer to when they suggest that the quality of the care-giving environment determines which children will flourish, even in the face of biological catastrophe.

In order to utilize a mother-infant interaction scheme as the basis for intervention, several steps might be taken. The first part of such an effort would be to carry out behavioral observations using a method that allows for sequence and duration of behaviors to be recorded for both mother and infant. A variety of such methods is available (e.g., Anderson, Vietze, Faulstich, & Ashe, 1978; Bakeman & Brown, 1977; Kaye, 1977). An alternative to such sequential observation methods would be to develop rating scales that incorporate items describing the form, timing, and sensitivity of mother-infant interaction. Observations should be carried out in a setting that is similar to the usual or natural setting the parent and child experience. When possible, attempts should be made to sample from different parts of the day and week in order to derive the broadest view of the transactions that take place between mother and infant. Following this initial observation, the data can be analyzed, and conclusions about the style of interaction that the dyad display can be made. These conclusions would then form a basis for planning the intervention to alter the interaction style or for the decision not to intervene at all.

According to Bronfenbrenner (1974) as well as others (e.g., Clarke-Stewart, 1977), it appears that the optimal intervention in the area of mother-infant interaction would be a home-based program. Such an intervention would consist of a series of contacts between a trained home visitor and the mother-infant pair. The mother would be given a set of tasks, problems, and activities designed to encourage greater flexibility in interaction style for both infant and mother. Although the focus of the intervention would be on fostering increased flexibility for both dyad members, the mother would be the agent of change for the child, being encouraged to help the child develop a more flexible interaction style. Thus, the parent would have to play two roles — the role of interaction partner and the role of change agent for the child. This perspective has been difficult to incorporate into past parent-centered intervention programs; rather, the child has been the focus of intervention for the intervener, not the mother. The information provided by the initial assessment of interaction style would provide the tools and language for the intervener in communicating about the strategies and goals of intervention with the mother.

It is expected that the success of intervention based on classification of initial interaction style would lie in the fact that emphasis would not be placed on providing mothers with prescriptions for specific behaviors such as vocalization or active tactile stimulation. Rather, the intervention program would stress the importance of initiating and maintaining the child's involvement with its physical and social surroundings by varying the form and timing of behaviors and increasing maternal sensitivity to infant state and to the interactional setting. In addition, it would be emphasized that the child plays an active role in the interaction, and the importance of allowing for the child to "have a turn" and of observing the components of the child's "turn" would be stressed.

EVALUATION OF INTERVENTION

It is expected that the outcomes of such an intervention strategy would be enhanced interest on the part of the child in exploration, greater activity and variation in the way the child interacts with the mother, and a change toward a more flexible maternal interaction style. Although it might be tempting to predict that the immediate effect of an early intervention program that was aimed at enhancing exploratory behavior might be to show increases in summary scores on standardized infant tests, such evaluation is strongly discouraged. Rather, it is expected that the immediate effects of the intervention would be to show changes in interaction style for both infant and mother. Indirectly it might be shown that the intervention program could result in changes in exploratory behavior as assessed by one of the experimental methods reported in the child development literature (e.g., Rubenstein, 1967; Riksen-Walraven, 1978). It might also be found that an intervention program designed to alter interaction style would enhance performance on cognitive-motivational variables such as problem solving, goal directedness, and secondary-circular reactions based on item clusters from the Bayley Scales (Yarrow, Rubenstein & Pedersen, 1975).

SUMMARY AND CONCLUSIONS

The area of mother-infant interaction has attracted attention from researchers and practitioners alike during the past 2 decades. With this interest have come attempts to understand how the infant's capacities to respond to stimulation affect the way in which mothers behave with them. Although early attempts to study mother-infant interaction were focused on how the parent affected the infant in the interactional context, more recently this focus has shifted. First the effect of the infant on the mother became an important way of considering early social interaction. However, most recently, the bidirectional nature of mother-infant interaction has assumed the greatest salience. This shift in focus has allowed researchers to consider a variety of interventions that might affect early mother-infant interaction. Such areas as early contact between mother and infant in the lying-in period have become controversial topics of study. The present chapter has reviewed some of the results of research indicating that young infants are sensitive to stimulation in all modalities, especially as provided by care givers. In addition, we have shown that research relating mother-infant interaction and infant developmental outcome finds a number of variables to be most effective. These include the contingency that might exist between infant and mother in interaction as well as the variety of stimulation offered by the mother to the infant. A way of applying mother-infant interaction measures to intervention efforts was outlined in the context of styles of mother-infant interaction.

The present chapter leads to the conclusion that the early postnatal period may be an important one for providing contact between infants and their mothers. The consequences of not providing such early contact *may* be detrimental to the development of the child. However, it should be noted that infants have been shown to have great capacity for stimulus input and are extremely resilient. Attempts to intervene in the mother-infant interaction system might well focus on the structure of the interactions rather than the content. Emphasis should probably be on timing of behavior in relation to infant behavior and sensitivity to infant cues. It appears that variety, flexibility, and reciprocity are central to any attempt to facilitate the development of the mother-infant dyad.

REFERENCES

Ambrose, A. *Stimulation in early infancy.* New York: Acad Pr, 1969.

Anderson, B. J., & Vietze, P. Early dialogues: The structure of reciprocal infant-mother vocalization. In S. Cohen & T. J. Comiskey (Eds.), *Child development: A study of growth processes* (2nd ed.). Itasca, Illinois: Peacock Pubs, 1977.

Anderson, B. J., Vietze, P. M., & Dokecki, P. R. Reciprocity in vocal interactions of mothers and infants. *Child Development,* 1977, *48,* 1676-1681.

Anderson, B. J., Vietze, P. M., Faulstich, G., & Ashe, M. L. Observation manual for assessment of behavior sequences between infant and mother: Newborn to 24 months. JSAS *Catalog of Selected Documents in Psychology,* 1978, *8,* 31. (Ms. No. 1672)

Bakeman, R., & Brown, J. V. Behavioral dialogues: An approach to the assessment of mother-infant interaction. *Child Development,* 1977, *48,* 195-203.

Barnett, C. R., Leiderman, P. H., Grobstein, R., & Klaus, M. H. Neonatal separation: The maternal side of interactional deprivation. *Pediatrics,* 1970, *45,* 197.

Bateson, M. C. Mother-infant exchanges: The epigenesis of conversational interaction. *Annals of the New York Academy of Sciences,* 1975, *263,* 101-113.

Beckwith, L. Relationships between infants' social behavior and their mothers' behavior. *Child Development,* 1972, *43,* 397-411.

Beckwith, L., Cohen, S. E., Kopp, C. B., Parmelee, A. H., & Marcy, T. G. Caregiver-infant interaction and early cognitive development in preterm infants. *Child Development,* 1976, *47,* 579-587.

Bell, R. Q. Stimulus control of parent or caretaker behavior by offspring. *Developmental Psychology,* 1971, *4,* 63-72.

Bijou, S. W., & Baer, D. M. *Universal stage of infancy (Child development, Vol. 2).* New York: Appleton, 1965.

Birch, H., & Gussow, G. D. *Disadvantaged children.* New York: Grune, 1970.

Bloom, K., & Esposito, A. Social conditioning and its proper control procedures. *Journal of Experimental Child Psychology,* 1975, *19,* 209-222.

Bowlby, J. *Attachment.* New York: Basic, 1969.

Brazelton, T. B. *Neonatal behavioral assessment scale.* Philadelphia: Lippincott, 1973.

Brazelton, T. B., Koslowski, B., & Main, M. The origins of reciprocity: The early mother-infant interaction. In M. Lewis & L. A. Rosenblum

(Eds.), *The effect of the infant on its caretaker (The origins of behavior,* Vol. 1). New York: Wiley, 1974.

Brazelton, T. B., Tronick, E., Adamson, L., Als, H., & Wise, W. Early mother-infant reciprocity. In *Parent-infant interaction.* Ciba Foundation Symposium 33. New York: American Elsevier, 1975.

Bronfenbrenner, U. *Is early intervention effective? A report on longitudinal evaluations of preschool programs* (Vol. 2). Washington, D.C.: D.H.E.W. Office of Child Development, 1974.

Bruner, J. The ontogenesis of speech acts. *Journal of Child Language,* 1975, *2,* 1-19.

Casler, L. The effects of extra tactile stimulation on a group of institutionalized infants. *Genetic Psychology Monographs,* 1965, *71,* 137-175.

Casler, L. Perceptual deprivation in institutional settings. In G. Newton & S. Levine (Eds.), *Early experience and behavior.* Springfield: Thomas, 1968.

Clarke-Stewart, K. A. *Child Care in the Family,* New York: Acad Pr, 1977. Characteristics and consequences. *Monographs of the Society for Research in Child Development,* 1973, *38,* (6-7, Serial No. 153).

Clarke-Stewart, A. *Child Care in the Family,* New York: Acad Pr, 1977.

Condon, W. S. & Sander, L. W. Neonate movement is synchronized with adult speech: Interactional participation and language acquisition. *Science,* 1974, *183,* 99.

Denenberg, V. H. Critical periods, stimulus input, and emotional reactivity: A theory of infantile stimulation. *Psychological Review,* 1964, *71,* 335-351.

Denenberg, V. H., DeSantis, D., Waite, S., & Thoman, E. B. The effects of handling in infancy on behavioral states in the rabbit. *Physiology and Behavior,* 1977, *18,* 553-557.

Dollard, J., & Miller, N. E. *Personality and psychotherapy.* New York: McGraw, 1950.

Eimas, P. D. On the processing of speech: Some implications for language development. In C. L. Ludlow & M. E. Doran-Quine (Eds.), *The neurological bases of language disorders in children: Methods and directions for research* (NINCDS Monograph). Washington, D.C.: U.S. Government Printing Office, in press.

Eisenberg, R. B. *Auditory competence in early life.* Baltimore: Univ Park, 1976.

Freud, S. *An outline of psychoanalysis.* London: Hogarth, 1938.

Friedman, S., Thompson, M. A., Crawley, S., Criticos, A., Drake, D., Iacobbo, M., Rogers, P. P., & Richardson, L. Mutual visual regard during mother-infant play. *Perceptual and Motor Skills,* 1976, *42,* 427-431.

Gewirtz, J. L. On designing the functional environment of the child to facilitate behavioral development. In L. Dittmann (Ed.), *Early child care.* New York: Atherton, 1968.

Gewirtz, J. L., & Boyd, E. F. Experiments on mother-infant interaction underlying mutual attachment acquisition: The infant conditions the mother. In T. Alloway, P. Pliner, & L. Krames (Eds.), *Attachment behavior.* New York: Plenum Pr, 1977.

Goldberg, S. Social competence in infancy: A model of parent-infant interaction. *Merrill-Palmer Quarterly,* 1977, *23,* 163-177.

Gordon, I. J. A home learning center approach to early stimulation. Gainesville, Florida: Institute for Development of Human Resources, 1971.

Harlow, H. F. The development of affectional patterns in infant monkeys. In B. M. Foss (Ed.), *Determinants of infant behavior.* London: Methuen, 1961.

Hasselmeyer, E. G. The premature neonate's response to handling. *American Nurses' Association,* 1964, *11,* 15-24.

Heber, R., & Garber, H. The Milwaukee project: A study of the use of family intervention to prevent cultural-familial mental retardation. In B. Z. Friedlander, G. M. Sterritt, & G. E. Kirk (Eds.), *Assessment and intervention (Exceptional infant,* Vol. 3). New York: Brunner/Mazel, 1975.

Hunt, J. McV. *Intelligence and experience.* New York: Ronald, 1961.

Jaffe, J., & Feldstein, S. *Rhythms of dialogue.* New York: Acad Pr, 1970.

Jones, S. J., & Moss, H. A. Age, state, and maternal behavior associated with infant vocalizations. *Child Development,* 1971, *42,* 1039-1051.

Karnes, M. B. *Research and development program on preschool disadvantaged children: Investigations of classroom and at-home interventions: Final report.* Washington, D.C.: U.S. Office of Education, 1969.

Kaye, K. Toward the orgin of dialogue. In H. R. Schaffer (Ed.), *Studies in mother-infant interaction.* New York: Acad Pr, 1977.

Kennell, J. H., Jerauld, R., Wolfe, H., Chesler, D., Kreger, N., McAlpine, W., Steffa, M., & Klaus, M. Maternal behavior one year after early and extended post-partum contact. *Developmental Medicine and Child Neurology,* 1974, *16,* 172-179.

Kennell, J. H., Trause, M. A., & Klaus, M. H. Evidence for a sensitive period in the human mother. In *Parent-infant interaction.* Ciba Foundation Symposium 33 (New Series). Amsterdam: 1975, Elsevier, 87-102.

Kirk, S. A. The effects of early education with disadvantaged infants. In M. B. Karnes, *Research and development program on preschool disadvantaged children: Final report.* Washington, D.C.: U.S. Office of Education, 1969.

Klaus, M. H., & Kennell, J. H. Mothers separated from their newborn infants. *Pediatric Clinics of North America,* 1970, *17,* 1015.

Klaus, M. H., & Kennell, J. H. *Maternal-infant bonding.* St. Louis: Mosby, 1976.

Klaus, M. H., Kennell, J. H., Plumb, N., & Zuehlke, S. Human maternal behavior at the first contact with her young. *Pediatrics,* 1970, *46,* 187-192.

Klaus, M., Kreger, N., McAlpine, W., Steffa, M., & Kennell, J. Maternal attachment: Importance of the first post-partum days. *New England Journal of Medicine,* 1972, *286,* 460-463.

Klaus, R. A., & Gray, S. W. The early training project for disadvantaged children: A report after five years. *Monographs of the Society for Research in Child Development*, 1968, *33* (4, Serial No. 120).

Korner, A. F. State as variable, as obstacle, and as mediator of stimulation in infant research. *Merrill-Palmer Quarterly*, 1972, *18*, 77-94.

Korner, A. F. The effect of the infant's state of arousal, sex and ontogenetic stage on the caregiver. In M. Lewis & L. A. Rosenblum (Eds.), *The effect of the infant on its caregiver*. New York: Wiley, 1974.

Leiderman, P., Leifer, A., Seashore, M., Barnett, C., & Grobstein, R. Mother-infant interaction: Effects of early deprivation, prior experience and sex on infant. *Research Publications for Research in Nervous and Mental Disease*, 1973, *51*, 154-175.

Levenstein, P. Cognitive growth in preschoolers through verbal interaction with mothers. *American Journal of Orthopsychiatry*, 1970, *40*, 426-432.

Lewis, M. State as an infant-environment interaction: An analysis of mother-infant interaction as a function of sex. *Merrill-Palmer Quarterly*, 1972, *18*, 95-121.

Lewis, M., & Goldberg, S. Perceptual-cognitive development in infancy: A generalized expectancy model as a function of mother-infant interaction. *Merrill-Palmer Quarterly*, 1969, *15*, 81-100.

Lewis, M., & Rosenblum, L. A. (Eds.) *The effect of the infant on its caregiver. (The origins of behavior*, Vol. 1). New York: Wiley, 1974.

Lewis, M., & Wilson, C. D. Infant development in lower class American families. *Human Development*, 1972, *15*, 112-127.

Lind, J., Vuorenkoski, V., & Wasz-Hockert, O. The effect of cry stimulus on the temperature of the breast in lactating primipara: A thermographic study. In Morris N. (Ed.), *Psychosomatic medicine in obstetrics and gynecology*. Basel: S. Karger, A. G., 1973.

Macfarlane, A. Olfaction in the development of social preferences in the human neonate. In *Parent-infant interaction*. Ciba Foundation Symposium 33 (New Series). Amsterdam: Elsevier, 1975, 103-117.

Moss, H. A. Sex, age, and state as determinants of mother-infant interaction. *Merrill-Palmer Quarterly*, 1967, *13*, 19-36.

Moss, H. A., & Robson, K. Maternal influences in early visual behavior. *Child Development*, 1968, *39*, 401-408.

O'Connor, S., Altemeier, W. A., Sherrod, K. B., Sandler, H. M., & Vietze, P. M. The effect of extended postpartum contact and problems with parenting: A controlled study of 301 families. *Birth and the Family Journal*, 1978, *5*, 231-234.

Pasamanick, B., & Knobloch, H. Retrospective studies on the epidemiology of reproductive casualty: Old and new. *Merrill-Palmer Quarterly*, 1966, *12*, 7-26.

Riksen-Walraven, J. M. Effects of caregiver behavior on habituation rate and self-efficacy in infants. *International Journal of Behavioral Development*, 1978, *1*, 105-130.

Ringler, N. M., Kennell, J. H., Jarvella, R., Navojosky, B. J., & Klaus, M. H. Mother-to-child speech at 2 years: Effects of early postnatal contact.

Journal of Pediatrics, 1975, *86*, 141.

Robson, K. S. The role of eye-to-eye contact in maternal-infant attachment. *Journal of Child Psychology and Psychiatry*, 1967, *8*, 13-25.

Robson, K. S., & Moss, H. A. Patterns and determinants of maternal attachment. *Journal of Pediatrics*, 1970, *77*, 976-985.

Rubenstein, J. Maternal attentiveness and subsequent exploratory behavior in the infant. *Child Development*, 1967, *38*, 1089-1100.

Sameroff, A. J., & Chandler, J. J. Reproductive risk and the continuum of caretaking casualty. In F. D. Horowitz, E. M. Hetherington, S. Scarr-Salapatek, & G. Siegel (Eds.), *Review of child development research* (Vol. 4). Chicago: U of Chicago Pr, 1974.

Schaefer, E. S. *Progress report: Intellectual stimulation of culturally deprived parents.* Washington, D.C.: National Institute of Mental Health, 1968.

Schaefer, E. S. Need for early and continuing education. In V. Denneberg (Ed.), *Education of the infant and young child.* New York: Acad Pr, 1970.

Schaefer, E. S. Parents as educators: Evidence from cross sectional, longitudinal and intervention research. *Young Children*, 1972, *27*, 227-239.

Schaefer, E. S., & Aaronson, M. Infant education research project: Implementation and implications of the home-tutoring program. In R. K. Parker (Ed.), *The preschool in action.* Boston: Allyn, 1972.

Skeels, H. M., & Dye, H. B. A study of the effects of differential stimulation on mentally retarded children. *Proceedings of the American Association of Mental Deficiency*, 1939, *44*, 114-136.

Skodak, M., & Skeels, H. M. A final follow-up study of 100 adopted children. *Journal of Genetic Psychology*, 1949, *75*, 85-125.

Sluckin, W. *Imprinting and early learning.* London: Aldine, 1965.

Solkoff, N., Yaffe, S., Weintraub, D., & Blase, B. Effects of handling on the subsequent development of premature infants. *Developmental Psychology*, 1969, *1*, 765-786.

Spitz, R. A. Hospitalism: An inquiry into the genesis of psychiatric conditions in early childhood. *Psychoanalytic Study of the Child*, 1945, *1*, 53-74.

Stern, D. N. Mother and infant at play: The dyadic interaction involving facial, vocal, and gaze behaviors. In M. Lewis & L. A. Rosenblum (Eds.), *The effect of the infant on its caregiver.* New York: Wiley, 1974.

Stern, D. N., Jaffe, J., Beebe, B., & Bennett, S. L. Vocalizing in unison and in alternation: Two modes of communication within the mother-infant dyad. *Annals of the New York Academy of Sciences*, 1975, *263*, 89-100.

Strain, B. A. Early dialogues: A naturalistic study of vocal behavior in mothers and three-month-old infants (Doctoral dissertation, Peabody College for Teachers, 1975). *Dissertation Abstracts International*, 1975, *75*, 22294. (University Microfilms No. 75-14168B)

Streissguth, A., & Bee, H. L. Mother-child interactions and cognitive development in children. In W. Hartup (Ed.), *The young child* (Vol.

2). Washington, D.C.: National Association for the Education of Young Children, 1972.

Tronick, E., Als, H., Adamson, L., Wise, S., & Brazelton, T. B. The infant's response to entrapment between contradictory messages in face to face interaction. *Journal of the American Academy of Child Psychiatry*, 1978, *17*, 1-13.

Tulkin, S. R., & Kagan, J. Mother-child interaction in the first year of life. *Child Development*, 1972, *43*, 31-41.

Vietze, P., Abernathy, S. R., Ashe, M. L., & Faulstich, G. Contingent interaction between mothers and their developmentally delayed infants. In G. P. Scakett (Ed.), *Observing behavior*. Baltimore: Univ Park, 1978.

Vietze, P. M., & Anderson, B. J. Styles of parent-child interaction. In M. Begab, H. C. Haywood, & H. Garber (Eds.), *Preventing psycho-social retardation*. Baltimore: Univ Park, 1979.

Vietze, P. M., Strain, B., & Falsey, S. *Contingent responsiveness between mother and infant: Who's reinforcing whom?* Paper presented at the annual meeting of the Southeastern Psychological Association, Atlanta, March 1975.

Walters, R. H., & Parke, R. D. The role of the distance receptors in the development of social responsiveness. In L. P. Lipsitt & C. C. Spiker (Eds.), *Advances in child development and behavior* (Vol. 2). New York: Acad Pr, 1965.

Wandersman, L. P. Stylistic differences in mother-child interaction: A review and re-evaluation of the social class and socialization research. *Cornell Journal of Social Relations*, 1973, *8*, 197-218.

Weikart, D. P. Preschool programs: Preliminary findings. *Journal of Special Education*, 1967, *1*, 163-181.

Weisberg, P. Social and nonsocial conditioning of infant vocalizations. *Child Development*, 1963, *34*, 377-388.

Wolff, P. H. The natural history of crying and other vocalizations in early infancy. In R. M. Foss (Ed.), *Determinants of infant behavior* (Vol. 4). London: Methuen, 1969.

Yarrow, L. J. Maternal deprivation: Toward an empirical and conceptual reevaluation. *Psychological Bulletin*, 1961, *58*, 459-490.

Yarrow, L. J. Research in dimensions of early maternal care. *Merrill-Palmer Quarterly*, 1963, *9*, 101-114.

Yarrow, L. J. Conceptualizing the early environment. In L. Dittman (Ed.), *Early child care*. New York: Atherton Pr, 1968.

Yarrow, L. J., Morgan, G. A., Jennings, K. D., Harmon, R. J., Gaiter, J. L., & Vietze, P. M. Mastery motivation: A concept in need of measures. *Educational Resources Information Center*, 1977, *129*, 415.

Yarrow, L. J., Rubenstein, J. L., & Pedersen, F. A. *Infant and environment: Early cognitive and motivational development*. New York: Wiley, 1975.

Yarrow, L. J., Rubenstein, J. L., Pedersen, F. A., & Jankowski, J. J. Dimensions of early stimulation and their differential effects on infant development. *Merrill-Palmer Quarterly*, 1972, *18*, 205-218.

Chapter 2

THE ROLE OF THE FATHER
IN CHILD DEVELOPMENT

MICHAEL E. LAMB AND ANN M. FRODI

THROUGHOUT recorded history as well as in most contemporary social systems, primary responsibility for the care of young children has been and is assigned to mothers. Fathers are typically deemed responsible for the economic support of the family but not for either child care or early socialization. Historically, this distribution of responsibilities on the basis of gender was rendered the most reasonable one by the restriction on movement imposed by childbearing and nursing and by the absence of any means whereby others could share in the feeding of young infants. These constraints forced women to remain near the family home. Since they *had to* assume responsibility for the care of young children until weaning, it seemed efficient for them to assume responsibility for the care of older children as well, even when the youngsters were no longer dependent upon lactating mothers for their survival. The normative practice around the world, thus, was and is for mothers to assume and retain responsibility for child rearing. It was only in later childhood that children — especially boys — received extensive guidance from their fathers. Not until the recent invention of the nursing bottle was any alternative pattern conceivable.

Meanwhile, popular theoretical assumptions have also assured that relatively little importance is attributed to fathers by developmental psychologists. Perhaps most influential has been the belief, popularized in the main by psychoanalysts, that early experiences are of especial importance. Given the prevailing caretaking practices, this necessarily involved attributing great importance to the mother-child relationship and giving limited attention to the father-child relationship. This tendency was further accentuated by the penchant of Freud and his followers for speculating extensively about early feeding experiences, proposing that it was via these experiences that infant-adult relationships developed. The psychoanalysts argued that infants came to love their caretakers (= mothers) because they were consistently associated with the pleasurable sensation of hunger reduction. Fathers, who were not responsible for early feeding, were obviously unable to attain so influential a status in the child's emotional life. Over the course of his professional life, Freud was to increase the relative importance attributed to the mother-child relationship. In a final summary statement (1940/1949), Freud argued that "a mother's importance [is] unique, without parallel, established unalterably for the whole lifetime as the first and strongest love-object, and as the prototype of all later love relations — for both sexes." (p. 45)

If anything, Freud's followers stressed the importance of the mother-infant relationship even more than he did. Their postulations were unaffected by the fall from favor of drive-reduction theories of learning (Dollard & Miller, 1950) and by Harlow's demonstration that infant rhesus monkeys preferred a terry cloth surrogate mother to a wire surrogate that provided nourishment (Harlow & Zimmerman, 1959). Bowlby's (1969) integration of psychoanalytic and ethological theory instated a new mechanism to replace the discredited secondary drive model but retained a focus on the primacy of the mother-child bond. Only with the dawning awareness of infant social competence and the appreciation that it is not the content (e.g., feeding) but the quality and quantity of interaction that are important have researchers come to attribute greater potential significance to the father-child relationship (Lamb, 1977d). Thus, until the late 1960s, little importance was attributed to father-child relations — particularly when infancy was under review. Not surprisingly, therefore, current knowledge and theoretical conceptualizations of paternal influences are both primitive and deficient.

This chapter is a selective and abbreviated review of the empirical research on fathers and their contributions to child development. We will pay most attention to the findings concerning fathers and young children, since the research in this area is more recent, more detailed, and is process rather than outcome oriented. There are four major issues around which we shall orient our discussion. First, are fathers responsive and sensitive to their children, and do they appear capable of nurturant, parental behavior? Once capacity has been determined, our next concern is with whether or not most fathers behave in such a way as to make themselves affectively salient and influential in their children's eyes. Third, we will examine outcome-oriented studies in order to determine what impact fathers have on their children's development and whether this varies depending on the degree of paternal involvement. Finally, we will speculate briefly about the likely changes that would follow the establishment of more egalitarian child-rearing and caretaking practices.

THE POTENTIAL FOR NURTURANT PARENTHOOD

To the extent that the parturient mother lactates and the father does not, one can argue that the female parent is biologically predisposed to assume responsibility for the care of her offspring. This fact appears to have popularized speculations about putative behavioral predispositions that impel the mother to behave maternally. Such speculation has also been fueled by the observation that females of almost all species assume primary responsibility for child care.

The evidence, however, does not support these conclusions. Even within species wherein males seldom assume responsibility for infant care, the potential for paternal nurturance can be shown to exist. Among primates, for example, mothers are usually the sole or exclusive caretakers, yet Suomi, Eisele, Grady, and Tripp (1973), Suomi (1977), and Redican (1975) showed that captive rhesus males were quite responsive to their offspring. Spencer-Booth and Hinde (1967) and Bucher (1970) showed that when rhesus mothers were removed from the group or surgically incapacitated, the males began to evince parental behaviors such as carrying the infant in the ventral-ventral position, grooming, or playing. In some species, of course, the degree of paternal involvement is greater than this, even under normal circumstances (cf. Redican, 1976; LeMaho, 1977).

Writers such as Klaus and Kennell (1976) and Money and Tucker (1975) have argued that the hormonal changes associated with pregnancy and parturition may prime the mother to be particularly nurturant and responsive to her infant. Moreover, these speculations are often couched in terms implying that deviation from the pattern laid down by biology may have dire consequences for the child. Such speculation appears unwise. The relevant data all refer to rats, and there is considerable question about their generalizability (Lamb, 1975). Hormonal mechanisms in species as closely related as rats and mice are vastly different, and this increases the extent to which inferential generalizations from rats to humans are quite suspect. In any event, even in rats hormones merely speed the onset of maternal behavior: Parenting can be induced in both males and females simply by exposure to newborn pups (Rosenblatt, 1969). Once parental behavior emerges, furthermore, the behavior patterns (with the exception of nursing) are identical, regardless of the route whereby they are initiated. Culturally socialized expectations assuredly provide a more parsimonious explanation than do speculations about hormonal mechanisms (cf. Lehrman, 1974).

However rigidly sex stereotyped was the assignment of child care responsibilities within human societies in the past, there is good reason to believe that sex role prescriptions are currently becoming more relaxed and that "deviations" are now more tolerable. Bem (1974) has suggested that many people are neither masculine nor feminine; instead, she proposed that they display components of both roles. This is referred to as *androgyny*. In a recent study of adult-infant interaction, Bem, Martyna, and Watson (1976) compared androgynous adults with those who were classified as either masculine or feminine. They found that the androgynous and feminine individuals (*regardless of sex*) kissed, touched, talked to, and smiled at the baby more than those rated as masculine. At least some males, then, appeared capable of responding nurturantly toward infants.

More directly relevant evidence concerning the capacity of males to interact sensitively and affectionately with infants comes from research conducted by Parke and his colleagues. In the first study, Parke, O'Leary, and West (1972) observed mothers and fathers interacting with their newborn infants prior to release from hospital. They found that fathers were just as likely as mothers to hold, touch, kiss and vocalize to their infants, and they were more likely to rock the infants than mothers were. Parke and O'Leary (1976) replicated their main findings in a second study in which the subjects comprised a less select middle-class sample. Even when the fathers had not participated in childbirth classes and were not present at delivery, they were quite as nurturant as the mothers on most measures. When both parents were present, in fact, the fathers exhibited more nurturant behaviors than the mothers did. Not surprisingly, other investigators have found that the fathers of newborn infants report strong feelings of affection toward their infants shortly after the child's delivery (Greenberg & Morris, 1974). Greenberg and Morris referred to this as a process of *engrossment*.

In later research, Parke and Sawin (1976, 1977) have attempted to compare maternal and paternal sensitivity during feeding sessions with infants of 3 to 4 months of age and younger. Again, they reported that fathers were just as responsive as mothers to infant signals such as coughing, sneezing, and spitting up — they competently adjusted their behavior in light of the infant's behavior. When the infants vocalized, fathers were most likely to increase their rate of vocalization, whereas mothers increased their touching of the infants. In all, while there were differences in interaction styles, fathers and mothers both responded appropriately, contingently, and nurturantly to their infants' cues.

Parke's research demonstrates quite convincingly that when appropriately motivated, fathers are quite as sensitive to their own infants as mothers are. Perhaps they would be more inhibited if they were confronted by someone else's baby. In fact, this appears to be the case. When subjects were observed interacting with a baby in a waiting room, Feldman and Nash (1977) found that the mothers of young babies interacted with the confederate baby more than their spouses did. Similar sex differences are found among young adolescents but not among 8-year-olds, childless married persons, or single cohabiting adults (Feldman, Nash, & Cutrona, 1977; Feldman & Nash, 1977; Frodi & Lamb, 1978). Responsiveness to babies, argue these researchers, is a culturally enforced sex-stereotyped behavior. At times when there are major pressures toward sex-typed behavior, we would expect to find sex differences emerging, whereas at times when gender role is secure and the pressures toward stereotyping are less intense, sex differences should, and do disappear. For the present purposes, the important finding is that despite social expectations that they be less responsive to babies than women are, fathers remain as sensitive as mothers to their own infants.

Further evidence against the existence of biologically based sex differences in sensitivity to infant signals was obtained in two experimental studies of the psychophysiological responses of young parents to infant smiles and cries (Frodi, Lamb, Leavitt, & Donovan 1978; Frodi, Lamb, Leavitt, Donovan, Neff, & Sherry, 1978). In these studies, fathers and mothers viewed videotape presentations of a baby who either cried audibly or smiled, cooed, and gurgled happily. In both studies, the crying baby elicited significant physiological arousal (heart rate acceleration, blood pressure increase, and increases in skin conductance) and self-reported negative feelings, whereas the smiling baby triggered no comparable arousal but pleasant subjective mood. The pattern of responses was the one predicted on the basis of a "functional ethological analysis" (Lamb, 1978b); most importantly, the same patterns occurred regardless of the subjects' sex. In a later study, Frodi and Lamb (1978) found that the same pattern of physiological responses occurred among 8- and 14-year-old boys and girls. Interestingly, however, the older girls interacted more with a live baby than did the boys.

In all, the results of a number of studies employing a variety of experimental procedures point toward a common set of findings. There appear to be no biologically determined sex differences in human responsiveness to infants. At various stages of the life cycle (including the first few months of parenthood), however, societal pressures are such that males behave as if they were less responsive or sensitive to the behavior of infants. Despite this, fathers appear quite as sensitive as mothers when interacting with their own infants. We can thus provide an affirmative answer to the question about the capacity or potential for sensitive and nurturant paternal behavior. This is an important conclusion, because there is a general consensus that the parent's sensitivity to his/her infant is either the major determinant of whether or not an infant-adult attachment will develop at all (Lamb, 1978c) or at least a determinant of what quality the relationship will assume (cf. Ainsworth, Blehar, Waters, & Wall, 1978).

Most of the relevant research on this score, unfortunately, concerns the development of infant-*mother* attachment, and most of the available data were gathered from one sample of infants. Ainsworth and her colleagues have shown that mothers who were more responsive to their infants' cries and to their cues in face-to-face interaction were likely to have infants who became securely attached to them (Ainsworth, Bell, & Stayton, 1974; Blehar, Lieberman, & Ainsworth, 1977). By contrast, the infants of less sensitive mothers developed insecure attachments to them. Other theorists tend to share Ainsworth's belief in the importance of parental sensitivity (Lamb, 1978c). Some evidence in support of this notion was gathered by Schaffer and Emerson (1964) in their study of the development of attachments. These investigators reported that the responsiveness of an adult to the infant's behavior was the most significant determinant of attachment formation. Responsibility for caretaking or feeding proved quite insignificant, and most infants developed attachments to noncaretaking fathers.

THE FORMATION OF FATHER-INFANT ATTACHMENTS

Although we do not know how much interaction is sufficient for an infant-adult attachment to form, it seems that most infants have at least the minimum necessary amount of interaction with their fathers. There is good evidence that most infants raised in traditional nuclear families do develop attachments to their fathers, despite the limited involvement of the fathers in caretaking or feeding. In an observational study of infant attachment behavior in the familiar home environment, Lamb (1977c, 1978a) found that most infants became attached to both their parents at about the same time (around 6 to 8 months of age). Between 7 and 13 months of age, furthermore, the babies showed no preferences for either parent over the other in the stress-free home situation.

Attachment theorists such as Bowlby (1969) and Ainsworth (1972), however, have argued that "true" preferences will be revealed only under conditions of stress. When infants are distressed, they should reduce their interaction with nonattachment and secondary attachment figures while increasing the display of attachment behavior toward primary attachment figures. Lamb (1976a, 1976c, 1976e, 1977c) has conducted a series of experimental studies involving observations of 8-, 12-, 18-, and 24-month-old infants in conditions of moderate stress. The findings of these studies have been quite unequivocal. In stress-free periods, infants generally displayed no preferences for either parent. Under moderate stress, infants increased the display of attachment behavior toward whichever parent was available. When both parents were present, however, both 12- and 18-month-olds clearly preferred their mothers. Somewhat surprisingly, the youngest and the oldest groups (8- and 24-month-olds) did not exhibit preferences for their mothers even when distressed. Under stress, therefore, it becomes clear that mothers are the primary attachment figures of young infants, if only during a narrow time span.

Lamb's naturalistic observational study also involved assessments of infant-parent attachments during the second year of life (Lamb, 1977a, 1977b). During home observations, it was found that boys of between 15 and 24 months of age overwhelmingly preferred their fathers. Girls as a group remained somewhat inconsistent, although the plurality preferred their mothers. The boys' preferences appeared related to the fact that fathers were twice as active in interaction with their sons as were mothers. The fathers also appeared to reduce temporarily the amount of interaction with their daughters. Mothers, meanwhile, continued to treat boys and girls similarly. The fathers' behavior thus served to increase their relative salience in the lives of their sons while slightly increasing the relative salience of the mothers in the daughters' lives. The preference patterns observed revealed that their behavior had a predictable effect.

Not surprisingly, the data indicate that in traditional families mothers spend more time with their infants than fathers do. After interviewing the parents of 6- to 21-month-olds, Kotelchuck (1975) reported that mothers spent an average of 9 hours per day with their children, while fathers spent 3.2 hours per day. Other investigators have reported lesser amounts of father-child contact, and consequently the ratio of child-mother to child-father time may be more dramatic than that reported by Kotelchuck (Parke, Power, & Gottman, 1978 and Lamb & Stevenson, 1978, review these data).

In any event, we have already noted that fathers need not be involved in caretaking activities in order to become attachment figures. Rather, it is the quality of the interaction between father and child that is the major determinant of attachment formation, and it is clear that infants form attachments to both parents. Instead of quarrelling about how much interaction takes place between fathers and infants, we need to ask about the relative importance of different types of interaction within the mother- and father-child relationships (Lamb, 1976b, 1977c, 1978a). Here we find that there is much less disagreement than there is about the amount of father-infant interaction.

Kotelchuck's (1975) interviews revealed that mothers spent 55 minutes a day (average) washing their infants and 2.3 hours playing with them. The corresponding figures for fathers were 9 minutes and 1.2 hours. In comparison to mothers, fathers clearly spent a greater proportion of their time in social activities such as play. Meanwhile, in his observational study of 7- to 13-month-olds interacting with their parents, Lamb (1976b, 1977c) found that when mothers and fathers played with their infants, they engaged in different types of play. Typically, the mothers in the study initiated conventional games like peek-a-boo and pat-a-cake and play involving toys. Fathers, however, were more likely to be physically stimulating and unpredictable in their play interaction. Recently, Yogman and his colleagues (1976) have shown that mothers and fathers adopt characteristically different styles of play as early as during the first months of their babies' lives.

The fact that mothers and fathers provide and represent different types of experiences for their children was also indicated by an analysis of the purposes for which babies were held by their mothers and fathers (Lamb, 1976b, 1977c). Mothers most often held their babies for caretaking purposes and in order to restrict the babies' explorations of "forbidden areas," whereas fathers were far more likely to hold the babies to play with them or because the babies simply wanted to be held. Clarke-Stewart (1977) found that fathers were rated better able than mothers to engage their children in play, were more involved in the play, and could maximize the children's enjoyment of the play. Perhaps because of this, the children were more cooperative, close, involved, excited, and interested in play with their fathers at 2 1/2 years of age. Lynn and Cross (1974) found that at 2 years of age, both boys and girls preferred to play with their fathers rather than their mothers. Only over the succeeding two years did girls shift their preferences from fathers to mothers.

In all, then, the results of several studies confirm that mothers and fathers come to represent different types of interaction for their young children. To our mind, these findings are important to the extent that they demonstrate how the sex-typed roles assumed by the parents are translated into differentiable styles of interaction with their infants. Thus, most infants not only have two attachments, they also have affective relationships with male and female role models. The possible importance of this for the child's development will be made evident shortly. Suffice it to say at this point that the sex-differentiated behavior patterns that characterize mothers and fathers are present regardless of the infant's sex.

THE DEVELOPMENT OF SEX DIFFERENCES AND SEX ROLES

It cannot be said, however, that the behavior of the two parents is completely unaffected by the sex of their infant or child. In general, fathers tend to show preferences for sons, while mothers show a greater protectiveness of and closeness to girls. This pattern has been reported in a variety of cultures (West & Konner, 1976) as well as among nonhuman primates such as rhesus monkeys (Redican, 1976). From the time of the child's birth, parents' perceptions of their children are influenced by the child's sex. Rubin, Provenzano, and Luria (1974), for example, showed that fathers described sons as larger, better coordinated, stronger, and more alert than daughters. The girls, in turn, were described as weaker, more awkward, more inattentive, softer, prettier, more cute, and more beautiful than boys. Mothers, too, had sex-typed perceptions, though they were less extreme than the fathers.

A survey of the United States carried out in 1975 revealed that parents desired sons rather than daughters by a ratio of 2:1, with the preference being more pronounced among men (Hoffman, 1977). Fathers are especially eager to have sons, and their preferential treatment of boys reflects this. Once they are able to interact with their infants, parents treat the infants somewhat differently depending on their sex. Parke and his colleagues (Parke & O'Leary, 1976; Parke & Sawin, 1976) found that within the first few days, fathers touched and vocalized more to firstborn boys than to either later-born boys or girls of any ordinal position. Over the succeeding months, fathers touched their sons more and were more interactive while feeding sons, whereas mothers showed analogous preferences for daughters on these measures. Fathers are even more tolerant of difficult temperaments in sons than in daughters, according to Rendina and Dickerscheid (1976). The only rather contradictory finding was that fathers held their daughters closer, more snugly, and longer than their sons, whereas mothers held their sons closely more often (Parke & Sawin, 1976).

Although both parents appear to treat boys and girls differently, fathers tend to be more empathic, and there is fairly substantial evidence that fathers are more concerned than mothers about the adoption of sex-appropriate behavior styles by their children (Bronfenbrenner, 1961; Lamb, 1976d). There is not yet consensus about the process whereby fathers influence sex role development in their children, but this is the aspect of child development that has been researched most thoroughly. We have noted that from early in the first year of life, the child is exposed to differentiable patterns of motherinfant (feminine) and father-infant (masculine) interaction; these may be as important as (or more important than) any explicit attempts on the part of parents to shape the behavior of their sons and daughters.

During the second year, there takes place a marked change in the fathers' behavior. Most notable is an increase in the amount of attention paid by fathers to their sons and a temporary withdrawal of fathers from their daughters (Lamb, 1977b; Lamb, Owen, & Chase-Lansdale, 1978). This may serve to increase the relative salience of the same-sex parent in the child's life and so increase the probability that the child will take the same-sex parent as its primary model. This pattern, which some observe early in the first year, remains evident as the children grow older. Margolin and Patterson (1975), for example, found that mothers treated their 5- to 12-year-old children similarly, whereas fathers directed twice as many positive responses to their sons as to their daughters.

Although fathers remain more concerned than mothers about sex-appropriate behavior (Block, 1978; Bronfenbrenner, 1961; Heilbrun, 1965), they tend to assign to mothers the primary responsibility for the appropriate socialization of daughters. Fathers retain a keener interest in the socialization of their sons, among whom sex-stereotyped behavior is established somewhat earlier than it is among girls. Block (1978) has recently shown that in several of the major Western cultures, a common pattern of sex-stereotyped expectations can be discerned. Fathers encourage competition, achievement, independence, and responsibility and tolerate aggression in their sons more than in their daughters. By contrast, they are concerned about truthfulness, trustworthiness, and "ladylike behavior" in their daughters.

Rather different mechanisms, it would seem, underlie the father's role in facilitating the adoption of masculine and feminine behavior by sons and daughters respectively. Fathers become more salient role models in the lives of their sons by increasing the amount of interaction with them, whereas they become influential in their daughters' development by their partial withdrawal. Their relative inaccessibility may force girls to *work* in order to obtain their fathers' approval and attention. One possible way to secure this approval is to pay attention to and imitate their mothers — females of whose behavior their fathers apparently approve (Lamb et al., 1978). In addition, fathers influence the types of demands that mothers make of their daughters and so have an indirect impact on their daughters' socialization.

Whatever the mechanisms involved, it appears that fathers may have a more consistent effect on their daughters' sex role development than on their sons'. Contrary to the predictions of identification theorists, research has not shown a correlation between the degree of masculinity of fathers and sons (see Lamb, 1976d, for a review). Instead, the literature in this area is quite confusing. The only fairly consistent finding is an unexpected one, namely, that the masculinity of the father is positively related to the femininity of his daughter. This finding is consistent with the notion of complementary, or reciprocal, role learning (e.g., Deutsch, 1944; Johnson, 1963; Hetherington, 1967), which proposes that roles can be learned not simply by imitating those who have adopted the role, but also by interacting with those who display a complementary role.

Some of the inconsistency in the research linking characteristics of fathers and sons may be accounted for by the failure of some researchers to take account of the *quality*, or warmth, of the father-child relationship. Boys tend to identify closely with their fathers (and thus take on the masculinity of their behavior) only when the fathers are not only masculine but also warm and nurturant (Mussen, 1973; Bandura & Walters, 1959). Warmth or nurturance is also important if the father is to influence the femininity of his daughter (Johnson, 1963). These data underscore the importance of the sensitivity or warmth of the father's behavior toward his family. Also important is the father's status in the family. The father is a more salient and influential role model when he is perceived as dominant within the household (Hetherington, 1967).

By far the greater proportion of research on "paternal effects" has involved studying children raised in families without husbands/fathers rather than studying patterns of father-child interaction and their correlates. The assumption is made that any difference between children raised in father-present and father-absent families indicates the dimension and type of paternal influence in normal circumstances. Many reviewers (e.g., Lamb, 1976d; Biller, 1974) have now criticized this assumption, noting that there are a number of ways (economic and social) in which father-absent families may differ from intact families. Variables such as age at the time of separation, reasons for the separation, the family structure, socioeconomic status, the mother's attitude toward her ex-spouse and toward men in general, and her reaction to the separation all modulate the impact of father absence on the children. Thus, it is impossible to assess the father's socializing role in any precise way by means of a study of father-absent families. In general, the father-absence literature suggests that boys raised without fathers either appear to be less masculine or else exhibit exaggeratedly masculine behavior, presumably in compensation (Biller, 1971, 1974; Lamb, 1976d). Also reported are "feminine" (nonanalytic) cognitive styles (Carlsmith, 1964).

There has been far less attention paid to the effects of father absence on girls, presumably because, unlike boys, girls do not lose a major role model when the father departs. The limited evidence available indicates that girls raised without fathers may later have difficulty interacting with males. When their parents are divorced, these girls appear unusually forward and promiscuous in their interactions with males, whereas those whose fathers have died are unusually shy and submissive (Hetherington, 1972). Among both boys and girls, early father absence appears most detrimental (Biller, 1974; Hetherington & Deur, 1972); the effects are not evident until adolescence in girls, whereas they are evident far earlier among boys.

MORAL DEVELOPMENT

Although there are some differences, most of the major theories of sex role development propose compatible and often similar mechanisms whereby fathers might influence their children's development. Unfortunately, the same is not true of theory in the area of moral development. Terminological inconsistency, confusion between moral judgment and moral behavior, varying operational definitions, and theoretical incompatibilities all combine to ensure that research in this area has been largely inconclusive.

In a major, though somewhat dated, review, Hoffman (1970) proposed that fathers who were interested and involved in child rearing had sons who identified with them and had an internalized (i.e., more mature) sense of morality. Likewise, nurturant fathers who were active participants in child care fostered altruism and generosity. Fathers who espoused love-oriented disciplinary techniques rather than punitive strategies had a greater impact on their children's morality. Delinquency in boys is often associated with father absence or the presence of fathers who are antisocial, unempathic, and/or hostile (Bandura & Walters, 1959). In general, however, there are more significant relationships between maternal behavior and child morality than there are between paternal behavior and child morality (Hoffman, 1970; Lamb, 1976d).

Although it is clear that considerably more research is needed in this area, one general theme bears restatement. As in the case of sex role development, it is the warmth, accessibility, and involvement of the father that critically determine whether he will have a profound and beneficial impact on his offsprings' moral development.

COGNITIVE DEVELOPMENT

The same factor appears to be important in modulating the father's impact on cognitive development in children. Until recently, most of our knowledge concerning paternal influence derived from studies of children raised without fathers. Most of these early studies revealed a negative impact on achievement and achievement motivation, especially among boys (Biller, 1971, reviews these data). Also reported were nonanalytic or "feminine" cognitive styles (Carlsmith, 1964). Boys normally perform better on tests of quantitative skills than on tests of verbal skills; father-absent boys showed the reverse pattern, which is the norm among females.

In the last few years, researchers in this area have turned from studies of father absence to observational studies of father-child interaction. In a recent study of toddlers, Clarke-Stewart (1978) found that children's performance on the Bayley Mental Development Index was related to their fathers' ability to engage them in play, the fathers' attitude toward the children, and the amount of interaction they shared. Quality of father-child play was more strongly related to the cognitive development of boys than of girls, whereas the amount of verbal interaction, positive expressiveness, and responsiveness was more highly related among girls. In interpreting her results, however, Clarke-Stewart suggested rather provocatively that it was the infants' characteristics that affected the fathers' behavior rather than the reverse. The major impact of fathers on their young children, she suggested, might be indirectly mediated via the fathers' effect on the mothers (Lewis & Weinraub, 1976). Clarke-Stewart's sample was very small, unfortunately, so it is hard to know how seriously to take her speculations.

Larger-scale observational studies involving preschoolers and their fathers have been undertaken by Radin (see Radin, 1976, for a review). Radin's research has shown that paternal nurturance facilitates the cognitive development of young boys. She postulated that paternal nurturance made it more likely that the boys would identify with their fathers. This should increase the child's motivation to learn and to perform, which in turn would contribute to cognitive development. Whether or not one agrees with her interpretations, Radin's data did show the predicted relationship between paternal nurturance and cognitive performance, at least among boys.

The evidence about paternal influences on preschool-aged daughters was more disturbing. Radin found that fathers tended to be inconsistent in their interactions with their daughters, as if they were unsure about the desirability of cognitive competence in females. As a result, they tended to inhibit rather than facilitate the competence of daughters. In addition, much of the impact appeared to be mediated indirectly via the mother rather than directly via the father-daughter interactions.

Other less comprehensive studies tend to confirm Radin's principal findings. Research involving older children suggests that underachieving boys have inadequate relationships with their fathers, whereas high achievers have good relationships with fathers who encourage achievement and are also dominant and democratic (Lamb, 1976d).

In a recent review, Lamb et al. (1978) pointed out that fathers may comprise one of the major barriers to the achievement and advancement of women in contemporary society. As noted earlier, it is they who have the greater commitment to traditional sex role prescriptions and who are more concerned that their children adhere to them. In their interaction with their daughters, as well as in the indirect effect mediated via the mothers, fathers communicate their disapproval of achievement orientation in females. The effect can be particularly profound when a warm father encourages femininity in his daughter yet believes that femininity and achievement are incompatible. In such cases, the girl is likely to adopt the values or beliefs of her father. This would help account for the fact that a major restraint on female advancement is posed by women's concerns about the desirability or appropriateness of achievement. These concerns probably derive from earlier socializing experiences.

DIRECT AND INDIRECT EFFECTS

In most of the preceding discussion, we have attempted to identify the ways in which fathers directly influence the development of their children, though we have repeatedly referred to the likelihood of indirect influential effects. There has recently been a great deal of speculation about the nature and potential importance of indirect effects. In fact, Lewis and Weinraub (1976) have gone so far as to argue that the major influence of fathers upon their children's development is indirectly mediated.

Parke, Power, and Gottman (1978) have provided the most extensive theoretical discussion of indirect effects. They propose four major ways (and some minor ways) in which indirect effects of fathers on children can be mediated. First, fathers may affect the quality or nature of mother-child interaction — perhaps by providing economic, social, and emotional support for their wives. This would relieve the women of certain concerns and responsibilities and thus improve the quality of their relationships with their children. Second, the fathers' attitudes and behavior toward the children may influence the development of characteristic behaviors or social styles in their children; these in turn may influence the way in which others will approach interaction with the children. Finally, the quality of the marital relationship may influence the way both parents behave toward their children (cf. Pedersen, 1975; Pedersen, Anderson, & Cain, 1976).

Appreciation of the potential importance of indirect effects has yet to make a significant impact on theorizing about the father's role or on the conduct of research and the interpretation of findings. As developmental psychologists come to pay greater attention to them, however, we may find that in focusing exclusively upon direct effects, we have been underestimating the extent of paternal contributions to child development.

PAST, PRESENT, AND FUTURE

Although we are neither historians nor prophets, we would be derelict if we closed this chapter without discussing the major reevaluation of paternal roles that is currently in progress. In much of the Western world, fathers have begun to assume or demand a larger role in the care and socialization of their children (cf. Levine, 1976). Increasing (though still small) numbers of fathers are seeking and being awarded custody of their children. Clearly, paternal roles are being reevaluated. Because of the recency of these developments, however, we can only speculate about their likely effects.

From the research reviewed earlier, we have learned much about the likely roles of mothers and fathers in children's sociopersonality development. There is one major limitation, however, and that is the exclusive focus on parental roles in traditional nuclear families. Although most children in Western societies are still raised in such families, an increasing number are being raised under some alternative child-rearing system, and there is mounting pressure for politicians as well as social scientists to take account of the changing practices. Advocates of nontraditional life-styles argue that by failing to study alternative family arrangements, social scientists perpetuate an unproven assumption that the traditional social structure must be preserved if the mental health of the next generation is to be assured. Persons who believe this assumption may well be correct if they simply mean that the process of socialization tends to ensure the development of individuals likely to fit into and perpetuate the existing social system. When the social system is evolving as rapidly as the present one, however, one would expect the socialization process to change accordingly. Rather than being maladaptive, then, alternative family styles might be viewed as the vanguard of social change.

Unfortunately, we lack the data on the basis of which to evaluate these propositions. The alternative contexts studies in and around Los Angeles by Eiduson and her colleagues (Eiduson, Zimmerman, & Bernstein, 1977) have proved to be exceptionally traditional where their infant care practices are concerned. Researchers such as the authors who have been eager to study infant development in cases where parents reverse maternal and paternal roles or share child care responsibilities have found it difficult to locate sufficient families for study. Perhaps many parents remain afraid of departing too far from the traditional pattern of infant care until more is known about the likely effects of unconventional patterns.

As a result of intensive government reforms, the situation that exists today in Scandinavia is somewhat different. To be sure, the adoption of nontraditional family roles has not proceeded as fast as many reformers had hoped or expected — perhaps because of the same fears that exist in the United States. Nevertheless, some families have seized the opportunity to raise their children differently. We are currently preparing to conduct research designed to compare the patterns of infant care and infant development in three types of families: mother as caretaker, father as breadwinner (the traditional family); father as caretaker, mother as breadwinner (the reversed-roles family); and mother and father sharing breadwinning and child-care roles (the shared-roles family). All families will be drawn from the same (middle-class) social strata in the same culture (Sweden) in order to permit us to isolate the influence of different child-rearing systems without having to deal simultaneously with the likely effects of different cultural milieux — a common problem in the interpretation of anthropological research on child-rearing. We believe that we will be able to complete a study whose findings will have theoretical and practical relevance not only to Sweden but to other Western countries as well.

In traditional families, we proposed earlier, the mother becomes associated in the infant's eyes with caretaking practices and gentle and/or conventional types of play. The father, by contrast, spends less time with his infant and assumes a minor role in the child's physical care. His major identification in the child's eyes is with play — notably boisterous, physical, and idiosyncratic types of play. This means that the sex roles assumed by the parents are translated into differential and sex-typed patterns of interaction that should be evident to the infant. Later, the parents' pattern of attention to boys and girls shifts in such a way as to focus the toddler's attention on the behavior of the same-sex parent. This may facilitate the adoption of appropriate gender identities by the children.

In both of the nontraditional family types we propose to study, this does not take place. Either both mother and father are associated with the feminine role or only father is. At least two key questions remain to be answered empirically. First, does the father's style of interaction reflect his masculine sex role, or does it reflect the style of interaction of a noncaretaking parent? If the former is true, the primary caretaking fathers and mothers should differ appropriately in their style of interaction, and the developmental process may proceed normally. If the latter is true, however, then the child's mother (rather than its father) would behave in a masculine fashion or else both parents would perform confused or undifferentiated types of roles. The normal development of gender identity might thus be compromised.

Regardless of the resolution of this issue, the consequences for the child are unclear for two reasons. First, the key determinant of with which parent the child identifies appears to be not the masculinity or femininity of the parents' behavior, but the change in their relative salience brought about by the fathers' increased attention to sons and withdrawal from daughters during the second year of life. If this occurs in nontraditional families (perhaps with the mothers' rather than the fathers' behavior being critical in channelling the infants' attention), then the children may still identify with the appropriate (i.e., same-sex) parent.

Second, while the parents in alternative families would be filling nontraditional roles, these roles would not be pathological. It is important, we believe, for the two parents to be secure in their gender identities — for the father to perceive himself as and be content to be a male and for the mother to perceive herself as and be content to be a female. Provided the parents themselves do not see their nontraditional behavior as incompatible with their gender identities, no harm to the children need be caused by the parents' adoption of nontraditional parental roles. When an individual's gender identity is secure, a wide range of sex roles can be assumed (Lamb & Urberg, 1978).

It is quite possible, therefore, that the events taking place within the nontraditional families may ensure that children adopt the appropriate gender identity while also ensuring that the sex roles they observe and start to imitate are nontraditional ones like their parents'. Such findings would support the position of the proponents of social change. On the other hand, if either of the two conditions outlined in the previous paragraph failed to be met, it would necessitate caution and would suggest that serious and potentially undesirable consequences might be expected. An alternative scenario is also conceivable: Perhaps nontraditional families have a completely different strategy for fostering psychological development.

Whatever the case, we believe that the issue is important enough to merit investigation. The number of nontraditional two-parent families is small today, but all the evidence suggests that their numbers will grow. At least within the Scandinavian countries, there is strong political encouragement of such life-styles. It behooves us as social scientists to gather descriptive information about the experiences of children being raised in a variety of contexts and to determine the extent to which the adoption of nontraditional parental roles positively or adversely affects personality and social development.

The uncertainties regarding the consequences of adopting nontraditional parental roles constrain our ability to make conclusive statements about the way fathers *should* behave in interaction with their children in order to facilitate the children's attainment of psychological health. Obviously, it is likely that as fathers assume a greater role in child care, their influence — both directly and indirectly mediated — will increase. Whether or not traditional roles are adopted, we believe that child rearing is likely to proceed more smoothly when both parents assume some of the responsibilities. We noted earlier that fathers clearly have the potential for sensitive and nurturant interactions with infants and young children. The issue, then, is not whether fathers are capable of raising children but whether society encourages them to view this as a legitimate and rewarding pursuit.

All the findings we have reviewed suggest that children benefit from interaction with fathers who are not only involved but also have a warm or nurturant relationship with and are accessible to their children. Contrary to popular belief, interpersonal warmth does not compromise individual masculinity!

In our opinion, however, paternal roles are most clearly in need of reevaluation where father-daughter relationships are concerned. Fathers may play an important role in establishing the debilitating concern of many young women that achievement, competence, and ambition are incompatible with traditional femininity. We believe that this belief is misguided and outdated. Fathers may need to play an especially important role in persuading their daughters that (for example) career and family aspirations are both legitimate and compatible, since there are currently few models of nontraditional femininity and the girls' mothers are likely to be inappropriate models.

REFERENCES

Ainsworth, M. D. Attachment and dependency: A comparison. In J. L. Gewirtz (Ed.), *Attachment and dependency*. Washington, D.C.: Winston, 1972.

Ainsworth, M. D., Blehar, M. C., Waters, E., & Wall, S. N. *Patterns of attachment: Assessed in the strange situation and at home*. Hillsdale, New Jersey: Lawrence Erlbaum Associates, 1978.

Ainsworth, M. D., Bell, S. M., & Stayton, D. J. Infant-mother attachment and social development: Socialization as a product of reciprocal responsiveness to signals. In M. Richards (Ed.), *The integration of a child into a social world*. Cambridge: Cambridge U Pr, 1974.

Bandura, A., & Walters, R. H. *Adolescent aggression: A study of the influence of child-rearing practices and family interrelationships*. New York: Ronald, 1959.

Bem, S. L. The measurement of psychological androgyny. *Journal of Consulting and Clinical Psychology*, 1974, *42*, 155-162.

Bem, S. L., Martyna, W., & Watson, C. Sex typing and androgyny: Further explorations in the expressive domain. *Journal of Personality and Social Psychology*, 1976, *34*, 1016-1023.

Biller, H. B. *Father, child, and sex role*. Lexington, Massachusetts: Health, 1971.

Biller, H. B. *Paternal deprivation: Family, school, sexuality, and society*. Lexington, Massachusetts: Health, 1974.

Blehar, M. C., Lieberman, A. E., & Ainsworth, M. D. Early face to face interaction and its relation to later infant-mother attachment. *Child Development*, 1977, *48*, 182-194.

Block, J. Another look at sex differentiation in the socialization behaviors of mothers and fathers. In F. Denmark (Ed.), *Psychology of women: Future directions of research.* New York: Psych Dimensions, 1978.

Bowlby, J. *Attachment (Attachment and loss,* Vol. 1). New York: Basic, 1969.

Bronfenbrenner, U. The changing American child — A speculative analysis. *Journal of Social Issues,* 1961, *17,* 6-18.

Bucher, K. L. *Temporal lobe neocortex lesion and maternal behavior in rhesus monkeys.* Unpublished doctoral dissertation, The Johns Hopkins University, 1970.

Carlsmith, L. Effects of early father-absence on scholastic aptitude. *Harvard Educational Review,* 1964, *34,* 3-21.

Clarke-Stewart, K. A. *The father's impact on mother and child.* Paper presented at the biennial meeting of the Society for Research in Child Development, New Orleans, March 1977.

Clarke-Stewart, K. A. And daddy makes three: The father's impact on mother and child. *Child Development,* 1978, *49,* in press.

Deutsch, H. *The psychology of women* (Vol. 1). New York: Grune, 1944.

Dollard, J., & Miller, N. E. *Personality and psychotherapy.* New York: McGraw, 1950.

Eiduson, B. T., Zimmerman, I. L., & Bernstein, M. *Single versus multiple parenting: Implications for infancy.* Paper presented to the American Psychological Association, San Francisco, August 1977.

Feldman, S. S., & Nash, S. C. The effect of family formation on sex stereotypic behavior: A study of responsiveness to babies. In W. Miller & L. Newman (Eds.), *The first child and family formation.* Chapel Hill: U of NC Pr, 1977.

Feldman, S., Nash, S., & Cutrona, C. The influence of age and sex on responsiveness to babies. *Developmental Psychology,* 1977, *13,* 675-676.

Freud, S. *An outline of psychoanalysis.* New York: Norton, 1949. (Originally published, 1940.)

Freud, S. Some psychological consequences of the anatomical distinction between the sexes. In S. Freud, *Collected Papers,* Vol. 5. London: Hogarth, 1950.

Frodi, A. M., & Lamb, M. E. *Physiological and behavioral responses to infant signals: A developmental study.* Paper presented to the Iowa Academy of Science, Cedar Falls, Iowa, April 1978.

Frodi, A., Lamb, M. E., Leavitt, L., & Donovan, W. Fathers' and mothers' responses to infant smiles and cries. *Infant Behavior and Development,* 1978, *1,* 187-198.

Frodi, A., Lamb, M. E., Leavitt, L., Donovan, W., Neff, C., & Sherry, D. Fathers' and mothers' responses to the faces and cries of normal and premature infants. *Developmental Psychology,* 1978, in press.

Greenberg, M., & Morris, N. Engrossment: The newborn's impact upon the father. *American Journal of Orthopsychiatry,* 1974, *44,* 520-531.

Harlow, H. F., & Zimmerman, R. R. Affectional responses in the infant monkey. *Science,* 1959, *130,* 421-425.

Heilbrun, A. B. An empirical test of the modeling theory of sex-role learning. *Child Development*, 1965, *36*, 789-799.

Hetherington, E. M. The effects of familial variables on sex typing, on parent-child similarity, and on imitation in children. In J. P. Hill (Ed.), *Minnesota symposia on child psychology*, Vol I. Minneapolis: U of Minn Pr, 1967.

Hetherington, E. M. Effects of father-absence on personality development in adolescent daughters. *Developmental Psychology*, 1972, *7*, 313-326.

Hetherington, E. M., & Deur, J. L. The effects of father absence on child development. *Young Children*, 1971, *26*, 233-248.

Hoffman, L. W. Changes in family roles, socialization and sex differences. *American Psychologist*, 1977, *34*, 644-657.

Hoffman, M. L. Moral development. In P. H. Mussen (Ed.), *Carmichael's manual of child development* (3rd ed., Vol. 2). New York: Wiley, 1970.

Johnson, M. M. Sex role learning in the nuclear family. *Child Development*, 1963, *34*, 315-333.

Klaus, M. H., & Kennell, J. H. *Parent-infant bonding*. St. Louis: Mosby, 1976.

Kotelchuck, M. *Father caretaking characteristics and their influence on infant-father interaction*. Paper presented to the American Psychological Association, Chicago, September 1975. ·

Lamb, M. E. Physiological mechanisms in the control of maternal behavior in rats: A review. *Psychological Bulletin*, 1975, *82*, 104-119.

Lamb, M. E. Effects of stress and cohort on mother- and father-infant interaction. *Developmental Psychology*, 1976, *12*, 435-443. (a)

Lamb, M. E. Interactions between eight-month-old children and their fathers and mothers. In M. E. Lamb (Ed.), *The role of the father in child development*. New York: Wiley, 1976. (b)

Lamb, M. E. Parent-infant interaction in eight-month-olds. *Child Psychiatry and Human Development*, 1976, *7*, 56-63. (c)

Lamb, M. E. The role of the father: An overview. In M. E. Lamb (Ed.), *The role of the father in child development*. New York: Wiley, 1976. (d)

Lamb, M. E. Twelve-month-olds and their parents: Interaction in a laboratory playroom. *Developmental Psychology*, 1976, *12*, 237-244. (e)

Lamb, M. E. The development of mother-infant and father-infant attachments in the second year of life. *Developmental Psychology*, 1977, *13*, 637-648. (a)

Lamb, M. E. The development of parental preferences in the first two years of life. *Sex Roles*, 1977, *3*, 495-497. (b)

Lamb, M. E. Father-infant and mother-infant interaction in the first year of life. *Child Development*, 1977, *48*, 167-181. (c)

Lamb, M. E. A reexamination of the infant social world. *Human Development*, 1977, *20*, 65-85. (d)

Lamb, M. E. The father's role in the infant's social world. In J. H. Stevens & M. Mathews (Eds.), *Mother/child, father/child relationships*. Washington, D.C.: National Association for the Education of Young Children, 1978. (a)

Lamb, M. E. The influence of the child on marital quality and family interaction during the prenatal, paranatal, and infancy periods. In R. M. Lerner & G. B. Spanier (Eds.), *Child influences on marital and family interaction: A life-span perspective.* New York: Acad Pr, 1978. (b)

Lamb, M. E. Social interaction in infancy and the development of personality. In M. E. Lamb (Ed.), *Social and personality development.* New York: HR & W, 1978. (c)

Lamb, M. E., & Stevenson, M. B. Father-infant relationships: Their nature and importance. *Youth and Society,* 1978, *9,* 277-298.

Lamb, M. E., Owen, M. T., & Chase-Lansdale, L. The father-daughter relationship: Past, present, and future. In C. B. Kopp & M. Kirkpatrick (Eds.), *Growing up female.* New York: Plenum, 1978.

Lamb, M. E., & Urberg, K. A. The development of gender role and gender identity. In M. E. Lamb (Ed.), *Social and personality development,* New York: HR & W, 1978.

Lehrman, D. S. Can psychiatrists use ethology? In N. F. White (Ed.), *Ethology and psychiatry.* Toronto: U of Toronto Pr, 1974.

LeMaho, Y. The emperor penguin: A strategy to live and breed in the cold. *American Scientist,* 1977, *65,* 680-693.

Levine, J. *And who will raise the children?* Philadelphia: Lippincott, 1976.

Lewis, M., & Weinraub, M. The father's role in the child's social network. In M. E. Lamb (Ed.), *The role of the father in child development.* New York: Wiley, 1976.

Lynn, D. B., & Cross, A. R. Parent preference of preschool children. *Journal of Marriage and the Family,* 1974, *36,* 555-559.

Margolin, G., & Patterson, G. R. Differential consequences provided by mothers and fathers for their sons and daughters. *Developmental Psychology,* 1975, *11,* 537-538.

Money, J., & Tucker, P. *Sexual signatures.* Boston: Little, 1975.

Mussen, P. H. *The psychological development of the child.* Englewood Cliffs, New Jersey: P-H, 1973.

Parke, R. D., & O'Leary, S. E. Father-mother-infant interaction in the newborn period: Some findings, some observations and some unresolved issues. In K. Riegel & J. Meacham (Eds.), *Social and environmental issues (The developing individual in a changing world, Vol. II).* The Hague: Mouton, 1976.

Parke, R. D., O'Leary, S. E., & West, S. Mother-father-newborn interaction: Effects of maternal medication, labor and sex of infant. *Proceedings of the American Psychological Association,* 1972, 85-86.

Parke, R. D., Power, T., & Gottman, J. M. Conceptualizing and quantifying influence patterns in the family triad. In M. E. Lamb, S. J. Suomi, & G. R. Stephenson (Eds.), *Social interaction analysis: Methodological issues,* Madison: U of Wisc Pr, 1978.

Parke, R. D., & Sawin, D. B. The father's role in infancy: A reevaluation. *The Family Co-ordinator,* 1976, *25,* 365-371.

Parke, R. D., & Sawin, D. B. *The family in early infancy: Social interactional and attitudinal analyses.* Paper presented to the Society for Research in Child Development, New Orleans, March 1977.

Pedersen, F. A. *Mother, father and infant as an interactive system.* Paper presented at the Annual Convention of the American Psychological Association, Chicago, September 1975.

Pedersen, F. A., Anderson, B. J., & Cain, R. L. *A methodology for assessing parental perception of infant temperament.* Paper presented to the Southeastern Conference on Human Development, Nashville, Tennessee, April 1976.

Radin, N. The role of the father in cognitive, academic, and intellectual development. In M. E. Lamb (Ed.), *The role of the father in child development.* New York: Wiley, 1976.

Redican, W. K. *A longitudinal study of behavioral interactions between adult male and infant rhesus monkeys (Macaca mulatta).* Unpublished doctoral dissertation, University of California, Davis, 1975.

Redican, W. K. Adult male-infant interactions in non-human primates. In M. E. Lamb (Ed.), *The role of the father in child development.* New York: Wiley, 1976.

Rendina, I., & Dickerscheid, J. D. Father involvement with first-born infants. *The Family Co-ordinator,* 1976, *25,* 373-379.

Rosenblatt, J. S. The development of maternal responsiveness in the rat. *American Journal of Orthopsychiatry,* 1969, *39,* 36-56.

Rubin, J. Z., Provenzano, F. J., & Luria, Z. The eye of the beholder: Parents' view on sex of newborn. *American Journal of Orthopsychiatry,* 1974, *43,* 720-731.

Schaffer, H. R., & Emerson, P. E. The development of social attachments in infancy. *Monographs of the Society for Research in Child Development,* 1964, *29* (Whole No. 94).

Spencer-Booth, Y., & Hinde, R. A. The effects of separating rhesus monkey infants from their mothers for six days. *Journal of Child Psychology and Psychiatry,* 1967, *7,* 179-197.

Suomi, S. J. Adult male-infant interactions among monkeys living in nuclear families. *Child Development,* 1977, *48,* 1255-1270.

Suomi, S. J., Eisele, C. D., Grady, S. A., & Tripp, R. L. Social preferences of monkeys reared in an enriched laboratory environment. *Child Development,* 1973, *44,* 451-560.

West, M. M., & Konner, M. J. The role of the father: An anthropological perspective. In M. E. Lamb (Ed.), *The role of the father in child development.* New York: Wiley, 1976.

Yogman, M. W., Dixon, S., Tronick, E., Adamson, L., Als, H., & Brazelton, T. B. *Development of infant social interaction with fathers.* Paper presented to the Eastern Psychological Association, New York, April 1976.

Chapter 3

THE WORKING MOTHER IN
THE INTACT FAMILY:
A PROCESS MODEL

Michael E. Lamb, Margaret Tresch Owen,
and Lindsay Chase-Lansdale

POPULAR notions regarding the effects of maternal employment on the development of young children are deeply rooted in cultural expectations concerning the responsibilities of parenthood. Historically, parental responsibilities have been divided in a sex-typed fashion. In North America, the earliest white colonists came from and sought to reestablish societies that prescribed for men primary responsibility for economically supporting their families and for women the responsibility for caring for and raising their offspring. Similar expectations characterized the social structure existing among the Native Americans who antedated the whites and within the African tribes from which our black population was drawn. These traditional sex role prescriptions did not require nor presume that married women and mothers be economically unproductive, however. On the contrary, our foremothers, like the women in contemporary hunter-gatherer societies, played a major role in the domestic economy. Proximity to and supervision of young children did not preclude responsibility for home care, gathering of fruits and berries, and the cultivation of fields within range of the home. No society could afford to consider child care as a full-time occupation for its women.

Increasing specialization, urbanization, and the decline of subsistence agriculture all had a major impact on family structure and organization. Economically productive work became something that could seldom be performed at or near the home. As a result, the opportunities for women to combine child care and working roles diminished, and fathers had to assume an increasing proportion of the responsibility for economic support of their families. Work and family roles thus became competing demands on women, whereas they had formerly comprised compatible demands. None doubted

59

which of the demands was more important. The first, major, and primary responsibility of women was to raise their children. This expectation was communicated by conventional wisdom, religious dogma, and official and unofficial guides for parents. Full-time motherhood became the goal toward which every woman was expected to strive.

The emergence of a new discipline — developmental psychology — served to enhance the perceived inviolability of these expectations. Sigmund Freud, a leading figure in establishing the area, developed a deterministic theory of child development that effectively proscribed alternative choices for responsible mothers. Freud proposed a normative theory of psychosocial development that assumed the existence of a traditional family structure, comprising a stern, aloof, breadwinning father and a nurturant, caretaking mother. Any deviation from the normative developmental pattern, argued Freud, would have dire consequences for the psychological health of the child. To further dramatize the importance of any such deviations, Freud introduced a principle that became an unquestioned tenet of subsequent theories of psychosocial development: the concept that early experiences play an especially important formative role in an individual's development.

The emergence of psychoanalysis and scientific psychology sharpened the issues regarding the roles and responsibilities of motherhood. A caretaking mother had to do more than maximize the chances of her offsprings' survival (itself a demanding task until comparatively recently); she was also responsible for shaping the personalities of the children in her care. This was a new and awesome responsibility. Consider Freud's claim, in one of the last books he was to write (1940/1949), that "a mother's importance [was] unique, without parallel, established unalterably for a whole lifetime as the first and strongest love object and as the prototype of all later love relations — for both sexes." (p. 45) If a woman failed to provide the care and experiences that only she (as full-time mother) could provide, she would probably have a major, enduring, and detrimental impact on her child's development. Traditional sex role prescriptions thus acquired a scientific justification, and the legitimate options of women were foreclosed.

·Freud's theory, for all its enormous popularity and impact, was developed on the basis of clinical experience with a few patients, none of whom were children. The emphasis on early experiences derived from the recollection of adult patients. Consideration of and experience with children seemed necessary, however, and several of Freud's followers became involved in the direct study of children. None of them came to dispute Freud's belief in the importance of early experiences.

To many clinicians and researchers, the observations now known collectively as *the maternal deprivation literature* comprised the most persuasive documentation of Freud's claim regarding the importance of the early mother-child relationship (Bowlby, 1951). The two world wars and the societal upheavals that racked Europe earlier this century orphaned numerous infants and young children. The majority of the children concerned were admitted to institutions and foundling homes. To the alarm of the well-meaning administrators, however, many of the children reared in these environments simply failed to thrive. There were repeated reports of affectless children, unwilling to interact, listlessly displaying no interest in their surroundings. This condition seemed especially common among children who were institutionalized in infancy. It was said to occur because the children concerned did not have consistent contact with an individual caretaker; each child, argued commentators like Bowlby, needed the exclusive love and care of a mother or mother-figure in order to develop psychologically. This interpretation achieved wide currency among psychoanalysts and nonanalysts alike. Most persons in the field thus came to view the data as substantial and dramatic evidence of the need for exclusive mother-infant relationships — the types of relationships that were precluded by maternal employment. More cautious theorists (Rutter, 1972) pointed out that institutionalized infants and children were deprived of more than mother-love (e.g., fathers, toys, visual and social stimulation), but they had little impact. As recently as 1975, it was argued that "many repetitions of minor separation [e.g., day care] may have effects similar in form to major separation" (Blehar, 1975, p. 294). Like institutionalization, the argument proceeds, maternal employment takes mothers away from their children, and the consequences may be similar.

In retrospect, one can state with some assurance that the interpretation by analogy was specious. Many of the effects of institutionalization appear to stem from general social and perceptual understimulation, not from maternal deprivation per se (Rutter, 1972). The analogy between day care/nursery school and institutionalization is an extremely poor one since it focuses on superficial similarities between children whose experiences have been totally different. Nevertheless, the psychoanalytic assumptions and the empirical findings appeared consistent with the societal values and prescriptions. Together they comprised a powerful inhibitor of maternal employment. It was not until the late 1950s that any substantive research was focused on the children of working mothers. The children involved in most of the early studies were of school age; there were, presumably, too few infants and preschoolers whose mothers were employed to make investigation possible.

The findings of the empirical studies of working mothers and their children will be reviewed in the section that follows. Our literature review will be selective and illustrative rather than comprehensive: Hoffman (1974) and Etaugh (1974) have recently published more detailed reviews of the evidence to which the interested reader is referred. The brevity of our review reflects our assessment that the research has not been particularly revealing. Research in this area has been scattered, scanty, and nonprogrammatic. As Hoffman (1974) noted, the field lacks articulated theories of the processes whereby maternal employment might affect children. In addition, she pointed out that most investigators have erroneously presumed that working mothers and nonworking mothers comprise homogeneous groups. Our primary goal in this chapter is to articulate a coherent theoretical framework within which the effects of maternal employment can be considered most profitably. We believe that both working and nonworking mothers comprise heterogeneous groups and propose (a) that women differ in their attitudes and values about work, career, and family; (b) that these factors interact in affecting the women's behavior; and thus (c) that they modulate the effect of maternal employment status upon children's development. Elucidation of the processes involved will be our major focus.

REVIEW OF THE LITERATURE

In the present section, we will briefly review the empirical literature on the effects of maternal employment. We will first review the evidence relating maternal employment to the development of infants and preschoolers before proceeding to a discussion of grade school, high school, and college students. Following the review, we will indicate why we feel that findings in this area have been so inconsistent and have revealed so little about the processes whereby effects on child development are mediated.

Most commentators continue to view employment of the mothers of infants and preschoolers as potentially more harmful than the employment of mothers of older children. This evaluation derives from the belief that young children require consistent and uninterrupted care from their mothers, and working mothers are, of course, absent from a large portion of the child's day. This has led psychologists to emphasize the daily separations and their likely effects on the mother-child relationship when discussing the effects of maternal employment. As noted earlier, some (e.g., Blehar, 1975) have gone so far as to regard daily and long-term (as in hospitalization and institutionalization) separations as qualitatively similar.

Most of the relevant studies have simply compared children enrolled in day care centers with those raised at home by their mothers. With one major exception (Blehar, 1975), these studies have found day care to have no demonstrable effect on the child-mother attachment (e.g., Brookhart & Hock, 1976; Feldman, 1974; Moskowitz, Schwarz, & Corsini, 1977; Roopnarine & Lamb, 1978; Doyle, 1974; Lieberman, 1976). A smaller number of studies have examined the effects of day care (and hence early extended exposure to peers) on the social skills and peer relationships of young children. Several reviews have suggested that group care leads to increased aggressiveness and/or self-assertiveness and independence (Bronfenbrenner, 1976; Ricciuti, 1976; Schwarz, 1975). Lieberman (1976) and Owen and Chase-Lansdale (1978), however, found that day care experience was unrelated to "peer competence," although Lieberman found that the amount of exposure to peers in the home neighborhood was related. The longitudinal study undertaken by Moore (1975) should have been revealing, since he followed his subjects for many years after the early group care experience. Unfortunately, however, Moore's finding that the instability and nature of alternate care in the preschool years predicted later maladjustment is rendered uninterpretable by the fact that caretaking instability was confounded with the instability of the families. In all, then, there is no evidence that early group care has a consistent or predictable effect on child development.

The studies of the relationship between adjustment and maternal employment in grade school children have yielded similarly inconsistent findings. Dits and Cambier (1966, cited by Etaugh, 1974) found poorer adjustment in the sons of working mothers than in the sons of nonworking mothers. On the other hand, Schreiner (1963, cited by Etaugh, 1974) reported no group differences, and Rabin (1965) reported that the children of working mothers were better adjusted than were the children of unemployed mothers! Further evaluation of these studies and their mutually incompatible findings is precluded by the fact that they refer (respectively) to Belgian, German, and Israeli children and are not really comparable.

The potential for paper-and-pencil assessments has ensured that many more studies of adolescents than of younger children have been reported. Unfortunately, the findings concerning adolescents are also inconsistent. For example, Brown (1970, cited by Etaugh, 1974) reported that eighth- and ninth-grade children whose mothers worked were more poorly adjusted than the sons of nonworking mothers. Nelson (1971), however, found the adjustment of ninth graders to be unaffected by maternal work status, and Fish (1970, cited by Etaugh, 1974), who used the same measuring instrument as Brown did, found no difference between college girls with working and nonworking mothers. Meanwhile, three studies (Farley, 1968; Nelson, 1971; Whitmarsh, 1965) have reported that maternal employment has favorable effects on the adjustment of adolescents. Clearly, the hypothesis that maternal employment will induce poor adjustment is inadequately substantiated by the evidence.

Another hypothesis proposes that maternal employment will adversely affect achievement by boys but will not affect achievement by girls (Nye & Hoffman, 1963). Several studies have indeed shown that the sons of working mothers perform more poorly than boys with nonworking mothers (Burchinal, 1963; Brown, 1970; Dits & Cambier, 1966; Frankel, 1964; Gold & Andres, 1978). On the other hand, several studies have shown maternal work status to be unrelated to measures of school achievement on both boys and girls (e.g., Burchinal, 1963; Keidel, 1970; Nelson, 1969; Roy, 1963; Schreiner, 1963), and Banducci (1967) found higher achievement among the sons of skilled workers and laborers and lower achievement among the sons of professionals. More importantly, several studies have shown that effects on achievement can be traced, not to maternal employment per se, but to the prestige of the mother's job and her level of education (Frankel, 1964; Jones, Lundsteen, & Michael, 1967). Since these factors are usually unassessed or uncontrolled, we do not know whether group differences on such variables might account for the inconsistency of the research findings. Again, then, we do not yet have available the evidence against which to evaluate the hypothesis relating maternal employment to filial achievement.

The evidence is fairly consistent only where it concerns the effects of maternal employment on children's sex role concepts. Since working mothers provide less traditional female role models than nonworking mothers do, one would expect children whose mothers work to have less traditional sex role attitudes than children whose mothers are full-time housekeepers and caretakers. Vogel, Broverman, Broverman, Clarkson, and Rosenkrantz (1970) found that the sons and daughters of working women attributed similar traits to men and women more than the children of nonworking mothers did. Traits that are generally gender specific were seen as characteristics of both sexes by the working mothers' children. Gold and Andres (1978) also found that grade school aged children held more egalitarian sex role attitudes when their mothers were employed than when they were unemployed. Baruch (1972) found that college women evaluated feminine competence more highly when their mothers were employed, and Douvan (1963) found that adolescent girls scored lower on the scale of traditional femininity when their mothers worked. On the other hand, two recent studies among college students (Baruch, 1972) and among the wives of graduate students (Lipman-Blumen, 1972) found no differences in sex role ideology related to maternal employment status. Only Meier (1972) found predicted differences in a study of college students. Even the evidence concerning effects on sex role attitudes and values, then, is not as consistent as one would expect.

Evaluation

Viewing together the evidence concerning adjustment, achievement, and sex role perceptions, we have to conclude that there is too much inconsistency and ambiguity for us to specify *the effects of maternal employment on child development.* One can identify several reasons why the research has been so confusing.

First, almost all the studies involving infants and preschoolers have been studies of day care rather than studies of maternal employment. The two are not synonymous — not least of all because only a small fraction (about 10%) of the substitute or alternate care used by families involves enrollment in day care centers rather than care provided by private babysitters, relatives, or *family day care* facilities. In addition, the restriction of attention to the *effects of day care* has precluded the investigation of other potentially important experiences associated with maternal employment. Children's social adjustment and their relationships with their parents are surely influenced by what occurs at home. It is thus necessary to explore those factors that are likely to influence patterns of parent-child interaction, factors such as whether the mothers work, whether they are satisfied with their work and/or with their maternal roles, how the husbands feel about their wives working, whether they participate in child care, and so on. All of these factors have been ignored in studies of day care. In fact, although these studies are believed to elucidate the effects of maternal employment, most do not even report whether the children's mothers are employed at all, let alone how long they have been employed and whether a full- or part-time job is involved.

Second, the researchers concerned make implicit assumptions about the homogeneity of the groups of children enrolled in day care. Similarly, they assume that different programs are likely to have undifferentiated effects. A few studies illustrate the untenability of these assumptions. Schwarz (1975) has pointed out that preschoolers in day care may have been cared for in a variety of facilities or modes since infancy. Prior experiences may greatly affect how children respond to day care, although pre-enrollment differences are usually not taken into account. Lieberman (1978), meanwhile, has shown that the quality of the mother-child relationship (which varied within both her day care and non-day care groups) was related to the degree of social competence evinced by the child when interacting with a peer, whereas day care enrollment was not. Finally, Owen and Chase-Lansdale (1978) found that working mothers differed in their perceptiveness of the effects on their children and that highly perceptive mothers had children who were more socially competent in interaction with peers. Viewed together, these studies confirm that the families of working mothers comprise a more psychologically heterogeneous group than past studies have implied.

The studies of older children have similarly been built upon the assumption that working and nonworking mothers comprise homogeneous groups. A common operational assumption is that all children whose mothers have ever worked at any time in the children's lives can be classified together as *children with working mothers*. The nature of the mothers' employment, the reason for it, and how long they have worked typically remain unspecified and unexplored. In fact, the children's backgrounds may differ widely in relation to these factors.

The fact that working mothers comprise a heterogeneous group has only been recognized in a *post hoc* fashion. Thus, for example, it has been reported that the daughters of working mothers favor dual-career marriages only when their mothers seemed successful in both maternal and work roles (Baruch, 1972). Yarrow, Scott, DeLeeuw, and Heinig (1962) found that role satisfaction predicted "adequacy of mothering" scores better than employment status did. Hoffman (1963) found that the children of working mothers who were satisfied with work differed from the children of nonworking mothers. It is intuitively reasonable that women's satisfaction with their role or combination of roles should allow one to differentiate among mothers regardless of their employment status. It is disturbing, however, that satisfaction is so hazily and so inconsistently defined: It has been viewed, for example, as an aspect of role strain (Douvan, 1963) or of guilt in employed mothers (Hoffman, 1963). Inconsistencies in the definition of such constructs renders inevitable the reporting of apparently inconsistent findings. Thus, satisfaction has been related to poor school performance and negative teacher ratings (Hoffman, 1963) as well as to higher academic achievement (Gold & Andres, 1978). It is evident, in other words, that meaningful research involving variables such as these must include precise and consistent operational definitions as well as clearly articulated predictions rather than *post hoc* explanations.

Summary

Most of the research reviewed in this section was undertaken with a view toward demonstrating differences between the children of mothers who work and the children of those who do not. When the researchers concerned could not find group differences, many proceeded to ask whether the children of *some* working mothers appeared to deviate from the norm. Thus, investigators have been forced to acknowledge that working mothers comprise a remarkably heterogeneous group. Unfortunately, repeated *a posteriori* recognition of this fact has not led to the design of studies in which the heterogeneity is rendered a focus of the research. Since the criteria that differentiate subgroups of working mothers attain major importance after the data are gathered rather than before, they tend to be measured less rigorously and less reliably than one would like. In addition, there tends to be inconsistency from study to study in definition of the critical differentiating variable(s). Both of these factors operate against methodological and empirical advance in this area.

We believe that the field lacks a conceptual framework that takes into account the structural variables (e.g., amount of time mother works outside the home, age of child at time of first maternal employment) and psychological variables (e.g., ideology about maternal employment, attitudes about child rearing and child development) that differentiate *both* working and nonworking women. Such a framework is essential if progress is to be made in this area, for it would permit the articulation of clear hypotheses that could be subjected to empirical scrutiny. Consequently, we will briefly outline a heuristic conceptual framework in the next section.

THE EFFECTS OF MATERNAL EMPLOYMENT
A PROCESS MODEL

In an earlier publication (Lamb, Chase-Lansdale, & Owen, 1978), we outlined a model in which elements in the decision about whether or not to work related to variations in maternal behavior and thus to effects on the child's development. Our model was originally designed to make predictions regarding maternal work status and social development in infancy, but in the pages that follow we will elaborate upon it in such a way that it makes predictions concerning the effects of maternal employment on the development of older children as well. It is, we should emphasize, only a heuristic model: The reader knows from the abbreviated review presented earlier that sufficient data do not yet exist to permit substantiation of any of the predictions. More importantly, ours is a *process* model, and the literature (as Hoffman, 1974, noted) has treated process with remarkable superficiality. Finally, we differ from most of our peers in believing that, where effects on the child's development are concerned, it is of little consequence whether or not the mother works. More important are why she chooses to work or not to work, how she feels about that decision, what arrangements are made for the child's substitute care, and how perceptive the woman is of the potential effects of working/not working on her mothering and upon her children's development.

Our presumption is that each of these affects the woman's behavior, which in turn affects her children's development. For the purposes of the present discussion, we will propose that the attitudes and values concerned exert their major impact on children via their effect on maternal sensitivity. We have developed a model with parental sensitivity as the major process variable purely in the interests of simplicity. We acknowledge readily that there are other variables that mediate parental impact on children's development. None of the candidates is as thoroughly and persuasively documented as is parental sensitivity, however, and none appears as important in mediating effects on children of such diverse ages as infants and adolescents. Furthermore, both empirical and conceptual considerations suggest that other salient dimensions of parental behavior and influence are correlated with the sensitivity dimension (Lamb & Easterbrooks, in preparation). Finally, we are attempting to present a simplified model for heuristic purposes: Empirical validation of the skeletal model will, doubtless, facilitate the development of more elaborate and complicated successors.

The key quality of sensitivity is the parent's empathic perception, understanding, and response to the immediate and age-appropriate needs of the child. Parental sensitivity thus affects the style and content of the adult's behavior in interaction with the child. Individual differences in parental sensitivity have predictable consequences for the child's development that differ depending upon the age of the child.

In infancy, parental sensitivity involves the ability to interpret the baby's signals accurately and to respond appropriately. A baby whose parents are sensitive will come to trust in their reliability and predictability and as a consequence will develop secure attachments to them (Ainsworth, Bell, & Stayton, 1974). The security of infant-parent attachment has important implications for the child's present and future development. Securely attached infants show a greater willingness to interact with other people than do those infants who are insecurely attached. As a result, securely attached infants are likely to benefit from a broader range of social experiences and will thus become more socially sophisticated. In addition, they may broaden their trust in their parents to a generalized trust of other people. Securely attached infants are also likely to be more attentive to the socializing efforts of their parents. Specifically, Lamb has argued that "the warmth that characterizes attachments increases both the salience of attachment figures as models and the reinforcing potency of their attempts to encourage or discourage its behavior . . . . In other words, secure attachments between parents and infants facilitate the types of socializing experiences stressed by learning theorists and increase the likelihood that they will have the desired effects" (Lamb, 1978, p. 38). This, of course, applies to infancy as well as to childhood.

Sensitivity toward older children is reflected in the *authoritative parenting style* described by Baumrind (1975). The authoritative parenting style is characterized by the same empathetic understanding of the child that comprises parental sensitivity in infancy. Authoritative parenting involves a willingness on the part of the parents to "meet their children as persons and maintain sufficient flexibility in the face of their children's individuality that they can learn from the latter the kind of parenting to which they will best respond" (Lamb & Baumrind, 1978, p. 54). Effective and sensitive parents are capable of guiding their children and encouraging the development of individual propensities, instead of trying to socialize by imposing alien standards. Authoritative parents are able to make age-appropriate demands and to grant the child the degree of independence (as well as the degree of support) that it is ready to assume (Lamb & Baumrind, 1978). This style of parenting stands in sharp contrast to the two other parenting styles examined by Baumrind: the authoritarian and the permissive. These two styles, although vastly different from one another in their philosophical underpinnings as well as in their implementation, represent insensitive parenting to the extent that the parents grant the child too little or too much opportunity to moderate its own behavior and to create its own principles and standards.

As with infants, sensitive parenting of older children predicts healthy social development. Baumrind's research shows that the children of authoritative parents are more socially responsive, more independent, more achievement oriented, and less aggressive than the children of either authoritarian or permissive parents.

The dimension of parental behavior that we have labelled *sensitivity*, therefore, is of central importance when discussing the consequences of effective parenting. We proposed that parental sensitivity is not an immutable personality trait; instead, we perceive it was a characteristic that is affected by attitudes, values, and the experience of parenthood. In the next several pages we will discuss those factors that are especially likely to determine the sensitivity of women who are deciding whether or not to combine work and family careers.

There are three classes of influences on maternal sensitivity that must be taken into account. First, there are factors that have to do with the woman's ideology — her attitudes regarding both maternal employment and traditional feminine goals — and the ideology of her husband, intimate peers, and the social milieu in general. Second, there are those attitudes related to the woman's opinions about the nature of child rearing and parenthood. In this latter category we are concerned, not with whether or not the woman wishes to be a mother, but with the degree of commitment she feels toward the parenting role. Third, the characteristics of the child should be taken into account. In the following section, we will briefly describe how variations in these attitudes may affect parental sensitivity.

Attitudes About Traditional and Nontraditional Career Goals

In the recent past, as noted in the introduction, women were expected to stop work outside the home from the time of their marriage or from the time that their first child was born until the completion of maternal responsibilities decades later. Sometimes this meant the resumption of part-time work upon entry of the youngest child into grade school. More often, however, it meant that employment would not be sought until the youngest child entered high school or college. In either case, there was a clear presumption that the woman's primary allegiance and responsibility were to her family and children. Child rearing was presumed to be personally satisfying and the primary source of self-esteem. Social status and career-related esteem were to be derived vicariously from her husband's career rather than from the woman's own.

A myriad of barriers to female advancement still remain, but the Women's Liberation Movement has effected major changes where women's attitudes are concerned. Where once full-time motherhood was assumed unless dire economic straits rendered this impossible, contemporary mothers and mothers-to-be must make a conscious decision about whether or not to remain employed. Motherhood remains important to most young women today; that is not the issue. What has changed is that other sources of self-esteem have become salient. It is the existence of two significant "pulls," coupled with the fear that the two roles (that of working woman and that of mother) cannot be combined successfully, that make the decision so painful and difficult. The decision itself is a complex one, typically involving several components: when to stop work, when to resume work, at what level of involvement, and so on.

Many women work because being employed contributes to their perceived self-fulfillment. Deciding to work after becoming a mother involves determining how much personal self-esteem is derived from employment (nontraditional aspiration) and how much self-esteem could be obtained by assuming and excelling solely in the maternal role (traditional aspiration). Employment may be important to some (for example, to professional women) because the job itself contributes to their sense of fulfillment. Others may find it important to feel that they are contributing to their family's financial well-being. To give up employment in either case would represent the loss of a significant source of positive self-regard. For a woman with traditional aspirations, of course, deciding not to return to work after the birth of her first child need not result in a net loss of self-esteem, since so much self-esteem is derived from successful fulfillment of the maternal role.

Several factors other than the woman's desire for self-fulfillment also affect her decision about whether or not to work. The most important of these are economic need, the age of the child(ren), and the attitudes of her husband.

Inflation and rising aspirations have combined to make a second income appear necessary to many families. Maternal employment has thus become not simply a source of self-fulfillment or "pin money," but a financial necessity. Perceived or real economic need, we should emphasize, has become a salient motivational force, not only within the lower socioeconomic classes, but also among the decidedly middle class, for whom the suburban home, second car, summer vacations, and college-educated children have become oppressively expensive for one (male) breadwinner.

Second, societal expectations, which have an important bearing on the woman's decision to work and on her evaluation of that decision, vary depending on the age of the children concerned. There is general consensus that women should not work when they have infants, whereas there is greater tolerance of maternal employment (especially part-time employment) when school-age children are involved. As a result, it is important to take the age of the child into account when evaluating the types of effects that may be involved and the extent of both personal conflict and societal pressures. The mother of school-age children is likely to experience less conflict in deciding to return to work than the mother of an infant. On the other hand, the non-working mother of older children may feel societal pressures to do more since she need not spend as much time parenting.

Paternal attitudes are also extremely important. Because this chapter has as its focus the employed mother, we will have little to say about fathers/husbands and their roles. We want to emphasize at this point, however, that husbands' attitudes are often crucial in determining how content women feel with their employment decision and how readily they are able to satisfy the seemingly incompatible demands upon them. When the husband is supportive of the wife's desire to work, he is likely to assume greater than normal responsibility for sharing child care and household chores and to be more tolerant of the inevitable lapses in performance of these tasks. When both husband and wife agree that mothers ought not to work, of course, the self-esteem of the woman who does not work will be less affected by withdrawal from employment.

Traditionally, fathers have participated less in the care and rearing of infants than in that of older children, especially older boys. Whether or not their participation is affected by maternal employment, therefore, one would predict that fathers would assume a greater proportion of parental responsibilities the older the children concerned. Needless to say, this would relieve the strain encountered by women attempting to fill two demanding roles.

The Mediating Variables

In the preceding paragraphs, we have discussed several major influences upon maternal self-esteem, resentment, and guilt in working women. In the present section, we will explain how these variables affect parental sensitivity and thus child development. We will focus only upon maternal sensitivity in this chapter, although we are well aware of the important contributions made by fathers to their children's development (*see* Chap. 2). In addition to the father's direct contributions, furthermore, the supportive attitudes and practices of a husband have a major impact on the maternal variables with which we are most concerned. If a husband is unsupportive of his working wife, she may feel guilty about her employment. Similarly, the husband's disapproval may make the nonworking woman feel unfulfilled and resentful of her infant. The effects of paternal attitudes upon maternal behavior are discussed more fully by Lamb, Frodi, Chase-Lansdale, and Owen (1978).

Any decision regarding maternal employment that results in a net loss of *self-esteem* promises to affect the woman's behavior adversely. We propose that high self-esteem is likely to be related to high parental sensitivity because the "woman who feels fulfilled is freed from self-destructive introspection and is able to focus empathically on the needs and emotions of others" (Lamb et al., 1978, p. 13). This means that the woman who chooses to return to work in order not to jeopardize her sense of personal worth may behave more sensitively when with her baby than the woman who wishes to return to work but fails to do so, perhaps because of the unsupportive attitudes of her husband, family, and/or friends. Our prediction is that self-esteem will be adversely affected by a decision to be a full-time mother unless the woman's values are such that motherhood is a source of greater self-esteem than employment is.

The woman who wishes to work but fails to do so is likely to experience, not only lower self-esteem, but also resentment of the infant. "*Resentment* is inimical to the sensitive empathic monitoring of infant signals and the execution of appropriate and contingent responses that are critically important" (Lamb et al., 1978, p. 13). Presumably, resentment occurs where there exists greater commitment to nontraditional aspirations (career) than to traditional aspirations (motherhood). The child becomes the focus of the resentment since it stands between the woman and pursuit of the goals she cherishes most.

Finally, the working woman who is committed to motherhood and believes in the formative importance of parental care is likely to feel *guilty* about her decision to work and about the possible effects of maternal employment on the child's development. The amount of guilt the woman experiences will be related to the degree of understanding and emotional support she obtains from significant others and to her own assessment of how well the maternal role is being fulfilled. We predict that, like those experiencing resentment and declining self-esteem, women who feel guilty about their employment are likely to be less sensitive in interaction with their children than women (whether employed or not) who do not experience guilt. Women who feel guilty about abandoning their children or entrusting them to someone else's care are likely to overcompensate when they are with their children. Behavioral insensitivity in these cases will be manifest in the mothers' tendency to dominate interaction with their children and to be insensitive both to age-appropriate needs for independence and to the children's signals and cues.

In sum, we propose that the individual's level of self-esteem, any resentment she feels of her children, and any guilt she feels about her employment decision together mediate the effects of the woman's attitudes and values upon her behavior in interaction with her children. The behavioral changes, in turn, affect the children's development.

Characteristics of the Child

In our view, the parents' degree of *commitment* is most likely to affect the child's development via its relationship to maternal self-esteem and guilt. Specifically, we presume that a woman who values parenthood highly is far more likely to feel that the role is fulfilling than is a woman who attributes less value to parenthood. Even when she is highly motivated to return to work yet fails to do so, a woman who is committed to parenthood is likely to experience less decline in self-esteem as a result of her unemployed status than a peer who is less committed. This is because the highly committed mother believes strongly in the importance of what she is doing.

In addition to examining the attitudes and values of the mother, it is also important to take into account the characteristics of the children concerned, particularly those characteristics loosely termed *aspects of temperament*. Parents who are looking forward to the experience of raising a child are especially likely to be distressed when faced with an intractably difficult child. What is at stake here is the parent's evaluation of her *effectance* as a mother. Any woman who has adjusted her career goals in order to perform the maternal role is likely to suffer a major decline in net personal esteem if she has a difficult child and concludes that she is performing the maternal role ineffectively. By contrast, the woman who reluctantly became a full-time mother yet is rewarded by interaction with a pliable, attractive, and even-tempered child is likely to find mothering more rewarding than anticipated. Such a woman should have her self-esteem bolstered and will be less resentful of the child than would otherwise have been the case. Notice, incidentally, that perceived effectance is determined not only by the (objectively determined) competence of the mother, but also by the characteristics of the child.

The child's temperament continues to exert a significant influence on parents' attitudes beyond the infancy period (Thomas & Chess, 1977), although the effects that occur in infancy are likely to be most dramatic. A temperamentally difficult child is likely to affect its mother's view of her competence and effectance, as well as her evaluation of how rewarding motherhood is to her.

Where perceived effectiveness as a parent is concerned, the child's developmental stage may also be an important variable. Parents may be more eager for and better suited for interaction with preschoolers than with infants, or with grade-schoolers than with adolescents. A different pattern of parenting is called for in each of the phases of childhood, and there is no reason to expect persons to be equivalently competent or satisfied at every phase.

Summary

In the preceding section, we have discussed a number of factors that, directly or indirectly, affect the mother's sensitivity to her children regardless of whether or not she is working. The factors comprise a highly interrelated complex of considerations that together influence the adult's behavior toward the child and thereby affect the child's development. To reiterate an argument made in our earlier publication (Lamb et al., 1978):

> It is clear that the most sensitive mother is one who feels that her aspirations (whether traditional or non-traditional) are *fulfilled,* who is *committed* to her [child's] development, who perceives herself as an *effective* caretaker, and who does *not* feel *guilty* about her employment status nor *resentful* of her [child's] dependency. The most sensitive mother is not necessarily the traditional non-working mother. Likewise, working and non-working mothers do not comprise homogeneous groups of insensitive (working) and sensitive (non-working) parents [as popular misconceptions propose]. (p. 22)

Macrosocietal and Extrafamilial Factors

Thus far, we have focused on the individual attitudes of the woman and her husband, with a view to elucidating how these are translated into changes in behavior that in turn affect the child's development. In the present section, we wish to explore (a) how economic factors and societal attitudes affect individual attitudes and the decisions to which they relate and (b) how the individual attitudes discussed earlier affect the choice of extrafamilial caretaking facilities.

In an earlier section, we suggested that perceived economic need may have an important bearing on how a woman and those around her evaluate her employment decision. Perceived economic need is a salient motivating factor for most young women in contemporary America. Many women feel compelled to work in order to support their families, even if their values make them have reservations about this. Our prediction is that women with both traditional and nontraditional attitudes would feel less guilty about their decision to work if it could be attributed to family financial need rather than to the goal of personal self-fulfillment. The former can be viewed as altruistic motivation, whereas the latter may be deemed selfish. *Perceived economic need*, however, is by definition a relative term, and among middle class families one could envision doubts about the reality of the perceived needs. In the lowest socioeconomic classes (i.e., in conditions of genuine poverty), we would not expect any such doubts.

The model we have elaborated is one that describes a quasi-rational decision about whether and when a mother ought to work. It would clearly be unrealistic to propose that such a process occurs under conditions of financial distress, since where there is no real choice, a decision model is irrelevant. On the other hand, we believe that some of the attitudinal variables we have described may play a salient role in a poor woman's evaluation of the effects of her employment on the child's development. Thus, these factors remain important considerations when determining why and in what way maternal employment affects child development.

In addition to differences in economic circumstances, there exist social class dissimiliarities with respect to prevailing attitudes and values. Most of the relevant data suggest that traditional definitions of women's roles are more prevalent among those from lower socioeconomic backgrounds. This means that a woman who grows up in such a milieu is likely to have traditional values herself; that is, she is likely to place a greater value on the traditional goals of motherhood than on nontraditional occupational aspirations. This increases the likelihood of role conflict and stress if economic considerations make employment desirable or necessary. Barring real (i.e., consensually defined) economic need, the husband, peer group, and community in general are likely to be supportive of traditional decisions (i.e., not to seek employment) by the lower-class woman. Thus, when a woman reluctantly chooses not to work, the attitudes of those around her may be sufficiently supportive of the decision that her self-esteem is buoyed and she is less likely to resent the child's intrusion into her life. For similar reasons, family and friends are likely to disapprove of decisions to seek or resume employment. This disapproval increases the likelihood of guilt on the part of a woman who chooses to work anyway. As in any social class, the disapproving and traditional expectations of her husband also ensure that this woman is likely to receive less help in performance of child care and household chores. Thus she is likely to be more harrassed, under greater strain, and less accessible (emotionally and temporally) to her children. She is, in short, likely to become less sensitive in interactions with her children. In addition, financial constraints undoubtedly ensure that the family is unable to afford quality child care. Therefore, the children's experiences are likely to be suboptimal both at home and in care facilities.

Up to this point, we have said little about the extrafamilial experiences of the children of working mothers. As implied by the preceding paragraph, the choice of appropriate care is another area in which the heterogeneity within the class of working mothers becomes apparent. We wish to identify, albeit cursorily, the factors that need to be taken into account when determining how various alternative care experiences may differentially affect the child's development. Before doing so, however, we want to point out that the values and attitudes discussed earlier not only predict how parents will treat their children, but also how carefully and appropriately they will select alternative care facilities. The sensitive working mother, we submit, is likely to be especially careful in her choice of a substitute care facility. She is also more likely to be perceptive of its potential effects and of the effects of her employment on the child's development (e.g., Owen & Chase-Lansdale, 1978).

By general consensus, quality substitute care involves stable, devoted, nurturant, and sensitive caretakers. In addition, difficulties are least likely to arise when the caretaker's philosophy is compatible with (or at least respectful of) the parents' child-rearing philosophy. These characteristics remain salient whether the "facility" involved is a day care center, a family day care arrangement, a private babysitter, or a resident relative. The ideal care environment affords the child as much (or more) opportunity for social interaction as its home would, as well as the opportunity for independent exploration of the environment. Compared with the average home, most caretaking arrangements permit the child to interact with and form relationships with a greater variety of individuals. In day care centers, for example, children have to learn to interact with a variety of adults, rather than just with their parents. They are also exposed to several children, of a variety of ages, from different backgrounds. Empirical and theoretical considerations indicate that these experiences are likely to have a beneficial impact on the child's development (Hartup, 1977). Before one can predict what effect extrafamilial experiences will have on young children, however, one must take into account the stability and quality of the caretaking staff, the ratio of caretakers to children, the age at which the children were enrolled, the age and number of other children, the match between the parents' and the institution's philosophies, and the degree of respect each shows for the other's competence, responsibilities, and beliefs.

The heterogeneity among the extrafamilial environments to which children are exposed is likely to be especially impressive where infants and preschoolers are concerned. School-age children, regardless of their mothers' employment status, spend most of their days in the care of a monolithic child care facility, the public school. Schools provide almost a full day's worth of care that is very similar regardless of the attitudes and values of the children's parents.

CONCLUSION

In this chapter, we have cursorily reviewed the available evidence concerning the effects of maternal employment on child development. The inconclusive and inconsistent nature of the evidence precludes the authors' making practical suggestions on social policy recommendations based on the empirical evidence. The only statement one can make with confidence is that maternal employment per se does not affect child development in any predictable or consistent fashion. We believe that it is unprofitable for developmental psychologists to ask whether or not a woman is employed when seeking information about effects on the child's development. Instead, we need to ask why she is employed, what her attitudes are, how she feels about her performance of work and family roles, what her family's economic circumstances are, and what sorts of relationships she has established with her spouse and children. The availability of data of this nature will permit us to elucidate the processes whereby maternal employment affects child development. When the processes are better understood, we will be in a better position to discuss implications and to offer informed recommendations to legislators and others involved in social policy formation.

REFERENCES

Ainsworth, M. D., Bell, S. M., & Stayton, D. J. Infant mother attachment and social development: Socialization as a product of reciprocal responsiveness to signals. In M. P. Richards (Ed.), *The integration of the child into a social world.* Cambridge: Cambridge U Pr, 1974.

Banducci, R. The effect of mother's employment on the achievement, aspirations, and expectations of the child. *Personnel and Guidance Journal,* 1967, *46,* 263-267.

Baruch, G. K. Maternal influences upon college women's attitudes toward women and work. *Developmental Psychology,* 1972, *6,* 32-37.

Baumrind, D. *Early socialization and the discipline controversy.* Morristown, New Jersey: Gen Learn Pr, 1975.

Blehar, M. C. Anxious attachment and defensive reactions associated with day care. In U. Bronfenbrenner & M. A. Mahoney (Eds.), *Influences on human development* (2nd ed.). New York: HR&W, 1975.

Bowlby, J. *Maternal care and mental health.* Geneva: WHO, 1951.

Bronfenbrenner, U. *Research on the effects of day care.* Unpublished manuscript, Cornell University, 1975.

Brookhart, J., & Hock, E. The effects of experimental context and experiential background on infants' behavior toward their mothers and a stranger. *Child Development,* 1976, *47,* 333-340.

Brown, S. W. *A comparative study of maternal employment and non-employment.* Unpublished doctoral dissertation, Michigan State University, 1970.

Burchinal, L. B. Personality characteristics of children. In F. I. Nye & L. W. Hoffman (Eds.), *The employed mother in America.* Chicago: Rand, 1963.

Dits, A., & Cambier, A. L'absence de la mère tors du retour de l'enfant de l'école. *Enfance,* 1966, *1,* 99-111.

Douvan, E. Employment and the adolescent. In F. I. Nye & L. W. Hoffman (Eds.), *The employed mother in America.* Chicago: Rand, 1963.

Doyle, A. B. Infant development in day care. *Developmental Psychology,* 1975, *11,* 655-656.

Etaugh, C. Effects of maternal employment on children: A review of recent research. *Merrill-Palmer Quarterly,* 1974, *20,* 71-98.

Farley, J. Maternal employment and child behavior. *Cornell Journal of Social Relations,* 1968, *3,* 58-71.

Feldman, S. S. *The impact of day care on one aspect of children's social-emotional behavior.* Paper presented to the American Association for the Advancement of Science, San Francisco, February 1974.

Fish, K. D. *Paternal availability, family role structure, maternal employment, and personality development in late adolescent females.* Unpublished doctoral dissertation, University of Massachusetts, 1970.

Frankel, E. Characteristics of working and non-working mothers among intellectually gifted high and low achievers. *Personnel and Guidance*

Journal, 1964, *42,* 776-780.

Freud, S. *An outline of psychoanalysis* (1940). New York: Norton, 1949.

Gold, D., & Andres, D. Developmental comparisons between ten-year-old children with employed and non-employed mothers. *Child Development,* 1978, *49,* 75-84.

Hartup, W. W. Peer interaction and the processes of socialization. In M. J. Guralnick (Ed.), *Early intervention and the integration of handicapped and non-handicapped children.* Baltimore: Univ Park, 1977.

Hoffman, L. W. Mother's enjoyment of work and effects on the child. In F. I. Nye & L. W. Hoffman (Eds.), *The employed mother in America.* Chicago: Rand, 1963.

Hoffman, L. W. Effects of maternal employment on the child — A review of the research. *Developmental Psychology,* 1974, *10,* 204-228.

Jones, J. B., Lundsteen, S. W., & Michael, W. B. The relationship of the professional employment status of mothers to reading achievement of sixth grade children. *California Journal of Educational Research,* 1967, *18,* 102-108.

Keidel, K. C. Maternal employment and ninth grade achievement in Bismarck, North Dakota. *Family Coordinator,* 1970, *19,* 95-97.

Lamb, M. E. Social interaction in infancy and the development of personality. In M. E. Lamb (Ed.), *Social and personality development.* New York: HR&W, 1978.

Lamb, M. E., & Baumrind, D. Socialization and personality development in the preschool years. In M. E. Lamb (Ed.), *Social and personality development.* New York: HR&W, 1978.

Lamb, M. E., Chase-Lansdale, L., & Owen, M. T. The changing American family and its implications for infant social development: The sample case of maternal employment. In M. Lewis & L. A. Rosenblum (Eds.), *The child and its family.* New York: Plenum Pub, 1978.

Lamb, M. E., & Easterbrooks, M. A. Individual differences in parental sensitivity: Some thoughts about origins, components, and consequences. In M. E. Lamb & L. R. Sherrod (Eds.), *Infant social cognition: Empirical and theoretical considerations,* Hillsdale, New Jersey: Lawrence Erlbaum Associates, in press.

Lamb, M. E., Frodi, A. M., Chase-Lansdale, L., and Owen, M. T. *The father's role in the non-traditional family context: Direct and indirect effects.* Paper presented to the American Psychology Association, Toronto, September 1978.

Lieberman, A. F. *The social competence of preschool children: Its relations to quality of attachment and to amount of exposure to peers in different preschool settings.* Unpublished doctoral dissertation, The Johns Hopkins University, 1976.

Lieberman, A. F. Preschoolers' competence with a peer: Relations with attachment and peer experience. *Child Development,* 1977, *48,* 1277-1287.

Lipman-Blumen, J. How ideology shapes women's lives. *Scientific American,* 1972, *226,* 34-42.

Meier, H. C. Mother-centeredness and college youths' attitudes toward social equality for women: Some empirical findings. *Journal of Marriage and the Family*, 1972, *34*, 115-121.

Moore, T. W. Exclusive early mothering and its alternatives. *Scandinavian Journal of Psychology*, 1975, *16*, 255-272.

Moskowitz, D. S., Schwarz, J. C., & Corsini, D. A. Initiative day care at three years of age: Effects on attachment. *Child Development*, 1977, *48*, 1271-1276.

Nelson, D. D. A study of school achievement among adolescent children with working and nonworking mothers. *Journal of Educational Research*, 1969, *62*, 456-458.

Nelson, D. D. A study of personality adjustment among adolescent children with working and nonworking mothers. *Journal of Educational Research*, 1971, *64*, 328-331.

Nye, F. I., & Hoffman, L. W. (Eds.). *The employed mother in America.* Chicago: Rand, 1963.

Owen, M. T., & Chase-Lansdale, L. *Maternal employment and its relationship to the peer competence of preschoolers.* Unpublished manuscript, 1978.

Rabin, A. I. *Growing up in the Kibbutz.* New York: Springer-Verlag, 1965.

Ricciuti, H. *Effects of infant day care experience on behavior and development: Research and implications for social policy.* Unpublished manuscript, Cornell University, October 1976.

Roopnarine, J., & Lamb, M. E. The effects of day care on attachment and exploratory behavior in a strange situation. *Merrill-Palmer Quarterly*, 1978, *24*, 85-95.

Roy, P. Adolescent roles: Rural-urban differentials. In F. I. Nye & L. W. Hoffman (Eds.), *The employed mother in America.* Chicago: Rand, 1963.

Rutter, M. *Maternal deprivation reassessed.* Harmondsworth, England: Penguin, 1972.

Schreiner, M. Auswirkungen mutterlicher Erwebstatigkeit auf die Entwidklugen von Grundschulkindern. *Archiv fur die Gesamte Psychologie*, 1963, *115*, 334-382.

Schwarz, J. C. *Social and emotional effects of day care: A review of recent research.* Paper presented to the study group on The Family and Social Change, Ann Arbor, Michigan, October 1975.

Thomas, A., & Chess, S. *Temperament and development.* New York: Bruner/Mazel, 1977.

Vogel, S. R., Broverman, I. K., Broverman, D. M., Clarkson, F. E., & Rosenkrantz, P. S. Maternal employment and perception of sex roles among college students. *Developmental Psychology*, 1970, *3*, 384-391.

Whitmarsh, R. E. Adjustment problems of adolescent daughters of employed mothers. *Journal of Home Economics*, 1965, *57*, 201-204.

Yarrow, W. R., Scott, P., DeLeeuw, L., & Heinig, C. Child-rearing in families of working and nonworking mothers. *Sociometry*, 1962, *25*, 122-140.

Chapter 4

GENERAL ISSUES IN WORKING WITH PARENTS OF HANDICAPPED CHILDREN

FRANK J. CANINO AND RONALD E. REEVE

INTRODUCTION

I T is common knowledge that our society includes a number of children with unusual physical or psychological limitations for whom traditional methods of education are inappropriate and/or insufficient. Certainly this is not a new insight. Only within the past 10 years, however, has this recognition been followed through to the point of action in the form of mandatory special educational programming for all handicapped children. Even less societal and professional attention has been directed toward the equally obvious difficulties involved in *parenting* an unusual, atypical child. Few parents feel adequately prepared for the challenges offered in raising normal children. Clearly the special problems involved in parenting when the child is not normal can make the already difficult task of being a good parent seem to be an impossibility. These parents of special children often need help.

The purpose of this chapter is to provide an orientation to the psychological reactions and continuing psychological needs of parents of handicapped children. The children are regarded as "exceptional" because their intellectual, emotional, physical, and/or social needs are sufficiently different from the majority of children within our society that they call for modifications of the usual child-rearing practices and professional services offered (e.g., medicine, psychology, guidance, education, and vocational training). The significance of an exceptionality, especially if diagnosable at birth, lies in part in its ability to drastically alter parents' perceptions of themselves and, consequently, their behavior toward the child. By focusing on the dynamic interplay between parental attitudes, values, and expectations with family processes, it will become clear that the impact of the child's condition and the parents' and siblings' perception of it are inextricably linked such that anything that affects the child also influences the child's family.

PARENTAL REACTION TO THE BIRTH
OF A SERIOUSLY HANDICAPPED CHILD

It is difficult to understand the significance of giving birth to a handicapped infant without recognizing the impact of a healthy child on the lives of parents. The meanings that parenthood acquires — its expectations and goals, its joys of giving and sharing — come about as a result of the parents watching the mystery of life unfold and knowing that they are in a critical sense responsible for it.

In the preparation for parenthood, both parents develop an expectation of what the child will be like. As Solnit and Stark (1961) have suggested, this is a normal anticipatory process in which the parents' image of the expected infant represents an amalgam of perceptions of self and significant other people in their past (e.g., mother, father, spouse, siblings, and previous children). Because of the powerful psychosociological influences and cultural values, expectant parents are deeply motivated to anticipate the birth of an "ideal" child. Their stereotypical beliefs will imbue the infant with a broad range of idealistic attributes, qualities, and expectations necessary for the child to "compete successfully and to assume the roles society assigns him and his parents' fantasy for him" (Ross, 1964, pp. 55-56). Parents typically hope that their child will surpass their own accomplishments and attain a higher level of sociocultural achievement.

For parents, the birth of a child represents a product of labor, a personal achievement: "Look what we've made!" In the case of the birth of an obviously handicapped child, a dramatic discrepancy exists between the "expected" and "real" infant, and an intense emotional crisis almost invariably develops (Baum, 1962; Irvine, 1974; Meadow & Meadow, 1971; Solnit & Stark, 1961; Wolfensberger, 1967). Parents frequently respond to the sudden loss of their desired "ideal" child as if they had experienced the death of a healthy child. Quite often, the birth of a handicapped child elicits strong internalized feelings of resentment and self-depreciation: "We've failed!" "We aren't any good." A child in many ways represents an extension of a parent's self. The capacity to produce unimpaired offspring is psychologically and culturally important for the parent's sense of personal adequacy.

In the literature, an almost infinite variety of parental reactions to having a handicapped child are posited, e.g., alarm, ambivalence, anger, avoidance, confusion, death wishes, denial, depression, disappointment, envy, fear, grief, guilt, helplessness, mutual dependency, self-blame, suicidal-homicidal impulses, etc. The list is not exhaustive, nor is it exclusively peculiar to parents of exceptional children. Rather, it serves to illustrate the diversity between and within normal individuals in responding to an external threat to their own personality integration (Baum, 1962; Meadow & Meadow, 1971; Telford & Sawrey, 1977; Wolfensberger, 1967). For the purposes of this review, several of the more prominent parental reactions will be discussed as they are significant to an understanding of the adjustment process.

Ross (1964) is one of several authors (e.g., Solnit & Stark, 1961; Baum, 1962; Tisza, 1962) who view *mourning* as a parental reaction to the birth of a defective baby. In classical Freudian psychology, grief and its behavioral manifestation, mourning, are normal reactions to the sudden loss of a valued object (in this case, the expected ideal child) (Freud, 1917/1957). Mourning the loss of the normal baby they had anticipated, the parents temporarily withdraw from the outside world to allow their egos (considered to be the core of the personality) to concentrate on withdrawing psychic energy (cathexis) from the lost object in which they had invested so much energy.

The mourning or grieving process is conceptualized as consisting of a series of stages in a recurring sequence. During the mourning process, highly charged parental longings for the idealized child are recalled, intensely experienced, and gradually discharged to reduce the impact of the loss. The amount of time required to complete the mourning may vary markedly from person to person, most commonly taking a year or two, and the resolution may never be complete. Stages usually included are shock and denial, grief, guilt, anger and hostility, withdrawal and overprotection, and eventually realistic acceptance and some semblance of stability.

Whether or not "mourning" occurs in the classical sense, it is clear that many parents do experience one and usually more of the responses included in that process.

When parents are first told that they have a retarded or otherwise handicapped child, their initial reaction is frequently one of *denial*. Through denial they are able to treat the obvious as though it does not exist. The reaction is "The doctor is wrong." Apparently some families in this situation then begin looking for a doctor who will tell them that their child is normal. As the child grows older, parents may cling to denial by telling themselves "He'll grow out of it."

Individuals who speak of fantasy cures, relatives (e.g., grandparents) who stress the child's assets while ignoring limitations, family members who are looking for someone to blame or scapegoat, or professionals who emphasize diagnostic imprecision and limitations of knowledge significantly contribute toward postponing the parents' confrontation with reality by increasing their uncertainty (Gayton, 1975). Unwittingly raising false hopes, these individuals compound the concerned professional's difficulty in assisting parents in coping with the realistic problems of rearing an exceptional child. Consequently, the task of recognizing and helping parents to work through their intense negative feelings is often lost in the process.

Feelings of *grief* are invariably present. Grief is a profound sadness born out of the realization that one's hopes, dreams, expectations, and anticipated joys of parenthood have been abruptly altered. Because it is unexpected, the experience is traumatizing. Once the initial shock and denial wear off, grief normally follows. Weeping and other signs of grief should not be considered as unhealthy responses. In fact, the omission of grief is as much a variation from normal as are excessively prolonged or intense reactions. Some evidence exists from psychoanalytic studies that unmanifested grief often is expressed in some other way and could result in a state of severe, continuing anxiety (Hollingsworth & Pasnau, 1977).

Probably the most pervasive reaction, one that is at least partly evident in every other reaction, is the feeling of *guilt*. The parents alone were responsible for the child's conception, and if the infant is abnormal, then there is an understandable tendency for them to feel that the fault is theirs. Although it is a rare occurrence, sometimes the parents are the actual cause of the defect, as in instances where they have attempted abortion and thereby damaged the fetus. More often, the guilt centers around less realistic acts or omissions, such as sexual activity during pregnancy, alcohol consumption, smoking, falls early in pregnancy, etc.

With the passage of time and the acknowledgment that their child is handicapped, parents begin to feel the stirrings of *anger*, and if not controlled, the anger grows into *hostility*. Unlike grief or guilt, hostility is an emotion that is directed outward. For this to occur, a reason to blame someone for having committed a mistake needs to be found. Parental attention thus turns to ascertaining the cause of their child's deficiency and the person responsible — doctor, therapist, teacher, spouse, relative, or even the child.

Unchecked feelings of hostility seldom simply go away. Rather, without help, such feelings may intensify. In the case of parents of handicapped children, anger results in hostility because with each new crisis or frustration, parents are unable to find a rational way to blame the child. This results in parental feelings of resentment toward the child for having so drastically changed their lives, which may then be translated into a conscious and overt wish that the child would die or never have been born (Pueschel & Murphy, 1975). The hostility, in some cases, is expressed directly in the form of excessive punishment of the child's misdeeds. Less direct expression may occur when parents aggressively administer unpleasant medications or insist on the child's slavish adherence to an overly vigorous physical therapy routine. Such behaviors represent direct or indirect expressions of parental resentment toward the child.

Hostility toward the child also evokes tremendous guilt. The child may indeed be frustrating, but chronic anger toward one's handicapped child is psychologically unacceptable. The parents feel a need to deny that they are angry at the child, and they therefore turn the anger inward, producing guilt.

The frustration and anger generated by the handicapped child's presence all too often becomes directed by parents toward the normal siblings. These children frequently are accused of being uninterested in, lazy regarding assistance in the care of, and insensitive to the needs of their handicapped brother or sister. Thus, they may become scapegoats for the negative feelings parents have toward the handicapped child and/or toward themselves. In this regard, it is interesting and disconcerting to note that, while there are too few services available for parents of handicapped children, such services are almost nonexistent for normal siblings of such children.

Even in the best of parents, and even with normal children, ambivalent feelings of acceptance and rejection toward children are common experiences. Despite the presence of love, empathy, forgiveness, and gentleness, parental attitudes typically have undertones of resentment, indifference, faultfinding, and selfishness. For the parents of a handicapped child, ambivalent emotions (usually unacknowledged and unconscious) give rise to disguised forms of parental rejection culminating in parental attitudes and behaviors that are detrimental to the child (Schild, 1971). Here, parents are torn between wanting to consciously atone for their negative reactions and unconsciously wanting to rid themselves of their child (Pueschel & Murphy, 1975).

Several manifestations of ambivalence are common. Parental refusal to recognize the child's condition as permanent by mistaking a spurt in growth as evidence that their child is not handicapped, or that the condition has been overcome, may result in parents' rejecting plans for the child's rehabilitation or training. Less obvious is the instance of the parent who sacrifices everything for the sake of the handicapped child, leading in effect to a life of parental martyrdom.

Closely related to this, and sometimes a component of parental martyrdom, is a lack of parental affection toward the child. This lack of affection, however, may be subtly disguised as good care or concern, which the parents consciously or unconsciously feel to be adequate substitutes for love.

Two other commonly mentioned reactions are often coincidental. The first, *withdrawal*, may occur immediately following the birth of the abnormal child. Sometimes the initial shock is so severe that the parents are unable to function at home or in the community (Kozier, 1957). The parent may try to leave the baby in the hospital indefinitely or may deny the baby's physical needs. Such withdrawal could also be called *disorganization*, and it is closely related to denial. When the parents begin to recover their ability to function, they may still withdraw from the community. In this case, *overprotection* is common. Due to a combination of other reactions — denial, hostility toward self and toward child, and guilt — the parents may devote themselves so completely to the child that they cut themselves off from all other life experiences.

Overprotection may take the form of preoccupation with the care of the child. The parents may become extremely compulsive concerning punctual administration of medications, supervision of prescribed exercises, careful cleaning of the child, etc., even to the exclusion of considerations regarding their other children's needs. This reaction may be an unconscious attempt to make up for whatever they have done to cause the child's defect. It is an attempt to "undo," by overprotection, the damage they have "caused."

Whenever parents invest an extraordinary amount of time devoting themselves entirely to satisfying the needs of their child, a condition of mutual dependency can develop. Parents of handicapped children are exceedingly prone to feel overanxious, which can readily foster overdependency in the handicapped child. Maternal overprotection stems from a distortion of the realistic needs of the child. A number of antecedent parental feelings (e.g., guilt, anger, and frustration) are responsible for initiating parental behavior that is neither habilitative nor psychologically healthy for the child. Excessive care only fosters a self-perpetuating cycle that, while satisfying the parents' neurotic insecurities, will lead to inadequate growth for the child. Moreover, as the child grows, s/he will respond to this dependency system by emphasizing incapacities, ceasing to perform activities of which s/he is capable, accentuating parental guilt, and becoming more demanding (Telford & Sawrey, 1977). Once this behavior becomes incorporated as part of the child's functional dependency system, the cycle is deeply entrenched and exceedingly difficult to change. Ultimately, a real dependency ensues as a consequence of physical and emotional atrophy.

Though the psychological loss of the idealized child can be considered as functionally equivalent to the death of a child, there is an important difference in the case of the birth of a handicapped child. That difference makes the mourning reaction more difficult to work through. The difference, of course, is that in the case of a stillbirth, the parents are able to resolve their grief in peace. In the case of the birth of an exceptional child, the parents must work through the crises raised by the discrepancy between the anticipated idealized child and the reality of their defective offspring while simultaneously adapting to the needs of their child. Frequently, the demands of love and attention by the abnormal child overwhelm parents, so that there is no time to work through the loss of the idealized infant.

Some controversy exists among investigators in this area about whether or not fathers and mothers differ in the type and intensity of their reactions to the birth of a handicapped child. It is clear that, by the nature of the reproductive process, the mother is more involved in the pregnancy and birth process. Mothers often report, for example, that they felt an emotional attachment to their child even prenatally as a result of carrying the child throughout pregnancy. Given the mother's significantly greater part in producing the child, it is reasonable to expect that the intensity of her reaction to the birth of a defective child will be greater. She is more likely to view herself as damaged or unworthy of motherhood. She may see the child as something she produced for the husband, a gift for him, and society does not condone imperfect gifts. Thus it would be expected that the mother's reaction be more severe and prolonged than is the father's. Either parent, of course, may see the child as a symbol of status as an adult, as proof of manhood or womanhood. Especially if the handicapped child is their first, they may feel crushed, unworthy, and perhaps impotent. Sexual advances may be rejected (Wentworth, 1974). Feelings such as these place a tremendous strain on the husband-wife relationship.

The reaction of parents to the birth of a handicapped child depends, not only upon the parents' past experiences and personalities, but also on the implicit meaning that the exceptional child symbolizes for them. The various psychological responses provide an opportunity for the ego to regain its integrity during the crisis period. "Mechanisms of defense become organized and called upon during the period and the end of mourning will bring with it the reestablishment of a homeostatic personality balance which is manifested by the appearance of individually suited defensive modes" (Ross, 1964, p. 61).

In some cases, the ego may become so overwhelmed and unable to cope with crisis that an extended period of postpartum depression develops. In relation to this, Olshansky (1962) suggested that parents of handicapped children are continually overwrought with "chronic sorrow" throughout their lives. Unable to gain respite from their child's incessant demands and unrelenting dependency needs, relief from such despair comes only in their death or the death of the child. Often parental guilt, anger, and denial are intertwined with chronic sorrow.

Despite the insight provided by Olshansky's "chronic sorrow" concept, it appears that many parents of handicapped children are able, given time and a reasonable amount of support, to move to a final stage in response to their child. This final stage, which can be called *adjustment*, is marked by parental ability to meet the crises of personal frustration and conflict in a realistic, well-integrated way, much as they meet other challenges and stresses in their lives. The major factors in coping successfully with the problems of the handicapped child seem to be that the child is accepted as s/he is by both parents; that the child not be excluded from family activities nor hidden from the outside world; that each parent continue to function in his/her usual manner, maintaining outside interests and associations with friends; that each partner nurture the wife-to-husband relationship by sharing responsibilities and seeking to understand each other's feelings; and that both parents meet the needs of their normal children as well as those of the exceptional child (Telford & Sawrey, 1977).

In this section, the focus has been on a classic situation, the reactions of parents to the birth and childhood of seriously handicapped children. This rather narrow focus is justified, it is felt, because of the dramatic and sustained impact that results from these situations and because such cases are not uncommon. However, it is important to note that many children who are considered handicapped by the time they reach school age never appeared markedly different from normal, at least not in the dramatic manner of those discussed earlier. Certainly parental reactions to these milder, less obvious handicaps would be quite different.

Very little literature is available describing how parents respond in cases of milder handicaps. Certainly the mourning reaction, resulting from the sudden loss of a highly valued object, does not occur, at least not in the classical sense. Some minimal mourning response may follow the identification and labeling of the handicap, however. Many parents appear to respond with something similar to the denial-grief-anger-guilt-ambivalence-adjustment process characteristic of parents' reactions to severe handicaps diagnosable at birth. However, the intensity of the response is much less severe, and the duration is much shorter. The adjustment process is thus significantly less difficult in these situations.

The relatively easier adjustment in cases of mild handicaps also may be in part because the parents have had a number of years of experience with the child during which their suspicions about the child's difficulties have had a chance to develop. It is a common experience for school-related personnel (school psychologists, special educators, school social workers), when they meet with parents to inform them that their child is handicapped and in need of special educational programming, to learn that the parents had harbored strong indications of such problems for years. This opportunity for gradual recognition of their child's deficiencies clearly lessens the shock value of the "handicapped" diagnosis.

IMPACT ON FAMILY INTEGRITY

It is becoming increasingly clear that the presence of a handicapped child importantly influences family stability. Tew, Payne, and Laurence (1974) have found a marked deterioration of the marital relationship over the years in families of spina bifida children. Of the 59 couples interviewed, only 1 in 4 appeared to be free of marital difficulty. The divorce rate in these families was twice that of controls and of the national average. The findings of this study and others (e.g., Begab, 1971; Wentworth, 1974) strongly suggest that the stresses of raising a handicapped child increase the risk of matrimonial disharmony and predispose the couple to separation or divorce.

In a recent review by Soeffing (1975), the consequences of a failing marital relationship associated with the demands of raising a handicapped child were seen as suspected factors in the physical abuse and psychological neglect of handicapped children. To date, no major research has linked the existence of a handicap as a direct, causative factor of abuse and/or neglect. However, the studies reviewed by Soeffing indicated a correlation, suggesting that the handicapped child qualifies as an abuse risk. This was attributed to the finding that abused children are often seen by their parents as different and difficult to raise.

Studies of parents' attitudes toward their handicapped children have supported the aforementioned statement and have indicated that such attitudes may become reflected directly in parental behavior (Worchel & Worchel, 1961). Wetter (1972) observed that among 70 couples with learning problem children — physically handicapped, emotionally disturbed, and mentally retarded — greater indications of parental overindulgence and rejection toward the child·were present than among controls. Similarly, Bryant (1971) found that the most frequently observed parent-child relationships among parents of hand-icapped children were acceptance, rejection and compensation. Of these, compensation, a combination of acceptance and rejection of the child's problem, impeded habilitation and rehabilitation the most.

Parental self-concept appears to influence maternal acceptance, liking, and respect of the .child (Irvine, 1974; Ross, 1964; Wolfens-berger, 1967). Fishman and Fishman (1971) found that a mother's level of self-esteem was specifically related to the point at which she learned of the handicap, her willingness to talk openly with the child about his/her handicap and related issues, and her desire to encourage the child's movement toward independence and achievement.

Finally, family stability is frequently jeopardized when the handi-capped child continually intrudes on the lives of family members. Cleveland and Miller (1977) determined that the existence of a severely retarded sibling influenced the life commitments and attitudes of older siblings. A questionnaire constructed to elicit childhood and adolescence recollections while also soliciting information about the effect their retarded brother or sister had on their own marriage, family, and career was given to 90 men and women. The results of the study provided two major findings. The first indicated that, as re-membered by these siblings, most parents apparently possessed ade-quate resources to cope with the problems of a retarded child while at the same time providing a supportive environment for the proper development of their normal children. This study also supported earlier work (e.g., Love, 1970; Begab, 1971; Wentworth, 1974) that suggested that siblings are apt to reflect the parents' attitudes, values, and conflicts.

The second important finding of the Cleveland and Miller study was a sex role difference in the adjustment and career orientation of siblings. The responses of males revealed that they were uninformed about their retarded sibling's condition during childhood and that this relative ignorance continued into adulthood. Conversely, females demonstrated more direct and continuous involvement in caring for their mentally handicapped brother or sister. This was found to be especially true for the oldest female sibling in the family. She was more likely to function as a surrogate parent, and she later demonstrated a preference for choosing a "helping" career in adulthood. However, the data from this study indicated that the increased responsibility assumed by the oldest female produced some adverse effects. She was more likely to be in need of counseling or to have sought professional help in the past. Overall, female siblings of the retarded reported experiencing more stress and less parental attention in their childhood years than males. This conclusion could be interpreted as placing females at risk psychologically due to their more intense exposure to the retarded child. In relation to this, Telford and Sawrey (1977) have suggested that the risk of emotional disturbance among normal siblings is greatest when the exceptional child monopolizes parental attention to the exclusion of other siblings.

The following conclusions can be drawn from the literature dealing with the emotional adjustment of nonhandicapped siblings. There is no strong evidence to suggest that the siblings of the handicapped are either better or more poorly adjusted than siblings of normal children (Wolfensberger, 1967). Whether the impact of a handicapped child is to be detrimental to a sibling's development appears to depend on the attitudes exhibited by the parents (Love, 1970). This is because the reaction of siblings in large measure depends on their perception of parental attention or lack of attention. As described by Wentworth (1974), the nonhandicapped child's personality development depends on such factors as consistency of parental affection, parental recognition of each of their children as separate identities, parental honesty, and a recognition that siblings do experience the same basic reactions (resentment, hostility, shame, denial, guilt, and grief) as parents, but that they may manifest their feelings differently.

MITIGATING PSYCHOSOCIAL FACTORS

It is important to emphasize that there is no such thing as a "typical" parent of a handicapped child. Reactions to the birth of an abnormal child vary greatly. Among the factors that have been found to alter the initial reaction and subsequent adjustment process are the following: social class and socioeconomic status (Farber & Jenne, 1963; Holt, 1958; Meadow & Meadow, 1971) religion (Liberthson, 1968; Telford & Sawrey, 1977; Zuk, 1959), birth order (Solnit & Stark, 1961; Wolfensberger, 1967), parental age (Meadow & Meadow, 1971), sex of the handicapped child (Wolfensberger, 1967), nature and type of handicap (Telford & Sawrey, 1977; Wentworth, 1974), and the presence of other siblings (Begab, 1971; Cleveland & Miller, 1977; Telford

& Sawrey, 1977; Wolfensberger, 1967). The literature in this area is far from conclusive and not without methodological imperfection. Nonetheless, some generalizations follow.

Though many exceptions have been noted, it appears that, in general, the greater the degree of handicap and the higher the social class of the family, the more difficult the initial adjustment process (Davis, 1963; Downey, 1963). This probably is because middle- and especially upper-class parents have higher expectations for their children. Also, with lower-class parents, the problems associated with having an exceptional child must "get in line" to compete for attention with other concerns, such as paying the bills.

With respect to parents' age, there is a greater chance that older mothers will give birth to a handicapped child. This child, especially if not planned, may cause more serious disruption in the stability of the marriage than if born to younger parents (Meadow & Meadow, 1971). On the other hand, younger parents are more likely to be faced with financial difficulties and the imperatives of establishing careers, thus increasing their burdens. Overwhelmed by feelings of inadequacy, they may rush to have another child to prove that they are fit parents, thereby further complicating matters.

The nature of the handicap (e.g., physical versus intellectual) importantly influences the severity of parental reactions (Ross, 1964; Telford & Sawrey, 1977). Ambiguous handicaps, that is, those that are less socially visible (e.g., mild hearing impairment or borderline intellectual capacity) are also less stigmatizing and therefore easier to deal with than ones of high visibility (e.g., blindness or orthopedic dysfunction). Yet even low-visibility handicaps present unique problems for these parents, who frequently believe that their children would be normal if only they tried harder. Telford and Sawrey (1977) commented that the general public similarly attributes a minimally handicapped child's poor performance to lack of interest or attention or to sheer apathy. Consequently, the child who deviates least from what is expected is increasingly prone to encounter less understanding and support from significant others in his/her life.

The degree to which families can avail themselves of professional assistance beyond that of family support significantly influences their ability to cope. The role of religious orientation in this process as yet remains poorly defined (Meadow & Meadow, 1971). Early research indicated that Catholics adjusted easier than members of other religious groups (Zuk, 1959), but contradictory evidence has appeared (Wolfensberger, 1967). Religion probably provides a degree of solace, and at least it often offers another organized support system in the community (Wentworth, 1974).

The presence of normal children in the home generally seems to be beneficial to the parents' adjustment (Telford & Sawrey, 1977). Normal children provide an outlet for the parents' needs for vicarious success experiences, other children may assist in caring for the handicapped child, and they help the parents to a more realistic understanding of the degree of handicap present in the exceptional child by providing a yardstick of normal development for comparison.

PARENT-PROFESSIONAL RELATIONSHIP

The literature in this area suggests that the parent-professional relationship is frequently unfortunate and too often quite destructive. Poor professional conduct ranging from well-meaning but misinformed or misdirected behavior by psychologists, physicians, and special educators (Clements & Alexander, 1975; Gayton, 1975) to negligence and even outright malpractice has led parents to become rather suspicious and distrustful of professionals (Weintraub & Abeson, 1975).

By the time the parents of an exceptional child have sought professional assistance from school-related personnel, they are usually painstakingly aware that their child is different. Confused, anxious, and indeed frightened, they entertain a host of secret fears and erroneous beliefs. At this time, parents are exceedingly vulnerable to criticism or to questions about their parental fitness. A professional who fails to recognize the torment and frustration the parents have already experienced may unknowingly chastise them or interpret their anxiety as psychological instability (Kaplan, 1971). Consequently, these parents may feel unable to share their worries, concerns, or ambivalent feelings and thus may remain unsupported (Gorham, 1975).

At the time of the diagnosis, the most persistent questions parents have are, "What's wrong with my child?" and "What can we do about it?" Parents have specific preferences as to how they would like to be informed. Both Gayton (1975) and Gorham (1975) stress the need for the intervening professional to inform both parents together, and as soon as possible, what the diagnosis is and, most importantly, what it means specifically. In dealing with the parents of an exceptional child, some professionals tend to emphasize a child's deficits rather than strike a balance between the child's strengths and limitations (Schild, 1971). The effective professional is one who addresses the parent's questions honestly without distorting his/her communications. Pragmatically informing the parents about their child's future does not mean that the professional is insensitive to parental feelings and fears. Parents want the professional to speak forthrightly and to provide them with directive information. As Gorham (1975), a parent of an exceptional child, noted, the psychologist or physician who is able to provide a family in need with a list of community resources and ancillary support services as well as ways to manage and educate their child importantly enhances his/her credibility. Moreover, the professional who coordinates all available information for parents to consider has laid the first building blocks of a trusting parent-professional relationship. Few parents of exceptional children are ever this fortunate.

A common belief among professionals is that parents will "shop around" for a pediatrician or psychologist who will provide them with a less painful diagnosis. The available research suggests that this is not the case (Clements & Alexander, 1975; Gayton, 1975; Wolfensberger, 1967). Anderson (1971) and Gorham (1975) suggest that shopping is a learned response to unsatisfactory contacts with professionals. It results from the initial failure of the professional to attend to the parents' emotional concerns and to demonstrate that they have been heard. When parents cannot understand their child's diagnosis, special treatment, or educational placement, they then will become dissatisfied and seek other assistance (Feldman, Byalick, & Rosedale, 1975; Warfield, 1975).

What are the major complaints parents have about their contacts with professionals? The following is a list derived from reviewing the literature examining parental concerns as expressed by parents of exceptional children (Brown, 1977; Gayton, 1975; Gorham, 1975; Rhodes, 1977; Telford & Sawrey, 1977; Wolfensberger, 1967):

1. Inappropriate use of screening procedures, criteria, and instruments for special class placement.
2. Failure to involve parents in the diagnostic process and in the planning of services to be rendered, despite the ultimate responsibility parents bear for deciding what services the child actually will receive.
3. Lack of accountability for the quality of services provided.
4. Failure to monitor and inform parents of the child's progress (seen as resulting from fragmentary services).
5. Failure to clearly specify educational or therapeutic objectives or implications for future management and prognosis.
6. Failure to inform parents regarding the duration of treatment and cost of services provided.

7. Frequent prevention of the parents from reading the contents of their child's reports or records for bureaucratic or professional reasons while strangers are permitted to do so.
8. Instruction of the parents to institutionalize handicapped children, only to have them find that institutions are the least equipped to help.
9. In the past, chastising of the parents if they did not institutionalize; now, causing of guilt feelings in the parents if they do institutionalize.
10. Ignorance on the part of professionals of ancillary support services for the exceptional child and his/her family.
11. Unwillingness by professionals to listen or apparent lack of concern about the parents' situation and feelings because of professionals' obsessive preoccupation with demonstrating how much they know about a particular handicap.
12. Failure of legislators to fulfill their promises to provide community services that will meet the needs of exceptional children.
13. Espousals by legislators that children have the constitutional right to a free education, while failing to provide the necessary appropriations to realize such an objective for exceptional children.
14. Finally, if a label must be applied, failure on the part of professionals to inform the parents that the diagnosis is not unchanging.

Sentiments such as these were prime factors in the passage of Public Law 94-142. More than half of the items listed here are dealt with specifically in that law. The flood of judicial (Telford & Sawrey, 1977; Theimer & Rupiper, 1975) as well as legislative decisions concerned with the rights of handicapped children and their parents has dramatically changed the legal status of the "special" citizen. Since 1967, litigation initiated by parents has resulted in landmark decisions in favor of the plaintiffs involving "right to education," "right to placement," "due process," and "professional accountability." While the attainment of a full education for all handicapped children will only be realized if professionals within the educational community adhere to the spirit and guidelines of the laws, it is becoming increasingly clear that parents of handicapped children are no longer content to remain a "silent minority." They are insisting, with strong legal support, on assuming the role of full partners with professionals in the education and treatment of their children.

INTERVENTION

The overall responsibility of the professional is to provide the family with ways to cope with the problems a handicapped child may present. In this section, several of the more prominent types of *parent involvement* and *parent counseling* will be discussed. The former relates to parents who have already come to recognize that their child requires special services. These parents have passed through the initial adjustment period and are ready to work with educators and other professionals in planning for their child's future. The latter approach, here called *counseling*, deals with parents for whom the adjustment process is incomplete. For these parents, counseling is designed to meet highly specific needs. Most often, this means answering their questions, helping them to recognize that their emotional reactions are not abnormal, and providing them with appropriate educational information and management skills to cope effectively with the child.

Parent Involvement

As described by Simches (1975) and Feldman et al. (1975), parent involvement reflects the emergence of a new relationship between parents and professionals. Involvement of parents has expanded beyond the traditional PTA role to viewing parents as teachers, advisors, and advocates. In large measure, this change resulted from mounting parental pressure to have a voice in the placement and programming decisions that affect their children. A positive by-product has been the emergence of constructive parental involvement in preschool and early educational settings that utilize didactic interchanges between parent and child. Preliminary evaluations by Warfield (1975) and Kelly (1973) indicated that several forms of parental involvement — parent-teacher discussion groups (Bricklin, 1970; Rossett, 1975), parents as aides, or parents directly instructing their child — result in better scholastic achievement for exceptional children.

Though more definitive findings are not yet available, it appears that when given an opportunity, parents can become a potent educational force and can develop mutual respect with professionals. For parents, this has resulted in a growing sense of control over their child's destiny and a sense of accountability jointly shared between parents and professionals. Thus, parent involvement seems to have lessened the distance between the goals of the school and those of the child's home.

Parent Counseling

Three major counseling strategies, or models, have evolved from work with parents of handicapped children. The first is *informational counseling*. This occurs, for example, when the physician tells parents that their child is handicapped, when the psychologist informs the parents of the results and implications of his evaluation, or when the teacher discusses the child's academic status.

The task of informing parents that their child has a defect is one of the most emotionally agonizing experiences a professional is likely to face. Learning to deal with this issue necessitates that the professional honestly examine his/her own feelings and attitudes concerning exceptional children. At times, the presenting handicap elicits intense personal anxieties in the professional. If s/he is unaware of them or unwilling to recognize their existence, the professional's conflicts can only operate to distort communication with the child's family.

The findings of Buscaglia (1975), McWilliams (1976), Ross (1964), Telford and Sawrey (1977), and Wolfensberger (1967), taken together, present a comprehensive review of therapeutic objectives during the information stage. They include the following:

1. Honesty, the ability to share relevant information without distorting or withholding information, is essential.
2. Imparting a meaningful diagnosis means that the professional presents the problem specifically and knowledgeably.
3. The effective relationship is one that encourages parents to participate in the decision-making process, seek information, and question recommendations.
4. Professional responsibility dictates that parents be provided with manageable plans as well as realistic goals. The effective professional anticipates parental defenses, questions what they say and do, and evaluates their ability to carry out recommendations.
5. Finally, listening nonjudgmentally to parental feelings while remaining sensitive to the role of unconscious motivations that seek expression through behavior helps in understanding parental needs.

Among the resources for parents of which professionals should be aware is *Closer Look*. A parent information service operated by the National Information Center for the Handicapped, Closer Look was established in 1970 in response to the need for information on services for handicapped children (Dean, 1975). Closer Look provides information to parents of handicapped children, to professionals who work with the handicapped, to students who are looking for career information, to parent groups seeking advice on how to make their organization work, and directly to the disabled individual. The information provided by this service covers such things as (a) explanations of state laws or public education programs for the handicapped child; (b) a guide to finding state or local services for handicapped children; (c) information tailored to the needs of children and young adults with specific handicapping conditions, including descriptions of parent organizations and reading lists; and (d) reports issued periodically to help keep parents informed about new developments that may affect their handicapped child. For additional information, inquiries should be sent to Closer Look, Box 1492, Washington, D.C., 20013.

The second major mode of counseling is *psychotherapy*, with the two most prominent forms of intervention being *behavior modification training* and *reflective counseling*.

Traditionally, the application of "behavioral" techniques has been reserved for clinical, institutional, and classroom settings (Kazdin, 1975). Contemporary research in behavioral psychology, however, indicates that parent groups or individual parents and siblings can learn to apply the principles of learning theory and behavior modification within the confines of their home to alter a handicapped child's behavior in a simple and practical manner (Bidder, Bryant, & Gray, 1975; Clements & Alexander, 1975; Fishman & Fishman, 1975; Kogan & Gordon, 1975; Mash & Terdal, 1973; Miller & Cantwell, 1976; Rinn, Vernon, & Wise, 1975; Schaefer, Palkes, & Stewart, 1974; Seitz & Terdal, 1972; Townsend & Flanagan, 1976; Tymchuk, 1975).

Despite some encouraging results, a rating of the overall efficacy of training parents or siblings as therapeutic agents is subject to several qualifiers. First, the mere use of behavioral interventions will not insure behavioral generalization across situations. As Miller and Cantwell (1976) have discussed, generalization is dependent on environmental consistency from the training situation (e.g., home) to diverse stimulus conditions (e.g., school). It would be illogical to assume that behavioral change could be maintained without consistent support from both home and school. For this reason, Clements and Alexander (1975) as well as Johnson and Katz (1973) have suggested that behavioral training programs be evaluated with respect to the critical variables of (a) identifying training techniques, (b) describing application procedures, (c) measuring behavior, (d) testing for generalization, and (e) providing follow-up data.

Reflective counseling generally seeks to resolve the parents' dissonance caused when normal parental expectations are markedly altered by the birth of the handicapped child. The implication is that the reconciliation of the parents' feelings will somehow translate into their acceptance of the child and his/her condition. Space does not permit discussion of all of the strategies involved in accomplishing this. For the most part, psychodynamic therapy has been the treatment of choice, but family therapy is proving itself a useful alternative as it gains in popularity and influence (Watts, 1969).

A continually popular adjunct to or substitute for reflective counseling with individuals is group therapy (Lewis, 1972). It is most appropriate for helping parents who are basically mature and emotionally stable. Group therapy experiences are not appropriate for certain individuals because of their monopolistic control of the group leader. Those for whom group therapy should not be recommended include individuals with highly specific needs (e.g., strong emotional dependency issues), masochists, oppositional types (e.g., passive-aggressive persons), or those with psychotic personalities (Ross, 1964).

Parents who participate in groups may do so for several reasons (Appell, Williams & Fishell, 1964; Bitter, 1963; Heisler, 1974). First, groups provide for a sharing of information, opinions, suggestions, and experiences concerning a mutual problem, i.e., difficulties involved in parenting a handicapped child. Group identification is exceedingly helpful during the initial adjustment period. A certain amount of support comes from knowing that other parents have similar problems, perhaps even some that are worse, and that they are coping realistically. Group therapy also tends to be an emotionally corrective experience for parents with the need to project and intellectualize. As a result of the overall group process, parents appear to perceive their child differently and learn to deal with their child's condition more effectively.

Critical reviews by Ramsey (1967), Sternlicht and Sullivan (1974), Tretakoff (1969), and Wolfensberger (1967) indicate that studies that reported helping parents with group therapy were so poorly designed that their conclusions lack scientific value or they fail independent verification. Most neglected to provide a comprehensive description of such factors as population variables that might be related to outcomes; leadership qualities, selection criteria, and training level of group leaders; participant selection criteria; the nature of the group's structure, function, and goals; objective measurement of participants' needs; and follow-up.

Based upon the cumulative findings of these reviews, however, it appears that parents do appreciate and feel that they profit from an opportunity to jointly share and explore their feelings. Groups seem to provide a forum for attitude change. However, the conditions that foster the changes cannot be ascertained because of the poorly designed research. Recent reviews by Tavormina (1974, 1975) provided some new evidence indicating that both behavioral and reflective group counseling are effective interventions with many types of behavior problems and with divergent populations. Behavioral training appeared to be the most effective method of teaching parents to manage their children, while reflective counseling approaches helped them to become aware of and to understand their feelings. When behavioral and reflective techniques were used in combination, parents responded very enthusiastically (Tavormina, Hampson, & Luscomb, 1976). Parents not only acquired specific management skills, but also reported gaining a more sensitive understanding of their retarded children. This combined format merits further consideration as an important technique for parents of handicapped children.

Parent Education

A burgeoning area of interest and involvement in work with parents of the handicapped is parent education or parent training. Various programs have been used for several years in work with normal children and are now being adopted for application to handicapped populations. By emphasizing the dynamics of the parent-child interaction, the strategies taught are designed to promote better communication between parent and child.

Two of the most widely recognized approaches are described in *Between Parent and Child* by Ginott (1969) and *Parent Effectiveness Training* by Gordon (1970). Both stress the role of active listening and appropriate ways for parents to respond to their children. Another technique, filial therapy, attempts to open lines of communication through the medium of play (Guerney, 1969). *Filial therapy* is a program designed to teach parents how to play with their children and, by doing so, to better understand their children's feelings.

An interesting group approach is the C-Group developed by Dinkmeyer and Carlson (1973). It is designed to teach parents problem-solving skills. The *C* in *C-Group* refers to its components: collaboration, consultation, clarification, confrontation, concern and caring, confidentiality, and commitment to change. Through group participation, parents share ideas for solving problems. The program is action oriented: It requires that the couple who present a problem make a public commitment to apply the solution derived by the group.

Lillie, Trohanis, and Goin (1976) provide a comprehensive guide to alternative parent training programs, detail the dimensions of training, and discuss the efficacy of home-based and center-based training.

Training programs for parents of handicapped children have proliferated despite a paucity of research supporting their value. Levitt and Cohen (1975) analyzed 13 parent intervention programs. They found them to be conducted in an informal and subjective fashion. The majority of the programs failed to assess parental needs with any standardized instrument or to apply appropriate statistical tests when evaluating outcomes. It appears that more rigorous study is required before parent training programs merit vigorous professional advocacy. However, several preliminary efficacy studies (Kroth, 1975; McDowell, 1976) have indicated that such programs may prove to be quite valuable.

CONCLUSIONS

The impact of a disability is felt by the child with the handicap, his/her parents, and those with whom the family comes in contact. Feeling confused, anxious, and perhaps fearful, angry, or guilty, parents of exceptional children are usually poorly prepared emotionally and intellectually to face the complexities inherent in raising their children. The literature reviewed points to the need for providing parents with some understanding of the nature of their children's problems as well as the importance of involving parents directly in the diagnosis, treatment, and educational and social management of their children. For parents of exceptional children, the solicitation of parental involvement is an absolutely essential prerequisite for establishing meaningful therapeutic services for their children. Professionals must take a leadership role in interacting with these parents by demonstrating an understanding of the parents' experience *and* supporting their right to participate in the education of their children as full partners with professionals.

REFERENCES

Anderson, K. The shopping behavior of parents of mentally retarded children: The professional person's role. *Mental Retardation*, 1971, *9*(4), 3-5.

Appell, T., Williams, C., & Fishell, K. Changes in attitudes of parents of retarded children effected through group counseling. *American*

Journal of Mental Deficiency, 1964, *68*(5), 104-108.

Baum, M. Some dynamic factors affecting family adjustment to the handicapped child. *Exceptional Children,* 1962, *28*(8), 387-392.

Begab, M. Mental retardation and family stress. In F. Menolascino (Ed.), *Psychiatric aspects of the diagnosis and treatment of mental retardation.* Seattle, Washington: Spec Child, 1971.

Bidder, R., Bryant, G., & Gray, O. Benefits to Down's Syndrome children through training their mothers. *Archives of Disease in Childhood,* 1975, *59*(5), 383-386.

Bitter, J. Attitude change by parents of trainable mentally retarded children as a result of group discussion. *Exceptional Children,* 1963, *30*(4), 173-177.

Bricklin, P. Counseling parents of children with learning disabilities. *Reading Teacher,* 1970, *23*(4), 331-338.

Brown, L. Parental involvement in diagnostic testing. In W. Rhodes & D. Sweeney (Eds.), *Alternatives to litigation: The necessity for parent consultation.* Ann Arbor: U of Mich, Department of Education, 1977.

Bryant, M. Parent child relationships: Their effects on rehabilitation. *Journal of Learning Disabilities,* 1971, *4*(6), 325-329.

Buscaglia, L. (Ed.). *The disabled and their parents: A counseling challenge.* Thorofare, New Jersey: C. B. Slack, 1975.

Clements, J., & Alexander, R. Parent training: Bringing it all back home. *Focus on Exceptional Children,* 1975, *7*(5), 1-12.

Cleveland, D., & Miller, N. Attitudes and life commitments of older siblings of mentally retarded adults: An exploratory study. *Mental Retardation,* 1977, *15*(3), 38-41.

Davis, F. *Passage through crisis: Polio victims and their families.* Indianapolis: Bobbs, 1963.

Dean, D. Closer look: A parent information service. *Exceptional Children,* 1975, *41*(8), 527-530.

Dinkmeyer, D., & Carlson, J. (Eds.). *Consulting: Facilitating human potential and change process.* Columbus, Ohio: Merrill, 1973.

Downey, K. Parental interest in the institutionalized, severely mentally retarded child. *Social Problems,* 1963, *11*, 186-193.

Farber, B., & Jenne, W. Family organization and parent child communication: Parents and siblings of a retarded child. *Monograph of the Society for Research in Child Development,* 1963, *28*, No. 7 (Whole No. 91).

Feldman, M., Byalick, R., & Rosedale, M. Parent involvement programs — A growing trend in special education. *Exceptional Children,* 1975, *71*(8), 551-554.

Fishman, C., & Fishman, D. Maternal correlates of self esteem and overall adjustment in children with birth defects. *Child Psychiatry and Human Development,* 1971, *4*(1), 255-265.

Fishman, C., & Fishman, D. A group training program in behavior modification for mothers of children with birth defects: An exploratory program. *Child Psychiatry and Human Development,* 1975, *6*(1), 3-14.

Freud, S. Mourning and melancholia. In S. Freud, *The standard edition of the complete psychological works of Sigmund Freud*, Vol. 14. London: Hogarth, 1957. (Originally published, 1917.)

Gayton, W. Management problems of mentally retarded children and their families. *Pediatric Clinics of North America*, 1975, *22*(3), 561-570.

Ginott, H. *Between parent and child*. New York: Avon, 1969.

Gordon, T. *Parent effectiveness training: The no-lose program for raising responsible children*. New York: McKay, 1970.

Gorham, K. A lost generation of parents. *Exceptional Children*, 1975, *41*(8), 521-525.

Guerney, B. (Ed.). *Psychotherapeutic agents: New roles for nonprofessionals*. New York: HR&W, 1969.

Heisler, V. Dynamic group psychotherapy with parents of cerebral palsied children. *Rehabilitation Literature*, 1974, *35*(11), 329-330.

Hollingsworth, C., & Pasnau, R. (Eds.). *The family in mourning: A guide for mental health professionals*. New York: Grune, 1977.

Holt, K. Home care of severely retarded children. *Pediatrics*, 1958, *22*(4), 744-755.

Irvine, E. The risks of the register: Or the management of expectation. In E. Anthony & C. Koupernik (Eds.), *The child in his family: Children at risk*. New York: Wiley, 1974.

Johnson, C., & Katz, R. Using parents as change agents for their children: A review. *Journal of Child Psychology and Psychiatry*, 1973, *14*(3), 181-200.

Kaplan, B. Counseling with mothers of exceptional children. *Elementary School Guidance and Counseling*, 1971, *6*(1), 32-36.

Kazdin, A. *Behavior modification in applied settings*. Homewood, Illinois: Dorsey, 1975.

Kelly, E. Parental roles in special educational programming: A brief for involvement. *Journal of Special Education*, 1973, *7*(4), 357-364.

Kogan, K., & Gordon, B. A mother instructor program: Documenting change in mother-child interactions. *Child Psychiatry and Human Development*, 1975, *5*(3), 189-200.

Kozier, A. Case work with parents of children born with severe brain defects. *Social Casework*, 1957, *38*, 183-189.

Kroth, R. *Communicating with parents of exceptional children*. Denver: Love Pub, 1975.

Levitt, E., & Cohen, S. An analysis of selected parent-intervention programs for handicapped and disadvantaged children. *Journal of Special Education*, 1975, *9*(4), 345-365.

Lewis, J. Effects of group procedure with parents of mentally retarded children. *Mental Retardation*, 1972, *10*(6), 14-15.

Liberthson, E. Helping families live with and for the mentally retarded child. *Journal of Rehabilitation*, 1968, *34*, 24-36.

Lillie, D., Trohanis, P., & Goin, K. (Eds.). *Teaching parents to teach: A guide for working with the special child*. New York: Walker, 1976.

Love, H. *Parental attitudes toward exceptional children.* Springfield: Thomas, 1970.

Mash, E., & Terdal, L. Modification of mother-child interactions: Playing with children. *Mental Retardation,* 1973, *11*(5), 44-49.

McDowell, R. Parent counseling: The state of the art. *Journal of Learning Disabilities,* 1976, *9*(10), 614-619.

McWilliams, B. Various aspects of parent counseling. In E. Webster (Ed.), *Professional approaches with parents of handicapped children.* Springfield: Thomas, 1976.

Meadow, K., & Meadow, L. Changing role of perceptions for parents of handicapped children. *Exceptional Children,* 1971, *38*(1), 21-27.

Miller, N., & Cantwell, D. Siblings as therapists: A behavioral approach. *American Journal of Psychiatry,* 1976, *133*(4), 447-450.

Olshansky, S. S. Chronic sorrow: A response to having a mentally defective child. *Social Casework,* 1962, *43,* 190-193.

Pueschel, S., & Murphy, A. Counseling parents of infants with Down's Syndrome. *Postgraduate Medicine,* 1975, *58*(7), 90-95.

Ramsey, G. Review of group methods with parents of the mentally retarded. *American Journal of Mental Deficiency,* 1967, *71*(5), 857-863.

Rinn, R., Vernon, J., & Wise, M. Training parents of behaviorally disordered children in groups: A three years' program evaluation. *Behavior Therapy,* 1975, *6*(3), 378-387.

Rhodes, W. Parent consultation: A healing process. In W. Rhodes & D. Sweeney (Eds.), *Alternatives to litigation: The necessity for parent consultation.* Ann Arbor: U of Mich, Department of Education, 1977.

Ross, A. *The exceptional child in the family.* New York: Grune, 1964.

Rossett, A. Parenting of the preschool exceptional child. *Teaching Exceptional Children,* 1975, *7*(4), 118-121.

Schaefer, J., Palkes, H., & Stewart, M. Group counseling for parents of hyperactive children. *Child Psychiatry and Human Development,* 1974, *5*(2), 89-94.

Schild, S. Counseling services. In R. Koch & J. Dobson (Eds.), *The mentally retarded child and his family: A multi-disciplinary handbook.* New York: Brunner/Mazel, 1971.

Seitz, S., & Terdal, L. A modeling approach to changing parent-child interactions. *Mental Retardation,* 1972, *10*(3), 39-43.

Simches, R. President's page. *Exceptional Children,* 1975, *41*(8), 565-566.

Soeffing, M. Abused children are exceptional children. *Exceptional Children,* 1975, *42*(3), 126-133.

Solnit, A., & Stark, M. Mourning and the birth of a defective child. *Psychoanalytic Study of the Child,* 1961, *16,* 523-527.

Sternlicht, M., & Sullivan, I. Group counseling with parents of the MR: Leadership selection and functioning. *Mental Retardation,* 1974, *12,*(5), 11-13.

Tavormina, J. Basic models of parent counseling: A critical review. *Psychological Bulletin,* 1974, *81*(11), 827-835.

Tavormina, J. Relative effectiveness of behavioral and reflective group counseling with parents of mentally retarded. *Journal of Consulting and Clinical Psychology,* 1975, *43*(1), 22-31.

Tavormina, J., Hampson, R., & Luscomb, R. Participant evaluations of the effectiveness of their parent counseling groups. *Mental Retardation,* 1976, *14*(6), 8-9.

Telford, C., & Sawrey, J. *The exceptional child.* Englewood Cliffs, New Jersey: P-H, 1977.

Tew, B., Payne, H., & Laurence, K. Must a family with a handicapped child be a handicapped family. *Developmental Medicine and Child Neurology,* 1974, *16*(6, Suppl. 32), 95-98.

Theimer, R., & Rupiper, O. Special education litigation and school psychology. *Journal of School Psychology,* 1975, *13*(4), 324-334.

Tisza, V. Management of the parents of the chronically ill child. *American Journal of Orthopsychiatry,* 1962, *32*(1), 53-59.

Townsend, P., & Flanagan, J. Experimental preadmission program to encourage home care for severely and profoundly retarded. *American Journal of Mental Deficiency,* 1976, *80*(5), 562-569.

Tretakoff, M. Counseling parents of handicapped children: A review. *Mental Retardation,* 1969, *7*(4), 31-34.

Tymchuk, A. Training parent therapists. *Mental Retardation,* 1975, *13*(5), 19-22.

Warfield, G. Mothers of retarded children review a parent education program. *Exceptional Children,* 1975, *41*(8), 559-562.

Watts, E. Family therapy: Its use in mental retardation. *Mental Retardation,* 1969, *7*(5), 41-44.

Weintraub, F., & Abeson, A. New education policies for the handicapped: The quiet revolution. In H. Dupont (Ed.), *Educating emotionally disturbed children.* New York: HR&W, 1975.

Wentworth, E. *Listen to your heart: A message to parents of handicapped children.* Boston: HM, 1974.

Wetter, T. Parental attitudes toward learning disabled. *Exceptional Children,* 1972, *38*(6), 490-491.

Wolfensberger, W. Counseling parents of the retarded. In A. Baumeister (Ed.), *Mental retardation: Appraisal, education, and rehabilitation.* Chicago: Aldine, 1967.

Worchel, T., & Worchel, P. The parental concept of the mentally retarded child. *American Journal of Mental Deficiency,* 1961, *65*(6), 782-788.

Zuk, G. Religious factor and role of guilt in parental acceptance of the retarded child. *American Journal of Mental Deficiency,* 1959, *64*(1), 139-147.

Chapter 5

WORKSHOPS AND PARENT GROUPS

R. R. ABIDIN AND BRYAN D. CARTER

IN recent years the professionals concerned with child development and mental health have come to recognize that the key point of intervention for children is through the parenting system. To some, this recognition is the discovery of the obvious. Yet most of the services and funds expended in the areas of child development and mental health during the 1950s and 1960s involved programs of professional and paraprofessional intervention directly with the child. The parent, while often acknowledged as a "source of the child's developing deviance," was rarely seen as the keystone of any treatment or intervention.

Work in the area of the cognitive development of children and the recognition of the relative ineffectiveness of traditional mental health services represent the basis for the resurgence of the focus on the parenting system as the major element in changing children's behavior.

The concept of working with parents for the benefit of their children is actually a very old one. Orville Brim, in his work *Education for Child Rearing* (1959), traces the origins of efforts to work with parents in the United States to the 19th century. A. S. Makarenko (1921) of the Soviet Union describes his role as parent educator during the period immediately prior to and after the Soviet Revolution.

For the most part, parent education efforts until 1965 centered around lecture/discussion models of parent training that focused on a specific set of ideas presented to parents by professionals. In the child development area, the program of *Parenthood in a Free Nation* (Kawin, 1963) typified the efforts. This program consisted of a structured discussion course characterized by an intellectual analysis of children's development and a consideration of "basic principles." The individual parents themselves were expected to work out the mechanics of when and how to implement the concepts. While this type of discussion group has some benefits for certain populations of parents, its major problem has been that it is overly general. Parents typically express the need for greater specificity of instruction with focus on their particular concerns.

In the mental health area, the work of S. R. Slavson (1958) typified the group guidance model of working with parents. The method described by Slavson, while more clinically oriented, nevertheless suffered from many of the same limitations as were found in the child development parent discussion groups. The parent participants were required to be verbal individuals who had a history of a fair degree of success in problem solving through the application of basic principles or concepts. The minority group parent, the uneducated parent, and the parent of low socioeconomic status would often be unable to handle or feel comfortable in such a program, given the initial skill and attitude demands required by such an approach.

Parents Learn Through Discussion, by Aline B. Auerbach (1968) represents both (a) the zenith of the parent group education approach using discussion as the primary methodology of education and (b) the transition to the more focused and skills-oriented approach that typifies the work of most of the authors in this volume. The research studies summarized by Auerbach essentially confirmed the findings reported by Brim (1959) that the use of lecture/discussion groups failed to show significant changes in the behavior and attitudes of parents. The most sophisticated evaluation study reviewed by Auerbach was that of the Westport-Weston Group (Westport-Weston, Connecticut, Mental Health Association, 1959). This project utilized the discussion methodology and procedures specified by the Child Study Association of America. The designs included the random assignment of self-selected individuals to experimental and control groups. The parents were pre- and post-tested on a wide range of criterion variables, e.g., child development knowledge, parent attitudes, decision-making skills, etc. None of the criterion variables revealed a statistically significant influence due to the discussion group experience.

The evolution of parent group education gradually began to move in the direction of a skills development approach in working with specific target populations of parents and children. This trend had the result of producing significant changes in parental attitudes and behaviors with concomitant modifications in the childrens' behaviors (Tavormina, 1974).

The remainder of this chapter will focus on the practical issues involved in conducting parent education groups. The guidelines presented are aimed at assisting the parent educator in developing an effective program of parent education or parent intervention training. It should be noted that before embarking on a parent education project, the parent educator must consider the basic purpose and assumptions behind the process of parent education.

THE BASIC PURPOSE OF PARENT EDUCATION

A program of parent education must result in two general, yet major, outcomes: (1) the parents' self-respect should be enhanced and (2) the parents should believe and experience themselves as being more competent in their role as parents as a result of the parent education experience. The activities of the training program must therefore have the dual effect of releasing human potential while developing specific skills and attitudes. The parents need to be provided with the opportunity to explore options in terms of methods and approaches to assisting their child's growth and development and in terms of methodologies and skills for managing the child's behavior. Above all, they should not be approached as potential converts to a particular point of view.

One of the most tragic and counterproductive consequences, which is a not infrequent outcome of some parent education programs, is when parents begin to think that the methods of parent-child interaction presented are the "right way." The author has listened to many parents describe how, after attending a particular parent education program, they came away feeling more depressed and inadequate than before they entered the program. Such an outcome seems to occur not because the concepts and methods being presented in such programs are ineffective or of minimal potential value, but rather due to the group leader's (as well as the program's) failure to recognize the general outcomes of enhanced parental self-respect and competence. Effective parent educators attempt to maintain cognizance of the fact that what they say and do in the program should enhance the parents' self-respect and increase the parents' sense of competence in their child-rearing role.

Helpful Basic Assumptions

1. Parents want to learn how to do the best they can in their role of parent.
2. People who find themselves as parents often don't have the necessary parenting skills in one area or another and must either learn them by trial and error or in some educational format.
3. The parenting role includes expectations, attitudes, behaviors, and problem-solving strategies, all of which must be considered in any parent education program. The parent group leader must

therefore help the group maintain a balance between the emotional, intellectual, and behavioral components of the learning experience.

4. Parents learn best what they are most interested in. This means that the subject matter of the parent education group should be close to their immediate life experiences. Ideally, the parents have decided to participate in the group knowing the general focus of the program, e.g., developmentally delayed children ages 0 to 6. Learning is further facilitated if the parents can be involved in developing the group's agenda.

5. The parent group must provide the parents the opportunity to integrate their new learnings into their own style. The idea that there is only one right way should both implicitly and explicitly be avoided.

6. Parents can and do learn from each other. The group leader should facilitate and encourage the communication and exchange of ideas and solutions between parents.

CHARACTERISTICS OF THE
PARENT GROUP LEADER

Knowledge Background

The parent group leader needs to bring to the group a fundamental knowledge of child development. The leader's familiarity with the processes of growth and change through which each child passes and the implications of these for the parent is essential to ensure adequate communication and understanding. Among the dangers inherent in the lack of background knowledge in child development is that the leader will be unable to recognize inappropriate parental expectations of their children and unable to empathetically respond to pressures placed on parents by the state-appropriate changing demands of the developing child.

Experential Background of
the Parent Group Leader

Parents often express the idea that a parent group leader must be an experienced parent to be able to adequately handle the responsibilities of the role. While in some cases the experience of having been a parent may enhance the group leader's effectiveness, this in itself is not an essential background element. In fact, the parenthood experiences of the group leader can have the negative effects of limiting the group's perspective or enveloping them in a set of ideas and approaches that happen to fit the leader's parenting style and family situation.

While the author is not aware of any research data that bears on the question of parenthood of the parent group leader in relation to his/her effectiveness, some clinical observations may be useful. Parent group leaders with a broad base of different life experiences without children of their own seem to have no particular difficulty as long as they possess other basic qualities essential to the helper/group leader role. The childless group leader who appears to have the most difficulty is the young idealist who holds the tabula rasa view of children and sees the role of group leader as rebuilder and sanctioner of "appropriate parenting behaviors."

In addition to acquiring knowledge of child development through reading and academic experiences, the parent group leader needs to have some direct experience with children. The source of this direct experience is not the most important factor. It may come from work in day camps, teaching school, babysitting, day care, etc. The essential element of these experiences is that the group leader has had sufficient interaction with children to become aware of the complexities and issues involved in trying to form relationships with children, in teaching and directing children, in rewarding and recognizing children, and in disciplining and placing limits in adult-child interactions.

In situations in which the group leader is working with parents of a special population of children, it is essential that the leader be familiar with relevant developmental issues and the specific characteristics of this child subpopulation. While this may seem obvious, it is surprising how often a mental health professional or parent educator becomes involved in work with a parent group involving special children with whom the leader has little familiarity. Parent groups for preschool children who are mentally retarded, hyperactive, and physically handicapped are illustrative of the need for direct experience by the group leader. While the focus of the group leader may be on the common developmental characteristics of all children, this does not mean that knowledge of general principles will always suffice. The leader must be familiar enough with the children under consideration to translate the general knowledge into a more relevant form.

Family systems concepts and the differing cultural backgrounds of parents are two other areas in which the parent group leader needs to be prepared. We are all members of a particular family system, which is imbedded in a particular culture and ethnic group. This experience, while useful in some situations, may actually be a limitation in others. On the other hand, parent group leaders cannot be expected to develop familiarity with all possible family systems or cultural backgrounds, but leaders must have enough experiences with different families and cultural groups to develop a sophisticated and cosmopolitan view that acknowledges a wide variety of parental expectations and goals. The group leader needs to be comfortable with the independence and social distance of children fostered by one family system and culture and with the conformity and social sensitivity expected in another. While direct exposure to the family life of a wide range of family systems may not always be possible for the parent group leader, one useful way of developing a broader perspective is for prospective parent group leaders to share their childhood experience in initial training sessions prior to working with parents as a parent educator.

A variety of techniques, e.g., role-playing and family sculpting, can be employed in the context of a group training format to provide prospective parent group leaders the experience of how their colleagues' families handled typical family issues such as aggression and affection. These stimulations often enable group leaders to explore more adequately the range of ways families cope with the same issues.

Knowledge of Group Dynamics and Group Process

The parent group leader's awareness of the fundamental principles of group dynamics is particularly helpful. Issues relating to group atmosphere, methods of facilitating communication, the roles various individuals in the group are playing, etc., are all important subjects. However, the one aspect of group functioning to which the parent group leader must be most sensitive is the issue of consensus and group pressures toward uniformity. While these ever-present pressures toward uniformity are helpful in work groups in maintaining group cohesion and moving the group along toward a common goal, in a parent education group they can be destructive forces that alienate group members. Members of parent groups are often unsophisticated regarding group dynamics, so individuals who are resistant to movement toward group consensus are placed under pressure to agree. The group leader's awareness of this and the use of corrective intervention can provide to all the group members a validating experience in which they can see the value and acceptability of their independent decisions. The group pressures most helpful within a parent group are those that urge parents to validate their ideas and approaches, both within the group and in the reality of their own family system. The group leader who is aware of these issues is in the position to facilitate learning for the individual group members.

Personal Characteristics of the Group Leader

The parent group leader must possess certain basic attitudes in order to deal effectively with his responsibilities as a parent group leader.

Acceptance

The group leader must see parents as responsible individuals and not as "sick" or "inadequate" people. Regardless of what the parents are currently doing, they must be seen as putting forth their best effort given their present situations and skills. The parents' current attitudes, expectations, and behaviors are to be respected as the parents attempt to raise their children in the way they believe will most likely make them happy and productive. Parent group leaders who do not hold these attitudes will communicate to the parents the message of the parents' unacceptability, which will eventually lead to the destruction of the parent group.

It is often surprising to witness the complex actions in which a parent educator may engage in attempting to gain the acceptance of the parent group members and yet witness how unsuccessful group leaders lack awareness of the parents' same need for acceptance. The kind of acceptance needed by the parent group leader is quite similar to that expressed by Carl Rogers (1951) concerning the therapeutic alliance. The acceptance is of the parents desire to be of value to and helpful to their child. It is not necessarily an acceptance of their ways of interacting with their child. It is an acceptance of the parents' becoming. It is an acceptance of the continued struggle to grow and develop and of the never-ending search for self-understanding. The other end of the acceptance continuum is the group leader's ability to be self-accepting. The self-accepting group leader views the parent group experience as a time when s/he can share some ideas and facilitate the learning of others. Unfortunately, some group leaders view all the transactions of the group as their responsibility and are overly concerned with their "performance." They are constantly judging and evaluating their performance from the inside out. While this behavior is always present to some degree, this orientation must be held to a minimum. One negative effect of this orientation is that a judgmental and critical self-orientation cannot help but be projected to the group; this posture usually becomes a barrier to communication and a roadblock to the parents' self-exploration. The second major negative effect of lack of self-acceptance in the group leader is difficulty in maintaining "other" orientation. Group leaders who are "other oriented" are able to maintain an alert openness and responsiveness to the comments and feelings of the parents. Typically these group leaders find maintaining group communication an easy task.

Interpersonal Reinforcement Rate

When one observes an experienced and effective parent group leader, one noticeable dimension is the high rate of positive reinforcement. The operant behavioral literature is replete with studies that document the efficacy of positive reinforcement in altering and shaping the behavior of children. The effective group leader has learned to be aware of the impact of abundant reinforcement and the diverse ways one individual can reinforce another. While it would not be appropriate or possible to list all the ways a group member can be reinforced, some of the most common should be mentioned:

1. Verbal Praise: Describe the specifics of what a person did and its effect on the group. "Mary, when you took what I said and gave an example from your family, that really helped everyone understand what I was trying to say."
2. Nonverbal Communications: Smiles, eye contact, and head nodding.
3. Physical Contact: A light touch, a handshake, or a pat on the back, where and when appropriate, can be highly encouraging and reinforcing to a parent. Such reinforcement, though, should be used in moderation and with regard to each parent's comfort with physical contact. Physical contact as a reinforcer can also serve to model affectional behaviors for the parent group members.
4. Concrete Token Rewards: Although the use of token rewards and economies has been detailed in the behavioral literature, their application by the parent educator should be used with tact and discretion. Parents may be given certificates, toys for their children, weekly tokens, etc., for completion of small and large steps in a program.

Before the First Meeting

Prior to conducting the initial session of the parent workshop, it is necessary for the group leader to make some basic decisions and arrangements for the ensuing sessions. While many of the points raised in this section seem obvious, failure to consider and plan for them often creates major problems for the inexperienced group leader.

What Will the Focus of the Parent Workshop Be?

Whether the group leader will be presenting a predesigned program for dealing with a specific body of knowledge and skills or whether s/he plans to conduct a group with a more open-ended format, consideration must be given to the population to be served and their needs. All too often, parent groups are begun on the basis of what a professional person has to offer rather than on the needs of the target groups or on the needs the target group is presumed to have. Decisions in this area are often critical to the success of a parent workshop and require a fair amount of self-examination and consideration of the needs of the population to be served.

Selection of Group Members

In some instances the group leader deals with groups that consist of a wide variety of parents. This approach is not advocated since it creates problems with the relevance of the overall program to the concerns of the individual parents. The most productive group experiences for parents are those in which the characteristics of the parents and their children are not widely disparate. The group leader can facilitate the learning of the parents by helping to define the focus of the group while making the initial selection of group members. If the group leader can speak with prospective group members about the group prior to the first session, then the group can progress to a focus with maximum relevance to the parents and their concerns. The pre-group interview also permits the group leader to deal with any anxieties, hostility, or apathy the group members may be feeling. This initial interview is very much related to subsequent group size and attendance, since the group leader can assess the motivation of the prospective group members earlier. In open-ended groups offered to the general public, it is very difficult to estimate the size of the group, and the lack of personal relevance often leads to erratic and dwindling attendance.

Group Size

In most workshop groups aimed at specific problems of child management in a preselected population, the ideal group size is from 6 to 10 individuals. Somewhat larger groups of from 10 to 20 members can be used if the focus of the group is to teach basic skills of parent/child interaction. Failure to control the size of the group usually reduces the relevance of the experience to the individual group members' concerns and interests. Attendance rates also diminish as the group size increases.

Frequency and Length of Meetings

The frequency of the meetings depends upon the purpose of the group. In groups designed to deal with specific problems of current intense concern to the parents, the group may meet two or three times weekly, with a reduction in frequency as the situations resolve themselves. This type of schedule is not at all uncommon for a parent group of a mental health center or as the initial phase of a long-term group for parents of mentally retarded children. The most common meeting schedule is once weekly for a fixed length of time, usually 6 to 10 weeks. Parent groups designed to deal with specific parenting skills, parent attitudes and values, or general developmental issues most appropriately fit this latter schedule.

The length of the sessions is dependent upon the nature of the tasks and issues to be dealt with by the group; as a general guideline, meetings should last from 1 1/2 hours to 3 hours. Discussion groups and those that focus on normal development can readily be handled in a 90-minute format. Groups designed to teach skills or deal with specific behavior problems usually require 2 or more hours per session. This additional meeting time is required in all groups in which role playing, demonstrations, and practice of skills are a part of the program. Group leaders must always be sensitive to the fact that each session has a unique aspect, and time must be provided for the sequential stages of warm-up, unfinished business, and a closing phase, as well as the main focus of the particular session.

The Meeting Place

The atmosphere and physical characteristics of the meeting place are an essential dimension of a successful parent group. The symbolic meaning of the meeting place can have a significant impact on parent behaviors. Holding the meeting in a church, mental health center, or classroom carries with it some initial parent biases that hinder or facilitate a particular group. In general, parent groups are facilitated if the sessions can be held in an informal living room environment in which the size of the room matches the number of people involved. Sharing between and among individuals is facilitated when the physical distance between individuals is not great and a conversational voice can be used. A circular arrangement of chairs (diameter less than 12 feet) further facilitates communication and an atmosphere of sharing. The room should suggest a sense of psychological security, which is facilitated by the provision of the following qualitative conditions:

1. Muted colors
2. Freedom from distracting noise
3. Carpeted floors
4. Soft chairs
5. Air conditioning
6. Good acoustics

Co-leader

It has been our experience that the use of a co-leader enhances the operation of a parent group, particularly when the leaders are of opposite sexes. A frequent theme that emerges in parent groups is the different perspectives traditionally attributed to men and women on issues related to child rearing and management. The presence of co-leaders of opposite sexes provides an opportunity for the modeling of divergences of viewpoint and the effective resolution and coordination of differences. This type of group leadership can also facilitate the communication of group members who have a history of difficulty in communicating across sexes. While the use of co-leaders of opposite sexes is helpful, the mere existence of a sex difference between co-leaders is not the primary value for their union as a co-leader team.

The co-leadership of a group provides a means whereby communication can be facilitated between the leaders and the group members. With co-leaders, the nonactive leader can strategically assess and monitor communication patterns in the group interaction while the other is speaking or demonstrating. This serves to insure that meaningful communication is taking place. Two leaders provide a more ready opportunity for demonstrating and modeling behaviors that can facilitate successful resolutions of problems in interpersonal interactions.

The presence of two leaders also insures continuity in the sequence of group sessions in the event one leader cannot attend a given session. Finally, the use of two leaders provides a good mechanism for the evaluation of the co-leader's group leadership behaviors. This potential for growth and improvement of the leader's skills is maximized when a debriefing period occurs immediately after the group session and the leaders can trade feedback.

Challenges to the Group Leaders' Credentials

Occasionally one finds young, relatively inexperienced parent group leaders or those without children of their own challenged by group members on the basis of this issue. These challenges may range from indirect questions concerning competence and knowledge to direct confrontations as to their ability to lead such a group in the absence of direct parenting experiences. Typical of these interactions are the following: "Have you run this kind of group before?", "Do you have any children?", and "What kind of qualifications do you have to run this kind of group?" Group leaders who are defensive and evasive in responses to these questions usually lose the confidence of the group. While the individuals who ask such questions may be seen as rude by some, it must be recognized that they have every right to ask these questions. The group they are involved with will consume their time and energy; as such, they have a right to evaluate whether or not they believe it will be worth spending their time and energy. The best response is a straightforward and matter-of-fact presentation of the information requested. In some instances, this may be followed by a statement to the effect that the success of the group is a shared responsibility of all involved.

The Silent and Apparently Noninvolved Group Member

For many inexperienced parent group leaders, the silent member is often seen as being uninvolved. It must be remembered that group involvement and participation are not necessarily indicators that learning and change are taking place. The silent group member's attendance, eye contact, and posture are often excellent clues as to whether the individual is truly uninvolved. The only major problems with a silent member result when the individual produces negative evaluative nonverbal feedback or refuses to interact in an exercise that requires the participation of the entire group. When either of these behaviors occurs, it is imperative that the group leader privately confront the group member involved about the incident and the issue. In some parent groups, it is essential that all members participate in the exercises for the benefit of the other members. In such cases the group member's continued attendance in the group may be conditional upon a certain degree of participation. This issue is usually easily resolved, particularly if the group leaders indicate their support to the silent member and listen to any concerns or apprehensions s/he may express.

Handling Problem Behaviors

While most of the group leaders' functions are aimed at creating a positive group atmosphere and facilitating participants' learning, on occasion the group leader will need to cope with behaviors that are disruptive to the learning process. This section attempts to address some of the more common problem behaviors group leaders may discover. The suggested approaches or solutions are not necessarily best or only ways of dealing with a given problem. Rather, they represent approaches that have been reported as being effective by experienced parent group leaders. In coping with problems in the group, the group leader should conceptualize the situation as an opportunity to demonstrate and model positive, nondestructive, and nonhurtful resolutions of conflict. In many ways the parents in the group will see the group leader's actions as a measure of the degree and kind of acceptance which they can expect from the leader. Thus the successful resolution of conflict can enhance the trust and security the parents feel in the group and this will maximize the potential for learning to take place. In coping with problem behaviors on the part of group members the leader must make the presumption of reasonableness and interpersonal caring with regard to the motives of all those involved in the interaction.

The Monopolizer

The actions of monopolizers are often based on a high need for personal acceptance and/or a large amount of anxiety about their adequacy. Paradoxically, the monopolizer often receives covert and, occasionally, overt disapproval messages from the group, which only further stimulates his/her need to speak. There are a number of steps that can be taken to assist with this problem. First, the group leader needs to initially and periodically raise the issue of equal "air time" for all group members. This is explained and reinforced as being a major goal of the group, since it produces the sharing and problem solving necessary for a successful group experience. Second, the monopolizer must not be put down or criticized by the group leaders, but should be validated and reinforced for his/her contribution. "Mr. Smith, it sounds as if you really have a good grasp of the principle we are discussing. Can anyone else see some other ways we can use the principle?" The group leader may interrupt and divert the focus of attention to other group members as suggested above, but not in so doing criticize the monopolizer. The third step in coping with monopolizers usually takes place after efforts along the lines of the first two steps have been taken but have failed to discourage and decrease this disruptive behavior. If, by the third session, a given group member is still monopolizing an excessive amount of the group's time, the group leader must speak directly to the member in private. Continued attendance may have to be made conditional upon more appropriate participation in the group.

Abusive Language or Criticisms

The use of abusive language or criticisms between group members usually has a chilling, if not totally destructive, effect upon the sharing, trusting, and mutual problem-solving atmosphere of the group. The group leader should immediately intervene when such behavior occurs and should presume a helpful intent on the part of the abusive or critical speaker. The following is one way this might be done:

> Mrs. Smith, I can see your concern about helping Mrs. Jones, but I am afraid your words may not be as helpful as you intended them to be. Why don't we stop for a minute and talk about helpful criticism. I would like to share with you an idea I have about helpful criticism. Helpful criticism to me has three parts. The first part is a brief description of what a person did. The second part is a description of the effect it had upon others. The third part is a request of the person to consider some other course of action. Mrs. Smith, when you told Mrs. Jones that what she said sounded dumb, I believe it upset Mrs. Jones and also may have upset some of the other group members. Would you be willing to try using the method of constructive criticism I have outlined to communicate your concern to Mrs. Jones? What were your concerns?

Crying and Emotional Upset

Periodically, a group leader is faced with a parent who becomes very upset and cries. The crying cannot and should not be ignored. The situation should be handled in a low-key manner, with the leader demonstrating patient reassurance, e.g., "Sometimes one needs to cry a bit before they can continue." Recognition of the emotions being experienced can also help the individual who is upset. If the upset continues for more than 5 minutes, the group leader may ask the member if s/he would like to take a break from the group for a few minutes. Ideally, one of the co-leaders should accompany the group member if s/he chooses to leave the group. While having the group member leave the group may be seen as inappropriate to those experienced in group therapy, this is not the case for a parent education group. It must be recognized that, in most parent groups, the parents do not conceive of themselves as patients, and the intrapsychic conflicts of other members of the group are not seen as their primary concern nor as an appropriate focus for the group.

The Presentation of Information and Skills in Prestructured Groups

In parent groups in which a part or the entire period of each session is centered around a predetermined curriculum or set of skills, it is necessary for the group leader to develop a structure for the sessions. The author has formulated a 5-step model for conducting groups with predetermined curriculums.

STEP I: The first task involves the group leader's organizing a presentation in which specific predetermined principles or skills are explained. This most often can be accomplished through the medium of a minilecture, i.e., a 5 to 10 minute presentation. The use of visual aids, such as an easel or blackboard, is often a very helpful device for listing the main ideas of the presentation. In developing the minilectures, the group leader must focus on clarity, brevity, and the use of simple language.

STEP II: The group leader should next present the group with examples of the principles or skills discussed in the minilecture. It is most helpful when the examples employed are relevant to the everyday interactions between the parents and their children.

STEP III: The group leader provides the group with examples that may or may not illustrate the principles or skills described earlier. The group as a whole must try to determine whether the examples provided by the leader fit and illustrate the principles and skills. Steps II and III are intermediate steps in the acquisition of the principles and skills to be learned. If the group members cannot handle these discriminations with a 95% level of accuracy, the group leader should not progress to step IV.

STEP IV: The group leader presents the group with problem situations in which the group must decide whether a given principle or skill would be appropriate. Part of the practice of analyzing the situations and deciding upon the applicability of a given principle or skill includes answering the following questions: Why is it applicable? Why isn't it applicable? Describe how you would apply the principle or skill.

STEP V: The group leader presents the group with a series of situations in which the principles or skills under study could be applied. The group members are requested to break down into small groups of 3 or 4 individuals and role-play their solutions repeatedly until all have participated and they have arrived at what they consider to be the best solution. This process usually takes from 15 to 30 minutes, during which time the group leaders move among the small groups and act as consultants. Following this exercise, the larger group is reassembled and the smaller groups are requested to present to the entire assembly their selected solution to the situation presented. The presentation of each of the smaller group's solutions is followed by a discussion and analysis of the proposed solutions by all of the group members.

The model presented is designed to maximize the parents' involvement with and commitment to learning the principles and skills. The traditional lecture/discussion format, which was used for years in parent education groups, while comfortable, often failed to engage the parents sufficiently to produce a familiarity and commitment to trying a given approach. The basic principles of social psychology suggest that the more energy an individual or group expends on a given idea, the greater the likelihood that they will value the experience and retain the information exchanged. The model presented uses graded steps to maximize parental involvement and to increase the probability that the material will be learned and integrated in the parents' response repertoires.

Problem-Centered Group Consultation

The problem-centered group represents a significantly different type of group experience for parents than either the prestructured group described earlier or a therapy group for parents. Problem-centered group consultation provides an experience in which parents are free to bring up problem situations they face at home with the expectation that the group will provide assistance with the solution of the problem. This type of group can readily degenerate into an "ask the expert" situation, in which all the questions are posed to the group leader. The group leader must be careful not to be seduced into this role, since it will defeat the value of the group consultation experience in giving the members practice in analyzing and solving problems in a more objective and rational fashion. Many times, the problems under consideration, while not burning issues to any given parent, are relevant due to a high degree of homogeneity in the ages of the children involved.

In problem-centered group consultation, the group leaders' role is that of a facilitator of the group problem-solving process. The basic steps in the process are provided as a guide to the group leader.

STEP I: The parent presents the problem to the group.

STEP II: The other group members restate the issues and problems back to the initiating parent. The parent initiating the problem is expected to clarify or correct any misconceptions. This phase continues until all involved feel comfortable in their understanding of the definition of the problem.

STEP III: The group engages in brainstorming in an attempt to arrive at the most probable causes for the problem. The group leader helps them analyze the cognitions, feelings, and behaviors of those involved in the situation. During this phase, the initiating parent's role is that of an information resource; this individual is requested to suspend any judgment as to the reasonableness or accuracy of the group's understanding. At the end of this phase, the initiating parent is asked to state what s/he thinks is the most reasonable understanding of the problem.

STEP IV: The group as a whole must now generate a list of possible solutions to the problem as stated by the initiating parent. The parent initiating the problem selects the most promising solution, and the group works on developing a description of how to implement the solution. This is followed by the group members acting out, in roleplay, the proposed solution.

Informal Unstructured Groups

Groups that meet informally and make no provisions for the structure of the sessions present perhaps the greatest challenge to the skills of the parent educator. As the life span of such groups is likely to be relatively short, the group leaders are required to employ all their knowledge and abilities in developing some focus for the experience and in rapidly assessing the needs and goals of the parents in attendance. Such groups are likely to consist of heterogeneous populations and are thus most difficult to fit into the parent education model presented here. General issues of relevance to all parents, e.g., stage-appropriate behaviors and problems, are most likely to meet with the greatest success in such situations. However, the inherent lack of structure in this type of group provides a heightened enticement for falling into the trap of assuming the "expert" role, in which all questions and issues are directed toward the parent educator, who is expected to provide the "answers."

One of the leaders' first tasks with unstructured groups is to provide the missing element: structure. It is important to come to a general group consensus of relevant topics and issues to be treated during the course of the parent education effort. This is often greatly facilitated by having each parent write on a piece of paper or index card a few topics of specific interest to him/her. The cards can be collected and the pool of topics written on a blackboard by the leader, with additional potentially appropriate topics being added by the parent educator. The parents can then vote for one or two topics of particular interest to them. Topics are then selected according to the outcome of the voting and the constraints of the time parameters of the parent education group experience. Such a procedure increases the assurance of the relevance of the parent training to the parent group. The last session or two of the groups' meeting schedule may be left open to treat topics whose importance emerges during the group meetings or to complete unfinished business.

Considerations

Considerable attention has been given in the literature to the notion of "meeting the client where he is," and this has relevance to parent education with informal and unstructured groups. Often the group, however diverse in certain immediately apparent respects, nonetheless shares areas of commonality, e.g., geographic location, aspirations for children, concerns with rising property taxes, etc. The group leaders facilitate the group interaction if they have taken the effort to familiarize themselves with these commonalities and are able to "speak the language" of the group. However, the leaders must be cautious not to overdramatize such characteristics to the point where it is perceived as a mockery or insult.

Individual members of the group typically demonstrate a preference for various ways of talking about their experience. If the group leaders listen closely to the predicates (verbs, adverbs, adjectives, and nominalizations) used by parents in discussing their own experiences, they can become aware of the primary representational system of each individual (Grinder & Bandler, 1976). For example, Don may describe an event he witnesses using such terms as, "Once I *perceived* what she was trying to do, it was very *clear* to me and I began to *see* the whole *picture*." Another group member might describe a similar event with the statement, "When I finally got a *feel* for what she wanted, I was able to *get a hold on* the situation and make *contact* with her." While the first group member described his experience in terms of what he saw (a *visual* representation of his experience), the second member discussed the event in feeling (a *kinesthetic* representation) terms. Experiences are also represented by group members from an *auditory* representational system, e.g., "I finally *heard* what she was making so much *noise* about, and then things *quieted* down considerably." Thus, people typically organize their world in terms of pictures, sounds, and/or feelings.

The importance of these processes lies in the fact that the group leaders' awareness of a member's way of representing experiences, e.g., visual, auditory, or kinesthetic, can serve to enhance clarity and accuracy of communication between group members, spouses, or between group member and group leader. When an individual believes that the leaders and/or group members understand his/her experience, a sense of trust is fostered. The parent who desperately states "Does what I'm saying to you sound right to you?" and is responded to with "Sure, I can see the picture you've drawn for us" is not likely to feel understood. By trying to match the response to the group members' most consistently used representational systems, feelings of misunderstanding and alienation between group members can be minimized. The parent educator who is able to assess an individual's most highly valued sensory channel of representation is in a position to enhance a state of empathy and to facilitate a positive learning experience.

Techniques for Stimulating Group Interaction

Often the lack of structure and organization in informal unstructured groups of parents serves to intimidate the already reluctant group members and further hamper meaningful self-expression and group interaction. It is crucial during the early phase of working with such groups that the activities be designed to be relatively nonthreatening and lead to the development of a sense of group cohesion.

While this is a crucial issue in virtually all groups, it is particularly true of unstructured groups, where there is a lack of task homogeneity, except in the most general terms, at the onset.

A sense of group identity is often fostered by the process of sharing among group members. This can be enhanced when the material shared is done so anonymously and involves the expression of feelings and experiences, as opposed to opinions or judgments. An example of such an icebreaker activity is to have each group member write down on identical pieces of paper the one thing that concerns or bothers him/her the most about being in groups like the present one. Each paper is folded and all are placed in a container and mixed together. Each member draws a slip of paper and reads the response written down, replacing it if it is his/her own. After the response is read, the group discusses it and adds comments. Comments by the trainer such as, "How do you think you would feel if you had this concern?" serve to encourage further exploration of these issues. This process can then be repeated with each group member writing a brief description of a happy or unhappy event s/he can remember from his/her own childhood on the paper. The person who draws the slip is then to express thoughts on how it would feel to have had that childhood experience. The slips of paper are collected and destroyed at the end of the exercise, without comment, to ensure confidentiality.

Role-playing is another technique or process that can be employed with unstructured and informal groups to facilitate the experience of the group members. Role-playing may be utilized to clarify and define a specific problem behavior the parent is dealing with and thus more closely approximates the *in vivo* situation. The various roles in the interaction can be played by the group leaders, the parents themselves, or any possible combination. Role reversal may aid in enhancing the parents' perspective-taking abilities in parent-child interactions. Behavioral rehearsal involving modeling and practice of desirable parenting behaviors can also stimulate the parents' involvement in the training experience.

The skillful and experienced parent educator comes armed with a repertoire of exercises and techniques that can be molded to fit the ever-changing needs of the unstructured parent group. Many parent groups require an extended warm-up phase in which a variety of family exploratory experiences can be shared. Often family photographs or albums, scrapbooks, or family projects can serve as springboards to discussion of a multitude of pertinent family issues. Such experiences can facilitate sharing, group cohesion, and pride in the family unit, as well as provide material relevant to parent training needs. Parents may be requested to bring in family trees so that an exploration of their family of origin may be conducted, which might further their understanding of how families function as well as encourage interest and participation.

Family sculpting, employing the patterns of communication elucidated by Virginia Satir (1972), is another process that can serve to foster active group participation. Many parents are intrigued by the concepts of the basic patterns, i.e., placating, blaming, computing, and distracting, as they readily see in themselves and their family members the manifestation of these roles and interactions. The actual experience of assuming a pattern in a role-played interaction can enhance self-awareness and serve as a point of departure for discussion of a variety of family issues related to role patterns, role complementarity and reciprocity, and role expectations. Patterns of communication games in which families engage become apparent through the use of such exercises. Group members can then be encouraged to employ various exercises at home in the context of their family interactions to further generalize the effects of the experience.

A note of caution is warranted regarding the use of these exercises and experiences. Parent trainers must employ practical judgment and tact when exploring potentially sensitive areas of family interaction through the use of such techniques. This appears to be particularly true in informal unstructured groups, as the very lack of structure is most conducive to diversion or regression to a group therapy process format.

While sculpting and role-play exercises often focus on specific events or material from a particular family, the parent educator's role is to extract from such vignettes general concepts, principles, or patterns relevant to as many parents as is possible. For example, a group leader may join a couple in role-playing a typical family scene, where they are trying to coax their independent-minded preschooler to bed. In the course of this enactment, the group leader becomes aware that the father is sending the child an incongruent message, the verbal content of his command communicating "Go to bed," while his teasing smile, engaging tone of voice, and lingering playfulness indicate his desire for the child to remain, despite the mother's authoritative insistence. Whereas a family therapist might probe for a deeper analysis of the dynamics of this particular family interaction pattern, e.g., the nature of the parents' contact when the child is not present, such a course of inquiry is not appropriate in the context of the parent education group. The parent educator might choose to discuss the interaction in terms of the need for husband and wife to have time alone together, the importance of being congruent when communicating, and effectively expressing both opposing feelings, etc.

Nonetheless, sometimes a group member may persist in engaging in inappropriate self-disclosure about problematic personal difficulties or family relationships. The parent educator can often minimize the impact of such behaviors by reframing the situation in a more positive or optimistic light for the parent, by providing support, and by tactfully directing the focus of the group toward another pertinent issue.

The parent group educator must be attuned to the multiple channels for communication available in the group training setting. Any of a large variety of techniques, methods, or processes, e.g., demonstration, lecture, group discussion, reading materials, self-disclosure, homework assignment, vivid metaphors, etc., may be employed to maximum advantage by the sensitive and skillful group leader. The purpose or goal of any technique or intervention may be to support a member, reframe a parent's statement or experience, explore an area in greater depth, divert attention from an explosive issue, etc., depending on the context and the manner in which it is employed. While the informal and unstructured group may present obstacles not present in more focused parent groups, it may also provide an opportunity for the deployment of creative and resourceful talents by the seasoned parent educator.

CONCLUSIONS

This chapter has attempted to provide an overview of what the authors perceive to be the general issues and specific considerations in conducting a parent education training group. The practical topics treated are felt to be relatively independent of the theoretical orientation of the parent group leader and to provide a framework for assessing and meeting the special needs of parents of exceptional subpopulations of children. While cognizance of these factors can serve to facilitate the acquisition of information and skills in leading parent training groups, it is acknowledged that the most effective method of learning is direct experience with parent groups themselves. With each experience, the parent educator acquires the sense of respect and humility necessary to become an effective collaborator and colleague in the difficult task of becoming an effective parent.

REFERENCES

Auerbach, A. B. *Parents learn through discussion.* New York: Wiley, 1968.

Brim, O. G. *Education for childrearing.* New York: Free Pr, 1959.

Grinder, J., & Bandler, R. *The structure of magic* (Vol. 2). Palo Alto, California: Sci & Behavior, 1976.

Kawin, E. *Parenthood in a free nation* (3 Vols.). New York: MacMillan, 1963.

Makarenko, A. S. *A book for parents.* Moscow: Foreign Languages Publishing House, 1921.

Rogers, C. *Client-centered therapy.* Boston: Houghton-Mifflin, 1951.

Satir, V. *Peoplemaking.* Palo Alto, California: Science and Behavior, 1972.

Slavson, S. R. *Child-centered group guidance of parents.* New York: Intl Univ Pr, 1958.

Tavormina, J. Basic models of parent counseling. *Psychological Bulletin.* 1974, *81* (11), 827-835.

Westport-Weston (Connecticut) Mental Health Association. *Evaluation study of a parent discussion group.* New York: Child Study, 1959.

Chapter 6

EVALUATION AND COMPARATIVE STUDIES OF PARENT EDUCATION

Joseph B. Tavormina

THE present volume illustrates the growing popularity of parent counseling as a preventive-educative-therapeutic intervention procedure. An ever-increasing body of theoretical and empirical literature demonstrates its widespread use. In fact, significant advances, although more theoretical than experimental, have occurred since the original publication of the "basic models" review, in which the issue of the relative effectiveness of different counseling strategies was addressed. This chapter presents an update of the earlier review as well as an analysis of the salient issues for subsequent research and development.

THEORETICAL STRUCTURES

Parent counseling fits into the family or systems theory perspective, with its emphasis on the parent as an active change agent in the parent-child-family interaction network. However, similar to the growth of family therapy as a popular strategy, parent counseling has developed many more adherents and practitioners than demonstrations and critical evaluations of its efficacy. Many definitions and types of parent counseling currently exist, but Graziano (1977) provided the best overall description, although taken from his particular theoretical perspective. He emphasized three factors: (1) the direct training of parents in (2) certain procedures that (3) they are to implement in their natural environment. This definition easily encompasses the often-confusing discrepancy between parent education and parent counseling, in which the former is preventive and the latter interventive in focus. However, the procedures used vary along three dimensions. The first two correspond to basic schools of psychotherapeutic intervention: One emphasizes feelings and the second emphasizes behavior as the primary starting point. The third model, the

---

This chapter is based in part on an earlier work, J. B. Tavormina, Basic models of parent counseling: A critical review. *Psychological Bulletin*, 1974, *81*, 827-835.

newest and gaining in popularity, employs a combination of the other two.

The first model is termed *reflective counseling* in light of the emphasis placed on parental awareness, understanding, and acceptance of the child's feelings (Auerbach, 1968; Ginott, 1957; Gordon, 1970). It uses cognitively mediated variables (feelings) as a means of affecting the child's behavior and the parent-child interaction. For example, the Ginott approach teaches parents the following trilogy: understand and reflect the child's feelings, then set an appropriate limit, and finally provide an alternative and more acceptable means for the child to express these feelings. The second method, *behavioral counseling*, attempts to reduce the emphasis on cognitive variables with its focus on actual behavior. Counseling is geared toward teaching parents to manipulate their responses to the child in order to affect the child's subsequent behavior (Patterson, 1971a; O'Dell, 1974; Graziano, 1977). As an example, parents are taught the basic principles of operant conditioning and how to apply them to their specific child-rearing problems.

The third *combination format* attempts to use the productive aspects of the first two. It is based on the assumption that parents need both to discuss their feelings and to learn new management tools; as such, it has bridged the gap between behavioral and reflective procedures by using elements of each separate method (Tavormina, Hampson, & Luscomb, 1976; Abidin, 1975; Schopler & Reichler, 1973). For example, the parents spend initial sessions confronting their own and their children's feelings; then the focus turns to solutions and strategies for specific child-rearing problems.

Both basic models have enjoyed a history of positive outcomes, in terms of testimonials and actual data. The combination format has gained its share of supporters, even without major empirical work; this is most probably due to its dual focus on attitudinal and behavior changes. Nevertheless, with these three divergent procedures, plus their multiple offshoots that depend on the preferences of individual practitioners or researchers, very few clear-cut conclusions can be reached as to which works best under which conditions or for which populations or target problems. In spite of the confusion, there is need to sort out the relative effectiveness of the three models as a guide for research and practice.

METHODOLOGICAL ISSUES

All three models are similar in that they focus on specific child-rearing issues. However, each takes a different perspective for defining and assessing counseling outcome. Although each has been used to deal with similar problems across similar populations, the focus of intervention, the issues addressed in counseling, and the criteria for measuring success differ widely. The behavioral model places a direct focus on concrete, observable behavior, while reflective techniques involve the use of cognitively mediated variables such as warmth and understanding. Change criteria for each follow from these assumptions: change in parental cognitions for the reflective model, and change in frequency of target behaviors for the behavioral counseling model. Arguments as to which is more effective in light of such criteria are meaningless. Furthermore, practitioners have provided parent testimonials and clinical impressions as demonstrations of the utility of their particular method, which leads to a strong statement that parent counseling is an effective tool, regardless of which strategy is employed.

In the face of the overall positive data, there is danger that "parent counseling" may become a new panacea, one used as a general interventive tool. Nevertheless, without specification of parameters (type of counseling, indications and contraindications for use, strategies for particular populations and problems), confusion and failure will result. Practical issues such as the needs of parents, the clinical constraints on practitioners, the lack of availability of enough clients with similar problems, difficulties with comparable control groups, and economic considerations all stand in the way of research on the efficacy of parent counseling. Consequently, as more clinicians adopt one or another of the available models, even without the necessary empirical safeguards, the failures of parent counseling will mount. However, such failures will reflect the limits of knowledge and application, rather than the paradigm itself.

In addition to these theoretical and pragmatic issues, differences in design and measurement techniques have been barriers to comprehensive evaluation of the various models. With respect to measures, problems have included those with validity and reliability, with the lack of comparable outcome measures across methods and across studies, and with the absence of standard measures to be used as general criteria for success. A multitude of measures have been used to assess outcome: parent reports, clinical impressions, attitudinal measures, observational measures, frequency counts of target behaviors, as well as measures of overall family interaction patterns. It seems that each researcher invents a new measure or two for each study. One need only add the fact that each study works with a slightly different population or range of subject ages or presenting problems, and the picture becomes even more confusing.

Design problems have also plagued research in the field. Little is known about the duration, maintenance, or generalization of counseling effects; very few adequate follow-up studies exist. Similarly, replication studies also are rare, as are suitable control conditions for many of the available studies. Instead, there is a multitude of studies, each with varying degrees of sophistication, most with positive results, but also with significant experimental flaws. Parent counseling as a science has reached the stage where methodological rigor is necessary: A phenomenon does exist; now it must be measured more precisely. Demonstrations of positive results are no longer sufficient; instead, attention must be paid to commonalities and comparisons across methods, populations, and problems addressed.

Consequently, it is time to develop common methodologies and measurement strategies. To provide a basis for comparison across methods or studies, it is feasible to incorporate measures typically used by the various counseling models as multiple criterion variables. A combination of parent report, attitudinal measures, and observer variables will provide a broad-based, more representative comparison of effectiveness. Furthermore, samples of the target behaviors across settings as well as evaluations of the frequency of selected additional, although non-targeted, behaviors will provide knowledge about generalizability and overall impact. Such a multimethod approach hopefully should minimize the effects of bias or distortion inherent in the use of single criterion measures (Lytton, 1971; Patterson & Reid, 1973; Tramantana, 1971). Even more importantly, a multimethod approach should help researchers broaden their scope of conceptualization about the parameters involved and highlight the need to specify these parameters beyond the limits imposed by theoretical allegiances.

Evidence for the Efficacy of Individual Models

While the aforementioned plea for a broader scope of analysis can be seen as a necessary next step, the field has not yet reached such a level of sophistication. With the exception of a handful of studies on comparative effectiveness across models, most work to date has focused on demonstrations of the efficacy of single models. Since much of this work has been reviewed elsewhere (Berkowitz & Graziano, 1972; Tavormina, 1974; Graziano, 1977), it will only be briefly summarized here.

Research on Reflective Counseling

The reflective counseling model offers many different approaches in terms of group size, homogeneity of membership, length of groups, number of meetings, and the process of the group (Gabel, 1972). There are some basic similarities (Auerbach, 1968; Brim, 1959; Ginott, 1957): (a) an exchange of information between parents; (b) development of a group agenda based on interests and problems specific to group members; (c) encouragement of the expression of feelings; and (d) creation of a climate of trust and safety in which all can participate freely and honestly. The basic goals are also similar: (1) understanding of the child's needs at various stages of growth; (2) examination of what group members expect of themselves as parents; (3) a focus on feelings within the parent-child interaction; and (4) recognition of the children as reacting and feeling individuals.

There have been three lines of research on this counseling model: parent testimonials and clinical impressions; evaluations of parental attitudes, knowledge, and feelings; and changes in parent and child behavior. Many nonsystematic, noncontrolled studies endorse the efficacy of reflective counseling. For example, Cary and Reveal (1967) cite clinical impressions of the benefits their program had in helping mothers gain an understanding of their children. Parental reactions to Bricklin's (1970) groups were highly favorable in terms of more reported understanding of their learning-disabled children. Nevertheless, in all of these studies, the absence of controlled measures significantly detracts from the scope and applicability of the reported results.

Shapiro (1955, 1956) was among the first to test the hypothesis that counseling affects parental attitudes and feelings. This study employed a design that has become typical for such evaluations: before and after intervention application of an attitude survey or similar instrument both to participants and some matched group of nonattendant controls. However, a number of negative outcomes (Balser, Brown, Brown, Laski, & Phillips, 1957; Gildea, Glidewell, & Kantor, 1967; Glidewell, 1961) counterbalanced the positive (Hereford, 1963; Gabel, 1972) ones that resulted from these designs. The mixed results from these studies may reflect the different instruments used to measure attitudes, the differences in group content, or the different types of group interactions. There is a need for systematic control and more rigorous definition of these variables in order to determine the effective components of the reflective procedure.

One may also question whether change in parental attitudes necessarily corresponds with or results in appropriate changes in either parental or child behavior. In fact, the available evidence has suggested a lack of correspondence in this regard. Friedman (1969) correlated parents' attitudes from the Hereford Parent Attitude Survey (1963) with their children's social behavior as assessed by raters who observed the children while they attended summer camp. Leadership in the child was correlated significantly with the attitude of parental trust. However, no other significant relationships were found between any of the other six rated areas and the five Hereford subscales. Similarly, Hereford (1963) reported that sociometric ratings of the children of counseled parents improved more than those of control children, but teacher ratings showed no change across groups. Swenson (1970) and Stearn (1971) reported similar results. Some parent attitude change also resulted in child improvement, but across all subjects, this improvement did not reach statistical significance. This lack of correspondence between attitudinal and behavior change casts some doubt on the utility of reflective counseling as a cost-effective intervention strategy.

Nevertheless, some investigations have shown that reflective counseling has a positive effect on child behavior, especially in a school setting. These studies have examined the effects on the actual school behavior of children after counseling their parents. Dee (1970) found that child-centered parent counseling enhanced the overall treatment effectiveness for 40 children with school adjustment problems, as measured by a personality questionnaire and a behavior rating scale taken at school and at home. McGowan (1968) divided 32 underachieving tenth-grade boys into 4 groups: a no treatment control, parent counseling only, student counseling only, and both parent and child counseling, each done separately. The focus of the parent groups was to help the participants better understand their children's behavior. All treatment groups improved on home improvement ratings and on the ability to express feelings, but *only* the boys whose parents received counseling significantly improved their academic achievement, which was maintained at a 5-month follow-up. Perkins (1970) and Perkins and Wicas (1971) reported similar results in their study of similar design of 120 ninth-grade male underachievers. Finally, Radin (1969) and Palmo (1971) found essentially the same results in their studies of the effects of parent counseling on school-related behavior. All these studies illustrated that counseling the parents to better understand the child's problems could result in changes in the child's behavior, at least within the school setting.

Consequently, reflective counseling can have a generalizable effect on the child's behavior, but it is very puzzling why such results occurred in one context (school issues) but not in others. Once again, the need to specify parameters of effectiveness across populations, presenting problems, and treatment settings must be underscored.

Reflective counseling has resulted in a number of positive outcomes, but enough critical data also exists to question its widespread utility. It is highly probable that some reflective counseling procedures are too vaguely defined or applied to have practical importance. The lack of precision in definition, the use of many different instruments to assess change, and the lack of a specific problem focus seem to interfere with the outcome of these counseling techniques. For example, Carkhuff and Bierman (1970) stress the need for greater specificity of focus as a practical necessity. They state that parents must be trained *directly* in ways of interacting with their children in order to effect actual behavior change. They add that one must work specifically on a particular problem in order to change it. Consequently, the reflective model presents a useful philosophy and outlook, which by itself can be helpful to parents, but it needs to be supplemented by greater specificity and a problem-solving focus in order to increase its applicability.

As an illustration of this specificity, Guerney's filial therapy (Andronico, Fidler, Guerney, & Guerney, 1967; Guerney, 1964; Guerney, Stover, & Andronico, 1967) attempts to bridge the gap between attitude change and resultant parent and child behavior. Parents are trained to conduct client-centered play therapy with their own children. The basic goal is to allow the child to work through his emotional problems via play in a therapeutic atmosphere of parental empathy and acceptance. Stover and Guerney (1967) attempted to evaluate the procedure by rating the tape recordings of sessions. Parents trained in filial therapy increased their reflective statements and decreased directive statements, while untrained parents did not change. In addition, the children of trained parents increased their verbalizations of negative feelings toward their parents, while control children did not. Hence, there is nothing inherent in the reflective counseling model to prevent the development of more specific application procedures; nevertheless, to date, that specificity has been rare.

Research on Behavioral Counseling

Behavioral counseling stresses the importance of the principles of learning theory in understanding parent-child behavior. Patterson

(1971a) isolates two critical steps in the process: (a) training parents to carefully observe and record the child's behavior and (b) training them to reinforce the child's behavior appropriately. The common denominators in the process are teaching the principles of conditioning and their application in specific circumstances.

As opposed to the group counseling format used frequently with the reflective method, a great deal of the work with behavioral counseling, especially the earlier studies, has used individual subject designs. Cone and Sloop (1971) reviewed 52 single-subject studies, all of which reported successful treatment outcomes for a variety of problem behaviors. Each study stressed the need to involve the parents in the treatment process by teaching them new ways of responding to the child. Many of these investigations pointed to the durability of change, typically over a 4- to 7-month follow-up. In addition, some authors suggested that there were beneficial side effects in the improvement of the quality of family functioning. Subjective reports on this issue included more warmth, more affection in the family, and an increase in parental self-esteem.

Other authors have highlighted the variety of problems and populations addressed by this model (O'Dell, 1974; Berkowitz & Graziano, 1972), each with very encouraging reviews. In the most comprehensive review to date, Graziano (1977) divided the targeted problems into the following categories: (1) somatic systems, which include general somatic problems, asthma, obesity, and enuresis and encopresis; (2) more complex issues, which include work with parents of retarded, psychotic, and autistic children across home, school, and institutional environments; (3) negativistic, noncompliant, oppositional, and aggressive behavior; (4) reduction of children's fears; (5) language and speech disorders; and (6) common home-based behavior problems that occur with high frequency but low intensity. The preponderance of positive outcomes across these divergent issues has presented strong evidence for the utility of the behavioral format, especially when dealing with specific, focused target behaviors.

In spite of these positive results, a number of critical questions merit exploration. First, the single-subject designs contrast with the no-treatment control and multisubject designs used to evaluate reflective counseling. Although these designs provide precise control and viably demonstrate the efficacy of work with single problems in single families, they do not provide a workable clinical model. On a very pragmatic level, working with single families is both costly and time-consuming for hard-pressed and understaffed clinics.

Second, there have been few systematic attempts to determine how the parents use their new knowledge in areas other than those targeted. The previously cited studies claim, but have not experimentally demonstrated, that the behavioral principles are put into generalized use. Target problems are dealt with, but whether the parents can or do use these problem-solving principles for subsequent issues remains an unanswered question. In other words, while the interventive aspect of work with single families has been highlighted, the preventive or educative aspects have not been demonstrated.

Third, the single subject designs do not address the issue of generalizability of techniques (O'Dell, 1974) from one family to another. What has been useful for one family may not hold for another even with similar problems, since the techniques were geared especially for the individual targeted family. Finally, even when parents become effective managers of the child's behavior at home, there is no guarantee (Wahler, 1969) of control over those behaviors in any other settings or with any other than the trained caregiver. For example, in contrast with the effects of reflective parent counseling on resultant child school behavior, the generalization of change from home to school has not been reliably demonstrated by behavioral counseling.

Until these issues are suitably addressed, one can only conclude that behavioral counseling may be limited in scope to dealing with specific target behaviors, rather than as a general educative tool for parents. Nevertheless, more recent work has begun to evaluate the utility of a behavioral group counseling format and to measure the effects of this method in areas other than those specifically targeted for change.

The basis of the group format is some presentation of didactic material or programmed texts that outline principles of reinforcement theory and child management. Two such texts were *Parents Are Teachers: A Child Management Program* (Becker, 1971) and *Families: Applications of Social Learning to Family Life* (Patterson, 1971b). However, Patterson emphasized that mere presentation or parental reading of these principles will not in itself change their behavior. The basic work of the group is the application of the didactic principles to the particular needs of each participating family. Theoretically, such a dual focus can cover both the educative and interventive aspects of parent counseling.

In his recent review, Graziano (1977) cited a number of studies of the behavioral group format, each with positive outcomes, but also with a great many shortcomings. Hirsch and Walder (1969), in a well-controlled study, found that treatment mothers gained a significant amount of knowledge about principles of behavior modification and decreased their frequency counts of inappropriate behavior. Neither group size nor maternal intelligence affected the outcome, a result suggesting that the process of behavioral counseling is both flexible and consistent enough to be applicable in a variety of situations. However, since improvement was also noticed for the no treatment control group, the authors felt that maternal reports (dependent measures were maternal responses to objective tests and maternal frequency of target behaviors) might have been a biased account. Perhaps mothers who want to see improvement will do so in spite of the circumstances. Indeed, it is possible that concerned parents might tend to report improvements, even when the target behaviors are not changing. This finding demonstrates the need for unbiased observations by impartial raters as more valid indices of change.

Similarly, Salzinger, Feldman, and Portnoy (1970) reported that 8 of the 15 parents of brain-injured children who attended their groups experienced success, while the rest were failures. They attributed these failures to the parents' inability or lack of motivation to carry out programs designed for them. They concluded, as did Patterson (1971b), that parents must be reinforced for their attempts, just as they are expected to reinforce the child's attempts to change his behavior. Since the parents, not their children, are the actual clients in these groups, they would benefit from more direct reinforcement, support, and encouragement, rather than merely being expected to apply new learning to difficult interactions with their children. Finally, McPherson and Samuels (1971) concluded that group methods may be useful, but they are not a panacea for parental child-rearing problems. As a result of their groups, parents of aggressive, hyperkinetic, and acting-out children reported feeling less helpless, but they added that the sessions were not enough to help them deal with the problems they were facing. The authors concluded that the group helped cue parents to some important dimensions, but such groups must be supplemented with play therapy for the child and reflective counseling for the parents to increase their effectiveness. Quite possibly, the group procedure may therefore lose some of the precision afforded by individual behavioral counseling, while at the same time it gains the advantage of wider applicability and a more general educative focus. This issue of a trade-off of education for intervention must be evaluated as a means to address cost-efficiency questions by use of these procedures.

A second line of innovative research has involved a greater sophistication in both group procedure and measurement methodology. One criticism of the behavioral group format has been the lack of specificity about what occurs within the group. A number of researchers have begun to clarify the nature of their interventions step by step. For example, Patterson and his co-workers (Patterson, 1971b) have developed a very specific program procedure that begins with home observations to gather baseline data on child behavior and parental modes of reinforcement. They then require the parents to study a programmed text on the principles of child management. After successfully passing a test on the didactic material, parents are taught to observe and record rates of target behaviors. Then training groups are formed to help parents set up and execute programs at home. Finally, repeated follow-ups are made to determine the stability of treatment effects. Not only has Patterson presented a model for specific program description, he also has paved the way for more methodological sophistication in terms of measurement. He was an early advocate of multiple outcome criteria, including parent ratings, parent frequency counts, and frequency counts by objective observers. For example, the 1973 study of 11 families of aggressive boys (Patterson & Reid, 1973) found significant improvement across all three variables. Nevertheless, Patterson still called for further development of various criterion measures to demonstrate the effectiveness of this procedure.

Another line of measurement improvement has been the focus on parent-child interaction patterns. In a series of papers, Mash and his associates (Cone & Sloop, 1971; Mash, Terdal, & Anderson, 1973) have developed a methodology to evaluate the antecedent-consequent relationship between parent and child. Observations are taken in a three-term contingency model, including parent starting an interaction, child responding, and parent reacting consequently. The authors directly trained parents how to command appropriately, reinforce compliance, and ignore noncompliance. Across a number of studies, they demonstrated that their observational system measured increases in child compliance and appropriate consequential parental behavior, while the control groups did not change significantly.

In a similar vein, Forehand and his associates (Forehand & King, 1974, 1975; Peed, Roberts, & Forehand, 1975) used both interactional and parent attitude measures to evaluate the efficacy of the Hanf parent training program (1968, 1969). This program entails a procedure of direct shaping of the mother's interactive behavior with the child. Results indicated not only that the attitudes and interactions improved in the lab setting, but they generalized to the home settings as well. These results highlight the importance of using multiple measures across settings to provide optimal assessments of outcome. In addition, the focus on interactional behavior allows for tests of parental ability to *use* the child-rearing procedures they have been taught, not only in areas specifically dealt with in the training, but in more generalized situations.

These developments have begun to demonstrate the potential utility of group behavioral counseling as an interventive and educational tool. Nevertheless, new research is necessary to incorporate the recent methodological improvements, notably the specificity of program description, multiple criteria assessment, and use of interactional systems as dependent variables, into more comprehensive designs.

Relative Effectiveness Across Models

As evidence for the efficacy of these individual procedures mounts, questions of relative effectiveness and cost-efficiency must be raised. The multiple criteria outcome strategy has eliminated one obstacle to such research, since measures typically used by each separate method can be incorporated into a broader-based evaluation package. Hence, the following issues have become more salient: Which approach is more appropriate for which population of parents, for which behavior problems, and for which types and ages of children? In addition, in a wider sense, comparative evaluation is necessary to determine how parent counseling will fare as an intervention/education strategy in contrast to the more traditional strategies, such as psychotherapy or behavior therapy for the child, or to the increasingly popular procedure of family therapy. Since the phenomenon of parent counseling has been shown to be effective, it is necessary to locate its place in the hierarchy of intervention modalities in terms of comparative utility and specific indications for its applicability.

Unfortunately, only a handful of studies of comparative effectiveness exist; more are desperately needed within the entire field of intervention as well as for parent counseling. Not only are method-versus-method comparisons important, but comparisons of methods-versus-alternative-potential-change factors also are necessary. It is unclear whether the parent counseling procedure, the group process, the characteristics of the leader, or the attention and expectancy variables have produced the positive outcomes in previous studies. In spite of the need for studies to identify the specific determinants of outcome for each procedure, only one well-controlled study currently exists. Walter and Gilmore (1973) contrasted the behavioral group counseling condition with a placebo treatment condition that emphasized the status-attention and expectancy variables inherent in the procedures. The group counseling method led to significant reductions in targeted deviant behavior as measured by both parent and observer frequency counts, while the placebo group did not improve. The authors concluded that the systematic and contingent application of behavioral principles, rather than therapist contact or parental expectancy of improvement, was crucial for successful counseling outcome. Consequently, this study presents an important first look at the within-intervention factors that could contribute to client improvement; hopefully others will follow.

Three lines of comparative effectiveness research exist; each provides different perspectives and conclusions. The first (Johnson, 1970) contrasted both parent counseling models with two traditional therapeutic intervention strategies for the children. Subjects were 45 essentially normal first and second graders, described by their parents as being obedience problems. Five conditions were studied: (a) reflective treatment of the mother; (b) reflective treatment of the child; (c) behavioral treatment of the mother; (d) behavioral treatment of the child; and (e) no-treatment control. Results on parent ratings of specific obedience behaviors showed that both behavioral and reflective treatments of the mother as well as behavioral treatment of the child resulted in child improvement. However, indices of general adjustment did not indicate significant change for any group. Therefore, each parent counseling mode had some but not universal positive effects, but the effects were no different than those from the child behavioral treatment condition. A number of possible explanations for these results exist. A population of normal children may be amenable to any intervention modality; in fact, the preventive/educative nature of any counseling for this population may be of primary importance, rather than specific child behavior change. Furthermore, within-intervention factors such as leader characteristics could account for the positive outcome, rather than the experimental conditions themselves. Finally, it is possible that different intervention strategies may achieve the same effects and be equally efficient with certain populations or problems, such that the very process of intervention may outweigh the effects of specific intervention contents. Whatever the case, the Johnson study has raised some very interesting issues to be clarified by subsequent research.

The second line of research, that of Alexander and his associates based upon their work with delinquent youth (Alexander & Parsons, 1973; Parsons & Alexander, 1973), has resulted in the strongest evidence for the superiority of the behavioral over any other treatment strategy. This research has provided significant methodological and measurement improvements as well as demonstrating very clear-cut results. Alexander pursued four main goals in this work, each of which stands as an important direction for all subsequent research in the area: (1) provision of a clear description of the intervention techniques; (2) description and evaluation of the changes in family process expected from the intervention (process measures); (3) use of clearly defined and nonreactive behavioral criteria to evaluate intervention effects (outcome measures); and (4) adequate controls for maturation and professional attention.

Four treatment conditions were contrasted: behavioral family counseling, client-centered (reflective) counseling; psychodynamic family counseling; and a no treatment control. Results across process measures (family interaction) and outcome measures (recidivism rates) strongly supported the superiority of the behavioral over any other method. The authors pointed to the specificity and problem-focus of the behavioral method as critical determinants of outcome.

Nevertheless, even with such a careful design and strong results, certain criticisms remain. Experimenter expectancy in favor of the behavioral method could have occurred: The behavioral was a new program, while the others were part of the more traditional intervention format for these youngsters. The therapists varied in training and perhaps most importantly in enthusiasm, factors that were not considered. Finally, specificity and problem-focus may have been the key change parameters, rather than type of counseling per se. Whatever the case, the overwhelmingly positive results point to the relative effectiveness of Alexander's specific behavioral method in contrast to the two other types of counseling for this population of families.

Essentially similar results were found in Tavormina's 1975 study of the relative effectiveness of behavioral and reflective group counseling of mothers with mentally retarded children. The behavioral and reflective conditions (two groups of each, each group led by different leaders with similar levels of experience) were contrasted with a no treatment wait control group. Results across the multiple outcome criteria (parent attitude, problem checklists, behavioral observations of mother-child interaction patterns, maternal target behavior ratings and frequency counts, and subjective maternal reactions) indicated that both treatment conditions resulted in significant improvement over the control group.

However, the data also demonstrated the superiority of the behavioral over the reflective method, since the behavioral groups resulted in significantly greater magnitudes of improvement in four of the six outcome areas. Furthermore, both individual behavioral groups resulted in similar magnitudes of change across measures, whereas the two reflective groups differed in some areas. Consequently, the leader probably becomes more of a pivotal figure in the outcome of the reflective groups, while in the behavioral groups the leader may be secondary to the method. In this regard, Alexander's notion of treatment specificity may be a critical underlying determinant of these results: The more specific the procedure, the less the outcome will vary due to extraneous influences such as characteristics of the leader.

This group of parents had significant child-rearing problems for which they desired solutions, and the behavioral format proved ideal for them. Nevertheless, the issue of generalizability of these results to other populations remains unclear. In an attempt to address this issue, Tavormina and his associates (Hampson, Tavormina, Grieger, & Taylor, 1977) replicated the previous design with a sample of lower socioeconomic status foster mothers. Once again, both the reflective and the behavioral treatment groups resulted in significant improvements over the no treatment controls. Once again, the behavioral method was more effective, but not to the extent demonstrated by the previous study. Along the lines of theoretical expectations, the behavioral groups resulted in greater improvement, especially on the observational and behavioral measures, while the reflective approach resulted in more significant gain in the attitudinal areas. Consequently, the reflective group had a significant impact most notably on parent attitudes, but it still lagged behind the behavioral in overall effectiveness. The authors suggested that some combination of the two approaches might affect both attitudes and behaviors in an optimal manner, such that a combination format might produce results across all criterion areas in a more efficient manner.

The Tavormina studies still lacked some necessary rigor: a lack of an adequate follow-up, no attempt to determine the generalizability of the results, especially to the home, and a possible confound of leader with method effects in the first study. Nevertheless, the results are strong and consistent in their demonstration of the overall efficacy of parent counseling and of the relative superiority of the behavioral over the reflective procedure. Coupled with the results shown in Alexander's work, they begin to provide considerable evidence on the comparative effectiveness issue. Each set of studies has individual shortcomings, but the power and similar direction of results with the strong methodological designs used by both authors demonstrate a phenomenon to be reckoned with in subsequent research and practice.

By no means is the relative effectiveness issue adequately answered as a result of these studies. Families of delinquents and families with mentally retarded children and foster children benefited greatly from the behavioral model. However, the foster parents also benefited from the reflective format in terms of growth in attitudes, and the parents of normal children in Johnson's study benefited from both types of counseling. In the long run, matching the particular format to the particular needs of the parents involved might help produce the most program efficiency.

The issue of intervention versus education/prevention also enters into this discussion, as does the question of specificity and problem-focus versus generalized format of the counseling procedure. In other words, the relative effectiveness dimension may revolve around the parameter of the original purpose of counseling for particular sets of parents. While both may be equally useful as general orientation tools, they may vary in effectiveness depending on the specific needs of given populations or individual parents. For example, the parents of delinquents and mentally retarded children needed and benefited from the specific child management tools provided by the behavioral model, whereas the parents of foster children had needs both for the tools and for more understanding of the children. Consequently, the needs of the parents when they enter counseling may account for many of the results, to the extent that attempts should be made to match the solutions offered by each strategy to the particular needs of parents as a prerequisite to counseling. Furthermore, one must take care not to generalize the results of these current relative effectiveness studies to any other populations of parents, without prior experimental investigation.

Not only are studies necessary to delineate the needs of other populations of parents and the relative effectiveness of counseling modes across these other populations, there is also need to contrast parent counseling as a strategy with other intervention strategies using methods such as those of Johnson (1970). As the data mounts for the efficacy of parent counseling, it has become more important to determine which populations and problems this intervention procedure (in general and in specific models) is most likely to benefit as the treatment of choice.

Finally, the relative effectiveness literature stands as a contrast in techniques; hence, it has not evaluated the underlying process variables that influence outcome, regardless of the technique employed. It will be important to determine which common denominators are effective across techniques so that these parameters can be highlighted. For example, specificity and problem-focus, leader characteristics, and patient needs and characteristics have been mentioned as influential factors. Other variables such as the group process or the group composition, the topics covered by the leader, and the quality of the interaction of specific leaders with specific groups all merit exploration as potentially influential factors. Consequently, it is necessary to broaden the scope of parameters of success beyond those provided by technique comparisons in order to develop a more complete understanding of the parent counseling process.

Attempts at Synthesis: The Combination Format

In order to develop a general educative and preventive tool for parents, recent attempts have been made to combine the behavioral and reflective strategies into one comprehensive package. Based on the premise that parents in general can benefit from skill training in child management areas, the combination formats emphasize both components as necessary parts of an overall parent education procedure. No single group or time-limited intervention, no matter how effective, can solve problems that have taken years to develop; consequently, the combination format attempts to build a foundation upon which other more specific interventions can be based. For example, the combination method seems to serve as a general introductory course; more advanced courses can be taken if other problems arise. Furthermore, the procedure is based on the premise that parenting is a skill, the learning of which parents can find helpful, especially in areas specific to their own needs.

The philosophy behind the combination models seems to follow directly from the generalist or eclectic intervention positions, which stress the need to match therapeutic endeavors to the particular needs of particular clients. It thereby represents an interesting and potentially useful innovation for the field of parent counseling, and it merits considerable attention both in program development and in outcome research.

The literature on this format, although limited in amount, presents some positive data for the efficacy of the model. Schopler and Reichler (1973) have developed a method termed *developmental therapy* that focuses on the emotional and specific skill needs of parents of autistic children. They emphasize parental realism in accepting and coping with their handicapped children. They then provide specific behavioral (mostly operant) procedures for the parents to use in working with their children. In addition, Schopler and Reichler rely heavily on modeling and therapist demonstrations as a means to show parents how to deal with their children, rather than merely telling them. This use of therapist modeling represents an important addition to their overall counseling procedure, since it provides parents with an opportunity to observe "experts" work with their children, from which they can learn new attitudes and specific approaches.

The limited outcome data on this project has been encouraging, as have been the authors' conclusions. Schopler and Reichler feel that realistic parental appraisals of the child contribute to parental freedom in dealing with the child and in helping the family to cope. Tavormina and his associates (Tavormina, Hampson, & Luscomb, 1976; Tavormina & Hampson, 1978) have voiced similar appraisals, based upon their work with the combination format with mothers of retarded children and with foster mothers. They emphasized the need for parents to face, express, and accept their feelings as a prerequisite to teaching them new child-rearing techniques. Specifically, once the parents have dealt with their feelings (helplessness, anger, frustration), they can be more receptive to new learning. In a comparison of the combination format for mothers of retarded children (initial sessions focused on expression of feelings; subsequent work on specific target behaviors with Becker's 1971 *Parents Are Teachers* as a guideline) in the previously mentioned behavioral and reflective groups (Tavormina, 1975), the combination participants (Tavormina, et al., 1976) voiced the greatest satisfaction with their groups. Actual data from the Tavormina, et al., 1976 study showed gains across measures for combination parents, but not to the extent produced by the behavioral groups themselves. In other words, the behavioral format led to more significant change on the specific outcome measures, but the mothers were more pleased with the combination format. Perhaps the trade-off of outcome for satisfaction may be helpful in the long run, but the absence of follow-up data does not allow for such conclusions. Whatever the case, the issue of relative utility of the combination method, especially across different outcome areas, must be clarified by subsequent research.

Along the lines pioneered by Schopler and Reichler, the addition of modeling procedures to the behavioral and reflective aspects of the combination method seems to strengthen outcome. In their program for foster parents of handicapped children, Tavormina and Hampson (1978) stress three components to their 10-week training groups: a reflective feeling focus geared to facilitate understanding and acceptance of parental and child feelings and behavior; a behavioral focus designed to teach new techniques to apply to specific problems; and a modeling focus in which members observe, participate, and are actively supervised in their attempts to use the new techniques. Preliminary data from this project have indicated significant behavioral and attitudinal change on the part of the parents, basically of the same magnitude as reported previously for the behavioral groups. However, this promising outcome must be supplemented by maintenance and generalizability data, as well as more specific comparisons with other procedures, before conclusions can be drawn. Furthermore, work with parents of the handicapped or foster children, who represent populations with very special needs, cannot be generalized to other different populations without some empirical support.

Only one other rigorous evaluation of the combination format exists with similar encouraging results (Sanders, 1975), but it too deals with a special population: children who were hospitalized for severe emotional problems. Sanders operationally defined and sought to increase parental warmth in terms of (1) lowered frequency of parental demands; (2) more acknowledgment of the child's feelings; (3) more positive feedback and less but more consistent negative feedback; and (4) encouragement of more spontaneity in the child. As a result of specific training in these areas, observational data revealed significant improvements in each of the four areas. The lack of control groups somewhat detracts from these results, but the use of before-and-after observations of parent-child interactions stands as a rigorous measure. Consequently, Sanders was able to operationally define a reflective concept and then was able to teach parents to implement this concept with their children. As such, this study represents a good model for the synthesis of existing procedures and for the specification of problems to be solved and of procedures to deal with them.

Without a doubt, the available data on the combination format points to the potential utility of the model. More research is needed, especially with other populations and types of child and parent problems. In addition, each author cited here has used a slightly different form of the combination procedure, so there is also need to specify and evaluate the important parameters of this new strategy.

CONCLUSIONS AND NEW DIRECTIONS

The positive and generally useful impact of the parent counseling intervention strategy has filled the experimental literature. On theoretical and pragmatic grounds, it has consistently demonstrated its overall importance. Nevertheless, a number of very crucial issues are still unanswered, and these stand as critical directions for subsequent theoretical and empirical advancement. Each will be considered separately.

1. Does the experimentally demonstrated change have practical significance as well? Here the relevant question becomes how much change is real change. Issues such as the statistical versus the practical significance of changes and the experimental control versus the practical utility dimensions must be addressed. For example, within the multiple outcome measurement strategy, which measures are most important? Should they be weighed in a hierarchial fashion? In addition, is more necessarily better in all cases, or does too much of a given behavior cause long-term negative effects? If parents are trained to the "appropriate" in response to their child's behavior, how appropriate is appropriate? Should it be 90 percent of the time or less or more? A number of studies have found that without training, most parents typically appropriately consequated their child's behavior 2/3 of the time (Wahl, Johnson, Johanson, & Martin, 1974; Tavormina, Kralj, & Hampson, 1978). Training to higher levels may make the parents too consistent and too contingent, to the point that their children are not prepared to deal with the inconsistencies and lack of contingency in their larger environments. Clearly, the field needs a delineation of the definition and direction of desired changes, especially in those areas where too much of a behavior may become just as problematical as too little of that same behavior.

2. Little attention has been paid to the negative and unintended effects of the counseling process on the family (Graziano, 1977). There are potential ripple effects from intervention with a subset of any system; as the equilibrium changes, other compensatory changes also occur. If these changes are not monitored, the issue of the overall impact of the counseling on the family system will remain unclear and potentially problematical since other unintended but negative consequences could result from positive changes in the subset that received the intervention. For example, most "parent" counseling really boils down to "mother" counseling, and the impact on the father of counseling the mother is not well known. Care must be taken to monitor the impact of parent counseling on the entire family system in order to provide badly needed information on the larger implications of counseling for the whole family.

3. Researchers and practitioners alike have experienced failures in some of their clients, but the literature has not dealt with the issue of the failures of parent counseling. The reasons for these failures, in terms of pragmatic errors, parent characteristics, and type of child problems faced, all merit experimental consideration. In fact, analysis of the cases of failures should help point to necessary design and application improvements. Unfortunately, the haste to prove the effi-

cacy of parent counseling procedures has also resulted in a relative avoidance of the factors involved when these procedures do not work.

4. The emphasis on parent counseling and parent education suggests some underlying model or definition about what it means to be a good parent. Is a "good" parent warm, contingent, accepting, or some combination of values? The implicit notions of good parenting expressed in various counseling procedures need to be made more explicit and tested empirically. Without such model building and validation, all counseling efforts stand on an unclear foundation, and the long-term implications for the grown children of previously counseled parents also are cast in doubt. Especially with the new trends to teach "parenting" courses as parts of high school curricula, there is need to clarify the necessary and positive components of parenting itself.

5. It is possible that different ages of the child require different types of parenting; parents of younger children need more of a behavioral focus, whereas parents of adolescents need more of a reflective focus. The changing demands of parenting across age and developmental stages of the child merit theoretical and experimental attention. Variables like the value of parental flexibility and tolerance in the face of continuously changing child problems should be considered.

To do justice to these issues, parent counseling must interface with developmental theory, in terms of both child and parent development over time and increasing age. The practical impact of parent counseling procedures must be considered with respect to their position in the life cycle of each particular family system as well as to the long-term implications of a particular intervention at a particular time in that life cycle. Consequently, the effects of parent counseling have been measured from a very narrow perspective; there is need to broaden that perspective to include an analysis of the developmental progression of the family system both as a determinant and as a result of the counseling intervention.

6. The preventive/educative and interventive aspects of the parent counseling strategy have been highlighted in this review as very different goals for the counseling process. It seems logical that different outcome criteria should be used to evaluate these different counseling types. Issues like individual versus group counseling, cost-effectiveness for the different goals, and area of impact resulting from each aspect should be considered by future researchers. For example, should more therapist time per success be expected for interventive counseling without its efficiency being questioned? Or, in general,

how should cost-benefit factors be weighed in light of the different scope of each counseling focus?

7. Most of the available literature has evaluated the effects of parent counseling as a result of variations in counseling technique. This focus, while important, has not allowed for an equally important focus on the process variables that may influence counseling outcome, regardless of technique. The impact of the leader on the outcome has not received enough attention with respect to the influence of leader ability, interest, and experience. Nor has the interaction of particular leaders with particular clients or groups of clients been evaluated as a potential outcome determinant. Finally, the role of group process variables and specific group behaviors should be considered when measuring outcome. In other words, factors other than techniques themselves must be evaluated to determine their contributions to counseling outcome.

8. One excellent indication of counseling outcome may be the initial level of the client at the outset of intervention. Yet, this topic has received little experimental attention. The potential influence of such issues as levels of parental psychosocial functioning; parental motivation for change; demographic characteristics such as age, education, and social class; specific parental attitudes and expectancies for the children; and relative amount of parental realism regarding their assessments of their children must be considered. Clearly, some parents are more amenable to change than others, a factor that varies with the different characteristics of the parents as they seek counseling. For example, what are the implications of couple parent counseling as opposed to mother counseling in terms of overall effectiveness? The role of the father in the system merits more of a focus, especially as he impacts on the outcome of any counseling procedure.

9. Finally, two issues frequently mentioned in the review should be reemphasized here. Too little work has been done on the maintenance and generalization of counseling effects. Little is known as to whether counseling serves as a temporary phenomenon or has lasting value for the family. Follow-up, replication, and generalization (to new settings and to other behaviors) studies are difficult to perform, but their difficulty should not serve as a complete deterrent to their use. Information is needed about the scope of counseling effects across time and across general areas and levels of family functioning.

The breadth of these recommendations serves as a final demonstration of the growth of parent counseling. As a field, it has begun to transcend mere evaluations of its utility. The phenomenon is clear; it is time to turn toward the development of an understanding of where it fits within the overall network of therapeutic strategies. Each recommendation points to an area in which the field of parent counseling must be broadened to determine its interface with other areas of theory and practice. Consequently, more comprehensive research is needed to supplement and synthesize the many research strands that currently dominate the field.

REFERENCES

Abidin, R. R. *Parenting skills: Trainers manual* (Vols. 1 & 2). New York: Behavioral Pubns, 1975.

Alexander, J. F., & Parsons, B. V. Short-term behavioral intervention with delinquent families: Impact on family process and recidivism. *Journal of Abnormal Psychology*, 1973, *81*, 219-225.

Andronico, M. P., Fidler, J., Guerney, B. G., & Guerney, L. The combination of didatic and dynamic elements in filial therapy. *International Journal of Group Psychotherapy*, 1967, *17*, 10-17.

Auerbach, A. B. *Parents learn through discussion.* New York: Wiley, 1968.

Balser, B. H., Brown, F., Brown, M. L., Laski, L., & Phillips, D. K. Further report on experimental evaluation of mental hygiene techniques in school and community. *American Journal of Psychiatry*, 1957, *113*, 733-739.

Becker, W. C. *Parents are teachers: A child management program.* Champaign, Illinois: Res Press, 1971.

Berkowitz, B. P., & Graziano, A. M. Training parents as behavior therapists: A review. *Behavior Research and Therapy*, 1972, *10*, 297-317.

Bricklin, P. M. Counseling parents of children with learning disabilities. *Reading Teacher*, 1970, *23*, 331-338.

Brim, O. G. *Education for child rearing.* New York: Russell Sage, 1959.

Carkhuff, R. R., & Bierman, R. Training as a preferred mode of treatment of parents of emotionally disturbed children. *Journal of Counseling Psychology*, 1970, *17*, 157-161.

Cary, A. C., & Reveal, M. T. Prevention and detection of emotional disturbances in preschool children. *American Journal of Orthopsychiatry*, 1967, *37*, 719-724.

Cone, J. D., & Sloop, E. W. Parents as agents of change. In A. Jacobs & W. W. Spradlin (Eds.), *Group as agent of change.* Chicago: Aldine-Atherton, 1971.

Dee, G. The effects of parent group counseling on children with school adjustment problems. *Dissertation Abstracts International*, 1970, *31*, 1008A.

Forehand, R., & King, H. E. Pre-school children's non-compliance: Effects of short-term behavior therapy. *Journal of Community Psychology*, 1974, *2*, 42-44.

Forehand, R., & King, H. E. *Non-compliant children: Effects of parent training on behavior and attitude change.* Unpublished manuscript, University of Georgia, 1975.

Friedman, S. T. Relation of parental attitudes toward child rearing and patterns of social behavior in middle childhood. *Psychological Reports,* 1969, *24,* 575-579.

Gabel, H. D. *Effects of parent group education and group play psychotherapy on maternal child rearing attitudes.* Unpublished doctoral dissertation, University of Rochester, 1972.

Gildea, M. C., Glidewell, J. C., & Kantor, M. B. The St. Louis school mental health project: History and evaluation. In E. L. Cowen, E. A. Gardner, & M. Zax (Eds.), *Emergent approaches to mental health problems.* New York: Appleton, 1967.

Ginott, H. G. Parent education groups in a child guidance clinic. *Mental Hygiene,* 1957, *41,* 82-86.

Glidewell, J. C. (Ed.). *Parental attitudes and child behavior.* Springfield: Thomas, 1961.

Gordon, T. *Parent effectiveness training.* New York: McKay, 1970.

Graziano, A. M. Parents as behavior therapists. In M. Hersen, R. M. Eisler, & P. M. Miller, (Eds.), *Progress in behavior modification* (Vol. 4). New York: Acad Pr, 1977.

Guerney, B. G. Filial therapy: Description and rationale. *Journal of Consulting Psychology,* 1964, *28,* 304-310.

Guerney, B. G., Stover, L., & Andronico, M. P. On educating disadvantaged parents to motivate children for learning: A filial approach. *Community Mental Health Journal,* 1967, *3,* 66-72.

Hampson, R. B., Tavormina, J. B., Grieger, R., & Taylor, J. R. *Relative effectiveness of behavioral versus reflective counseling with foster parents.* Presented at the American Psychological Association, San Francisco, August 1977.

Hanf, C. *Modifying problem behaviors in mother-child interaction: Standardized laboratory situations.* Presented at the Association of Behavior Therapies, Olympia, April 1968.

Hanf, C. *A two-stage program for modifying maternal controlling during mother-child interaction.* Presented at the Western Psychological Association, Vancouver, April 1969.

Hereford, C. F. *Changing parental attitudes through group discussion.* Austin: U of Tex Pr, 1963.

Hirsch, I., & Walder, L. Training mothers in groups as reinforcement therapists of their own children. *Proceedings of the 77th Annual Convention of the American Psychological Association,* 1969, *4,* 561-562. (Summary)

Johnson, S. A. A comparison of mother versus child groups and traditional versus behavior modification procedures in the treatment of "disobedient" children. *Dissertation Abstracts International,* 1970, *31,* 2989B.

Lytton, H. Observational studies of parent-child interaction: A methodological review. *Child Development,* 1971, *42,* 651-684.

Mash, E. J., Terdal, L., & Anderson, K. The response-class matrix: A procedure for recording parent-child interactions. *Journal of Consulting and Clinical Psychology,* 1973, *40,* 163-164.

McGowan, R. J. Group counseling with underachievers and their parents. *School Counselor,* 1968, *16,* 30-35.

McPherson, S. B., & Samuels, C. R. Teaching behavioral methods to parents. *Social Casework,* 1971, *52,* 148-153.

O'Dell, S. Training parents in behavior modification: A review. *Psychological Bulletin,* 1974, *81,* 418-433.

Palmo, A. J. The effect of group counseling and parent-teacher consultations on the classroom behavior of elementary school children. *Dissertation Abstracts International,* 1971, *32,* 1863A-1864A.

Parsons, B. V., & Alexander, J. F. Short-term family intervention: A therapy outcome study. *Journal of Consulting and Clinical Psychology,* 1973, *41,* 195-201.

Patterson, G. R. Behavioral intervention procedures in the classroom and the home. In A. E. Bergin & S. L. Garfield (Eds.), *Handbook of psychotherapy and behavior change: An empirical analysis.* New York: Wiley, 1971. (a)

Patterson, G. R. *Families: Applications of social learning to family life.* Champaign, Illinois: Res Press, 1971. (b)

Patterson, G. R., & Reid, J. B. Intervention for families of aggressive boys: A replication study. *Behaviour Research and Therapy,* 1973, *11,* 383-394.

Peed, S., Roberts, M., & Forehand, R. *Generalization to the home of behavior modified in a parent training program for non-compliant children.* Unpublished manuscript, University of Georgia, 1975.

Perkins, J. A. Group counseling with bright underachievers and their mothers. *Dissertation Abstracts International,* 1970, *30,* 2809A.

Perkins, J. A., & Wicas, E. Group counseling with bright underachievers and their mothers. *Journal of Counseling Psychology,* 1971, *18,* 273-278.

Radin, N. The impact of kindergarten home counseling program. *Exceptional Children,* 1969, *36,* 251-258.

Salzinger, K., Feldman, R. S., & Portnoy, S. Training parents of brain-injured children in the use of operant conditioning procedures. *Behavior Therapy,* 1970, *1,* 4-32.

Sanders, S. Corrective social interaction therapy: Role modeling. *American Journal of Orthopsychiatry,* 1975, *53,* 875-883.

Schopler, E., & Reichler, R. J. Parents as cotherapists in the treatment of psychotic children. In A. Davids (Ed.), *Issues in abnormal child psychology.* Monterey, California: Brooks-Cole, 1973.

Shapiro, I. S. Changing child-rearing attitudes through group discussion. *Dissertation Abstracts,* 1955, *15,* 538-539.

Shapiro, I. S. Is group parent education worthwhile? A research report. *Marriage and Family Living,* 1956, *18,* 154-161.

Stearn, M. B. The relationship of parent effectiveness training to parent attitudes, parent behavior, and child self-esteem. *Dissertation Abstracts International,* 1971, *32,* 1885B-1886B.

Stover, L., & Guerney, B. G. The efficacy of training procedures for mothers in filial therapy. *Psychotherapy: Theory, Research, and Practice,* 1967, *4,* 110-115.

Swenson, S. S. Changing expressed parent attitudes toward child-rearing practices and its effect on school adaptation and level of adjustment perceived by parents. *Dissertation Abstracts International,* 1970, *31,* 2118A-2119A.

Tavormina, J. B. Basic models of parent counseling: A critical review. *Psychological Bulletin,* 1974, *81,* 827-835.

Tavormina, J. B. Relative effectiveness of behavioral and reflective group counseling with parents of mentally retarded children. *Journal of Consulting and Clinical Psychology,* 1975, *43,* 22-31.

Tavormina, J. B., & Hampson, R. B. *A special foster care program for multi-problem children.* Presented at the American Psychological Association, Toronto, August 1978.

Tavormina, J. B., Hampson, R. B., & Luscomb, R. L. Participant evaluations of the effectiveness of their parent counseling groups. *Mental Retardation,* 1976, *14,* 8-10.

Tavormina, J. B., Kralj, M. M., & Hampson, R. B. *Behavioral observations of the quality of mother-child interaction patterns.* Unpublished manuscript, University of Virginia, 1978.

Tramantana, J. A review of research in behavior modification in the home and school. *Educational Technology,* 1971, *11,* 61-64.

Wahl, G., Johnson, S. M., Johanson, S., & Martin, S. An operant analysis of child-family interaction. *Behavior Therapy,* 1974, *5,* 64-78.

Wahler, R. G. Setting generality: Some specific and general effects of child behavior therapy. *Journal of Applied Behavior Analysis,* 1969, *2,* 239-246.

Walter, H. I., & Gilmore, S. K. Placebo versus social learning effects in parent training procedures designed to alter the behavior of aggressive boys. *Behavior Therapy,* 1973, *4,* 361-377.

SECTION II

WORKING WITH SPECIFIC POPULATIONS

Chapter 7

WORKING WITH PARENTS OF AGGRESSIVE CHILDREN

ARTHUR M. HORNE AND GERALD R. PATTERSON

THE AGGRESSIVE CHILD

CHILDREN who are out of control, disobey parental requests, fight, whine, tease, and argue probably comprise the single greatest source of frustration and complaints for parents (Patterson, 1964; Roach, 1958). Previous attention from child specialists, however, has centered upon areas they identified as serious and demanding attention, such as anxiety, withdrawal, and psychosomatic symptoms. Childhood aggression has generally been assumed to be a passing stage that would be outgrown during later childhood and adolescence. Follow-up studies of aggressive children, however, clearly indicate that out-of-control children are unlikely to "outgrow" their problems (Morris, 1956; Robins, 1966). Rather, children identified as in need of treatment for fighting, stealing, refusing to obey parental commands, and other aggressive acts were likely to be identified as deviant when they reached adulthood. They were associated with major crime, psychotic and neurotic behavior, and difficulty in maintaining employment much more than a matched sample of normal, nonaggressive children.

The aggressive child is identified as a child who demonstrates behavior normally associated with children, including crying, whining, temper tantrums, fighting, and refusal to obey parents, but at a much higher rate than is found in normal children (Patterson, Cobb, & Ray, 1973; Patterson & Reid, 1970). The aggressive child is very adept at coercing reinforcers from his/her environment, receiving the majority of reinforcers available in the family and giving very few in return. The process by which the aggressive child receives reinforcers has

The model presented in this chapter is the result of the efforts of all persons involved in the Social Learning Project over the past decade. Their contributions are recognized and appreciated. Matthew Fleischman provided significant contributions to this chapter, and his input is greatly valued. Appreciation is expressed to Rosie Coyle of Indiana State University and to Mary Perry of the Oregon Social Learning Center for their typing and manuscript preparation.

been identified by Wahler (1976) as a negative reinforcement trap. The child demands a reinforcer, such as candy in a grocery store, and, if refused, has a temper tantrum. In order to stop the crying, parents give the candy and thus are reinforced for complying because the child ceases his/her tantrum. Thus, the parents are "trapped" into complying with the child's wishes by their desire to terminate his/her noxious behavior.

PROGRAM DEVELOPMENT

1965-1973: Development of the Basic Technology

In the 1960s it became apparent that new and more effective methods of aiding families with child-rearing problems were necessary. This was, in part, evidenced by the fact that nearly 1/3 of all referrals by teachers and parents for mental health services were for children who were aggressive or out of control (Roach, 1958). The necessity of developing more effective child management programs was made more evident by Bahm, Chandler, and Eisenberg (Note 1), who found that of those referred for mental health services, only a small fraction of the conduct-disordered were offered services. Levitt (1971 pp. 474-494) reported that for those who did go to mental health services and were accepted for treatment, the treatment offered typically was individual, traditional therapy, which resulted in little effectiveness for socially aggressive and out-of-control children and left much to be desired in terms of effecting lasting change in the inappropriate behaviors of children (Meltzoff & Kornreich, 1970; Teuber & Powers, 1953). Further, children with conduct problems, it was found, tended *not* to change for the better if left untreated (Beach & Laird, 1968; Morris, 1956; Robins, 1966).

Since 1965, a group of research psychologists in Oregon have been studying the application of social learning theory to the treatment of aggressive children. Initially their treatment began by accepting for treatment families who were referred for treatment and included at least one boy who was socially aggressive or was out of control.

In its earliest work, the project pursued a series of single case studies in an effort to develop a feasible treatment methodology. Almost immediately, efforts centered on training parents and others in the child's environment to act as the treatment agents. At first, procedures included a heavy reliance on candies and buzzer boxes, but they quickly moved toward using elementary point systems, time-out, modeling, and contingent attention (Patterson & Brodsky, 1966; Patterson, Jones, Whittier, & Wright, 1965; Patterson, McNeal, Hawkins,

& Phelps, 1967). Concurrently, the project began experimenting with a procedure for observing deviant behavior in natural settings. With results in both the methodological and treatment areas showing promise, additional families were accepted for treatment. In each family there was a socially aggressive or out-of-control child. Prior to intervention with each family, observational data of behavior and interactions were recorded 10 times over a 2- to 3-week period. Following the observations, treatment was offered, then additional observations were conducted for posttreatment analyses of the effects of treatment. At this time, the Total Deviant Behavior score was developed, a score that identifies the total number of deviant behaviors the individual child engages in per minute while under observation. The treatment results of this stage of family therapy research indicated there was 60% to 75% reduction of inappropriate behavior from baseline to termination, with an average of 22.8 hours of professional time per family required for treatment purposes (Patterson, Cobb, & Ray, 1973).

Because in-school behavior was also often a problem (Patterson & Brodsky, 1966; Patterson et al., 1965), procedures were developed based on social learning theory using peers and teachers as change agents. Data collected showed that the resultant changes in the child were achieved with little cost to the teacher and persisted through follow-up (Patterson, Shaw, & Ebner, 1969).

Encouraged by these results, beginning in 1968, 27 new families with extremely aggressive, out-of-control boys were recruited for treatment. Referrals were taken on a limited basis from the local community. The children were typically from lower socioeconomic classes, with 8 from father-absent homes and 5 being treated with medication with accompanying diagnoses of minimal brain damage. During this time, the treatment procedures were refined and became more standardized. Programmed materials were given to parents, and tests were given over the material contained in the programmed materials. Prior to moving on to advanced-level work, parents were required to demonstrate mastery of the material presented at each level. In the previous work, therapists had attempted to alter only one or two behaviors, but with this phase of treatment, they began to work with a large number of clinical problems. Treatment generally encompassed all of the child's out-of-control behaviors of concern to the parents and referring agent. An average of 31.5 professional hours was required to produce changes in home-observed problem behaviors. Approximately 2/3 of the treated boys evidenced reductions of at least 30% in their output of aggressive behavior as measured by home observations. In addition, parents provided daily reports on the occurrence of symptoms of primary concern to them. These data also showed significant reductions from a 63% reported occurrence at baseline to 33% reported occurrence at termination. One year of follow-up data showed persistence of the effects along both measurement dimensions. In many cases, however, brief booster treatments were necessary.

It should be noted that the client population did not suffer from the attrition rates of between 56% and 70% experienced with more traditional treatment (Eideson, 1968; Hunt, 1961; Overall & Aronson, 1963). Of the 35 referrals, 8 (23%) dropped out during the intake/baseline, and 6 others left treatment prior to therapist recommendation. However, these latter 6 cases, who were seen by a therapist, were counted as treated (i.e., counted in the sample of 27). Both the lower attrition rate and the effectiveness of the treatment are particularly encouraging given demographic and clinical characteristics of the sample. In terms of referral categories, aggressive youngsters are typically less successful clients than their withdrawn or neurotic peers (Levitt, 1958, 1971; Robins, 1966), and in terms of client socioeconomic status, families of low socioeconomic status are the most likely to drop out of treatment shortly after intake (Overall & Aronson, 1963). This is not to say that family socioeconomic status or single-parenthood had no impact on the treatment. Both the study of 27 families (Patterson, 1974b) and a replication (Fleischman, Note 2) showed that single mothers and impoverished families are more difficult to treat, require longer treatment times, and comprise a greater proportion of the failures. Overall, however, the data suggested that such families are amenable to a social learning approach.

Analysis of the effects of treatment on the target child's siblings (Arnold, Levine, & Patterson, 1975) showed significant decreases in observed deviant behavior by termination — improvements that endured through 1 year of follow-up. This improvement in the siblings' behavior occurred whether or not the therapists extended treatment directly to the siblings and seems to substantiate the notion that treatment provides the parents with skills that generalize to other members of the family.

Of these 27 out-of-control cases, 14 also required classroom intervention. The classroom procedures developed included using feedback devices placed on the desk so that children would be able to identify when they were engaging in appropriate classroom behaviors. These were later changed to a less conspicuous work card that was designed for recording points earned for appropriate behaviors. The programs were initially developed and conducted by therapists but were later turned over to teachers for implementation and maintenance; it was found that, with practice, only a few minutes each day were required for teachers to effectively carry out treatment. For some families, where learning deficits were quite extensive, parents were taught to work as remedial teachers for their children (Patterson, Reid, Jones, & Conger, 1975).

For treatment of classroom behavioral problems, observational data were collected using a reliable measure of appropriate and inappropriate classroom behaviors. At completion of treatment, 2 out of 3 of the treatment group boys equalled or excelled the baseline performance of the normal peer classmates in the same room. The improvement continued on into the follow-up period. The average treatment time required of a therapist for classroom intervention was 28.6 hours per case (including remedial work).

In the early 1970s, the home and school intervention procedures were described in a single volume by Patterson, Reid, Jones, and Conger (1975). The general stance was that of the therapist working with individual families. The emphasis was upon working with the entire family as a system, with a particular focus upon training family members to learn negotiation skills in bringing about changes in each other's behavior. It immediately became clear that the book provided inadequate coverage of certain key concepts. To partially remedy this situation, audio tapes were developed for parents that detailed how to and how not to use such processes as contracting, time-out, negotiation, and positive reinforcement (Patterson & Forgatch, 1975, 1976). Even more detailed descriptions of the treatment processes are badly needed and are currently in preparation.

Controlled Studies

The clinical research described in the previous section was on treated families only. In order to conduct comparative clinical research, control measures were added to the next phase of program development. In the first controlled study conducted, 12 families who were referred for treatment were compared; 6 families received treatment, and 6 families became part of a waiting list control group. The 6 treated families showed significant reductions in acting-out and aggressive behavior, while the 6 untreated waiting list control families showed no reductions in inappropriate behavior (Wiltz & Patterson, 1974). In this study the first 6 consecutive families being seen were assigned to the treatment group and the next 6 consecutive families served as the waiting list control group.

In order to conduct research following a tighter experimental design, another comparative study was undertaken, this time incorporating random assignment to control for bias. The 6 families randomly assigned to treatment received the therapy program, while the remaining 6 families were administered a placebo therapy group model. After 5 weeks, the treatment group significantly reduced socially aggressive behaviors. The placebo therapy group had a slightly *higher* level of acting-out behavior *after* treatment than before (Walter & Gilmore, 1973). Both groups of families reported satisfaction with counseling, however, indicating that parental judgment may not be the best indicator of success.

At this point it was tentatively concluded that a behavioral treatment program had been developed that satisfied some criticisms of behavioral approaches to parenting. Generalization and maintenance were demonstrated, and in the two control group studies conducted — one involving assignment to a waiting period equal to the average treatment duration (Wiltz & Patterson, 1974) and the other to a placebo treatment (Walter & Gilmore, 1973) — neither control group showed any reduction in their total deviant behavior.

1973-1977: Review and Replication

The majority of work described thus far was directed toward families with socially aggressive children, children showing behaviors such as teasing, noncompliance, hitting, temper tantrums, etc. In 1972, in addition to families with socially aggressive children, families with a child who was a high-rate stealer were included. Analysis of the first study indicated that the earlier treatment had been less successful with children who committed low-rate behaviors (Reid & Patterson, 1976 pp. 123-145). In addition, family training procedures were expanded to incorporate these new behaviors, and additional criterion measures for success of treatment were developed. In 1972, 32 families with a stealer were being seen.

In the treatment program for families who had a stealer, in addition to training parents to deal with common tantrums and noncompliance, parents were taught to attend to even the mildest forms of stealing, such as unexplained borrowing or finding. As a result of teaching parents to track their child and to react mildly without being overly concerned about having total proof, the low-rate behaviors became amenable to treatment. The analysis by Reid, Rivera, and Lorber (Note 3) showed that this stealer sample was as effectively helped as the original, more heterogeneous sample of problem children (Patterson, 1976; Reid, Rivera, & Lorber, Note 3). It has been found in studying court records that treated aggressive children have almost no police records over a 2-year period (Moore, Chamberlain, & Mukai, Note 4). Children who are stealers, however, have presented a different picture. The data demonstrated a high offense rate for young stealers who were treated, though the treated rate levels off at about 30% committing police offenses. The offense rate for *untreated* stealers, on the other hand, did not level off and in fact accelerated drastically, reaching a 3-year accumulated rate of 80% committing police offenses (Patterson, 1976).

Another major task was to attempt to replicate the first study (Patterson's 1974 results) with an entirely different group of therapists. To do this, and to maintain some distance between the replication workers and the original team of researchers, an administratively distinct unit called the Family Center was created within the Oregon Research Institute (Fleischman, Note 5). Besides conducting the replication, it was hoped that the Family Center could become a demonstration model upon which to base other programs for aggressive children. An effort was made to further standardize the treatment, with particular emphasis on a group format for training parents (Fleischman & Conger, Note 6). A team was selected including a director, two clinical assistants, a school specialist, and three technical assistants. The director and clinical assistants had received prior intensive training from Patterson and his colleagues. The school specialist was a doctoral student in special education, with skills in classroom intervention and academic remediation. The technical assistants were undergraduate students trained in home observation and data collection methods.

Outcome data for the first 19 families to complete treatment are now available and are promising. Observed deviant behavior changed from a baseline mean of .844 per minute ($SD = .557$) to .462 at termination ($SD = .484$) ($t = 2.79$; $df = 18$; $p < .01$, one-tailed). Patterson's (1974a) sample of 27 children had a baseline average of .749 and a termination average of .402. The second major outcome measure, the proportion of targeted problem behaviors reported by parents, fell from 56% ($SD = 15\%$) to 23% ($SD = 14\%$) ($t = 6.02$; $df = 11$; $p < .01$). Patterson's sample showed an equivalent reduction from 62% to 35% of reported occurrences. An additional measure — change in the rate of negative and positive behaviors selected, observed, and recorded by the parents — also showed significant changes. Negative behavior decreased from .035 per minute ($SD = .02$) during baseline to .018 ($SD = .01$) at termination ($t = 4.34$; $df = 18$; $p < .001$), while positive behaviors increased, though nonsignificantly, from .029 per minute

(SD = .02) to .038 (SD = .03) (t = 1.09; df = 18). A detailed report is currently being prepared by Fleischman (Note 5).

It appears that in replicating Patterson's earlier work, not only was the effectiveness of the basic social learning model affirmed, but the steps taken to standardize and streamline the process did not impair its effectiveness. The only apparent major difference between the studies is that the Family Center's staff, using the refined treatment, achieved their results in 15.1 hours of professional time compared to Patterson's 31.5.

PROCEDURES

The procedures used to treat families with aggressive children have evolved over the last decade as a result of the empirical testing of a family intervention model derived from social learning principles. Elements of the model that have proven effective have been retained in the therapy manual by Patterson et al. (1975). Diverse therapeutic approaches have influenced the model such that methods consistent with a social learning orientation have been incorporated into the treatment services offered to parents. The result is a therapeutic model that is continually evolving; it is not complete, nor is it anticipated that it will be finished in the near future. When the model ceases to develop, it means that people have probably ceased to collect data evaluating it. Thus, the procedures that follow are offered as a snapshot of a growing model rather than the final picture of a treatment approach.

Program Format

The core program begins with a referral and an intake interview, followed by a baseline period for observations. After the baseline period is completed, 2 sessions are conducted with the parents of the aggressive child. Following the 2 sessions with the family, later sessions that are of a more structured nature may include parents from several families to form a group. In settings with a large client turnover, the use of a group parent instruction model provides for an efficient use of trainer time, for it is possible for an individual trainer to provide instruction to parents of as many as five families at one time during the group sessions.

Intake

The parents and the target child come for an intake interview, but they are seen separately. It is important that the initial meeting be warm, supportive, and understanding, for the tenor of all future contacts is determined by the first meeting at the Center. An emphasis on change occurring within the family is presented during the intake session, and it is emphasized that all family members will contribute to the change process — the child is not expected to do all of the work.

During the intake process, the parents and child have separate interviews. In the parent interview, the parents are given an overview of services and of the treatment model to be used. There is a discussion of the amount of involvement required of parents and of the types of concerns that are treated as well as the fees charged. If it is determined at that point that the social learning model is not appropriate or not desired, assistance in identifying other community services is provided.

If the parents indicate a desire for training, they are requested to complete an assessment package. The complete package is presented in Patterson et al. (1975), including samples of the inventories used. The assessment includes having the parents complete the Adjective Checklist (Becker, 1960), the Symptom Checklist (Patterson et al., 1975), and a Family Fact Sheet (Patterson et al., 1975), along with self-report information about the child's behavior, both past and present. The parent's self-report information includes specifying precisely what problems exist, descriptions of examples of parental consequation for the problems, including the forms of punishment used, who administers punishment, the consistency with which parents consequate misbehavior, and related information. At this point, also, the parents' ideas about the causes of the child's problems are explored. Parents' beliefs about causes of behavior (e.g., environmentally determined, the result of bad genes, the consequence of early trauma, or a function of organic damage) are important in determining the manner in which the program is presented. Observation procedures, which comprise a major element of assessment, are described to parents, and an appointment is set for the first home observations to occur. Counseling does not begin until 6 observations have been conducted in the home.

While the parents are being interviewed, the child is seen by another intake worker. The child interview is used to rule out brain damage, extreme retardation (IQ less than 50), and psychotic behavior. The Wide Range Achievement Test (Jastak, Bijou, & Jastak, 1965), the Wechsler Intelligence Scale for Children vocabulary test (Wechsler, 1949), and the Piers-Harris Scale for the measurement of self-concept (Piers & Harris, Note 7) are used, along with intake worker observations of cooperation, to assess the child. Through an open-ended interview process, the child is asked to describe changes in the family that s/he would like to see. The child's presentation is later incorporated into the treatment program to the extent possible.

Following the intake interview, baseline data are collected for a period of approximately 2 weeks. Data are collected using the observational coding system and a daily telephone report of data the parents collect. Observations in the home over the 2-week baseline period provide objective, reliable information about family interactions that are not available from other measurement sources. Additionally, the use of observations conducted at regular intervals throughout treatment provides the trainer with objective information concerning changes occurring within the family. This is important in light of research that indicates parents perceive improvement even when such improvement does not occur. Walter and Gilmore (1973) found that 67% of parents studied reported improvement in their children's behavior even when the behavior was not treated and when observations indicated that behavior had become worse.

This regular data feedback from observers provides the therapist with knowledge of when families are changing and, therefore, when treatment methods are effective. This leads to continual revision of the program offered parents, as directed by the objective information gathered through the observations. The use of observational procedures also provides an accountability system for the community to allow evaluation of services provided.

The observational system is described in detail by Reid (1978). Observations supply information about the total deviant score of family members. The total deviant score is comprised of 14 behaviors: Command Negative, Cry, Destructive, Dependent, Disapproval, High Rate, Humiliate, Ignore, Noncomply, Negativism, Tease, Whine, Yell, and Physical Negative. The remaining items in the code are positive or neutral behaviors in which family members may engage. Extensive evaluation studies of the observational data indicate that interaction patterns of normal children may be altered by instruction; that is, parents of normal children, when instructed to make their children look good or bad for observers, were able to do so. Parents of aggressive children, however, were not able to make their children look good for observers, indicating that the aggressive child truly is out of control and that the observational coding system is an accurate assessment of his/her behavior (Jones, Reid, & Patterson, 1975).

In addition to the observational procedures, telephone reports from parents are used for baseline as well as treatment assessment information. During the intake interview, parents complete a checklist of aggressive behaviors engaged in by their child. Following the intake interview, the parents are contacted daily, before training has begun, by a data clerk or secretary. In the course of the phone interview, parents are asked about specific behaviors that had been previously checked as bothersome and the setting in which the behaviors occurred. Discussion of the training process never occurs during these interviews, and interviewers are careful to emphasize that the purpose of the contact is for data collection only. After baseline, calls are reduced to 2 per week. The parent phone report serves as a second source of data about the aggressive behaviors being treated.

The baseline data collected through observations and telephone interviews is plotted on a graph in order to provide the therapist with a clear picture of the behaviors of the family. Data graphing provides the therapist with information to guide treatment and to later evaluate performance of the family and the therapist. The data collected after the 2-week baseline period will help show changes if they are occurring and will lead to examination of procedures should the data indicate changes are not occurring.

Session 1

For sessions 1 and 2, the therapist meets with the parents of an individual family. Group sessions may begin with session 3.

The initial session with the therapist is designed to lay a firm foundation for the intervention procedures. Parents are helped to feel comfortable in seeking treatment, and there is a clarification of general and specific problems the parents are having with their children. The family is then given an explanation of why the social learning model is appropriate (or why it is not, in which case a referral to another agency is initiated) for the treatment of concerns they have expressed. Time and energy requirements for the program are again explained.

A major function of the initial session is to develop enthusiasm for the program and to motivate parents to actively involve themselves in the process of family change. Basic active listening skills of empathy, warmth, caring, genuineness, and concreteness are essential in this, as they are in all following sessions.

During this session, the therapist inquires about any concerns the parents may have regarding therapy and the intake process, including observations and telephone contacts. There is then a review of the parents' purposes of seeking treatment, using the intake form as a guide and reviewing the positive and negative behaviors of the child, as well as the occurrence of low-rate events such as stealing, vandalism, and firesetting. Parents are asked to identify changes that have occurred since the intake interview and to report other problems they have encountered or become aware of since the intake occurred. Other areas that are examined at this time include school performance, medical problems, difficulties with siblings, problems siblings may be experiencing, adults in the home other than parents, and other care givers within the child's environment.

Parents are also asked to describe the disciplinary methods they use and any parental disagreements regarding child management. Parental marital concerns are explored as well as other current stresses that the family may be experiencing. With this information, the therapist then reviews in detail the social learning program. An explanation is given of why the focus of treatment is on the parents and about the amount of parental effort required for the program. Following this explanation, parental commitment is requested, and if it is given, a parental responsibility contract with specific treatment goals is developed and signed by the parents and the therapist. The session closes with a scheduling of the next session and a statement of encouragement.

Sessions 2 and 3

The parents are instructed to bring the target child with them for the 2nd session. At this session, the therapist explains the purpose of the treatment the family is receiving in such a way that the child does not feel blamed. Rather, the training the family is receiving is presented as a learning process that many families experience, and it is stated that one of the goals is for the family to learn ways of getting along better at home. Following that, the therapist reviews the problems presented by the child to the intake interviewer and explores what other problems the child seems to have at home and school, along with what other changes the child would like to see in himself/herself and in other people s/he is with often. Generally, children are able to identify changes they would like to see, such as not having parents fuss so much, to be given more responsibility, and to spend more time with parents.

The therapist reviews with parents how to behaviorally define the actions of the child and then discusses with them any problems they had with the child during the previous week. Then the therapist begins the instructional phase of the social learning treatment model.

The general format may be presented to parents of individual families or groups of parents. The purpose is to help them learn to examine problem situations related to having the child follow commands. They are taught specific ways of approaching the situations in order to avoid conflicts with the child. This includes giving commands in a firm voice, stating clearly and precisely what is wanted and by when. They are also taught to specify desirable and undesirable behaviors of the child related to situations in which commands are given.

Obeying of commands is selected as an initial teaching unit because most parental complaints may be redefined as a failure of the child to follow stated or implied rules or commands. For example, parents who complain of fighting as a difficulty with their child may restate the problem as disobeying a no-fighting rule in the house. A child who dawdles at bedtime is failing to obey the command to go to bed on time. Most aggressive child problems may be defined in terms of the child not obeying a parent command or family rule.

By the end of the 3rd session, parents should be able to give commands to their children that are more likely to be obeyed. This involves having parents practice in the session giving commands, first having the child's attention, presenting the command in a firm but pleasant manner, saying exactly what they want done, and specifying when they want it completed. Parents next identify what appropriate and inappropriate child behavior would be for that specific command, and they write out several commands they may give during the coming week. The commands are related to the problem areas that were defined in the 2 previous sessions. Further, parents write out examples of what compliance and noncompliance of the commands would be, in clearly defined terms, so that the parents will be able to record whether the child carried out the command or not. The parents are then instructed that when they arrive home, they are to explain to the child what is meant by obeying. Then the parents and child are to role-play several examples of obeying and not obeying so that all members of the family understand what is expected. Parents are asked to observe the child for 1 hour each day, during which approximately 5 commands are given, and to record the number of times s/he obeys commands as well as the number of times s/he disobeys.

Arrangements are made for the therapist to call the next day to determine how the assignment is proceeding for the family. It is very important at this point that phone calls be placed in order to establish that parents are indeed carrying out the assignments and that they are experiencing success.

Parents are also given a copy of *Families* (Patterson, 1971) or

Living with Children (Patterson & Gullion, 1968) and are assigned readings specifically related to observing behavior.

Session 4

Session 4 begins with a review of the work attempted during the previous week. It is important to not move on to further instruction without the parents having mastered the basic parenting skill of defining what is expected from the child and being able to track the child's compliance or noncompliance through observations.

After establishing that parents are able to identify appropriate and inappropriate child responses, the therapist then introduces the next element in examining problem situations: reinforcement. Good and poor social reinforcers are identified, and parents are asked to identify appropriate and inappropriate social reinforcers in role-played situations presented by the therapist. The main emphasis is on social reinforcers (hugs, kisses, pleasant expressions, playtime together, etc.), but the concept of backup reinforcers (television time, desserts, toys, etc.) is also introduced. The use of a point system to record and administer backup reinforcers is explained to parents, and the remainder of the session is devoted to assisting parents in establishing a point system for their child related to the child problems they presented previously. The assignment parents are given at the end of the session is to continue giving commands, observing and recording compliance on their weekly chart, and to reinforce obeying with the point system and social reinforcers. Parents are also given a reading assignment in one of the parent texts relating to setting up a point system.

During the week, the therapist maintains contact with the families by phone each day. If parents are experiencing difficulties that cannot be ameliorated by phone, the therapist may make a home visit.

Session 5

The previous two sessions taught parents how to observe behavior and to record compliance and noncompliance, as well as how to reinforce, both socially and with a point system, appropriate behavior. The 5th session introduces the use of time-out as a mild punishment for noncompliant behavior. Parents have difficulty ignoring coercive action by children (Patterson, Cobb, & Ray, 1973). Combining time-out with a reinforcement program has been found by other researchers to lead to desirable changes in aggressive behavior (Hawkins, Peterson, Schweid, & Bijou, 1966; Johnson, 1971). Wahler (1969) found that the reinforcement value of parents themselves increased for children as a function of parental use of time-out and differential attention. Parents and children became more cooperative and enjoyed each other's company more (Wahler). Furthermore, time-out is a humanitarian alternative to the child abuse resorted to by about 1/3 of the Oregon Social Learning Center sample.

Time-out involves having parents select a room that is away from people and devoid of interesting things to do. It also involves having parents remove the child to the time-out room immediately upon failure to follow a command and requires that parents not threaten the child with time-out, but actually use it, each time and without arguing.

After the guidelines for the use of time-out are given, parents are asked to describe situations from their experiences of the previous week in which their child did not comply with a command. The therapist then demonstrates the use of time-out with the parents role-playing the part of the child, illustrating both appropriate and inappropriate uses of time-out. Parents are then asked to demonstrate through role-playing their ability to satisfactorily carry out the time-out procedure.

The assignment given parents for the 5th week includes continuing the activities from previous weeks — giving commands, observing, rewarding compliance — and adding time-out to the process. Readings in *Families* (Patterson, 1971) on the use of time-out are assigned, and parents are instructed to role-play time-out with their child. Arrangements are made for the therapist to contact the parents by phone the next day to carefully review their application of the procedure. Again, home visits by the therapist may be necessary. Implementation of time-out is one of the most difficult steps for parents, and careful supervision and support is essential.

Session 6

Session 6 is an evaluation unit. Parents are instructed to bring to the session the charts they have been maintaining on their child's behavior. During the session, the charts are examined to assess the effectiveness of the program to date and to identify problems parents are having in implementing the skills covered. The aggressive behaviors recorded and graphed for a period of 5 weeks should demonstrate a definite decrease by this time. Generally this session is conducted as a problem-solving activity and provides the parents and the therapist an opportunity to review progress and practice any skills that are not satisfactory.

Parents are instructed to continue using the child management skills during the coming week and to incorporate any changes that were developed as a result of the 6th training group.

Session 7

The first 6 weeks of treatment concentrate on a limited number of problem areas, generally 2 specific problems that the parents were having with their child. During the 7th week, parents are asked to expand the program they have been using with their child by adding other behaviors they are interested in changing. Previously, behaviors under study had occurred predominantly in the home, and aggressive behaviors outside the home, such as in school, on shopping trips, or at relatives' or friends' homes, were not treated. During the 7th week, these out-of-control behaviors may be added to the treatment program. Parents, having experienced success in home-related problems, now have the skills necessary to implement the social learning model in a more difficult setting. Phone contact and more home visits, if necessary, are still carried out so that close supervision and immediate aid are available for parents with difficulties or concerns.

Following Sessions

At this point, the basic child management units have been presented to parents, and the parents have been instructed in the process of developing and maintaining a program of effective behavior change for their children. Approximately 50% of the families treated are able to demonstrate dramatic changes in the target child's aggressive behavior by the 8th week. Generally, they receive some additional contacts to insure maintenance. The maintenance period lasts for several weeks, depending upon the continued progress of the family. For the remaining 50% of families, additional work is necessary. The focus of future work may be upon special child problems such as school-related problems, bedwetting, stealing, or firesetting. It may also include the slow working through of conflicts that interfere with one or both parents using child management methods. Some parents are reluctant to apply the procedures, for reasons idiosyncratic to them, but continue to receive extended treatment, which may last up to a year or more.

A topic that many parents need additional assistance in managing is the building of new behaviors, as opposed to altering or modifying behaviors already in the child's repertoire. Many parents experience frustration over a child's lack of ability to complete tasks that are age-appropriate. The skill of shaping through breaking down the final behavior into small steps is one that is seldom mastered by many parents. In essence, the purpose of the module is to teach parents to be more effective teachers, resulting in less frustration for their children and themselves.

One of the most critical modules is training in negotiation. This is particularly true for families with out-of-control adolescents and parent-to-parent conflicts. The latter situation probably characterizes about 1/2 to 2/3 of the families. For the remainder, straightforward training in child management skills is sufficient, i.e., an educational stance. For the others, however, it is necessary to provide a means for resolving the severe conflicts that interfere with problem-solving efforts. The skills taught include both communication and problem-solving skills. They are taught via role-playing, supervised practice sessions at the clinic (including video feedback), and monitoring of *in vivo* sessions at home by use of tape recordings.

Program Implementation Problems

The social learning model for treating families as described has been demonstrated to be effective in changing families with aggressive children. More than a decade of experimental manipulations of components of the treatment program has led to identification of a basic social learning model for helping families. In a review of follow-up literature on parent training, Patterson and Fleischman (1978) showed that there is a substantial data base for believing that the effects persist for at least 12 months following training. However, the outcome studies consistently show that the various training programs, including the ones at the Oregon Social Learning Center, are not successful with 1/4 to 1/3 of the families. It is the question of why these are failures that concerns us here.

Parent Implementation Problems

Even though the program is explained to parents prior to entering treatment, many parents do not expect the model that is presented. The popular model of therapy portrayed on television and in books and magazines requires little active involvement on the part of parents. Rather, traditional therapy frequently emphasizes talking about problems within the family in general and with children specifically, and it often focuses on historical antecedents of problems.

Many parents enter social learning therapy with the expectation of a cathartic experience wherein they will describe the problems of the family, describe their frustration of attempting child rearing in today's society, identify childhood experiences they had, and then leave their child to be treated by the professional. When they learn that social learning therapy emphasizes parent involvement, action rather than talking, and dealing with the present rather than past history, some parents terminate therapy. The model has not met their expectation.

For parents expecting a talking therapy that emphasizes emotional release and psychological insight into the nature of problems, a careful discussion of the purposes of treatment and the advantages of the model presented often suffices as a motivational source to have them commit their time and effort to the social learning model. For other families, a referral to another community service that comes closer to fulfilling their expectations of therapy is appropriate, for the parents are more likely to experience success when the services offered are consistent with their expectations of therapy.

Some parents, upon learning they will become actively involved in the therapy process and in fact will serve as the primary change agent, withdraw from therapy. This problem is particularly evident in families referred by agencies such as schools, police, court, or child welfare offices. These parents often indicate a lack of interest in putting forth the amount of effort required by the social learning model. To them, coming for help is fulfilling requirements of others; the therapy is not generally a service they were interested in obtaining. The family referred by another agency presents the major motivational problem for treatment and comprises the largest dropout category.

Parents who come for therapy after being referred by another agency often do not see that there is a problem with their children, nor do they see a need for change. Rather, therapy is seen as an interference in their lives. When these families come under orders, as from police or the courts, the therapist accepts their resentment and attempts to let the parents know that the feeling of intrusion is understood. Through developing an understanding relationship with the family, the therapist attempts to be seen as supportive of the family members as they identify ways to manage the imposed requirement of therapy. The solution to the problem is usually to begin therapy and be as successful as possible as a means of removing the order for therapy. This leads to the family and therapist working as a team to experience success, with the primary goal being to fulfill other agency requirements and the side product being more satisfactory family management. When success is experienced by these parents, they are usually able to maintain the effects of training for two reasons — there is less harassment from outside agencies, and family life, particularly child management, is more enjoyable.

For low-income, single-parent families, the effort required for treatment is at times greater than the parent may be able to exert. If a single, low-income working mother attempting to support several children does not have enough energy to work, clean house, and care for children, she is unlikely to have the resources to add additional tasks to her life, regardless of the possible value. Unlike the clients referred from other agencies, she may have motivation to change and recognize the value of the services being offered, but may lack the ability to experience success.

Attempts to aid low-income and single parents have proven to be very helpful in reducing the dropout rate. One procedure that demonstrated high success was a parenting salary for low-income families (Fleischman, Note 2). In examining the effects of parenting salary upon cooperation and success in therapy, Fleischman found that for low-income single- and two-parent families, a doubling of the cooperation of participants occurred when a parenting salary was offered. The parenting salary had little effect, however, upon middle-income families.

Other activities used to increase the level of cooperation and success of this category of parents have included providing transportation to and from therapy, furnishing a playroom and staff to supervise children while parents are occupied in training, and even providing telephone service for families unable to afford it. Treatment for low-income families is not likely to be successful without a telephone to provide regular monitoring and support. In addition to the resources available through the Center, other community resources have been used as assistance for these families, including aid in locating legal services, unemployment compensation, welfare, child-care placement, and alternative employment opportunities. Counselors and other members of the helping professions seeking success with this population must expect to devote time and effort to aiding these parents beyond the basic training program.

A fourth category of families that experience difficulties implementing the program includes families in which parents have demonstrated little interest in their children, as when the children were unplanned or undesired, and families that have busy work and recreation schedules such that parents see the required involvement of being the change agent as an intrusion into their lives. In this situation, parents may see their children as limiting their lives more than previously and may develop even greater resentment toward their children than existed before beginning training.

When social learning therapists encounter the program of parents who resent their children, rather than proceeding with the program, attention is directed toward the family relationships and effort is made toward helping parents understand the effects of their feelings upon the entire family structure. Alternative directions for the family may be considered, including the possibility of foster homes or adoption. Frequently parents indicate they are aware that difficulties will develop if the resentment continues and express a desire to learn more effective methods for living with their children. When this occurs, the program is reinstated, with an emphasis placed on more enjoyable parent-child relationships. It is encouraging to these parents to learn of the Patterson (1971) work, which indicates that families successfully completing training experience greater satisfaction with family membership.

These problems are most often identified during the intake procedures, and attention is given to the expected difficulties during the intake session or during the first meeting with the parents. The intake interviewer or therapist frequently is able to recognize difficulties and begin the necessary steps to manage the problems during the first contact, rather than waiting for parents to begin dropping out of treatment or fail to experience success with the program.

Some parents who seek training to aid them in child management concerns are also experiencing other family problems of such a nature that the other concerns interfere with the effectiveness of the program. Included in this category are families with marriage problems, alcohol and drug abuse concerns, and in-law interference. Parents who cannot devote attention to the program due to excessive concern over these other problems will not benefit from the program. When other family problems make themselves known to the therapist, usually through a lack of progress in reduction of inappropriate child behaviors, the therapist stops the program and discusses the problems with the family. For marriage problems, for example, the therapist may negotiate with parents to work through the program cooperatively, with marriage counseling offered afterwards. At times, marriage counseling is offered in conjunction with the child management program. Other problems are managed in a similar way.

Another problem with parent implementation of the program involves interference from outside sources. When parents work and leave children with other child-care personnel such as day-care centers, babysitters, grandmothers or others, the caretaker often not only fails to follow the program at the parents' request, but at times even goes contrary to the program by reinforcing coercive and out-of-control behavior.

During the initial interview, the therapist should be aware of outside personnel who have contact with the children of the family. By being aware in advance, sometimes it is possible to think of ways of presenting the program to caretakers in order to elicit their help. At times it has been necessary to make contact with the caretaker in order to emphasize the importance of the program. Instructional lessons have also been given to caretakers to better equip them to participate in the program.

A similar problem is demonstrated by the fact that many parents have difficulty working with their children in a variety of settings. It is best to begin working with behaviors that are amenable to change in a home setting rather than away from home. Parents who attempt to begin behavior change in a grocery store, at a neighbor's home, or in the car are likely to experience frustration and stop the program. After experiencing success at home, the likelihood of success away from home is much greater.

Therapist Implementation Problems

The social learning model for helping families has been organized so that persons without extensive training in a social learning theory treatment model may effectively use the materials. Presently there is a shortage of personnel to deliver child mental health services, while there is a high potential demand for such services given the number of aggressive children in our society. Thus, the program has been organized in such a manner that it may be used by psychologists, counselors, social workers, community volunteers, and paraprofessionals. Several studies (Mira, 1970; Paul, McInnis, & Mariotto, 1973; Wahler & Erickson, 1969) suggest that treatments incorporating a social learning framework may be implemented effectively by such workers.

It has been necessary, however, to determine that in addition to mastering the content of the social learning program, the therapists should have a high level of basic active listening skills such as empathy, warmth, and genuineness and an understanding of family dynamics. This has resulted in the necessity of training in skills in addition to the use of parenting materials for some therapists working with families.

A second area of difficulty that therapists have experienced is that of being nonlinear in their work. Social intercourse is enjoyable for most persons, and particularly for therapists. The general pattern of social intercourse is to respond to the person talking so that the conversation moves imperceptibly from one topic to another. Consequently, many therapists respond to stimulus material imbedded in a parent's presentation of the problem, which results in a "branching" program of problem solving rather than a "linear" program. This occurs particularly with therapists accustomed to listening for language cues that imply underlying conflict. The result is that the therapist may follow these cues and spend an entire hour in detective practices identifying the conflicts, to find that only a few minutes remain to teach the parenting materials. Intensive supervision with early cases is necessary to remediate this problem with parent therapists.

A third area of difficulty experienced by therapists who attempt to implement the social learning model independently is that there is an erosion of skills when the setting in which these skills are employed does not provide reinforcement for their maintenance. Therefore, a greater probability of success may be expected when a team is trained with a common core of skills. The use of case staffings and team implementation of the social learning program is a way of developing a pool of expertise within an agency.

Agency Implementation Problems

The social learning model was developed within a research setting. In moving to an applied setting, alterations in the program are necessary. A key element of the model as used at the Oregon Social Learning Center is data collection, particularly emphasizing use of the observational coding system. In order to maintain data collection as a therapeutic tool and yet provide for a less expensive procedure, two innovations have been suggested. The first is to use an aide-level technician to handle data collection, intake procedures, and client-processing work. This results in a considerable time savings for therapists but still provides therapists with necessary information. The second innovation involves use of the telephone sampling procedure rather than observations in the home. Home observations are very expensive. Three studies to date have demonstrated that the phone system correlates significantly with home observations. Patterson (1974c) found a correlation of .67 between the two measures, and this was replicated by Fleischman (Note 2), who obtained a correlation of

.42, and by Reid (1976), with a correlation of .58. In each of these studies, telephone sampling and direct home observation yielded the same statistical inferences about overall treatment effectiveness.

Fleischman and Horne (1979) are currently exploring the problems encountered in translating this treatment program into a form usable in on-line social agencies. The program centers around an educative approach detailed by Fleischman and Conger (Note 6). In an intensive 8-week training session, therapists in three social agencies are trained to apply some components of the Oregon Social Learning Center model. The therapists are supervised by on-site visits from the Oregon Social Learning Center trainers, by telephone contacts, and by samples of therapy tapes. Each site has trained observer/data collectors who assess families prior to, during, and following therapy. Families of aggressive children are randomly assigned to either traditional or social-learning-trained staff. The outcome of this extremely important study will tell us much about the problems involved in translating the treatment model from the laboratory to the community.

REFERENCE NOTES

1. Bahm, A., Chandler, C., & Eisenberg, L. *Diagnostic characteristics related to service on psychiatric clinics for children.* Paper presented at the 38th Annual Convention of Orthopsychiatry, Munich, 1961.
2. Fleischman, M. J. *The effects of a parenting salary and family SES in the social learning treatment of aggressive children.* Unpublished doctoral dissertation, University of Oregon, 1976.
3. Reid, J., Rivera, E., & Lorber, R. *A social learning application to the outpatient treatment of children who steal.* Manuscript in preparation, 1978.
4. Moore, D., Chamberlain, P., & Mukai, L. *Children at risk for delinquency: A follow-up comparison of aggressive children and children who steal.* Manuscript submitted for publication, 1978.
5. Fleischman, M. J. *A replication of Patterson's treatment of conduct problem children.* Manuscript in preparation, 1978.
6. Fleischman, M. J., & Conger, R. E. *An approach to families of aggressive children: Procedures for didactic parent training groups.* Unpublished manuscript, Oregon Social Learning Center, Eugene, Oregon, 1978.
7. Piers, E. V., & Harris, D. B. *The Piers-Harris self-concept scale.* The Pennsylvania State University, University Park, Pennsylvania, 1963.

REFERENCES

Arnold, J. E., Levine, A. B., & Patterson, G. R. Changes in sibling behavior following family intervention. *Journal of Consulting and Clinical*

Psychology, 1975, *43,* 683-688.

Beach, D., & Laird, J. Follow-up study of children identified early as emotionally disturbed. *Journal of Consulting and Clinical Psychology,* 1968, *32,* 369-374.

Becker, W. C. The relationship of factors in parental rating of self and each other to the behavior of kindergarten children as rated by mothers, fathers and teachers. *Journal of Consulting Psychology,* 1960, *24,* 507-527.

Eideson, B. Retreat from help. *American Journal of Orthopsychiatry,* 1968, *38,* 910-921.

Fleischman, M. J., & Horne, A. M. Working with families: A social learning approach. *Journal of Contemporary Education,* 1979, in press.

Hawkins, R. P., Peterson, R. F., Schweid, E., & Bijou, S. W. Behavior therapy in the home: Amelioration of problem parent-child relations with the parent in a therapeutic role. *Journal of Experimental Child Psychology,* 1966, *14,* 99-107.

Hunt, R. G. Age, sex, and service in a child guidance clinic. *Journal of Child Psychology and Psychiatry,* 1961, *2,* 185-192.

Jastak, J. F., Bijou, S. W., & Jastak, S. R. *Wide Range Achievement Test (WRAT).* Wilmington, Delaware: Guidance Associates, 1965.

Johnson, J. Using parents as contingency managers. *Psychological Reports,* 1971, *29,* 703-710.

Jones, R. R., Reid, J. B., & Patterson, G. R. Naturalistic observation in clinical assessment. In P. McReynolds (Ed.), *Advances in psychological assessment* (Vol. 3) San Francisco: Jossey-Bass, 1975.

Levitt, E. A comparative judgmental study of defection from treatment at a child guidance clinic. *Journal of Clinical Psychology,* 1958, *14,* 429-432.

Levitt, E. Research on psychotherapy with children. In A. E. Bergin & S. L. Garfield (Eds.), *Handbook of psychotherapy and behavior change.* New York: Wiley, 1971.

Meltzoff, J., & Kornreich, M. *Research in psychotherapy.* New York: Atherton Pr, 1970.

Mira, M. Results of a behavior modification training program for parents and teachers. *Behavior Research and Therapy,* 1970, *8,* 309-311.

Morris, H. H. Aggressive behavior disorders in children: A follow-up study. *American Journal of Psychiatry,* 1956, *112,* 991-997.

Overall, B., & Aronson, H. Expectation of psychotherapy in patients of lower socioeconomic class. *American Journal of Orthopsychiatry,* 1963, *33,* 421-430.

Patterson, G. R. An empirical approach to the classification of disturbed children. *Journal of Clinical Psychology,* 1964, *20,* 326-337.

Patterson, G. R. *Families: Application of social learning to family life.* Champaign, Illinois: Res Press, 1971.

Patterson, G. R. Interventions for boys with conduct problems: Multiple settings, treatments and criteria. *Journal of Consulting and Clinical*

Psychology, 1974, *42*, 471-481. (a)

Patterson, G. R. Retraining of aggressive boys by their parents: Review of recent literature and follow-up evaluation. In F. Lowry (Ed.), Symposium on the seriously disturbed preschool child. *Canadian Psychiatric Association Journal*, 1974, *42*, 471-481. (b)

Patterson, G. R. Multiple evaluations of a parent training program. In T. Thompson (Ed.), *Proceedings of the First International Symposium on Behavior Modification*. New York: ACC, 1974. (c)

Patterson, G. R. The aggressive child: Victim and architect of a coercive system. In L. A. Hamerlynck, L. C. Handy, & E. J. Mash (Eds.), *Theory and research* (Vol. 1) *Behavior modification and families*. New York: Brunner/Mazel, 1976.

Patterson, G. R., & Brodsky, G. A behaviour modification programme for a child with multiple behaviour problems. *Journal of Child Psychology and Psychiatry*, 1966, *7*, 277-295.

Patterson, G. R., Cobb, J. A., & Ray, R. S. A social engineering technology for retraining the families of aggressive boys. In H. E. Adams & I. P. Unikel (Eds.), *Issues and trends in behavior therapy*. Springfield: Thomas, 1973.

Patterson, G. R., & Fleischman, M. J. Maintenance of treatment effects: Some considerations concerning family systems and follow-up data. *Behavior Therapy*, 1978, in press.

Patterson, G. R., & Forgatch, M. *Family living series, Part I*. Champaign, Illinois: Res Press, 1975.

Patterson, G. R., & Forgatch, M. *Family living series, Part II*. Champaign, Illinois: Res Press, 1976.

Patterson, G. R., & Gullion, M. E. *Living with children: New methods for parents and teachers*. Champaign, Illinois: Res Press, 1968.

Patterson, G. R., Jones, R. R., Whittier, J., & Wright, M. N. A behaviour modification technique for a hyperactive child. *Behaviour Research and Therapy*, 1965, *2*, 217-226.

Patterson, G. R., McNeal, S. A., Hawkins, N., & Phelps, R. Reprogramming the social environment. *Journal of Child Psychology and Psychiatry*, 1967, *8*, 181-195.

Patterson, G. R., & Reid, J. B. Reciprocity and coercion: Two facets of social systems. In C. Neuringer & J. Michaels (Eds.), *Behavior Modification in clinical psychology*. New York: Appleton, 1970.

Patterson, G. R., Reid, J. R., Jones, R. R., & Conger, R. *A social learning approach to family intervention* (Vol. 1) *Families with aggressive children*. Eugene, Oregon: Castalia Pub, 1975.

Patterson, G. R., Shaw, D. A., & Ebner, M. J. Teachers, peers, and parents as agents of change in the classroom. In F. A. M. Benson (Ed.), *Modifying deviant behaviors in various classroom settings*. Eugene, Oregon: U of Oreg Bks, 1969, No. 1, pp. 13-47.

Paul, G. L., McInnis, T. L., & Mariotto, M. J. Objective performance outcomes associated with two approaches to training mental health technicians in milieu and social learning programs. *Journal of Abnormal Psychology*, 1973, *82*, 523-532.

Reid, J. B. (Ed.). *A social learning approach to family intervention* (Vol. II) *Observation in home settings*. Eugene, Oregon: Castalia Pub, 1978.

Reid, J. B., & Patterson, G. R. The modification of aggression and stealing behavior of boys in the home setting. In A. Bandura & E. Ribes (Eds.), *Behavior modification: Experimental analyses of aggression and delinquency*. Hillsdale, New Jersey: Lawrence Erlbaum Associations, 1976.

Roach, J. L. Some social-psychological characteristics of child guidance clinic caseloads. *Journal of Consulting Psychology*, 1958, *22*, 183-186.

Robins, L. N. *Deviant children grown up: A sociological and psychological study of sociopathic personality*. Baltimore: Williams & Wilkins, 1966.

Teuber, H., & Powers, E. Evaluating therapy in a delinquency prevention program. *Psychiatric Treatment*, 1953, *21*, 138-147.

Wahler, R. G. Oppositional children: A quest for parental reinforcement control. *Journal of Applied Behavior Analysis*, 1969, *2*, 159-170.

Wahler, R. G. Deviant child behavior within the family: Developmental speculations and behavior change strategies. In H. Leitenberg (Ed.), *Handbook of behavior modification and behavior change*. Englewood Cliffs, New Jersey: P-H, 1976.

Wahler, R. G., & Erickson, M. Child behavior therapy: A community program in Appalachia. *Behaviour Research and Therapy*, 1969, *7*, 71-78.

Walter, H., & Gilmore, S. Placebo versus social learning effects in parent training procedures designed to alter the behavior of aggressive boys. *Behavior Therapy*, 1973, *4*, 361-377.

Wechsler, D. *Wechsler intelligence scale for children (WISC)*. New York: Psychological Corporation, 1949.

Wiltz, N. A., Jr., & Patterson, G. R. An evaluation of parent training procedures designed to alter inappropriate aggressive behavior of boys. *Behavior Therapy*, 1974, *5*, 215-221.

Chapter 8

WORKING WITH PARENTS OF HYPERACTIVE CHILDREN

Robert H. Willoughby

THIS chapter is written for the practitioner working with hyperactive children and their parents. In selecting its content, the author attempted to address questions and issues pertaining to childhood hyperactivity that the practicing clinician is likely to encounter in interacting with these children and their parents. Because of this decision, several of the multitude of laboratory investigations conducted with hyperactive children have necessarily had to be excluded. Those interested in reading further in this area are referred to more complete works by Albiso and Hansen (1977), Baxley and LeBlanc (1976), Cantwell (1975), Fine (1977), Ross and Ross (1976), Routh (1978), and Safer and Allen (1976).

WHAT IS A HYPERACTIVE CHILD?

One of the first questions faced by the professional working in this area is, What exactly *is* childhood hyperactivity? Unfortunately, the clinical and research literature on this topic is often confusing. This confusion is reflected in the number of different labels applied to childhood hyperactivity. Thus, one reads about the *hyperkinetic syndrome,* the *hyperkinetic impulse disorder,* and the *hyperactive child syndrome* (American Psychiatric Association, 1968; Burks, 1960; Knobel, 1962; Laufer & Denhoff, 1957; Stewart, 1967; Werry, Weiss, Douglas, & Martin, 1966). Or, in other instances, where underlying neural dysfunction is presumed, labels such as *minimal brain dysfunction, organic deviation,* or *organic learning and behavior disorder* may be encountered (Bradley, 1957; Clements, 1966; Millichap & Fowler, 1967; Wender, 1971).

It seems that much of the confusion regarding childhood hyperactivity could be avoided if the focus were directed to the child's *behavior* and not merely to a diagnostic label. One of the most salient behaviors of this disorder is the child's excessive motor activity (Chess, 1960; Laufer & Denhoff, 1957; Werry, 1968). However, most author-

185

ities in the area also emphasize the hyperactive child's difficulty in inhibiting activity when the situation demands it (Routh, 1978; Ross & Ross, 1976), and not his/her activity level per se. In addition, hyperactive children have difficulty in sustaining attention, respond impulsively (Campbell, Douglas, & Morgenstern, 1971), and have deficient planning skills (Palkes, Stewart, & Kahana, 1968). Thus, before labeling a child *hyperactive,* one must consider factors beyond the activity level alone. Indeed, the significance of a high activity level depends upon several factors, including the child's age (Routh, Schroeder, & O'Tauma, 1974) sex, (Willoughby, 1976a), the situational appropriateness of the behavior, and the child's ability to inhibit the hyperactive behavior when requested to do so (Ross & Ross, 1976). All of these factors must be taken into consideration in arriving at a final diagnosis of childhood hyperactivity.

An especially important index of hyperactivity is the child's tendency to react inappropriately to specific situational demands. Thus, parents or teachers rarely complain about a hyperactive child's general activity level, but rather about overactivity in specific situations. For example, a child who is behaving quite appropriately on the playground during recess may be unable to "turn off" his/her activity upon returning to the classroom. Such observations have led investigators to emphasize the *social inappropriateness* of the hyperactive child's behavior rather than the actual behavior itself (Ross & Ross, 1976; Werry, 1968; Zenthall, 1975).

This view of hyperactivity has some important diagnostic implications, for it suggests that some hyperactive children may not appear unduly troublesome during a brief clinic visit but may present extreme difficulties in other settings, such as the home or the classroom (Kenny, Clemmens, Hudson, Lentz, Cicci, & Nair, 1971).

In conclusion, a hyperactive child is a child who (1) fails to respond appropriately to the situational demands for activity inhibition, (2) has difficulty sustaining attention to task-relevant stimuli and ignoring task-irrelevant stimuli, and (3) shows evidence of impulsive decision making (Routh, 1978). These "core" characteristics of childhood hyperactivity are frequently accompanied by school problems (largely related to poor concentration and the inability to sustain attention) and sometimes by aggressive, antisocial behaviors (Cantwell, 1975; Rapoport & Benoit, 1975).

Using these criteria, the number of hyperactive children of school age in the United States has been estimated as between 500,000 and 1.5 million (Eisenberg, 1973). Other estimates have ranged from a low of 3% (Freedman, 1971) to a high of 10% (Huessy, 1967) of the elementary school age population. For some reason not yet adequately explained, the male/female ratio in these studies ranges between 4:1 and 9:1.

WHEN DOES HYPERACTIVITY FIRST APPEAR?

Can an infant be hyperactive? There is little question that the answer to this question is yes. A substantial amount of evidence, largely drawn from the retrospective accounts of parents of hyperactive children, indicates that these children showed a tendency to be irritable and difficult to manage even as infants (Werry, Weiss, & Douglas, 1964). Indeed at least one retrospective account of the early behavior of hyperactive children places the number showing difficulties in infancy at nearly 60% (Stewart, Pitts, Craig, & Dieruf, 1966). These findings have led certain investigators such as Werry (1968) to conclude that many children are developmentally hyperactive. In such cases of *developmental hyperactivity*, the child shows a history of hyperactive behavior virtually since infancy, with no evidence of brain dysfunction, mental retardation, or childhood psychosis. These clinical observations of hyperactive children resemble the findings from studies of infant "temperament" (Thomas, Chess, & Birch, 1968; Thomas & Chess, 1977), in which individual differences were observed on dimensions such as the activity, rhythmicity, distractibility, attention span, and persistence even during the early months of life. While no direct relationship between these early measures of infant "temperament" and later childhood hyperactivity has been established, the parallels between this research and clinical reports of infant activity are certainly worth further investigation.

Regardless of early developmental history, the diagnosis of childhood hyperactivity is most likely to be made during the elementary school years. Undoubtedly this is because of the new demands placed upon the hyperactive child in the school setting. Upon entering this new environment, the hyperactive child is faced with a number of rules, many of which pertain directly to his/her problem areas — restraining activity and paying attention. Such new demands are often too taxing for hyperactive children and lead to a variety of educational and behavioral difficulties.

Thus, we may conclude that although hyperactivity may have its origins in early life, it usually becomes a significant problem when the child first faces the demands of an educational setting. It is during these early school years that the parents are likely to become aware that their child is more than just "full of excess energy" and that s/he cannot meet the academic and social demands of the classroom. It is also during this period that the child is most likely to be referred for assessment and possible treatment.

DO CHILDREN "GROW OUT OF" HYPERACTIVITY?

While the answer to the question of whether children outgrow hyperactivity is not complete, one thing seems certain: The problem of hyperactivity, so frequently observed in middle childhood, does not disappear in adolescence as some earlier investigators have indicated (Laufer & Denhoff, 1957; Laufer, 1962). Hyperactive children do not simply "grow out of" their problem. While it is true that activity level is likely to diminish with age (Rutter, 1968), the problems of inattention, impulsive decision making, and consistently poor school achievement are likely to remain (Weiss, Kruger, Danielson, & Elman, 1975). Moreover, since most hyperactive children have school difficulties dating back to their earliest years, feelings of low self-esteem and strained peer relations typically persist, and may get worse, during adolescence. Indeed, some authorities (Ross & Ross, 1976) have proposed that adolescence, *not* middle childhood, may be the most troublesome time for most hyperactive children.

The results from most studies of hyperactive children during adolescence agree with the aforementioned observations (Quitkin & Klein, 1969; Weiss, Minde, Werry, Douglas, & Nemeth, 1971; Mendelson, Johnson, & Stewart, 1971; Hoy, Weiss, Minde, & Cohen, 1972; Huessy, Metoyer, & Townsend, 1974; Maletzky, 1974). A summary of the results of these studies indicates that most parents of "hyperactive" adolescents report (1) a shift in symptoms from hyperactivity during middle childhood to increased rebelliousness in adolescence, (2) no real change in distractibility and continued difficulty with concentration, (3) impulsiveness in daily decision making, (4) continued underachievement, (5) low self-esteem, and (6) in some instances, difficulty with the law.

These findings clearly indicate that treatment of hyperactivity should *not* be discontinued during adolescence. Rather, this developmental period may be among the most important times for psychological and educational intervention.

WHAT IS THE CAUSE OF HYPERACTIVITY?

Investigations of childhood hyperactivity throughout the years have clearly shown that there is no single cause for this problem. Furthermore, it is becoming evident that there is not a single ("true") hyperactive child but several different subgroups of children who manifest various combinations of behaviors mentioned earlier (Conners, 1972, 1973; Porges, Walter, Korb, & Sprague, 1975).

Organic Determinants

One persistent, but incorrect, belief is that *all* hyperactivity has an organic basis. Thus, it has been proposed by some earlier investigators (Pasamanick, Rogers, & Lilienfeld, 1956; Millichap, 1968) that hyperactivity is the product of brain damage at birth or encephalitis early in infancy. Although there is some early evidence linking encephalitis with hyperactivity (Ebaugh, 1923), not all hyperactive children have a history of this disorder. In fact, estimates are that less than 10% of all children referred for hyperactivity come from histories even suggesting brain injury (Stewart & Olds, 1973). Studies comparing children with documented brain damage to controls (Werry & Sprague, 1970; Chess, 1972) report no greater incidence of hyperactivity in the brain-damaged children. Thus, there is absolutely no evidence that brain damage *causes* hyperactivity, although some hyperactive children may also be neurologically impaired.

Another interpretation is that hyperactivity results from brain *dysfunction*, not brain damage (Denhoff, 1961; Laufer & Denhoff, 1957). Such dysfunction is presumed to occur in the diencephalon, which functions to inhibit incoming sensory impulses from subcortical areas of the brain to the cerebral cortex. A deficiency in this neural inhibitory mechanism is proposed to account for the observation that hyperactive children often appear to be overwhelmed by a highly stimulating environment, largely because they cannot "gate out" irrelevant stimulation.

Other theorists have approached the hyperactive child's poor inhibition from a neurochemical standpoint. Thus, Wender (1971) has proposed that hyperactive children are deficient in certain neurotransmitters, specifically norepinephrine, which accounts for the decrease in their inhibitory system. This would explain why specific medications (e.g. dextroamphetamine) that have chemical structures similar to norepinephrine might serve to increase neural inhibition and have a calming effect upon certain hyperactive children.

An entirely different interpretation of hyperactivity is presented by Satterfield and his colleagues (Satterfield, Cantwell, Saul, & Lesser, 1973). Satterfield has argued that hyperactive children are, in actuality, neurologically *underaroused*. This notion is based upon laboratory observations that hyperactive children showing the greatest response to stimulant medication are those who show abnormally *low* levels of autonomic arousal, for example, low skin conductance levels.

Criticism has been directed to all of these organic explanations of hyperactivity (see Sroufe, 1975) because of a lack of convincing evidence. However, it is clear that some children showing evidence of hyperactive behavior may, in fact, possess some of these structural or metabolic defects proposed. Unfortunately, at this time, such dysfunction is almost always present as a *post hoc* explanation of why a child who shows a positive response to stimulant medication did so in the first place.

Psychosocial Determinants

It is clear that much of what is termed *childhood hyperactivity* may also have a psychosocial basis. Thus, investigators such as Marwit and Stenner (1972) have conceptualized certain children not as hyperactive, but as hyper-*reactive*. The use of this term is to emphasize the child's reaction to pressures, both external and internal, with an increased activity level. There appear to be two primary contributors to this process: anxiety and depression.

Anxiety and Hyperactivity

It is often observed that a child's heightened activity level reflects his/her way of dealing with or working through anxiety. Interestingly, such children exhibit what Ayres (1972) has termed *tactile defensiveness* and may use their activity as a method of keeping people at a distance. Such children are likely to become overly active or agitated when people come too close.

Although there is some evidence (Henderson, Dahlin, Partridge, & Engelsing, 1973) that certain children appear to avoid tactile contact in early childhood, or even in infancy, the vast majority of children whose hyperactivity has an emotional basis typically does not show the early behavioral patterns of developmentally hyperactive children. More often, their behavioral difficulties can be traced to clear signs of acute familial stress or even more lasting psychopathology. It is therefore not surprising that investigators (Kenny et al., 1971) have reported that 64% of the families containing "hyperactive" children seen in a pediatric outpatient setting showed some evidence of increased familial stress.

Certain authorities (Fine, 1977) have proposed that such children often serve as the repository of family tension and are engaged in a desperate search for boundaries. Fine attributes this difficulty with *ego boundaries* to a vascillating and unsupportive parent-child relationship, which often leads to heightened anxiety. The author's experiences with several so-called hyperactive children agree with Fine's interpretation. In addition to the limit testing and noncompliance, which are the trademarks of hyperactive children, one often sees evidence of obsessive, ritualistic behaviors in these children that apparently serve as a source of stability in a threatening environment. Often other signs of anxiety such as tics or other nervous mannerisms may be evident as well. Needless to say, such children are absolutely the worst candidates for stimulant medication; yet, once the children are labeled as *hyperactive,* such medication may be prescribed without even considering the possible psychosocial contributors to their problem.

Some investigators have even discovered that the mere presence of a parent or other evaluative agent may lead to increased anxiety and lowered performance in hyperactive children (Gelfand, 1973). A reasonable interpretation of these findings is in terms of the child's *evaluative anxiety.* Interestingly, in Gelfand's study, *no* such performance deficits were observed with a nonevaluative, possibly less threatening, adult.

Depression and Hyperactivity

Not infrequently one finds heightened activity level as a technique for combating depression (Palmer, 1970). Here, as in the case of the child with intense anxiety, hyperactivity serves to defend the child against potentially unpleasant thoughts, which may be more accessible when one is in a less active state. Much as an adult may bury himself/herself in work as a means of defending against feelings of loss, some children will show increased agitation and restlessness after experiencing loss. In the author's experience, such obvious losses as death or divorce, or even less obvious ones such as moving or parental inaccessibility due to change in employment, are often recognizable antecedents to changes in the child's activity level.

Changes in family stress level may even cause behaviors previously thought to be well under control to reappear. Even instances where there is not actual loss but a relative loss of accessibility to a desired person, hyperactive behavior may be fostered through *negative attention seeking.* Thus, one commonly sees children whose parents are largely inaccessible to them engage in behaviors such as noncompliance with requests, frequent interruptions, or in some extreme cases, self-injury in an attempt to obtain attentional reinforcement. While it is difficult to see such youngsters as depressed, it is clear that their heightened activity levels and noncompliance with accepted social sanctions are often directly related to significant reduction or loss of parental contact.

In summary, it is clear that there are several reasons — organic, psychological, and social — why a child may show signs of hyperactivity. From these observations one can only conclude that because there is not a single cause for hyperactivity, there is also no "truly" hyperactive child. This means that in assessing children for possible hyperactivity, one must be aware of the vast individual differences between them, not only in terms of specific target behaviors, but also in terms of potential contributors to their present condition.

HOW IS HYPERACTIVITY ASSESSED?

The program for assessing and treating hyperactive children at the University of Virginia Medical Center is one of many different approaches. It is based upon much of the research discussed in the preceding sections. An underlying assumption of the program is that there is no single hyperactive child, but rather several different subtypes of hyperactive children. This position agrees with the findings of several investigators (Baxley & LeBlanc, 1976; Routh & Roberts, 1972; Sroufe, 1975), which call into question the existence of a single, unitary hyperactive child "syndrome." From the standpoint of the practitioner, this means that no two children given the label of *hyperactive* should be expected to demonstrate the same, or even similar, profiles on a series of psychological or behavioral measures. Moreover, since this is the case, it is unlikely that the same treatment plan will be sufficient for all children referred to as hyperactive.

This viewpoint has led the author to develop a battery of behavioral measures that is used in the differential diagnosis of childhood hyperactivity. The rationale behind using a series of measures rather than a single measure, such as an activity rating, is to obtain a profile on the target child that clearly differentiates those behaviors on which s/he may differ from other, nonhyperactive children. These behaviors serve as the targets for eventual intervention.

Consistent with most definitions of childhood hyperactivity, this battery provides measures in each of the following areas: (1) activity level, (2) activity inhibition, (3) sustained attention, (4) impulsivity, and (5) planning ability. A description of the individual measures contained in the battery is presented in the following section.

The Hyperactivity Battery

All children referred for possible hyperactivity are evaluated on the following measures.

Activity Level

The child's activity level is measured by using a task similar to that used in other studies of open-field activity (Hutt and Hutt, 1964; Pope, 1970; Routh, Schroeder, & O'Tauma, 1974). The child is left alone in an activity room 15 by 15 feet that is visibly divided into four equal parts. Within each of the quadrants is a table, on which are six toys (each table contains an identical set of toys). Three of these toys are "active" toys (a Nerf® ball, a toy car, and a toy drum), while the three remaining toys are "passive" toys (an Etch-A-Sketch®, Tinker Toys®, and crayons and paper). The child is permitted to play with any of the toys within any of the quadrants during a 15-minute free activity period. Throughout that time, unseen observers record the number of quadrant changes made by the child during each minute, the number of contacts s/he makes with the same toy, and his/her number of toy changes.

Activity Inhibition

The measure of activity inhibition is adapted from a study by Routh, Schroeder, and O'Tauma (1974) with nonhyperactive children. Here, the child is brought into the activity room and informed that s/he should select *one* toy to play with for the entire 15-minute period and that s/he should restrict his activity to *one* single quadrant of the activity room. Once again, the measures of interest are the number of quadrants entered during each minute, the number of toy contacts, and the number of toy changes.

Impulsivity-Reflectivity

One characteristic associated with hyperactive children is their tendency to act impulsively. The selected measure of impulsivity in the present battery is the Matching Familiar Figures Test (MFF). The MFF is an instrument developed by Kagan (1965) and provides a measure of the child's cognitive "style" or "tempo." The task requires the child to match one of six comparison figures, which are highly similar, to a sample figure. Measures of interest include the accuracy of the child's matching (as reflected in errors) and the latency to his/her first response, with specific combinations of these two measures assumed to reflect the child's style in approaching the matching task. Thus, certain children, whom Kagan has termed *impulsives*, typically show brief response latencies combined with a high rate of errors, while other children, termed *reflectives*, have longer latencies accompanied by lower error rates. The MFF has been used in other investigations with hyperactive children (Campbell, Douglas, & Morgenstern, 1971) and is reportedly sensitive to measuring the effects of medications such as methylphenidate on changes in response latency and errors.

Sustained Attention

Another frequently reported characteristic of hyperactive children is their inability to sustain attention for any length of time (Sykes, Douglas, & Morgenstern, 1973). As a measure of sustained attention, the battery includes a variation of the Continuous Performance Test (CPT) used in previous studies with hyperactive populations. However, the CPT used in this battery differs from the traditional studies of vigilance, which typically used *visual* stimuli, by requiring that the child attend to tape-recorded *auditory* stimuli for a designated period. In this task the child is required to selectively respond to the name of a particular animal (e.g., duck) embedded within a list of other animal names (e.g., dog, cat, cow, etc.). Thus, the task demands that the child selectively attend to the designated stimulus while ignoring other stimuli that serve as distractors. In this regard, the CPT is similar to the traditional signal-detection task where the objective is to respond only to a relevant signal and ignore other irrelevant signals. Consistent with this interpretation, two measures are obtained on the CPT, one that reflects signals missed (*omission errors*) and one that reflects "false alarms" to signals not present (*commission errors*).

Planning Ability

The Porteus Mazes Test is incorporated into the battery as a measure of planning ability. Hyperactive children have been shown to do poorly on this measure, a finding that is interpreted as reflecting their deficient planning and impulsive approach to the task (Palkes, Stewart, & Freedman, 1972). Maze performance has also been shown to improve in some samples of hyperactive children under medication.

Additional Means of Assessment

Activity Level Ratings

All children referred for activity assessments are also rated by both parents on a standardized activity questionnaire, the Werry-Weiss-Peters Activity Scale (Werry, 1968).

In addition to this battery of performance measures, all children evaluated for hyperactivity are administered a standardized test of intelligence, such as the Wechsler Intelligence Scale for Children (WISC-R) or the Wechsler Preschool and Primary Scale of Intelligence (WPPSI).

Normative Information

After the referred child has been administered the activity battery, his/her score on each of the measures is compared to those children from a nonhyperactive control group, all of whom have previously been evaluated on the above measures (Willoughby, 1976a, 1976b). This norm group consists of a sample of 160 children, 40 at each age level between 4 and 7 years, none of whom have ever been suspected of being hyperactive. Since normative information is still being obtained on older children, those children ages 8 and above evaluated on the battery are now compared to 7-year-old norms. In the case of a child whose mental age is significantly below his/her chronological age, comparisons are made on the basis of mental age.

The child's score is seen as being significantly elevated when that score is above +2 standard deviations above the mean on any of the above measures (–2 SD in the case of MFF latency) as compared to the appropriate norm group. Clinically, a child is usually judged as being significantly at risk for hyperactivity when three or more of the measures, including the parent rating, are in excess of +2 SD above the mean when compared to the appropriate norm group.

It is important to clarify that the objective of administering a battery of this type is not simply to categorize a child as *hyperactive* or *normal* based upon the extent to which s/he deviates from a specified norm. Rather, it is to designate potential problem areas for the individual child. To do this, information beyond that obtained on these quantitative measures is also accumulated. This includes interview data and behavioral observations of the child in informal social interactions with his/her parents. Thus, the parent of a young child may sometimes be asked to remain in the activity room with him/her as a source of security but is asked to resist any attempts by the child at social interaction. Since several of the younger children in the nonhyperactive norm group also would remain in the room only if their mothers were present, this procedure is not entirely unusual. While initially done out of practical necessity, this procedure has proven extremely useful in helping to formulate a clearer impression of the parent-child interaction as well as to provide some indication of the child's activity level.

Some Examples of Characteristic Activity Profiles

This section presents the performance profiles of a representative sample of children seen by the author for assessment of hyperactivity. They are presented to illustrate how children, all of whom were rated as highly active by their parents, may show wide variability on measures comprising the hyperactivity battery.

Case 1 (M.S.)

Table 8-I portrays a child who fits most individuals' expectancies of the "truly" hyperactive child. He shows some significant elevation on both activity measures, demonstrates a very impulsive style, and receives a very high activity rating from both parents. However, it is interesting that his ability to sustain attention is within normal limits, whereas his tendency to be impulsive is further demonstrated by a high number of commission or "false alarm" errors on the CPT. A further suggestion of an impulsive style is seen in his below-average performance on the Porteus Mazes Test, which measures planning ability.

Table 8-I

Case	M.S.	
Age	7-8	
Sex	Male	
IQ		
	Verbal	103
	Performance	75

Activity

Free	118 quadrant changes	(M = 17.3; 7-year-olds)
Restrictive	17 quadrant changes	(M = 2.3; 7-year-olds)

MFF

Errors	35	(M = 14.2)
Latency	4 seconds	(M = 13.4)

CPT

Omissions	8	(M = 9.1)
Commissions	18	(M = 2.3)

Porteus

Age Equivalent	6 years

WWP Rating

Mother	44	(M = 9.9)
Father	44	(M = 9.9)

Case 2 (L.T.)

Case 2 (Table 8-II) is in marked contrast to the previous one. Although this child's parents also rated her as highly active, there is little behavioral evidence that she is hyperactive. The suggestion here is that this youngster is either selectively hyperactive or that the parents' high rating reflects some underlying process other than those

Table 8-II

Case	L.T.		
Age	7-3		
Sex	Female		
IQ	102 — WISC-R	Info. (5)	
		D.Span (7)	
Activity			
Free	1 quadrant change	(M = 17.3)	
Restrictive	1 quadrant change	(M = 2.3)	
MFF			
Errors	18	(M = 14.2)	
Latency	11 seconds	(M = 13.4)	
CPT			
Omissions	3	(M = 9.1)	
Commissions	3	(M = 2.3)	
Porteus			
Age Equivalent	9 years		
WWP Rating			
Mother	38	(M = 9.9)	
Father	NA		

typically associated with hyperactivity, possibly a reaction to familial stress or possibly anxiety.

Case 3 (M.A.)

The record presented in Table 8-III more clearly reflects signs of underlying anxiety than hyperactivity. Notice that although his activity level is not high, he has a very rapid response latency on the MFF accompanied by a high number of commission errors on the CPT. Moreover, the pattern of his omission errors is very unusual. Thus, rather than showing the typical increase in errors over time, his attentional abilities actually improved as the task went on. This observation alone would cause one to question whether this child's problem is really one of inattention or one of underlying anxiety.

Table 8-III

Case	M.A.		
Age	7-6		
Sex	Male		
IQ	102 — Raven		
Activity			
	Free	19 quadrant changes	$(M = 17.3)$
	Restrictive	2 quadrant changes	$(M = 2.3)$
MFF			
	Errors	32	$(M = 14.2)$
	Latency	3.5 seconds	$(M = 13.4)$
CPT			
	Omissions	12*	$(M = 9.1)$
	Commissions	14	$(M = 2.3)$
Porteus			
	Age Equivalent	7 years	
WWP Rating			
	Mother	19	$(M = 9.9)$
	Father	20	$(M = 9.9)$

*10 errors first 10 minutes; 2 errors last 5 minutes.

Case 4 (M.C.)

The child whose record is shown in Table 8-IV demonstrates an interesting pattern of a heightened activity level accompanied by what appears to be difficulty in auditory information processing. Notice that on those tasks requiring visual information processing (the MFF, the Porteus, and the performance section of the WISC-R), the scores are within normal limits. In comparison, those tasks with an auditory component (the CPT and certain verbal subtests of the WISC-R) are significantly depressed. There would appear to be some difficulty with auditory attention, or possibly auditory memory, which needs to be explored in greater detail. Clearly, this child's problem is not just hyperactivity; he may also have an accompanying learning disability.

Table 8-IV

Case	M.C.				
Age	7-2				
Sex	Male				
IQ					
	Verbal	90 — WISC-R	Info.	(6)	Coding (15)
	Performance	109	Arith.	(6)	
			D.Span	(6)	
Activity					
	Free	80 quadrant changes			(*M* = 17.3)
	Restrictive	9 quadrant changes			(*M* = 2.3)
MFF					
	Errors	13			(*M* = 14.3)
	Latency	10.5 seconds			(*M* = 13.4)
CPT					
	Omissions	29			(*M* = 9.1)
	Commissions	0			(*M* = 2.3)
Porteus					
	Age Equivalent	8 years			
WWP Rating					
	Mother	40			
	Father	38			

Hopefully, these case examples have conveyed to the reader the wide variability of children referred for evaluations of their "hyperactivity." Despite the fact that all of these children had elevated parent activity ratings, they present very different composite profiles, which suggest very different problems, often with very different approaches toward remediation.

HOW IS HYPERACTIVITY TREATED?

There have been three predominant approaches to treating hyperactivity: (1) medication, (2) behavior modification, and (3) dietary management.

Drugs

Stimulant drugs have been used for over 40 years in treating hyperactivity, dating back to Bradley's (1937) original report of the use of amphetamine (Benzedrine®) as a treatment for this disorder. However, only since the mid 1960s have well-designed, adequately controlled studies of the effects of stimulant medications upon children's behavior been conducted (Conners & Eisenberg, 1963; Conners, Eisenberg, & Sharpe, 1964; Conners, Eisenberg, & Barcai, 1967). The majority of these early studies were conducted to determine the effects of two medications, methylphenidate (Ritalin®) and dextroamphetamine (Dexedrine®), upon the behavior of hyperactive children. However, in recent years, two more stimulants, caffeine (Garfinkel, Webster, & Sloman, 1975) and magnesium pemoline (Cylert®), have also been investigated (Conners, Taylor, Meo, Kurtz, & Fournier, 1972; Knights & Viets, 1975).

In most of these studies, the index of drug effectiveness has been either lower score on a parent or teacher rating scale or improvement on laboratory tasks such as the CPT, the Matching Familiar Figures Test, or the Porteus Mazes (Conners & Eisenberg, 1963; Conners, 1966) or, more recently, performance on a paired-associate learning task (Swanson & Kinsbourne, 1976). In general, most of these studies indicate that when compared to a placebo, methylphenidate, dextroamphetamine, and pemoline all lead to statistically significant improvement on teaching ratings and performance on these laboratory tasks. The exception to this general improvement is caffeine, which apparently has no positive effect on performance.

However, in light of the preceding discussion of individual differences in hyperactivity, one may question the *clinical significance* of these findings. Baxley and LeBlanc (1976) have pointed out the fallacy of using group statistics to compare the performance of subjects such as hyperactive children who are widely heterogenous. Among the difficulties encountered in such studies are the measures used to determine a drug's effectiveness, a variable in which subjects may have differed widely to begin with (Conners, 1972). For example, the findings of a study by Porges et al. (1975) showed that methylphenidate had a very beneficial effect upon the reaction time of hyperactive children known to have attentional problems but virtually no effect upon the reaction times of hyperactive children who did not show pretreatment attentional difficulties.

Such findings imply that one may always anticipate a drug-by-subject interaction when examining the effects of medication upon a hyperactive child's behavior. This causes general statements about the benefits of medication and even specific statements about dosage level to be imprecise and often clinically useless. In light of the suspected side effects of stimulant medications upon height and weight (Safer, Allen, & Barr, 1972; Safer & Allen, 1973) and their known side effects on eating and sleep patterns, being more cognizant of idiosyncratic reactions to the same levels of medication is certainly an important consideration.

Behavior Modification

Behavior modification has proven very beneficial in intervening with hyperactive children both in home and classroom (Allen, Henke, Harris, Baer, & Reynolds, 1967; Ayllon, Layman, & Kandel, 1975; O'Leary, Pelham, Rosenbaum, & Price, 1976; Patterson, Jones, Whittier, & Wright, 1965; Rosenbaum, O'Leary, & Jacob, 1975). These studies avoid the difficulties associated with idiosyncratic responses to intervention by typically working with a single hyperactive child rather than a heterogenous group of hyperactive children. In addition to traditional operant learning techniques, some studies have employed techniques such as systematic desensitization with hyperactive children (Micklick, 1973). This combination of operant and respondent procedures may prove especially beneficial for children whose hyperactivity has an emotional basis.

One problem often found in studies of behavior modification is poor generalization. Several investigators have attempted to deal with this problem by using procedures designed to increase the hyperactive child's self-control. The methods used are typically based upon the cognitive behavior modification procedures of Meichenbaum (1977), in which the hyperactive child is taught to gain control over his/her own behavior by the use of self-verbalization. A variation of this procedure was first used about 10 years ago in training hyperactive children to improve their decision-making and planning skills on the

Porteus Mazes (Palkes, Stewart, & Kahana, 1968). A short time later, Meichenbaum and Goodman (1969) showed that they could improve the performance of highly impulsive children on a simple motor task by having the children talk aloud to themselves. More recently, a number of investigators (Douglas, Parry, Marton, & Garson, 1976; Finch & Kendall, 1978; Kauffman & Hallahan, 1979), have developed extensive intervention programs for children with attentional disorders and hyperactivity based upon these cognitive behavioral principles. Although still in its early stages, addition of cognitive processes such as self-instruction to well-established behavioral procedures such as reinforcement for attending or time on task would appear to hold a great deal of promise for intervention with hyperactive children.

Diet

Feingold (1975) has contended that a highly effective treatment for hyperactivity is the removal of artificial colors and flavors and natural salicylates from the child's diet. Attempts at dietary treatment of hyperactivity have eight not supported Feingold's hypothesis at all (Adams & Witt, 1978; Harley, 1976; Williams, Cram, Tausig, & Webster, 1976) or given only slight, but unconvincing, evidence (Conners, Goyette, Southwick, Lees, & Andrulous, 1976). The author is aware of only one experimental study indicating that diet may be an effective treatment for hyperactivity (Rose, in press); however, the generalizability of these findings is questionable because of the small sample size employed ($N = 2$) and the sex of the subjects (both were females). At this time, one must conclude that although dietary manipulation may be an effective treatment for *some* hyperactive children, its benefits for the large majority of such children are still very much in question.

SUGGESTIONS FOR WORKING WITH PARENTS OF HYPERACTIVE CHILDREN

The purpose of this section is to share with the reader some of the author's experiences in working with the parents of hyperactive children. An attempt has been made to provide suggestions that are practical and can be implemented by the practicing clinician at each phase of the diagnostic-treatment process; the referral, the interview, the interpretive, and the treatment stages.

The Referral Process

Clarifying the Referral

Perhaps the earliest problem in working with hyperactive children is that the referral is often unclear and sometimes even conflicting. In treating a hyperactive child, the therapist is working, not just with the parents, but with a poorly defined, yet existent, "team" of professionals who have interacted with the child and who may have widely differing views regarding the nature and extent of his/her problems. This group almost always includes the child's pediatrician and teachers and often includes other specialists such as a learning disabilities teacher, speech therapist, or child psychiatrist. The therapist who accepts a referral to see a hyperactive, or allegedly hyperactive child, should be aware that s/he has immediately become incorporated into this larger system and is not working with the child and his/her parents alone. *The first step in the diagnostic-treatment process is to determine how the individuals comprising this system view the child's problem.* Uncovering potential areas of disagreement between "team" members before seeing the child assists the therapist in more clearly defining the problem or problems to be worked on, thereby accelerating diagnosis and treatment. In addition, it also enables the therapist to determine what role s/he will play in the diagnostic-treatment process.

It is increasingly more common for therapists to receive referrals directly from the parents of children suspected of being hyperactive. Undoubtedly, this is related to the increased volume of newspaper and magazine articles on childhood hyperactivity to which parents are exposed. In dealing with a parent-initiated referral, the therapist should immediately determine whether the parent is "working alone." Has the problem been discussed with the child's pediatrician? If so, has a diagnosis of hyperactivity been made? A reply like "I have discussed Johnny's problem with Doctor X, but he says that Johnny's just a normal, healthy growing boy" obviously suggests some degree of disagreement between parent and physician regarding the magnitude of the child's problem. Although there is a natural tendency to do so, the psychologist receiving this type of reply from a parent should avoid taking sides. The fact is that both parent and pediatrician may be correct in their observations! As stated earlier in the chapter, many children who are very hyperactive in one setting — for example, at school — may present as normal, even relatively calm, youngsters in a pediatrician's (or psychologist's) waiting room, especially if the visit is brief and nonthreatening. Thus, even the most sensitive and concerned pediatrician may see the child at his/her "best" during an office visit and be unaware of the child's disruptive potential in a more demanding situation.

Often a more informative question is how the child's teacher views his/her behavior in the classroom. Children with difficulty in attending and inhibiting their activity are typically unable to mask these problems under the demands of a classroom, as they might in a brief office visit to their pediatrician. Thus, discovering that a child is *not* seen as a problem at school but is virtually "unmanageable" at home should immediately arouse suspicion about the appropriateness of a diagnosis of childhood hyperactivity.

It is more likely, however, that the child is being referred *because* of school difficulties. Indeed, even though the referral may be "initiated" by the parents, it may be under pressure from the child's teachers. This is not an uncommon occurrence in referrals about children suspected of being hyperactive. Referrals that are not truly initiated by parents often create problems later in the treatment phase of the program, simply because the parent may deny, or even genuinely not have, any significant problems managing the child in the home. In such instances, parents rarely implement treatment recommendations. It is, therefore, of great benefit to the therapist accepting a referral on a hyperactive child to determine whether the parents are in agreement with other professionals, especially the child's teacher, that a problem actually exists. There is no poorer prognostic sign for the outcome of a recently referred case of hyperactivity than to have the parents inform the therapist in the initial interview that they are here because "the school sent us." This agenda should be clarified when taking the referral itself, preferably not during the initial interview.

When this situation occurs, it is often a good idea to contact the child's teacher or, if possible, observe the child in the classroom before conducting a parental interview. This should only be done, of course, with the parents' knowledge and consent. Another early maneuver that often proves beneficial in clarifying the objectives of the referral is to arrange a meeting among those adults concerned with the child's problem (parents, teachers, and other specialists) to discuss how each of these individuals perceives the problem. It is often wise to conduct such a meeting in a "neutral" place such as the therapist's office, rather than at the school, which many parents do not view as neutral. Often, it is impossible for the school personnel to meet elsewhere. In such an instance, a school meeting is certainly preferable to no meeting at all, regardless of the parents' initial suspicions. Obviously, time constraints make this approach impractical in some cases referred for assessment. However, in those cases in which the therapist detects a genuine disagreement between the parents and school personnel in regard to the child's problem, bringing all parties together to present their views often engenders an atmosphere of mutual cooperation that was heretofore absent.

Regardless of the specific circumstances underlying a referral, the therapist should accumulate as much relevant information about the child and his/her problem as possible. Ideally, this information should be received well before the initial contact with the child or the parents. In addition to obtaining the child's medical and school records, it is always a wise idea for the therapist to talk directly with the child's pediatrician and teacher. In some instances the pediatrician will supplement the child's records with a letter describing the problem. However, one cannot reliably count on this happening; often the therapist receives a thick volume of medical records that makes little or no sense. In such cases, phone contact with the pediatrician is usually very beneficial. The therapist should determine the physician's diagnostic impressions of the youngster, whether s/he is currently on medication for hyperactivity, and, if so, the type and dosage. Gathering such information before the initial interview can be extremely time saving for the therapist and often alters the course of the interview significantly.

The Interview

Initially, See the Parents Alone

There are several different ways of conducting the initial interview once a referral is accepted. The author's preference is to interview both parents without the child present. There are several reasons for this. A hyperactive child often proves so disruptive to the interviewing process that gathering pertinent information is made extremely difficult. Although having the child present may provide the interviewer with the opportunity to observe him/her in action or to note how the parents manage disruptive behavior, a great deal of valuable interview time may be lost if the parent spends most of the time chasing the child around the therapist's office.

Another reason for excluding the child is to give the parents total access to an attentive and caring professional. This may be the first time since the child's birth that the parents have had the undivided attention of another adult to whom they can relate "their side of the story." Few professionals who spend an hour with a hyperactive child in a clinical setting really appreciate the enormous stress that the parents of such a child must live with 24 hours a day. Moreover, the defenses of the professional are often such that s/he cannot even begin to confront, let alone answer, the question, "What would I do if I had to face this kid all day long?" The first step in the interview process, then, is to attempt to appreciate and accept the parents' intense frustration and often hostile feelings about their child. The parents must be able to relate their story in an uninterrupted fashion, without feeling that this anger and frustration toward their child will cause them to be branded as "bad" parents by another adult.

Be Nonjudgmental

For the therapist unacquainted with hyperactive children, it often comes as a shock to find that these parents often do not like their children. This does not refer to the technical point of liking the child but disliking his/her behavior — it gets far more personal than that. Many of these parents are plagued by the impulse to injure their children or have intense guilt feelings about actually acting upon such an impulse. They are concerned with how "normal" parents could have such feelings about their own child. These parents need genuine acceptance, not judgmental attitudes from the therapist, in order to progress in any program of therapy.

Often the therapist finds the parents' seeming obsession with recounting only the negative aspects of their child's behavior very upsetting. It is as though the entire session is for the purpose of venting negative feelings about the child with nothing constructive being contributed. Even more frustrating is that when the therapist attempts to determine some of the child's positive qualities, these attempts are often ignored by the parent, who is still obviously angry. The only way to deal with such anger is to let it happen. Any attempt to shut it off prematurely will only serve to frustrate the parent further and cast the therapist into the role of another uncaring professional. A good idea is to wait quietly for a break in this sequence. A parental comment like "Well, after all that, I guess that you think I must really hate my child" provides the therapist with the opportunity to reassure the parent that these feelings are not only understandable but acceptable. At the same time, the parent's statement may provide an opening for a comment like "Can you think of anything that Johnny does that pleases you?" Most parents can come up with at least one or two recent examples of their child's behavior that they approve of.

Provided that the timing is appropriate, this attempt at redirecting the interview can provide the therapist with some important information to be used later during the treatment phase of the case. There may be a few of the child's behaviors that the parent recognizes as positive; the therapist can document these for later use to build on later in the treatment. Prior to any intervention, most interactions between parents and hyperactive children are negative and rely upon coercion by the parents to be even minimally effective. This makes for an extremely tense and negative relationship between parent and child. The first step in working with the parents is for the therapist to show them that s/he understands and accepts their negative feelings toward their child. The second step is to help them pinpoint some positive behavior in their child's repertoire that can be built upon.

Do Not Assume Both Parents Agree About the Child's Problem

A final benefit of interviewing the parents alone is that when the child is present, his/her disruptive behavior may serve as a convenient buffer between them, thus making it possible for the parents to avoid any possible conflict or disagreement. In such instances, one parent often assumes the role of distracting or entertaining the child, sometimes to the point of becoming uninvolved in the interview. Seeing the parents alone and directing equal attention to each of them circumvents this problem and forces any conflict they may have about the child's problem into the open. The interviewer *should not immediately assume that both parents of a potentially hyperactive child are in agreement about the severity of the problem and the need for professional intervention.* There are occasions where one parent may disagree markedly with the other as to the nature and extent of the child's problem. This is where obtaining activity ratings from each parent before the initial session often proves highly beneficial. Whereas one parent may rate a child's activity level as excessive, the other may rate it as falling within the normal range. If such a discrepancy does occur, the author has found that it is usually the mother who is most likely to rate the child as excessively active, with the father providing the lower rating. Perhaps this is related to the higher incidence of hyperactivity in boys and the father's different expectancies regarding his son's activity level. Or, quite possibly, it is related to the observation (Cantwell, 1975) that the fathers of hyperactive boys often recall similar problems during their own childhood. In such cases, it is not uncommon to have the father defend his lower activity rating with comments such as "I'm sure he'll grow out of it; I did" or "I guess I turned out all right." Comments of this type go beyond a strong identification between father and son and often indicate an overidentification or fusion between these two individuals. This may prevent the parent from accurately seeing a problem requiring immediate intervention, as well as engendering conflict between the parents about seeking such intervention.

When the therapist detects such conflict, s/he should deal directly with it rather than trying to avoid it, for the very conflict about the severity of the child's problem and how to manage it may be a major contributor in increasing the child's symptom expression.

Obtain a Thorough History

As has been pointed out several times in this chapter, there are a myriad of reasons that a child may show hyperactive behavior. The parents of some hyperactive children report that the child has been "on the go" since birth, while the parents of other hyperactive children may equate a specific cause — for example, the loss of a person close to the child, or when s/he first entered school — with the onset of the problem. In order to obtain a clearer picture of the antecedents to the problem and their potential contributions, a thorough history is essential. Thus, the therapist should obtain pertinent information in the following areas: (1) The child's *developmental history*, including the pre- and perinatal course, the possibility of prematurity, and the attainment of developmental milestones at appropriate ages. (2) The child's *early temperament*. Was s/he an active or a calm infant? Were his/her sleep cycles regular or erratic and unpredictable? Did s/he have colic? (3) The child's early *psychosocial history*. Had s/he ever been separated from the parents for a prolonged period? If so, how did s/he react? Has s/he lost a significant person to death or divorce? Has s/he moved about a great deal, living with several different families, etc.?

In addition to obtaining information about the child's history, it is important to acquire relevant information about his/her current living conditions and family structure. The therapist should ascertain the number of persons residing in the home and the child's relationships to them. Does the child have an adequate play area, or is it overcrowded? Has the family relocated, and if so, how is the child adjusting to the move? Is there evidence of family tension related to the parents' work, to financial difficulties, or to marital discord? All of these areas should be explored in searching for specific contributors to the child's difficulties. (For a more complete discussion of these topics, the reader is referred to Cantwell, 1975, Chapter 2.)

Help Parents to Pinpoint

In addition to obtaining a thorough history, the therapist should attempt to determine those *immediate antecedents* that are likely to precede activity problems in the child. This can best be done by having the parents relate a recent real-life experience in which the child lost control or otherwise proved disruptive. While there are some children who are continually active from dawn until midnight, requiring little or no sleep and rarely engaging in any quiet activity, there are other children referred to as "hyperactive" who, according to the parents, can sit and watch television or even work on complex tasks for relatively lengthy periods but who are virtually unmanageable on other occasions. It is important for the therapist to attempt to pinpoint the events, persons, or tasks that might "set the child off." Pinpointing antecedents not only benefits in making a determination about the child's diagnosis and subsequent treatment, but it may also assist the parent to recognize that reordering events or altering levels of stimulation in the child's environment may have a bearing upon his/her behavior. All too often parents enter into a session with the false notion that hyperactive behavior is invariably the result of some underlying neurological dysfunction or brain damage and that there is nothing they themselves can do to help their child short of giving him/her a pill. Having the parents become more sensitive to the immediate antecedents to the child's disruptive behavior, even in this initial session, forces them to think of their child's problem in a new and potentially changeable way.

When working with children who are currently taking medication, it is important to sensitize parents to potential changes in their child's behavior at different times during the day. It is common to see a child's behavior deteriorate as the medication becomes less effective. Thus, a parent whose child is taking such medication should be aware that s/he may have times during the day that are likely to be more difficult than others and that such times may be related to the medication schedule. Often the therapist can assist the parents in restructuring the child's daily activities so that highly arousing or stressful events do not occur during these low periods to thereby avoid what were in the past significant behavioral problems.

Interpreting Findings to Parents

One of the least-investigated areas in any of the health care professions is how clinicians go about communicating their diagnostic findings to parents. Unfortunately, there is an overabundance of jargon in most professions that serves only to confuse the parents of a hyperactive child. The following are suggestions for professionals working with hyperactive children to assist them in better communicating findings to their parents.

Avoid Technical Terms Whenever Possible

The use of technical terms tends only to confuse parents about what is really wrong with their child. The best example of a term to be avoided, at all cost, is *minimal brain dysfunction*. This term almost always gets translated as *brain damage*, no matter what great pains are taken to adequately explain it. This often causes parents to view the child's activity problem as having an organic basis and, therefore, an organic solution, such as medication. Often such an interpretation only interferes with implementing the treatment plan.

Be as Specific as Possible

A term like *hyperactive* spans a wide spectrum of problems and conveys little information. The precise nature of a child's problem should be spelled out to the parent in terms more exact than "Johnny is hyperactive." Thus, if the youngster's problem is primarily the inability to sustain auditory attention or the tendency to be highly impulsive but not to demonstrate an excessive activity level, the differences should be pointed out to the parents. It is helpful to provide examples of the child's specific problem from test data and behavioral observations.

Have Some Idea of the Treatment Plan

It is important for the therapist to have some notion of how s/he plans to treat the child before entering the interpretive session. Most parents, when provided with findings about their child's problem, ask the question, "What can be done about it?" No one expects the therapist to have an ironclad, fully defined treatment plan at this time; however, s/he should have some notion of the steps to be taken to get help for the child. It is important not to overload the parents with too many details of the treatment plan at this time. Merely knowing that the therapist has an understanding of the problem and has a course of action in mind is likely to be sufficient to reduce the parents' apprehension.

Do Not Be Afraid to Say "I Don't Know"

It is a safe wager that virtually every interpretive session that has been conducted with parents of children showing any disability has included the question "What caused this problem?" or something akin to it. For some reason, many professionals have difficulty admitting that they do not know the cause of a problem, so they invent one. The proliferation and use of the ill-defined term minimal brain dysfunction is perhaps the best example of this.

In fact, in many cases of "hyperactivity," there is no clear etiology, and the professional should readily admit this. Even in cases where hyperactivity appears to occur in families, no clear mode of genetic transmission has been determined. And while it appears that certain complications of pregnancy and birth increase the risk of later hyperactivity, there is certainly no direct cause-effect relationship between such child complications and hyperactivity in each individual case. What parents are often asking when they inquire about etiology is whether they could have done something to prevent their child's problem. The therapist should be attuned to this underlying message and provide the parents with the reassurance that nothing they did directly or indirectly is likely to have caused their child's problem.

The therapist must also be prepared to deal with parents who are dissatisfied with the findings reported and who wish further evaluations done, so that they can get "the real answer" to their child's problem. Typically, such parents will want a fuller neurological evaluation, an EEG, or even a CAT scan.

Although such evaluations often contribute little new information to the understanding of the child's problem and its subsequent treatment, it is generally unwise for the professional to spend a great deal of time convincing the parents of the low payoff likely to occur from their efforts. Rather, the therapist should attempt to understand that the parents' need to know what caused their child's present problems may be rooted in intense and long-standing guilt and that the search for additional explanation is something they must do. Often it is only when the parents have worked through such guilt feelings and ended their search that the process of treatment can begin. In such cases, there are no ready solutions — only understanding and patience on the part of the therapist.

Treatment

The first point that must be made regarding the treatment of hyperactivity is that *there is no single treatment* for this disorder. Children referred to as *hyperactive* typically show markedly different constellations of behaviors and equally diverse etiologies to their present problems. Almost everyone would agree that there is a profound difference between a child who has been "on the go" since toddlerhood and a child who has shown signs of heightened activity since losing a parent by death, even though both may appear hyperactive. Furthermore, it is clear that the techniques used in treating these two children are unlikely to be the same. Thus, the first step in treating the hyperactive child is to do a definitive assessment of the child's problem using some of the procedures discussed earlier in this chapter. Based upon the results obtained from these formal measures, observations of the parents and the child in interview sessions, a thorough examination of medical and educational records, and contact with the child's teacher and pediatrician, diagnosis and a subsequent treatment plan can be established.

It is the author's view that the most reasonable approach to treating hyperactivity is a *multimodal* one. Most recent research findings indicate that combining intervention techniques like medication and behavior modification is generally more effective than using a single procedure alone (Gittleman-Klein, Klein, Abikoff, Katz, Gloisten, & Kates, 1976). Thus, an approach to intervention might combine behavior modification with medication, where deemed necessary, augmenting these procedures with a special educational placement for the child. Simply because a multimodal approach does draw from several areas, it is important for the parent to recognize that medication alone is not sufficient to alter many of the child's undesirable behaviors. On the other hand, it may be that medication will assist particular children in being initially more responsive to a treatment like behavior modification.

When initiating a program of intervention with the parents of the hyperactive child, it is important to clarify that hyperactivity is not a disease that can be "cured" by giving their child a pill every 4 hours. Rather, from the very earliest part of treatment, the parents should be made aware that for treatment to be effective, both of them will be required to follow a consistent program of intervention in the home, and they will probably be required to work very closely with the appropriate personnel at their child's school.

Enlisting Parental Involvement

The message of parental involvement should be conveyed in the first therapy session by arranging a time when both parents can attend the treatment sessions. This often means that the therapist will be asked to hold sessions in the late afternoon or evening to accommodate working parents. Thus, the therapist must decide whether meeting such scheduling demands is possible or even desirable.

A second technique of conveying the message of parental involvement in treatment is to contract with the parents about the number of treatment sessions and to clearly spell out their responsibilities in those sessions. It is important to communicate to the parents that once the number of sessions contracted for has been met, either the parents *or* the therapist can elect to stop treatment. At this time, the therapist should clarify that a lack of parent involvement with the therapy program or a failure by the parent to follow through on recommendations for treatment would be among the reasons for contract termination.

A third technique for increasing parental involvement is to give the parents homework assignments. These may be didactic, such as having the parents read some material on child management, or they may be more interpersonal, such as requiring the parents and child to have a family meeting or contracting session. The author has found that an excellent combination of these two approaches to homework — the didactic and the interpersonal — is to have the parents listen to an audio tape of a particular intervention procedure together and then discuss how this procedure might be used with their child.

These procedures are not merely a "power play" by the therapist over the parents. Without this early communication of parental involvement, the parents of hyperactive children are very likely to place the burden of responsibility to cure their child on the therapist and take on little or no responsibility for management beyond giving the child his/her daily pill. Therapists new to this area should be aware that the allocation of responsibility to the professional is especially likely to occur with the parents of hyperactive children who have expectancies based upon their previous experiences with physicians and a medical model of intervention (see Whalen & Henker, 1976). For such parents, the therapists' goals are (1) to redefine the child's problem as a behavioral and educational one, rather than solely a medical one, and (2) to redistribute responsibility for its treatment between the therapist and the parents.

Where to Begin?

A good first step in most intervention programs with hyperactive children is to restructure the parent-child relationship. Simply stated, the therapists' objective is to replace a negative, coercive relationship between parent and child with a positive, more reinforcing one. This is best accomplished by beginning a program of compliance training, in which the child receives reinforcement for complying with the parents' requests. One reason for beginning a program of compliance training is that it is easily implemented and therefore is likely to be attempted by the parent. If it is even modestly successful in the initial stages, the program typically serves to attenuate the tension in the parent-child relationship, with the incidence of coercive procedures diminishing sharply. The parents of children who are beginning to show some increase in their compliance frequently make statements like "I enjoy being with him more," or "I feel more confident that I can handle him now," or "For the first time in his life, he actually listens to me." Thus, not only are there changes in the parents' *behaviors* toward the child, but also some clearly demonstrable changes in the parents *feelings* about the child.

Training the Parents

The parents of children who are on a compliance training program are given a series of forms like the one shown in Figure 8-1. Prior to filling out the forms at home, the parent is trained in how to record the child's compliance by observing the therapist work with the child and having an assistant demonstrate the recording procedure. The parent is requested to record the child's compliant and noncompliant behaviors, when possible, in the home setting. Parents are reassured that no one expects them to record all of the child's behavior throughout the day, but that they should record as much behavior as is possible without this task interfering with the daily routine.

In addition to giving training in recording the child's compliance, the therapist presents the rationale for the program. Here, the principle of positive reinforcement is discussed, with the parents receiving a reading assignment and/or audio tape assignment on the use of positive reinforcement in managing behavior. No mention is made of punishment or time-out. In most cases, the urgency of the parents' problems is such that intervention in the form of positive reinforcement begins immediately, with pretreatment baseline recording eliminated.

NAME_____   DATE_____
RECORDER_____

DAY	TIME	REQUEST/PERSON	Obey (O) Disobey (D)	RESULT

Figure 8-1. A recording sheet for compliance training.

"Troubleshooting" the Treatment Plan

The design of the recording sheet permits the therapist to explore possible areas of difficulty in the training program. For example, inspection of noncompliant behaviors may indicate that the child is especially uncooperative at various times during the day, or in specific settings, or with particular individuals. The therapist should be attuned to all of these potential relationships and assist the parents in exploring why they occurred. Often simple reprogramming of the events in the day of a hyperactive youngster can help to resolve these difficulties, once they are detected. This issue is discussed more thoroughly in a later section of the chapter.

If a program of compliance training is not working, however, the most likely reason is the parents' inability to spontaneously reinforce the child's cooperative behaviors. For some reason, many parents show strong reluctance to reinforce the child for something s/he "should be doing anyway" and for which s/he does not "deserve" a special reward. A way of dealing with this reluctance is to interpret positive reinforcement as a manner in which the parent shows appreciation to the child for his/her cooperative behavior. An interpretation of positive reinforcement as a gesture of parental appreciation can accomplish two things. First, it confronts the parents with the paradox of their being willing to help the child but being unwilling to show appreciation for the child's efforts. Second, it forces the parents to conceptualize positive reinforcement in social, interpersonal terms rather than in material terms. This is especially helpful for those parents who feel that they are bribing their hyperactive children to be good and who feel uncomfortable doing so.

The author's observation of children on these programs indicates that one of the most powerful reinforcers for hyperactive children is *accessibility* to their parents. This procedure, used successfully by other investigators (Wright, 1975), consists simply of granting the child free time with the parent of his/her choice for a designated period during the day, usually 30 minutes to an hour, with the child able to select the activity s/he desires. Using this social reinforcement procedure has several advantages. First, the parent who ostensibly cares about his/her child can hardly object to spending some time with that child. Second, engaging in an action that is likely to be mutually reinforcing for both parties enhances the quality of the parent-child relationship.

Aversive Control

Beginning the intervention program with positive reinforcement for compliance does not mean that aversive control procedures are never used. Parents of hyperactive children frequently must use aversive procedures in managing their child's behavior. The author has found that the two most effective procedures are time-out and response cost, where privileges are withdrawn or lost after undesirable behavior. However, it is wise to invoke these aversive procedures only *after* compliance has begun to increase and stabilize beyond the pretreatment level.

Helping Parents to Cope

A major contributor to the failure of therapy programs with hyperactive children is that parents become so undone by the sheer intensity of their child's behavior that they "blow" the program and retreat to earlier, less effective management strategies. Even parents who are well versed in the principles of behavior management sometimes find themselves engaging in behaviors they know are incorrect and counterproductive for their children. The therapist working with parents of hyperactive children should expect statements like "I really blew it. Before I knew what was happening, I was back screaming at him again" or "He really knows how to get to me." In situations where this happens frequently and the program appears to be suffering because of the parents' low tolerance for the child's behavior, it is often a productive strategy to work directly in strengthing the parents' coping skills. Teaching specific skills such as those in the stress innoculation procedure developed by Meichenbaum (1977) and techniques for anger management developed by Novaco (1975) is especially recommended. The author has utilized these procedures in working with parents of hyperactive youngsters and has found them to be a valuable adjunct to traditional behavior management training.

Restructuring the Child's Environment

In addition to these behavioral management suggestions, the therapist should be aware of other procedures for working with hyperactive children. One of the most straightforward of these is the restructuring of the child's physical and, to some extent, his/her social environment. If a child in treatment is having difficulty at a particular time of day or in a particular setting, it is likely that there are antecedent events that are "setting off the child's behavior." For example, it may be that the dinner hour is a stressful time for all family members, but it is the hyperactive child who reacts with the greatest intensity to this stress. Or perhaps the other children in the family can settle down to sleep after a friendly wrestling bout with the father, but the hyperactive youngster simply cannot. These problems, which are directly related to the hyperactive child's tendency to get easily agitated but be unable to return to an appropriate baseline behavior once stimulation has ceased, can often be easily remedied. The therapist should assist the parent in pinpointing those events that are likely to be over-arousing to the hyperactive child and attempting to curtail or eliminate them entirely. Thus, the nightly wrestling match may be replaced by a quieter activity, or dinner may be rescheduled for a less stressful time. In cases where the child is showing stress-related behaviors at a time when medication is wearing off, reprogramming may simply consist of recommending to the child's physician that a different medication schedule be considered.

Confronting Failure

There are occasions when, no matter how well it is conceptualized, the program of intervention appears to be going nowhere. In most instances, this is because parents are not following the prescribed treatment plan, and usually are not getting involved in the homework assignments. When this occurs, the therapist must confront the parents with their reluctance to implement the treatment plan.

The therapist should raise the question of whether the hyperactive child's behavior poses a *real* problem to the parents and, if so, why are they not implementing the therapist's recommendations? A confrontation of this kind between the therapist and parents will sometimes alter the course of treatment dramatically. Often it is the single most important interaction between these individuals up to this time. Areas of disagreement between parents and therapist, or between the parents themselves, may be uncovered. These frequently relate to disagreement about the extent of the child's problem, a question of whether professional intervention is really needed, or a statement by one parent that s/he is carrying out the program with little assistance from the other parent.

It is in this session that a therapist may also begin to suspect that having a "problem child" may be very important for the functioning of the parents' own relationship. Perhaps having a common problem

— the child — permits the parents to avoid facing difficulties in their own relationship. Thus, should the child's problem diminish, the parents' own difficulties may become increasingly more visible. Or perhaps the parents simply have never been able to plan and work together on matters related to child rearing, and the pressure to do so by the therapist has made this painfully evident. Whatever the reasons behind failure to implement the prescribed program, confronting the parents usually provides invaluable information to the therapist.

Therapists working with the parents of hyperactive children should therefore never be reluctant to make strong treatment recommendations, so long as they are soundly rooted in empirical findings and clinical experience. For even if the parents are unable or unwilling to act upon these recommendations, their very failure to do so may provide the needed impetus to move the course of treatment in a positive, although possibly very different direction.

REFERENCES

Adams, W., & Witt, R. *The effect of Feingold K-P diet violations.* Paper presented at the 86th Annual Convention of the American Psychological Association, Toronto, Ontario, August 1978.

Alabiso, F. P., & Hansen, J. C. *The hyperactive child in the classroom.* Springfield: Thomas, 1977.

Allen, K. E., Henke, L. B., Harris, F. R., Baer, D. M., & Reynolds, N. J. Control of hyperactivity by social reinforcement of attending behavior. *Journal of Educational Psychology*, 1967, *58*, 231-237.

American Psychiatric Association. *Diagnostic and statistical manual of mental disorders* (2nd ed.). Washington, D. C.: American Psychiatric Association, 1968.

Ayllon, T., Layman, D., & Kandel, H. J. A behavioral-educational alternative to drug control of hyperactive children. *Journal of Applied Behavior Analysis*, 1975, *8*, 137-146.

Ayres, A. J. Types of sensory integrative dysfunction among disabled learners. *American Journal of Occupational Therapy*, 1972, *26*, 13-18.

Baxley, G. B., & LeBlanc, J. M. The hyperactive child: Characteristics, treatment and evaluation of research design. In H. W. Reese (Ed.), *Advances in child development and behavior.* New York: Acad Pr, 1976.

Bradley, C. The behavior of children receiving benzedrine. *American Journal of Psychiatry*, 1937, *94*, 577-585.

Bradley, C. Characteristics and management of children with behavior problems associated with organic brain damage. *Pediatric Clinics of North America*, 1957, *4*, 1049-1060.

Burks, H. F. The hyperkinetic child. *Exceptional Children*, 1960, *27*, 18-26.

Campbell, S. B., Douglas, V. I., & Morgenstern, G. Cognitive styles in hyperactive children and the effect of methylphenidate. *Journal of Child Psychology and Psychiatry*, 1971, *12*, 55-67.

Cantwell, D. P. (Ed.). *The hyperactive child*. New York: Spectrum Pub, 1975.

Chess, S. Diagnosis and treatment of the hyperactive child. *New York State Journal of Medicine*, 1960.

Chess, S. Neurological dysfunction and childhood behavioral pathology. *Journal of Autism and Childhood Schizophrenia*, 1972, *2*, 299-311.

Clements, S. D. *Minimal brain dysfunction in children*. (NINDS Monograph No. 3, U.S. Public Health Service Publication No. 1415). Washington, D. C.: U.S. Government Printing Office, 1966.

Conners, C. K. The effects of dexedrine on rapid discrimination and motor control of hyperkinetic children under mild stress. *Journal of Nervous and Mental Diseases*, 1966, *142*, 429-433.

Conners, C. K. Symposium: Behavior modification by drugs. II. Psychological effects of stimulant drugs in children with minimal brain dysfunction. *Pediatrics*, 1972, *49*, 702-708.

Conners, C. K. Psychological assessment of children with minimal brain dysfunction. In F. F. de la Cruz, B. H. Fox, & R. R. Roberts, Minimal brain dysfunction. *Annuals of the New York Academy of Sciences*, 1973, *205*, 283-303.

Conners, C. K., & Eisenberg, L. The effects of methylphenidate on symptomatology and learning in disturbed children. *American Journal of Psychiatry*, 1963, *120*, 458-565.

Conners, C. K., Eisenberg, L., & Barcai, A. Effect of dextroamphetamine in children. *Archives of General Psychiatry*, 1967, *17*, 478-485.

Conners, C. K., Eisenberg, L., & Sharpe, L. Effects of methylphenidate (Ritalin) on paired-associate learning and Porteus Maze performance in emotionally disturbed children. *Journal of Consulting Psychology*, 1964, *28*, 14-22.

Conners, C. K., Goyette, C. H., Southwick, D. A., Lees, J. M., & Andrulous, P. A. Food additives and hyperkinesis: A controlled double-blind experiment. *Pediatrics*, 1976, *58*, 154-166.

Conners, C. K., Taylor, E., Meo, G., Kurtz, M. A., & Fournier, M. Magnesium permoline and dextroamphetamine: A controlled study in children with minimal brain dysfunction. *Psychopharmacologia*, 1972, *26*, 321-336.

Denhoff, E. Emotional and psychological background of the neurologically handicapped child. *Exceptional Children*, 1961, *27*, 347-349.

Douglas, V. I., Parry, P., Marton, P., & Garson, C. Assessment of a cognitive training program for hyperactive children. *Journal of Abnormal Child Psychology*, 1976, *4*, 398-410.

Ebaugh, F. G. Neuropsychiatric sequelae of acute epidemic encephalitis in children. *American Journal of Diseases in Children*, 1923, *25*, 454-462.

Eisenberg, L. The overactive child. *Hospital Practice*, 1973, 28, 1-10.

Feingold, B. J. *Why your child is hyperactive*. New York: Random, 1975.

Finch, A. J., & Kendall, P. C. Impulsive behavior: From research to treatment.

In A. J. Finch & P. C. Kendall (Eds.), *Treatment and research in child psychopathology*. Hollings Wood, New York: Spectrum Pub, 1978.

Fine, M. J. Hyperactivity: Where are we? In M. J. Fine (Ed.), *Principles and techniques of intervention with hyperactive children*. Springfield: Thomas, 1977.

Freedman, D. X. Report on the conference on the use of stimulant drugs in the treatment of behaviorally disturbed young school children. *Journal of Learning Disabilities*, 1971, *4*, 523-530.

Garfinkel, B. D., Webster, C. D., & Sloman, L. Methylphenidate and caffeine in the treatment of children with minimal brain dysfunction. *American Journal of Psychiatry*, 1975, *132*, 723-728.

Gelfand, S. C. The effects of an altered interpersonal environment on minimally brain damaged children. *Dissertation Abstracts International*, 1973, *34*, 1274B-1275B.

Gittleman-Klein, R., Klein, D. F., Abikoff, H., Katz, S., Gloisten, A. C., & Kates, W. Relative efficacy of methylphenidate and behavior modification in hyperkinetic children: An interim report. *Journal of Abnormal Child Psychology*, 1976, *4*, 361-379.

Harley, J. P. *Diet and behavior in hyperactive children: Testing the Feingold hypothesis*. Paper presented at the 84th annual meeting of the American Psychological Association, Washington, D.C., August 1976.

Henderson, A. T., Dahlin, I., Partridge, C. R., & Engelsing, E. L. A hypothesis on the etiology of hyperactivity with a pilot-study report of related non-drug therapy. *Pediatrics*, 1973, *52*, 625.

Hoy, E., Weiss, G., Minde, K., & Cohen, N. J. *Characteristics of cognitive and emotional functioning in adolescents previously diagnosed as hyperactive*. Unpublished manuscript, McGill University, 1972.

Huessy, H. R. Study of the prevelance and therapy of the choreatiform syndrome of hyperkinesis in rural Vermont. *Acta Paedopsychiatrica*, 1967, *34*, 130-135.

Huessy, H. R., Metoyer, M., & Townsend, M. 8-10 year followup of 84 children treated for behavior disorder in rural Vermont. *Acta Paedopsychiatrica*, 1974, *40*, 230-235.

Hutt, S. J., & Hutt, C. Hyperactivity in a group of epileptic (and some non-epileptic) brain damaged children. *Epilepsia*, 1964, *5*, 334-351.

Kagan, J. Impulsive and reflective children: Significance of conceptual tempo. In J. D. Krumboltz (Ed.), *Learning and the educational process*. Chicago: Rand, 1965.

Kauffman, J. M., & Hallahan, D. P. Learning disability and hyperactivity (with comments on minimal brain dysfunction). In B. B. Lahey & A. E. Kazdin (Eds.), *Advances in clinical child psychology* (Vol. 2). New York: Plenum Pr, 1979.

Kenny, T. J., Clemmens, R. L., Hudson, B., Lentz, G. A., Cicci, R., & Nair, P. Characteristics of children referred because of hyperactivity. *Journal of Pediatrics*, 1971, *79*, 618-622.

Knights, R. M., & Viets, C. A. Effects of pemoline on hyperactive boys. *Pharmacology, Biochemistry, and Behavior*, 1975, *3*, 1107-1114.

Knobel, M. Psychopharmacology for the hyperkinetic child — Dynamic considerations. *Archives of General Psychiatry*, 1962, *6*, 310-321.

Laufer, M. W., Cerebral dysfunction and behavior disorders in adolescents. *American Journal of Ortho-Psychiatry*, 1962, *32*, 501-506.

Laufer, M. W., & Denhoff, E. Hyperkinetic behavior syndrome in children. *Journal of Pediatrics*, 1957, *50*, 463-474.

Maletzky, B. M. *d*-Amphetamine and delinquency: Hyperkinesis persisting? *Diseases of the Nervous System*, 1974, *35*, 543-547.

Marwit, S. J., & Stenner, A. J. Hyperkinesis: Delineation of two patterns. *Exceptional Children*, 1972, *38*, 401-406.

Meichenbaum, D. *Cognitive-behavior modification*. New York: Plenum Pr, 1977.

Meichenbaum, D., & Goodman, J. Reflection-impulsivity and verbal control of motor behavior. *Child Development*, 1969, *40*, 785-797.

Mendelson, W., Johnson, N., & Stewart, M. A. Hyperactive children as teenagers: A followup study. *Journal of Nervous and Mental Diseases*, 1971, *153*, 273-279.

Micklick, D. R. Operant conditioning procedures with systematic desensitization in a hyperkinetic asthmatic boy. *Journal of Behavior Therapy and Experimental Psychiatry*, 1973, *4*, 177-182.

Millichap, J. G. Drugs in management of hyperkinetic and perceptually handicapped children. *Journal of the American Medical Association*, 1968, *206*, 1527-1530.

Millichap, J. G., & Fowler, G. W. Treatment of "minimal brain dysfunction" syndromes. *Pediatric Clinics of North America*, 1967, *14*, 767-777.

Novaco, R. *Anger control: The development and evaluation of an experimental treatment*. Lexington, Massachusetts: Heath, 1975.

O'Leary, K. D., Pelham, W. E., Rosenbaum, A., & Price, G. H. Behavioral treatment of hyperkinetic children. *Clinical Pediatrics*, 1976, *15*, 510-515.

Palkes, H., Stewart, M., & Freedman, J. Improvement in maze performance of hyperactive boys as a function of verbal training procedures. *Journal of Special Education*, 1972, *5*, 337-342.

Palkes, H., Stewart, M., & Kahana, B. Porteus Maze performance of hyperactive boys after training in self-directed verbal commands. *Child Development*, 1968, *39*, 817-826.

Palmer, J. O. *The psychological assessment of children*. New York: Wiley, 1970.

Pasamanick, B., Rogers, M., & Lilienfeld, A. M. Pregnancy experience and the development of behavior disorder in children. *American Journal of Psychiatry*, 1956, *112*, 613-617.

Patterson, G. R., Jones, R., Whittier, J. H., & Wright, M. A. A behavior modification technique for the hyperactive child. *Behavior Research and Therapy*, 1965, *2*, 217-226.

Pope, L. Motor activity in brain injured children. *American Journal of Orthopsychiatry*, 1970, *40*, 783-794.

Porges, S. W., Walter, G. F., Korb, R. J., & Sprague, R. L. The influence of methylphenidate on heart rate and behavioral measures of attention in hyperactive children. *Child Development,* 1975, *46,* 727-733.

Quitkin, F., & Klein, D. F. Two behavioral syndromes in young adults related to possible minimal brain dysfunction. *Journal of Psychiatric Research,* 1969, *7,* 131-142.

Rapoport, J. L., & Benoit, M. The relation of direct home observations to the clinic evaluation of hyperactive school age boys. *Journal of Child Psychology and Psychiatry,* 1975, *16,* 141-147.

Rose, T. L. The functional relationship between artificial food colors and hyperactivity. *Journal of Applied Behavioral Analysis,* in press.

Rosenbaum, A., O'Leary, K. D., & Jacob, R. G. Behavioral intervention with hyperactive children: Group consequences as a supplement to individual contingencies. *Behavior Therapy,* 1975, *6,* 315-323.

Ross, D. M. & Ross, S. A. *Hyperactivity: Research, theory, action.* New York: Wiley, 1976.

Routh, D. K. Hyperactivity. In P. R. Magrab (Ed.), *Psychological management of pediatric problems* (Vol. 2). Baltimore: Univ Park, 1978.

Routh, D. K., & Roberts, R. D. Minimal brain dysfunction in children: Failure to find evidence of a behavioral syndrome. *Psychological Reports,* 1972, *31,* 307-314.

Routh, D. K., Schroeder, C. S., & O'Tauma, L. A. Development of activity level in children. *Developmental Psychology,* 1974, *10,* 163-168.

Rutter, M. Lésion cérébrale organique, hyperkinesie et rétard mental. *Psychiatrie de l'Enfant,* 1968, *11,* 475.

Safer, D. J., & Allen, R. P. Factors influencing the suppressant effects of two stimulant drugs on the growth of hyperactive children. *Pediatrics,* 1973, *51,* 660-667.

Safer, D. J., & Allen, R. P. *Hyperactive children: Diagnosis and management.* Baltimore: Univ Park, 1976.

Safer, D. J., Allen, R. P., & Barr, E. Depression of growth in hyperactive children on stimulant drugs. *New England Journal of Medicine,* 1972, *287,* 217-220.

Satterfield, J. H., Cantwell, D. P., Saul, R. E., & Lesser, L. I. Response to stimulant drug treatment in hyperactive children: Prediction from EEG and neurological findings. *Journal of Autism and Childhood Schizophrenia,* 1973, *3,* 36-48.

Sroufe, L. A. Drug treatment of children with behavior problems. In F. D. Horowitz (Ed.), *Review of Child Development Research* (Vol. 4). Chicago: U of Chicago Pr, 1975.

Stewart, M. A. Hyperactive child syndrome recognized 100 years ago. *Journal of the American Medical Association,* 1967, *202,* 28-29.

Stewart, M. A., & Olds, S. W. *Raising a hyperactive child.* New York: Har-Row, 1973.

Stewart, M. A., Pitts, F., Craig, A., & Dieruf, N. The hyperactive child syndrome. *American Journal of Orthopsychiatry,* 1966, *36,* 861-867.

Swanson, J. M., & Kinsbourne, M. Stimulant-related state-dependent learning in hyperactive children. *Science,* 1976, *192,* 1354-1357.

Sykes, D. H., Douglas, V. I., & Morgenstern, G. Sustained attention in hyperactive children. *Journal of Child Psychiatry and Psychology,* 1973, *14,* 213-220.

Thomas, A., & Chess, S. *Temperament and development.* New York: Bruner/Mazel, 1977.

Thomas, A., Chess, S., & Birch, H. G. *Temperament and behavior disorders in children.* New York: NYU Pr, 1968.

Weiss, G., Kruger, E., Danielson, U., & Elman, M. Effect of long-term treatment of hyperactive children with methylphenidate. *Canadian Medical Association Journal,* 1975, *112,* 159-165.

Weiss, G., Minde, K., Werry, J. S., Douglas, V., & Nemeth, E. Studies on the hyperactive child. VIII. 'Five year followup. *Archives of General Psychiatry,* 1971, *24,* 409-414.

Wender, P. H. *Minimal brain dysfunction in children.* New York: Wiley, 1971.

Werry, J. S. Developmental hyperactivity. *Pediatric Clinics of North America,* 1968, *15,* 581-599.

Werry, J. S., & Sprague, R. L. Hyperactivity. In C. G. Costello (Ed.), *Symptoms of psychopathology.* New York: Wiley, 1970.

Werry, J. S., Weiss, G., & Douglas, V. Studies on the hyperactive child. I. Some preliminary findings. *Canadian Psychiatric Association Journal,* 1964, *9,* 120-130.

Werry, J. S., Weiss, G., Douglas, V., & Martin, J. Studies on the hyperactive child. III. The effect of chlorpromazine upon behavior and learning disability. *Journal of the American Academy of Child Psychiatry,* 1966, *5,* 292-312.

Whalen, C. K. & Henker, B. Psychostimulants and children: A review and analysis. *Psychological Bulletin,* 1976, *83,* 1113-1130.

Williams, J. I., Cram, D. M., Tausig, F. T., & Webster, E. *Determining the relative effectiveness of dietary and drug management of hyperkinesis: A preliminary report of findings.* Unpublished manuscript, 1976.

Willoughby, R. H. Behavioral evaluation of hyperactivity: Implications for diagnosis and treatment. Paper presented at symposium, *The Hyperactive Child: Research Perspectives and Clinical Applications,* Charlottesville, Virginia, June 1976. (a)

Willoughby, R. H. Activity level, attention and impulsivity: A look at some potential interrelationships. Paper presented at the 84th annual convention of the American Psychological Association, Washington, D.C., September 1976. (b)

Wright, L. Handling the encopretic child. *Professional Psychology,* 1975, *6,* 137-144.

Zenthall, S. Optimal stimulation as theoretical basis of hyperactivity. *American Journal of Orthopsychiatry,* 1975, *45,* 549-563.

Chapter 9

WORKING WITH PARENTS OF LEARNING DISABLED CHILDREN

J. Jeffries McWhirter

INTRODUCTION

ALMOST all of those who work with children recognize the importance of parent cooperation in the education of children. Parent Teacher Associations came into being to meet this need for cooperation. Educators in the area of early childhood education have consistently found that parent involvement facilitates effective preschool programs (Calvert, 1971). Professionals serving disadvantaged and ethnic minority students have found that extensive parental involvement is crucial if they are to realize their goals (Lopate, Flaxman, Bynum, & Gordon, 1970). Child guidance clinics have long recognized the important role of parents in the therapy of children. Many require the child's parents to participate with the child in the therapeutic process; others train parents to aid in the treatment of the child (Clement, 1971; McPherson & Samuels, 1971; Berkowitz & Graziano, 1972; Johnson & Katz, 1973).

The tremendous influence of parents and family on the personality of the child has been acknowledged and documented by numerous authorities over the years (Adler, 1927; Freud, 1929; Baruch, 1949; Ginott, 1965; Gordon, 1970; Patterson, 1975). The family provides an array of early experiences and circumstances that influence and mold the development of the child. Parents as models of social values and behavior are particularly important. The parents' behavior sets the atmosphere of the home — cheerful or depressing, peaceful or warlike, ego enhancing or ego deflating.

Parents in general, and parents of learning disabled children specifically, need to be involved in a real partnership with the school. Parents can become partners-in-education if educators listen to them when they try to communicate their ideas, hopes, and feelings. They can become partners if they are involved in school programs as volunteers and as implementers of home study programs. They can become partners if they are provided support, counsel, information and direction in meeting the needs of their children. Educators must find ways to actively enlist the involvement and support of parents in cooperatively sharing the mutual responsibilities of the learning process.

Because of the particular problems encountered by learning disabled children and the resultant educational and emotional-social difficulties, educators must enlist each significant adult — especially the parents — in assisting the learning disabled child in his/her total growth process. Parents of children with learning disabilities carry an important key in helping their children achieve emotional, social, and educational mastery in spite of their disabilities. Parents of children with learning disabilities want to do a good job of parenting; they want their children to lead useful lives, to be happy, to be successful. The schools need to help them help their children meet these goals. There have been a number of reports (Barsch, 1969; Brown, 1969; Adamson, 1972; Bryant, 1973; DeGenaro, 1973; Kelley, 1973; Munsey, 1973; Neifert & Gayton, 1973; Stewart, 1974; McWhirter, 1976a, 1976b) that support the value of working with parents of learning disabled children. While there has been little hard empirical research in this area, the heuristic and descriptive research that has been done consistently supports the notion of parent contact and parent involvement.

The purpose of this chapter is to identify important elements in working with parents of learning disabled children and to highlight strategies that offer promise in ameliorating problems faced by learning disabled children and their parents. No one approach to helping parents offers a panacea. In fact, this chapter will consider both individual and group issues as well as educational and psychological strategies. The underlying thrust of an effective parent program is to design the program to aid parents in resolving the conflicts and frustrations they experience in their roles as care givers to their children. Sometimes it is necessary to consult, counsel, and encourage parents on an individual basis; at other times, the use of counseling and educational groups is most effective. Helping parents understand and support educational approaches may at times be indicated; on the other hand, emotional-social and psychological concerns may be at issue. School personnel need to be open to a variety of helping approaches.

WHO IS THE LEARNING DISABLED CHILD?

The term *learning disabilities* is relatively new in special education. Because the concept of learning disabilities presents special problems to parents and those working with parents, it needs to be defined here. The National Advisory Committee on Handicapped Children of the United States Office of Education (1968) developed for a congressional bill the following definition:

> Children with special (specific) learning disabilities exhibit a disorder in one or more of the basic psychological processes involved in understanding or in using spoken or written language. These may be manifested in disorders of listening, thinking, talking, reading, writing, spelling, or arithmetic. They include conditions which have been referred to as perceptual handicaps, brain injury, minimal brain dysfunction, dyslexia, developmental aphasia, etc. They do not include learning problems which are due primarily to visual, hearing, or motor handicaps, to mental retardation, emotional disturbance, or to environmental disadvantage. (p. 34).

While this and other definitions are useful to most professionals and many parents, some parents need an interpretation that is less technical. A more pragmatic definition is as follows: A learning disability is a perceptual problem of probably unknown cause that leads the child to perceive the world in one or more of the sensory modalities (usually visual, auditory, or psychomotor) in a unique way. That is, the child experiences a developmental or perceptual lag that causes him to see, to hear, or to respond to various stimuli in a unique way. The learning problems are not, at least primarily, created by disadvantaged circumstances, emotional disturbance, mental retardation, or physical handicaps.

This definition and interpretation imply educational remediation that is teacher-learner oriented, suggesting a program of positive action and appropriate teaching. The definition is relatively nonstigmatizing and suggests a specific deficit in children who are basically normal. Rather than being concerned with etiology and labeling, the definition and interpretation highlight the child's specific deficiencies and suggest the need for appropriate remedial procedures. Because of these factors, they offer encouragement to parents.

WHO ARE THE PARENTS OF
LEARNING DISABLED CHILDREN?

Parents of children with learning disabilities are not unlike most parents. As a group, they have heterogenous intelligence, achievement, background, and attitudes. They cannot be stereotyped. Although there are often general principles and guidelines in understanding them by virtue of the problem they and their children face, it would be erroneous to assume they are alike. Indeed, it is the premise of this chapter that a parent program for parents of learning disabled children must be broad based and comprehensive in order to meet the many needs and diverse values, attitudes, and characteristics of these parents.

There are elements, especially of an affective nature, that are common to parents of learning disabled children. Frequently, parents of learning disabled children experience similar feelings of confusion, frustration, anger, blame, guilt, and intolerance. In order to be helpful and effective with parents, school personnel must be cognizant of and sensitive to these feelings.

CONFUSION: Parents of learning disabled children are often bewildered and confused about the problems that beset their child. Barsch (1969) points out that the child with a learning disability is not a static set of fixed characteristics. In addition, disagreement exists even among professionals regarding the issue of an acceptable definition of the term *learning disability*. If the professional world of education lacks clarity of definition, if college programs are only recently beginning to emerge and develop, if the technical and clinical terminology sometimes confuses the professional, and if teacher qualifications for educating the learning disabled are vague and nonspecific, no wonder that the parents of these children are bewildered and confused. School personnel need to clarify to parents the areas that create confusion.

FRUSTRATION: Not infrequently, the confusion and bewilderment of parents result in frustration for them. Frustration is often increased by the child's inconsistent behavior. Different parents, of course, respond in different ways to this frustration. Some respond with anger and hostility; some with guilt; some with apathy, withdrawal, and apparent indifference. Others are able to channel the frustration into positive action. Many have become members of organizations such as the Association for Children with Learning Disabilities. Recent federal and state legislation that has greatly helped the cause of learning disabled children has been furthered by grass-roots parent involvement as well as the involvement of concerned professionals. School personnel need to look for ways to channel parental frustration into constructive pursuits.

ANGER: Some parents react to their learning disabled child with anger and hostility. When the anger and hostility are directed toward the child, the learning disability is compounded; the child's problems become more severe, and remediation becomes more difficult. Schools need to develop parent, child, and family counseling approaches that will help vent the anger and ease the hostility.

BLAME: Sometimes the anger is expressed by blaming the school, the teacher, the counselor, or the psychologist. Needless to say, this scapegoating interferes with needed cooperation between home and school. School personnel need to cultivate a nondefensive stance, allowing parents to drain off their need to blame. When parents have a legitimate grievance, appropriate action must follow the complaint. When the grievance is inappropriate or unfair, the miscommunication must be clarified with understanding.

GUILT: Frequently the parent — often the mother — blames herself for the child's disability. Often parents are their own harshest critics, taking all the blame for the impulsive, disruptive and antisocial behavior of their child. Unfortunately, guilt acts as a burden that interferes with parents' taking effective action in dealing with the child. It is as if the guilt is so heavy because of past transgressions that the parent cannot try new methods because they will also be noneffective and will result in even more guilt. Parents need to provide good examples, good training, and learning opportunities, but they should not take all of the blame when things do not go right all of the time. School personnel need to communicate this attitude to parents.

INTOLERANCE: Many parents of learning disabled children are caught in a perplexing dilemma. Their child is of average intelligence, and in many ways his/her performance and behavior are normal. The disability is somehow more pronounced precisely because in most regards s/he is normal or average. This frequently creates an enormous intolerance toward the child's special problems and sometimes toward the child as a person. McCarthy and McCarthy (1969) call this response the "taste of honey" phenomenon. The contrast of the subnormal with normal abilities create a potential source of constant irritation for the parents. Because the child is normal in many ways, the parent pressures him/her in ways that may be unreasonable, given the disability, and then resents the child's inability to respond. Similarly, the parent pressures the professional for the educational, medical, or psychological treatment that will lead to complete normalcy. The "honey" of normalcy tasted by the parents creates a yearning for more. School personnel need to help parents to build on the strengths of their child and to redirect their intolerance and pressure into more constructive pursuits.

Because of the feelings experienced and exhibited by parents of learning disabled children and because of the negative behavior that often arises from these feelings, school personnel need to develop counseling and educational programs for parents. The issues, pressures, and concerns that differentiate these children and these parents from other children and other parents need to be placed in a proper context. The unique character of learning disabilities needs to be defined and communicated clearly to parents. Educational strategies that might help parents deal more effectively with their children need to be presented. Psychological procedures that have a demonstrated efficacy need to be highlighted. In short, school personnel must assist parents so they can more adequately deal with the problems of their child.

The rest of this chapter will deal with those elements of a parent program that have been most helpful to parents. Contact with individual parents through conferences and counseling will be discussed. Group approaches of both an educational and counseling nature designed for working with parents will be highlighted. Special attention will be given to the notion of home involvement, using educational and psychological suggestions to aid the parent in working with the child's disability and to help the parent modify the child's inappropriate and self-defeating behavior.

In developing a parent program, one must remember that parents need help in a multifaceted way. The three major domains, cognitive, affective, and psychomotor, need to be considered. The first domain, the cognitive, relates to the intellectual manipulation of knowledge. Parents need facts and information. Certain aspects of a parent program should focus on providing such facts and information.

Second, one needs to be concerned about the affective domain. The emotional reactions mentioned earlier obviously need attention. Many parents need a place where they can go to talk about their feelings. Since an affective reaction of the parent to his/her child is constantly present, an individual designing a good parent program must recognize and respond with appropriate guidance.

The psychomotor domain is the final area to be considered in a parent program. Facts and feelings need to be put into action. The intent of a program is not simply to provide information for information's sake, but to provide a framework of understanding that leads to a different behavior. Parents are useful, productive people who need to be utilized in helping their children.

All three domains need to be considered in contacts with parents. They especially demand attention when considering the group dynamics of a parent training program. The educational approaches discussed later in this chapter are designed to provide parents with knowledge and skills so they can better help the child. Likewise, the counseling focus is intended to facilitate a more positive expression of emotion and more effective and facilitative communication. In both treatment modalities, parents are encouraged to behave and act in different and more productive ways.

PARENT CONFERENCES

The teacher and often the principal, counselor, or psychologist comes into contact with the individual parent in the context of parent conferences. These individual conferences are an integral aspect of an effective parent program. There are certain elements that are crucial to a good parent-teacher conference and are particularly important when the child has a learning disability. Those elements include (1) relating to and developing rapport with the parents, (2) demonstrating support for the parents, (3) sharing diagnosis with the parents, (4) home study programs, and (5) making suggestions for the parents.

Relating to the Parent

The first step in relating to the parent is the development of an attitude that recognizes the parent as the prime caretaker of the child. Too often in education professionals have acted as if they were the experts and parents had nothing to contribute. Educators have communicated subtly, and sometimes not so subtly, that if parents would simply adopt their values, advice, and suggestions, then the attitudes and behavior of the children would improve. While professionals do have information and knowledge that can be useful and are willing to help in the rearing of children, they must begin to communicate that their influence is not nearly as great in the child's life as is the parents' influence. Indeed, the most basic education of the child, the perceptions of himself/herself and others and attitudes toward life, are formed primarily in the home. The child's values and their behavioral expressions with negative consequences can best be modified through parental involvement. What is taught in school becomes more meaningful to the child when parents are interested and involved in their child's school learning. Recognition of these points leads to an attitude that facilitates improved communication between school personnel and parents.

The second aspect in relating to parents is the ability to listen. The teacher or counselor who is a friendly, noncritical listener, who respects the parent as an individual without making excessive demands, is acting in a therapeutic way with the parent. With such listening, many of the negative feelings parents experience that were discussed earlier can be resolved. This, of course, allows the parent to move on to more productive pursuits.

It is frequently helpful to paraphrase the parents' comments to demonstrate that they are being heard and to make sure that the listener really does understand what the parents are trying to communicate. Too often, school personnel spend time formulating answers when they ought to be attempting to fully understand the parents' point of view and feelings. The school person should listen to what parents are saying — really listen — and attempt to understand the emotional impact of the topics parents choose to raise, the problems they describe, the observations they make about their child, and the relationships among family members on which they comment.

Support for Parents

The second element important in the parent conference is support. Parents of learning disabled children need support from school personnel. Listening and relating to parents with a positive attitude and with understanding is supportive. Finding helpful ways within the interview to respond to parental feelings of confusion, frustration, anger, blame, guilt, and intolerance is also supportive. Often these methods of support will be adequate in helping the parents.

Sometimes, however, parents of a learning disabled child have adopted a defeatist attitude toward their child and his disability. Support in this case might take the form of encouragement. The teacher or counselor must focus attention on the hopeful facts: the child's strengths and his/her potential for improvement. Encouragement of this sort is closely related to helping the parents accept their child. Acceptance of the learning disabled child, as well as of the normal child for that matter, involves appreciation of his/her individuality, pride in his/her assets, and tolerance for his/her shortcomings. It is supportive to encourage the parent in a nonjudgmental, nonhostile way to more fully accept the child.

There are a variety of ways in which parents can be supported. Providing parents with action steps, that is, practical ways they can respond at home to help their child overcome a particular problem, shows support. In some instances, the parental attitude is so negative that individual, group, or family counseling is indicated. Providing these services or referring parents for further assistance is supportive. Support is also demonstrated when the school makes an attempt to provide educational experiences for parents. Later sections of this chapter deal in more detail with these programmatic ways of showing support.

Diagnosis and the Parent

The third area enhanced by the individual conference is diagnosis. Parents can often play a vital role in the collection of data for their child's diagnosis. A case history containing information on the child's development and background is normally an initial phase of the diagnostic process. Parents are usually able to provide the following information: the child's prenatal history, birth conditions, neonatal development, and the personal history, including health and medical factors. This information is potentially useful in the diagnosis. Also useful in diagnosis is the broader evaluation of the problem from the parents' point of view. How is the child's school problem a reflection of problems at home? How are family problems accentuated by the learning difficulties? How have the child and the family adapted and reacted to the specific learning disability? What have the parents observed about the way their child learns? Answers to these questions provide additional information concerning the environment and the learning style of the individual child.

Identification of learning style is an important aspect of providing appropriate treatment. DeCecco (1968) and Sperry (1973) provide direction for identifying the primary sensory modality through which the child learns best. The educator should question the parent about a recent movie or television program seen by the child. What did he remember most? What impressed him? The child's response may suggest a visual, auditory, or even kinesthetic mode of learning. The parent can also be asked to observe whether the child focuses on jokes he reads in the Sunday comics (visual) or on jokes he has heard (auditory). Does the child more easily remember anecdotes and discussions (auditory) or does he remember information from books (visual)? By asking appropriate questions, school personnel can utilize the store of information parents have about their children. In turn, the parents are sensitized to better understand the learning channels through which they can help their child.

A final aspect of diagnosis relates to the need for the school to provide constructive information for parents regarding the specifics of the learning disability. Because *learning disabilities* refers to such a wide array of disorders, the parents need to know the exact nature of their child's disability, the prospects for remediation, and suggestions for practical application for the parents and the child. Parents are more supportive of school programs and more involved in their child's progress when they have an understanding of the diagnosis and the remediation procedures flowing from it.

Home Study Programs

The fourth area in which the individual conference has value is in the provision of concrete and specific suggestions for parents to use at home to improve the social-emotional climate for themselves and the child and to further the educational aims of the school. Schools should provide home study programs. Ideally, a home program builds on diagnostic findings, details specific educational activities, and is monitored by a specialist in learning disabilities. In fact, the maximum benefit of any procedure, whether applied at school or at home, is to identify the specific area of dysfunction, determine the level of developmental lag, and structure a program of remedial tasks. Parents can be most useful when their efforts at home are coordinated with the school's efforts.

Home programs are useful as a practical way to involve parents in the treatment of the child's developmental lag or to modify the negative behavior of the child. It is necessary, however, to look at the total family process and to identify both strengths and weaknesses of the parents and family and then respond with an appropriate program. Some families seem less able to utilize home programs than do other families. Neifert and Gayton (1973) have identified the following family types and have suggested that creative intervention strategies, rather than home programs, are probably more appropriate for such families.

MOTHER-AWARE FAMILIES: In this group of families, the mother feels that something is wrong with the child but the father does not support her view. It is common for fathers to be initially less accepting of the notion of learning disabilities and to be more resistant in the early treatment. However, if this situation persists, the utilization of a home program, particularly of a remedial nature, is less effective. School personnel can make better use of their time educating the father in the specifics of his child's difficulty or counseling with both parents in areas related to their mutual conflict.

POWER STRUGGLE FAMILIES: Home programs are contraindicated in families where a serious power struggle exists between mother and child. In this situation, the home program itself becomes the object of the power struggle and contributes to potentially greater discord. Helping both mother and child understand the causes of the child's misbehavior and helping mother withdraw from her side of the conflict are necessary goals.

MULTIPROBLEM FAMILIES: If the family is beset with serious educational, financial, social, and health problems, it is difficult for the parents to have the resources, both physical and emotional, necessary for a regular home program. For such families, effective intervention needs to be on multiple levels — educational, economic, social, and medical. Unfortunately, most school districts have neither the finances nor the personnel to be helpful.

MARRIAGE PROBLEM FAMILIES: Home programs are generally not effective in families where marital conflict between the parents is severe. In some families, the child has developed behaviors that serve to further divide his parents; in other families, the parents use the child as a cudgel to batter each other. In both instances the home program might serve as another weapon. When marriage discord seems to be a primary factor, referral to an agency for marital counseling is the most appropriate response for school personnel.

LARGE AND DISORDERLY FAMILIES: When the family has many children, the parents usually cannot find time to monitor a home program. Because of the realistic demands on both father and mother in carrying out the functions of normal family life, little time or energy is left over for an educational program. This circumstance is exacerbated when there is little or no order in the home. School personnel would do better to devote their efforts to helping the family establish order. This is especially important since routine tends to be helpful to many learning disabled children.

Although parents are concerned most about their children, they must be approached and worked with realistically on the basis of *their* needs, concerns, and problems, not the needs of the school personnel. Home programs, of course, are more successful with some parents than with others; the benefits to the child are considerable when the strengths and weaknesses of a family permit the establishment of a home program.

With an understanding of the child's learning style and specific information about his educational functioning, parents should be encouraged to work with their child on specific and limited tasks. Frequent assessment of the child's level of achievement, close monitoring of the parents' activities, and appropriate adjustment of tasks are essential for an effective program.

A home program should not be used as a substitute for a strong school-based remedial program, but rather as a supplement to the child's educational experience at school. While a home program is not appropriate for the families just described, less comprehensive experiences may be recommended. Most parents and their learning disabled child could profit from some of the following suggestions. Many of these techniques could be used in a home program but also have benefit when used in a less systematic way.

Suggestions For Parents

This section provides some examples of ways to help parents help their learning disabled child. There are three primary areas in which suggestions have been most useful to parents: social-emotional, visual, and auditory.

Social-Emotional Areas

Since the emotional overlay is such a common problem with learning disabled children, suggestions in this area can be most helpful to parents. Consequently, the first segment consists of a few suggestions that have been useful to parents in providing structure in order to minimize the negative behavior of the child.

• Have parents encourage the auditory-deficient youngster to paraphrase or restate their commands. This actively engages the youngster and increases the probability that the message was received.

• Have parents modify their commands so that messages are given in smaller units. Often a series of commands (e.g., "Pick up your toys, dust your furniture, and vacuum your room.") is too complicated for the child to retain. What appears to be laziness or refusal to comply may be actually a behavioral manifestation of an auditory memory learning disability.

• Have parents suggest that the child look directly at them when the parents are talking or giving a command. This helps the communication process.

• Have parents use touch when communicating to their child. A gentle touch to the face or a friendly grasp of the arm helps get the message across.

• Have parents provide the visually learning disabled child with a quiet, stimulus-free environment so that the child can read, write, and study. Partitions, screens, and cubicles help block out distractions.

• Have parents shorten activities and tasks requiring attention. It is particularly important to accommodate the child with a short attention span. Later, they can increase the time gradually.

• Have parents minimize the competitive aspects of games and interactions between the learning disabled child and his peers and siblings. Particularly for the learning disabled child, competition is destructive.

• Have parents provide time structure for the task at hand. As much as possible, it is important that a specific task be done at the same time every day. There should also be a time limit for completion of a certain task. This imposed order is useful in providing limits for the child.

• Have parents point out feedback cues from the environment so that the child can learn to internalize standards.

• Have parents help the child anticipate *how, when, where,* and *why* related to a particular situation. This helps him learn to predict events and outcomes.

• Have parents provide alternatives for negative behavior such as fighting. Pillows, plastic punching toys, and punching bags are more appropriate targets for hitting, throwing, or kicking than are siblings or peers.

REMEDIAL-EDUCATIVE TASKS: The following activities represent games and tasks that can be suggested for parents to use at home with their learning disabled child. To repeat, these procedures should be used as a supplement to an educational program that has included accurate diagnosis and appropriate remediation. As a supplement, the suggestions have proved useful because they engage the parent with his or her child and may provide learning experiences to undergird school activities.

The learning disabilities most disruptive to school achievement are those in the visual and auditory modalities. Although other sense modalities can be engaged, sight and hearing are crucial for school success; difficulties in these two areas are the most common among children identified as learning disabled. Consequently, the following activities are divided into those most helpful to the visual or to the auditory learning disabled.

Visual Activities

These tasks might be useful with visually learning disabled children.

• Have parents encourage the learning disabled child to separate the knives, spoons, and forks; also try tools, buttons, nuts, bolts, nails, and screws.

• Have parents provide dot-to-dot pictures using either letters or numbers to form familiar objects and pictures.

• Have parents encourage the child to pick out letters and spell simple words from alphabet cereal.

• Have parents point out likenesses and differences in the shapes of letters and words. Later they can request that the child do this.

• Have parents provide comic strips that the child can cut into separate panels and then rearrange into proper sequence.

• Have parents encourage the child to make a scrapbook about common themes or elements using pictures or words clipped from magazines.

• Have parents play memory games with the child, e.g., "What did you have for breakfast this morning?," "What happened on that television program last evening?"

• Have parents play "concentration" with the child. A deck of cards is spread out face down on the table. The players alternately turn over two cards, attempting to find a match. If the cards are not matches, they are returned to the table face down. When a match is made, the player places both cards in his hand and continues. The winner is the player with the most cards at the end of the game. A variation is to have the child play by himself against time.

• Have parents engage the child in activities requiring cutting, pasting, drawing, and coloring. Provide media other than paper and pencil.

• Have parents encourage children's games that involve visual-motor integration such as jumping rope, ball and jacks, marbles, hopscotch, and so forth.

• Have parents play catch with the child using balls, bean bags, wadded paper, or balloons.

• Have parents involve the child in activities that increase awareness of left-to-right progression; point out left-right order when playing games and when reading stories and comic strips.

• Have parents allow the child to wear a ring on his right hand as a reminder of handedness. These last two suggestions are particularly important in developing laterality and directionality in the child.

Auditory Activities

These activities might be useful for parents to use with children who have auditory disabilities.

• Have parents initiate activities or games that require a response to sounds. Games such as "musical chairs" or "Simon says" may be useful in developing auditory attention skills.

• Have parents play rhyming games with their youngster. For example, they can ask him/her to think of words that rhyme with *car* or with *park*.

• Have parents ask the child to close his eyes and identify sounds, particularly in a noisy public place.

• Have parents recite the ingredients of a favorite dessert and ask the child to repeat them. They can wait several hours and then ask again. After the child knows the ingredients, he can be asked to verify the contents with one ingredient deliberately left out, which he is to identify.

• Have parents read a sentence and then ask the child to repeat it.

• Have parents tell the child what items are needed from the grocery and have him remember them.

• Have parents ask the child to remember one item of information he has heard during the day.

• Have parents, after naming several animals, encourage the child to make appropriate animal sounds in the sequence of the named animals.

• Have parents encourage the child to remember simple poems and jokes.

• Have parents sound out, discuss, and practice those sounds that cause the most trouble for the child. They can have him/her practice in front of a mirror and with a tape recorder for visual and auditory feedback clues.

• Have parents urge the child to use tongue twisters like "Peter Piper picked a peck of pickled peppers."

• Have parents suggest that the child respond in complete and correct sentences rather than with one or two word replies.

In addition to these tasks, parents should be encouraged to provide materials for their child that will lead to learning. Books, magazines, puzzles, and writing material are useful in creating a climate for learning. More specific games and materials and their learning functions are listed below.

VISUAL-MOTOR FINE MUSCLE COORDINATION: Pick-Up sticks®, marble games, Etch-a-sketch®, paint-by-number sets, yo-yo, and follow-the-dots books.

AUDITORY-VOCAL ASSOCIATION: Walkie-talkie, radio, tape recorder, Dr. Seuss books, and talking books.

VISUAL COORDINATION AND PURSUIT: Balloons, flashlight, moving target toy gun set, and Ping-Pong set®.

There are also many commercial games available that can be helpful. These tasks, toys, and games can be suggested to parents to supplement the school's program.

An additional source for practical techniques can be found in the present writer's book *The Learning Disabled Child: A School and Family Concern* (McWhirter, 1977). This book was written to provide parents, teachers, and counselors an understanding of the educational and psychological components of learning disabilities as well as practical techniques to help the child. Another source is Wallace and Kauffman's (1973) *Teaching Children With Learning Problems,* a text written primarily for teachers. Many of their suggestions for teachers can be adapted for parents. Both books provide a rich array of techniques, games, procedures, and activities that have proved helpful to parents and group leaders working with parents.

Home activities provide an avenue whereby the child receives the practice s/he needs in his weak area. Hopefully, s/he will also receive support, attention, and encouragement from his parents for engaging in learning-related tasks.

Parents must be advised that these activities should be approached as fun, enjoyable activities. Negative feelings are often engendered in parents when they try to help their child; they must recognize that they are approaching the child in areas where s/he has a handicap, which may create anxiety and frustration for him/her. If the parent can continue with patient and sensitive understanding, the activities can be beneficial. If the parent, on the other hand, finds him- or herself becoming upset, frustrated, or annoyed, it is best to stop the activity. An underlying principle is *do not pressure the child.* Parents must be made to realize that their child probably has low self-esteem. The home activities will be counterproductive if they decrease self-esteem even more.

PARENT COUNSELING

Individual Counseling

In addition to the parent conference, an effective program for parents of learning disabled children includes provisions for parent counseling. A good parent program is based in large part on recognition of individual differences between parents and the provision of activities to meet individual parent needs. The emotional handicaps of parents can be more serious than a child's learning disability if positive attitudes and constructive action are delayed too long. Counseling can help. The counselor's role of helping parents define and cope with their child's problems and the counseling process of facilitating the parents' exploration of feelings of helplessness, anxiety, and self-blame are extremely important.

It is beyond the scope of this chapter to detail all the elements of effective counseling. It is, however, important to identify trends that have validity and usefulness. Certainly, the need to relate to parents with a positive attitude, the skill of noncritical listening, and supportive encouragement are as important in the counseling interview as they are in parent conferences. Some parents need more time, support, and direction than is available in the parent conference. Individual counseling for such parents is indicated.

Individual counseling for parents is also important because some parents have severe difficulties in a group setting. Also, some problems are not particularly amenable to a parent counseling group or family counseling. Counseling in these situations can best be handled in individual contact, and such an arrangement should be provided.

Family Counseling

Another approach used within parent programs has been the use of the conjoint model of family counseling. The conjoint model follows the work by Virginia Satir (1964) and stresses the importance of more functional communication within the family. Individual families are seen as a unit, and the family members are confronted with their dysfunctional behaviors in an ego-enhancing and supportive way. Essentially, all family members are involved in an exploration of family problems.

Family Group Consultation

Family group consultation (McWhirter, 1966; Fullmer & Bernard, 1968; McWhirter & Kincaid, 1974) is a procedure that brings together several families for a number of sessions. Emphasis is placed on open communication among all members of the group to generate new knowledge about family interaction and new behavior within families.

Generally, there are three phases to the group process. The first phase provides for a discussion of events and identification of problems occurring in the home. Communication patterns within each of the families are explored.

In phase two, the total unit is broken down for small group counseling. There is no single best formula for the structure of this phase. Parents, older siblings, and younger siblings might constitute three separate small groups. The parents of one family might meet with the children of another. Separate family units might meet in a conjoint model. The learning disabled children might constitute one group, with their parents in another and their siblings in yet another. The critical issue is to provide a unique context from which to view problems and communication patterns.

In phase three, all members come together again in the large group to share information and to further explore problem areas. Usually, goals are set for family members to work on during the period between sessions.

Group Counseling

Parent counseling groups tend to revolve around parental feelings and attitudes. Although some information about learning disabilities and emotional problems is sometimes helpful, the main content of the session are the fears, pain, anger, guilt, and frustration experienced by parents of children with special problems.

Parents are encouraged to take part in open dialogue and to share their thoughts and feelings. It is important to create in the group an environment where parents can freely discuss their intimate feelings. The group provides an opportunity for parents to develop communication skills, enabling them to better understand and communicate with the child, each other, and significant others.

One of the primary advantages of counseling groups is that they provide parents with a mutual source of emotional support. Parents relate their experience to the experiences of other parents in the group. This leads to the realization that the parent is not alone in his fears, discouragement, or helplessness. Frequently one parent instinctively knows what to say to aid another parent, and the counseling group provides just the opportunity.

PARENT EDUCATION GROUPS

Another area where school counselors, teachers, and psychologists can be of assistance to parents is with educational groups. The intent underlying the educational offerings is to provide the participants with knowledge, information, or a skill they did not have previously. The assumption is that with this increased information, the parent is better able to deal with the problems the child presents.

Procedures

Before considering the potential content of education groups, the dynamics of these groups need to be considered. Certain procedures are most important in establishing an effective group (Dinkmeyer, 1973; Dinkmeyer & McKay, 1974). As one contemplates beginning an educational group, certain elements must be attended to by the group leader. Many of the following suggestions have relevance to the family and group counseling approaches, as well as parent education groups.

Planning

Two points need to be considered prior to actually beginning a parent group: attendance and organization. Both issues are accomplished in the planning stage and are very important in contributing to the success of a group.

Attendance is often a concern of parent educators and needs to be carefully considered. There are a number of ways in which attendance can be increased. Certainly the parents of newly identified learning disabled children need to be contacted directly by someone on the school staff and informed of group meetings. Other ways that have worked to improve attendance are the following:

1. Have the school counselor offer personal invitations, either in person or by telephone.
2. Seek referrals of appropriate parents from principals and teachers.
3. Meet with the parents of incoming students to discuss various aspects of the parent program.
4. Advertise in local newspapers or in the school newspaper.
5. Provide babysitting for parents with younger children.
6. Invite mothers to school for coffee and weekly discussions.
7. Put announcements of meetings in children's progress reports.
8. Present information about the parent program at PTA meetings.

Perhaps the most effective way to increase attendance is through the use of the innovative ideas of the school staff in designing a parent program with appropriate group experiences geared to meet specific needs. Through the accurate assessment of parental goals, experiences can be structured to fulfill the desired needs, with a resultant improvement in attendance.

Organization

Organizational issues are also important in conducting a parent group. If parents are made to feel welcome and comfortable, they are more likely to become involved in the group. Consequently, by organizing the meetings using the following suggestions, the group should proceed more smoothly.

1. Be sure that the meeting room has moveable chairs that can be arranged in a circle.
2. Make sure there is a chalkboard available.
3. Provide coffee and cookies.
4. Have parents put a big place card in front of them with the first names of the parents and the names and ages of their children.
5. Bring enough copies of handouts for each meeting.
6. Provide multiple copies of several books for parents to check out.

In addition to these preliminary activities, there are several skills that are more important for effective functioning as a group leader. These skills are not particularly difficult to learn, but they do require attention and practice.

STRUCTURING: Parent groups are usually most effective when the members are informed of the purpose and content of the sessions from the beginning. When parents understand the structure and guidelines, they tend to stray from the task less frequently. Of course, it is counterproductive if the format is too rigid; the leader must maintain enough flexibility to alter the direction of the group process if there is a perceived need to do so. But, setting the guidelines at the beginning and reminding the participants throughout the course of the meetings is extremely useful in providing direction.

Once guidelines have been established, the leader can note any deviations he sees and redirect the discussion. Another useful procedure is to ask the members "What guidelines are we failing to consider?" or "What is happening to our group?" These comments and questions should help keep the session within the appropriate limits.

BONDING: Particularly at the beginning of the group, the issue of inclusion is important. The group leader needs to create a climate that fosters feelings of inclusion and belonging. Encouraging members to use first names and to learn each others' names is one way to create such a climate. A useful exercise is to request several different group members, after they become slightly familiar with first names, to go rapidly around the circle and name everyone in the group. This serves as a practical warm-up to the group and helps encourage referring to each other by name.

Throughout the sessions, the leader needs to be conscious of identifying and facilitating common bonds between parents. These take the form of identifying similarities among parents, their children, problems, feelings, and ideas. For example, parents are requested to discuss problems they have in getting their children to do their homework. There will probably be at least two parents who express similar concerns or problems. The leader bonds them together with a comment such as "It seems, George, that your situation is similar to Sue's. You both seem to be saying that you feel frustrated when your children won't do their homework. Do the two of you see it this way?"

These two procedures, acquaintance with names and bonding, lead to inclusion of group members and provide links between parents that help facilitate greater communication. The techniques also promote interaction among members and provide a framework for universalizing.

UNIVERSALIZING: Parents of learning disabled children frequently feel that the problems and concerns facing them are unique. Sometimes this leads to a reluctance in sharing their personal difficulties. The group leader can help lower anxiety by pointing out that many parents share common concerns. When a parent brings up a problem or has difficulty applying a principle, the leader can universalize the example by asking "Who else has had a problem similar to this?" Universalizing helps unite the group. By sharing common concerns, group members begin to encourage and to learn from one another. In the process members are stimulated by the opportunity to help others in the group.

REDIRECTING: This skill helps to maximize group discussion and involvement. When a statement or question is expressed to the leader but needs to be discussed by the parents, the appropriate response is to redirect the comment. Questions like "What do others here think of that statement?" or "Does anyone else have a response to Larry's question?" help to facilitate group discussion. Parents are more influenced by group dialogue than by dialogue between leader and member alone.

FEEDBACK: By encouraging feedback from one member to another, the group leader helps parents learn how their behavior, feelings, and beliefs affect others. The feedback that members receive about their child-rearing practices helps them to develop greater self-awareness. Feedback does not require change, since it is up to the other person to decide what to do with the information. However, it is a powerful tool in helping the parent look at himself. When appropriate, the group leader should model the process. For example, the following feedback message, "In hearing how you talked to Mark, I found myself becoming frightened at your anger. Could it be that Mark feels this way, also?" might be most helpful in helping the parent understand some of the dynamics underlying the conflict with his son.

SPECIFYING: The group leader needs to avoid generalizations and help the parent focus on specific examples. When the parent asks a general question, request that he describe the specific situation. When a general statement is made, ask for a concrete example. Make sure that the parent include what the child did, the parent's response, and how the child reacted to the responses. Specific examples help the group understand the situation and facilitate the application of principles to specific problems.

SUMMARIZING: Summarization is necessary at various points in the group process to clarify the group involvement and bind together various threads of the discussion. Summaries can be used at the beginning of a session to refresh participants' memories or at the end of a discussion to provide a stopping point. The leader can summarize or request a summary at any point in the discussion if it appears to be valuable to the process. The summary may pertain to the content of the discussion, the feelings of the participants, or the degree of involvement and interest.

In addition to the aforementioned points, each session should be viewed from the perspective of "What is the parent to learn?" This question can usually be easily answered concerning the cognitive content — the information the parent gains in the session. More difficult, and yet just as important, is the affective content — what the parent experiences in the session. The group leader needs to be constantly looking for methods to help the parent experience and feel the information presented. For example, when discussing the relationship of laterality and directionality to balance and Kephart's notions of visual motor skills, providing a balance beam and a list of activities is most useful (Chaney and Kephart, 1968; McWhirter, 1977, p. 196). Role-playing, simulation exercise, specific examples, reading, and demonstrations can help parents both know *and* understand the important ideas being discussed. In addition, these techniques serve as motivators and greatly increase the interest and involvement of parents.

These techniques and skills are helpful in providing a framework so that parents can acquire knowledge useful to themselves and to their child. Knowledge is helpful in two ways. First, as parents come to know more about a particular problem or situation, the anxiety they experience is minimized. Often the unknown is more anxiety producing than the actual situation. For example, knowing the ramifications of the learning disability helps lower anxieties and often leads to more harmony in the home. The second way in which knowledge is helpful to parents is in providing alternate ways of responding to the child. As the parents better understand the problem, as they learn more effective child-rearing practices, as they develop specific parenting skills, they are better able to respond to the child in an effective, more helpful way.

Group Formats

A variety of educational group experiences has proved helpful to parents. The following is a description of educational offerings useful to many parents, including those whose child is learning disabled. Brief accountings will be devoted to a communication skills approach, an Adlerian/Dreikurs approach, a behavior modification approach, and a group offered specifically for parents of learning disabled children. The previously mentioned book, *The Learning Disabled Child: A School and Family Concern* (McWhirter, 1977), provides a detailed description and outline of procedures for implementing these various programs. Interested readers are referred to this source for further help in developing these experiences for parents.

Communication Skill Group

A major source of family problems is ineffective communication between parents and children. Parents and children often feel discouraged, frustrated, and misunderstood in their attempts to communicate with each other. The purpose of a communication group is to train parents to be better communicators with their children. This approach provides educational experiences to help the parent learn certain communication patterns. Relying heavily on skill training, the communication group has focus, goals, and processes that are considerably different from the client-centered, group-centered experience where the participant discusses problems in a safe, supportive atmosphere.

Several reports (Gordon, 1970; McWhirter & Kahn, 1974; Terkelson, 1976) have suggested that when parents are brought together for discussions and training in communication skills, more effective relationships within the family can be achieved. Poor communication between learning disabled children and their parents because of poor self-esteem, developmental factors, or perceptual difficulties makes the inclusion of a communication training group a necessity in a good parent program.

Adler/Dreikurs Study Group

Many parents have found the concepts proposed by Adler (1927) to be most beneficial when incorporated into their child-rearing practices. Much of Adler's work has been applied to American culture by Dreikurs (Dreikurs & Soltz, 1964), who has advocated child study groups. A number of articles (Agati & Iovino, 1974; Frazier & Matthes, 1975; Fears, 1976) have supported the utility of such groups.

The content of child study groups usually includes the fundamentals of Adlerian theory such as social interest, purposiveness of behavior, and striving for superiority. For parents of learning disabled children an understanding of the four goals of misbehavior (i.e., attention getting, power, revenge, and assumed inadequacy), is extremely useful. Furthermore, the notions of logical and natural consequences and encouragement provide helpful procedures in responding to the misbehavior and discouragement of the child.

Behavior Management Group

Parents can also profit from basic information on learning theory and behavior modification (McPherson & Samuels, 1971; McWhirter & Hudak, 1975; Frazier & Matthes, 1975), and a good parent program will provide instruction in ways of managing child behavior. Ideas such as the Premack Principle and home token economies are of great benefit to families and can easily be included as content in a behavioral group.

Some of the concepts identified with the behavioral approach are particularly important for the learning disabled child. For example, immediate reinforcement of small increments of improved behavior with emphasis on positive reinforcement is most helpful in modifying the learning disabled child's behavior. Most important, the concepts tend to build rather than lower the child's self-esteem.

Learning Disabilities Group for Parents

Parents need an overall understanding of learning disabilities and a specific grasp of their child's dysfunction. A group developed around the concept of learning disabilities serves a very worthwhile function, particularly for parents of a child who has recently been identified as learning disabled (McWhirter, 1976a, 1977). Parents are usually confused and bewildered at this time and most appreciative of information and contact from school personnel.

The program of a learning disabilities group should include information that clarifies the concept of learning disabilities. Because of their importance to the learning process, both the auditory and visual channels should be discussed and their possible dysfunctions detailed.

The relationship between learning disabilities and emotional problems of children needs to be highlighted. Where possible, specific disabilities of children should be discussed to give each parent a complete picture of the problem.

As parents gain relevant knowledge about the learning problems their child confronts, their extraneous anxiety is diminished. They can focus more in dealing with problems. Parents can learn to respond in ways to help the learning disabled child in his emotional-social adjustment. Parents can also be taught to provide supplementary learning experiences for the child, either building on his present knowledge or helping to remediate the area of deficiency. The previous section of this chapter on suggestions for parents is important here. By providing practical concrete suggestions for parents, the group leader utilizes the parents as a resource to assist their own child.

In addition to the parent groups described here, there is a variety of additional experiences that have potential benefits to parents. Groups can be structured around useful books such as Ginott's *Between Parent and Child* (1965) or Berne's *Games People Play* (1964). For some parents, knowledge of normal child development might be the most important content for an educational group. For others, information on values clarification has utility. In short, a good parent program includes a variety of educational components to help provide the parent with accurate and appropriate information.

Individual parent contact and parent counseling and educational groups, particularly for parents whose child is learning disabled, provide useful and necessary avenues for parent support and education. They also offer a potential resource that the school needs to tap. As the school and home become more closely united in the educational process of the child, the nonproductive friction and the apathetic withdrawal of parents will be lessened. As the contact becomes more productive, parents are helped to develop the necessary skills, information, and knowledge to more effectively rear their children. They also better understand their children and the school program. This understanding helps build a pathway of mutual trust between the parents and the school, a pathway that improves the educational environment of the child.

REFERENCES

Adamson, W. C. Helping parents of children with learning disabilities. *Journal of Learning Disabilities*, 1972, 5(6), 12-15.

Adler, A. *Understanding human nature.* New York: Fawcett, 1927.

Agati, G. J., & Iovino, J. W. Implementation of a parent counseling program. *The School Counselor,* 1974, *21*(2), 126-129.

Barsch, R. H. *The parent teacher partnership.* Arlington, Virginia: Coun Exc Child, 1969.

Baruch, D. *New ways in discipline.* New York: McGraw, 1949.

Berkowitz, B. P., & Graziano, A. M. Training parents as behavior therapists: A review. *Behavior Research and Therapy,* 1972, *10*(4), 297-317.

Berne, E. *Games people play.* New York: Grove, 1964.

Brown, G. W. Suggestions for parents. *Journal of Learning Disabilities,* 1969, *2*(2), 97-106.

Bryant, J. E. Parent-child relationships: Their effect on rehabilitation. *Journal of Learning Disabilities,* 1973, *6*(2), 102-105.

Calvert, D. R. Dimensions of family involvement in early childhood education. *Exceptional Children,* 1971, *37,* 655-659.

Chaney, A. B., & Kephart, N. C. *Motoric aids to perceptual training.* Columbus: Merrill, 1968.

Clement, P. W. Please, mother, I'd rather you did it yourself; Training parents to treat their own children. *Journal of School Health,* 1971, *61*(2), 65-69.

DeCecco, J. *The psychology of learning and instruction.* Englewood Cliffs, New Jersey: P-H, 1968.

DeGenaro, J. J. What do you say when a parent asks, How can I help my child? *Journal of Learning Disabilities,* 1973, *6*(2), 100-102.

Dinkmeyer, D. C. The parent "c" group. *Personnel and Guidance Journal,* 1973, *52*(4), 252-256.

Dinkmeyer, D. C., & McKay, G. D. Leading effective parent study groups. *Elementary School Guidance and Counseling,* 1974, *9*(2), 108-115.

Dreikurs, R., & Soltz, V. *Children: The challenge.* New York: Hawthorn, 1964.

Fears, S. L. Adlerian parent study groups. *The School Counselor,* 1976, *23*(5), 320-330.

Frazier, F., & Matthes, W. Parent education: A comparison of Adlerian and behavioral approaches. *Elementary School Guidance and Counseling,* 1975, *10*(1), 31-38.

Freud, S. *Group psychology and the analysis of the ego.* New York: Bantam, 1929.

Fullmer, D. W., & Bernard, H. W. *Family consultation.* Boston: HM, 1968.

Ginott, H. *Between parent and child.* New York: Avon, 1965.

Gordon, T. *Parent effectiveness training.* New York: McKay, 1970.

Johnson, C. A., & Katz, R. C. Using parents as change agents for their children: A review. *Journal of Child Psychology and Psychiatry,* 1973, *14*(3), 181-200.

Kelley, E. J. Parental roles in special education programming — A brief for involvement. *Journal of Special Education,* 1973, *7*(4), 357-364.

Lopate, C., Flaxman, E., Bynum, E. M., & Gordon, E. W. Decentralization and community participation in public education. *Review of Educational Research*, 1970, *40*, 135-150.

McCarthy, J. J., & McCarthy, J. F. *Learning disabilities*. Boston: Allyn, 1969.

McPherson, S. B., & Samuels, C. R. Teaching behavior methods to parents. *Social Casework*, 1971, *14*, 148-153.

McWhirter, J. J. Family group consultation and the secondary schools. *Family Life Coordinator*, 1966, *15*(4), 183-185.

McWhirter, J. J. A parent education group in learning disabilities. *Journal of Learning Disabilities*. 1976, *9*(1), 48-52. (a)

McWhirter, J. J. Special issue. *Devereux Forum*, 1976, *11*,(1), 1-77. (b)

McWhirter, J. J. *The learning disabled child: A school and family concern*. Champaign, Illinois: Res Press, 1977.

McWhirter, J. J., & Hudak, J. L. Parent groups on child management. *Devereux Forum*, 1975, *10*(1), 28-32.

McWhirter, J. J., & Kahn, S. E. A parent communication group. *Elementary School Guidance and Counseling*, 1974, *9*(2), 116-121.

McWhirter, J. J., & Kincaid, M. Family group consultation: Adjunct to a parent program. *Journal of Family Counseling*, 1974, *2*(1), 45-48.

Munsey, M. The parents' right to read. *Journal of Learning Disabilities*, 1973, *6*(6), 394.

National Advisory Committee on Handicapped Children. *Special education for handicapped children: First annual report*. Washington, D. C.: D.H.E.W. Office of Education, January 31, 1968.

Neifert, J. T., & Gayton, W. F. Parents and the home program approach in the remediation of learning disabilities, *Journal of Learning Disabilities*, 1973, *2*(2), 85-89.

Patterson, G. R. *Families*. Champaign, Illinois: Res Press, 1975.

Satir, V. *Conjoint family therapy*. Palo Alto: Sci & Behavior, 1964.

Sperry, L. Counselors and learning style. *Personnel and Guidance Journal*, 1973, *51*(7), 478-483.

Stewart, J. C. *Counseling parents of exceptional children: Principles, problems and procedures*. New York: MSS Educational Publishing Company, 1974.

Terkelson, C. Making contact: A parent-child communication skill program. *Elementary School Guidance and Counseling*, 1976, *11*(2), 89-99.

Wallace, G., & Kauffman, J. M. *Teaching children with learning problems*. Columbus, Ohio: Merrill, 1973.

Chapter 10

WORKING WITH PARENTS OF ABUSED AND NEGLECTED CHILDREN

HAROLD P. MARTIN

THROUGHOUT this chapter, the term *abusive parents* is used to refer to parents who significantly mistreat their children. Much of what will be directed toward abusive parents will also be true for parents who neglect, emotionally deprive, or sexually molest their children. Indeed, the same concepts may be applicable to parents who, without such dramatic behavior, are inadequate in parenting their children. This approach conceptualizes abusive parents as a rather heterogenous group, all of whom, however, have in common their inability to adequately parent their children. Abusive parents are similar in many respects. Some abusive parents neglect their children, while the majority do not. Most reports of abusive families describe families of low socioeconomic status, while the group also includes adults of advantage. Some abusive parents are highly invested in their children, albeit for distorted reasons; others have minimal emotional investment. While the literature makes only oblique references to an association between physical and sexual abuse, there are data that suggest considerable overlap in these two seemingly distinct entities.

Two points derive from this view. The first is that abusive parents are not all the same and cannot be approached in identical fashion. There is variation among the population of abusive parents just as there is with parents who treat their children well.

The second point to be noted is that there is less discrete uniqueness than is generally thought in the various syndromes that all fit under the spectrum of "mistreatment of children." While this recognition may make the task of spelling out how to help such parents more difficult, it is also a warning that individualization must be used in planning help for any abusive parent.

CHARACTERISTICS OF ABUSIVE PARENTS

Despite the disclaimer noted above, it nonetheless seems logical that

252

before one can hope to intervene effectively with abusive parents, one must have some idea of the constellation of unifying characteristics that have been found to typify this population. This is especially 'critical when trying to help an adult deal with his/her own behavior. This is different from helping a parent deal with the child's behavior, i.e., deal with the child with a handicap, asthma, learning disabilities, etc. In the abusive situation, one is trying to help an adult deal with something that, for the most part, is internal. Parent education, casework, or whatever form of help is being considered is ultimately directed at helping the adult understand and change abusive and neglectful behavior.

While keeping in mind the admonition to recognize variability in abusive adults, one will find certain characteristics recurring time and time again. For example, it is very unusual to find an abusive parent who had a happy childhood. Most abusive parents were mistreated themselves as children — abused, neglected, or emotionally deprived. The abusive adult typically has not had models of good parenting from his/her own family. Below is a paraphrased summary of common characteristics of abusive parents as conceptualized by Brandt Steele (1975).

1. Social isolation. The parent is usually quite emotionally isolated from family, friends, or neighbors. The abusive family as a nuclear unit has few contacts outside its boundaries.
2. Low self-esteem. The abusive parent has a concept of himself/ herself as inadequate, unlovable, incompetent, and worthless. Usually this stems from a childhood in which the person perceived those messages from his/her own parents. Low self-concept precedes abusive behavior and is reinforced by acknowledgment of mistreatment of one's own child.
3. Most abusive adults are immature and dependent. Problems are faced and dealt with in a very immature fashion. The dependence is shown in the adult's intense wish for someone to play a parent-surrogate role and take care of him/her.
4. There is very little joy or pleasure in the life of abusive parents. Most have come from very barren, unhappy childhoods. They may demonstrate anger, sadness, or aggression but rarely exhibit fun and joy in age-appropriate activities.
5. Many professionals have been impressed at how frequently the abusive parent has highly distorted perceptions and unrealistic expectations of children. This may reflect a pervasively distorted understanding of children's development in general, or it may only be a distortion in respect to a specific child.

6. Many, if not most, abusive parents have an aversion to the idea of spoiling their child and also believe in punishment, especially physical punishment, as a means of helping a child to learn things. This is evident in minimal nurturing behaviors and frequent physical punishment.

7. There seems no question that most abusive and neglectful parents are severely limited in their ability to empathize with others. This is seen most clearly in their inability to empathize with their own children. It can also be noted in an apparent insensitivity to other people. People, including his/her own children, are viewed primarily in terms of their capacity to meet the needs of the abusive adult. As will be noted, this is a manifestation of a severe deviation or delay in the development or relatedness-to-people from early childhood.

What one finds, then, when working with abusive parents, are adults who are lonely, unhappy, isolated, and insensitive and who take little pleasure in life and feel that they probably do not deserve such pleasure. They feel lonely, unloved, and unlovable. They make others feel sad, angry, and concerned. One quickly senses the seemingly bottomless pit of abusive adults' need for care and attention.

Throughout the remainder of this treatise, the term *therapy* shall be used in a rather unconventional manner. The author uses the word *therapy* to connote helping. The adjective *therapeutic* does not suggest formal therapy (e.g., psychotherapy, physical therapy, etc.) but refers to activities and interchanges that have a beneficial and helpful effect. It is in this sense that the noun *therapy* is considered. Hence, therapy for the parent may take the form of talking, empathizing, teaching, or any number of other procedures of assistance.

PRINCIPLES FOR HELPING

Perhaps the most important principle for any type of work with abusive adults is the idea that the *relationship* between the helper and the parent is the critically important component of the therapeutic process. The relationship is the bedrock of what will help and what will make help possible. The relationship *is* the therapeutic agent. The content of what one says or does is primarily important as it shapes the relationship between the professional and the abusive parent. The abusive parent wants someone to care, someone to understand, and someone to be available. It will be essential for the professional to care, to try to understand, and to be available to help the parent change his/her life when the parent is so motivated.

Timing is a second and critically important variable in providing help to an abusive adult. Early in the helping process (and the early stage may last for months or years), the abusive adult is apt to be angry and suspicious. So-called "helpers" have wanted, and perhaps succeeded, in taking away the child. "Helpers" have accused this person of criminal behavior. Helpers have come in and out of his/her life and have not stayed around in any type of long-term commitment.

Early in the course of treatment, the abusive parent does not have a real investment in changing. The parent may want life to be better. The parent wants the child to behave better. There may be an intense interest in changing many things in life. But, typically, there is no real deep sense of wanting to change himself/herself.

The abusive parent wants help, but s/he is not aware, early on, that some types of help are only possible through work by and on himself/herself. And so, early in the course of treatment, the abusive parent is not interested in learning about child development or homemaking. S/he wants help and relief from pain and loneliness. S/he is interested in the child acting better, but not in learning different methods of child care that might make that possible. In response to this, the professional must make an assessment of what stage the parent is in so as to know what may be possible and helpful at that particular time.

Eventually, the helping person will want to assist the parent in changing. This change may include understanding himself/herself and the child better; learning new ways of coping with the child; dealing with low self-esteem, etc. But before this can happen, the professional needs to move very slowly and cautiously to help the abusive adult move into a position of *wanting* to change. This will only be possible after the abusive adult feels s/he is *capable* of changing. If one feels completely worthless and inadequate, there is a sense of futility at even trying to develop new knowledge or new skills. Motivation to change can only occur after the adult has developed some sense of trust in the helper. There will be a period of testing and gauging behavior during which the abusive parent will make judgments as to whether the professional is truly interested in him or whether the professional has a hidden agenda of goals unrelated to the parent.

The issue of timing is especially important for the abusive adult who feels coerced into treatment. Treatment may be court ordered, i.e., it may be a condition of the court for the parent to retain custody of the child or to escape criminal prosecution. Even without court orders, the abusive adult may legitimately feel coerced into treatment by a child protection agency, by family, or by various professionals. The professional is often faced, then, with a recalcitrant adult who is either disinterested in insight or who defiantly says, "Help me if you can." If the professional is used to dealing only with highly motivated clients or students, it takes some adjustment to adapt to the abusive adult who attends class or treatment but demonstrates little interest in becoming actively involved in the learning process.

Abusive adults need various forms of help and different people to help. As one comes to be trusted by the abusive parent, the demands for nurturance and signs of caring may become overwhelming or too burdensome for most individuals. The emotional drain of working with abusive parents is probably the principal reason for the tremendous turnover rate in child protection services, which not uncommonly approaches 100% turnover per year. "Burn-out" is so common as to be almost universally discussed at any meeting of child abuse workers. For the professional to be able to maintain a helping stance with the abusive client, there must also be others available to the client for help and nurturance.

The abusive parent needs various types of help. As will be discussed, the parent needs a friend or parent-surrogate, a psychological therapist, and someone to help him/her learn new ways of dealing with children. The parent may need help with housing, employment, job training, and child care options. There may be legal problems to unravel. Marital problems need attention. It is this author's opinion that no one single professional can deal with all of these problems. No one form of help can successfully meet all of these important needs of the abusive adult.

Treatment for the abusive parent will not be successful if it is traditional and office based. The frightened, lonely, abusive adult requires more outreach and signs of caring than traditional patients. A lesson might be taken from the early work of Brandt Steele, a psychoanalyst and psychoanalytically oriented therapist. It has been remarkably instructional to see this man learn quite early that to be effective with abusive patients, he would make home visits, take phone calls at erratic hours, and keep up correspondence with his "graduates" for years after termination of treatment. Teachers, group leaders, caseworkers, and lay therapists have learned that the abusive client cannot be successfully helped by seeing the client only in the office or classroom. The client transferentially puts the helping professional into the role of a parent-surrogate and makes requests and demands much as a child does of its parent. This drain on human energy must be shared by some group or cadre of helpers.

It should be clear from these comments that treatment for the abusive parent cannot be short-term. Individual components may be time limited, but help and treatment of various sorts will be required by most abusive adults over a long period of time. Someone or some group of people must be prepared to provide help for months or years.

Finally, the professionals who work with abusive parents must be prepared to deal with their own feelings, which will inevitably be stirred up. In working with an adult who uses physical aggression to deal with frustration and anger, the professional may find that behavior repugnant. The professional will have to deal with his own memories and feelings surrounding the physical punishment he received as a child. The tremendous tug and pull by the abusive client to put the professional into a parent-surrogate role must be recognized and worked through by the therapist. When the professional does not acknowledge these personal touchstones, s/he reacts to the client with fear, anger, or over-protectiveness. There is a seductive pull for the abusive client to become, symbolically, a member of the family of the professional: his child, his parent, his sibling. These special problems are not insurmountable, but they certainly require a keen sense of self-observation by the professional.

GOALS OF HELP

From a child-oriented perspective, the ultimate goal of help for abusive parents is to significantly alter child-rearing practices. However, from another perspective, it can be seen that the abusive adult needs help completely independent from the child's welfare. One might take this to the ultimate position of maintaining that even if all of the children of a particular adult are being permanently removed from his custody and parental rights are being permanently severed, then we are left with an adult who still needs a multiplicity of help. Except in the relatively rare case of the psychotic or borderline psychotic adult, abusive parents do not feel good about their abusive behavior. They do not want to be cruel or thoughtless to their own children. As noted in the previous section, the typical abusive adult is a lonely, unhappy, isolated person with low self-esteem who deals with stresses of life in inappropriate, maladaptive, and often self-punishing ways.

Some of the goals for the abusive adult will include the following.

1. Help the adult feel better about himself/herself, i.e., develop an

appropriate self-concept that includes an acknowledgment of one's strengths and abilities as well as one's deficits.

2. Help the adult to develop lifelines with people who are trusted enough to turn to when life's stresses and indignities arise.

3. Help the adult learn to extract pleasure from life in forms other than using people for need gratification.

4. All of these points revolve around helping the adult to become less isolated. This will require an improved self-concept, developing a sense of trust in others, and learning the socialization skills that most adults take for granted as part of a normal growing-up process.

5. All of the suggestions above speak to the goal of helping the abusive adult learn more adaptive ways of dealing with stress. The common responses of anger, depression, or withdrawal need to give way to less self-destructive means of grappling with stress. One would hope that friends and professionals could be turned to for nurturance and support.

6. Realistic self-expectations should reflect a more accurate view of himself/herself by the abusive adult. Paradoxically, the abusive adult often has such high self-expectations that no one could attain such grandiose goals. If one's self-esteem is tenuous, then it is difficult to admit to limitations or shortcomings, as they merely reinforce the basically negative view the adult has of him- or herself.

7. Appropriate ways to discharge anger must be learned. Acting out in the form of verbal or physical violence as an automatic means of discharging anger must be replaced by more personally and socially acceptable behaviors.

8. Help must often include assistance with some real life stresses such as employment, housekeeping, education, job training. child care, etc. In addition to alleviating the handicap a parent has when faced with such social disadvantage, assistance in these areas can do a great deal to help the abusive adult develop a sense of trust, self-esteem, and optimism for a better future.

9. The abusive adult will need help in making some decisions about his/her desire and capacity to adequately parent the children. This requires that the counselor hold no particular bias for the parent. In some instances, possibly the most healthy and helpful stance for the parent would be to accept that s/he does not want to retain custody of the child or that s/he feels that s/he will not be able to adequately parent the child. More often, the parent will decide in the opposite direction, in which

case s/he will need a great deal of help in learning how to go about the process.

10. This leaves us to deal, then, with the ultimate goal of helping the abusive parent alter and improve his/her child-rearing behaviors. This goal has two components. The first has to do with the adult changing his/her feelings toward the child, and the second is related to changing behavior toward the child. Both must be worked on for abusive and neglectful parents to feel good about their own parenting ability.

FORMS OF HELP FOR ABUSIVE PARENTS

A rather large number of forms of help have been employed with abusive adults. Perhaps the wide variety reflects the relative lack of success found with any one particular form of intervention. Most abusive parents need some combination of forms of help consisting of at least two or three of the following. It should be stated from the outset that there has not been sufficiently adequate documentation as to the effectiveness of any of the following methods of treatment, nor any particular combination of them, with abusive adults. The literature expresses various biases or experience, but clearly defined and researched answers are not forthcoming to guide us in knowing which types of adults will benefit from which types of intervention. Nor is there adequate documentation of which goals can and cannot reasonably be expected to be achieved by each modality. The few brief comments about each form of treatment are taken from the experience of the author and from the many professionals who have written and spoken of their clinical experience. The various modalities described here do not constitute an exhaustive or complete list of all types of help available to abusive parents but do include the forms of assistance this author feels are most beneficial and accessible in most communities.

Casework

This approach, the most common help given abusive parents, should provide aid in organizing and managing a household, including the children. The caseworker functions as a triage agent, assisting the parent and family members in obtaining various types of specific help as needed. Typically the caseworker visits the parents at home. While this is partially to monitor the progress of the family, it also affords the opportunity of a more personal approach than one that is centered in a professional's office. The caseworker places heavy emphasis on helping the family to more adequately utilize available social systems, be they food stamps, ADC funds, job training, child care, etc. The caseworker delivers concrete help to the family while also attempting to be supportively psychotherapeutic by listening and helping the parents sort out their feelings and options for solutions to problems. The emphasis is on problem solving with a minimum of insight-oriented treatment.

Homemaker Services

Homemaker services are especially valuable as real assistance to families where large family size and overwhelming stress make it very difficult to manage the household. This is not a free maid service, but it does provide a person who will not only help the mother in managing and caring for the home, but who will assume a large educational role in helping the mother learn more efficient ways to maintain a household on her own.

Individual Psychotherapy

Individual psychotherapy was suggested early in the history of child abuse by the Denver group, i.e., Brandt Steele and C. Henry Kempe. It is their feeling that most abusive and neglectful parents have long-standing psychological problems. The psychodynamics of the adult are conceptualized as stemming from the parent being ill parented himself. The Denver group focuses on the insight-oriented therapy while stressing the importance of the therapist as a trusted confidant. The actual form of therapy varies and may range from psychoanalytic to behavioral in nature. This form of help highlights the need for abusive adults to understand themselves and to learn through a therapeutic relationship how to develop an appropriately trusting liaison with another adult.

Lay Therapy Program

A lay therapy program was developed at the National Center in Denver many years ago. The lay therapist is a nonprofessional who is relatively mentally healthy, who has successfully parented children, and/or who has been well parented himself. The role of the lay therapist is a mixture of being a friend, a surrogate parent, and a surrogate sibling to the abusive parent. The therapist visits and talks with the parent several times a week. His/her role is to listen, to be supportive, and to befriend the abusive adult. There is no expectation on the part of the lay therapist to help the parent gain insight, nor is there any admonition to monitor parenting behaviors. In the National Center's experience, the lay therapist develops a close and long-term relationship (friendship) with the abusive adult. This relationship may last for years and includes being available for crises as they arise. Socialization may include such things as shopping together or even joint recreational activities. With some abusive adults, the lay therapist is basically a foster-parent, while at other times, the friendly peer relationship is more prominent.

Group Therapy

Group therapy has been utilized for many reasons with abusive adults. Some persons find it easier to obtain help from a group rather than on a one-to-one basis with an individual therapist. Many individuals find it comforting to realize that there are many other people with similar problems. One key advantage of group therapy is that the individual abuser not only obtains help from others, but also *gives* help to others. This subtle difference may make a tremendous difference in self-esteem, as the abusive adult sees that he can be of assistance to other abusive parents. The other important aspect of group therapy is the relationships that develop between parents in the group. Many groups deliberately include socialization activities as part of the therapeutic model.

Self-Help Groups (for example, Parents Anonymous)

Much of what has been noted under group therapy also holds true for Parents Anonymous. Started by Ms. Jolly Kay, herself an abusive parent, a typical chapter is made up of self-referred adults who have abused their children or who are concerned that they might abuse their children in the future. Originally, there was no professional involvement with most chapters. More recently, however, provisions have been made for a sponsor for each group, usually a mental health professional. Modeled in some fashion after Alcoholics Anonymous, the chapter typically meets weekly and members give considerable support to each other with problems and crises.

Residential Care

Residential care has rarely been utilized except for the hospitalization of severely disturbed adults. However, a few child abuse centers, including the National Center in Denver, have had residential treatment programs at various times (Lynch & Ounsted, 1976). One of the rationales for a residential model is the opportunity to provide intensive therapy of a variety of sorts over a short time period. A second advantage is the therapeutic use of the mileu of the residence. At a minimum, the residential program offers the abusive adult some respite from most of the stresses of running one's own home and all that it entails. The program offers nurturance, surcease from the outer world, and an organized program that typically focuses on various forms of therapy, including parent education and attention to child-rearing behaviors. The expense of such programs is prohibitive for most communities. There are some other problems in residential care that are not insurmountable, such as the typical regression of the patients, acting-out behaviors, and the difficult reintroduction of the adults back into their "normal" lives.

Marriage Counseling

Marriage counseling is often an adjunct to other forms of help. The marriages of abusive adults are typically troubled. It is very unusual for an abusive adult to have a satisfying, close marriage. Since coping with interpersonal relations is the prominent problem of most abusive adults, it is to be expected that the relationship of marriage partners is not spared but is also troubled.

Family Therapy

Family therapy has been utilized very seldom by agencies serving the abusive parent. There is an appeal for this type of therapy, as abuse or neglect or sexual abuse is most commonly seen as a signal of pathology throughout the entire family structure. However, shortly after the community gets involved with an abusive family, there is usually so much anger and rejection directed toward the target child that family therapy is not thought safe for the child from a psychological standpoint. And yet, some communities have utilized it. There are definite indications that it can be an effective intervention when the timing is right. The family as a unit must come to grips with the various pathological relationships within its structure, which is very difficult to attain with each member of the family receiving some therapy or help apart from all of the other members (see Beezley, Martin, & Alexander, 1976).

Treatment for the Child

Treatment for the child must be mentioned here because the therapy may be indirectly helpful to the parents. The child may need a variety of types of help, such as medical care, physical therapy, speech therapy, infant stimulation, or educational therapy (preschool or day care). A significant advantage deriving from such assistance includes the benefit of respite for the mother by having certain times of the week when someone else is taking care of the child. Child behaviors that are stressful to the parent may be altered and improved through such treatment. Therapy directed toward the child helps obliterate the idea that only the parent has problems and acknowledges that the child may not be a completely normal, gratifying child.

Direct Help with Parent-Child Relationship

This is a key part of any program of help for abusive parents and a form of therapy most often ignored. Regardless of what is done to assist the abusing adult, if the child is to remain with the biological parent, direct help in altering the parenting of the child is essential. It is possible that some of this work can be done as an integral part of psychotherapy, group therapy, or casework. However, it may be necessary for a professional to take on this job quite separately from other types of help being given the parent. At the National Center in Denver, a number of approaches have been utilized to help the parent feel differently and behave differently toward his child. The most fruitful approach is to have a mental health professional work directly with the parents and their child together. The professional helps the parents see and understand which of their behaviors are successful and which are self-defeating in managing their child. It has been our experience that the intervention cannot focus exclusively on behaviors, but must also include helping the parents understand the *meanings* of their child's behavior, as well as the meanings and reasons for their own responses. This is not, then, a trade school to learn the crafts of parenting, but a system that combines the teaching of techniques and strategies along with helping the parent gain insight into the meanings and reasons for behavior. This type of intervention takes various forms in different communities. Some have found approaches such as Parent Effectiveness Training of value. It may be possible for day-care workers or preschool teachers or other types of child care professionals to offer this form of assistance.

It remains this author's bias, however, that special training and experience in changing parenting behaviors are required for optimal help for the abusive parent. The abusive parent, after all, is primarily identified as an adult who cannot, or has not been able to, adequately relate to his/her child. It is generally believed that this specific area requires the most expert of therapists. The parent needs to change his/her behavior toward and with the child. S/he also needs to change feelings for the child. These are the most difficult and yet the most critical goals of the entire helping process.

The question frequently arises as to when the professional can feel with some confidence that the parent-child relationship has improved to the point where it can be assumed that adequate parenting is available in the home. This question must be addressed when considering when to return the child to the home. It relates to the goals of the professional directing efforts at improving the parenting of the abusive adult. While there might be any number of criteria utilized, the following are given as guidelines for signs of potentially adequate parenting.

EVIDENCE THAT THE PARENT ENJOYS THE CHILD: The pleasure the parent takes in the child should not be exclusively focused around "pleasing" behaviors, that is, the parent taking some pleasure in the child only when the child is minding, behaving, or meeting the expectations of the parent. Rather, the goal refers to the parent truly enjoying the child, taking delight in seeing and fostering age-appropriate behaviors in the child, such as the child's play, learning, and development. It would be worrisome if the parent continued to view the child as a burden or a challenge to be met through shaping and molding behavior.

APPRECIATING THE CHILD AS AN INDIVIDUAL: A child should not be primarily an extension of the parent. An adult's worth or lack of worth cannot be measured in terms of a child's behavior. When a child is viewed primarily as an extension of the parent, the dynamics exist for the adult to project onto the child his/her own wishes, impulses, or self-assessment. In such a situation, for example, the child may be viewed as having many of the bad characteristics of the parent. Conversely, the child may be used in a pathological way for primary need gratification by the adult. When the child is appreciated as an autonomous individual, the parent will not be inclined to personalize misbehavior of the child as if it were deliberately directed at the parent. The child will be enjoyed for who s/he is, a young person struggling with the inevitable stresses and joys of growing up.

DEVELOPING REASONABLE EXPECTATIONS: The abusive parent should develop appropriate and reasonable expectations of the child. This will only be possible if the parent has some knowledge of what constitutes reasonable and appropriate behavior for children at different ages and if the parent can accept his/her child as not needing to be unusually good or unusually bad. This change in the parent is essential for the professional to feel optimistic that abuse and neglect will not recur.

REDUCTION IN TESTING BEHAVIORS: A further sign of improved parent-child interaction would be a diminution of provocative behavior by the child. Most children, when uncertain as to the investment of a parent or parent-surrogate, will engage in testing behaviors; this is a very common complaint of foster parents of abused children. However, as the child senses the permanence of an adult's attachment and bonding, the provocative testing behaviors should decrease. This may require some therapy directed toward the child when his emotional development has been significantly altered. A minimum of provocative child behaviors is not only an important indirect measurement of a good parent-child relationship, but it also decreases the potential for the abusive adult to mistreat the child. Unfortunately, by the time society becomes involved in most abusive families, the children from such homes have often incorporated a style of relating to adults that includes anger-provoking behavior. Such a child may test the patience of any adult. The child needs to learn to trust adults and learn alternate ways of obtaining attention and confidence.

TOLERATION OF NEGATIVE BEHAVIOR: Related to the previous goal is the need to see that the abusive parent has learned to tolerate and deal with the child's anger and negative behavior in some manner other than physical or verbal abuse. This will require the attainment of new techniques of responding to negative behavior, as well as an understanding and acceptance of anger and aggression as a part of all normal children.

EXPRESSION OF POSITIVE FEELINGS: The professional might also look for signs that the abusive adult is able and willing to express positive feelings for the child. This may take the form of verbal or physical nurturance. There is very little loving behavior or verbalization in most abusive homes. To see such overt expressions of loving and caring would fulfill the therapist's wish to see the abusive parent enjoy the child and take pleasure in him/her.

ENCOURAGING OUTSIDE ATTACHMENTS: A further sign of movement away from a symbiotic relationship between parent and child is the parent's willingness to allow the child to attach emotionally to other adults. This is a difficult task for many parents, seeing their child develop friends and develop healthy and loving relationships with adults such as teacher, neighbor, therapist, etc. When the parent is able to allow, or actually encourage, such attachments, it is a sign of selflessness that connotes the parent's appreciation of the child, not as *just* his/her child, but as an individual with strivings, wishes, and gratifications independent of the nuclear family.

One of the implications of considering these criteria for assessing the parent-child relationship is a need to look at the behaviors of the parent that reflect feelings and attitudes toward the child. Such criteria are based on the assumption that the parent has learned to view the child differently and that the parent has developed the ability to respond behaviorally to the child in a growth-promoting way.

Parent Education

In a sense, most of what has been discussed as intervention in the parent-child interaction could as easily be placed under the heading of parent education. However, this requires the conceptualization of parent education as more than the teaching of facts or skills, but as including a form of intervention that will impact on the parents' view of themselves and of their children.

Parent education refers minimally to learning what parenting involves and how to parent children. It includes learning about children and about child development, and hopefully, it includes learning about one's own children. It may also involve learning about parents, which can be extended so that a mother learns about being a woman, a wife, and a mother. It encompasses an accumulation of facts or knowledge but should go further to include changes within a person as to how s/he feels about self and how s/he feels about others. Self-concept and self-esteem are involved, as well as empathy and understanding of others.

As noted earlier, parent education can be valuable to abusive parents, but it must be preceded by other forms of help. When the abusive adult is in the midst of angry confrontation with agencies or is hurting or depressed, s/he is not receptive to educational intervention. Actually, in some senses, all help and intervention has an educational component. Psychotherapy should be educational, at least in the sense of the patient learning about himself. Any form of intervention affords the opportunity for the abusive adult to learn about relationships and how s/he can more satisfactorily interact with other persons. It really is a matter of focus. The educational or learning value of many types of intervention is subtle and indirect and is not the major contracted focus of the treatment process. In parent education, however, the teaching and learning processes are primary and focused, while insight and internal psychological change in the parent are indirect and covert, albeit of equal value to the client.

Thistleton (1977) has recently described a parent education program for abusive and neglectful parents. It should be stressed that in her program, the parents also receive psychotherapy and homemaker services. The parent education program maintains the goal of having the parents learn about child growth and development and the techniques of home management. Sessions are arbitrarily divided into two phases. The first phase includes a curriculum of (a) nutrition, (b) home safety, (c) child growth and development, and (d) use of toys by children in play. This is preceded by an initial nurturing session directed at helping the mother learn something about personal grooming. The second phase of ten sessions focuses on discipline and problem solving in issues of children's behavior. Anecdotal reports indicate that this program is helpful with some abusive parents. It seems that in addition to the content, an important component of this parent education program involves *giving* to the parent. Indeed, the first phase is set up so that the parent is paid for attending. The giving element shifts from very concrete forms, i.e., money and assistance, to the provision of help and support by the parent educator.

Carter and his co-workers (1975) describe a program of parent education predicated on the premise that inadequate parenting is attributable to the mother's lack of child-rearing skill and knowledge, with a resultant overreliance on inconsistent physical punishment. Long- and short-term groups seemed to benefit equally, although there were inadequate measurements of direct changes in parenting behaviors in this study. The curriculum focused on such issues as home management, safety, and nutrition, as well as on parent's responses to children's behaviors.

Justice and Justice (1976) took a broader scope in working with parents. They identified six areas of concern on which their intervention strategies are based: (a) symbiosis, (b) isolation, (c) talking and sharing with mate, (d) impatience and temper, (e) child development and management, and (f) employment.

Family life education has been proposed as a potential deterrant to inadequate parenting. A major thrust of the federal government program has been to develop curricula for school children that would prepare youngsters for their roles as parents; hopefully, such learned techniques would decrease the likelihood of recurrent abuse. There is truly no data to support or refute such hypotheses.

It seems reasonable to assume that abusive behavior might be prevented in some persons through preparation for parenthood. It also seems clear that such preparation must include more than just learning facts about children and parenting. In the best such programs, the school child is exposed to *in vivo* experiences of what it actually feels like to have children in his/her care. This may involve a practicum in a preschool setting or having responsibility for the care of infants under supervision in the school. It is only through such a hands-on approach that a teenager can truly feel what it is like to play the role of a parent. The frustrations and joys of child care must be experienced to be truly appreciated. When such practical experiences are joined with group discussion of the affective responses to children, a teenager may be in a position to really anticipate what parenting would be like. Without such experiences, a family life education program can only hope to approach remediating the cognitive deficits of the parent-to-be.

There has been less experience in family life education for abusing parents. Such an approach would be based on the hope that education would decrease the risk of repeated abuse and neglect. It is assumed that materials and curricula for abusive parents could not be identical to those developed for school children. Parents, abusive or not, know what it is like to have a child in their care. An approach similar to those described by Carter, Thistleton, and Justice and Justice would be more appropriate. The leaders of a group course in parent education or family life must be trained to anticipate that they will inevitably be faced with abusive parents discussing their own deviant parenting at some length. The group leaders must be prepared to hear abusive adults alternately justify and criticize their own parents' behavior. It is essential that a nonjudgmental stance be maintained by parent educators. In a sense, the abusive parent participants will use such an educational forum as catharsis, group support, and a form of psychotherapy. The therapist will be dealing with adults whose models of parenting have been deviant yet who need to justify and rationalize the abusive and neglecting parenting behaviors to which they were exposed as children. In medicine, there is a time-honored cliché that states, "No one ever had a bad internship." No young physician wants to admit, even to himself, that his year of training might have been wasted, inferior, or second rate. Similarly, most adults, especially ill-parented adults, are loathe to allow criticism of their upbringing. It taxes the skills of the parent educator to help such abusive parents give up the models they had as children without attacking or denigrating those models.

SUMMARY

The task of planning helping strategies for abusive parents is a difficult challenge indeed. Success is possible, but the professional must be prepared for the special problems encountered throughout such a therapeutic course.

We are dealing with a difficult population. The abusive parent is a lonely, unhappy adult. S/he has little capacity or reason to trust others. S/he feels worthless. S/he has been accused of behavior that makes his/her self-esteem even lower. S/he has had poor models of parenting and has not learned to solve problems in adaptive ways, but relies on self-destructive means of dealing with disappointment and stress. S/he is in great need of nurturance and acceptance, basically, in need of good parenting even as an. adult.

Experience has shown that change in the abusive adult is slow in coming and difficult to attain. A recent report from the NSPCC research team (Baher, Hyman, Jones, Jones, Kerr, & Mitchell, 1976) acknowledged that the majority of mothers had not changed their parenting behaviors, even after 21 months of treatment. Preparatory work akin to a corrective emotional experience may be necessary before insight or learning can be possible by the parent.

The treatment of abusive adults requires special energy, patience, and skills from the professional. The abusive parent may want to learn things and may want to change himself/herself. But more prominently, s/he will want someone to provide love, understanding, caring and availability — parenting. S/he will have to deal with anger toward others and self-directed anger. S/he may view attempts at assistance or suggestions as criticisms that reinforce his/her own poor self-image.

It seems clear to this author that abuse and neglect are multifactorial phenomena. No single cause can be isolated, treated, or prevented. There are at least three major views of the background of abuse. The psychodynamic view is that abusive behavior is rooted in the psychological makeup of adults who have been ill-parented themselves as children. This view emphasizes the importance of psychotherapeutic help. A second view emphasizes the social and environmental stresses of abusive parents. Those who see this as the predominant factor in child abuse stress programs of alleviation of such social stresses and the need for the entire society to view and portray violence as unacceptable behavior. Finally, there is a view that inadequate parenting is primarily rooted in lack of knowledge and skills. Many who espouse parent education or preventive family life education come from such a philosophical paradigm.

It seems inescapably true to this author that there is validity in each of these three views. Polarization to the point of exclusive attention to only one of these three factors dooms to failure therapy or prevention.

Any professional who works with abusing adults must play many roles. The psychotherapist will sometimes find him or herself functioning like a caseworker; the lay therapist will need to include home management in his/her intervention armamentarium; and the parent-educator will have to combine many functions to be effective.

Parent education, defined quite broadly, can be a critically essential component of helpful intervention for the abusive adult. Only exploratory attempts have been made to include this treatment modality into the helping strategies for inadequate parents. There will be few guidelines for the parent educator concerning either content or process. It is hoped that understanding of abusive parents and their needs, coupled with the parent educator's experience with a wide variety of clients, may prepare him/her for the challenging and gratifying task of helping the abusive adult grow and develop.

REFERENCES

Adamowics, D. (Ed.). *Child abuse and neglect: The problem and its management: The community team — An approach to case management and prevention* (D.H.E.W. Publication No. (OHD) 75-30073). Washington, D. C.: U.S. Government Printing Office, 1975.

Baher, D., Hyman, C., Jones, C., Jones, R., Kerr, A., & Mitchell, R. *At risk: An account of the work of the battered child research department, NSPCC.* Boston: Routledge & Kegan, 1976.

Beezley, P., Martin, H., & Alexander, H. Comprehensive family oriented therapy. In R. E. Helfer & C. H. Kempe (Eds.), *Child abuse and neglect: The family and the community.* Cambridge, Massachusetts: Ballinger Pub, 1976.

Blumberg, M. L. Treatment of the abused child and the child abuser. *American Journal of Psychotherapy*, 1977, *31*(2), 204-215.

Carter, B., Reed, R., & Reh, C. Mental health nursing intervention with child abusing and neglecting mothers. *Journal of Psychiatric Nursing and Mental Health Services*, 1975, *13*(5), 11-15.

Ebeling, N., & Hill, D. (Eds.). *Child abuse: Intervention and treatment.* Acton, Massachusetts: Publishing Sci, 1975.

Franklin, A. (Ed.). *Child abuse: Prediction, prevention and follow-up.* New York: Churchill Livingstone, 1977.

Greene, A. A psychodynamic approach to the study and treatment of child-abusing parent. *Journal of American Academy of Child Psychiatry*, 1976, *15*(3), 414-429.

Jeffery, M. Practical ways to change parent-child interaction in families of children at risk. In R. E. Helfer & C. H. Kempe (Eds.), *Child abuse and neglect: The family and the community.* Cambridge, Massachusetts: Ballinger Pub, 1976.

Justice, B., & Justice, R. *The abusing family.* New York: Human Sci Pr, 1976.

Kempe, C. H. Approaches to preventing child abuse: The health visitors concept. *American Journal of Diseases in Childhood,* 1976, *130,* 941-947.

Kreindler, S. Psychotherapy for the abusing parent and the abused child. *Canadian Psychiatric Association Journal,* 1976, *21*(5), 275-280.

Lynch, M., & Ounsted, C. Residential therapy: A place of safety. In R. E. Helfer & C. H. Kempe (Eds.), *Child abuse and neglect: The family and the community,* Cambridge, Massachusetts: Ballinger Pub, 1976.

MacLachlan, E., & Cole, E. The Salvation Army Education for Parenthood Program. *Children Today,* 1978, *7*(3), 7-11.

Margrain, S. Review: Battered children, their parents, treatment and prevention. *Child Care Health Development,* 1977, *3*(1), 49-63.

Martin, H. *The abused child: A multidisciplinary approach to developmental issues and treatment.* Cambridge, Massachusetts: Ballinger Pub, 1976.

Steele, B. *Working with abusive parents from a psychiatric point of view* (D.H.E.W. Publication No. (OHD) 75-70). Washington, D.C.: U.S. Government Printing Office, 1975.

Thistleton, K. The abusive and neglectful parent: Therapy through parent education. *Nursing Clinics of North America,* 1977, *12*(3), 513-524.

Chapter 11

DIVORCE COUNSELING:
A COMMUNITY SERVICE FOR FAMILIES
IN THE MIDST OF DIVORCE

JUDITH S. WALLERSTEIN AND JOAN B. KELLY

A conceptual framework for the development of child-centered, preventive clinical services for divorcing families is presented. The structure and components of an intervention service — including treatment strategies, successful interventions, failures, therapist role, transference and countertransference responses, and professional dilemmas — are discussed.

THIS paper and a companion piece to follow[4] describe an experimental intervention program, developed in relation to the needs of an emerging and rapidly increasing subgroup of the population, namely children and parents in divorcing families. The intervention models evolved as part of a research project aimed at exploring the experience of divorce among normal children and adolescents, and tracing its effects on their psychological and social development, with particular regard to the vicissitudes of the parent-child relationship at three checkpoints — the parental separation, one year later, and four years later. In a sense, the interventions were secondary to the research goals, and provided a way to gain access to the intimate functioning of the divorcing families at the peak of stress and thereafter. The overarching goal of the investigation, however, has been to recommend or develop psychological, social, and educational measures to alleviate distress and diminish psychopathological outcome.

Because of the extraordinary dearth of systematic study of this population in the social and behavioral sciences, we initially flew blind in planning our services. We drew heavily upon crisis intervention

Reprinted from the *American Journal of Orthopsychiatry*, 47(1), January 1977. Courtesy of publisher. Presented at the 1976 annual meeting of the American Orthopsychiatric Association in Atlanta, Georgia. Research was supported by a grant from the Zellerbach Family Fund of San Francisco.

theory and on the literature on loss and mourning. We reasoned that a) divorce constitutes a time-limited crisis in the life of the child and the adult, during which the usual coping and adaptive mechanisms are in disarray; b) the adult's capacity to parent is diminished at such time; c) the child and adolescent might benefit from the opportunity to talk with an objective and psychologically informed adult who might help to clarify feelings, sort out fantasy from reality, and enable the young person to place his feelings and the situation within an appropriate perspective; d) the same would be true for our counseling with the parent; and e) counseling within a time-limited psychotherapy model represented the treatment of choice.

After 5 years of work with 60 families whose 131 children were between the ages of 3 and 18 at the time of the divorce, our knowledge of divorce and its sequelae has greatly increased, and our conception of the nature of the divorce process itself has changed. We have generated a set of observations and hypotheses regarding expectable responses related to age, sex, and family constellation in children and adolescents of divorce.[3, 6, 7, 8] Moreover, we have acquired a new set of findings that have continued to inform and shape our interventions; some of these, central to the development of clinical programs, are as follows:

1. Divorce is a disorganizing and reorganizing process in a family with children. The process extends over time, often several years. Although it has, like most life events and crises, the potential for growth and new integrations, the road is often rocky and torturous, and many people underestimate the vicissitudes and difficulties of the transition. Our study confirms findings[9,10] that we may reasonably expect a period of several years of disequilibrium before new, more gratifying job, social, and sexual relationships can become stable enough to provide comfort and a renewed sense of continuity. Perhaps change extending over time is characteristic in adulthood and therefore should not be surprising. It is important to keep in mind that 2 or 3 years of disequilibrium in the life of a child may represent a significant proportion of his entire life experience. These observations are relevant to the timetable of an intervention program.

2. One of our central findings is that the entire postseparation period, rather than just the predivorce period or the divorce events themselves, and the functioning of the custodial parent following the divorce, are the central determinants in the young child's well-being at the end of the first year of separation.[7] Therefore, the parent's functioning following the divorce, especially in the instance of the young child, is of crucial importance to the child's continued devel-

opment and bears on the approach and timing of the intervention service.

3. We found, further, that, among older children and adolescents, the youngster's capacity to maintain his developmental stride, while not as closely dependent on the psychological and social functioning of the custodial parent, is nevertheless related inversely to the parent's need to lean heavily on the child for emotional and social sustenance and to involve the child in continuing battles and recriminations with the divorced spouse.[6, 8] It appears that there may be an optimum emotional distance between the older child and the parent that provides mutual support, yet allows for sufficient separation to protect the integrity of development. This distance can be breached all too readily by a continuation of the chaotic events and intense angers of the divorce and by continuing demands for alignment with the parent after the divorce. Such findings also affect the timing and content of counseling.

4. The period immediately following separation seems particularly useful, in terms of return on intervention efforts. Relationships are shaking loose from their moorings, considerable anxiety is generated in this process, and, in accord with crisis theory, the chances for effecting change in a fluid system are greatly enhanced. More particularly, divorce, as seen in our study, represents a nodal point of change in the parent-child relationship, for the custodial as well as the noncustodial parent. In fact, the changes in the parent-child relationships in some age groups are at times startling and not predictable from earlier, predivorce modes of relationship.*

Many decisions made during the divorce in regard to the subsequent structuring of relationships, including custody and visitation, have long-term consequences for the future of the child and the parent-child relationship. Yet, often the impetus and direction for these changes derive entirely from the stress-laden interaction of the family disruption. It would seem of considerable importance to provide the opportunity at this time for thoughtful consideration of consequences and alternatives. On the positive side, it appears that many parents, despite their own preoccupations, are relatively accessible to interventions regarding their children immediately following the parental separation; this is due to genuine concern, as well as to guilt, real and exaggerated, over what they perceive as past and present hurts inflicted on their children. Many, feeling they have

---

*Some 40% of the fathers of preschool children in our study improved their relationship with their children in the first year following the divorce, with 40% of the mothers in the same group having deteriorated relationships with their preschool children.[7]

wasted important years in an unhappy marriage, see the divorce as a second chance for themselves and for their children. Thus, the divorce period produces a three-cornered potential — a crisis-engendered capacity for (potentially helpful) change; the external demand for major decisions regarding future parent-child relationships; and a (sometimes) heightened motivation for improvement. Where these coexist, they can be brought together uniquely at this time to serve the best interests of the child.

5. Divorce has been compared to loss from death, in part because death and mourning have been widely studied in recent years. Loss is, indeed, a common denominator in both situations. Divorce shares with death the psychic and developmental hazard that loss in the external world will not be fully assimilated within the inner world of the individual, as a result of unresolved ambivalence and intense unmodified need for the lost object. Unlike death, however, divorce presents for the child the continued availability of the departed parent as a live object for intense living-out of conflict and longing. Many children in our study were, at 4 years after the separation, holding fast to fantasies of reconciliation.

The complex psychological tasks imposed by the divorce are only partially resolved by the acceptance of the circumscribed loss. Beyond this, both child and adult must achieve new and complex changes in intimate relationships and self-concept, without the structural support and role assignments of the family system. These achievements ultimately involve the completed mourning of the loss of the predivorce family (and the renunciation of the aspirations attached to it), acceptance of the now circumscribed relationship with the noncustodial parent, and adjustment to the revised relationship with the custodial parent — all combined with the capacity to make use of newly fashioned substitute relationships for growth. Such complex and painful adjustments can only take place over time, and it is unlikely that the child can achieve them without considerable help from parents or others.

6. Although many parents who came to our service had been in psychological treatment of many persuasions for varying lengths of time, it was uncommon for their psychotherapy to have focused in depth or detail on the parental relationship with the children at the time of divorce. By and large, it centered upon the parent's own life decisions and directions, perhaps in part because many therapists have limited training in work with children and are not able to offer specific guidance. Thus, the need for the development of divorce intervention dealing with children and the parent-child relationship

seems relatively unaffected by parental participation in an ongoing psychotherapy.

With these considerations, evolved from our study, establishing our conceptual framework, the balance of this paper will be devoted to the structure of the intervention service, and to an analysis and an assessment of its various components, including treatment strategies, applications, role of the therapist, successful interventions, and failures.

STRUCTURE OF DIVORCE COUNSELING SERVICE

The Children of Divorce Project has been located since 1971 at the Community Mental Health Center of Marin County. Lying immediately north of San Francisco, Marin is a predominantly white, affluent, surburban community with one of the highest incidences of divorce in the nation.* The project has, from the start, provided a separate gateway offering only divorce-related counseling, maintaining highly confidential records, and relying on its own outside grant funding. No fees have been charged. The interdisciplinary clinical team of six had training and experience in clinical work with children and families.

Parents in the process of divorce were referred by attorneys, school psychologists, teachers, social agencies, and the community at large. A preparatory period of carefully planned community education and personal contact with these sources provided the foundation for their referrals. A limited number of cases were referred by the court when the investigative worker was hopeful that litigation over custody or visitation could be avoided through counseling. The service was advertised as preventive and applicable to all families with children undergoing divorce, and not addressed to families in special distress or unusual circumstances. Parents came with the understanding that our work was child-centered, preventive, and planning-oriented.

Since our interest was in examining the nature of the divorce experience within a nonclinical population, and developing services for normal children, children with a history of psychological difficulty and psychiatric treatment, or whose general psychological, social, or intellectual functioning fell significantly below the developmentally appropriate norms, were screened out. This screening gained in importance as referring agencies, particularly schools, who were reluctant to suggest psychotherapy for troubled children, referred

---

*In 1973, the divorce rate per 1000 population for the United States was 4.4; in 1974, it rose to 4.6. For the same period, California reported 5.7 and 5.8.[2] Corresponding figures for Marin County were 6.8[1] and 6.6.[5]

chronically disturbed children to our service if a divorce occurred in the family. By and large, we referred such children to the main Community Mental Health Center door. This initial impression — that a brief intervention, based primarily on the divorce experience, is not suitable in the treatment of chronic, long-term disturbance — has been strengthened by our accumulated experience.

The intervention model was time-limited from the outset. Parents came for an initial period of 6 weeks of counseling for themselves and their children. The constraints of the 6-week period contributed to the intensity of the experience and accelerated the development of the relationship. The brevity of the intervention also dictated rapid assessment and early choice of strategy. We did not, however, hold rigidly to the time limit; where it appeared that more counseling sessions were indicated, we extended the intervention time. Our total experience suggests that a three-month counseling period is more realistic and effective in many situations. Each parent and each child was seen separately by the same therapist three to six times. (Where there were more than three children in the family, two therapists were sometimes assigned.) During the divorce an average of 14.2 hours was spent with each family in the Project. In addition, one staff member was employed in visiting the schools to obtain information directly from teachers. Families were invited to return for continued consultation at the end of the year. They were informed that the staff member would be available during the intervening year, should they wish to consult the service. Of 60 families, 58 were seen at the end of the first year. (The 4-year follow-up is currently underway.)

The intervention was predicated on working with families at the time that the divorce decision and parental separation were current and central to the life of the family, constituting an intensive, focal event, especially for the children. This time was initially conceptualized as the period extending up to 1 year following the legal step of filing. Our experience places the optimum intervention time for the children at between 1 and 6 months following the parental separation. We found that early intervention can sometimes handicap the effectiveness of counseling. Often, it is not useful to intervene in the period of initial shock, disbelief, and denial. Sometimes the divorce decision and filing are accompanied by behavior totally untypical of divorce. If parents have not physically separated, it is difficult, if not impossible, to help the children understand and accept the divorce. In the absence of legal filing, one may find oneself intervening in a marital dispute that may not become an actual divorce. Counseling delayed, however, beyond the initial 6-month period may be too late to affect both the legal and the less formal aspects of the decision-making process, or may find symptomatic behaviors and parent-child alignments consolidated and strongly defended. Delay in counseling may also unnecessarily extend confusion and suffering for both parent and child.

With the exception of families with chronically troubled children, we accepted all who met our broad requirements. Sometimes, only the custodial parent came (in our sample, all but one of the custodial parents were mothers), and fathers often appeared initially reluctant. As our technical skill increased, fewer fathers stayed away. In 60 families, we saw 59 mothers and 46 fathers.

We were, from the start, brought face to face with some serious professional and ethical dilemmas regarding our offer of service to the general divorcing population. In some families the divorce occurred following the death of a grandparent, the diagnosis of a serious or fatal illness in a child, or a serious accident in the family. Such divorce decisions seemed precipitated by one parent in full flight from a reactive depression, rather than in response to marital stress, and often evoked strong opposition and bewilderment in the other parent. We found it very difficult to refer, delay, or otherwise dissuade such persons from rushing headlong into divorce, although there was available psychological help for them in the community. Another group that generated concern were those mentally ill parents for whom the divorce filing appeared to be yet one other symptom in a more generalized or accelerated acting-out or general decompensation. With both these family groups, the leverage of the intervention and referral was necessarily limited, and the children, for the most part, appeared at especially high risk. Our service was not, in our view, suitable to their needs, yet we were uneasy in turning them away. It is likely that family disruptions that are related only secondarily to marital stress will increase as divorce becomes both socially and legally more accessible.

INITIAL PHASE OF COUNSELING

Clarification of the service goals and structure was followed by a careful, although necessarily telescoped, history-taking which began with the courtship, the vicissitudes of the marriage, its balance of gratifications and strains, and finally the escalating events and feelings that preceded the decision to divorce. We were interested in ascertaining the dominant style of family life and interaction, the history of psychotherapy for the parents, which parent initiated the divorce, whether either opposed it, and to what extent the decision had been gradual or represented a sharp discontinuity with the past.

We discovered that many parents quickly led us to the core of the marital problem through their accounts of their marriage.

> Mr. O. began with a half-hour recitation of his wife's many faults, which he characterized as "appalling." He opined that she never attended to the little things that mattered, that she was careless and slovenly, and just "a sexual animal." The children were not fed and ready for bed when he arrived home from work. She was unable to balance a checkbook. He said, "The last thing I want to do is to talk to somebody at the end of a busy day." He added, reflectively, "If you look at basic drives, I suppose the sexual drive wasn't satisfying for her." He admitted that they had engaged in sexual intercourse once yearly during the past five years, because he could not tolerate being touched by her.

We attempted to map out the current situation of each parent, economically and legally, their respective educational and employment histories, their current life plans, expected continuities and change. We were interested in the presence or absence of other relationships, and we were interested in the events and ambience of the marital dissolution, particularly in the eruption of anger and physical violence at that time. Out of these data we attempted to formulate an early impression of the central psychological impact of the divorce experience, especially on self-esteem, and of the defensive and varying coping responses to loss. We endeavored, as well, to make some estimate of the more customary level of functioning and capacities.

The disorganizing impact of divorce, which can sometimes be obscured by a flurry of what appears, on the surface, as new and organized behavior, was evident in several parents. For example,

> Mrs. C. reported that she had recently organized her life in a single-handed effort to convince personnel directors to provide day-care centers in industry and hospitals, and that her calendar was filled with appointments related to this project. Mrs. C. lacked training and a job and had no employment experience, except as a volunteer. As the interviews progressed, she began to report fatigue, frequent crying spells, and feelings of helplessness and total defeat regarding her capacity to deal with her own school-age children. Gradually, it became apparent that she was having a great deal of difficulty in making the simplest connections, and that she was depressed, disorganized, and acutely frightened.

A different example of the intensity of grief in response to divorce was evident in our first interview with Mr. M., in which the therapist reported,

Mr. M. then put his hands over his face. When he raised his face after a few minutes of silence, he said, movingly, that he would like my help in counseling him as to how to accept the fact that he was losing his son. He has to face the fact that his boy will probably be living under the direction of some other man some time soon. His eyes filled with tears as he said he would like me to think about what it does to a guy to lose his son.

The second focus of the history-taking dealt in a more traditional way with each of the children, but with special emphasis on the present conflict, the divorce response, the parents' relationship with the particular child, and parental expectations and plans for the future. This history-taking combined with the first focus of the active counseling process. Parents were asked about the child's understanding of the divorce, how much the child had shared in the decision-making and the concomitant feelings of the parents, how much he or she had also been party to fights and to angers, what explanations had been offered and by whom, and what the child's response had been in words and in behavior. In this way, we quickly established ourselves in a direct helping and advisory role, with our paramount concern being the child, although by no means exclusively so; we addressed the parent from the start in her or his parenting role, and began to make psychological connections between new behaviors and divorce-induced stress.

By the third interview, we expected to have a tentative diagnostic formulation sufficient to establish priorities in the counseling process. By this third interview with the parent, the therapist would have seen each child at least once and would have received a full school report of academic and social performance during the preceding year. From these data it was possible to put together multifaceted assessments of the child, the parent, and the parent-child relationship, as well as other significant and supportive relationships of the child's environment, within the context of the divorcing and reorganizing family system. The counseling agenda and strategy would be delineated at this time, and, where appropriate, shared with each parent.

COUNSELING AGENDAS

Parents brought crowded agendas from many aspects of their lives in which they were experiencing bewilderment, anxiety, pain, and relief or euphoria. The questions uppermost in their minds devolved from the many lacunae consequent to the family disruption, from the absence of structure and defined ground rules (and customs), and from their need to make important decisions and establish new behavior precedents. Therefore, they asked many practical questions and required specific advice. One common question was how to relate newly established social and sexual relationships to the children. In addition, parental agendas were very much influenced by their respective roles in the divorce-seeking process. Parents who had initiated the divorce generally perceived the children as relatively intact, and wanted these perceptions confirmed by us. Similarly, parents who felt injured or abandoned saw their children as more troubled and damaged by the divorce process and wanted confirmation for these contrary perceptions. The psychological substrata to many parental concerns were conscious and unconscious fears, guilt, and preoccupation with possible damage to themselves and to their children, combined with loneliness, depression, and fears of being overwhelmed by homosexual, heterosexual, and intense aggressive impulses no longer contained by the marital structure. For some, the divorce proceeding brought relief and a sense of emancipation, and these parents characteristically were seeking aid in making better and more informed choices in the use of their new freedom. Sometimes, on the other hand, the central agenda was a desperate wish for help in restoring the broken marriage.

Many of the most acute conflicts were displaced onto or otherwise reflected in the parental relationships with their children. For example, some mothers began to worry intensely about sexual promiscuity in their teenage daughters, in the absence of any visible evidence of basis for this new concern. Other parents became concerned regarding their children's continued contact with the other parent, whom they saw as dangerous, seductive, or destructive to the children. Sexual and incest fantasies projected onto the divorcing partner were abundant at such times, and were sometimes told to the children. Some parents were indeed deficient in appropriate judgment in their new conduct with their children. One father, who during weekend visits slept on a waterbed with his 7-year-old daughter, was both annoyed and surprised when she resented being displaced on the bed occasionally by his current girlfriend. Several custodial mothers, on the other hand, instructed their children, when visiting, to search through the father's belongings for evidences of a sexual partner; they subsequently interrogated their children regarding the sexual liaisons of their divorcing husbands. Some custodial parents, disregarding the impact on their children (and seemingly oblivious to it) of their efforts to catch up on many years of sexual and social deprivation, engaged in a frenzied social-sexual life in ways that were both stimulating and anxiety-arousing to these young and teenage children.

Parallel to the spilling of sexual impulses into the relationship with the child, parents also often, consciously and unconsciously, used the children as extensions of their angers and their wishes for vengeance. By and large, these concerns were brought to us by the parent who was the target of these angers and who felt attacked, bewildered, and helpless under the ruthlessness of the assault. More often than not, the parent was one who had felt relatively close to the now attacking child. Children, with some coaching from the sidelines, called their mothers Jezebel or whore, and scolded them for not pulling down their skirts. One adolescent, with the custodial parent's support, threw rocks at the home of the divorcing parent's lover. Other children participated in gathering evidence that might be useful in litigation. Sometimes parents described their own social and emotional isolation following the family disruption and their almost total dependence on their children.

Because of these fluid boundaries between internal repercussions within the parent and spilling over onto or coercive involvement of the child, it was often necessary throughout the counseling process both to clarify the focus and to shift it repeatedly from parent to child.

These findings also dictated a strategy that was in no way committed to following the expressed parental agendas. Our own explicit position as advocate for the child conferred on us the freedom to speak actively and directly for the children's need, and to make interpretations and suggestions in the interest of an improved parent-child relationship. The eventual strategy that emerged with each case thus came out of this complex meshing of our own agendas and goals with those of the parents.

INTERVENTION STRATEGIES

The interventions can be conceptualized as primarily child-centered, relationship-centered, or adult-centered, although all reflect admixtures of these differing emphases to various degrees. These strategies can, at the same time, be ranged along a concomitant spectrum from those predominantly educational in impact to those predominantly clinical. Interventions that dealt primarily with the child and with the interpretation of the child's needs to the parents, where we taught the parent to observe, to make psychological connections, and to employ particular techniques to change behavior or alleviate distress, fall toward the educational end of the spectrum. Interventions that dealt primarily with the parent-child relationship combine both educational and psychotherapeutic focus. Efforts at encouraging psychological change primarily within the parent, in order to increase parenting capacities, fall more closely within a clearly psychotherapeutic modality.

CHILD-CENTERED INTERVENTION

Most parents were concerned with explaining their decision to divorce to their children. This constituted an unsurmountable problem for the parents of many preschool children; 80% of those in our study had found the task too difficult, and — whether out of shame, guilt, misplaced concern for the child, or inability to communicate with their very young child — had offered no explanation. As a consequence, the youngest children were allowed to suffer helplessly with the departure of one parent from the household, without the support that probably would have been forthcoming in a relatively minor crisis. The widespread regressions, symptomatic behaviors, and fearfulness which we observed in the youngest children can, at least in part, be attributed to the absence of explanations and assurance of support from their parents. Much of this behavior was alterable when we taught parents to understand and deal with their preschool children appropriately.

Mr. D., a 25-year-old custodial father of two young children, is an employed blue-collar worker. He is an intelligent young man whose young wife left after many months of bitter quarreling. He still loves his wife and cannot talk about her without tears. Mr. D. describes his 3-year-old son, John, as confused, tearful, wakeful, anxious, and irritable. No explanation had been offered the child regarding the mother's departure. Father at first thought the child would be too young to understand, but was very responsive to detailed suggestions regarding the importance of an appropriate explanation, coupled with repeated assurances in a variety of daily contexts that the child would be cared for.

At our second meeting, Mr. D. reported that he had, in accord with our advice, carefully explained to the child that his parents were not going to continue to live together because they were unhappy and fought. Referring to quarrels the child had witnessed, he assured the child that the quarrels would not continue but explained that he, the father, was most able to care for John at this time and would continue to do so without fail. This discussion enabled the child, for the first time, to ask many questions about his mother's whereabouts and to ask to see her. On the way home from a visit with the mother, which the father had arranged, the child began to cry. Father said, "I know. I understand that it's hard when Mommy isn't coming back home to live with us." John responded. "Daddy, can we have another talk?" Shortly thereafter, the child's behavior and mood began to improve.

We made many suggestions to support a continuing relationship between the child and the noncustodial or visiting parent. Our efforts in this endeavor were refueled along the way by repeated observations regarding the suffering and intense longing that so many children experience in regard to the departed parent, and by our finding that enhanced ease of access to the visiting parent led consistently to a lessening of the child's distress.[3] One of the major contributions of the intervention was to provide bewildered fathers with suggestions regarding the planning of visits, holidays, and vacations with their children. We were surprised to find that many of the fathers carefully wrote down all of our suggestions, and amazed to learn that they often followed them in full for the entire year that followed.

Many custodial parents were perturbed at the anger of their school-age children, or hurt at the withdrawal of adolescent children with their seeming coldness and disinterest in the parental plight. In dealing with these concerns, we drew heavily upon our research to clarify age-appropriate responses, to explain behavior in detail, and to suggest specific approaches by the parent. Sometimes we counseled that feelings had to run a natural course to some resolution. We explained that underlying the anger were the many fears of the children that they would be lost in the shuffle, and their conflicted sense of loyalty to both parents, which was very troublesome to them. We told startled parents that children worry about them. We talked with parents about the moral concerns of their adolescents, and about the advisability of sometimes permitting their adolescent youngsters the "strategic withdrawal" which we found often correlated highly with continued unimpaired psychological development.[6] Often, we found parents responsive to these broad educational explanations and relieved to find that the problems they faced were not unique.

Occasionally we employed anticipatory guidance in our child-centered interventions, sometimes boldly venturing into a discussion of contingency plans for the future.

> Much of our counseling with Mr. S. centered around our shared concern that his high-spirited young adolescent daughter would be living her adolescent years with the strict old-fashioned value system of his divorcing wife and without the countering support his presence would have provided for her, had the divorce not occurred. We discussed ways in which he still might be able tactfully to serve as an important resource for the girl during the years ahead, ways that might be both acceptable to his wife and useful to his daughter.

Sometimes we educated a parent to relieve symptomatic behavior via parental interpretation.

> Mary, age 4, refused to lie down at bedtime. Prior to the separation, her parents regularly fought in the evenings after the child had presumably been asleep. The mother was advised to explain to Mary that she could now go to sleep comfortably, that the fights would not occur, and that the purpose of the divorce was precisely to avoid such angry fighting. She was advised to tell the child repeatedly that her mother would care for her, and that her father would continue to visit. The child's symptoms disappeared following this explanation.

Though all of these are examples of primarily educational child-centered interventions, it is clear that they simultaneously provide ramifying access to the inner world of the parents as well, relating particularly to issues of restoring self-esteem in the parenting role.

RELATIONSHIP-CENTERED INTERVENTION

Relationship-centered intervention was the strategy of choice for those parents whose deficit was not primarily in knowledge but in their capacity to respond effectively. Caught in conflict whereby the tugs of the distressed child-parent relationship mirrored intrapsychic and interpersonal pressures and ambivalence, many parents felt immobilized. Sometimes, for example, custodial mothers of school-age and young adolescent children became the targets of angry campaigns designed to discourage or destroy their attempts to establish a new social life and to force instead a return to the marriage. This behavior often immobilized those parents whose misgivings and low self-esteem found expression in the strident voices of the angry children. The children's needs expressed in the interaction sometimes coincided with the superego projections of the conflicted parent.

> Mrs. V. complained that she was harrassed and victimized by her 10-year-old daughter, Alice, who was controlling her and her household. She felt that she would have to discontinue her very limited social life because Alice made her feel so guilty. She would have liked to be firmer, but had always been afraid to be so. Alice was openly pressing for a reconciliation between her parents. This caused the mother to waiver, because she agreed that children need two parents. At the same time, she recalled bitterly that her husband abused her physically over the years and inveterately gambled away their savings.
>
> In our third interview, Mrs. V. described the conversation she had had with Alice following our discussion. She was able for the first time to make clear to the youngster that she would on no account

return to the marriage. Alice screamed for an hour, threatening to
run away, but she then settled down suddenly and said, "Mom, I'm
so unhappy." Alice confessed that she felt that she was the only one
who loved her father. She loved them both and could not bear to
choose between them. Following this, at our suggestion, mother and
daughter began to talk regularly, at scheduled intervals. Temper
tantrums began to lessen.

Of interest in this example is that the mother had been driven into
repeating with her abusing daughter the relationship with the departed abusing husband, in the face of which she had felt helplessly
victimized for years. The focus of the counseling, presumably on the
coercion by the daughter, also helped her to resolve the continuing
conflict of ambivalence and neurotic adaptations to her former husband. This phenomenon was not uncommon in our experience, that
the marital conflict from which the individual was painfully extri-
cating himself or herself was silently reinstalled in the consequent
alterations of the parent-child relationship. This whole complex psychological reenactment is maximally accessible to interpretive intervention at this time, just because it is still in *status nascendi.*

The intervention strategies in such instances contained several in-
terweaving components: a) an explanation of the underlying dynamics of the child's behavior to the parent; b) continued and
appropriately timed interpretations of the parent's internal conflicts
and consequent immobilization and difficulty in exercising proper
parental function; and c) supporting the painful, slow beginning
efforts of the parent to move to regain parenting capacity and to curb
the youngster's destructive and self-destructive behavior. This combination of strategies, often very effective, is clearly a mix of educational
and psychotherapeutic measures.

Much of the work with fathers regarding visitation falls under the
same rubric of relationship-centered intervention. Many fathers, especially those whose wives had taken the initiative in seeking the divorce, had, for several months, ceased to visit their children out of
anger at their wives, out of hurt, out of shame, out of grief, out of
sense of their own unimportance and expendability. Often, fathers
who had been rejected by their wives presumed that they were equally
unwanted and unneeded by their children.

The counseling task was twofold, namely to disengage the relationship with the children from the marital struggles, and at the same
time to validate for the fathers their continuing importance to their
children. The strategy involved encouraging the father's motivation
to continue his relationship with his children and to help create a
visitation structure that would facilitate these contacts. Our efforts in

this were refueled by repeated observations regarding the intense longing that so many children experience in regard to infrequent or nonvisiting parents.[3] We were surprised to find that fathers who had not visited for many months before our intervention began to visit regularly, after we helped unravel the neurotic reenactments they had fallen into and emphasized their importance to their children. One of the central contributions of this intervention program may be the number of fathers who visited their children regularly and frequently following our contact, and continue to do so.

> Mr. H. had not visited his three young children in the 6 months following the separation. At issue was his insistence that he would not pick up his children at his former house, where his divorcing wife was living with his former best friend. He expressed intense anger about the house, which he had built for his wife. After considerable work with both parents, in which the symbolism of the hated house was not interpreted, an agreement was reached for the mother to bring the children weekly to the paternal grandparents' home, to meet their father there. Mr. H. followed with weekly visits, which were still being faithfully continued at the 3-year follow-up.

Sometimes we took an opposite approach. Where the relationship seemed hurtful to the child, we tried to help the noncustodial parent to disengage from the relationship, at least temporarily, within the immediate future. There are instances where the noncustodial parent's relationship with the child places that child in jeopardy with the custodial parent by aggravating angers and intense jealousies. Although this may be baffling and tragic for the rebuffed parent, the goal of the counseling is to help him or her accept the reality of a circumscribed, sometimes even permanent, loss of contact with his or her children. By helping the parent in these very difficult situations accept the loss, we have been guided by the conviction that temporary or even permanent loss of the relationship with one parent is preferable to ongoing litigation, which can become a way of life in some families, and which may serve continually to refuel the custodial parent's often paranoid accusations.

> We advised Mr. L., who had left his wife for a younger woman, that his repeated efforts to court his school-aged children — in the face of the wife's fury and the children's resentment — were futile at that time, and that the continued litigation he planned would only create further conflict and unhappiness for his children. Further, we suggested that the passage of time might result in a diminution of anger and might provide a later opportunity to seek and reestablish meaningful contact with the children. This advice was difficult to follow, in part because it involved an acceptance of loss and precipitated a

mourning response. There is, in fact, little doubt, from our findings, that one psychological meaning of continued litigation for the parent is the warding-off of depression.

Sometimes the goal was to help the parent disentangle his use of the child as an extension of parental behavior. This was possible when the use of the child in the marital conflict was not a deliberate part of the parent's plan.

> Mrs. A. described her meeting with her husband when he visited their home. She began to make fun of him, and her 8-year-old daughter followed suit openly, mimicking her father. As this teasing in tandem went on, the mother seized his glasses to prevent his departure, and the daughter then hid them. Suddenly, in total reversal, the mother wheeled upon the daughter and accused her angrily of disrespect for her father. Here, we took the initiative in bringing to the mother's attention her double messages to the daughter, of which she had been seemingly unaware. Mrs. A. was able to perceive her role in placing the child in a very difficult bind, and could then alter her own behavior.

Sometimes the concern of these relationship-centered interventions was not the resonance of the parents' intrapsychic constellations with stresses in the parent-child relationship, but rather involved aiding in the realistic assessment of a practical situation and its possible psychic consequences. One poignant example is the noncustodial parent whose spouse had suffered with recurrent mental illness, sometimes accompanied by severe depressions and suicide attempts, and who had intervened during the marriage to safeguard the children or to take over the household care and chores where necessary. The questions raised for us by such parents, which led to the development of particular counseling strategies, were whether they could continue, following divorce, to extend some protection to their children without undertaking custody.

> Mr. Q., a slender, soft-spoken young man, first wanted to know whether everything we talked about would be kept from his wife. Assured of confidentiality, he expressed deep concern about his wife's mental condition, with particular regard to her ability to take care of their children during recurrent crises. He described her many physical illnesses, her severe depression, her proneness on occasion to violent tantrums. He was very fond of his wife, and had not wanted the divorce. He spoke highly of her intuitive understanding and her capacity and tenderness as a mother when she was well. His primary concern was with the consistency of the care-taking she could offer to his children.
>
> Counseling with this father took, as its point of departure, our

agreement that his wife was, indeed, recurrently troubled and sick, and that his concerns were realistic. We discussed both specific visitation patterns and ways of maintaining his nurturant relationship with his children. We also endeavored to help him face the fact that the divorce would impose limitations on his ability to continue his earlier role. We were interested to find that Mr. Q. was continuing, 4 years after the marital separation, to implement some of the plans we had helped him to develop.

PARENT-CENTERED INTERVENTION

Primary emphasis ·on the parent and his or her needs was largely related to facilitating the transition to the single-parent role. Although most of the divorces in our study were sought by women, many of these women were emotionally unprepared for the stresses, pressures, and multiple discontinuities that follow the divorce decision and marital separation. Our findings suggest that even unhappy marriages can provide a modicum of mutual support and a division of labor and responsibility in regard to the children. The full contribution of these supports is often unrecognized until they disappear.

Many of the women who actively sought the divorce in a search for greater independence and psychological adulthood had, for many years, been relatively helpless and dependent upon their husbands. In these families, fathers had played a dominant role as provider, standard setter, decision maker, and disciplinarian for the children. Several women in this ·group had married at school graduation and had never lived independently from their families. For all of these women, the shift from the psychological role of older sibling to being the adult who carries full responsibility and has the obligation as well as the freedom to dictate the rules and routines of the immediate family was fraught with much anxiety. One fear shared by many new single parents was that of being unheeded by children not used to accepting their authority, and of being unloved and rejected by children who resented their new exercise of authority.

Some of the most effective counseling was done with these parents, despite their apprehensiveness, in part because many were hopeful, highly motivated, and eager to make full and immediate use of available knowledge to achieve the "second chance" they envisioned for themselves and their children.

Sometimes, however, this transition to single-parenthood moved very slowly and painfully, as if the divorce had depleted emotional reserves, and the parent needed to mark time prior to the next step. The technical problem of the counseling was to adapt the intervention to the individual capacity for change and to the idiosyncratic and varying tempo of this change.

Some parents were frantic, overwhelmed by worry and diffuse anxiety, and needed help in sorting out and organizing almost every segment of their lives.

> Mrs. X. described her situation vividly: "I feel like I'm treading water in a tidal wave." She had asked her husband to leave because she was so angry at his many delinquencies that she was afraid she might hurt him. She was worried about whether she would ever be able to be a good mother because she felt she was so impatient, and yelled all the time. Her recent request for a loan had been rejected by the bank, her car had been stolen, and she had been asked to work split shifts at her job. She was concerned about the effect of her new schedule on her children, and it was difficult for her to leave the house each day, when her children cried and asked plaintively whether they could expect her return.

Finally, in this third group were those persons in whom the divorce triggered disorganization of psychotic proportions. In these families we saw kidnapping, homicidal threats, and an uncontrolled eruption of primitive, angry impulses. With these persons, our intervention goals were limited. Our aim was to afford the child whatever protection was possible within the general disorder. We found that it was sometimes possible, by employing a combination of supportive techniques, interpretation, and referral, to curb some of the acting-out and maintain the parent over a period of time sufficient to permit us to set up protective safeguards or to construct a plan for the child.

> Mrs. Y., whose history revealed episodes of poorly controlled rage and depression, appeared very distraught in her first and subsequent interviews, and was often on the verge of violence. Our relationship with her peaked when she called the therapist at night in a highly agitated state, screaming that she was going to murder her husband. This outburst followed an incident she had witnessed, in which her school-age son knocked repeatedly on the father's closed car window in order to attract his attention, and the father had driven off, unheeding, leaving the weeping child. We took her threat seriously, instructed Mrs. Y. to refrain from any contact with her husband, and arranged to see her on an emergency basis. In the several interviews that followed, the therapist attempted, with a combination of support and interpretive comments, to defuse Mrs. Y.'s projective identification with her son and to help her to restore a modicum of control over her erupting angers, which we considered to threaten not only her husband, but her child, as well. Mrs. Y. was gradually responsive to this intervention and accepted a referral for psychotherapy for herself when we terminated, although she had strongly

resisted this idea previously. A year later, when we saw Mrs. Y., she was beginning, slowly, to reconstitute and to restructure her life. Her relationship with her child was gradually improving, and the child reported to us that he was no longer frightened of his mother, and no longer needed a special hiding place of his own.

TERMINATION

In the final interview with each family, plans for follow-up or referral for treatment were made, and a general summary of the situation was presented. Referrals for outside treatment at such times of crisis often did not take, and the patient would drop out after only an initial interview. This finding raises as a significant consideration in planning crisis-focused brief intervention service whether it is incumbent upon the service itself to provide for the possibility of internal treatment continuing. Where we were able to do this, the patients continued treatments. The planned follow-up was an essential component of the structure and the relationship, in that it clearly conveyed our continuing interest in the family and our continuing availability to the family, as well as the natural expectation of ongoing struggle, mastery, and resolution efforts during the forthcoming year.

ROLE OF THE THERAPIST

The various strands of the therapeutic relationship, namely the reality of the counseling, the therapeutic alliance, the transferences, the countertransferences, the displacements from the current outer environment, all significantly reflect the overarching divorce experience. Displacements from the divorce experience became almost immediately evident within the therapeutic relationship, affecting both the intensity and content of the interaction, and the countertransferences as well.[11] In a goodly number of instances, the clinician became the object of angers and jealousies, especially from women who were feeling abandoned. Some parents said what many felt, comparing their situation bitterly with their view of us, "Of course *you* have a good job, *you* have a good education, *you* have a profession, *you* have a husband (or so they assumed)." Others experienced anger with a young and attractive colleague. One mother said, "You're successful, pretty, young, and I hate you." A father said, "You're just like my wife, who left me."

These displacements, accompanied by anger, jealousy, raw hurt, and embarrassed admission, called forth complex and intense countertransferences. The guilt we began to experience is psychologically akin to the survivor guilt of those who work with the bereaved. Furthermore, we began to develop anxiety regarding the stability of our own marriages, as attractive, personable people, much like our own self-images, thronged our offices in the throes of divorce. On a regressed level, the countertransference response contained the fear of "the evil eye," in recognition of primitive and open angers and envy around us. On a more mature level, little separated us from our patients, and our own vulnerability was magnified, precisely because the patients were drawn from our own social, economic, and educational community. It appears that the less distance that obtains between patient and therapist on a variety of social and psychological measures, the greater the potentiality for projective identification and countertransference response. Thus, while it is no surprise that direct work with people in crisis is difficult and depleting of physical and psychic energy, the full impact was somewhat greater than expected. The narcissistic blows that so many of these people had sustained made for irritability, defensiveness, and combativeness. Also, the sense of having been injured and wronged led to their needing to invoke us to confirm their moral correctness or to restore their lessened self-esteem. All of the staff found the work intermittently draining and depressing. We met periodically to allay each other's anxiety, to offer each other support, and to strengthen wavering commitments. These observations are relevant not only to the mental health professions, but also to attorneys and judges, who are subject to similar pressures without the safeguards of psychological training. One conclusion we derived from this experience is that it is probably not feasible to do divorce counseling such as this effectively full-time.

The quality of the real relationship that obtained between therapist and family was also somewhat different than that which occurs in the more usual therapeutic context. This difference emerged with clarity at the 1-year and 4-year follow-ups, in the excited, affectionate way many people greeted us. We were, in turn, interested to find how clearly we remembered the minute details of our contact with them after several years, and we observed our own pleasure and pride when people did well and our personal concerns when they were floundering. These meetings also reflected a kind of camaraderie that is the unique possession of persons who have shared in a crisis together and emerged whole.

Our style of counseling was, from the start, open, direct, personal, and, as compared with the usual clinical pace, more advice-giving and directive. When it seemed appropriate, we did not hesitate to invoke our own personal concerns over a particular situation within the family, and to make these concerns known. Our advocacy on behalf of the child gave us considerable moral authority and leverage and made us, in turn, the advocates of the parenting role, as a logical extension of our conviction. In a sense, we accepted the overall transference to us as members of an extended idealized family and tried to meet what we considered to be the parents' legitimate expectations that in an ongoing crisis they could reach out and find competent advice, guidance, and support within the community. Implicit in our relationship was the health-model assumption, namely that these parents, no matter how disturbed at the time we saw them, were capable of more mature functioning; that reasonably conflict-free spheres of parenting did indeed exist; and that the incapacity, helplessness, and regression they were experiencing were likely to be of temporary duration. In helping parents perform their parenting role, we addressed them in their most adult role. And in contributing to enhancing their parenting, we contributed directly to raising self-confidence and self-esteem. Part of our effectiveness derived from the fact that, though we took a very active role in certain areas, these were carefully circumscribed, and that we correspondingly refrained scrupulously from intervening in problems that were not our primary concern.

TREATMENT FAILURE

The examination of failure is important, not only in the assessment of the applicability of these interventions, but because it highlights the plight of a significant part of the child population that is at high risk. As conceptualized here, counseling failure is twofold: namely, parents whom we have been unable to engage meaningfully in the parenting process, combined with a family situation of continuing high stress for the children.

Parents who were unable or unwilling to perceive their children's needs as psychologically separate from their own, and who were correspondingly unable or unwilling to use such perceptions to guide their behavior, were not discernibly affected by our intervention efforts. Essentially such parents came to counseling in order to consolidate an adversary position, or to force a reconciliation, or to protect their endangered interests. Sometimes parents were unable to distinguish their children's needs because the child's physical presence was essential in warding off the parent's threatening depression.

> Mr. T. said of his daughter, "She's a mood elevator for me. Without her I go down."

On occasion, the unwillingness to view the youngster's needs separately occurred because of the press of the parent's total dependence upon a child within a life-long history of social isolation and loneliness, and the parent's inability to make other social contacts to replace the now disrupted family. More often, however, parents who had opposed the divorce decision and who experienced the divorce as a humiliating, intolerable rejection following upon years of exploitation ("I put him through medical school! I made him what he is today!") consolidated a combative stance that soon became immutable, and that included sometimes one child and sometimes all the children within its shared boundaries ("He does not care about *us*. He left *us*."). These parents were preoccupied with a wish for revenge against the offending partner, and this soon became the central preoccupation and obsession of their lives. Realizing all too well that there was little they could do directly to hurt the departed spouse except via the children, they manipulated the relationship with the children in such a way that it became the chief instrument in their unremitting effort to inflict pain and punishment. In our study of the parents who fell into this group, we found two primary subgroups — those with a paranoid character structure or suffering with psychosis with paranoid features, and those whose continuing rage was in the service of warding off an intolerable narcissistic blow and a consequent serious depression. Many of these parents appeared in our follow-up, despite our inability to change their behavior, and we were again troubled to find that frequently the intensity of their anger was undiminished by the passage of time.

Sometimes parents who became caught up in a new life-style, and in a conscious plan to relive their adolescences and recapture lost opportunities, were also unable in their total self-preoccupation to distinguish their own needs from the needs of their children. Another group we failed to help consisted of those in whom the eruption of impulses was so strong that all pretense at rational thinking was abandoned; their family situation was one of chaos and extraordinary acting-out, including burglary, poisoning of household pets, vandalism, kidnapping of children, and brandishing of weapons. While some of these people were openly psychotic, others seemed to suffer with a time-limited derangement, triggered by the divorcing process, and theretofore had led fairly circumspect lives. Few of these people were able to make use of counseling at the height of the eruption; an additional number were able to do so a year later.

Difficulty in eliciting change in parental attitudes was also experienced among families in which, prior to the divorce, parent and child had created a close, mutually supportive relationship, predicated in the main on the parent's need and unhappiness. With improvement in the parent's general situation following the divorce, and especially with a remarriage or a new love relationship for the parent, the child was suddenly excluded, no longer needed by the custodial parent, and often remote from the noncustodial parent. It was often very difficult to clarify this complex phenomenon, and to bring it to the attention of the involved parent, within the constraints of the counseling process.

CONCLUSIONS

We have described the major components of a pilot project of intervention into the divorce process. Our purpose is not to develop a short-cut or substitute for intensive psychological treatment where that is needed. It is to develop a program and a body of technique appropriate to large segments of the population who are in need of planning and are likely to be temporarily disabled in their parenting capacity and function because of the formidable tasks and stresses that accompany divorce. A central dilemma for both parent and child at this time may be the temporary, but profound, conflict of interest between the child's need for continuity to safeguard and support his development and the parental decision to break up the family structure that has provided the child's main supports. It would seem that a social policy which increasingly facilitates divorce must properly also make provision for services that may be required by children and parents during and immediately following parental separation, and by single-parent families. The clinical intervention program described represents one part of the complex array of services which these children and their parents require.

REFERENCES

1. California County Fact Book. 1975. County Supervisors Association of California, Sacramento, Calif.
2. CALIFORNIA DEPARTMENT OF HEALTH. 1975. Vital Statistics, Marriages, and Marriage Dissolutions. Department of Health, Sacramento, Calif.
3. KELLY, J. AND WALLERSTEIN, J. 1976. The effects of parental divorce: experiences of the child in early latency. Amer. J. Orthopsychiat. 46(1):20-32.
4. KELLY, J. AND WALLERSTEIN, J. 1977. Brief interventions with children in divorcing families. Amer. J. Orthopsychiat. 47(1):23-39.
5. MARIN COUNTY. 1974. Records of licenses-to-marry issued and final

dissolutions granted, 1973. Office of the County Clerk, San Rafael, Calif.

6. WALLERSTEIN, J. AND KELLY, J. 1974. The effects of parental divorce: the adolescent experience. *In* The Child in His Family. Vol. 3, E. Anthony and C. Koupernik, eds. John Wiley, New York.

7. WALLERSTEIN, J. AND KELLY, J. 1975. The effects of parental divorce: experiences of the preschool child. J. Amer. Acad. Child Psychiat. 14(4):600-616.

8. WALLERSTEIN, J. AND KELLY, J. 1976. The effects of parental divorce: experiences of the child in later latency. Amer. J. Orthopsychiat. 46(2):256-269.

9. WEISS, R. 1975. Marital Separation. Basic Books, New York.

10. WESTMAN, J. 1971. The psychiatrist in child custody contests. Amer. J. Psychiat. 127:1687-1688.

11. WHITAKER, C. AND MILLER, M. 1969. A reevaluation of "psychiatric help" when divorce impends. Amer. J. Psychiat. 126:611-618.

Chapter 12

WORKING WITH PARENTS OF
DISTURBED ADOLESCENTS

Edward L. Vogelsong and Bernard G. Guerney, Jr.

Developmental theory suggests that adolescence is a crucial time for identity formation (Erikson, 1968; McArthur, 1962). In our society, this transition between childhood and adulthood often involves emancipation from the family of orientation. The difficulty of this task is heightened, however, without the support and understanding of the adolescent's parents. A number of studies have suggested that lack of understanding and communication between adolescent and adult generations is a major factor contributing to disturbance among adolescents (e.g., Beavers, Blumberg, Timken, & Weiner, 1962; Ferreira, 1960; Franklin, 1969; Glaser, 1971; Khan, 1969; Morrison & Collier, 1969; Mosher, 1969; Satir, 1967, 1972; Stabenu, Tupen, Werner & Pollin, 1965; Watzlawick, Beavin, & Jackson, 1967; Weblin, 1962; Wellisch, Vincent, & Ro-Trock, 1976; Wise, 1970). Several survey studies of adolescents from normal families also reported communication dissatisfactions and difficulties (Dubbé, 1965; Earle, 1967). Walters and Stinnett (1971) reviewed approximately 200 articles on parent-child relationships and concluded that there is a positive relationship between parental communication of acceptance, warmth, and support and a child's emotional, social, and intellectual development. They also found that extreme restrictiveness, authoritarianism, and punitiveness without love, warmth, and acceptance are negatively related to a child's social and emotional development and positive self-esteem.

Parents who convey acceptance and openness toward their adolescent children can help provide an opportunity for expression of feelings regarding identity and independence that might otherwise be channeled in destructive and frustrating ways. Acceptance of adolescent children by parents can help adolescents be more accepting of themselves.

A variety of therapeutic techniques have been devised for fostering better relationships between parents and their adolescent children. Most of these approaches are rather traditional, in the sense that they

297

rely heavily upon diagnosis of family pathology. One interesting and innovative addition to this approach is to have several families meet together in what is called *multiple family therapy* (Benningfield, 1978).

We believe that the most productive and efficient method of working with parents of disturbed adolescents (and when feasible, the adolescents themselves) is to teach them specific skills that they can use to improve their relationships. This approach is based on a mass-educational, rather than a clinical-medical, model (Authier, Gustafson, Guerney, B., & Kasdorf, 1975; Guerney, Guerney, & Stollak, 1971/72; Guerney, Stollak, & Guerney, 1970; Guerney, Stollak, & Guerney, 1971). This approach began in the early 1960s with filial therapy (Andronico, Fidler, Guerney, & Guerney, 1967; Guerney, B., 1964; Guerney, L., 1976; Guerney, Guerney & Andronico, 1966; Stover & Guerney, 1967). Recently this approach has been extended to programs aimed at parents and their disturbed adolescent children (e.g., Patterson, 1976; Patterson, McNeal, Hawkins, & Phelps, 1967; Patterson, Reid, Jones, & Conger, 1975). In this approach, parents are taught skills to help them reduce deviant behavior and increase more positive behavior in their children. In the following section, we present another example of this type of program, the Relationship Enhancement Program. More complete descriptions may be found elsewhere (Guerney, 1977), but the approach is presented here in sufficient depth to allow the reader to obtain a full grasp of the nature and implications of using an educational model to remedy the problems of adolescents and their families.

THE RELATIONSHIP ENHANCEMENT PROGRAM

Relationship Enhancement (Guerney, 1977) is a therapeutic method designed to teach participants skills for improving interpersonal relationships. Both parents and adolescents are taught to be aware of and to express their feelings and thoughts in constructive ways and to respond to each other with understanding and empathy. By creating this environment of openness, respect, understanding, and lack of defensiveness, family members are able to avoid power struggles and, instead, work together toward a mutually satisfactory resolution of problem areas.

Relationship Enhancement is an *educational* program. It attempts to teach participants a carefully defined set of skills in a highly structured and systematic manner. Emphasis throughout the program is placed on learning and using these skills to improve interpersonal relationships. This educational orientation can help remove the stigma and resistance frequently associated with "treatment" or "therapy." It can be suggested to participants that they are participating in a course in which they are learning certain skills and behaviors, just as someone might take a course to learn to drive a car or play a musical instrument.

Yet where pathology exists, this program is *therapeutic* in its outcome. Numerous research studies have demonstrated a dramatic improvement in parent-adolescent relationships, in ability to communicate, and in satisfaction. A study of relationships between fathers and their adolescent sons by Ginsberg (1977) employed a variety of behavioral and self-report measures to test the effects of this program. Improvement was demonstrated in communication skills, communication patterns, the quality of the relationship, and self-concept. Coufal (1975) showed that similar changes occurred in a Relationship Enhancement Program for mothers and their adolescent daughters. When this program was compared with a more traditional program for improving parent-adolescent relationships, the Relationship Enhancement Program proved superior. In a 6-month follow-up of the Coufal study, Vogelsong (1975) found that gains made by mothers and adolescent daughters in the Relationship Enhancement Program were retained over time, whereas participants in the more traditional approach continued to function on the same level as before they had participated in the program. Over the past 3 years, we have been gathering data from families in which more than one parent and adolescent received Relationship Enhancement training. The conclusions of this research are similar to what was learned from the father-son and mother-daughter programs: Substantial positive changes result from participation in a Relationship Enhancement Program.

Another characteristic of this program is that it is *preventive.* In addition to new and constructive ways of dealing with problems that already exist, participants also learn to deal with potential problems before they become unmanageable. In this sense, Relationship Enhancement skills are useful to parents and adolescents who have a good relationship and want it to continue, as well as to families with a history of serious problems who want to break this pattern.

There are several values that are implicit in the Relationship Enhancement Program. We believe that these values should be made clear to participants, so that there is no misunderstanding of program goals. In fact, because this program is based on an educational philosophy and strategy, we see no reason to withhold any information or assumptions from clients. Although we do not require that participants fully subscribe to these values before entering the program, we do want them to know that this training will tend to foster the values that underlie it.

Relationship Enhancement assumes that *honesty* is the best policy and is a value that is always to be sought. Where there are attempts to hide or disguise the truth, the effects of therapy are diminished drastically. Relationship Enhancement training strives to create an environment between parents and adolescents that encourages people to be honest and straightforward with each other. By learning skills that reduce defensiveness and hostility, participants are able to be honest and open with each other without fear of being attacked or criticized. Not only is each person more comfortable in being honest with others, participants also value receiving honest feelings and perceptions from each other.

Compassion is a second value fostered by Relationship Enhancement training. We assume that it is good for parents and their adolescent children to love each other, and we want them to find useful ways of expressing this love. A very meaningful part of this program involves teaching people to discuss what they like about each other, not just what they do not like and want to change. It is our experience that relationships built on fear, punishment, and guilt are not nearly as satisfying as those that are built on compassion.

A third value underlying Relationship Enhancement is *equality*. We believe that adolescents' feelings are just as important as their parents'. If therapy is to be effective, each person's point of view must be considered seriously. This value does not mean that parents lose their authority; it does mean that they must encourage and respect their children's views and feelings. It does not mean that parents can be outvoted by their children, rather that their children's point of view must be given every consideration before any conflict can be resolved satisfactorily. Unless everyone's point of view is recognized as having validity, resentment and power struggles will be encouraged, and mutually satisfactory solutions to problems will be impossible.

Although Relationship Enhancement is a highly structured and systematic program, it is also highly flexible and is adaptable to a wide variety of client populations. In the rest of this chapter, we describe Relationship Enhancement skills, give examples of how they might be used in parent-adolescent conversations, and discuss a number of details that should help the practitioner to use this program with clients.

Basic Skills of Relationship Enhancement

Participants are taught *Expresser* skills, *Empathic Responder* skills, and techniques for *switching* between *Expresser* and *Empathic Responder* skills in a conversational way.

Expresser Skills

The Expresser chooses the topic for discussion and is taught to observe the following guidelines.

1. Imagine yourself in the other person's place and say things in a way that will make it easiest to listen and understand. By saying things in a way that is sensitive to others' needs and feelings, you are letting them know that you want to understand them. When people believe that you want to understand them, they will try harder to understand you.

2. Make it clear that you are not staking out an exclusive claim on the truth. Except when you are talking about your own emotions or about something you are absolutely certain is perceived by the other exactly as you perceive it, say something like, "In my view (judgment) . . . " or "As I perceived (understood) it . . . " In this way, if you are honest, you will also *always be accurate* and will avoid much disagreement and anger from the other person.

3. Talk about the *specific* behaviors of the other person that are important to you, rather than dealing with generalities. In this way you can avoid statements that question the character or motives of others and can pinpoint the issues in order to help bring about the exact effects you want.

4. Talk about how you view and react to these specific behaviors, what they make *you* think and feel. This will help the other person understand you and set the stage for allowing you to influence the other person's attitude and behavior.

5. When you have negative reactions or feelings toward another person, look for any pertinent positive feelings or attitudes you have toward that person and express them as well. Underlying positive feelings are often the very reason we have negative feelings. For example, "I'm hurt by what seems to me to be your indifference because I like you and want to spend more time with you." If positive elements are left out, the issue is less likely to be resolved in a satisfactory way. When you include your positive feelings, you help the other person be more receptive to the negative aspects of your views.

6. Present your *interpersonal message,* the specific new behavior pattern you wish to see, then describe the positive feelings and reactions you have or would have toward those behaviors.

7. Always be alert and sensitive to how the other person is reacting to what you are saying. If you are not making any progress, it may be time to stop expressing yourself and instead show your empathic understanding of the other person. You cannot force your opinion on others; if they are not listening, you are wasting time and increasing everyone's frustration. Sometimes the only way to increase their willingness to understand you is to clear away the interference in their minds and emotions by hearing them out.

Empathic Responder Skills

The Empathic Responder listens to the Expresser and tries to convey understanding and acceptance of what has been said. The Empathic Responder is taught to observe the following guidelines.

1. For the moment, put your own feelings and thoughts aside.

2. Put yourself in the other person's place. Listen to the words expressed by the other person, pay attention to the nonverbal components (voice level and affect, eyes, hands, posture), and listen for the feelings stated and implied. What's really going on inside this person? How would you be feeling if you were that person? What would you say *next* if you were that person?

3. Show understanding, acceptance, warmth, and a desire to understand by your *nonverbal* responses. Through your facial expressions, posture, gestures, and voice tone show interest, concern, a desire to understand, and appreciation that you are learning the other person's point of view.

4. Through your *words* show understanding, acceptance, and warmth by summarizing the main feelings and thoughts expressed or implied by the other person. Often this means trying to *say the next thing that would be said* if the other person were to go on talking in a way that displayed feelings and ideas very honestly and openly. Do not show *any* disbelief or disagreement. Do not question or try to influence the other person even subtly toward a view that you believe to be more valid than the one expressed.

5. Acceptance of another person should not be confused with agreement. You can disagree with others' perceptions or opinions and still accept their right to their own points of view. Although you

may think it unfortunate, unreasonable, self-destructive, or unfair for a person to have certain feelings, it is best to accept these
feelings as genuine and important to the person. The other
person will then be more inclined to understand and consider
your point of view if you later feel compelled to express how you
differ in your perception of the events and in the kind of behavior you would consider appropriate.

6. If you no longer can *stand* the idea of being accepting of the
   other person — for example, if you find yourself subtly trying to
   steer or influence the views of the other person by means of a
   supposedly empathic response — try to overcome your need to
   influence until you get an indication from the other person that
   you really have understood. Then switch to the Expresser skill to
   present your own point of view.

Switching Skills

Participants are taught the following rules for switching back and
forth between Expresser and Empathic Responder skills.

1. Make sure there is never any confusion about who is the Expresser and who is the Empathic Responder. There is only one
   Expresser at any given time. The other person is automatically
   the Empathic Responder. Where there is confusion about these
   roles, stop your conversation and clear up the ambiguity before
   proceeding.
2. When the Empathic Responder's own feelings are very strong, it
   is sometimes difficult to continue to listen. The Empathic Responder may ask to switch roles and become the Expresser at any
   time, so long as the last statement of the Expresser has been
   responded to accurately.
3. Sometimes the Expresser also will want to switch roles in order
   to learn the thoughts or feelings of the other person. This switch
   also first requires an empathic response by the Responder.

Example

The following dialogue is an example of how these skills might
be used in a conversation between a mother and her adolescent daughter.

MOTHER (EXPRESSER): I know you think I worry too much and you'd
    like me to trust you more [an empathic response] — and I really do
    want to trust you, honey — but I am worried about the guy you've

been dating [emphasis on own feelings]. I've never met him, and I don't want to be unfair to him, but I'd feel much more comfortable about your dating him if I could get to know him. You told me that he dropped out of high school and doesn't have a job [specific behaviors]. It's hard for me to get enthusiastic about your seeing him when the little that I know about him doesn't give me a very good impression of him [avoids stating anything about the boy's presumed characteristics, instead concentrates exclusively on subjective statements].

DAUGHTER (RESPONDER): You want to trust me, but don't want anything to happen to me [accepts and clarifies mother's views and feelings]. You'd like me to bring him home to meet you [reflects the unstated but clearly implied interpersonal message].

MOTHER (EXPRESSER): That's right. I find myself hoping that he won't ask you out again, and I'm not sure if that's fair to you or to him. I don't want to choose your friends for you, but neither do I want to see you get hurt. You're very important to me and I want to feel good about what you're doing [emphasizes underlying positive feelings].

DAUGHTER (RESPONDER): You think a lot of me and want to be fair to me and him [accepts and clarifies mother's views].

MOTHER (EXPRESSER): Exactly.

DAUGHTER (SWITCHING TO EXPRESSER): I'd like to be the Expresser. I'm so glad you want to meet him. From some things you've said before, I thought you never wanted him in the house. I never asked him to come in because I was afraid you would embarrass me by the way you treated him [emphasizes own perceptions, avoiding accusations].

MOTHER (RESPONDER): You're relieved to know that I would like to meet him. You were afraid that I would embarrass you if you brought him home [accepts feelings].

DAUGHTER (EXPRESSER): Yeah. I think he's really a nice guy and that when you get to know him you'll really like him. But let me warn you. He's very quiet. I think it would be better if you didn't try to pump him for a lot of information the first time he comes. Give him a chance to warm up and get comfortable.

MOTHER (RESPONDER): You don't want me to put him on trial the first time he comes.

DAUGHTER (EXPRESSER): Right. I would appreciate it if you were casual. I think it would be good to talk to him about music. I think he's a great musician [subjective expression of views].

MOTHER (RESPONDER): You really want me to like him [acceptance and clarification of feelings].

DAUGHTER (EXPRESSER): Sure.

MOTHER (SWITCHING TO EXPRESSER): I feel much better knowing what you've told me. I was afraid you didn't want me to meet him, and that made me more suspicious. I promise you that I'll try not to make life difficult when you bring him around.

DAUGHTER (RESPONDER): You were afraid I was trying to keep something from you and that's why I didn't bring him around. (SWITCHING TO EXPRESSER): I'm glad to know you want to be fair.

MOTHER (RESPONDER): Being able to talk about it like this was a big help [acceptance and clarification].

DAUGHTER (EXPRESSER): That's right.

Problem Solving in Relationship Enhancement

Problems in parent-adolescent relationships frequently create tension and power struggles. It often seems that the only options available are for parents to exercise their authority and make a decision or for them to give in to the wishes of their children. Neither of these options is really a satisfactory solution to the problem. Instead of creating better family relationships, they lead to resentment and estrangement. Power struggles pit parents and adolescents against each other, instead of encouraging them to work constructively toward creative solutions that will be acceptable to both.

The Relationship Enhancement Program is designed to give families skills for working together to achieve solutions that will bring parents and adolescents closer together. We frequently find that increased understanding and sensitivity are all that are needed to help participants think of solutions satisfactory to everyone. The dialogue that follows is an example of how problem solving of the simple everyday variety is accomplished using Relationship Enhancement skills.

SON (EXPRESSER): Dad, I'd like to use the car Saturday afternoon. A bunch of kids are going out to the state park to go swimming, and we don't have enough transportation. The weather is supposed to be perfect, and we're going to take along some hot dogs to cook for supper. Any reason I can't use the car?

FATHER (RESPONDER): You're really looking forward to going and hope you can drive.

SON (EXPRESSER): Right.

FATHER (SWITCHING TO EXPRESSER): I'd sure like to say yes, but I'm in a real bind. I promised your mother I'd go to the orchard this weekend to get some peaches to freeze, and the only time I have free is Saturday afternoon.

SON (RESPONDER): You're sorry, but you need the car Saturday afternoon. (SWITCHING TO EXPRESSER): Why do things always have to go wrong for me? Isn't there any way I can have the car?

FATHER (RESPONDER): You're really very disappointed. (SWITCHING TO EXPRESSER): I'm wondering if someone else could drive and you could go along with them.

SON (RESPONDER): You think one solution might be for me to get a ride with somebody else. (SWITCHING TO EXPRESSER): That just won't work, Dad. Neither Harry nor Bill can drive on Saturday, and they're depending on me for a ride.

FATHER (RESPONDER): So you really can't see any way to get there without our car.

SON (EXPRESSER): Yes. How about getting the peaches next weekend? I'd even go along to help.

FATHER (RESPONDER): You're suggesting that we wait till next weekend to get the peaches. (SWITCHING TO EXPRESSER): I wish that would work, but I'm afraid they'll be out of season by then. It's already late, and I know your mother's really going to be upset if we don't get any peaches this year.

SON (RESPONDER): So that won't work either.

FATHER (EXPRESSER): Maybe you could go for the peaches sometime this weekend.

SON (RESPONDER): Another possibility is for *me* to go get the peaches. (SWITCHING TO EXPRESSER): I don't see when I'd go. Sunday's completely out, and I wanted to go to the dance Friday night.

FATHER (RESPONDER): So you don't think you'll have any time this weekend either. (SWITCHING TO EXPRESSER): I don't know what to do. Your mother needs the peaches, and you need the car.

SON (RESPONDER): You'd like to help, but you can't think of any solutions. (SWITCHING TO EXPRESSER): If I could eat supper early Friday, I could go to the orchard and get the peaches and get back for the last half of the dance. How would that be?

FATHER (RESPONDER): You'd be willing to eat early and get to the dance late if you could get the peaches Friday night and then have the car Saturday afternoon.

SON (EXPRESSER): Yes.

FATHER (SWITCHING TO EXPRESSER): I don't see anything wrong with that. In fact, I'd be delighted if you got the peaches, because then I could work on straightening up the garage Saturday afternoon. I think it's a great idea.

SON (RESPONDER): You're all for it. (SWITCHING TO EXPRESSER): Great! Thanks, Dad.

For more difficult or complex problems for which solutions are not immediately apparent, participants are taught specific skills that help them arrive at a point of agreement. At all times they use Expresser and Empathic Responder skills and switch as necessary. There are six steps to problem solving.

1. Make sure that all sides of the problem are understood fully. Have the views and feelings of each person been expressed completely? Have each person's views been understood by the other people involved? If not, continue to talk with each other until all feelings are explored and understood.
2. Take time out to think of solutions that will satisfy the needs of everyone involved.
3. Make concrete suggestions to each other, and be sure that the Empathic Responder communicates understanding of a suggestion before reacting to it.
4. Be sure to work out all the details such as time, place, frequency, etc. Each person should understand exactly what is being "contracted."
5. Consider ahead of time ways in which exceptions and difficulties might arise and how they will be handled.
6. Set a time when everyone will get together again to evaluate the solution and suggest changes as necessary.

The Leader's Role

In the Relationship Enhancement Program, the leader (therapist, counselor) functions as an instructor to help participants learn Relationship Enhancement skills. The leader is not a person through whom family members communicate with each other, but someone who teaches family members skills they can use to communicate directly with each other. The leader is not the person who makes suggestions and comes up with solutions for family problems; instead, the leader teaches participants problem-solving skills they use to arrive at mutually satisfying compromises and resolutions. The leader teaches participants these skills by *explaining* them, *demonstrating* them, and *supervising* family members in learning and practicing them.

In *explaining* Relationship Enhancement skills, the leader gives participants a rationale for using these skills and a behavioral description of the skills. At the very beginning of the program, the leader explains the skills in a way that helps participants understand how these skills relate to their own problems and needs. As the training progresses, the leader reviews the skills, especially when participants are having difficulties. The leader never asks participants to do anything without giving them an explanation and a reason for what they are being asked to do.

By *demonstrating* Relationship Enhancement skills, the leader shows family members how they can use these skills in their relationships with each other. At the beginning of the program, the leader may demonstrate the skills in several ways.

1. A brief film or videotape may be shown in which Relationship Enhancement skills are demonstrated.
2. An audiotape of a conversation may be played in which Relationship Enhancement skills are used.
3. A co-leader can be used to demonstrate Relationship Enhancement skills in a "live" conversation.
4. The leader may give participants examples of the skills after they have been explained and demonstrate the various skills by conducting a conversation with one of the participants.

Sometimes it is helpful first to give a demonstration of a conversation without the use of Relationship Enhancement skills and then contrast that with a conversation on the same topic using Relationship Enhancement skills. As the training progresses, the leader can continue to demonstrate these skills when participants are having difficulty learning them or when certain changes or refinements are desired.

In *supervising* participants as they practice Relationship Enhancement skills, the leader reinforces appropriate behavior and helps participants improve in their ability to use Relationship Enhancement skills. It is important for the leader to recognize and reinforce every effort that participants make to learn Relationship Enhancement skills. At the beginning of the program, this means that they will be reinforced for rather elementary behavior, such as not asking questions, not giving lectures, and not making accusations or character judgments of each other. Initially, participants are reinforced for any attempt they make to improve their communication skills and to follow the directions of the leader. As they become more sophisticated and proficient in their use of these skills, the leader reinforces them at that level of functioning. When participants respond inappropriately, the leader structures the situation for them again by explaining the appropriate rationale and behavior and sometimes by demonstrating the skill. In order to refine a particular statement or response, the leader models for the participants by suggesting to them words to use or by modeling a particular posture, voice tone, etc.

Throughout the training program, the leader's attitude is one of encouragement and support toward the participants. Instead of criticizing the mistakes they make, the leader explains to them again what to do. The leader constantly looks for examples of appropriate behavior to reinforce in order to demonstrate pleasure to the participants for whatever attempts they make to learn these skills.

The leader always is neutral in any issue or disagreement between family members. The leader's role is not to take sides or make decisions, but to help family members understand each other and arrive at their own decisions. There are several implications in this attitude that are very important for the leader to understand and implement.

First, the program is essentially ahistorical. It is not necessary for the leader to have a complete social history of the family in order to train them in interpersonal skills. Nor is it the leader's goal to consider past events for the sake of the family's insight and understanding. The emphasis of Relationship Enhancement skill training is to make decisions regarding the present and future. If family members find it useful to explore past feelings and events, they should not be discouraged from doing so, but the leader should not require exploration as a matter of course. An interest in the past on the leader's part is viewed as harmful because generally it leads clients to *think* that a diagnostic procedure is taking place that involves fault-finding and blaming. In our view, an interest by the therapist in the past generally impedes progress significantly because it consumes time better spent in skill training, increases client defensiveness, and saps motivation for self-improvement and change.

Second, the leader should avoid all temptations to find fault or blame any participants for family problems. It is not the leader's role to determine whether people have acted appropriately or inappropriately, but only to help participants learn ways of talking with each other more openly and constructively. By doing this, we believe the leader greatly improves the chances that the family will learn to adopt behaviors most appropriate for their own welfare and happiness.

Third, the leader never takes sides with any participants or engages in any discussion about who is right; the leader's opinion is irrelevant and more harmful than useful. If participants view the leader as the "authority" or "the one who knows what is right," they will compete with each other for approval and thus defeat the main purpose of the program — to understand each other and come to their own decisions and solutions. Few therapists or trainers ever take sides directly. We believe that many take sides *indirectly*, however, through the type of questions they ask, the information they provide, the anecdotes they tell, etc. Relationship Enhancement leaders follow procedures that protect them from following the predisposition that most of us have to take sides.

Fourth, the leader shows respect for the feelings and points of view of each participant and is thus a good model for everyone in helping them achieve this same goal.

Program Format and Length

The Relationship Enhancement method can be used with a single pair or with a group comprised of members from one or more families. The Relationship Enhancement Program also lends itself to a variety of formats, ranging from weekly meetings of 1 or 2 hours to intensive marathon sessions. The format selected and the length of the program will depend upon the goals of the client and the program leader, the severity of the problems, and the amount of time available.

The format with which we have the most experience is that of meeting weekly with clients. If participants from several families are meeting in a group, the sessions usually last about 2 hours. If we are working with only one family, the meetings usually last from 1 to 1 1/2 hours. This period of time gives each of the participants an opportunity to practice and receive supervision in the skills they are trying to learn and perfect. It also allows sufficient time for participants to deal intensively with the issues that are introduced and at least to begin working on some solutions to conflicts and problems.

A more intensive format is advisable when clients are seeking help in the midst of a crisis. Under these circumstances, it is helpful to meet with clients for longer periods of time and more frequently than once a week in the early weeks. Another possibility is to have an intensive weekend session of 8 to 10 hours a day. In these extended periods of time, the clients can move very quickly into working on and resolving difficult areas. The weekend format is also appropriate for clients who are seeking enrichment for an already satisfying relationship.

Whether or not the clients are seeking help in the middle of a crisis, we favor an extended session for the first meeting. In a 3- to 4-hour period of time, the leader can go far beyond what is normally done in an intake interview. We believe that this first meeting should include an assessment of client needs, an explanation of how the Relationship Enhancement Program can help meet those needs, a demonstration by the leader (either live, on tape, or on film) of the skills of Relationship Enhancement, and an opportunity for the participants to practice those skills. With this understanding of client needs and demonstration and practice of skills relating to those needs, the chances are increased substantially that the clients will return for further help in learning skills for resolving their conflicts. Through this extended first session, it is possible for the leader to give participants a full understanding of what the program entails and to begin the therapy process by having them practice some skills before they leave. The leader makes a special point of showing each participant how learning these skills can be useful in improving relationships with other family members and with other people in life.

The amount of training recommended depends upon the participants' ability to learn, the severity of problems, and the level of skill proficiency they desire. We never recommend less than 16 to 20 hours of training. We have found that with shorter periods of training, many clients have difficulty in using the skills outside the sessions in their daily lives and in continuing to use the skills regularly once the sessions are over.

Topic Selection

The Relationship Enhancement Program is designed to help family members deal in constructive ways with topics that are important in their relationships with each other. Although Expresser and Empathic Responder skills can be learned and practiced in almost any conversation, it is far more important to help participants realize that these skills can be applied to significant relationship issues. Therefore, participants are asked to practice their skills while talking about family relationships that are of central importance to them.

Another important consideration in determining what topics are appropriate to discuss in any session is whether participants' skill levels are adequate to deal with the topic. During the early sessions of training, emphasis is placed on learning skills rather than on solving difficult problems. Only after participants have obtained proficiency in using Relationship Enhancement skills are they permitted to use these skills in discussions that deal with highly emotional subject matter. Topic selection, therefore, progresses from easier topics in the early sessions to more difficult subjects as the training continues.

At the very beginning of training, participants' attention should be focused entirely on learning skills, not on subject matter. For this reason, the first topics selected for practice are ones that have nothing to do with family relationships. The leader first demonstrates Empathic Responder skills by engaging one of the family members in a conversation about a subject that does not involve the other family members. During this conversation, the leader's statements are limited to Empathic responses, and participants are told to follow this model when they practice their Empathic Responder skills. The leader then chooses appropriate topics and talks to each person present in turn, asking him or her to make Empathic responses to the leader's statements. Each of these conversations should last about 5 minutes. These conversations are kept short so that each person has an opportunity to practice this skill as quickly as possible. As time permits, another round of these conversations can be conducted.

After participants have demonstrated that they can respond reasonably well to the leader's Expresser statements, they are asked to practice with each other. Once again, the topic of conversation is limited to an area that has nothing to do with other family members. The Expresser selects the topic and the Empathic Responder makes appropriate statements to demonstrate understanding and acceptance. While the Expresser and Responder are practicing these skills, the leader provides supervision through coaching, modeling, and reinforcement, while the other participants observe. After one dyad has completed a conversation, another dyad begins to practice the skills. This pattern is continued until everyone has had a chance to be both Expresser and Empathic Responder.

After participants have demonstrated an ability to use their skills in talking with each other about issues outside their family relationships, they are asked to talk with each other about positive areas in their relationships. At this time, the leader reviews the guidelines for Expressers and gives several examples of good and bad Expresser statements. Once again, participants practice in pairs, with the leader providing supervision and other group members observing.

In the next stage of training, participants are asked to discuss with each other problems in their relationships — areas in which they would like to see some changes made. When appropriate, the leader reviews problem-solving skills and asks participants to use these skills in working toward a resolution of their conflict. By the time participants have reached this level of training, they are fairly proficient in their ability to use Relationship Enhancement skills and can deal constructively with the main problem areas in their family relationships. The leader continues to provide active supervision in order to help participants refine their skills and encourages them to become more active in the process of facilitating each other. As their skills increase, the leader gradually becomes less active.

Generalization to Home Life

One of the main goals of the Relationship Enhancement Program is to help participants use these interpersonal skills in their daily lives. In the Relationship Enhancement Program, such generalization to the home is not left to chance. Rather, generalization is regarded as having to be taught in the same manner as any other skill may be taught. There are a number of ways in which this is accomplished. Perhaps the most important of these is that of teaching participants *Facilitator* skills.

In this context, Facilitator skills are a means of instructing and helping others to change their behavioral patterns in ways that are mutually desired and agreed upon. In practice, this means that participants are taught to behave toward each other and other members of their families in the same way that the group leader behaves toward the participants. The concepts of demonstration, modeling, prompting, reinforcing, and setting an appropriate example at all times are explained to the participants. They are encouraged to observe and model their own behavior after the behavior of the group leader. They are then given practice in basic instructional sessions in using these Facilitator skills. They are encouraged to use these same skills to help other members of the family learn to employ successfully the Relationship Enhancement skills in the context of the home. Such skills are employed both when specific time has been set aside by the family members to work on problems and in the course of spontaneous daily interactions. An example of the kind of statement that one participant might make to another when it is already understood that both are intending to use Relationship Enhancement skills would be, "I believe you have just made an expressive statement without responding empathically to my statement. It would make me feel better if I heard you respond empathically now." An example of the kind of statement that might be made in the course of spontaneous interactions would be, "It would be easier for me to react well to what you are saying if you would restate what you just said as opinion rather than as fact" or, "I recognize that you are very angry with me. It would help me to respond constructively if you could make your point again but instead of talking about what you think my motives are, tell me specifically what I did that annoyed you so much."

Another way in which generalization to home life is encouraged in

Relationship Enhancement Program is by giving participants specific assignments for using and practicing their skills at home.

An important consideration in any assignment made is to be sure that participants can meet with success in what we ask them to do. The Relationship Enhancement leader, therefore, discourages participants from practicing the skills at home until it seems certain that they can do a relatively good job without supervision. Generally, this means that there will be several hours of skill practice with the leader before participants are asked to begin practicing on their own.

When it is recognized that family members have adequate performance skills, the leader asks them to agree on a particular time at home when they will sit down with each other and practice. At first, this time is limited to 15 or 20 minutes to avoid an extended conversation in which participants might forget to use their Relationship Enhancement skills and digress into their more familiar patterns of communication. During these first home practice sessions, the topics of conversation are also limited to subjects that do not involve the relationships of family members. In this way, intense emotions are avoided so that participants can be free to concentrate their attention on the skills they are learning. Initially, participants are asked to practice at home on topics such as "Something I like about myself" or "Something I am looking forward to." The leader stresses that if people have difficulty in using their skills at home, they should immediately stop practicing and report the difficulty to their leader during the next meeting. As time goes on, and as participants become more proficient in the use of Relationship Enhancement skills, the leader encourages them to extend practice time at home and to talk about increasingly difficult subjects.

The structured time for home practice is a very important part of helping family members relate more effectively to each other. By knowing that they have set aside a specific time during each week when there will be an opportunity to talk about important issues, a great deal of pressure is removed from daily family interactions. It should be stressed that these weekly meetings are important, both throughout the program and after participants are no longer meeting regularly with the leader. Families should be encouraged to continue to meet on a regular basis in order to be able to deal most constructively with important issues. One way the leader can stress the importance of these regular home practice sessions is by discussing them at the beginning of each meeting with the clients. The leader should inquire how the practice sessions went, what topics were discussed, and how successfully participants were able to use their Relationship

Enhancement skills. The leader also uses this time for trouble-shooting any difficulties that have occurred during the home practice sessions. When participants indicate they have problems, they are asked to reconstruct the particular situation that caused them difficulty so that the leader can help them work through it successfully. In this way, the leader helps participants work out difficulties they experience in using their skills so that they will know how to deal more skillfully when a similar situation occurs again.

In addition to this structured time in which family members are asked to sit down with each other and practice their Relationship Enhancement skills, the leader also encourages participants to use their Relationship Enhancement skills on a daily basis at any time that seems appropriate and helpful. Participants are expected gradually to develop an attitude in which they want to speak constructively to each other and to understand each other's point of view at all times. Participants are encouraged to keep in mind the guidelines for Expresser skills when they make any statement to another family member. They should also be encouraged to listen in an empathic way when someone else is saying something important to them.

Relationship Enhancement skills can be used occasionally around the dinner table, when people are working, making decisions, or playing together. But clients are taught that the skills are always appropriate and helpful when they are making difficult decisions, when there are disagreements or different points of view, when there is confusion, and at any time when there is a strain in interpersonal relationships. Any time there is unhappiness, conflict, or frustration in a relationship, it means that the skills should have been used in the past and should be used again as soon as possible.

The leader can help family members generalize their Relationship Enhancement skills to daily situations by encouraging them to use these skills regularly. Whenever feasible in terms of the family's abilities, family members are asked to keep a log or journal of times when they use Relationship Enhancement skills in their relationships with each other and of times when it would have been helpful to use these skills but they did not. In each meeting with a family, the leader should ask for a report about these logs or, if there are no logs, a verbal report covering the same ground. The leader should praise them and give them reinforcement when they have used their skills, help them reenact some situations in which the skills were not used but now could be, and in general help them to see opportunities for using these skills that may not have been obvious to the families.

The leader can also encourage family members to help each other in their use of Relationship Enhancement skills in their daily lives. Participants should be reminded that when they attempt to be constructive in their conversations, others will also be encouraged to be constructive.

In one other area family members are asked to do some work at home to increase their benefit from participation in this program. At the beginning of the program, all participants are asked to make a list of the topics they want to discuss during the program. This list should include some positive things that they enjoy in their relationships with other family members, as well as the most important areas they would like to change. The leader should emphasize that this list can be revised regularly. Participants may add items at any time and may also remove items at any time. In preparation for each meeting, participants are asked to review their lists and to select a topic that they will initiate as Expresser. By making regular use of this list, the leader increases the chances that the time spent with participants will be used to discuss significant issues. This list prevents participants from coming to a meeting and not knowing what to talk about and also prevents them from talking about things that are important to them at the moment merely because they occurred recently and currently elicit strong feelings but have little enduring significance. Instead, it encourages clients to work on deep problems and conflicts — ones that are central to establishing a trusting and reciprocally satisfying relationship that can have effects far into the future. Assurance is always given that participants will not be required to talk about any subject that they do not want to talk about. Each participant is able to indicate on his/her list the particular topics s/he feels ready to discuss and those s/he does not feel ready to discuss.

Working Only with Parents

In this chapter, we have described a Relationship Enhancement Program in which parents and adolescents participate together. We believe that this format is the most effective way of improving relationships within families. However, we recognize that there are times when it is not possible to involve adolescents, either because they refuse to participate or because they are institutionalized or unavailable for some other reason. In such instances, parents can be taught Relationship Enhancement skills that they can use in their relationships with their adolescents.

Just as it is possible to work with one parent and one adolescent or a small group of parents and adolescents, so it is possible in this format to work with one parent, two parents from one family, or a small group of parents from several families. Once again, a variety of formats can be used, ranging from an intensive, concentrated period, such as a weekend, to meetings held once a week.

The leader's role in these sessions, as in the parent-adolescent sessions, is to provide explanation, demonstration, and supervision to help participants learn Relationship Enhancement skills. The selection of topics for practice in these sessions is also progressive, starting with easy topics and moving to more difficult ones as participants' skill proficiency increases. In the area of homework, also, participants are encouraged to use the skills they have been practicing whenever possible and appropriate.

The main adaptations required when working only with parents are described in more detail elsewhere (Guerney, 1977). A major aspect of this adaptation is the extensive use of role-playing. When instructing only one parent, as in a private practice situation, the leader sometimes plays the role of the parent and sometimes the adolescent. In the former instance, the leader demonstrates how a parent would use Relationship Enhancement skills; the latter role is used to provide the parent with practice. (By discussing the adolescent with the parent and by observing the parent play the role of the adolescent, the leader should be able to play the role of the adolescent in a realistic way.) In a situation in which several parents are learning Relationship Enhancement skills together, different group members can play the roles of either adolescents or parents.

The leader must be sure to emphasize to parents that they cannot expect immediate changes in their adolescent just because they are learning and using Relationship Enhancement skills. Parents should be encouraged to use these skills in their relationships with their adolescents but must recognize that, because the adolescents have not been trained, they will not respond in the same way. Parents must therefore exercise far more patience and tolerance to achieve the kind of positive results that are achieved when the adolescent also participates. The role of the Facilitator can increasingly enhance the adolescent's skills, however, even when the adolescent does not participate. The use of this Facilitator skill is role-played extensively with the leader.

General Guidelines for Leaders

There are several principles or attitudes that the educator working with the parents of disturbed adolescents will almost always find appropriate and useful when following an educational approach to remediation (Guerney, Guerney, & Stover, 1972). The therapeutic educator should do whatever possible to be perceived by parents as an individual who understands the difficulties, problems, needs, and emotions of the parent; welcomes and respects the opinions and views of the parent even while attempting to encourage change and experimentation based on a different point of view; does not try to identify past deficiencies, thereby avoiding the possibility that the parent will feel blamed; and regards the parent as a vital helper in trying to improve the well-being of the adolescent. Thus, the parent educator should observe the following guidelines.

AVOID AN HISTORICAL DIAGNOSTIC ORIENTATION: We suggest that parent educators ignore any predisposition they or the parents might have to explore what went *wrong* in the past. Instead, they should concentrate on what can be made to go *right* in the future. In our view, this omits nothing of significance, saves time, reduces defensiveness, and enhances motivation.

SEEK TO BRING ABOUT FAVORABLE CIRCUMSTANCES IN THE FUTURE: We believe it is important in this regard for the educator to realize that the parent does not have to be free of conflicted needs, distorted self-images, or other pathologies in order to bring about circumstances favorable to healthy growth within the family. Such growth requires only that the parent not express any existing pathologies in such a way as to deny the child understanding and fulfillment of his basic psychological needs and learning experiences.

ADOPT A TASK ORIENTATION TO THE EXPIRATION OF PROBLEMS AND DIFFICULTIES: Do not be distracted by abstract issues. Use the time available to teach parents skills that will help them to understand themselves and their children better. Deal with concrete instances instead of abstract questions and issues.

ATTEMPT TO TRAIN FOR GENERALIZATION: Do whatever possible to bring the home situation into the training context and the skills being taught into the home situation. Use logs, homework, discussion, replays of home events, and identification of occasions for skill use at home to produce generalization. Until a pattern has been developed in which clients regularly use these skills at home successfully to resolve problems and enrich relationships, we believe that the skills will tend to atrophy. However, as these skills are used and they lead to positive results, they will tend to be used more frequently in the future.

ADOPT A FOLLOW-THROUGH APPROACH: Although an educational program is often time limited, we believe it is useful for the leader to engage in follow-up procedures. This can be useful to provide feedback as to when, where, and how educational efforts are and are not working. In addition, the leader can use follow-through in the fashion of a "booster" program by telephoning the family or by meeting with them periodically to review their use of skills and make further suggestions (Vogelsong, 1975).

The rewards of being a parent educator are indirect rather than direct. Such leaders must adopt the attitude that has been identified with successful parenting: The desire to be nurturant and to be directly helpful must be tempered by the goal of producing eventual self-sufficiency, independence, competence, and confidence on the part of the client.

REFERENCES

Andronico, M. P., Fidler, J., Guerney, B., Jr., & Guerney, L. The combination of didactic and dynamic elements in filial therapy. *International Journal of Group Psychotherapy*, 1967, *17*, 10-17.

Authier, J., Gustafson, K., Guerney, B., Jr., & Kasdorf, J. A. The psychological practitioner as a teacher: A theoretical-historical practical review. *The Counseling Psychologist*, 1975, *5*(2), 31-50.

Beavers, W. R., Blumberg, S., Timken, K. R., & Weiner, M. F. Communication patterns in the families of schizophrenics. *Journal of Nervous and Mental Disease*, 1962, *135*, 419-424.

Benningfield, A. B. Multiple family therapy systems. *Journal of Marriage and Family Counseling*, 1978, *4*(2), 25-34.

Coufal, J. C. *Preventive-therapeutic programs for mothers and adolescent daughters: Skill training versus discussion methods.* Doctoral dissertation, The Pennsylvania State University, University Park, Pennsylvania, 1975.

Dubbé, M. C. What parents are not told may hurt: A study of communication between teen-agers and parents. *Family Life Coordinator*, 1965, *14*, 51-118.

Earle, J. R. Parent-child communication, sentiment and authority. *Sociological Inquiry*, 1967, *37*, 275-282.

Erikson, E. *Identity: Youth and crisis.* New York: Norton, 1968.

Ferreira, A. J. Semantics and the context of schizophrenic language. *Archives of General Psychiatry*, 1960, *3*, 128-138.

Fidler, J., Guerney, B., Jr., Andronico, M., & Guerney, L. Filial therapy as a logical extension of current trends in psychotherapy. In B. Guerney, Jr. (Ed.), *Psychotherapeutic agents: New roles for non-professionals, parents, and teachers.* New York: HR&W, 1969.

Franklin, P. Family therapy of psychotics. *American Journal of Psychoanalysis*, 1969, *25*, 50-57.

Ginsberg, B. Parent-adolescent relationship development program. In B.

Guerney, *Relationship Enhancement: Skill-training programs for therapy, problem prevention, and enrichment.* San Francisco: Jossey-Bass, 1977.

Glaser, K. Suicidal children — management. *American Journal of Psychotherapy,* 1971, *25,* 27-36.

Guerney, B., Jr. Filial therapy: Description and rationale. *Journal of Consulting Psychology,* 1964, *28*(4), 303-310.

Guerney, B., Jr. *Relationship Enhancement: Skill training programs for therapy, problem prevention and enrichment.* San Francisco: Jossey-Bass, 1977.

Guerney, B., Jr., Guerney, L., & Andronico, M. P. Filial therapy. *Yale Scientific Magazine,* 1966, *40,* 6-14.

Guerney, B., Jr., Guerney, L., & Stollak, G. E. The potential advantages of changing from a medical to an educational model in practicing psychology. *Interpersonal Development,* 1971/72, *2*(4), 238-245.

Guerney, B., Jr., Guerney, L., & Stover, L. Facilitative therapist attitudes in training parents as psychotherapeutic agents. *The Family Coordinator,* 1972, *21,* 275-278.

Guerney, B., Jr., Stollak, G. E., & Guerney, L. A format for a new mode of psychological practice: Or, how to escape a zombie. *The Counseling Psychologist,* 1970, *2*(2), 97-104.

Guerney, B., Jr., Stollak, G. E., & Guerney, L. The practicing psychologist as educator — An alternative to the medical practitioner model. *Professional Psychology,* 1971, *2*(3), 276-282.

Guerney, L. Filial therapy program. In D. H. L. Olson (Ed.), *Treating relationships.* Lake Mills, Iowa: Graphic Pub, 1976.

Khan, A. U. A therapeutic technique based on the interpersonal theory and family dynamics. *Psychotherapy and Psychosomatics,* 1969, *17,* 226-240.

McArthur, A. Developmental tasks and the parent-adolescent conflict. *Marriage and Family Living,* 1962, *24,* 189-191.

Morrison, G. C., & Collier, J. G. Family treatment approaches to suicidal children and adolescents. *Journal of the American Academy of Child Psychiatry,* 1969, *8,* 140-153.

Mosher, L. R. Schizophrenogenic communication and family therapy. *Family Process,* 1969, *8,* 43-63.

Patterson, G. R. Parents and teachers as change agents: A social learning approach. In D. H. L. Olson (Ed.), *Treating relationships.* Lake Mills, Iowa: Graphic Pub, 1976.

Patterson, G. R., McNeal, S., Hawkins, N., & Phelps, R. Reprogramming the social environment. *Journal of Child Psychology and Psychiatry,* 1967, *8,* 181-195.

Patterson, G. R., Reid, J. B., Jones, R. R., & Conger, R. E. *A social learning approach to family intervention* (Vol. 1), *The socially aggressive child.* Eugene, Oregon: Castillia Pub, 1975.

Satir, V. *Conjoint family therapy.* Palo Alto, California: Sci & Behavior, 1967.

Satir, V. *Peoplemaking*. Palo Alto, California: Sci & Behavior, 1972.

Stabenu, J. R., Tupen, J., Werner, M., & Pollin, W. A. A comparative study of families of schizophrenics, delinquents and normals. *Psychiatry*, 1965, *28*, 45-49.

Stover, L., & Guerney, B. G., Jr. The efficacy of training procedures for mothers in filial therapy. *Psychotherapy: Theory, Research and Practice*, 1967, *4*(3), 110-115.

Vogelsong, E. L. *Preventive-therapeutic programs for mothers and daughters: A follow-up of relationship enhancement versus discussion and booster versus no-booster methods*. Doctoral dissertation, The Pennsylvania State University, University Park, Pennsylvania, 1975.

Walters, J., & Stinnett, N. Parent-child relationships: A decade review of research. *Journal of Marriage and the Family*, 1971, *33*, 70-111.

Watzlawick, P., Beavin, J. H., & Jackson, D. D. *Pragmatics of human communication: A study of interactional patterns, pathologies and paradoxes*. New York: Norton, 1967.

Weblin, J. E. Communication and schizophrenic behavior. *Family Process*, 1962, *1*, 5-14.

Wellisch, D. K., Vincent, J., & Ro-Trock, G. K. Family therapy versus individual therapy: A study of adolescents and their parents. In D. H. L. Olson (Ed.), *Treating relationships*. Lake Mills, Iowa: Graphic Pub, 1976.

Wise, L. J. Alienation of present-day adolescents. *Journal of the American Academy of Child Psychiatry*, 1970, *9*, 264-277.

Chapter 13

WORKING WITH BLACK PARENTS

JAMES P. COMER AND CAROL M. SCHRAFT

INTRODUCTION

Overview

THIS chapter will present issues and strategies for mental health professionals working with low-income black families. We will begin with an overview of black parents in America today, focusing on the special problems of poor families. We will next discuss existing programs about both education for improving parenting and participation in institutional decision making.

In the second section, we will describe our work in a school intervention program in a low-income black community. Integrating parents into all aspects of school life is a major component of the program. Some of the strategies used are parent education and counseling, parent participation in school policy and decision making, and parent involvement in the day-to-day life of the school as aides, tutors, and classroom assistants. The final section will focus on the implications of these approaches for program planning and practice.

Black Parents in America Today

As a result of slavery and exclusion from the mainstream job market, a disproportionate number of blacks are poor. The country's "War on Poverty" did not begin until 1965. While we invested almost 200 years in legal forms of discrimination, we dismantled this modest effort that could have overcome some of the effects of slavery for many in less than a decade. The principle of affirmative action, a small conservative attempt to correct racism on the job market and in higher education, was only introduced in 1972 and has been under constant bombardment ever since. The point here is that yesterday's racism is today's poverty, and both complicate the job of child rearing for black parents.

Race-related problems exist, not only for blacks who have failed to gain entry into mainstream America, but for black doctors, lawyers, military personnel, business executives, university professors, members of Congress, Olympic gold medal winners, and recipients of the Nobel Peace Prize as well. It is very hard for black parents to prepare and motivate children for long-range goals and tasks when their own chances have been short-circuited by racism and poverty or when success has been achieved at significant personal or psychic cost.

Racism and its effects on black families are insidious. On the evening news, one is more likely to hear about a black mother defrauding the state welfare system for a few hundred dollars than about medical professionals defrauding Medicaid for millions; more likely "reverse discrimination" than affirmative action; more likely "genetic inferiority" than the debilitating effects of poverty; more likely black school dropouts than black graduate students; more likely blacks looting in the ghetto than the contributions of black leaders. Though it is claimed that these are the stories that "sell," it is interesting to note that "Roots," the saga of a courageous American black family through six generations of slavery, had the largest viewing audience of any program ever shown on television.

As one almost trivial example of the insidious ways that racism pervades our daily lives, a school newsletter in a Connecticut town with a reasonable-sized middle-income black population announced that schools would be closed on Martin Luther King's birthday *in compliance with* state law. It went on to say that schools would also be closed on two subsequent dates *in honor of* Abraham Lincoln and George Washington. So routine are such attacks on the black psyche that even the most talented, socially secure, and economically stable black parents cannot fully protect their children from racism in our society.

The impact of racism, of course, is greatest for undereducated and poor families. These families lack access to the most basic support systems all parents need to raise healthy children. These resources are (1) a reasonable sense of economic security and the ability to provide one's family with adequate food, clothing, shelter, medical care, and other basic needs; (2) an understanding of child development and the kinds of parent attitudes and behaviors that will facilitate it; and (3) a knowledge of mainstream institutions such as schools and the political system and how to influence these institutions to one's advantage.

The behavior or survival mechanisms displayed by many parents with inadequate resources is commonly misunderstood. Parents raising their children in overcrowded decaying ghettos are themselves often blamed for the circumstances forced upon them by the society. Popular phrases such as "the culture of poverty" or "the welfare mentality" imply that given access to a full range of life-styles and cultural expression, this portion of the population consciously chose to live and raise their children under inadequate circumstances.

It is important to differentiate between black culture and low-level survival mechanisms forced on some black people. Culture refers to the adaptive beliefs, attitudes, values, and ways that a people develops in the course of coping with life. A culture offers group members intellectual, social, and emotional sustenance, enabling the culture to thrive from one generation to another. When members of a cultural group are thrust into an alien environment with no control over policies and practices for several generations, many of its adaptive ways are destroyed, modified, or diminished in effect. The affected persons turn to a variety of survival mechanisms.

In an effort to cope first with almost 250 years of slavery, then with approximately 100 years of legal segregation and abuse, and finally with *de facto* segregation and abuse, blacks developed multiple coping mechanisms. The black church, colleges, fraternal organizations, music, dance, drama and other art forms, and extended family bonds are examples of prosocial adaptations or high-level survival mechanisms. These are the institutions, customs, and behaviors — plus relationship, expression, or style remnants from Africa — from which a positive Afro-American culture has been forged. Through institutions of this culture, blacks find comfort away from the abuses of the larger society and develop the social skills and power needed to participate in it more successfully.

These institutions cannot, by themselves, compensate for the major inequities of the American social, political, and economic system. They cannot provide adequate resources for the large numbers of blacks who are shut out of the mainstream. Blacks who have not had desirable developmental experiences and who do not see the possibility of living-wage jobs, education, decent housing, or recreation are often forced to turn to low-level survival mechanisms. Acting dumb, being passive, playing Uncle Tom, being supercool or supertough, and "ripping off" mainstream institutions are examples of ways that some blacks seek to survive in a society where reasonable access to the mainstream has been denied.

Such behavior often leads to difficult family and child-rearing conditions. Children from such circumstances are more likely to participate in crime, drug, and alcohol subcultures. These are low-level survival mechanisms or antisocial, maladaptive behaviors that do not promote long-term group advancement. However, they do prevent immediate psychic stress and depression for the individuals employing them.

These very oppressed, alienated, and troubled families are those most frequently referred to mental health and social welfare professionals. The charge is to change or modify their difficult behavior. The attitudes, values, and ways are too often erroneously referred to as black culture. As outlined above, the behavior, attitudes, and circumstances of these families are the result of a complex interaction among intrapsychic, economic, social, political, historical, and educational conditions imposed on them. They are not conditions these families would choose. All of these factors need to be considered when planning and implementing programs for low-income black parents.

PROGRAMS FOR BLACK PARENTS

Black parents have been the subjects of numerous research studies, social welfare services, and mental health and educational programs. While each project may improve the lives of a few families, none has been effective in significantly altering the decaying pattern of life in low-income black communities. Intervention programs tend to function in isolation. The result is a fragmented network of uneven, inadequately funded, sometimes overlapping programs and projects rather than a comprehensive, integrated system that will lead to the kind of community development that will improve the circumstances of poor black families.

In this section, we will examine three critical components of a comprehensive approach to serving low-income black parents. The first, *education for improved parenting*, focuses on programs about child development and the kinds of parent behavior that will enhance children's growth. This component addresses parent change and is an approach frequently used by mental health professionals. The second approach, *participation in institutional decision making*, concentrates on enabling parents to develop the skills needed to change social systems affecting their lives. This component focuses on social, educational, and political change. It is an approach that was popular during the civil rights movement of the 1960s. The third component is economic support. In the section *economics and black parents*, the ways in which poverty impacts both parent change and institutional change approaches will be discussed. Together, these three components form the foundation of a comprehensive mental health service delivery for black parents.

Education for Improved Parenting

There is a mass of available advice on how to be a better parent. While much of the data are conflicting, there is agreement on two basic points. First, each child needs consistent care by a person who functions as his or her "psychological" or permanent parent (Bowlby, 1951; Goldstein, Freud, & Solnit, 1973). Second, there is a particular kind of parenting behavior that more often leads to success in school. Ira Gordon (1977) reviewed the major research across cultures on parenting behaviors related to school success. He wrote:

> (The data) all show that the variables are not magical. They have to do with, among others, whether: 1) parents see themselves as teachers of their children; 2) they talk with them, not at them; 3) they take them to the libraries or the museums or the parks; 4) they sit around the dinner table and share and plan; 5) they listen; 6) they display a child's work on the refrigerator or the wall; 7) they themselves read and talk about what they read. (p. 75)

This information is important for all parents. Mainstream parents are likely to learn these skills through modeling, reading child care books and periodicals, attending lectures and courses, and consulting with specialists such as pediatricians and teachers. Low-income black parents often lack access to these avenues of information. The task for the mental health professional or educator is to enable the low-income parents to gain the same skills readily available to mainstream parents. Opportunities to learn must be presented in ways so that these parents can understand the concepts and incorporate them into day-to-day behavior with their children.

The selection of a particular strategy should be based on both the extent of the parent's isolation from the mainstream and the particular resources and skills available to the worker. Three basic methods have been utilized to transmit child care information to black parents: home-based programs, discussion groups, and parent education courses.

Several home-based programs have been described by Lane (1975). This approach recognizes the parent's isolation from the mainstream and brings the mainstream directly to the home in the form of a parent educator or counselor. This person visits mothers and their preschoolers on a regular basis to teach specific skills about child rearing. The programs usually provide parents with toys, books, or kits with which to work with their children.

Another method is a parent discussion group, rap session, or an informal workshop series. These groups are most useful when they are integrated into natural settings such as schools, well-baby clinics, or churches. Many standard parenting group programs such as Parent Effectiveness Training (Gordon, 1970) or Family Life Education (Family Service Association of America, 1976) are available for this purpose.

A third approach is to offer a child development course for high school equivalency or college credit. This is a helpful strategy for relatively well organized parents who, in addition, are sometimes able to use such a course as a stepping-stone toward a college or career program.

There are two important problems in the approaches suggested here. First, these programs often operate on the assumption that problems faced by black children are the result of their parent's inadequacies. They imply that the parent, rather than the school, welfare system, or housing authority, needs to be changed. Second, parenting programs are frequently bent on advocating a particular method or way of relating to the child. They fail to fully appreciate the differences of opinion in the child development field. In addition, they ignore the sense of alienation many black parents feel.

The interactions between parents and their children take place in a given social and economic context. By focusing on the parent's failings, social and educational institutions can be diverted from examining their own shortcomings. This is a very common practice in schools, for example, where mental health professionals are frequently called upon to "shape up" deviant families to meet the standards of teachers and administrators. The question is rarely one of how the school can change its programs, rules, and customs to better meet the needs of troubled families.

The second problem, that of the differences of opinion within the child care and parent education field itself, represents special conflicts for black parents. Most professionals would agree that there is not one "best" or "right" way to care for a child. Rather, successful child rearing is more likely when most of the people relating to the child hold similar views toward desirable behavior, the child's place in society, and expectations for him/her as an adult.

Mainstream parents have some assurance that their values and ways will be reinforced by other people caring for their children such as teachers, health workers, and recreation leaders. These parents may be friends, colleagues, or neighbors of the people who work in schools, community centers, and the medical profession. A disproportionate number of low-income parents are at a great social and economic distance from the people who operate mainstream institutions.

For example, a child may come home from school and tell his mother that the teacher punished him. If the mother and the teacher know and respect one another and view each other as relative equals, it is likely that the mother may say to the child, "Your teacher punished you because she wants you to behave and learn." If the child continues to be upset, the mother who feels comfortable dealing with the school people may call the teacher, stop by the class, or send a note. The child learns that there is a certain consistency of expectation and support between home and school.

If, on the other hand, the mother has been made to feel uncomfortable at the school and inadequate by the school's standards, as is more often the case with low-income black parents, she may instead say, "What do you expect, *those* people at the school don't like *us* (poor people, black people) anyway." If, under these circumstances, the mother comes to the school at all, it is likely to be in an angry defensive manner that generates a great deal of noise and confusion but does little to help the child.

Programs must take into account that low-income black parents are often functioning and raising their children in one world and sending them to school and other child-caring institutions in a world they feel rejected and alienated from. Because low-income black parents are often in a social and economic situation different from the mainstream, any given set of "advice" on how to be a good parent must be viewed from a perspective that appreciates *both* realities and the long social distance between them. Behaviors that are functional in the larger society may be dysfunctional in their situation. For example, school success is dependent on the ability to be thoughtful, reflective, and goal oriented. Survival on the street, on the other hand, is often dependent on being quick, impulsive, and action oriented in order to avoid being a repeated victim. Child-rearing education for low-income parents must respect that reality while enabling parents and children to have greater flexibility of movement and participation in the society. It is also important for low-income parents to learn more effective strategies and methods for changing handicapping conditions.

Participation in Institutional Decision Making

Because many black parents have had limited access to the mainstream, they may lack the social and political skills needed to make "the system" work to their own advantage. Research studies have repeatedly shown that an ability to control one's own fate is critical to successful parenting. Studies show that low-income black parents feel far more impotent in controlling their environment than mainstream parents (HARYOU-ACT, 1964; Coleman, 1966).

Skills required to successfully negotiate the mainstream include a knowledge of bureaucratic organizations and how they operate, strategies of political influence, voting, budgeting, letter writing, decision making, and parliamentary procedure. Opportunities for poor blacks to learn these skills are limited. While many programs serving minorities have specific provisions for parent participation in some aspect of governance or policymaking, systematic education about developing strategies of influence and power is rarely provided.

Much of what has passed for "parent participation" has, in fact, been "parent manipulation." Arnstein (1971) and others have differentiated levels of parent participation in mainstream institutions. The range includes placing parents on powerless rubber stamp "advisory" committees; diverting parents from criticizing the institution by organizing institution-enhancing activities such as neighborhood clean-ups; and informing and consulting with parents, allowing a token voice but no real authority in major programmatic decisions.

As Arnstein notes, "Since those who have power normally want to hang onto it, historically it has had to be wrested by the powerless rather than proffered by the powerful" (p. 84). One way to appear to share power without doing so is to permit parent participation without helping parent leaders acquire organization and management skills.

While parent participation was intended in all of the Office of Economic Opportunity programs, the interpretations and actual outcomes have varied from site to site. Since 1971, parent participation in public education has been mandated through Parent Advisory Councils as part of Title I of the Elementary and Secondary Education Act (E.S.E.A.). In both programs, participation has been limited to low-level participation. Many grassroots groups simply do not have adequate knowledge of the political systems needed to survive. More powerful levels of participation — partnership, delegated power, and community control — require greater parent initiative, organization, and management skills.

Moreover, there is an inherent contradiction in Title I programs. On the one hand, the program operates to compensate for the inadequacies of the home. On the other, it mandates participation by the very parents designated as inadequate in order to carry out program policies. Davies (1978) reports that there are 60,000 Title I

Parent Advisory Councils with about 900,000 members. Although this represents the largest group of organized parents in the country, it has little power and little impact. The Stanford Research Institute report on parent involvement in compensatory education (Stearns & Peterson, 1973) pointed to the lack of substantive, specific, and necessary roles for these groups. One of a number of reasons that this is so is that low-income parents lack the skills to significantly impact the system.

A particular conflict for professionals working with Title I and similar parent participation groups is that the professional is a part and an advocate of the very program s/he is asking parents to reform. For this reason, most function to "sell" the parents on whatever it was the institution wanted to do in the first place. For parents to help bring about reform or change, a significant number of the professionals involved must be committed to it.

Parents who are already alienated from the mainstream require a process of "political socialization." Frustrated and intimidated by the larger social system, it is often hard for such parents to see how attending program policy meetings or even voting in public elections will readily change their lives. Mainstream institutions often exploit the hopelessness of low-income blacks rather than providing them with participation skills and an opportunity to be involved in a program committed to change or improved institutional operation. Saliterman (1971), Davies (1978), and others have described ways that mainstream institutions keep parents at low levels of participation. Such tactics include delaying and changing meetings, referring final decisions to other groups, fact-finding, consulting with other parents, tabling items until a later date, and giving parents incomplete information or information in complicated legal jargon. When parents cannot keep pace with such machinations and stop coming to meetings, the school, community center, or tenants' organization can say, "We tried to involve parents, but they weren't interested."

Economics and Black Parents

Extreme poverty is often a bar to good parenting even when intentions are good. A mother may, for example, take part in a program designed to improve parent-child relations. She learns that certain specific ways of relating to a child promote better development. Let us say that she comes to understand that talking *with* a child enables him/her to develop internal controls, whereas talking *at* a child makes him/her dependent on an external authority. If the parent finds herself living in poverty, the probability of employing this concept consistently is not great. If this mother comes home from a long day of work where she herself was ordered about in a degrading way, while not earning enough to pay essential bills, it is unlikely that she will have the energy and attitude to say, "Let's all sit down together and plan a picnic for Saturday," not to mention having the time and energy to actually go on a picnic. Because of the stress caused by poverty and the related hard realities of her own life, she may more often say, "Shut up before I beat your behind. Can't you see I'm trying to cook supper?"

Marcus Foster (1971) commented on the effects of poverty on parents as follows:

> Poor people aren't dumb, but they are often tired, their energies drained in the struggle to provide the basic things for their children and their household. They have little time left to sit around in a school and talk about readiness activities. When the housing is poor and people are uncomfortable, when the winter is cold and there is a problem with rats, it's not easy to grapple with strategies for changing the educational system or the social structure. (p. 86)

During New York's Ocean Hill-Brownsville project, a brief experiment in community control in a poor black school district, parents were surveyed about their participation in school programs (Gottfried, 1970). While parents wanted education for their children, had visited their children's school, supported the experimental district, and wanted to participate more actively themselves, their abilities to promote the project were greatly diminished by the debilitating conditions of slum life. "When parents were asked which they thought were the three biggest problems facing people like themselves in Ocean Hill-Brownsville, they ranked housing and slums first; crime, robberies, and vandalism second; and addiction and dope to be the third most crucial problems." (p. 9). Issues such as education and schools were thus ranked only fourth and fifth.

Although low-income black parents have been the recipients of numerous social welfare and educational programs, few have provided them with more money. Educational opportunities and living-wage employment have been available for only a very few.

The opportunities available for poor parents are rarely a legitimate route out of poverty except for the few who found work in the now greatly reduced poverty programs. Poor black parents often face a no-win choice. They can suffer the degradation of being "on welfare" and regarded by the larger society as lazy, immoral, and incompetent or they can seek marginal employment.

Parents working in marginal jobs are often faced with yet another complicated problem of making arrangements for substitute child care. As Fraiberg (1977) notes, the child care facilities available to the poor are all too often "child storage houses, staffed by caregivers who are mostly indifferent and often outrageously neglectful." Thoughtful and comprehensive day care programs such as "Children's House" described by Provence, Naylor, and Patterson in *The Challenge of Daycare* (1977) are unusual exceptions.

The long-range solutions to the complicated problems of unemployment and poverty, compounded by racism, will require a significant reformulation of national policy and reallocation of resources. However, it is possible for small groups of professionals working in individual schools, community centers, day care centers, mental health clinics, and public assistance offices to organize effective parent programs addressing the problems presented here.

YALE CHILD STUDY CENTER SCHOOLS PROGRAM

Yale Child Study Center has, since 1968, collaborated in a school development program in a principally black section of New Haven. The program started in two elementary schools and continued for 5 years, during which time it was supported by the Ford Foundation and Title I funds. In 1973, Child Study Center withdrew from one school because of internal conflicts. Since 1975, the Center for Minority Group Studies of the National Institute of Mental Health has supported a comprehensive parents' program of development of a social skills curriculum in the Martin Luther King School, a 350-student K through 4 institution. Starting in 1977, a field test of the intervention process has been conducted in a third school.

Ours is a preventative mental health approach that focuses on the complex network of relationships among *all* the players in the school — administrators, teachers, support staff, children, and parents. We were particularly concerned with developing a mutuality of purpose among school people, parents, and university staff. Recognizing that there is no "quick fix" to the complicated problems of inner city schools, the choice was to develop long-term strategies for institutional change by working closely with one or two schools, eventually moving the process throughout the New Haven school system and to other systems.

In our 10 years at King, there has been a gradual neighborhood change from a population with a small core of middle-income black families to a predominantly low-income group with a disproportionately high number of transient and very troubled families. In 1969, King School ranked 32nd of the 33 New Haven elementary schools on the Metropolitan Achievement Test in reading and math. There was a high student and teacher absentee rate and much conflict between children, between children and staff, and between parents and the school.

In 1976 and 1977, with a population of many more poor and marginal families, King students who had been in the program 2 years or more, using the median, scored at grade level on the Metropolitan Achievement Test in reading and math. Including all students, they had the highest scores of any Title I school in the city. The school had the 3rd best citywide attendance in 1976 and the 2nd best in 1977, a significant indicator of positive school climate. While there are, of course, many factors that account for the change, the involvement of parents and subsequent improvement of the relationship between the school and its community has perhaps been the most significant.

Like many 1960s school intervention programs involving collaboration between mainstream institutions and poor black communities, this one had a disastrous 1st year. Conflicts about open education, race, and decision-making authority were but a few of the issues around which problems developed. Conflict erupted on all possible fronts, perhaps most vocally from parents who resented their children being used as "guinea pigs" for a project from "downtown." Downtown was the New Haven Public Schools, Yale, and others from "the system." Parents were angry with the system, "the establishment," whose members enjoyed prestige, power, and privilege without improving the quality of education, opportunities, and conditions of life for people in poor and minority neighborhoods.

The initial engagement with the parents was heated, potentially all-consuming, and destructive to the program, but also the energy source that eventually made the program work. The very parents most involved in the initial fighting about whether or not Yale should be involved in their school became the first parents to participate in child development and parenting programs and to work on decision-making committees and special projects they helped to develop.

The struggle between parents and professionals, whether expressed actively or by the passive hostility of noninvolvement, is not a *necessary* ingredient for successful parent participation in a school program, but it is *common*. A longer, closer period of preprogram collaboration and planning, better organization, and other situational factors might have prevented this struggle. The point here, however, is that the program leaders were willing to give and take with the parents, to understand their initially difficult and hostile ways of interacting as their disappointment in and frustration with mainstream institutions, rather than as a personal attack or as a symptom of mental illness.

Program leaders engaged in arduous discussions, which at times appeared to be going nowhere. They were also willing to negotiate with the parents and to make the necessary organizational and staffing changes necessary to stabilize the school. As a result, by the end of the 2nd year, the school had moved from an unstable situation overburdened by "innovation" to an orderly albeit more traditional educational setting. Although in actuality, only a very few parents were intimately involved in this *process*, the *results* were visible to the entire community. This small group of about six parents was involved in the school in two basic ways: as members of the school governing board and in workshops with staff.

As with most intervention programs of that era, parents were included on the steering committee, the project governing board. While parents on this committee participated in program policy at various levels, one of their most meaningful and helpful contributions was participation in personnel selection. Principals, teachers, and prospective staff members continuously commented on the fairness and wisdom of parents in these determinations. As parents became engaged in this task and saw that their point of view would be given real consideration, the anger was gradually converted into productive energy.

During the summers, parents and staff participated in workshops and school planning *together*. It was through these *joint* activities where parents, school staff, and Child Study Center personnel were all equal participants that the parties came to know each other as people, rather than as parents vs. professionals, or blacks vs. whites, or Yale vs. school system. By engaging in these tasks together, common values and goals were recognized.

These events provided the foundation for a comprehensive parents' program. However, it was not until the school had reached a level of reasonable stability, basic organization, reasonable child behavior, and beginning curriculum development strategies that professional energy could be directed toward a comprehensive parents' program.

At the beginning of the 4th year, the principal, a community relations worker from the school staff, and the social worker from the Child Study Center worked with the core group of six parents from the steering committee and the summer workshops to develop programs for all the parents. Thus, the professional energy was largely directed toward the more stable, well-integrated, and most interested parents.

This is different from the clinical and/or deficit approach, which concentrates on the school's most difficult families. We recognized that the school needed *both* clinical and systems intervention. In previous years, a large portion of Child Study Center social work time was spent in intensive casework with a handful of troubled disorganized families. This was time-consuming work with little pay-off. Our goal was to rearrange the balance between the two so that as the parent involvement program developed, it would, in and of itself, serve as a support system for all parents.

This required a different use of clinical skills. First, it meant providing the technical and organizational support for the parent-staff organization. The parents wanted to form an independent group, which they called the Parent-Teacher Power Team. The group's name, the decision not to be part of the nationally affiliated PTA, and the experience by the organizing parents on the project steering committee all supported the expectation of parents to have a major voice in school policy and decision making.

The parents *also* wanted a traditional, respectable, mainstream parents' group. They planned a formal dinner dance, a gospel choir concert, a potluck supper, bake sales, and so forth. Many of these activities were familiar from the church, fraternal organizations, and other cultural groups in the black community. We recognized them as activities that could bring large numbers of previously alienated parents to the school in a friendly, positive way.

It is not usually considered fashionable for clinicians to invest themselves in such "superfluous" activities as fashion shows, dinners, or book fairs. Relegating parents to the White Elephant booth is the very strategy utilized to keep middle-status parents busy and out of the educator's hair. Many professionals see operating a parents' therapy group, parenting course, or high-level policy group to be of more noble purpose and therefore a more appropriate use of their training and time. We believe that broad-based activities such as those described serve vital functions. First, they are useful vehicles through which one can help parents develop important skills — how to conduct a meeting, make decisions, plan events, and develop publicity. They also help parents learn how to become more effective in collaborating with the school staff.

The King parents developed increasing competence and organizational skill as they gained practice operating their own group. For example, it took no less than ten meetings to plan the Parent-Teacher

Power Team's first family night dinner. One entire meeting was spent on the kind of paper goods to buy. A year later, all the details of the potluck supper were worked out in less than an hour.

Another important purpose of these activities is their potential for stimulating school spirit, or a warm, caring school climate. What differentiates the broad-based activities of the Parent-Teacher Power Team from those of many traditional parent groups is their intention in this regard. The intention of the former is to recruit parents who are afraid of the school, who feel intimidated by establishment professionals, and who often lead boring, pleasureless lives. When these parents come into the school and find a warm and respectful welcome, their alienation from the mainstream is reduced. When parents visit the school regularly for positive reasons, they come to see themselves as important helpers in the educational process. Such a parent is more likely to be responsive when there is a problem. This is an altogether different purpose than thinking up activities to keep the parents busy.

The formation of a broad-based parents' organization and an active calendar of parent-staff-student events was recognized as the first level in the comprehensive parents' program. The second level involved a strategy to integrate parents more fully into the day-to-day life of the school in a way that would bring teachers and parents into a collaboration that would be highly visible to the children. We realized that fewer parents could participate at this level than in the general activities. As we discussed this level of involvement with parents and presented several feasible alternatives, they decided on an ongoing bimonthly workshop series that they called *Coffee and Conversation Hours*. All the parents in the school are invited to the coffee hours through flyers and phone calls.

The initial purpose of these meetings was for parents to familiarize themselves with school operations and curriculum. The teaching staff presented workshops in various academic areas. The parents requested local teachers rather than bringing in outside experts because they wanted to become more familiar with their own staff and program. This served to improve parent-staff relationships. Had the program been conducted by outside experts, the parents would have learned no more meaningful information about given methods or techniques. Further, a valuable opportunity to enhance ongoing relationships would have been lost.

The format of the coffee hours varied over the years. The first year, workshops were presented by grade level; later, much of this material was presented again by subject area. We developed a parents' guide to children's learning, which included a schedule for classroom observation, questions for parents to ask teachers at conferences, and suggestions for parents at home. Because the teaching staff was active with the parents, they supported these activities. Since 1971, coffee hours have covered virtually every aspect of elementary school curriculum, methods of effective parenting, and social, political, and economic community issues.

Each year, several meetings are concerned with child development. The Parent-Teacher Power Team requests a group leader from Child Study Center with expertise around their particular concerns. These cover a broad range of common concerns for all parents including discipline, sexuality, drugs, alcohol, the effects of television, and habit disorders. The programs have always been organized in response to parent requests, rather than as the considered opinion of the experts about what parents need. The parents are, however, consistently receptive to suggestions from both school and Child Study Center staff and, in fact, look to the professional staff for ideas about format, organization, and materials.

As parents became more and more comfortable in the school, teachers encouraged them to volunteer in the classrooms. This started off on an irregular basis, around special events such as parties and trips. Eventually, several parents became effective classroom assistants and tutors. However, regular volunteer work was usually not feasible for King parents. Few low-income parents have excess time. A routine pediatric visit at a crowded clinic may take the better part of a day. The realities of poverty caused many parents to place a priority on earning money over activities at the school. A part-time job or keeping children for a working neighbor often took priority over volunteer work for King parents.

In response to this dilemma, we developed a program that would pay parents a small stipend for their regular participation in day-to-day school and classroom activities. This approach allowed parents to earn money in a relatively high status activity that brought them closer to education and enabled them to develop skills to help their children at home. About 15 to 20 parents are active in this program at any one time. This constitutes about 10% of the 175 families in the school. It is program policy to find an activity for every parent wishing to participate, regardless of the parent's skill level. Parents have functioned as classroom assistants, tutors, cafeteria helpers, game leaders at recess, library aides, and clerical assistants. Some parents are in the school building taking part in the educational program for children every school day. We believe it to be an important, positive lesson for the children in community-school relations.

The parent stipend program has the additional advantage of vastly increasing the resources of the school at a limited cost. Many children have received daily tutorial sessions, individual and small group support from parents that would not be available otherwise. The presence of parents gives tangible support for the activities, values, and ways of the school and larger society.

Parent participation in school governance is the third or most complex level of participation. By participating in the management of the Parent-Teacher Power Team, parents acquire organizational skills. By taking part in a wide variety of educational programs and participating in day-to-day activities, they learn about school operation, curriculum, and methods of better parenting. As parents participate in many varied ways, they become increasingly effective decision makers. Thus, while only a few parents at any one time are able to make the investment of time and energy required for participation in decision making, those that do so operate from a sound knowledge base.

A knowledge of the institution and how it functions combined with competency in basic organizational strategies are the most important ingredients for successful parent participation in decision making. Placing poor minority parents on a decision-making body without providing the underpinnings of a substantive parent program may increase parent alienation, promote conflict behavior, and threaten the school administration and staff. This was a major cause of many early problems with our program, the Ocean Hill-Brownsville program, and other educational change approaches.

At all levels, there is joint planning by staff and parents. Just as it is unfair to expect parents to participate in and endorse a program designed for them by experts, so is it unfair to expect teachers and other professional staff members to capitulate to parent control. Thus, we advocate shared decision making as contrasted with control by any one group, be they parents, staff, administration, or mental health professionals.

The philosophy of shared decision making and shared responsibility has facilitated a different view of clinical intervention. Rather than attributing problems to either the parents or the school staff, a "no-fault policy" developed. The emphasis is on changing everyone in the system to make the school more effective. In this atmosphere, even very troubled parents whose children are experiencing serious difficulties with the school have become more cooperative. Less time is wasted on broken appointments, blaming and recriminations, crises, and failure to follow through.

We have recently begun a field test of this process in another inner city school, although we began quite differently than at King. This was a different community, a different school staff, a different social and political climate, and most important, 10 years later in our own experience. Our approach, was low-keyed, low profile, low on publicity, and far more realistic in promise. We have helped the school begin the development of a parent-staff organization, supported broad-based activities initiated by staff and parents, and provided funds for a parent stipend program. That school, too, is beginning to experience the promise and power brought to the school by parents.

CONCLUSIONS

Summary

The racism in American society complicates the task of child rearing for black parents in all social and economic groups. Low-income and undereducated blacks are the most vulnerable. They lack access to the supports all parents need to raise healthy children — community security and the ability to provide for a family's basic needs, a knowledge of child development and the kinds of parent attitudes and behaviors that will facilitate it, and a knowledge of mainstream institutions and how to influence these systems to one's advantage.

While black parents have been the recipients of many social welfare programs, none has significantly altered the decaying pattern of poor minority communities. Most intervention projects function in isolation rather than as integrated parts of a total program to improve the living conditions of poor black families. Insufficient attention is paid to the complex interaction among historical, economic, political, cultural, social, educational, and psychological factors contributing to the circumstance of these families.

We have identified three components of efforts to serve black families that we consider critical — education for improved parenting, participation in institutional decision making, and income opportunity or support.

Information to improve child-rearing skills is important for all parents. The difficulty with this approach for poor, minority parents is that it tends to focus on changing the behavior of individual parents rather than the attitudes and actions of the social institution in question. These programs are often designed by professionals and prescribed for a given parent group. Our own work suggests that education for improved parenting can be most successful when it is part of a total program of institutional change and development.

The goals and strategies for such a program should be determined by a collaborative effort among the primary service agents in the setting (in our case, teachers and principal), the mental health professionals providing support for parents and staff, and the parents. While each of these groups has individual training needs, we found it helpful to plan regular joint parent-staff sessions.

A number of programs have provisions to involve low-income and minority parents in decision making with the intent of increasing their ability to influence the institution and the larger social system. Such programs often face difficulties because most low-income parents lack the training, exposure, and resources to be effective in these roles. Most often, institutions initiate parent participation programs under a funding mandate. The intention is to comply with the guidelines, give parents a limited voice, but leave the basic power structure of the institution intact.

We found that parents are effective participants in decision making when they have knowledge about the functioning of the institution. This was made possible in our program through their participation in its day-to-day routines. The institution provided real opportunities for parents to learn effective participatory strategies. Substantive parent participation in our program grew out of a comprehensive effort to involve parents in all aspects of school life, including social events, classroom activities, fund raising, personnel selection, budget determinations, school policy, and the management of their own organization.

Even when parent education and participation programs are thoughtfully planned and well managed, their effectiveness can be diminished by poverty. Inadequate economic conditions can severely tax the capacities of parents with the best intentions. Volunteerism and participation in planning and policy committees are ideas resting on the assumptions of excess time and the availability of supportive resources such as transportation and babysitters.

In our program, recognition of the value of parent participation is given by concrete supports such as child care for preschoolers, educational materials for use at home, and a stipend for regular participation as classroom assistants, cafeteria aides, tutors, and clerical helpers. Thus, while the intent of our program is parent participation as contrasted to regular employment, allocation of some program funds to the direct economic support for parents demonstrates an appreciation of the difficulties inherent in the participation of the poor.

In developing programs for low-income black parents, it is important to consider all three of these factors: transmitting parenting skills, stimulating participation in institutional decision making, and providing economic or material support. By focusing on potential strength rather than weaknesses or pathology, real parent power and support for the educational program were mobilized.

Implications

The following points are important for mental health professionals and parent educators developing programs through the approach suggested here. First, any program for parents should be planned as an integral part of the overall development of the institution. A governing or planning group comprised of the regular actors in the system (teachers, principals, nurses, day-care workers, etc.) and parents should plan programs based on an assessment of both needs and available resources. The mental health professional facilitates this collaborative planning process rather than prescribing any given program, training course, or project.

Second, supports must be provided to stimulate participation by poor, minority, and isolated parents. Included here are material resources such as transportation, child care, and income, as well as personal support and encouragement conveyed by phone calls, home visits, letters, and so forth. Third, we as mental health workers must recognize and redefine our roles as representatives of the mainstream or "the system." This often requires being less clinician and teacher and more facilitator and coordinator. It is always easier to attribute program failure to bureaucratic ineptitude or funding regulations than to acknowledge that some of our traditional ways of thinking and working are inadequate.

Facilitating Collaborative Programs

Effective parent participation programs grow out of an assessment of needs, problems, and concerns on the one hand and available resources, strengths, and supports on the other. A planning group made up of parents and other regular participants in a given institution must identify the needs and resources and develop problem-solving strategies.

The majority of staff and/or parents may not be interested in investing time and energy in this process initially. The concept of shared decision making and planning is unfamiliar in most bureaucratic settings. Staff are accustomed to taking orders from the top. As discussed previously, poor minority parents often feel impotent with respect to controlling their environment. However, it is usually possible to locate at least a few supportive staff members and parents in any setting. Assessment and planning can begin with this nuclear group.

The role of the mental health professional is to facilitate the collaborative process rather than to direct the group or prescribe solutions. As illustrated in our work at King School, the parent program grew out of long hard discussion and debate among all of the players in school life — administrators, teachers, mental health staff, and parents. The program was successful because *everybody* in the system of the school participated and changed, not just the parents. As one of the parents said, "Everyone here has a piece of the action and a stake in the outcome."

The collaborative process is developed through joint activities. At King School, the summer workshops, policy committees, school governance group, and personnel selection committee were all joint parent-staff activities. Parents and school staff came to know and respect each other as people through these activities. A regular calendar of events such as potluck suppers, book fairs, fashion shows, and gospel choir concerts planned and attended by both staff and parents serves to sustain and solidify this bond.

The selection of particular parent education programs should facilitate participation by parents and staff. Such programs should reflect day-to-day concerns. One year at King School, a new primary teacher started a system for teaching mathematics involving the use of cubes and blocks. At a planning meeting, one parent voiced concern about children "playing" instead of "doing their work." We suggested that parents ask the teacher to explain her approach and then helped the teacher plan some workshops for parents during the regularly scheduled coffee hours.

In the course of the workshops, we had a good opportunity to present some of Piaget's ideas about the development of children's thinking regarding numbers. The teacher, along with several children from the class, explained the use of her particular system. Parents received suggestions and made materials to help children at home. Through this process, parents came to support a teacher about whom they had initial reservations. Parents both improved their child-care skills and learned how to negotiate constructively with teachers. Because the workshop grew out of a real parent concern, it was much more valuable and well received than it would have been had it been proposed out of our notion of what would be good for the parents.

Parent participation in institutional decision making is the natural outcome of a collaboratively planned program. Parents at King School are effective in negotiating with the school system and other community agencies because of skills developed in planning and carrying out internal school programs with the staff. In the 1977 school year, for example, King parents successfully went to bat to hire a particular teacher, generated $2,000 in funds for a new playground, and obtained approval for a new schoolwide security system from the Board of Education. These were all solutions to problems identified within the parent-staff school governing group.

It may be easier for the worker (and for the institution as well) to advocate a particular training program, project, or course than to engage parents and staff in a collaborative planning process. Such programs are often very useful to the particular parents who are able to take advantage of them. But they do not permit the orderly search for effective methods and the kind of individual and group growth and system change our approach promotes.

Stimulating Participation

Stimulating and sustaining participation among low-income black parents can be difficult for reasons related to the institution and to the situation of the parents themselves. Institutions may be fearful about losing power to parents, being accountable to parents, and being interfered with by parents. Factors inhibiting parents include social and educational distance from the mainstream, preoccupation with economic survival, and a psychological sense of being controlled by others rather than controlling one's own fate. When parent participation programs fail, it is easier to say, "The parents weren't interested" than "Our efforts weren't good enough."

Both parents and institutions are capable of a wide range of responses in their interactions with one another. We have worked with many parents at King who have had such poor relationships with schools and similar systems that their characteristic response is either passive resistance or attack.

One parent was well known to another school in the community for violent outbursts with staff. This school had placed one of her children on homebound instruction because of disruptive behavior and was in the process of completing a diagnostic evaluation on a second child with similar difficulties at the time the family moved to the King district. This mother had learned to expect the worst from schools, the welfare office, the clinic, and everyone else in "the system." When she came to register her children at King, she announced that neither she nor her children were "crazy," and that the child on homebound instruction had been excluded from school unfairly. She was surprised when no one disagreed or retaliated.

The principal, in fact, offered to register the homebound child in a regular class. The parent was taken to talk with all of the teachers with whom her children would be placed. A regular plan of communication was arranged with each teacher. We invited her to the next parents' meeting, offering our babysitting service for her preschooler. Within a few weeks, this mother approached Child Study Center staff for help with personal and child management problems. She later told us that we were the first mental health people who didn't act as if she were "mentally disturbed." Eventually, this woman became active in the school, worked as a classroom assistant, and was one of our best advocates in the community.

A confrontation with this mother would have been easy. An initial stance of referring her for counseling, refusing to register the homebound child, or continuing the diagnostic evaluation of the second child were all school responses that would have intensified her hostility. Our approach reduced her hostility and feelings of isolation, both factors which mitigate against parent participation.

Even when programs reach out to parents through newsletters, phone calls, home visits, and material supports, it is still often hard to sustain participation by poor, isolated parents. It is important for institutions to consider the terms on which parents are being recruited. Parents are quick to see when an advisory board is a powerless rubber stamp. They cannot be expected to sustain interest in a parenting course that advocates methods impossible in their own situation.

Parent participation programs are effective to the extent that parents are able to see how their participation will contribute to an outcome they consider desirable. Such outcomes include personal career, educational, and/or financial gains; evidence that parent participation improves the well-being of their own children; and concrete improvements in the institution in which they have participated.

Parent Educators and the System

We as parent educators and mental health professionals must accept responsibility for helping to make mainstream social and educational institutions more responsive to the communities they serve, finding ways to succeed in spite of obstacles and resistances. All too often, workers complain about problems without taking the initiative to develop solutions. If the mental health worker is unable to identify resources or supports for program development, there is no useful role for him/her in that setting. For example, one worker felt that her school had a weak Title I Parent Advisory Council because the school did not provide transportation to meetings. The worker continuously badgered a harried, disorganized school principal to provide transportation and complained about his lack of interest.

We suggested that the worker take the initiative to form carpools, personally pick up parents, or ask other supportive staff to provide rides. This kind of positive action enables discouraged people to see that change is possible. It is easier to attribute problems to "the guidelines," "the Board," "the system," "those who don't care," than to change the structure or develop ways to work within it more effectively. We are all part of the system and, as such, can choose to perpetuate its difficulties or develop strategies to make it better.

Finally, professionals working with poor black parents need to remember that these families have the same goals, dreams, and aspirations for their children as everyone else. The parents with whom we work want their children to succeed in school, to be contributing members of the work force, to help improve conditions in their community. What differentiates these parents most from mainstream parents is access to the resources that would make these aspirations more readily attainable.

REFERENCES

Arnstein, S. R. A ladder of citizen participation. In E. S. Cahn & B. A. Passett (Eds.), *Citizen participation effecting community change.* New York: Praeger, 1971.

Bowlby, J. *Maternal care and mental health* (World Health Organization Monograph No. 2). Geneva: World Health Organization, 1951.

Coleman, J. S. *Equality of educational opportunity.* Washington, D.C., U.S. Government Printing Office, 1966.

Davies, D. *An overview of the status of citizen participation in educational decisionmaking.* Washington, D.C.: Institute for Responsive Education and the Education and Human Resources Development Division of Optimum Computer System, Inc. for the Group on School Capacity for Problem Solving of the National Institute of Education, 1978.

Family Service Association of America. *Overview of findings of the Family*

Service Association of America task force on family life education development and enrichment. New York: Family Serv, 1976.

Foster, M. *Making schools work: Strategies for changing education.* Philadelphia: Westminster, 1971.

Fraiberg, S. *Every child's birthright: In defense of mothering.* New York: Basic, 1977.

Goldstein, J., Freud, A., and Solnit, A. *Beyond the best interests of the child.* New York: Free Pr, 1973.

Gordon, I. J. Parent education and parent involvement: Retrospect and prospect. *Childhood Education,* 1977, *54*(2), 71-79.

Gordon, T. *Parent effectiveness training.* New York: McKay, 1970.

Gottfried, F. A survey of parental views of the Ocean Hill-Brownsville experiment. *Community Issues,* October, 1970.

HARYOU-ACT, Harlem Youth Opportunities Unlimited. *Youth in the ghetto: A study of the consequences of powerlessness and a blueprint for change.* New York: HARYOU-ACT, 1964.

Lane, M. B. *Education for parenting.* Washington, D.C.: Nat Assn Child Ed, 1975.

Provence, S., Naylor, A., & Patterson, J. *The challenge of daycare.* New Haven, Yale U Pr, 1977.

Saliterman, G. Participation in the urban school system: A Washington case. In E. S. Cahn & B. A. Passett (Eds.), *Citizen participation effecting community change.* New York: Praeger, 1971.

Stearns, M. & Peterson, S. Parent involvement in compensatory education programs: Stanford Research Institute Report. Washington, D.C.: Office of Planning, Budgeting and Evaluation, U.S. Office of Education, 1973.

SUGGESTED READINGS

Books for Black Parents

Comer, J. P. & Poussaint, A. F. *Black Child Care.* New York: Simon & Schuster, 1975.

This easy to read book presents basic information about child development from infancy to adolescence for black parents. Strategies for enabling parents to more effectively deal with racism in schools and other institutions are presented. Since *Black Child Care* is available in paperback (New York: Pocket Books, 1976), we have used it as a basic text for group discussions and workshops with low-income black parents.

Ross, P. H. & Wyden, B. *The Black Child — A Parent's Guide.* New York: Peter H. Wyden, Inc., 1973.

A useful handbook that explores racism and the ways in which it is manifested in our day-to-day life. The book focuses on the ways in which adult racial attitudes are transmitted to children, on methods of discipline, and on psychosexual development.

McLaughlin, C. J., in collaboration with Frisby, D. R., McLaughlin, R. A., & Williams, M. W. *Black Parents' Handbook: A Guide to Healthy Pregnancy, Birth and Child Care.* New York: Harcourt Brace Jovanich, Inc., 1976.

    A clearly written factual book about pregnancy and child care. Information about conception, diet, medical care, and medical problems common to black pregnant women and children are presented.

References for Professionals Working with Low-Income Black Parents of Preschool Children

Fraiberg, S. *Every Child's Birthright: In Defense of Mothering.* New York: Basic Books, Inc., 1977.

    A thoughtful and comprehensive book on the importance of parent-child relationships and how parenting can be undermined by poverty. Helpful for professionals working with parents on welfare and "working poor" parents.

Lane, M. B. *Education for Parenting.* Washington. D.C.: National Association for the Education of Young Children, 1975.

    A good source of program ideas for parent education and training. A variety of approaches is presented for both in-school and home-based approaches. Contains an excellent annotated bibliography of reading materials, descriptions of programs, and films.

Provence, S., Naylor, A., & Patterson, J. *The Challenge of Daycare.* New Haven: Yale University Press, 1977.

    This landmark book describes the multiple considerations involved in providing a comprehensive day care program for low-income and minority children. The work is based on the operation of "Children's House," a demonstration project at Yale Child Study Center from 1967 to 1972. The chapter "Working with Parents" is particularly useful for professionals wishing to develop more effective strategies for enabling poor, alienated parents to become more effective with their children.

References for Developing Parent Participation Programs

Institute for Responsive Education, 704 Commonwealth Avenue, Boston, Massachusetts, 02215.

    The Institute for Responsive Education disseminates research and other information helpful to both professionals and laymen engaged in developing parent participation programs. Of particular interest is the I.R.E. newsletter, *Citizen Action in Education,* and the comprehensive annotated bibliography, *Citizen Participation in Education,* 1978.

Schraft, C. M. & Winters, W. G. *Developing Parent School Collaboration: A Guide for School Personnel.* Connecticut State Department of

Education Bureau of Pupil Personnel and Special Educational Services, 1977. Available from Yale Child Study Center, New Haven, Connecticut.

This is a manual for practitioners developing parent programs in low-income schools. It describes how to develop parent participation at increasing collaborative levels from broad-based parent school events to parent involvement in the day-to-day life of the school to parent participation in school governance.

References on the Black Experience in America and Black Culture

Billingsley, A. *Black Families in White America.* Englewood Cliffs, New Jersey: Prentice-Hall, Inc., 1968.

Carmichael, S. & Hamilton, C. V. *Black Power, The Political Liberation in America.* New York: Random House, 1967.

Clark, K. B. *Dark Ghetto: Dilemmas of Social Power.* New York: Harper & Row, 1965.

Comer, J. P. *Beyond Black and White.* New York: Quadrangle Books, 1972.

Grier, W. H. & Cobbs, P. M. *Black Rage.* New York: Bantam Books, 1969.

Chapter 14

FROM CONSUMER TO MIDDLEMAN: EMERGING ROLES FOR PARENTS IN THE NETWORK OF SERVICES FOR RETARDED CHILDREN

Louis J. Heifetz

The story of the handling of parents of the retarded by professionals is a very sad one. While many unfortunate episodes have been the result of ill-advised but well-meaning management, others have been due to callousness and outright malpractice.

Wolf Wolfensberger (1967, p. 350)

Mental retardation is widely regarded as a hopeless condition; yet it is hard to think of a human affliction as amenable to productive intervention.... But a radical reconceptualization of the problem is required.... The mental health specialist must be trained in ways to multiply his effectiveness by working through less extensively and expensively trained people.

Nicholas Hobbs (1964, pp. 827-828)

IMAGINE a list of behaviors so utterly abnormal that they would be considered deviant in any culture, in any historical period, and under any conceivable set of circumstances. Or, conversely, imagine a list of behaviors so basically normal that they would be regarded as acceptable regardless of their cultural, historical, and situational context. For several years, I have posed these complementary challenges to students in a course on psychopathology. Among their candidates for either list, none has required more than a minute to prompt another student's convincing counterexample. The purpose of the exercise is to dramatize how fundamentally and subtly time- and culture-bound are our conceptions of normative behavior and deviance and how thoroughly these societal and historical forces will shape our efforts at prevention and treatment of abnormality (Opler, 1959; Szasz, 1970; Zilboorg & Henry, 1941). As a particular category of abnormality, mental retardation must inevitably be viewed

349

through the highly variable lenses of time and culture (Rosen, Clark, & Kivitz, 1976; Sarason & Doris, 1969). To remove the distortions completely is impossible, since the very efforts at correction will also be time- and culture-bound. But clarity can be increased through a heightened awareness of the idiosyncratic nature of our aggregate as well as our individual world views. And there may be no better aid to greater understanding than a cautious skepticism about ever completely achieving it.

A major thesis of this chapter is that professionals can not work truly effectively with parents unless they are acutely aware of their own conceptual framework, understand the broad outline and finer details of each parent's framework, and begin to anticipate the manner in which the two frameworks interact as the parent-professional relationship evolves.

The frameworks that guide the activities of professionals in the field are similar in many ways to the frameworks that shape the activities of professionals in the natural sciences. The nature of these frameworks and their role in the evolution of various scientific disciplines have been lucidly analyzed by Kuhn (1970), a philosopher of science. What he calls *paradigms* are constellations of premises, beliefs, theories, values, procedures, and techniques shared by the practitioners of a given scientific discipline. A paradigm outlines the appropriate region of scientific inquiry, provides the concepts to be used in the pursuit and interpretation of data, and specifies the instruments and methodology that are legitimate for the generation and analysis of relevant data. Some of the most important elements in a paradigm are the concrete and exemplary problem-solutions that provide models for the investigation and solution of other problems that arise within the paradigm. Thus, a paradigm fulfills the sociological function of defining a community of scientists who are bound by a shared commitment to the same beliefs, concepts, values, and standards, thereby permitting "the relative fulness of their professional communication and the relative unanimity of their professional judgments" (p. 182). Equally important, a paradigm serves a heuristic function by furnishing, through its exemplary problem-solutions, "past scientific achievements . . . that some particular scientific community acknowledges for a time as supplying the foundation for its further practice" (p. 10).

Paradigms are a prerequisite for the birth and growth of any coherent tradition of scientific inquiry. As long as the basic elements of the paradigm are accepted, its community of adherents can go about the business of elaborating and refining the paradigm, cumulatively exploring its territory and solving its problems in what Kuhn has called "normal science." Periods of normal science may be extremely long-lived, as in the classic example of the Ptolemaic paradigm, which dominated astronomy from the second until the sixteenth century. But sooner or later, a paradigm's reign must end. In some cases, new and irreconcilably contradictory data will appear. In other cases, nonscientific factors (like changes in the religious, political, or cultural milieu) will make a paradigm untenable. In still other cases, a newly proposed paradigm may be far more parsimonious than its predecessor, as was the Copernican system that supplanted the Ptolemaic paradigm. Eventually, a new period of normal science will emerge, but the transition may be protracted and chaotic. A long-established paradigm may be refuted, leaving its discipline fragmented, with each subarea spawning its own "native son" as an inadequate candidate for a successor paradigm. On the other hand, a fairly unified paradigm may come forth to challenge the incumbent, but with the complementary pattern of each paradigm's relative strengths and weaknesses, the battle for supremacy may engage the discipline in a drawn-out civil war. In contemporary psychology, this is exemplified by the conflicts between the psychoanalytic and behaviorist schools of thought. In fact, the field of retardation is one of the many arenas in which these two paradigms have clashed. Moreover, there is good reason to expect that the impact and incidence of paradigm clashes are on the increase.

At the present time, there is more extensive and sophisticated involvement — by a larger array of scientific and clinical disciplines — than at any other time in the history of mental retardation services (e.g., Mittler, 1977). A review of these multiple disciplinary perspectives would indicate that service providers as a whole are not involved in anything resembling a period of "normal science." Because of the previously noted tendency of paradigms to restrict as well as to focus the process of inquiry, the light shed by a particular discipline has a blinding effect as well as an illuminating one upon its disciples. As a consequence, the individual practitioner of a given paradigm is destined to approach the needs of a family in a simplistic and fragmentary fashion. The problem is further complicated by the fact that families often interact with many diverse professionals in their travels through the service network. It is not surprising to find that paradigm clashes are not confined to scholarly journals and debates; nor are the stakes limited to the rise and fall of academic reputations. The hard fact is that children and parents provide the major fields of paradigmatic battle. And they are the true casualties of the cross fire, needing reassurance and stability, but faced with a service system in which the perspectives are multiple, changing, and often incompatible.

Obviously, these problems will not disappear until the field of mental retardation enters another period of normal science. In the interim, however, the problems may be significantly reduced by cultivating several forms of heightened awareness among professionals. The present chapter is intended as one small contribution to such "consciousness raising."

To begin with, we often behave as though the basic premises of our paradigms were absolute truths, even when they are nothing more than working hypotheses needing periodic reappraisal. We also need to regularly review the assumptive sources of conflict among our paradigms. These conflicts are often based upon seriously outdated images of the opponents, which may delay the synthesis of originally antithetical paradigms.[1] Finally, the importance of parental frames of reference cannot be overemphasized. Just as the clash of paradigms will radically influence the evolution of a science, so will the interplay of professional and parental frameworks shape the development of the consumer-provider relationship. As a first step toward understanding a parent's framework, professionals must be aware of the great complexity and variability of the elements of that framework.

PARENTS AND PROFESSIONALS
SOME DEVELOPMENTAL ISSUES

Long before we actually become parents, our script for that role has already been largely determined. From birth, our genetic endowment imposes some absolute physiological limits and, with them, an array of behavioral predispositions that are the first vague outlines of our life script. Almost immediately thereafter, we begin to navigate the inevitable straits and channels of psychosocial and cognitive development, the regularities of which have been so thoroughly charted by Freud, Erikson, and Piaget. Here our various childhood environments, family and school primary among them, interact with genetics as collaborative scriptwriters. The amount of growth that is fostered at each maturational stage and the adequacy or inadequacy with which each transitional crisis is resolved profoundly affect the evolving script, not only in broad outline, but also in some areas of fine detail. We emerge from adolescence rather well defined for the present and

---

[1]For example, the success of cognitive behavior therapy would have been impossible if the behavior therapists and insight-oriented therapists had all conformed to or believed their respective stereotypes as devotees of the "black box" or "intrapsychic supremacy."

with an aggregate momentum pointing us toward a narrowed range of likely futures. A large number of once possible roles have effectively been ruled out by this point. However, despite the enormous degree to which personality has already been determined, despite the great detail in which our lives have been defined, despite our awareness of limited options available in designing the remainder of our lives, there is still one role that is, with minor exception, open to all — the role of parent. This is arguably the most important role in the human repertory, yet it is the least selectively cast: We bring to the role no particular equipment or preparation. Instead, we carry the infinitely varied baggage of our birth, childhood, and adolescence: collections of facts and distortions; memories sharp or vague; constellations of attitudes with or without consistency; information-processing mechanisms of varying efficiency; expectations that have little or every chance of being confirmed; and strategies for living and decision making that range from the highly effective to the severely maladaptive. And it is from this welter that the role of each individual parent emerges.

For most parents, the creation of their role is more a matter of replication than innovation. Their children will likely show the same general progression from dependence to independence as they themselves did. In rearing their children, they will perform innumerable functions that draw on years of observational learning of the functions performed by parents and surrogates in their nuclear and extended families. There will even be similarities from one family generation to the next in overall styles and patterns of child rearing. In a sense, the new parent is playing variations on the previous generation's themes; when inspiration fails, the original score will usually do.

The situation is quite different for a parent of a retarded child. Even the most general developmental expectations are suddenly open to question. Many parents have had no prior experience with retarded children; certainly, those with any previous familiarity with retardation never perceived that experience as preparation for their own parenthood. And their current repertoire of parenting skills, whether at the embryonic level of observational learning or more thoroughly developed through the raising of other children, will be grossly insufficient for this new set of child-rearing tasks. The parents are suddenly cast in a role that they never expected, that they probably did not want, and for which they had never been psychologically prepared. The task of the professional, then, is to help the parents in understanding the role and the various ways it can be played, to support them in their struggle to define the role for themselves, and to furnish them directly and indirectly with resources that will enable them most effectively to play their role.

As the quotation from Wolfensberger that prefaced this chapter suggests, professionals as a whole have not acquitted themselves well in their task. Indeed, what emerges from his comprehensive review (Wolfensberger, 1967) is a most bleak assessment: Parents of retarded children cannot adequately design their role without professional help, but professional involvement in their situation is often of no help whatsoever and can even be damaging.

Before embarking on a review of parental dynamics, a brief history of professional strategies of family intervention, and a closer examination of some very recent and promising trends in family services, it will be helpful to introduce a conceptual framework for integrating these separate areas. Key elements in this framework are the *developmental needs* of the parents as well as the child and the activities or *functions* engaged in by service providers (including parents, professionals, and others) in order to fulfill those needs. Within this framework, one can define the parental role as *the set of functions that the parent performs on behalf of the child* (supplemented, perhaps, in a more detailed definition by a specification of conditions under which each function is performed).

The professional role may be similarly defined but further differentiated into three subroles: those functions that are performed directly for the child (e.g., diagnostic testing); those that are performed directly for the parent (e.g., individual psychotherapy); and those that are performed indirectly for the child through the parent (e.g., training in home management techniques). Notice, by the way, that this formulation explicitly identifies the parent as an active generator of services as well as a recipient of services. Therefore, in this chapter, the term *consumer-provider relationship*, which is frequently encountered in the literature of human services, should be read as shorthand for a relationship between a service provider (the professional) and a service consumer/provider (the parent). At issue are the ways in which such relationships develop and the possibilities for efficiently cultivating their more productive forms.

Most consumer-provider relationships are built upon the answers to four questions:

1. What is the basic nature of the problem; what *needs* for service have been identified?
2. What are the known remedies or palliatives for the problem; what *functions* exist to fulfill these needs?
3. Who is *capable* of adequately performing these functions?

4. Who has the *obligation* to perform these functions?

The responses to these questions, i.e., *assessment, prescription, competence,* and *responsibility*, will not only guide the parent's search for professional assistance, but will also influence the manner in which the service functions are likely to be shared between parent and professional. In other words, the answers to these questions define roles for professionals as well as for parents.

In the area of mental retardation services, answers to the four questions are far from consensual. Indeed, some of the most fierce and durable controversies in the field have stemmed from these questions, e.g., developmental vs. impairment models of etiology (Ellis, 1969; Milgram, 1969; Zigler, 1967, 1969); medical vs. psychoeducational strategies of intervention (Bijou, 1966; Freeman, 1966; Itard, 1932; Louttit, 1965); institutionalization vs. normalization (Baker, Seltzer, & Seltzer, 1977; Begab, 1963; Blatt, 1970; Blatt & Kaplan, 1966; Feuerstein & Karasilowsky, 1972; Kugel & Wolfensberger, 1969; Zigler & Balla, 1977); parents as neurotic victims vs. parents as competent teachers (Berkowitz & Graziano, 1972; Solnit & Stark, 1961). And these debates are more than simple historical curiosities. The long-term shifts in attitudes and philosophies that the field as a whole has displayed over the decades are all simultaneously visible in a cross-section of present-day consumers and providers. In a given consumer-provider relationship, this diversity may offer helpful pluralism or maladaptive chaos.

Three patterns may occur in a consumer-provider pairing. In the first type, there are large differences between the parent's and the professional's assumptions and expectancies about their relationship (i.e., their answers to the questions of assessment, prescription, competence, and responsibility). This lack of congruence can produce an uncomfortable, unstable, and (if dissonance is not resolved) unproductive relationship. In the second, there is basic agreement between parent and professional, but it is partly founded on faulty, albeit shared, assumptions (e.g., the belief that Down's syndrome children have no potential for learning and are best cared for in a custodial institution). Here the relationship is comfortable and probably stable, but far from maximally productive. The third kind of relationship is based on assumptions that are not only shared, but also accurate. Such a relationship is the most conducive to comfort, stability, and, for parent and child alike, growth.

The most important questions are related to parental competence in meeting their children's special developmental needs. Here the professional should include an assessment of present parental capability, their potential for becoming more capable, and their self-perceptions of present and future competence. These questions are not just important for each individual case. In addition, the aggregated answers will tell much about the overall ability of our service delivery system to meet the needs of retarded children and their families. Because of the severe limits on professional resources, the success of the service network will depend heavily upon its willingness and ability to incorporate parents as service *providers* as well as service *consumers*.

PERSONNEL SHORTAGES AND THE PARAPROFESSIONAL MOVEMENT

The current recognition of mental retardation as a major social problem in the United States is rather recent and only began as a postscript to World War II. As Sarason and Doris (1969) have observed, "There is apparently (and unfortunately) nothing like a war to force a society to look at its human resources" (p. 10). Among the more than 5 million draft-age men rejected from service as being unfit physically, mentally, morally, or emotionally, more than 1 out of 7 were declared mentally deficient. Analysis of the demographic characteristics of the rejectees served to distinguish cases of "primary" mental deficiency from cases produced by educational deprivation. Also demonstrated were the connections among minority status, education of restricted quantity and quality, poverty, and mental retardation (Ginzberg & Bray, 1953). A decade later, the importance of social, economic, and cultural variables in the prevalence of retardation was highlighted by the President's Panel on Mental Retardation (1962). National concern for the retarded was also enhanced by the overall impetus of the "war on poverty" (Sarason & Doris, 1969). In a similar way, some educational and cultural aspects of the problem were made salient through the civil rights movement, beginning in 1954 with the landmark decision in *Brown v. Board of Education* (Robinson & Robinson, 1976). The creation (in 1950) and growth of the National Association for Retarded Children as an advocacy voice of monumental impact (Begab, 1975) combined with these other social developments and brought retardation into national focus as a community problem.

This new prominence of retardation as a problem requiring nationwide human services efforts served to dramatize the inadequacies and inequities of the existing services (President's Panel on Mental Retardation, 1962). These issues were hardly unique to retardation and had received a great deal of attention within the mental health fields in general. Data collected for the Joint Commission on Mental Illness and Health (Albee, 1959) showed a huge gap between the demand for mental health services and the supply, indicated that the gap was widening, and suggested that the most optimistic estimates of increases in professional personnel would still fall far short of the need, a prediction that has stood the test of time (Albee, 1970). Albee criticized the variations on the private practice paradigm that were the predominant models for clinical psychology, psychiatry, and allied professions; he recommended the exploration of new models that would greatly increase the effective power of the mental health professionals by means of programmatic multiplier effects.

Albee's findings had followed close on the heels of Hollingshead and Redlich's (1958) classic study of the relationships among social stratification, mental illness, and its treatment. In public as well as private agencies, socioeconomic status (SES) was found to be a stronger determinant of type of treatment than was diagnosis: The higher a patient's SES, the more extended, expensive, and personal the treatment; the lower the SES, the more perfunctory, inexpensive, and impersonal the treatment. With the demand for services outrunning the supply, it was no great surprise that the more privileged elements in society would receive a disproportionate share of services. In the field of retardation services, the shortage was underscored by Lindsley's (1966) somber statistics: 1 child psychiatrist, 2 child psychologists, and 10 special education teachers for every 5,000 retarded children. A parent's search for these and other rare resources often became a long, expensive, and basically fruitless quest (Greenfeld, 1970). And as Baker (1976) has noted, "Access still depends on where one lives, whom one knows, how much money one has — and just plain luck" (p. 693).

Writing in 1964, Hobbs persuasively reiterated and extended the critiques that Albee had made for our service delivery systems. In particular he urged that professionals recognize the small sphere of influence to which they would be restricted as long as they reserved for themselves the role of direct service provider, that by investing substantial time in the training of paraprofessionals as therapeutic agents, the professionals could serve a much wider clientele. Such recommendations fly directly in the face of "professional preciousness" (Sarason, 1972), the tendency to define problems in ways that require the services of traditionally trained professionals. With the increasing awareness that these parochial formulations render the supply-demand problems insoluble, the paraprofessional movement has grown significantly (Guerney, 1969; Sobey, 1970). Teachers, ward attendants, aides, volunteers, and other kinds of paraprofessionals and nonprofessionals have been trained effectively to deliver forms of therapeutic service that had previously been the exclusive domain of mental health professionals.

Lindsley (1966), noting that about 95% of retarded children live at home, suggested that parents be viewed as potential providers of psychoeducational services who could be trained to take on an active and expert role in their children's training and development. This was the most radical form of "manpower engineering" (Hobbs, 1964) being proposed in retardation services. Other new definitions of service providers either blurred the distinctions among service functions performed at different levels in the professional hierarchy (e.g., nurse practitioners) or drew on sources of personnel that had not been involved in service delivery (e.g., foster grandparents). Parents, however, had always been involved in the service network, but in their traditional role as *consumers*, not *providers*. What Lindsley was advocating was a provocative rewriting and partial reversal of the parental role. Instead of being exclusively at the receiving end of a hopelessly understaffed service system, parents could be equipped to function as "middlemen" between the professional network and their children. However, while Lindsley's argument was numerically impeccable — each child would be served by 1 or 2 parents in addition to .0002 psychiatrists, .0004 psychologists, and .002 special education teachers — it was bound to generate massive resistance from the ranks of the professionally precious. Yet the roots of this resistance went deeper than mere professional elitism. At stake was the integrity of a widely endorsed model of parental psychodynamics, some long-held theories on the nature of retardation and their derivative schools of treatment. In short, a complex and interwoven paradigm would have to be challenged in order to act on Lindsley's suggestion.

THE IMPAIRMENT MODEL AND FAMILY INTERVENTION

Among the many fictions and half-truths about retardation, one of the most prevalent and pernicious is the idea that the observable "symptoms" are invariably linked to some specific defect or pathology of the central nervous system (Menolascino, 1970). This impairment is presumed to exist even when it cannot be directly demonstrated, is considered chronic and untreatable, and is thought to place severe (if not absolute) constraints on the utility of remedial education. This viewpoint emerged toward the end of the nineteenth century (Bourneville, 1893), along with the rise of the "medical model" of mental illness, which had been spurred by the discovery of the relationship between syphilis and the common type of insanity called general paresis (Zilboorg & Henry, 1941). Just as the movement for "moral treatment" of the insane fell into decline with the influx of medically oriented approaches (Adams, 1964), so too did the humane educational approaches to retardation that had been pioneered by Seguin (1846) and Howe (1850) fall victim to the impairment model, which appeared and rose to preeminence within a mere 20 years, 1880 to 1900 (Menolascino, 1970). Shortly thereafter, the impairment model was neatly complemented by the development and often spurious applications of intelligence tests in the early 1900s. The close correspondence of these tests with clinical judgment (Goddard, 1910) and their comparative ease of application (Kuhlman, 1912) led to their being excessively relied upon as a diagnostic index of retardation. Their high test-retest reliability and other statistical characteristics (Terman, 1916) lent further credence to the concept of inherently fixed intelligence and the implied futility of educational intervention. Finally, it was a small step from the low IQ scores of delinquents (Goddard & Hill, 1911), criminals (Pintner, 1923), and prostitutes (McCord, 1915) — never mind the flaws in test validity, sample selection, test administration, and logical inference — to attribute to all retarded persons the innate tendencies toward immorality and violent crime (Fernald, 1912). These findings provided "scientific" confirmation for a growing alarmist attitude toward the retarded and launched the trend toward segregated institutionalization that has been the primary professional-societal response to retardation in America in this century (Blatt, 1970).

The impairment model of the retarded child spawned a corollary model of the retarded child's parent. With the alleged futility of educational and developmental intervention for the child, the only needs that could be met were those related to "creature comfort." Institutional placement was a very logical response under the impairment model. But, with institutional places available for only about 5% of the retarded, the majority of parents were, by elimination, placed in the role of custodian. Thus, parents were faced with a long-term (perhaps lifetime) responsibility for maintaining a child who was not likely to meet many of their expectations, but who would require a great deal of their time, energy, and attention. Moreover, they would find their regular child-rearing skills irrelevant or insufficient to many of the daily problems of home management and to the promotion of the child's cognitive growth; nor was there much assistance to be had in these areas from professionals. Instead, the typical response of the mental health professions has been some form of psychodynamic therapy or counseling, usually focused on parents' emotional reactions and the maladaptive and nonadaptive behaviors that accompany them (Wolfensberger & Menolascino, 1970).

A significant literature on parental dynamics and professional intervention did not begin to appear until the early 1950s (Wolfensberger, 1967). The dominance of psychoanalytic thought in psychiatry, clinical psychology, and social work at that time virtually guaranteed that the problems of parents of the retarded would be conceived of in terms of neurotic reactions to anxiety and stress and that strategies of treatment would be formulated accordingly. In particular, the pessimistic view of the child portrayed by the impairment model confronted parents with a situation considered too painful to be completely accepted. As a result, various defense mechanisms of neurotic proportions were expected to come into play.

Beddie and Osmond (1955) emphasized the impact of institutionalization, which they viewed as a deathlike loss with no societally standardized mourning rituals. Consequently, the necessary "grief work" might be delayed until the child's actual death, consigning the parents in the interim to a painfully extended period of "mourning." In a similar vein, Solnit and Stark (1961) wrote that the birth of a retarded child, with its tragic demolition of parental expectancies, would be seen by them as a crucial "object loss," thus severely exacerbating the stresses attendant upon a normal birth. The intensely emotional impact of guilt, depression, and "narcissistic injury" could often lead to either of two extreme reactions. With guilt uppermost, the parents could be driven to a neurotic, relentless commitment of time and resources to the child's welfare. On the other hand, their "narcissistic injury" and intolerance of the child's retardation might impel them to "deny" the child's existence in order to escape the stigma of his/her relationship to them. Within this psychoanalytic perspective, many parents were seen as suspended between the neurotic poles of denial and guilty recognition, a state that Solnit and Stark called *chronic mourning*.

Wolfensberger (1967) has catalogued 45 parental reactions mentioned in the literature, none of them positive, with guilt being the most widely cited. Representative positions from this literature have been presented by Baum (1962), who saw guilt as a multiply determined product of severe parental anxiety, anger, and other factors, and by Schild (1964), who believed that parental guilt had to be dissipated before successful counseling could begin. In general, contributors to this literature have suggested that parental guilt lacks a base in reality and tends to generate maladaptive behavior.

Essentially, parents were viewed within this paradigm as the neurotic victims of the child's untreatable impairment, with the primary wounds inflicted by guilt and grief. Therefore, the goals of counseling and therapy were to explore the true feelings underlying the various neurotic distortions (e.g., denial, projection, reaction formation, over-identification, self-blame, mourning), to clarify and help parents to understand these feelings, to provide emotional support and reassurance and, ideally, to engineer parental acceptance of the child and his/her impairment. Beyond this, there was little to do but recommend institutionalization in the cases where, even with therapy, the parents could not adjust to the child's continued presence in the home. In the event that a scarce opening could be found, the final function of the professional was to reconcile the parents to the need for placement, a process that has often been described in simplistic and cavalier fashion (e.g., Reed, 1963).

This neurotic model, although recently predominant and still widely endorsed, has been subject to increasingly critical reappraisal, ranging from small revisions to outright rejection. Several writers have questioned the primary importance assigned to parental guilt. Patterson (1956) has suggested that a situational form of "regret" associated with occasional instances of negative behavior toward the child is more common among parents than is trait-level guilt. McDonald (1962) has noted that the "guilt" observed during an intake interview may well be an artifact of inept interviewing, in which the professional's history-taking questions may inadvertently take on an accusatory tone. Olshansky (1966) questioned the high frequency of reports of parents' "denial" of their child's retardation; because of our cultural constraints against persistent grieving, what parents are more likely denying is their "chronic sorrow," "an understandable nonneurotic response to a tragic fact" (p. 21).

Other critics have charged that the neurotic model is itself "neurotic" in its apparent denial of the realistic pressures upon parents, the often normal nature of parents' stressful reactions, and the extensive resources and coping skills that parents can bring to bear upon their difficult situation. Mackinnon and Frederick (1970) cautioned against prematurely making the same assumption with parents of retarded children that is often made with parents of emotionally disturbed children — namely, that the focus of treatment should be upon the pathological family dynamics, of which the child is only a symptom. Parental resentment is certainly justified when professionals automatically offer "therapeutic programming in response to their request for a limited and realistic service" (p. 495). A graphic illustration of the damage that can result is provided by Kysar (1968), the psychiatrist-father of an autistic and retarded child.

Parents are not always emotionally overwhelmed, but may instead be in need of honest information about their child, the implications for his/her future, and concrete strategies for coping with his/her special needs as "essentially mature and rational people" (Matheny & Vernick, 1968, p. 953). Menolascino (1968) has suggested that the persistent emphasis on parental feelings is often a consequence of professional inability to manage practical problems. Still subscribing to an impairment model of retardation, these professionals may distort the request for management assistance into a need for dynamic counseling. "Professional ignorance all too quickly reifies the child's 'untreatability,' increases parental frustration and sense of helplessness, and ultimately legitimizes the need for psychotherapy" (Heifetz, 1977a, p. 205).

PSYCHOEDUCATIONAL CHALLENGES
TO THE IMPAIRMENT MODEL

An assumption of the impairment model is that the behavior of retarded children, in particular, their difficulties in learning, is a direct function of their low intelligence. However, in the last 20 years, a large body of research has accumulated that heavily implicates emotional and motivational factors in retarded performance. The role of these factors has been comprehensively reviewed by Windle (1962) and Zigler (1971). Of particular importance is the retarded child's history of learning, in which failure has predominated over success (Bijou, 1966). This experience establishes the expectancy of failure and conditions the child to escape or avoid the historically aversive learning situations (House & Zeaman, 1960; Kass & Stevenson, 1961). Another finding has been that the problem-solving strategies used by retarded children tend to rely on external cues and feedback more heavily than do the strategies used by nonretarded children (Turnure & Zigler, 1964). In addition, mere knowledge of being correct, which is a powerful reinforcer for middle-class children of normal intelligence, has been found to be a much less effective incentive for retarded children (Zigler & DeLabry, 1962). And, as another by-product of the retarded child's learning history, it has been shown that punishment paradigms are only modestly effective in comparison with contingencies of positive reinforcement (Cromwell, 1959; Stevenson & Zigler, 1958).

These research findings have tremendous implications for the way in which we approach the questions of *assessment* and *prescription* discussed earlier. It is probably not possible, at present, to alter basic intellectual capacity or to exceed the absolute limits that capacity imposes on the speed and extent of a child's learning. However, by realizing that task performance is a joint function of intellective and motivational factors (Zigler, 1971), it becomes possible, through the careful construction of special learning environments, to realize more thoroughly the child's innate potential for growth.

In the last 15 years, educational approaches to retarded children have been revolutionized by behavior modification, a variety of techniques that stress "the functional relationships between behavior and its environmental antecedents and consequences and seek to rearrange the child's environment in order to shape and maintain adaptive behavior patterns and to reduce or extinguish maladaptive ones" (Heifetz & Farber, 1976, p. 21). Behavior modification with retarded children draws on two major kinds of learning theory: Principles of operant conditioning (Skinner, 1966) are the most widely used, but Bandura's (1969) principles of social/observational learning have become increasingly influential. The reader is referred to reviews by Gardner (1970), who attributes to these techniques "behavior change of a range, degree, and rate which most psychiatric, psychological, and educational personnel had not thought possible owing to the limitations imposed by the term 'mental retardation'" (p. 250), and Robinson and Robinson (1976, Chap. 15), who conclude that behavioral approaches "have contributed enormously to the success of teachers, parents, therapists, and others concerned with the care and education of retarded children" (p. 302).

A comparison of these two enthusiastic appraisals suggests that the emergence of behavior modification as a technology of teaching retarded children has only begun to revise the view of parents' place in the service delivery system. The studies reviewed by Gardner dealt almost entirely with institutionalized persons (who were, for the most part, severely or profoundly retarded) or with retarded children in carefully engineered classroom environments. Procedures were designed by highly trained professionals who either directly administered or closely supervised them. Nowhere in the review were parents identified as potential treatment agents, although they were implicitly included in the cautionary concluding citation:

> . . . we must be sure that there are scientists (research personnel) to provide the necessary thinking through and analysis of the techniques used by applied personnel. . . . behavior therapy, with its worthy social goals, its theoretical simplicity (deceptive though it

may be), and its empirical success (under certain circumstances), will attract many psychotechnicians. It is, therefore, a field in danger of being ruined by amateurs. (Bachrach & Quigley, 1966, p. 510)

In other words, while some behavioral exponents were demonstrating a remarkably effective approach, they were also, at this stage of development, restricting its use to a group of professional practitioners whose numbers, as previously discussed, were woefully inadequate. Certainly they were not to be criticized for being scrupulously scientific in monitoring the effectiveness of these learning theory applications. But one could also discern a real reluctance to deal with parents as potential providers of services. Perhaps the prospect of clients as collaborators did too much violence to the self-image of some professionals. Among certain behaviorists, then, professional preciousness marched on in the guise of "science."

A welcome trend appeared in the years between the Gardner (1970) and Robinson and Robinson (1976) reviews, as the behavior modification and paraprofessional movements began regular cross-fertilization in the area of parent training. Initial reports often involved one highly motivated parent (typically the mother), a specific target behavior of the child's, and a substantial professional role in treatment, which often occurred in a clinic or hospital setting (Berkowitz & Graziano, 1972). Some formats gave a bit more autonomy to parents by having them replicate procedures at home that were originally used in the clinic (Nolan & Pence, 1970; Terdal & Buell, 1969). Other formats also included training in general principles of behavior management in order to equip parents to design future management programs (Pascal, 1973).

Paralleling earlier trends in professional applications, parent training no longer focused exclusively on the management of circumscribed surplus behaviors (O'Dell, 1974), but also prepared parents to modify various deficits in their children's skill development, including language acquisition (Simeonsson & Wiegerink, 1974). Some investigators even found that parents could, with proper training, be more effective than professionals as teachers of their own children (Schopler & Reichler, 1971). Such findings were not surprising to those who had argued that parents, as the most potent source of reinforcement in the child's natural environment, were ideal candidates for teachers (Tharp & Wetzel, 1969). Programs like the Portage Project (Shearer, 1974), the Model Preschool Center (Hayden, 1974), and the Infant, Toddler and Preschool Project (Bricker & Bricker, 1976) all furnished comprehensive forms of parent training, often as part of a smoothly integrated home-school program.

As parents were found capable of assuming increasingly varied and sophisticated responsibilities in behavioral teaching, children's learning environments were significantly enriched. Many professionals spent less time as direct providers of children's services and more time working through the parents they had trained. Just as professional use of behavior modification had recast the questions of *assessment* and *prescription*, so did parental ability with these techniques offer a radically different reply to the questions of *competence* and *responsibility*, as mentioned previously. A new and hopeful paradigm of parent-professional collaboration was taking shape. Ultimately, though, it would .have to confront the same shortages in professional personnel that had proved so limiting to models of direct service provision. In order to exploit the potential of parents as teachers, high priority would need to be placed on improving the efficiency of the parent-training process.

One strategy was to borrow the group formats often used for parent counseling or therapy under the assumptions of the impairment model and adapt them to the more didactic purposes of the psychoeducational model. In the last several years, group formats have become widely and successfully used (Berkowitz & Graziano, 1972; O'Dell, 1974). Typically, these groups contain 4 to 10 parents or couples trained by 1 or 2 professionals. This added efficiency is most encouraging, but because of the shortage of competent professional trainers, it contributes only a few more drops to the bucket. Moreover, as training goals become more complex and ambitious, it may be difficult for trainers to provide instruction adequate to each family's individual needs without reducing the efficiency that groups offer over one-to-one training formats.

The need for direct professional contact could theoretically be reduced by giving parents self-instructional materials for shaping and managing their children's behavior. While only a few investigators have emphasized the use of written instructions in their reports (e.g., Pascal, 1973; Salzinger, Feldman, & Portnoy, 1970), the preparation of written programs, guides, and summaries has been common practice in group and individual training formats. Also, some general "how-to" books on behavioral approaches to parenting have been available for about a decade (Becker, 1971; Patterson & Gullion, 1968; Vallet, 1969). However, there have been virtually no rigorous attempts to evaluate these instructional materials directly or to compare their effectiveness with other approaches to training that require substantial amounts of professional time.

THE READ PROJECT:
INSTRUCTIONAL MANUALS AND
SUPPLEMENTARY TRAINING FORMATS

Baker and his colleagues have recently developed a series of training manuals specifically tailored for parents and caretakers of developmentally disabled children (Baker, Brightman, Heifetz, & Murphy, 1976, 1977; Baker, Brightman, Carroll, Heifetz, & Hinshaw, 1978). Manuals focus upon three major areas, teaching self-help skills, developing receptive and expressive language, and managing behavior problems, with manuals in a given area corresponding to different levels of development. Each manual is constructed to be self-contained and includes sections on choosing a target skill or identifying a behavior problem, setting the stage for teaching sessions, behavioral principles, data-keeping procedures, and answers to questions frequently asked by parents. Each manual also contains "mini-case studies" highlighting central points in setting up and carrying out programs, many explanatory illustrations, and a large number of step-by-step program outlines. During the several stages of designing, developing, and testing the manuals, scores of parents served as testers and editorial consultants. Each of these developmental stages included elements of formative evaluation research. In addition, the final versions of the manuals were given a comprehensive, summative evaluation in one of the largest (160 families) parent training studies reported to date (Heifetz, 1977b). Because of the scope of this study, the extent to which its findings testify to latent ability of parents as teachers, and the issues it raises for further evolution of parent-professional collaborations, it will be described in some detail.

Participants in the Read Project were 160 families with a retarded child living at home. Children ranged from 3 to 14 years of age; 96% were receiving some form of ongoing schooling at the time of their participation in the study. Most of them were classified as organically retarded, with levels ranging from mild to severe; none met the usual criteria for cultural-familial retardation. The parents were quite heterogeneous in terms of educational background and annual income; families were evenly distributed over the entire middle-class range, with some participants from the upper and lower social strata as well. The 20-week training period emphasized the programming of self-help skills, but also provided an introduction to the teaching of language skills and the management of behavior problems, with opportunities for interested parents to begin programs in those areas. In order to test the manuals as a self-supporting resource and as part of three other training formats that provided increasing amounts of professional assistance, families were randomly assigned to the following experimental conditions:

MO (*M*anuals *O*nly) parents used the instructional manuals with their children but received no other form of training or professional assistance (cost per family, $38).[2]

MP (*M*anuals with *P*hone consultation) parents used the manuals and received telephone consultations every 2 weeks from a staff member ($77 per family).

MG (*M*anuals with *G*roup training) parents, while using the manuals, participated in 8-family training groups that met every 2 weeks with 2 staff members ($118 per family).

MGV (*M*anuals with *G*roup training and home *V*isits) parents, in addition to having all the elements of the *MG* condition, received a 1-hour, in-home consultation from a staff member between group meetings ($211 per family).

Control group parents were trained at the end of the experimental period, using an *MG* format.

Trainers in conditions *MP*, *MG*, and *MGV* had backgrounds in clinical psychology, special education, or nursing. All were familiar with the theory and practice of behavior modification and had previously worked with retarded children and their families. During the training period, other ongoing services to the children and parents in each condition proceeded uninterrupted. Thus, the four training formats were actually being tested for their *marginal effectiveness* over and above the preexisting services.

The outcome of the Read Project study was both encouraging and in some ways surprising. On the whole, the training formats were effective in fostering expertise in the mothers and gains in the children. Contrary to expectations, the *MO* condition was equal or marginally superior to the more expensive formats in these two areas, especially in comparison to the *MP* format. Conditions *MG* and *MGV*, however, did show some scattered evidence of the benefits of professional involvement in training.

On a written test of behavior modification principles, mothers in conditions *MO*, *MG*, and *MGV* showed significantly greater pre-/post- gains than mothers in the control group, with *MO* mothers showing the greatest gains of all. *MP* mothers, on the other hand,

---

[2]These costs were covered by the research grant. Parents, all of whom were volunteers solicited through media announcements and contact with various human service agencies, incurred no expense.

were not statistically different from the control mothers. For fathers, pre-/post- gains varied directly with the amount of professional involvement in their training format. *MGV* fathers significantly outgained control group fathers, and there was also a trend-level superiority of *MG* fathers over the controls. Fathers in the *MP* and *MO* conditions showed less improvement and, in fact, were not significantly different from the control fathers.

Children in each of the four training conditions (*MO, MP, MG,* and *MGV*) made significantly greater gains in self-help skills than did the control children. And the four training formats did not differ significantly on this overall measure of self-help improvement. A finer-grained analysis looked separately at *programmed* skills (those that the parents had specifically taught during the training period) and *unprogrammed* skills (those that had room for improvement but that the parents had not chosen to teach). The total gain in *programmed* self-help skills for the four training conditions equaled or surpassed the total gain in *all* self-help skills for the control group. Thus, even without professional assistance or training, parents' programming efforts had made a direct and demonstrable impact on their children's development.

The data on unprogrammed skills gave a reassuring answer to the question of *symptom substitution,* the possibility that gains in programmed skills would be offset by losses in unprogrammed skills. Each of the training conditions had a higher rate of improvement than the control group on unprogrammed skills, although for conditions *MP, MG,* and *MGV,* the rate was significantly higher. The *MO* format, however, did have a significantly higher rate, which indicated a significant *generalization effect* of self-help programming in addition to the specific effects shown by all the training conditions.[3]

On several other dimensions, the direct-contact conditions (*MG* and *MGV*) seemed to offer some real advantages. Parents had been encouraged to fill out one-page *teaching logs* for each day of formal teaching; families in the *MG* and *MGV* formats made log entries about 1/3 more frequently than families in the *MO* and *MP* formats. Similarly, the direct-contact families were almost twice as likely to begin programs in areas other than self-help skills (especially behavior problems) when those opportunities for diversification were offered in the latter part of the training period. Also, conditions *MG* and *MGV* fostered greater involvement by fathers, who averaged 70%

---

[3]With no consultants to offer specific suggestions, *MO* parents had to learn general principles from the manuals and then tailor them to their own situations. This generalized level of learning is most encouraging and might explain their children's improvement on skills not addressed in specific teaching sessions.

attendance at training group meetings and, as already noted, showed significant pre-/post- gains in knowledge of behavior modification. Finally, *MG* and *MGV* families, on a post-training attitude questionnaire, expressed greater confidence in their ability to teach new skills and manage behavior problems, particularly when compared to *MO* families. Each of these advantages of *MG* and *MGV* would seem to bode well for the extent and quality of future efforts at teaching their children.

PARENTS AS TEACHERS:
DEVELOPMENTAL CONSIDERATIONS
FOR PROFESSIONALS

The remarkable performance of the Read Project families makes a statement about the potential of parents as effective teachers that is too powerful to be ignored, even by the most skeptical of professionals. Nevertheless, there is a need for some caution in drawing generalizations from this study. As was shown, the image of parents as overwhelmed emotionally and reacting neurotically is far from universally valid. Still, the stresses upon parents are prevalent, their severity is undeniable, and parental coping strategies are often less than adaptive. Also, the Read Project parents were not very representative of the total population of parents of retarded children. Above all, they were a voluntary sample who had gone through several stages of self-selection before the project had even begun. They had shown an alertness to new resources, a willingness to undertake a nontraditional role toward professionals and toward their children, and the motivation and confidence to play that role effectively for five months, even in the absence of professional assistance. In a sense, then, they had already arrived at a stage of *maturational readiness* that enabled them to take advantage of the Read Project training formats.

Parents vary widely in their readiness to assume a proactive teaching role with their children. This variability reflects different levels of understanding of their children's condition and different stages of evolution in their attempts to define a role for themselves in relation to their children. There appears to be some regularity in the sequence of reactions and coping strategies displayed by parents (e.g., Farber & Ryckman, 1965; Rosen, 1969). Professionals should be aware of these sequences in order to design their resources, and the structure of the consumer-provider relationship, in accordance with a family's developmental stage and needs.

Drawing extensively on Farber's sociological model of the retarded child's impact upon his family, Wolfensberger and Menolascino have described an operational framework for professionals to use in managing a wide range of family problems and situations (Menolascino, 1968; Wolfensberger, 1967; Wolfensberger & Menolascino, 1970). Their framework identifies three major stages of parental reaction — *novelty-shock crisis, crisis of personal values,* and *reality crisis* —, outlines the set of management needs associated with each stage, and suggests a wide range of service strategies for meeting those needs, including many options not often employed by professionals.

Novelty shock accompanies the sudden awareness of the child's retardation. More important than the specifics of his/her condition is the general demolition of parental expectancies about the child and his/her future. The degree of novelty shock depends greatly upon the way in which the unexpected event is interpreted to and by the parents. What is needed here is a context of substantial emotional support in which to calmly and accurately convey facts and information about the child's condition. The uncertainty of detailed longitudinal predictions should be acknowledged, and realistically positive elements should be stressed. Contact with effectively coping "veteran" parents can be very helpful.

A crisis of personal values occurs when the presence of a retarded child violates some important elements in the parent's social, subcultural, or personal hierarchy of values. Descriptions of parents in value crisis are reminiscent of the psychoanalytic model of the neurotic parent, whose only solace is the distortion via defense mechanisms of an unacceptable reality. The crisis of personal values can be both long-term and recurrent. The most important need here, according to Wolfensberger and Menolascino (1970), is for *existential management* to resolve the conflict between parental values and the symbolic meaning of their child's retardation. This purpose may not be especially well served by traditional psychodynamic forms of therapy. As possible alternatives, they suggest forms of counseling that "are not oriented toward psychodynamics and unresolved childhood fixations but toward the meaning of life and its ultimate values" (p. 484).

Reality crises stem from the extraordinary day-to-day demands of raising and caring for the child; such crises are viewed for the most part as normal, understandable reactions to situational stress. The most relevant services here might include day-care placement; services of a visiting nurse or homemaker; training in behavioral approaches to teaching skills and managing behavior problems; special equipment to facilitate child care and promote development; and competent, persistent referral and advocacy to guide parents to these and other resources and insure that they obtain them.

To accompany their analysis of parental reactions and needs, the authors propose a general management strategy with three stages. In stage 1, the presence or absence of novelty shock is assessed. If present, the resources discussed above under novelty shock are provided. If absent, stage 2 comes into play, beginning with an assessment of the realistic, situational demands upon the family. Where these exist, the family should receive concrete, immediate resources that will alleviate some of the situational stress with minimal delay and will continue to reduce and even prevent similar stress. At this point, sufficient time should be allowed to pass for the stage 2 interventions to take effect. One by-product of relieving situational stress may be a reduction in the psychopathology caused or exacerbated by that stress. Stage 3 assesses the extent of value conflicts and the degree of *primary psychopathology*, problems stemming from other sources, but possibly aggravated by the presence of the child. Primary psychopathology can be managed with the same sort of therapy/counseling resources that would be appropriate for families without a retarded child. For value conflicts, the previously suggested existential management strategies should be invoked.

PROFESSIONAL AND SOCIAL NETWORKS: INFLUENCES ON PARENTAL HELPLESSNESS AND COPING

The major goal of any family management framework is to help parents adapt to the demands and stresses of raising a retarded child. Parents vary widely in their reactions to these stresses. A problem that is handled routinely by one family may require special effort from a second family and even overwhelm a third. Individuals differ innately in their susceptibility to stress, and this contributes to individual differences in patterns of coping with stress. Obviously, there is little a professional can do about a parent's innate level of physiological vulnerability. However, an individual's prior experience with stress will greatly determine how effectively s/he copes with a currently stressful situation. A professional who is attuned to a parent's history of stress and coping attempts will be in a better position to help the parent develop more effective coping skills. However, professionals should also be aware of the ways in which they may limit a parent's ability to cope by inadvertently shaping him/her into patterns of helplessness.

Seligman and others (summarized in Seligman, 1975) have shown the importance of a person's belief in his/her ability to predict or control the occurrence and duration of stressful events. When exposed to stresses that are unaffected by any of the person's actions, s/he may conclude that the stresses are beyond control. Repeated exposure to uncontrollable stress often produces a psychological state of *learned helplessness,* which has three major manifestations. There are various signs of emotional distress, including anxiety and depression. Motivation to act seems to be generally undermined, especially in subsequent exposures to similar stressful situations, where individuals make few attempts to deal with the sources of their stress. Finally, their ability to learn new coping skills seems to be attenuated. For example, when placed in situations in which the source of stress is in fact controllable, they are slow to learn that some of their responses are functionally related to the onset and offset of the stressful events.[4]

For parents of retarded children, there is no shortage of opportunities for learning helplessness. At the very outset, their need to find a clear-cut explanation for their child's retardation may be overwhelming, yet a specific cause will be found in only a tiny minority of cases. Another recurrent source of stress is contained within the final question of how to provide for the child's needs after the death of the parents. The frustrations associated with child-rearing tasks may reduce parenting to little more than day-to-day custodial care. After all, if most attempts at teaching self-care skills to the child have failed, it is understandable for parents to feel helpless and hopeless as teachers and to find a greater sense of efficacy as competent, caring custodians. Similarly, if the child's behavior problems rarely respond to parents' attempts at management, it may well be easier for them to become resignedly tolerant of the disruptions. In addition to these home-based sources of stress, parents face the frustrating search for effective educational, psychological, medical, and other professional services. And as frustration comes to outweigh endurance, their feelings of helplessness increase again.

Helplessness is not just haphazardly learned, it is also systematically taught. Unfortunately, our service network contains many effective instructors in helplessness, i.e., professionals who subscribe to outdated theories of the limited learning ability of retarded children; pediatricians who are unaware of remedial education programs for preschool-age children; and counselors who recommend the form of therapy that *they* are best equipped to provide, regardless of the *parents'* need for entirely different forms of assistance. In a sense, each of

---

[4]An individual's predisposition to learned helplessness appears to be related to the personality variable of "internal versus external locus of control" (reviewed in Lefcourt, 1976). "Internals" see themselves as having power over what happens to them, while "externals" have a fatalistic view of their lives being shaped by chance or other forces beyond their control. "Internals" are more likely to accept personal responsibility for their lives, while "externals" are more prone to fall into helplessness and hopelessness.

these professionals is passing on to parents his/her own piece of learned helplessness.

It is unrealistic to expect professionals to be entirely up-to-date in all the disciplines, theories, and practices involved in serving retarded children and their families. However, one professional's area of ignorance is another's area of competence. Hence, it would seem reasonable for individual members of the service network to be mutually informative and thereby complement one another's efforts at service delivery. But this sort of exchange does not happen regularly within human service networks, for several reasons (Sarason, 1976; Sarason, Carroll, Maton, Cohen, & Lorentz, 1977). Although the professional network contains an enormous number of potential relationships, the number of actual relationships is comparatively small. Network members drastically underestimate the possibilities of activating connections that are secondhand, thirdhand, or even more distant. They are only vaguely aware of the extent of their interconnections and are thus not very skilled at "networking." Professional preciousness exaggerates the problem, with members of one discipline often reluctant to seek consultation from members of another discipline, even within a single agency.

Preciousness not only undermines relationships among professionals, it also defines the parent-professional relationship in helplessness-inducing terms. Parents' potential for active, effective partnership in service delivery, which has been so extensively documented in the behavioral training literature, is denied, particularly by paradigms that routinely assume the existence of psychopathology in the parents. "The relationship between the 'ill' person and the 'healer' is structured so as to foster feelings of helplessness, passivity, and dependency on the part of the former, while generating inappropriate illusions of omnipotence on the 'healer's' part" (Roos, 1972, p. 139).

In their travels through the service network, it is virtually impossible for parents to avoid all the opportunities for learned helplessness. Even families as active and effective as the Read Project participants are not impervious. Consider, for example, the experience of families in the Manuals Only format. [To review briefly, parents were trained in behavioral approaches to child teaching and management under one of four different formats: *MO* (written *Manuals Only*); *MP* (*Manuals* with *Phone* consultation); *MG* (*Manuals* with *Group* training sessions); and *MGV* (*Manuals* with *Group* training and home *Visits*).] In terms of gains in children's self-help skills and mothers' knowledge of teaching principles the *MO* format was as effective as the other three despite their greater amounts of professional assistance. But in contrast with the objective evidence of their competence as teachers, *MO* mothers expressed significantly less confidence in their teaching ability than the other mothers. It was as though they could not truly perceive their own achievement without a professional expert's "seal of approval" confirming their success. Such a deeply ingrained or thoroughly conditioned attitude of dependence on professionals raised questions about the parents' ability to continue active, independent teaching at home.

These questions arose again in a 14-month follow-up study of the Read Project families (Baker, 1977). Mothers in each of the training conditions had basically maintained their knowledge of teaching principles; their children had retained the advances in skill development made during the Read Project and were making further progress. On the other hand, the regularity of planned, formal teaching sessions (emphasized in the manuals) had declined over the 14 months. There was, however, widespread incorporation of good teaching principles into the daily routine; over 60% of families were involved in some degree of skill-teaching and/or behavior-managing activities that appeared technically sound and beneficial. Among the four training formats, *MO* families showed somewhat less consistency and quality in their teaching and management; they also made the least continued use of the manuals. In short, while the positive effects of the Read Project were still very much in evidence more than a year later, the parents had to varying extents retreated from their advanced positions as consistent, precise, and effective teachers. And the *MO* families, as advanced as the others 14 months previously, had retreated the furthest. Although the 20 weeks of the Read Project had enabled these parents to play a nontraditional role competently, it had not made them comfortable enough in the role to play it indefinitely. There are few instant role reversals in a service delivery system whose most overlooked by-product is helplessness.

We would do well to reconsider the fundamental purpose and structure of the parent-professional relationship, with special attention to the accumulating data on (1) recently developed, highly effective techniques of remedial education that recognize the retarded child's behavior as a joint function of capacity and emotional/motivational factors; (2) parents' potential to undertake significant (albeit quite variable) responsibility for their child's developmental remediation; and (3) the myriad ways in which we conspire — bluntly or subtly, by intention or by accident — to ignore, to deny, and, ultimately, to annihilate that potential.

The professional service network is only one important contributor to parents' learned helplessness. Of comparable importance is the set of social networks in which parents are naturally embedded: nuclear families and larger kinship systems; neighbors, friends, and co-workers; and subcultures defined along ethnic, religious, political, or other lines. When a parent is cast in the unexpected role of care giver to a retarded child, it is only natural for this role to be significantly shaped and interpreted by these social networks. A parent's social networks might be able to counteract some of the damage wrought by an inept professional or exacerbate it, complement and enhance a professional's effectiveness or undermine it. Unfortunately, neither the positive nor the negative influences of parents' social networks are regularly noticed by professionals, who all too often restrict their attention to the small universe in which they and the affected family are the sole inhabitants. The clergy provide a prime example of the consequences of this neglect.

An estimated 42% of people seeking psychological assistance turn at some point to the clergy (Joint Commission on Mental Illness and Health, 1961). Pastoral counseling might be very helpful to parents experiencing novelty shock or existential crisis over their child's retardation. "The most basic values of many people are mediated to them by religion. Religion provides them with a rationale for living and an emotional as well as an intellectual framework wherein to explain events. Particularly during times of distress, individuals tend to seek solace and support in religion, even when they were not otherwise particularly devout" (Wolfensberger, 1967, p. 384). Yet despite the clergy's potential for critical and unique forms of family assistance (Hulme, 1974; Robertson, Maholick, & Shapiro, 1969), their actual participation is meager (Ames, 1971; Golden, 1962). Insight into this phenomenon is also meager, since the activities of the clergy in retardation are less well documented and researched than those of other service providers. Empirical studies are few and tend to focus on isolated parts of the clergy's involvement: referral patterns (Mannino, Rooney, & Hassler, 1967); attitudes about retardation (Peterson, 1970); role conflicts of clergy-as-counselors (Klausner, 1964); and, only rarely, actual patterns of clinical practice (Stubblefield, 1964).

A recent study (Heifetz & Franklin, 1978) explored the clergy's relationships to parents and retardation professionals in the provision of services. One phase of the study asked clergy to indicate the "appropriate division of responsibility" for various services. Of particular interest were the data on "religious teaching" activities (rated among the highest responsibilities for clergy and parents, but among the lowest for professionals) and "secular teaching" activities (rated among the highest responsibilities for professionals and parents, but among the lowest for clergy). It was encouraging to find the clergy giving so central a role to parents in their children's education. But it was troubling to find that they viewed themselves as irrelevant to secular education and the professionals as irrelevant to religious education.

Perhaps clergy could be trained as competent referral agents for parents in search of educational placements or other services outside the usual expertise of the clergy. Those clergy who occasionally made such referrals, however, reported a typical lack of feedback from the professional; they also mentioned the nearly total lack of referrals *to* clergy *from* professionals. At a more ambitious level, religious special education would seem to offer a natural arena for clergy-professional collaboration. This will require a clergy to realize that the specialist's education techniques are as applicable to a religious curriculum as they are to a secular one. Similarly, professionals interested in training parents should recognize that parents who are hesitant to adopt the teaching role may be much more responsive to a church/synagogue-based program oriented toward religious special education, especially if religious values are central to their life. In short, the collaborative potential of the clergy and professional networks is great, but it is seriously jeopardized by the mutual preciousness that currently separates them.

NORMALIZATION, ADVOCACY, AND PARENT TRAINING TOWARD A SYNTHESIS

In the last 10 years, the ideology of normalization has wrought a profound change in the evolutionary course of human services for the retarded (Wolfensberger, 1972). Nirje (1969) has expressed its operational guideline as "making available to the mentally retarded patterns and conditions of everyday life which are as close as possible to the norms and patterns of the mainstream of society" (p. 181). As a consciousness-raising philosophy, normalization has spurred the move toward deinstitutionalization, stimulated the political activities of parent organizations and other advocacy groups, and promoted more integrated forms of special education, culminating in the passage of Public Law 94-142 (the Education for All Handicapped Children Act).

Although normalization and behavior modification emerged in mental retardation services at about the same time, they have had minimal overlap, which is regrettable but not altogether surprising. In the realm of human services, normalization is strongly identified with humanism, while humanism and behaviorism are typically seen as antagonistic schools of thought. This "conflict" has become a classic example of two paradigms stereotypically exaggerating their differences and overlooking their vast potential for productive synthesis. Fortunately, there are signs of an embryonic rapprochement (e.g., *Humanism and Behaviorism: Dialogue and Growth*, Wandersman, Poppen, & Ricks, 1976). Roos (1972) has succinctly shown the conceptual compatibility of normalization and behavioral approaches to teaching and training. As a service ideology and a clinical technology, they are very well matched.

The Roos article focused on professional uses of behavior modification through 1970. In light of advances made in behavioral parent training since then, it is possible to extend his argument for behavioral approaches to normalization. As an example, one goal of parent training is to systematize the haphazard forms of strategies of selective reward that are a regular practice of child rearing, i.e., a normative process that can be used to develop more normative self-care, cognitive, and interpersonal skills. Equally important is the way in which behavioral training can help to normalize the parent's role. Well-trained parents can effectively reassume responsibility for many child-rearing tasks that would otherwise be abdicated to the professionals or simply neglected.

Behavioral training can also enhance the advocacy roles (Kurtz, 1975) of parents within the normalization movement. In the Read Project, for example, trained parents were significantly more confident than control group parents in their ability to evaluate the quality of their children's school services. Being trained as competent producers of services had apparently made them more discriminating as consumers. And this evaluative capacity should enable them to give or withhold their consent in a more truly "informed" manner.

Finally, it is important to realize the dangers that exist when parent-as-advocate means little more than parent-as-plaintiff. Such a model ignores the fact that the total supply of direct professional resources is hopelessly inadequate and that legislatively mandated equal access assures nothing more than egalitarian inadequacy. Such a model denies the potential of parents to become service providers who could help to close the demand-supply gap and also runs the risk of having parents put professionals into a defensive state of siege. The long-term negative consequences for normalization and educational mainstreaming should be obvious.

Instead, advocacy should be substantially directed toward the exploration, design, and critical evaluation of models of clinical collaboration between parents and professionals. Such models could greatly increase the magnitude and effectiveness of services, enhance parents' sense of efficacy as child rearers as well as service-network travelers, and forge between parents and professionals the psychological sense of community that is the unifying ethos of the normalization movement.

REFERENCES

Adams, H. B. "Mental illness" or interpersonal behavior? *American Psychologist*, 1964, *19*, 191-197.

Albee, G. W. *Mental health manpower needs*. New York: Basic, 1959.

Albee, G. W. The uncertain future of clinical psychology. *American Psychologist*, 1970, *25*, 1071-1080.

Ames, T. Ministering to the mentally handicapped and their families in the community. *Journal of Pastoral Counseling*, 1970-1971, *5*, 51-55.

Bachrach, A. J., & Quigley, W. A. Direct methods of treatment. In I. A. Berg & L. A. Pennington (Eds.), *An introduction to clinical psychology* (3rd. ed.). New York: Ronald, 1966.

Baker, B. L. Parent involvement in programming for the developmentally disabled child. In L. L. Lloyd (Ed.), *Communication assessment and intervention*. Baltimore: Univ Park, 1976.

Baker, B. L. Support systems for the parent as therapist. In P. M. Mittler (Ed.), *Research to practice in mental retardation* (Vol. 1) *Care and intervention*. Baltimore: Univ Park, 1977.

Baker, B. L., Brightman, A. J., Heifetz, L. J., & Murphy, D. M. *Steps to independence: A skills training series for children with special needs (Early self-help skills; Intermediate self-help skills; Advanced self-help skills; Behavior problems)*. Champaign, Illinois: Res Press, 1976.

Baker, B. L., Brightman, A. J., Heifetz, L. J., & Murphy, D. M. *Steps to independence: A skills training series for children with special needs (Toilet training)*. Champaign, Illinois: Res Press, 1977.

Baker, B. L., Brightman, A. J., Carroll, N. B., Heifetz, B. B., & Hinshaw, S. P. *Steps to independence: A skills training series for children with special needs (Speech and Language: Level 1; Speech and language: Level 2)*. Champaign, Illinois: Res Press, 1978.

Baker, B. L., Seltzer, G. B., & Seltzer, M. M. *As close as possible: A study of community residences for retarded adults*. Boston: Little, 1977.

Bandura, A. *Principles of behavior modification*. New York: HR&W, 1969.

Baum, M. H. Some dynamic factors affecting family adjustment to the handicapped child. *Exceptional Children*, 1962, *28*, 387-392.

Becker, W. C. *Parents are teachers*. Champaign, Illinois: Res Press, 1971.

Beddie, A., & Osmond, H. Mothers, mongols, and mores. *Canadian Medical Association Journal*, 1955, *73*, 167-170.

Begab, M. J. *The mentally retarded child: A guide to services of social agencies.* Washington, D.C.: U.S. Government Printing Office, 1963.

Begab, M. J. The mentally retarded and society: Trends and issues. In M. J. Begab & S. A. Richardson (Eds.), *The mentally retarded and society: A social science perspective.* Baltimore: Univ Park, 1975.

Berkowitz, B. P., & Graziano, A. M. Training parents as behavior therapists: A review. *Behavior Research and Therapy,* 1972, *10,* 297-310.

Bijou, S. W. A functional analysis of retarded development. In N. R. Ellis (Ed.), *International review of research in mental retardation.* New York: Acad Pr, 1966.

Blatt, B. *Exodus from pandemonium.* Boston: Allyn, 1970.

Blatt, B., & Kaplan, F. *Christmas in purgatory: A photographic essay on mental retardation.* Boston: Allyn, 1966.

Bourneville, D. *Recherches cliniques et thérapeutiques sur l'hystérie et l'idiotie.* Paris: Bureau du Progres Medical, 1893.

Bricker, W. A., & Bricker, D. D. The infant, toddler, and preschool research and intervention project. In T. D. Tjossem (Ed.), *Intervention strategies for high risk infants and young children.* Baltimore: Univ Park, 1976.

Cromwell, R. L. A methodological approach to personality research in mental retardation. *American Journal of Mental Deficiency,* 1959, *64,* 333-340.

Ellis, N. A behavioral research strategy in mental retardation. Defense and critique. *American Journal of Mental Deficiency,* 1969, *73,* 557-566.

Farber, B., & Ryckman, D. B. Effects of severely retarded children on family relationships. *Mental Retardation Abstracts,* 1965, *2,* 1-17.

Fernald, W. E. The burden of feeble-mindedness. *Journal of Psycho-asthenics,* 1912, *17,* 87-111.

Freeman, R. D. Drug effects on learning in children: A selective review of the past thirty years. *Journal of Special Education,* 1966, *1,* 17-44.

Feuerstein, R., & Karasilowsky, D. Interventional strategies for the significant modification of cognitive functioning in the disadvantaged adolescent. *Journal of the American Academy of Child Psychiatry,* 1972, *11,* 572-582.

Gardner, W. I. Use of behavior therapy with the mentally retarded. In F. J. Menolascino (Ed.). *Psychiatric approaches to mental retardation.* New York: Basic, 1970.

Ginzberg, E., & Bray, D. W. *The uneducated.* New York: Columbia U Pr, 1953.

Goddard, H. H. Heredity of feeble-mindedness. *Journal of Psycho-asthenics,* 1909-1910, 48-54.

Goddard, H. H. & Hill, H. F. Delinquent girls tested by the Binet Scale. *Training School Bulletin,* 1911, *8,* 50-56.

Golden, E. S. Mental retardation: The church's neglect and challenge. *Pastoral Psychology,* 1962, *13,* 6-11.

Greenfeld, J. *A child called Noah.* New York: HR&W, 1970.

Guerney, B. G. (Ed.). *Psychotherapeutic agents: New roles for nonpro-*

fessionals, parents, and teachers. New York: HR&W, 1969.

Hayden, A. H. A center-based parent training model. In J. Crim (Ed.), *Training parents to teach: Four models. First chance for children* (Vol. 3). Chapel Hill, North Carolina: Technical Assistance Development Systems, 1974.

Heifetz, L. J. Professional preciousness and the evolution of parent-training strategies. In P. M. Mittler (Ed.), *Research to practice in mental retardation* (Vol. 1) *Care and intervention.* Baltimore: Univ Park, 1977. (a)

Heifetz, L. J. Behavioral training for parents of retarded children: Alternative formats based on instructional manuals. *American Journal of Mental Deficiency,* 1977, *82,* 194-203. (b)

Heifetz, L. J., & Farber, B. A. Modifying classroom behavior. *New York University Education Quarterly,* 1976, *7*(4), 21-29.

Heifetz, L. J., & Franklin, D. C. *Pastoral functions in service delivery: A study of role definition.* Paper presented at the Eighty-Sixth Annual Convention of the American Psychological Association, Toronto, 1978.

Hobbs, N. H. Mental health's third revolution. *American Journal of Orthopsychiatry,* 1964, *5,* 822-833.

Hollingshead, A. B., & Redlich, F. C. *Social class and mental illness: A community study.* New York: Wiley, 1958.

House, B. J., & Zeaman, D. Transfer of a discrimination from objects to patterns. *Journal of Experimental Psychology,* 1960, *59,* 298-302.

Howe, S. G. *Training and teaching idiots.* A report to the Governor of Massachusetts. Published as Senate No. 38, February 1850.

Hulme, T. Mental health consultation with religious leaders. *Journal of Religion and Health,* 1974, *13,* 114-127.

Itard, J. M. G. [*The wild boy of Aveyron*] (G. Humphrey & M. Humphrey, trans.). New York: ACC, 1932.

Joint Commission on Mental Illness and Health, Final Report. *Action for mental health.* New York, Basic, 1961.

Kass, N., & Stevenson, H. W. The effect of pretraining reinforcement conditions on learning by normal and retarded children. *American Journal of Mental Deficiency,* 1961, *66,* 76-80.

Kazdin, A. E. Issues in behavior modification with mentally retarded persons. *American Journal of Mental Deficiency,* 1973, *78,* 134-140.

Klausner, S. *Religion and psychiatry.* Glencoe, Illinois: Free Press of Glencoe, 1964.

Kugel, R. B., & Wolfensberger, W. (Eds.). *Changing patterns in residential services for the mentally retarded.* Washington, D.C.: President's Committee on Mental Retardation, 1969.

Kuhlman, F. The Binet and Simon tests of intelligence in grading feeble-minded children. *Journal of Psycho-asthenics,* 1912, *16,* 173-193.

Kuhn, T. S. *The structure of scientific revolutions.* Chicago: U of Chicago Pr, 1970.

Kurtz, R. A. Advocacy for the mentally retarded: The development of a new social role. In M. J. Begab & S. A. Richardson (Eds.), *The mentally retarded and society: A social science perspective.* Baltimore: Univ Park, 1975.

Kysar, J. The two camps in child psychiatry: A report from a psychiatrist-father of an autistic and retarded child. *American Journal of Psychiatry*, 1968, *125*, 103-109.

Lefcourt, H. M. *Locus of control.* Hillsdale, New Jersey: Erlbaum Associates, 1976.

Lindsley, O. R. An experiment with parents handling behavior at home. *Johnstone Bulletin*, 1966, *9*, 27-36.

Louttit, R. T. Chemical facilitation of intelligence among the mentally retarded. *American Journal of Mental Deficiency*, 1965, *69*, 495-501.

Mackinnon, M. C., & Frederick, B. S. A shift of emphasis for psychiatric social work in mental retardation. In F. J. Menolascino (Ed.), *Psychiatric approaches to mental retardation.* New York: Basic, 1970.

Mannino, F., Rooney, H., & Hassler, F. A survey of clergy referrals to a mental health clinic. *Journal of Religion and Health*, 1967, *6*, 66-73.

Matheny, A. P., & Vernick, J. Parents of the mentally retarded child: Emotionally overwhelmed or informationally deprived? *Journal of Pediatrics*, 1968, *74*, 953-959.

McCord, C. P. One hundred female offenders. *Journal of Criminal Law and Criminology*, 1915, *74*, 953-959.

McDonald, E. T. *Understand those feelings.* Pittsburgh: Stanwix, 1962.

Menolascino, F. J. Parents of the mentally retarded: An operational approach to diagnosis and management. *Journal of the American Academy of Child Psychiatry*, 1968, *7*, 589-602.

Menolascino, F. J. Psychiatry's past, current and future role in mental retardation. In F. J. Menolascino (Ed.), *Psychiatric approaches to mental retardation.* New York: Basic, 1970.

Milgram, N. The rational and irrational in Zigler's motivational approach to mental retardation. *American Journal of Mental Deficiency*, 1969, *73*, 527-532.

Mittler, P. M. (Ed.), *Research to practice in mental retardation* (3 Vols.). Proceedings of the Fourth Congress of the International Association for the Scientific Study of Mental Deficiency. Baltimore: Univ Park, 1977.

Nirje, B. The normalization principle and its human management implications. In R. Kugel & W. Wolfensberger (Eds.), *Changing patterns in residential services for the mentally retarded.* Washington, D.C.: President's Committee on Mental Retardation, 1969.

Nolan, J. D., & Pence, C. Operant conditioning principles in the treatment of a selectively mute child. *Journal of Consulting and Clinical Psychology*, 1970, *35*, 265-268.

O'Dell, S. Training parents in behavior modification: A review. *Psychological Bulletin*, 1974, *81*, 418-433.

Olshansky, S. Parent responses to a mentally defective child. *Mental Retardation*, 1966, *4*(4), 21-23.

Opler, M. K. (Ed.). *Culture and mental health*. New York: Macmillan, 1959.

Pascal, C. E. Application of behavior modification by parents for treatment of a brain damaged child. In B. A. Ashem & E. G. Poser (Eds.), *Adaptive learning: Behavior modification with children*. Elmsford, New York: Pergamon, 1973.

Patterson, G. R., & Gullion, M. E. *Living with children*. Champaign, Illinois: Res Press, 1968.

Patterson, L. L. Some pointers for professionals. *Children*, 1956, *3*, 13-17.

Perske, R. The pastoral care and counseling of families of the mentally retarded. *Pastoral Psychology*, 1968, *19*, 21-28.

Peterson, D. More than knowing: Clergymen: Their attitudes toward and knowledge of the mentally retarded. *Mental Retardation*, 1970, *8*, 24-26.

Pintner, R. *Intelligence testing*. New York: Holt, 1923.

President's Panel on Mental Retardation. A proposed program for national action to combat mental retardation. Washington, D.C.: U.S. Government Printing Office, 1962.

Reed, S. C. *Counseling in medical genetics* (2nd. ed.). Philadelphia: Saunders, 1963.

Robertson, R., Maholick, L., & Shapiro, D. The parish minister as counselor: A dilemma and challenge. *Pastoral Psychology*, 1969, *20*, 24-30.

Robinson, N. M., & Robinson, H. B. *The mentally retarded child*. (2nd. ed.) New York: McGraw, 1976.

Roos, P. Reconciling behavior modification procedures with the normalization principle. In W. Wolfensberger (Ed.), *The Principle of normalization in human services*. Toronto: National Institute on Mental Retardation, 1972.

Rosen, L. Selected aspects in the development of the mother's understanding of her mentally retarded child. *Mental Retardation*, 1969, *7*(5), 52-55.

Rosen, M., Clark, G. R., & Kivitz, M. S. (Eds.). *The history of mental retardation*. Baltimore: Univ Park, 1976.

Salzinger, K., Feldman, R. S., & Portnoy, S. Training parents of brain-injured children in the use of operant conditioning procedures. *Behavior Therapy*, 1970, *1*, 4-32.

Sarason, S. B. *The creation of settings and the future societies*. San Francisco: Jossey-Bass, 1972.

Sarason, S. B. Community psychology, networks, and Mr. Everyman. *American Psychologist*, 1976, *31*, 317-328.

Sarason, S. B., Carroll, C., Maton, K., Cohen, S., & Lorentz, E. *Human services and resource networks*. San Francisco: Jossey-Bass, 1977.

Sarason, S. B., & Doris, J. *Psychological problems in mental deficiency* (4th ed.). New York: Har-Row, 1969.

Schild, S. Counseling with parents of retarded children living at home. *Social Work*, 1964, *9*, 86-91.

Schopler, E., & Reichler, R. J. Parents as co-therapists in the treatment of psychotic children. *Journal of Autism and Childhood Schizophrenia*, 1971, *1*, 87-102.

Seguin, E. *The moral treatment, hygiene and education of idiots and other backward children.* New York: Columbia U Pr, 1846.

Seligman, M. E. P. *Helplessness.* San Francisco: Freeman, 1975.

Shearer, M. S. A home based parent training model. In J. Crim (Ed.), *Training parents to teach: Four models. First chance for children* (Vol. 3). Chapel Hill, North Carolina: Technical Assistance Development Systems, 1974.

Simeonsson, R. J. & Wiegerink. R. Early language intervention: A contingent stimulation model. *Mental Retardation,* 1974, *12*(2), 7-11.

Skinner, B. F. Operant behavior. In W. K. Honig (Ed.), *Operant behavior: Areas of research and application.* New York: ACC, 1966.

Sobey, F. S. *The nonprofessional revolution in mental health.* New York: Columbia U Pr, 1970.

Solnit, A. J., & Stark, M. H. Mourning and the birth of a defective child. *Psychoanalytic Studies of the Child,* 1961, *16*, 523-537.

Stevenson, H. W., & Zigler, E. F. Probability learning in children. *Journal of Experimental Psychology,* 1958, *56*, 185-192.

Stubblefield, H. The ministry and mental retardation. *Journal of Religion and Health,* 1964, *15*, 13-23.

Szasz, T. S. *The manufacture of madness.* New York: Har-Row, 1970.

Terdal, L., & Buell, J. Parent education in managing retarded children with behavior deficits and inappropriate behaviors. *Mental Retardation,* 1969, *7*(3), 10-13.

Terman, L. M. *The measurement of intelligence.* Boston: HM, 1916.

Tharp, R. G., & Wetzel, R. J. *Behavior modification in the natural environment.* New York: Acad Pr, 1969.

Turnure, J., & Zigler, E. Outer-directedness in the problem solving of normal and retarded children. *Journal of Abnormal and Social Psychology,* 1964, *69*, 427-436.

Vallet, R. E. *Modifying children's behavior.* Palo Alto, California: Fearon, 1969.

Wandersman, A., Poppen, P., & Ricks, D. *Humanism and behaviorism: Dialogue and growth.* New York: Pergamon, 1976.

Windle, C. Prognosis of mental subnormals. *American Journal of Mental Deficiency,* 1962, *66*. (Monograph supplement)

Wolfensberger, W. Counseling the parents of the retarded. In A. A. Baumeister (Ed.), *Mental retardation: Appraisal, education, and rehabilitation.* Chicago: Aldine, 1967.

Wolfensberger, W. *The principle of normalization in human services.* Toronto: National Institute on Mental Retardation, 1972.

Wolfensberger, W., & Menolascino, F. J. A theoretical framework for the management of parents of the mentally retarded. In F. J. Menolascino (Ed.), *Psychiatric approaches to mental retardation.* New York: Basic, 1970.

Zigler, E. Familial mental retardation: A continuing dilemma. *Science,* January 20, 1967, *155*, 292-298.

Zigler, E. Developmental versus defect theories of mental retardation and the problem of motivation. *American Journal of Mental Deficiency*, 1969, *73*, 536-555.

Zigler, E. Motivational aspects of mental retardation. In R. Koch & J. C. Dobson (Eds.), *The mentally retarded child and his family.* New York: Brunner Mazel, 1971.

Zigler, E., & Balla, D. The social policy implications of a research program on the effects of institutionalization on retarded persons. In Mittler, P. M. (Ed.), *Research to practice in mental retardation* (Vol. 1) *Care and intervention.* Baltimore: Univ Park, 1977.

Zigler, E., & DeLabry, J. Concept-switching in middle-class, lower-class, and retarded children. *Journal of Abnormal and Social Psychology*, 1962, *65*, 267-273.

Zilboorg, G., & Henry, G. W. *A history of medical psychology.* New York: Norton, 1941.

Chapter 15

WORKING WITH PARENTS OF PRESCHOOL CHILDREN

ALICE STERLING HONIG

IT is refreshing to note that a proliferation of programs, both at federal and community levels, during the past decade,
makes possible a current survey of the wide variety of ways in which
parents have been and can be involved in the education and optimal
rearing of their preschool children. Our country during these years
has seen much "consciousness raising" concerning the importance of
parents in the education of their children and the rearing of competent, likeable, successful human beings. It is an ironic twist of history
that 200 years ago, during the Puritan period, Americans were also
very "conscious" of how crucial a parent's role was — in breaking the
"will" of a young child or for punishing any "evil" tendencies a child
might exhibit!

Once, parents were politely and not so politely shunted aside by
professional early childhood educators from any involvement with a
young child's early schooling or learning. Now, parents are regarded
as positive partners to be enlisted by preschools and other community
programs to enhance family development and enrich a child's
learning career.

A Historical Look at the New
Perspectives on Parenting

What is the history of this change in perspective with regard to the
importance of parent involvement? Prior to 1960, most nursery
schools typically enrolled middle-class children. In the early 1960s,
several pioneer education programs were developed, designed particularly for preschool children from low-income families. Head Start is
perhaps the most famous of such programs. Many educators involved
in these early projects tried to think through the ways in which traditional nursery school values and practices might or might not be
appropriate with young children from low-income homes.

During that period, project personnel were trying to create curricula for babies, toddlers, and older preschoolers. In addition, they

were busy training care givers to understand and apply theories such as those of Piaget and Erikson to their programs. Many were so busy creating curricula and training care givers that not enough attention was paid to the importance of parent participation for supporting any gains the children might make while in the program. Without such parental sustenance, many programs found their initial score gains were "washed out" several years after children graduated from programs.

Times have changed. Today, for any federally funded program, a parent involvement component is essential. Federal interagency day care guidelines (1968) mandate that parents must have the opportunity to partake in making decisions concerning the operation of and selection of staff for a program. Much has been learned about the process of parenting and the outcomes of different styles of parenting that increases awareness of the important and profound influence of parents as educators of their young children. For those who want to work successfully with parents, a knowledge of parental values, beliefs, and habits is as important as it is for any anthropologist seeking to understand the socialization patterns of child rearing and associated cultural customs that characterized adult citizens of any specially studied society. Thus, we shall look first at a review of research as it illuminates the relation of parenting practices to child outcomes for preschoolers. Second, we shall examine a variety of program models and types, narrowly or broadly based, that have systematically or peripherally tried to involve parents in enhancing living and learning experiences for their young children. Third, we shall look in more specific detail at a particular parent involvement program, the Family Development Research Program, that offered comprehensive services to families in Syracuse, New York. Finally, we shall offer suggestions to parent involvement personnel. What has worked? What aspects and conditions must one be sensitive to in working with groups of parents or individual parents of preschoolers? How can difficulties be overcome in implementation of program goals in training parent educators or in sustaining the initial motivation of parent educators once problems arise? How can the parent involver "match" his/her offerings within the program to the special needs of each family served? What creative ideas have different projects found to encourage parental participation?

RESEARCH EVIDENCE FOR THE IMPORTANCE OF PARENTING

In 1951, Milner interviewed mothers and children and found that children who achieved higher language scores on the California Test of Mental Maturity were read to more often, had more mealtime conversations with parents, and received less harsh physical punishment than children who were not doing as well. The higher-scoring children came from predominantly middle-class homes. That is, their families made a fairly good living, could afford to buy toys and books, and could take their children places and feed them well. Such research differences, when replicated, led Strodtbeck (1965) to refer to the *hidden curriculum* of the middle-class home. Laosa (1977) studied Mexican American mothers teaching their children. Mothers with twelfth-grade educations employed a teaching strategy characterized by fewer commands and more frequent questions. They were less likely than mothers with sixth-grade educations to do the task for their young children. Thus, we became aware that children come into schools and day-care centers with very different interactional and instructional histories with parents. But finding that socioeconomic or educational differences are related to children's school performance is not particularly useful. *Status* variables such as parental income or education level may be difficult to change. *Process* variables such as the kinds of family interactions with preschoolers that encourage children's developmental achievements and social skills with peers and adults have been found to be far more important predictors of later child functioning. Schaeffer (1972) reviewed a variety of longitudinal and cross-sectional studies of parenting and concluded that family process was more highly related to intelligence and achievement than were social class or school quality variables.

Indeed, Ainsworth, Bell, and Stayton (1972) suggest that mothers who raise children in low-income families but have babies doing well on developmental tasks at 1 year have had close, loving, responsive relationships with their infants. These mothers have given appropriate prompt attention to infant needs and "floor freedom" for babies to explore their environment. Secure attachment of baby and mother seems to provide "insurance" that a baby will do well developmentally.

Klaus and Kennell (1976) have focused research efforts on the long-range social and intellectual effects of early synchronous, mutually satisfying mother-infant interactions. In their many studies, mothers and babies who "bond" well show long-range differences in interaction patterns. Such mothers use more positive language later in talking with their toddlers. They give fewer commands. If babies are born prematurely, the findings are that early maternal contact and close bonding will eventuate in more normal IQ scores by 4 years of age than are attained by premature babies whose mothers did not have enriched early contact and opportunities for early bonding.

Child competence seems to occur more certainly where the care giver and baby are able to participate in mutually positive interaction games. Cohen (1977) videotaped preterm infants in interactional tasks with their mothers. The tasks involved dramatic ball play, book reading, putting on mittens, and making block designs. Competence in the 2-year-olds studied was measured by the Gesell Developmental Schedules, a receptive language test, and by the Bayley Mental Scale. When the mothers and toddlers functioned well together in eliciting positive behaviors from each other, competence was found to be superior, despite the fact that each of these children had been born prematurely.

Beckwith's findings (1972) with adopted infants at 1 year of age are similar. Mothers who gave their babies fewer restrictions and lots of talking, loving interactions had infants who did better on the Cattell Infant Intelligence Scales at 1 year.

Why is mutual interaction pattern between infants and parents so important? Maternal responsiveness to signals fosters the development of the child's *communication* skills. The child develops increasing surety and confidence in his/her ability to have needs met. S/he can then use energies for exploring, for learning about how the world works, and for becoming competent. S/he feels efficacious: if s/he cries, somebody comes. The world is an orderly place; people are trustable.

Sroufe (1977) views early positive attachment as an asset in helping the preschooler pursue constructive social and exploratory goals. He describes recent work by Matas, who classified 50 infants as to the quality of their attachment with their mothers at 1 year. When tested at 2 years of age, children not securely attached 1 year earlier performed more poorly on tool-using problems and tasks. Well-attached babies showed more persistence in trying to solve these toddler tasks. Well-attached babies were less easily frustrated and were able to use the adult as a source of help. Less well-attached babies gave up easier, threw temper tantrums, and were less able to use the parent for assistance. Thus, the importance of early positive attachments between parent and child may have long-range significance for later problem-solving skills. Such research has significant lessons for those who are parent involvers.

The importance of a close, warm, affectionate relationship between parents and child has been shown in other studies of older preschoolers who are high achievers. Loving relationships and successful learning are closely intertwined in the early years.

Positive Parenting and Child Competence

Carew, Chan, and Halfar (1976) observed parents and children in their homes during the first years of life as families went about their daily activities. They were able to document the kinds of parenting interactions that produced more-competent and less-competent children by 3 years of age. The critical variables were not socioeconomic status nor ethnicity nor religion. Parenting style turned out to be critically related to competence outcome in the preschoolers.

Honig (1978) has summarized Carew et al.'s findings regarding the parenting environment that supports competence.

1. When children were the most competent, the mother turned out to be a good organizer and arranger and shaper of the child's experiences and routines.
2. Homes of competent preschoolers had toys that were typical of a nursery school — crayons and papers and scissors and such.
3. Competent children were allowed to help a lot with household chores — dusting, hammering, raking leaves, helping to sort laundry.
4. Fathers in the families of the competent preschoolers spent more positive interaction time with their children. All the families were two-parent families, incidentally.
5. Competent children were allowed access to what we would call more messy and perhaps even slightly dangerous items. There were blunt scissors in the homes of these children. Parents allowed their toddlers to help with washing up dishes, even though a puddle might have to be sponged up from the kitchen floor. Indeed, there is no one more enthusiastic at helping wash dishes than a 2-year-old. Have you ever watched a "two" wash dishes with soapsuds up to his shoulders!
6. Regular *reading* to children daily. There is so much research now that confirms the importance of early regular reading for later cognitive competence. Reading (with expression, interest, change of voice tone, and conversing about the story) correlated with later intellectual achievements.
7. TV differences. In the most competent children's homes, TV was *severely* limited and supervised. The children could watch 1 hour of a program such as "Sesame Street." In the least competent infants' homes, children watched 6 hours a day if they wanted, and viewed any program.

8. Mothers of competent children *modeled* appropriate activities for the children. If the parents wanted a child to do something, they showed him/her how.

9. The mother was a good *observer*. She kept an eye out to see where the child was developmentally, what the child was doing, and in which part of the house. The mother gauged her responses and activities according to her observations of the child's interests, abilities, and temperament.

10. The mother praised, encouraged, suggested, permitted, and facilitated — she was a facilitator. Where the mother was highly restrictive and punitive, the child's competence was severely damaged. The children from such families were in the least competent group. Mothers of competent infants often *participated* with the child during activities.

11. Competent children's parents had firm, consistent household rules. They provided reasons for their rules.

12. The mothers of competent preschoolers behaved as *teachers*. The mothers conversed, posed questions, transmitted information, and helped their children to solve problems. They helped their children to understand what they didn't understand. If you remember, Smilansky (1968) in her classic study of sociodramatic role play differences among advantaged and disadvantaged children observed that few low-income parents see themselves as teachers. And of course, parents are the most precious teachers of all.

13. The mother as dramatizer. Mothers of competent preschoolers engaged in dramatic play. For example, one day the researcher arrived and found mother with her 16-month-old in the kitchen. Both had toy badminton rackets in their hands and were playing pretend badminton. Did you ever play fantasy tea parties with young children? Did you ever see your little one hiding in your closet among your clothes and say, "Where's Joan? I've lost Joan! What will Daddy say when he comes home? Where can Joan be?" All the while Joan, in full visibility in the closet, is entranced with joy at this pretend game. Role-playing games help promote cognitive competence. Other games and entertainments of these parents often had intellectual content. Entertainment by parents of less competent infants often involved just physical, rough and tumble play. (pp. 19-21)

In a study of positive parenting, Swan and Stavros (1973) interviewed the parents of 5- and 6-year-old children. These 40 children, from black low-income families, were doing exceptionally well in the Title I classrooms of their New Orleans Elementary schools. The children were not afraid to try new games and activities. They worked independently and used information from teachers and peers. Teachers reported that the children asked meaningful and appropriate questions and enjoyed learning and skill mastery for their own satisfaction rather than to please someone or get external rewards. The parents of these successful, self-confident, and socially poised children reported a philosophy of child rearing that encouraged independence for the children and understanding and respecting the child's feelings and point of view. The parents expressed feelings of competence at raising their children. Most of the parents read and discussed stories with their children and expressed great interest in what their children were doing. Fathers and mothers in these predominantly two-parent families involved their children in meaningful chores at home. The parents saw their children in a very competent and positive light and talked a great deal with their children.

Bradley and Caldwell (1976) found that "maternal involvement with child," "provision of appropriate play materials," and "emotional and verbal responsivity of the mother," which were measured when children were 2 years old, correlated highly with Stanford Binet IQ scores at 54 months.

Such studies throw light on some of the specific parent behaviors, expectancies, attitudes, interactional patterns, and attachments that foster optimal development in preschoolers.

PARENTING PROGRAM MODELS

Partly in response to research findings about parent needs, and certainly in response to a basic belief in the indispensability of positive parental involvement for helping a child to grow well, a variety of program models and services have been developed (Honig, 1975).

Parent Group Meetings

One of the best-known methods of involving parents in the education of their children is to invite them to parent group meetings, usually at the school the child attends. At the elementary school level, the PTA has a long history.

Programs that involve parents of preschoolers in groups have sometimes opted for cognitive emphasis — teaching mothers how to improve children's language skills, for example. Other parent groups have focused on topics such as increasing parental self-awareness, knowledge of ways to motivate children, expression of parental needs, home management skills, making and learning to use inexpensive home learning materials, increasing self-esteem in the family, and helping parents acquire job skills.

Toy Lending and Demonstrating

One of the most widely used models for helping parents use toys to teach their children was created by Nimnicht and his colleagues (Nimnicht, Brown, Addison, & Johnson, 1971) at the Far West Parent/Child Toy Library Program. Parents are involved in eight 2-hour sessions, usually meeting once a week. Child development topics are discussed, and a new toy is introduced at each meeting. The toy as a means to boost children's problem-solving skills is demonstrated, discussed, and illustrated in films. Parents at the group meeting role-play with each other the many ways they could use a toy to promote thinking and problem solving. They use these ideas later at home with the toy to help the child make discoveries and increase his skills.

Stevens (1973) has reported that an 11-week program of small group parent meetings that included toy/book demonstration and lending produced significant IQ gains for children of project participants. He suggests that the parent consultants would have been even more effective had they provided feedback to a parent during his/her interaction with a child in the home.

Improving Children's Language Skills

Working with Mexican American mothers in an Arizona Follow-Through program, Garcia (1972) modeled techniques whereby the mothers could help their young children ask more questions, particularly during storybook time. Mothers role-played with each other. They learned to use cueing techniques, to use contingent praise to reward a child's questions, and to use hand counters to record the numbers of questions asked by their children. Later, the mothers were asked to reward causal questions particularly. Many mothers became aware of the potential importance of a young child's talking and asking questions through the program. Similar success has been found with Papago Indian mothers and children (Henderson, 1974).

One parent group meeting plan to help parents encourage language development from infancy through the preschool years is called *Teach Your Child to Talk* (Pushaw, 1969). Parent workshops are carefully programmed with slides, cassette-illustrated vocalization examples, and written materials for workshop leaders.

Programs for Teenage Mothers

Badger (1977) has provided charismatic leadership and innovative programming by bringing groups of low-income teenage mothers to group meetings in a hospital setting during evenings, when the teenagers are not at jobs or continuing their schooling. Her program offers a wide variety of information and skills at levels that these very young mothers can understand. Demonstrations of infant competencies, talks on good nutrition and infant care, and encouragement of affectionate mother-infant contact are among the activities. Badger's own enthusiasm for positive parenting practices is a major ingredient in encouraging some of these young mothers to become involved in more appropriate feeding, cuddling, and stimulation techniques with their babies.

The Girl Scouts of America and other groups have begun to provide handbooks and training materials to assist group leaders in involving young parents, particularly in fostering the education of their youngsters. The National Federation of Settlements and Neighborhood Centers has a recommended "How To" program guide (1976) for a curriculum to provide low-income youth with an opportunity to explore a variety of adult roles related to family life and to acquire problem-solving skills and knowledge necessary to function effectively in those roles. Such curricula for adolescent parenting groups have become even more crucial in light of current United States statistics that 1 of every 5 babies is being born to a teenage parent.

Exploring Childhood

This program, originally developed for junior and senior high school students, is a multimedia model that is useful in work with parent groups. The program provides learning concentrated on three modules: working with children, seeing development, and family and society. Parents, with an appropriately trained group leader, can not only learn more about their children's development, but also gain insight into themselves as people who are learners too. Program emphasis on the development of observation skills and the keeping of a journal help to increase parental awareness of how children grow and learn in families and a variety of learning situations.

Parent Effectiveness Training (P.E.T.)

Perhaps the most popular and widespread program for involving parents in groups to help them understand and deal better with their children is the Parent Effectiveness Training system, P.E.T., developed by Dr. Thomas Gordon (1976). Several very important principles are taught to parents, who participate in a series of weekly classes. P.E.T. techniques are designed to help parents discard their usually unsatisfactory ways of handling conflicts with children and develop more effective "no-lose" conflict-resolution methods. P.E.T. instructors teach parents to stop sending ineffective "You-messages" (such as "You've made a real mess in my living room!") and learn to send "I-messages" (such as "I feel real upset when my living room looks messy and I am afraid company may drop in.") when the behavior of a child interferes with the parents' lives. Dr. Gordon teaches that the most effective message for motivating children to change behavior that bothers parents is a simple sharing of how their behavior makes the parent feel and how it affects the parent's life. P.E.T. advocates "active listening" on the principle that when children encounter difficulties and want to share their troubles, they need parents to listen, not to talk or preach at them. You-messages can be sent that assure the child that his feelings count, that the parent really cares. For example, if Joey comes home from playing outside and kicks at the front door and looks very grumpy, the parent participating in a P.E.T. group learns to say something like, "It sure looks like you had a tough time today. Looks as if maybe you had some troubles out there."

Systematic Training for Effective Parenting (STEP)

Materials are provided by Dinkmeyer and McKay (1976) for nine parent group sessions. Group discussion centered around playlets presented via audiotape by the group facilitator covers the following topics during nine parent training sessions:

1. Understanding the goals of children's behavior and the goals of misbehavior
2. Understanding how children use emotions to involve parents
3. Encouragement
4. Communication: Listening
5. Communication: Exploring alternatives and expressing your ideas and feelings to children
6. Developing responsibility

7. Decision making for parents
8. The family meeting
9. Developing confidence

STEP proponents feel that the group process helps parents provide support and encouragement for each other. The handbooks, posters, audiotapes, and charts come in a large carrying case easy to transport.

Avoiding the pitfalls of either permissive or authoritarian parenting is difficult for some parents. Baumrind's research (1971) has shown that loving yet authoritative parents, who are consistent and firm in discipline, have preschoolers who are more self-reliant, secure, and effective children. Some of the "packaged" programs described above attempt to teach parents specific techniques for meeting their own needs as adults and solving their problems in more satisfactory ways with their children.

Interpersonal Cognitive Problem Solving (ICPS)

Shure and Spivack (1978) have taken a problem-solving approach to training low-income parents to teach their own children to generate solutions to interpersonal problems and to foresee consequences of their own behaviors in such a way that the children can make better adjustments. The authors describe their findings to date:

> We learned that after only three months' time, overly impulsive children in normal inner-city preschools and kindergartens displayed less impatience, overemotion, and aggression. Overly inhibited children became more socially outgoing, became better liked by their peers, and showed more awareness of others' feelings ... To date, the most powerful ICPS mediator in young children appears to be the ability to conceptualize multiple solutions to interpersonal problems and, secondarily, the ability to anticipate the consequences of acts. (pp. 7-8)

These findings among trained preschoolers continued to hold up in comparison to control children 1 year later. The authors report that in their work with mothers and their preschool children, those mothers who consistently applied problem-solving techniques when actual problems came up had children who most improved in ICPS thinking skills and subsequent behavioral adjustment. The kinds of dialogues and scripts that are taught, of course, require that parents acquire new thinking skills of their own. "Training parents to think through solutions to interpersonal problems and to anticipate the consequences of acts helps them appreciate the very thinking process they in turn learn to transmit to their children" (p. 38).

Building Children's Self-Esteem

Washington (1977) has developed a systematic program, SUCCESS, designed to help urban parents improve their effectiveness as educators and builders of self-esteem in their children by setting and resetting clear, attainable learning goals. Sometimes a parent gets angry that a child is not "obeying" or "trying." In reality, the adult may have given vague clues as to what the desired behavioral goal is or how to tackle a requested task. Sometimes a parent may set a task too difficult developmentally for the child at a particular level of functioning. Clarity and specificity help a child to "zero in" on aspects of a problem s/he is expected to solve. The SUCCESS program seems a logical social application of findings from Hess and Shipman's Chicago study of black mothers from four different income levels in learning task interactions with their preschool children. Those mothers who were better educated and whose children successfully completed the Block Sorting and Etch-A-Sketch Designs tasks gave "specific directions and feedback, worked to elicit the child's cooperativeness, accompanied their requests for physical response with verbal explanations, and used elaborated rather than restricted language styles" (Hess, 1969, p. 4).

Innovative program models for working with parents in groups have proliferated in recent years. Some of these models have been tested in research designs. Other programs have concentrated on service delivery rather than validation of the model in any systematic research program. Sometimes the parent group model has involved informal telephone networks. Sometimes the groups receive thorough and systematic training with a particular focus.

Job Training for Parents

Heber's program for infants of mothers with IQ under 75 has demonstrated how remarkably well tutorial developmental care from birth can offset "predictable" cognitive deficits (Heber, Garber, Harrington, Hoffman, & Fallender, 1972). Program children achieved a mean IQ of 126 vs. 95.7 for control children by 66 months of age. Mothers were involved in vocational training, mostly on-the-job training programs, for 26 weeks at private nursing homes. Also, they took adult education classes designed to provide basic academic tools necessary for vocational adaptability. This group training engendered

... a group spirit which was serving to enhance positive attitudes for work and achievement. Those mothers who were having difficulty adjusting to a didactic milieu for various (oftentimes familial) reasons were frequently enjoined in some manner by the other group members into participating. In many ways the result was a therapeutic situation for the group. The defenses with which some of the mothers entered the program were quickly dismantled. For example, one mother, who never in her life had held a job for longer than three weeks, would often verbally attack her teacher and peers during the initial stages of the academic training program. Like other women in the program, she had been reluctant to join, not only because of her children at home, but because she felt that her inability to read well would preclude ever obtaining a job — a problem that nothing could rectify. She even acknowledged at a later time that she had convinced herself that she could not hold a job because of her academic deficits. . . . The mothers gathered around this woman and through long, heated, usually emotional conversations, which many times interrupted classroom instructions, talked over her fears and other problems. Sometimes, on weekends, they talked over coffee in one of the mother's homes. Finally, she began to realize that she did have the ability to finish the program. She concluded the training with a high skill rating and is currently employed as a nursing assistant. (pp. 12-13)

Parent Groups and Children at Risk

When people share their troubles in raising normal children, when they hear someone else's problems, they often feel less isolated and more able to cope. This is the premise on which many parent group models are based. For parents of handicapped children, group supports may be even more critical. Bassin and Drovetta (1970) report that parent-to-parent contacts with trained parents of other developmentally delayed children have been particularly helpful when a handicapped baby is born. Perhaps only parents who have reared handicapped children can honestly say, "We've been there, can we help?" The objectives of this St. Louis program are for parents to work with new parents of handicapped infants to: (1) explain in jargon-free terms about a given disability, (2) assist in locating community resources, (3) provide helpful hints on home training, (4) share ideas about ways to tell relatives and friends about the disability, and (5) help new parents understand and accept their own attitudes and feelings about having a disabled child.

Home Visitation

Ira Gordon (1971) was one of the pioneers of the home visitation model. Essentially, this model provides a trained professional or para-professional home visitor for each family. The home visitor brings games and skills and understandings about child development and parent-child interactions to the family. Usually, exercises and games appropriate to the developmental level of the child are taught each week. Often, sample sheets describing a game, how to play it, and what the aim of the game is are left with the parent. Gordon's home visitors concentrated on teaching mothers how to provide facilitating sensorimotor experiences and language games for infants. The home visitor focused on the parent as the important person to do work with, rather than with the baby. Although activities and how to carry them out were demonstrated with the young child, the home visitor tried to move quickly to encourage the mother to try the game or activity with the child. Lambie, Bond, and Weikart (1974) also provided a home visitation program for low-income mothers of infants. The main objective was to increase a mother's awareness of and her ability to enhance her infant's cognitive growth through the use of toys and a Piagetian-based curriculum.

Susan Gray (1971) and Bettye Jean Forrester (1972) of the Demonstration and Research Center for Early Education (DARCEE) project developed a home visitation program for mothers of preschoolers. Their goal was to provide mothers with coping skills and assurance needed to handle the job of being their preschool child's primary teacher. This program is notable for encouraging the mother to work with all of her children, not just with a special target child. Special skills are needed when a home visitor has to plan for and carry out activities with a mother and several children of different ages. Another important DARCEE goal was to help the mother become an independent planner of her children's activities — whether puzzle play or a trip to a local park — as quickly as possible.

The Mother-Child Home Program Project (Levenstein, 1977) uses the home visitation model to encourage mothers to stimulate their children's intellectual development through verbal interactions involving two dozen specifically chosen toys and books called Verbal Interaction Stimulus Materials (VISM). Toy demonstrators receive intensive training and careful supervision. This program has registered gains in children's developmental scores on successive years whether the toy demonstrators were volunteer middle-income and college-educated women or paid paraprofessionals who had earlier been recipients themselves of this home visitation program. The toy demonstrator's role is not that of a counselor, but it requires the development of a warm relationship with mother and child, the demonstration of how to use each toy and book to stimulate child language, and the development of maximum participation by the parent. Mothers are encouraged to elicit and extend conversations with the child and to read to and play with the child between home sessions, which occur twice weekly.

Home visitation as a model has the advantage of being able to be tailored to the ecology, culture, and circumstances unique to each family. For isolated rural families where no preschool programs are available or feasible, the home visitor with his or her materials model may provide a high point of the week for parents and youngsters.

This model has been used with particular success to help parents of handicapped preschoolers in rural Wisconsin. Parents involved in the Portage Project (Shearer and Shearer, 1972) are taught how to keep daily frequency records of child behaviors being learned. Parents are shown how to write a behavioral prescription, such as "Child will hop on one foot five times, without help." They are taught what to reinforce and how to shape behaviors by the technique of initially providing and then "fading out" reinforcements. Each child is assigned an individual goal that can be achieved in 1 week, regardless of severity of handicap. The home teacher leaves materials to be used, written instructions, and charts to record progress. One of the strong points of this project is that "the home teacher draws on resources the parent has at hand for ideas to increase a child's experiences, discoveries and skills. The home teacher meets the mother on territory she is familiar with and that she is in charge of — her own home" (Honig, 1975, p. 21).

For migrant farm families, whose members often work long hours, the home visitation model may be a necessity. Segner and Patterson (1970) brought a suitcase with toys for different developmental stages and skill levels to the homes of Mexican migrant workers in Colorado. Each toy was neatly stored and labeled in a colorful drawstring pouch. The home visitation model here acknowledges the importance of moving programs to where the parents are comfortable.

Home visitation provides considerable feedback for the parent involver. Often the worker becomes much more sensitive to special family conditions, needs, and circumstances that will require modification of lesson plans or attention to special cultural factors in planning or in modeling interactions and activities with parents.

Sometimes the home visitation model is the only model that will work for a project until trust is built between project personnel who visit the home and the families involved. For example, Johnson and

Leler (1975) found that fathers in Mexican American families would only allow mothers enrolled in the Houston, Texas Parent Child Development Center (PCDC) to go outside the home and participate as aides in the child care program offered during the second year of the program. During the first year, Spanish-speaking home visitors and community liaison workers built trusting relationships as they worked with each family. The home visitation model served as a bridge, a resource that provided positive experiences with the kinds of program activities that would later be offered for mother and child in a center setting with other mothers and children.

Often, beginning a program with a home visitation model allows parents to develop skills and expertise with young children so that they can in turn become either home visiters or day care teachers. The Gordon Back Yard project, which followed his initial home visitation program, created mini day care centers in the back yards of mothers who had been previous program recipients. These mothers were in charge of the program, and graduate students from the project were then assigned as assistants to the mothers.

The home visitation model must remain sensitive to community mores. In some communities, it may be impossible to hire men as parent involvement personnel because of community suspiciousness of males visiting mothers who are alone at home. In other groups, male home visitors may find their role comfortably accepted. Indeed, Scheinfeld, Bowles, Tuck, and Gold (1969) found that fathers of low-income families in an urban housing project could be more actively involved with their preschool children's educational experiences when male home visitors tailored their program specially for the fathers.

Another difficulty that has been faced occurs when the home visitor focuses too narrowly on the special cognitive goals of a program without ensuring that the parent's emotional needs for support are also met. Adkins (1971) found that few parents managed to be home at the agreed hour for home visitors in programs in Hawaii. The home visitors were trained to bring language or mathematics materials from a specific curriculum being carried out in special preschool programs with disadvantaged children. One home visitor was more successful than others in finding parents at home. Her secret? She made sure to allow the parent to talk about family troubles and parent concerns, as well as spending time on the curricular materials the parent was to use at home to supplement the preschool program.

Where a program simply mandates home visits without training staff adequately in conceptualizing the goals of the program, without provisions for training outreach staff either in child development or in skills for working with the particular group targeted, then trouble may arise. One supervisor asked for help because his social work aide had been told by a 16-year-old unwed mother not to bother coming back for any more home visits. He bored her, was not useful, and "interfered" with her television soap opera viewing besides. The supervisor explained that his outreach people had not been trained in home visitation techniques nor in understanding stages of child development, nor did they provide any curricular guidelines or specific activity ideas. A willingness to reach out to parents may not be sufficient for successful parent involvement. Clear goals and sensitive, flexible, specific ways to meet these goals need to be part of a successful home visitation effort.

Home Visits with Disturbed Mothers

Dr. Selma Fraiberg (Fraiberg, Adelson, & Shapiro, 1975) has used the home visitation model in a unique "kitchen therapy" approach to reach abusive mothers, who alternately neglect the baby or treat it severely and inappropriately.

> Fraiberg has found that only as you deeply reach into the personal experience of the mother, into the past parenting that the young woman herself went through — *her* rage, *her* grief, *her* pain — will you help her to feel with and for her baby. A mother may tell you, "I hated it when my mom took the strap to me." But does the mother *feel* or just say it? When the therapist gets to the feeling part, Dr. Fraiberg reports something that sounds quite miraculous. As the young woman reaches through to these deep buried feelings in herself of pain and rage and hatred, all of a sudden she hears that her baby has been screaming for 20 minutes in that living room. She runs and picks it up and catches the baby to her breast. (Honig, 1978, p. 28)

Home Visits with Linkages to Other Services for Families

The most comprehensive federal demonstration program to deliver home-based services to families of Head Start eligible children is Home Start. Home Start programs identify and use existing community resources and services, as needed, to provide nutritional, health, social, and psychological services for children and their families. Table 15-I gives an idea of the range of jobs and activities that a home visitor does or arranges for in the Home Start program. Results of the 3-year demonstration project (Love et al., 1976) found the following.

1. The home-based delivery system was as effective as Head Start in delivering services, including medical and dental services, to children. The operating costs of both programs were comparable.

2. Compared to a control group, Home Start parents were more involved with their children through verbal interaction, provided more books and read more to their children, and used more questioning to encourage their children to think.

3. Compared to control children, Home Start children were more ready for school and more task oriented.

4. Paraprofessionals trained as home visitors provided effective service to families.

Table 15-I

SOME ACTIVITIES THAT A HOME START HOME VISITOR DOES

Introduce a toy (or book or creative experience) that will necessarily involve the parent in a developmental experience with the child.

Help the mother make homemade toys improvised from household items to foster development.

Help the mother with a household chore (such as washing dishes, making biscuits, or peeling potatoes) and, by involving the child, demonstrate how the activities that normally make up the fabric of each day can be used as constructive learning experiences for children.

Talk with the mother about each child and the things she is doing to further his/her development, praising her for gains made and making occasional suggestions.

Introduce activities that involve the older children or that encourage the older children to work with and help the younger ones.

Budget some time to give the mother an opportunity to talk about her own achievements, needs, or problems.

Take time from more serious purposes for a snack or sociable chat, perhaps while helping a busy mother dry dishes or fold diapers.

Read and evaluate the newspaper's food ads with mother.

Help mother make a shopping list.

Go food shopping with mother and child.

Assist family in taking steps to obtain donated or commodity foods.

Arrange for local home economists to demonstrate preparation of inexpensive but nourishing foods.

Cook supper with mother and child, showing mother (by example) how child can be involved — noting colors, textures, and shapes of food and kitchen equipment, counting eggs, spoons, etc., and talking.

Take mother with child for child's physical and dental examinations.

Set up appointments at free clinic for mother's physical examination.

Set up family first aid course for Home Start staff and parents.

Mark height of each family member on wall in home.

Arrange for exterminator to come.

Help parents assess home with regard to safety precautions — exposed poisons, electrical outlets, lead paint, etc.

Make sure that all follow-up health care is provided for identified health needs.

Call on local doctors to tell them about Home Start and ask their help.

Show mother how to check for worms.

Provide toothbrushing kits and instructions for all family members.

Read with mother the health columns in local newspapers.

Use local telephone book as a directory of resources, showing mother how resources are listed.

Take mother or parents to the resource facility, walking through entire process with parent(s).

Use "Parent Effectiveness Training" to prevent communications problems within families.

Help families team up with neighbors or relatives who own transportation.

Hold program-wide picnics or other social affairs for parents or entire families.

Take parents to local libraries and show shelves with books on child rearing.

Arrange for Home Start staff and interested parents to take courses on child rearing, such as "Parent Effectiveness Training."

Hold mothers' group meetings to use one another as resources in finding solutions to child-rearing problems.

Prepare simple guides to accompany children's television programs shown locally, to make television watching less passive and more active.

Suggest ways to turn everyday events into learning experiences, such as going to the grocery store and playing a "color game" on the way or peeling vegetables and teaching the child size and color concepts at the same time.

Obtain films on child development or child rearing to show to groups of parents.

Cut out pictures in magazines and help parents make games — classifying objects, counting, etc.

Obtain tools and materials such as plywood scraps and dri-wall, so parents (especially fathers and older brothers) can make wagons, insert puzzles, storage chests, bookshelves, and other items for their own families.

Adapted from *Parent Involvement in Early Childhood Education* by A. S. Honig, Washington, D.C., National Association for the Education of Young Children, 1975, pp. 25-26.

Parent Involvement in Addition to Preschool

Many preschool programs, whether providers of service or additional research and demonstration programs, offer child care plus a parent involvement component. In many communities, Head Start programs are run 4 days a week; on the 5th day, teachers go into the community and work with families at home. One of the curriculum components of Weikart's Perry Preschool Project for children included parent involvement. "Children visited at home scored significantly higher on standardized tests of achievement than did a comparison group of children" (*Carnegie Quarterly*, 1978, p. 9).

Parent Child Centers and Parent Child Development Centers

Innovative ways of involving families as well as providing services to children have been developed by the federally funded PCC and PCDC. For example, at the New Orleans PCDC, parents are provided with a spiral-bound notebook entitled *In the Beginning: A Parent Guide of Activities and Experiences for Infants from Birth to Six Months* (Rabinowitz, Weiner, & Jackson, 1973). The notebook provides important information for new parents. Noticing skills are sharpened by suggested ideas for observation of the new baby. Crossword puzzles and dot-to-dot puzzles to be solved by the parent help reassure that the program ideas and activities are indeed understood by the parent. Puzzles, drawings, and the use of multicolored pages and simple clear text help make such a notebook easy to read as well as fun for a parent to follow as baby grows and the parent's skills and understandings with the child also grow.

The Houston, Texas PCDC already mentioned provides a wide range of services for the Mexican American families in the program, such as helping mothers who wish to learn English or to learn how to drive a car. A weekend retreat house was used from time to time to bring families together for meals, games, social interactions, and talks together about family and child-rearing concerns.

Parent involvement in the Birmingham PCDC (Lasater, Briggs, Malone, Gilliom, & Weisberg, 1975) is strictly center based. Mother-child pairs attend the center together. After 15 months of participation on a part-time basis, the mother is eligible for model mother (teaching mother) status, which requires a regular 40-hour week. Stanford Binet IQ scores for program males and females at 4 years of age are 99.5 and 104.2 respectively, compared with randomly assigned control males and females, who score at 85.5 and 90.2 respectively.

The positive child outcomes found in these programs are encouraging in view of the variety of models and methods by which parent involvement, in addition to quality child care, is accomplished.

Brookline Early Education Project (BEEP)

With the avowed goal of developing school competence for each child, BEEP is an interdisciplinary program that provides basic and elaborate diagnostic services to families (who are recruited prenatally), support for parents in the rearing of their children, and direct preschool educational programs. BEEP program objectives also include an evaluation of the benefits of these services to assess the comparative value of the educational programs, which differ in intensity and cost depending on the needs of individual families. Evaluation is also ongoing to determine the value of the thorough diagnostic procedures in predicting later learning and health problems. Two other major innovative goals of BEEP include the following:

1. To determine whether a public school, a pediatric center, and a graduate school of education can develop new ways of working together to raise the quality of diagnostic and educational service for young children and their families.

2. To determine how such a program of diagnosis and education is received by various elements of the community — by parents, school teachers, family doctors, local pediatricians, community agencies, and the general citizenry (Pierson, 1973, p. 1).

Thus, BEEP does not attempt to train parents directly in the manner of many other projects, but provides diagnostic and educational support systems plus staff personnel supports to enable parents to optimize the development of their children.

Parent Involvement and Television

Some programs attempt to link their parent involvement efforts with educational television programs for young children, such as "Captain Kangaroo" or "Sesame Street." Television programs for young children without cooperative interest and participation by the parents may not produce the cognitive and prosocial learning that has been so carefully programmed and planned for.

In Appalachia, the Home-Oriented Preschool Education (HOPE) project (Alford, 1972) has used 30-minute 5-day-a-week televised lessons called "Around the Bend" as a springboard to encourage preschool-age children to want to learn and to develop skills for learning. HOPE instructs parents through a home visitation program in ways to use these special television programs so that positive parent-child interactions are promoted and parents can become effective teachers with their children. The outlay and operating costs average to about $270 per year. A home visitor once a week delivers to parents guides to the television program activities. S/he provides materials for parent and child to use together to supplement and enlarge upon the TV lessons. Additionally, s/he carries out some learning activity with the parent and child. A mobile preschool comes to the community several half-days per week so that children also have a chance for group experiences with a preschool teacher who coordinates the group's learning activities with home and television activities.

The Child and Family Resource Program (CFRP)

Among the latest innovative efforts to involve families of preschoolers in enhancing living and learning conditions for their children is CFRP, a national Head Start Demonstration program, which was initially funded in June, 1973. CFRP uses Head Start as a base for developing a community-wide service delivery network.

> The CFRP process begins with the enrollment of the family, which is followed by an assessment of the needs and strengths of the family unit. On the basis of discussions between family members, CFRP staff, and community resource specialists, the unique goals and needs of each family are assessed, and ways are discussed in which both the family and CFRP staff can contribute to an overall Family Action Plan for meeting identified needs. (O'Keefe, 1978, p. 1)

Each CFRP receives approximately $130,000 for a 12-month period and serves at least 80 low-income families.

Key features of the CFRP programs are their flexibility and thoroughness in meeting family and child needs. This individualization and tailoring of programs to fit each family is a strength that argues well for the success of CFRP programs. Most research and demonstration models funded earlier could only take families willing to fit the model of that particular program. Now there is a federal model to fit families. Another excellent feature of the CFRP programs is the attempt to link resources in each community to serve the diagnostic and remediation needs of family members. A third admirable feature of this program is the provision of continuity of services from the prenatal period through early elementary school years. Unfortunately, funding of many projects with excellent preschool curricular and parent involvement efforts often stops abruptly when the child enters elementary school. Some families require continuity of service. Some children and some school systems may find their adjustment to one another far better where CFRP personnel help provide continuity of care and continuity of resources should they be needed by an individual family. The fourth objective of CFRP is to enhance and build upon the strengths of the individual family as a child-rearing system with distinct values, culture, and aspirations.

THE FAMILY DEVELOPMENT RESEARCH PROGRAM (FDRP)

This section will describe a particular omnibus intervention model with which the author was associated as program director for a decade. The major goal of the FDRP was the support of child and familial behaviors that sustain growth and development after intervention ceases. The family was the primary focus of the program (Lally & Honig, 1977a).

Saul Alinsky's theory of community organization influenced the way the program conceptualized its role in the community served. Alinsky has pointed out that if you try to provide programs for people without giving them a say in what is happening to them, more often than not, they will suffer from your gift.

The FDRP offered comprehensive services to 108 families that were low in both income and education. None of the program mothers had a high school diploma at time of birth of the target child. Child care services, a major part of the program, were provided at the Syracuse University Children's Center for children from 6 to 60 months. The center program for children was seen by the project director as the backup to family services rather than as the major input of the project. The program dealt directly with the families and encouraged the individuality of each family with its inherent cultural background. The Children's Center staff provided relief from daily pressures without assuming the entire burden of family responsibilities or trying to be substitute parents. Emphasis on family involvement stemmed from an awareness that when most child-centered intervention programs ceased, the children from the multiproblem families were soon found to be indistinguishable from their peers in intellectual functioning. The emphasis on family involvement was based on the beliefs that affective bonds between parent and child are extremely important to early learning and that a child's identification with attitudes and values of parents is much more likely to occur than identification with attitudes and values of others.

For the home visitation program, a conscious choice was made to select child development trainers who were indigenous to the low-income community they served. An omnibus approach to intervention was taken because of the broad objectives of the program. The role of the child development trainers (CDTs) changed constantly, becoming more and more relevant as the program progressed. The longer a CDT worked with a family, the more s/he became aware of the family's needs and problems. The CDT's role expanded to include the following activities:

1. Promotion of health and nutrition needs and good family diet.
2. Promotion of a rich quality of positive affectionate interaction between mother and child and between family and child.
3. Provision of information, games, toys, and ideas relating to stages of child development.
4. Dissemination of sex education information.
5. Sharing with families and numerous positive and effective ways to discipline children, including P.E.T. methods.
6. Leadership of group meetings whe.e mothers could learn about and discuss issues of interest to themselves.
7. Liaison work with teachers. CDTs alerted teachers to situations at home that could change a child's sociableness or responsiveness to adult expectations.
8. Data collection. The CDTs recorded the family's interest in and involvement with the target child during each weekly visit.
9. Active leadership roles in planning the weekly parent workshops held every Friday morning at the Children's Center. The projects carried out included sewing clothes, making cardboard furniture for preschoolers, and turning castoffs such as orange juice cans and egg cartons into stacking and nesting toys or into mobiles or educational toys.
10. Liaison agent with community facilities that could provide needed referral services to families for job training, schooling to achieve a high school equivalency diploma, health services, legal aid, etc. Whenever possible, the CDT helped parents to become aware of various programs and services available within the community, so that the parents could enhance their own personal development in career opportunities, economic independence, and positive self-concept.
11. Provision of an effective model for adult-child social and intellectual transactions. The CDT often modeled appropriate and pleasurable ways to play with a child and to facilitate a child's increased attention to a task or perseverance at a task.
12. Promotion of the parent's active and decisive participation in the learning experiences and development of the child. Mothers were particularly encouraged to find ways to make learning and language experiences a part of the daily routines of the family. CDTs praised the mother as she tried out new learning games each week. Activity sheets were left with the family each week, and the mother was encouraged to play these Piagetian and language learning games daily. Promotion of an educationally

facilitative role for the parents included helping them to make contacts with the public schools as preschoolers graduated from the FDRP and encouraging parents to visit classrooms and teachers. Promotion of the parent's education role also included taking parents on trips to the airport, zoo, libraries, and parks with their children, so that they could gain experience with community facilities that would help them in their work of enhancing the horizons of their children.

Program services to families extended to include service to unborn infants. The paraprofessional CDTs made weekly home visits to expectant parents, starting 3 to 6 months before the child was born. These visits were continued as long as the child was in the program, that is, until the child entered elementary school. Family problems, financial, emotional, social, nutritional, etc., were dealt with as they appeared. The severity and complexity of these problems reinforced the center staff's deep conviction of the need for comprehensive or omnibus family-oriented child care services (Lally & Honig, 1975).

A major component of the Children's Center was the "Infant-fold" for children ranging from 6 months to 15 to 18 months of age. The infants attended a center-based program on a half-day basis. Four infants were assigned to one care giver for special loving care, cognitive and social games, and language stimulation. Materials, persons, and environment were jointly used to promote sensory and motor skills. For example, a loving care giver could blow colorful bubbles for his/her toddlers. S/he could exclaim about the rainbow colors and the floating and bursting and urge those who were walking to try to locomote toward and reach for the bubbles. Feeding times were used as happy sociable occasions to teach food names, textures, and colors and to reinforce the finger dexterity required for a baby to pick up tasty, nutritious, and safe food tidbits from his/her feeding table.

Teachers followed a curriculum based on the developmental theories of Jean Piaget and Erik Erikson. In both these theories, one stage builds on its predecessor, and early stages are integrated into future stages. Basic emotional-social conflicts and basic cognitive processes and achievements are experienced and refined throughout life. Changes in cognitive functioning often provide explanations for changes in social-emotional level, and social-emotional advances often permit advancement in cognitive understandings (Lally & Honig, 1977b). Play materials for the infants and toddlers were used to help children develop means-ends relationships, object permanence, causality, and spatial concepts in a climate of basic trust. The level of a task presented was matched perceptively by the care giver to the developmental level of each child. See Honig (1974) for a description of the infant curriculum.

One consistent emphasis for teachers and CDTs was the use of routine daily activities such as diapering and feeding, whether at home or center, to promote joyful emotional encounters, positive self-concept, and language experiences.

Preschoolers (18 months to 60 months) attended a full-day, multiage group experience called the Family Style Program. This program was modeled after the philosophy of the British Infant School. The concepts of freedom of choice, encouragement of creativity, and creation of an environment that facilitates exploration and enjoyment of learning experiences were central to our program. Integration of intellectual and affective development was a goal of the Family Style Program. The men and women care givers in family-style groups provided four special activity areas:

1. Small-muscle games, such as puzzles, pegboard, bead stringing, marble games.
2. Sensory experiences, such as tasting, smelling, listening to stories and records, feeling gerbils, materials, and textures, and watching plants, animals, and filmstrips.
3. Large muscle games, such as tumbling, jumping, running, and balancing.
4. Expressive play (with water, clay, finger paints, rice, Pla-Doh®, and sawdust) and dress-up role-playing.

Children could choose which area to enter. They moved freely from one area to another and decided on the amount of time they wished to spend on any one activity. Of course, teachers often provided interesting special activities in a particular area that could lure a child who preferred, for example, large muscle play consistently to all other activities.

During the year prior to kindergarten entrance, tutorial experiences with carefully sequenced Piagetian activities to promote preoperational competencies were introduced. Two or three children were worked with intensively for about 20 minutes several times a week. The tutorial groups promoted positive social relationships, patience, and camaraderie among the children as well as cognitive skills.

Teacher input and transactions with toddlers and preschoolers were assessed in ongoing evaluation. Table 15-II shows the kinds of adult behaviors assessed by the ABC checklists (Adult Behaviors in Caregiving) that were used during the program years.

Table 15-II

SPECIFIC SKILLS ASSESSED IN TEACHERS OF TODDLERS

I. Facilitates Language Development

Converses
Models language
Expands language
Praises, encourages
Offers help and solicitous remarks,
  or makes verbal promises
Inquires of child or makes request
Gives information
Gives culture rules
Labels sensory experiences
Reads or identifies pictures
Sings or plays music with child
Role-plays with child

II. Facilitates Development of Skills:
Social-Personal

Promotes child-child play
  (cognitive and sensorimotor)
Gets social games going
Promotes self-help and social
  responsibility
Helps child recognize his own needs
Helps child delay gratification
Promotes persistence, attention span

Physical

Small-muscle perceptual motor
Large-muscle, kinesthesis

III. Facilitates Concept Development

Arranges learning of space and time
Arranges learning of seriation,
  categorization, and polar concepts
Arranges learning of number concepts
Arranges learning of physical causality

V. Preferred Social Emotional
Negative Behaviors*

Frowns, restrains physically
Isolates child physically — behavior
  modification
Forbids, negative commands

Inappropriate Social-Emotional
Negative Behaviors*

Criticizes verbally, scolds, threatens
Ignores child when child shows need
  for attention
Punishes physically
Gives attention to negative behavior
  that should be ignored

VI. Caregiving: Child

Diapers, toilets, dresses, washes,
  cleans
Gives physical help, help to sleep,
  shepherds
Eye-checks on child's well-being
Carries child

VII. Caregiving: Environment

Prepares and serves food
Tidies up room
Helps other caregiver(s)
Prepares activities, arranges environ-
  ment to stimulate the child

VIII. Qualitative Categories

IV. Social-Emotional: Positive

Smiles at child
Uses raised, loving, or reassuring tones
Provides physical loving contact
Uses eye contact to draw child's
    attention

Encourages creative expression
Matches tempo and/or developmental
    level of child
Actively engages child's interest in
    activity or activity choice
Follows through on requests, promises,
    directions, disciplines

---

*Our teachers are instructed that all social-emotional negative behavior can be decreased by concentration on social-emotional positive behavior and by providing an interesting environment. Some behaviors under the category of "social emotional negative behaviors" are preferred over others. Some are considered inappropriate.

Parents were often in attendance at the center. Small groups of parents met weekly either in their homes or at the center to discuss varying topics of interest. Some topics were teenage sexuality, preschoolers' sexuality and sex education for the preschool child, socialization techniques, fire prevention in the home, women's liberation, and children's literature. Mothers also made up classification and seriation games for their preschoolers. Parents often telephoned the center to discuss matters of concern. Other parents used CDTs as informational bridges to the center or to keep open lines of communication of concerns. The various parent meetings and workshops included very few fathers, and attendance was usually less then 50%.

The program had a strong in-service training component for all teachers and home visitors. The CDTs met weekly to increase their knowledge and skill base, to share information about their work with families, and to share successful techniques of parent involvement that might be useful to another home visitor. Close staff relations were furthered by frequent meetings to exchange ideas, to create new materials, and to obtain and discuss developmental assessment information that would help a care giver or a CDT to deal more effectively with the children.

Evaluation and dissemination of handbooks and materials were important components of the CFDP. A variety of child outcome measures including language, cognitive, and socioemotional adjustment with peers and adults were used. As well, the parents were asked to evaluate the effectiveness of the home visitor program via an interview questionnaire called PEPPER (Parent Evaluation of Program and Prognosis for Educational Responsibility). Some of the typical responses of mothers concerning the impact of their home visitor follow:

> "My CDT never puts me down. She has always been friendly and helpful in any way she could."

"She is patient. I'm awfully moody sometimes."

"Her greatest help is in trying to teach my child what she has. If left to me, I couldn't have done it all myself — working nights and all."

"She really made me see I could be a teacher and make toys for my child. I didn't need lots of money to buy toys."

"She really cares about my child and me."

An evaluation of parental efforts (to work with the child, to use positive discipline techniques, and to add explanatory reasons when punishments were given) was made based on the weekly and monthly reports filled out by the CDTs.

Nonobtrusive measures of parental change show that after 3 years in the program, more CFDP mothers have obtained their high school diplomas (37.3%) compared to contrast mothers (25%). Evaluation of care givers was the fourth component of the assessment program. The ABC checklists (Honig & Lally, 1975) were used to monitor classroom interactions of teachers with infants, toddlers, and preschoolers.

What have we learned from our work in the Family Development Research Program? We have learned that paraprofessional home visitors with intensive, ongoing training can provide to families a wide variety of services with sensitivity to the ever-changing needs of families as children grow and as crises or new problems arise. Care givers in the Children's Center were able to carry out a curriculum that integrated loving interactions, cognitive language stimulation, and opportunities for learning into daily routines. The family-style groups were able to build positive self-concept by encouraging choices, social skills, responsibility for own actions, and cognitive/language competence.

Parents liked the program and saw benefits for themselves as well as their children in the different facets of the program. Program children at 5 years of age were happy and intelligent (92% of program children were within the average range of intelligence and above, compared to 79.2% of carefully matched contrast children). Program children were sociable with adults and peers.

One troubling concern arose in following the children as families left the program. The learning environment represented by large first-grade classes, with teacher-dominated activities and little personalized individual attention, was correlated with follow-up findings of an abrupt change in program graduates' relations with adults. Through kindergarten, graduates compared with their matched classroom contrasts had been characterized by more positive bids to teachers and peers. In kindergarten, program graduates sought adult help, acted responsively to adults, communicated verbally, and acted friendly toward adults significantly more than their classroom matches. They were also significantly more task-persistent, self-actualized in activities, and verbally communicative (Honig, Lally, & Matthieson, 1979).

Program graduates in first grade sought adult attention through negative as well as positive bids. Toward other children, the program graduates continued to behave in positive ways. It is possible that preschool program youngsters were frustrated in their expectations for learning and for responsive adult interactions in the school classroom. It may be that provision for *continuity* of programming for preschoolers from low-education, low-income families is crucial for maintaining the kinds of positive social and cognitive gains found while preschoolers and their families are in the program. Some families and some children may need sustained personalized support systems such as are presently available in the new Child and Family Resource program.

PROCESSES, ACTIONS, METHODS, AND IDEAS TO HELP PARENT INVOLVERS IN THEIR WORK

For successful parent involving, the worker must be aware of the values and goals s/he holds for families and about the work of parent involving. Visits to the home, for example, may alienate rather than involve the parent if the home visitor always demonstrates how competent s/he is with the child in modeling and demonstrating activities and methods of interacting. The parent may get the idea that s/he is not so good at this process and give up on trying. Or the parent may feel resentment toward the home visitor. One home visitor reported that as she left the home, she saw the mother go to throw away the egg carton brought earlier to demonstrate a numerosity game using beans and numbers written inside the cardboard cups of the egg carton. In no way had the mother been involved in the planning or even in the carrying out of the activity. Small steps might have helped, such as asking the mother if she could possibly save an egg carton after use so that the visitor and parent together could number the cups and design number games for the preschooler.

Beliefs In the Job

Firstly and most importantly, the parent involver must believe and act on the hypothesis that the parent is the ultimate curriculum creator for the child. Parents are responsible for the development of their children. The parent must be seen as the responsible person by program personnel. Sometimes, indeed, parents are restrictive, interfering, harsh, or inappropriate with their children. The parent involver may find and honestly and matter-of-factly state that s/he finds a behavior inappropriate. But the message *still* must be that the parent is the important person. The parent involver must work with the parent, the child's first and most influential teacher.

Building Trust Takes Time

One of the mothers in our program said after several years that she would not have put up with someone who was as uncooperative and suspicious as she had been in the early months and years of our program. The child development trainer had come back again and again even when this mother did not stay at home for agreed upon appointments for the home visits. After several years, the mother remarked, "I really believe my child development trainer cares about us. It's not just a job for her." This mother started to meet appointments more regularly. She now had the shades in her apartment raised more often than not when the home visitor was due to come. As Honig (1975, p. 81) has written, "Patience is a virtue. Some parent involvement efforts take a lot more 'give' before they 'take.'" The parent involver may have to give extra services and accommodations, such as scheduling visits at 7 AM before the mother leaves for a factory shift. Building a caring relationship is fundamental to success in getting parent cooperation in facilitating cognitive lessons and more positive discipline approaches with the child.

Training for Parent Involving

Third, training for parent involvers is crucial. The parent involver should have detailed understanding of the stages of infant, toddler, and preschooler development. This means knowing the tasks and gains of the sensorimotor and preoperational periods. A worker who just has the know-how to introduce a toy-on-a-string game but cannot explain simply to the parent how the baby is advancing as s/he learns to use a string to pull in the desired toy is teaching rote activities. Parent involvement should generate pleasure and excitement in the parent. Learning means-ends relationships and learning to seriate all the shoes in the hall closet are developmental advances that reflect the curiosity and active learning of the child. The parent who understands just how new and difficult each task and stage of understanding and skill development is will be able to appreciate the effort of the child, even if child efforts sometimes result in spilled milk or towers of blocks that topple unsteadily.

But knowledge of how intelligence, language, and fine and gross motor skills grow and how typical is egocentric and animistic thinking in preschoolers is not enough. Skills must be learned along with understandings of development. These skills involve both the child and the parent. With the child, the parent involver must learn how to engage a child's interest and hold it. Changing voice tone, judicious of fingers to hold a puzzle board firm so that a toddler keeps trying to fit pieces in (despite temptations to dump the board and disorganize it), use of caressing words and gestures, and appropriate use of praise and encouragement are important skills. Helping children focus their attention and modeling ways to encourage persistence at slightly difficult tasks are skills the parent involver should learn through training sessions.

People need skills to help other people grow and change. Skills in working with parents will grow over time, but much help can be offered in preservice training sessions. Modeling skills, communication skills, and ways to encourage and build up parent self-esteem are crucial to success with families, unconventional though these may be. One home visitor in our FDRP project was becoming discouraged with the mess and chaos of one household. On a wet, snowy day, the home visitor arrived at the front door and asked the mother if she had some old newspapers. "I really want to wipe my boots from all this muddy snow," explained the worker. "I wouldn't want anybody to track mess into my house and I sure wouldn't want to dirty up your house. I would really appreciate your finding me some old newspaper so I can wipe my shoes thoroughly before coming in." The mother graciously complied with the worker's earnest request. Somehow a subtle message of valuing the mother's home was communicated in this simple, natural action. From then on, the mother began to make an effort to have the child clean and her apartment somewhat straightened up when the home visitor arrived.

Another home visitor, a preschool teacher 4 days weekly in a Head Start program, came for her weekly home visit. Although she knew well that this parent never found the time to take her child on trips, she complimented the mother. "You know, Tommy seems to recognize animals on our Lotto cards so well at preschool. You must really make an effort to show him picture books at home or to take him to the zoo. We are so proud of Tommy. He really knows so many animal names." The mother did not reply. Within 2 weeks, Tommy reported excitedly to his preschool teacher how his momma had taken him to the zoo, what a good time they had had together, and what he had seen. Sometimes, building a secure feeling of importance for the parent can further program goals for the child more than a multitude of didactic *dos* and *don'ts*. P.E.T. materials and Ginott's work (1965) on communications between parent and child should be helpful in training parent workers to improve parent communication skills as well as their own listening and communicating skills with parents.

Flexibility of the Parent Involver

Efforts to involve parents with their young child's learning and education must be varied to meet parental and child development needs. Some parents are ready for more sophisticated ideas, ready for group meetings, ready to grasp ideas about stage appropriate activities. Other parents need someone to confide in about their financial problems or their sexual entanglements. They will cheerfully tell the parent involver that they enjoy teasing the baby or that this child is "really stupid compared to his brother." Where parent sensitivities to the child are lacking, the parent involver cannot rush in with toy-making projects and chatter about activities exclusively. The parent's behavior may be shaped gradually by modeling appropriate interactions and as one notices and admires a parent's efforts to interact in loving or educationally stimulating ways.

Parent involvement means not only lessons, but a way of working with parents, children, *and* lessons. Flexibility is the key concept in changing and adapting task ingredients and games so that household resources and parent-child motivation and skill levels are taken into account. Parent involvers must meet the problem of the "match" between program goals and lessons and present family functioning and needs.

Using Community Resources

Using community resources and agencies to help the parent settle urgent family problems so that more attention and life energy can be focused on interactions with the child may be the first order of business in some cases. One mother, new in the program, was highly upset because her husband had moved out and started a relationship with another woman in the apartment house. Until the worker found new housing for the mother and children, the distraught lady could not focus on ideas that had to do with her children.

A parent involver will find his/her job role easier to define if liaisons are made with other services that can help meet family needs. Access to well-baby clinics, legal aid services, food stamp programs, housing agencies, literacy programs, and job training facilities are important. Some parent involvement projects have a special crisis service. If a family has a behavioral crisis, community personnel with expertise in interpersonal or emotional problems are on call to serve project families as the need arises. Sometimes ministers in a community will volunteer to assist in such crises. In one family, the grandmother got into a fight, pulled a policeman's gun from his holster, and threatened him. She was given a 1-year penitentiary sentence. Meanwhile, her two teenage daughters, who were enrolled with their babies in a parent involvement project, found themselves in a critical situation at home. A local minister was very helpful in allaying fears and allowing the parties concerned to talk out some of their anxieties with him. Parent involvers need not feel that they must carry the burden of all family problems. Other community resources may be far more suited to handle particular issues that are increasing family stress.

Process Is More Important Than Content

Specific activities or lessons can never be as important for parent involvement as the processes and sensitivity used in modeling cognitive transactions with children, in encouraging child language, and in setting limits and redirecting a child's attention while demonstrating a given lesson. A parent involver who notes that a parent loves to cook or garden or sew can pick up on these parent skills and invent ways in which parent and child together can talk about the activity and participate in some ways together. Matching socks fresh from the laundry is a more important and exciting visual discrimination and classification task than matching big and little circles carefully cut out by the worker. Helping a parent cook, set a table, or put away silverware in the appropriate trays makes the child feel so important and teaches classification skills as well. In all cases, the parent involver should be alert to admiring ways a parent may mention that a child "helped" at home and was also using good thinking and reasoning skills. White (1977) has pointed out time and again in his research that effective mothers of competent children respond appropriately to child initiatives, let children help in the house, and somehow deliver mini-lessons as part of the ongoing flow of household living all during the day.

Modeling is important. Every time the parent involver elicits competent behaviors, persistence at a difficult task, or attempts at new
developmental advances, s/he can voice delight and appreciation so
that the parent grows to feel "My child is O.K. — even A-1! I must be
pretty good to have a child like this." Training is thus very important. A well-trained parent involver will try to challenge and motivate
a child with tasks that are not too difficult but not so easy that they
bore the child or that the parent is unlikely to think that any special
effort was required for task success.

Parent involvers will also model how to carry out tasks and lessons
with a child. They must also model patience, curiosity, and delight in
children's tiny progresses, plus friendship and genuine caring for the
family.

Importance of Facing Family Realities

Part of the process of successful parent involving involves being
realistic. For example, Howard (1975) reports that a project to involve
teenaged unwed fathers was very unsuccessful in getting fathers to
meet on Saturdays, a day when they did not have school or jobs. It
turned out that the young fathers considered Saturday their special
time to get ready for dates, etc. Despite the fact that project personnel
thought they were being sensitive to job and schooling needs, the day
chosen did not fit the needs of the young fathers. Realistic choices
made together with parents will often help settle such problems and
avoid frustrations and failures. One obstetrician felt quite frustrated at
not being able to involve unwed fathers in any program, although the
teenage pregnant girls did come for checkups. Then he hit on the idea
of hiring a street worker who knew the youths' culture to lure the
young men into group meetings and discussions when they came to
hang around the clinic doors on days when their "girls" were having
pregnancy checkups.

Realistic appraisal of family situations and concerns may help project members make decisions that will increase the chance of success
for parent involvers. One project revealed that insistence on active
parent involvement efforts by preschool staff was not producing results. Frank discussion with some of the teachers revealed that some
were afraid of unleashed large dogs, others were intimidated by large
numbers of children in the home who snatched materials and made
working with the target parent and child quite difficult. A reality-
oriented solution was found when the staff decided to go home visiting in pairs. Fears were decreased. In homes with several children,

one parent involver concentrated on the mother and target child while the other provided activities and lessons for the other children.

Although participation in the home visitation program of our project was mandatory for families with children enrolled in the developmental day-care program, some young mothers did not answer their doorbells despite agreed-upon visiting dates and times. One ingenious home visitor, who heard giggling behind an apartment door, went next door, identified herself, and politely asked to use the telephone. She called the young mother who said, "Oh, did I forget about our appointment? Oh well, I'll see you next week then." The home visitor assured the young mother that she was so pleased that the mother now remembered the appointment, she was right next door and would be at the door in 1 minute! Ingenuity and facing reality together will help parent involvers find ways to solve some of the problems and difficulties that arise.

In another project, the group leader found that discussion of preschool activities and understandings was often sidetracked by parents bringing up problems with discipline, toileting accidents, etc. The group leader realistically explained that problems of this sort could be discussed with the staff social worker. She explained that in their weekly group meetings, she and the parents would work hard toward learning about how their children learned and how the parents could be the most effective and special teachers of their preschoolers.

Another way facing reality can help keep staff morale high is by analyzing, not what has been planned for a parent group meeting, for example, at a center, but what actually would motivate parents to come to meetings and ensure that the substance as well as the form of parent involvement occurs. Projects have frequently found that supper meetings are an effective way to increase family attendance. Another project found that meeting with groups of parents as they came to pick up their children one afternoon a week was a very workable method of reaching parents, provided that the staff presented a packaged dinner (for each family member) that the parents could take home at the close of the parent group meeting.

Another project found that preschoolers' parents would come to parent conferences and discussions if there were to be slides or movies of their children shown. Another group found that parents would attend meetings when they knew that their child would be in a little skit or performance as part of the planned activities.

One charismatic and energetic parent involvement project director reported that she had two methods that worked wonderfully. One was to promise a Bingo game right after parent group meetings. The other method that parents loved was a large cloth banner with the name of a new "Mother of the Week" that was draped over the back of the preschool bus each week. Mothers apparently asked their preschoolers what that special mother had done to get a banner for that week. Perhaps one had come in and baked bread with the children. Another had sewn smocks (for the water table) that were waterproof and easy for preschoolers to put on by themselves. In any case, meeting the needs of parents will often help offset some of the low attendance figures that must be realistically faced as preschool programs attempt to involve parents. Dr. Sprigle (1972), of the Jacksonville, Florida Learning-to-Learn program (for disadvantaged preschoolers), reported extremely high parent group attendance. The secret? Project staff stopped at each family's home on Sunday afternoon, helped parents get children ready, and picked up families for the afternoon family meetings.

Give Power to Parents

The more parents really feel that they are an integral part of their preschoolers' educational achievements and that they have the know-how and the skills to accomplish this job, the more likely they will be to carry out program goals set by parent involvers. How can power be given to parents? First, knowledge is power. Parents as citizens have rights to child development knowledge and skills, just as citizens have rights to literacy and job training for work and participation in society. Parent involvers might like to create a *Bill of Rights* for parents and provide adequately to meet the needs spelled out in that Bill of Rights. Here is one I have developed.

A Parents' Bill of Rights

1. *Parents need knowledge about how children develop.* Normative patterns and stages in physical, social, language, and sexual development as well as nutritional and health needs at various child growth stages should be part of the knowledge base for parenthood.
2. *Parents need observation skills.* They need to see their children with new eyes and listen to their children and themselves with new ears. When a child drops toys off his high chair tray, he may be practicing voluntary hand-release skills. He may be learning about near and far space as he watches with interest the way toys fall closer or farther away. He is not deliberately plotting to drive

a parent to distraction or interfere with a parent's housework! A parent cannot match learning games or language interactions effectively to a child's level of development unless noticing skills are sharpened so that the parent can better determine what the child's level of understanding or competence is at the present time.

3. *A parent needs alternative strategies for problem prevention and discipline.* Hit and scold are dreary old tricks in many parents' bag of discipline tricks. Parents need to know a whole array of techniques such as distraction or imaginary role-play or using positive rewards to shape desired behaviors. Parents need to learn how to become active listeners, to set firm limits with love, and to provide explanations as part of firmly set rules.

4. *Parents need to learn how to use their home for learning experiences.* Cooking times are wonderful for learning words like *mix, stir, wash, taste,* and *roll.* Laundry times, workshop times, and toy-cleanup times are fine for teaching words and concepts as well as having children feel they are important helpful family members. Every home should have plenty of TLC, that is, be a Total Learning Center with plenty of Tender Loving Care provided.

5. *Parents need language tools.* One of the most consistent scientific findings from child development research over the past two decades is that parents are crucial as language enlargers, language enrichers, and language boosters for their children. Reading frequently to preschoolers has been found to correlate with later school achievement. Maternal language style and paternal language style can be enriched. The parent who has learned to give names to the things a child notices, to respond positively and promptly to babbling and early talk, and to label the actions a child carries out and the feelings a child expresses has a powerful tool for helping that child advance in language skills.

6. *Parents need to feel that they are teachers, the first and most important early teachers of their children.* As Honig puts it (1975, p. 5), "Parents' paying attention, their pleasure expressed, their listening, their interest — all nourish the growing self of the child as food nourishes his or her body and as toys and sights, sounds and smells nourish the senses."

What specific techniques can be used to give parents power? One is that parents can be invited to case conferences at a center as "specialist informants" on the child. A parent knows what foods the child prefers, what will make the child smile most easily, and what kinds of activities the child enjoys best. The parent can serve as a privileged informant whose knowledge can be really useful to preschool teachers.

Another suggestion is to have parents create games and activities once they have been shown some sample activities and understand what the child is learning and what the aim of a particular game is. In our FDRP, parents who had learned to carry out classification and seriation games with their preschoolers enjoyed making up games for other mothers to use. The child development trainer would mimeograph a new activity sheet with the mother-author's name on it and distribute the sheet to other CDTs to give to their parents to try.

Another suggestion is to let parents share in suggesting topics for parent group meetings and parent workshops. Sometimes staff chooses important topics, but sometimes parents have special concerns too. For example, some of the fathers in our group forbade their wives to look for work while they had a preschool child. So exploring feelings and ideas about women working and about communicating feelings and specific ideas on this topic was a central topic at some of the parent meetings.

Encourage parents to visit elementary schools and teach parents how to assess the quality of interactions and teaching in a variety of kindergarten classrooms. As our project children approached 5 years of age, we taught interested mothers how to use the ABC checklists described earlier in this chapter. They went to different kindergartens and tallied the frequencies of care giver behaviors observed in classrooms. The mothers agreed remarkably well on which kindergarten teachers they thought would best carry out loving learning interactions with their children once the children left our program and went to school.

Build communication bridges to parents. The FDRP care givers safety-pinned a Memo-to-Mommy note to every child's outer clothing each day. The note kept the parent in contact with some aspect of the child's day, interests, or activities. "Jane built a 6-block tower today." "Harry did not hit anyone today." "Gerry was the best rester in his group today." There is always something positive to communicate to a parent so that the parent feels good about himself/herself and about the child.

Train the parents in advocacy. Teach them techniques to organize and articulate their needs to community agencies and educational institutions.

Parents may not believe that they can be teachers and toymakers, despite reassurances by project staff. Workshops where parents create toys can build a parent's confidence and often inspire delight that s/he can provide toys made from "beautiful junk" for the child. Making sure that the parent gets chances to carry out learning activities that were modeled in the home during each visit is another good way to increase parent feelings of competence and power in influencing the child's learning career.

Rotating a library of toys and books may be a good way to get parents active in teaching-learning experiences with the child. The parent feels that someone is not just giving advice about how to encourage the child in different areas and at different stages of development, but also providing the wherewithal on a regular basis.

Parent Involvers Need Materials and Supports and Need to Share Ideas

Project personnel need a library of materials of their own, both written and audiovisual. *Parents Magazine,* Guidance Associates, and Concept Media all have excellent filmstrip materials that would be useful for parent involvers to use with groups of parents. Most of these kits have discussion guides to help the parent involver. Compilations and descriptions of a variety of program models are available (Honig, 1975; Morrison, 1978) for personnel to find out about programs that work, problems that have been encountered, and how other programs dealt with their problems.

Parents who want extra information can be provided with lists of excellent reading materials in addition to books and articles already suggested. Knox's *Parents Are People Too* (1978), Dodson's *How to Parent* (1970), and Smith's grandmotherly *Survival Handbook for Preschool Mothers* (1978) are but a few of the fine books with suggestions to support and enlighten parents in that most creative, intellectually complex, and demanding job called *parenting.*

Parent involvers need a resource library to meet their special needs with parents. Does a parent have a deaf baby? The free booklets for parents published by the John Tracy Clinic (1968) are excellent materials to offer a family. Does a parent express concern about sexuality in the preschooler? Gordon's (1975) chapter "Before they go to school teach them everything they need to know (about sex)" is quite useful. Does the parent have a handicapped or retarded toddler? Sample copies of *The Exceptional Parent* magazine as a gift to the parents may provide a feeling of support from advice that really helps. The parent involver may want to use ideas from *A Step-by-Step Learning*

Guide for Retarded Infants and Children by Johnson and Werner (1975) or from Honig (1979). Is the parent involver having problems because the parent is very distressed at being alone? *The Single Parent,* the journal of Parents Without Partners, often provides insights and strengths to help single parents.

Is the parent involver trying to work with unmarried fathers? Then Pannor's work (Pannor, Massarik, & Evans, 1971) has some valuable tips. For example, when project personnel actively involved the unmarried mother to help reach the unmarried father, then 94.3% of the latter were reached. When the unmarried mother did not aid, then the project personnel reached only 12.1% of the unmarried fathers.

Access to major research books and articles as well as how-to manuals is important. Research data are important as a resource for parent involvers. Data can indicate what was tried and by whom, what problems were encountered, what worked for how long, with which populations, and in what settings. Knowledge about other programs helps parent involvers make wiser choices and helps to sharpen awareness of one's own goals and processes.

The major point to remember is that *parent involvers need support systems too.* They need resources, audiovisual as well as written. They also need an understanding supervisor who can listen well to problems and help the parent involvers evolve creative ideas for dealing with some of these problems or offer suggestions of other community resources to use as aids.

PARENTING PACKAGES: Many materials, written or multimedia, are now available for use in programs that involve parents. These materials could be used in home visits or in groups or be provided for individual parent use. For example, *Let Me Introduce Myself: The First 30 Months of Life: A Guide for the Parents of Infant Children* has been developed by Ligon, Barber, and Williams (1976) so that parents (with good reading skills) can teach themselves to understand their new little one's growth as seen through the child's eyes in this "autobiography" of sorts. For parents with lower literacy skills, Lally and Gordon (1977) provide a full set of activities for parents of infants.

The Southwest Educational Development Laboratory (1977) publishes a series of very short booklets written in large easy-to-read print. Each booklet focuses on a special activity that can help a parent enrich experiences with and for the preschool child. Some booklet titles are *Read to Your Child, Talking with Children,* and *Children Learn by Watching and Helping.* These booklets could be used in group meetings or home visits or could be distributed through television spot announcements of helpful materials available for parents of preschoolers through a community agency's sponsorship.

Cooperative Extension Services in many states provide booklets to help parents of preschoolers. Finch's brochure *Odds and Ends: Learning Activities for Preschoolers* is one such brochure for parents.

The Parents As Resources Project (P.A.R.) provides workshops for parents and parent involvers nationally to help teach techniques of play and group activity with preschoolers through the use of home-made materials. Some of their titles are *A Pumpkin in a Pear Tree, Recipes for Fun* (and *Recetas para Divertirse,* the Spanish version), and *I Never Saw a Purple Cow,* plus booklets on how to conduct parent involvement workshops and train others in activities with preschoolers (P.A.R. Project, 1971).

New parenting resources are constantly coming on the market. The Head Start program has recently tried out a new program with parent groups called *Exploring Parenting: A New Head Start Parent Education Curriculum.* The curriculum is built around the philosophy that you must first feel good about yourself before you can relate to others in a positive way. Parent participants keep a journal or diary of everyday events as they increase their awareness and knowledge of various aspects of rearing children.

Places and Populations

Parent involvers may need to learn more specifically about the particular linguistic, ethnic, or age group of parents their project is serving. Working with mountain people in Appalachia requires some special extra readings during in-service training, just as workers need special knowledge of adolescents when providing services to teenage mothers in an inner city clinic.

Staff may also want to think about the ways to interest the community in supporting parenting programs. Newspaper columns and TV spot ads may be suggested. Some libraries have sessions for parents and tots as well as toy- and book-lending kits for parents.

Stitt (1978) has recently reported on the Parent Place she founded 1 1/2 years ago. Distressed parents learn about the Parent Place through leaflets in supermarkets or from newspaper advertisements. A telephone crisis line plus a drop-in child care service are available when needed. It is encouraging to realize the number of innovative places and ways in which parent involvement efforts are being carried out. One of the latest places is the pediatric clinic playroom where parents bring their children for outpatient care routinely in many cities (Morris, 1973) or the private pediatrician's office at night (Jackson &

Terdal, 1978). In some communities, a preschool teacher brings a mobile van to neighborhoods. Parents and preschoolers have a chance to see and participate in activities and peer experiences that might be otherwise impossible in isolated areas.

CONCLUSION

What we have surveyed suggests the richness of materials, resources, and human creative energies for increasing our ability to work with parents, involving parents more intimately, more positively, and more responsively in the education and positive social-emotional learning of their children. Parent involvement is a new profession. We must keep a quality of humility and respect for the awesome job that parents have in raising youngsters wisely and well and a respect for parents' strengths and knowledge of their children, even as we share our skills and knowledge with parents. Parent involvement is a great adventure. May we discover more and more treasures among our parent and child citizens as we continue on this adventure, by whatever roads we take.

REFERENCES

Adkins, D. C. *Home activities for preschool children: A manual of games and activities for use by parents with their children at home, to foster certain preschool goals.* Honolulu, Hawaii: University of Hawaii Center for Research in Early Childhood Education, 1971.

Ainsworth, M. D. S., Bell, S. M., & Stayton, D. J. Individual differences in the development of some attachment behaviors. *Merrill-Palmer Quarterly,* 1972, *18,* 123-143.

Alford, R. D. (Ed.) *Home-oriented preschool education: Curriculum Planning Guide.* Charleston, West Virginia: Appalachia Educational Laboratory, 1972.

Badger, E. *Curriculum: Postnatal classes for high risk mother-infant pairs.* Cincinnati: Department of Pediatrics, University of Cincinnati College of Medicine, 1977.

Bassin, J., & Drovett, D. Parent outreach. *The Exceptional Child,* 1976, *6,* 6-9.

Baumrind, D. Current patterns of parental authority. *Developmental Psychology,* 1971, *4,* 1-103.

Beckwith, L. Relationships between infants' social behavior and their mothers' behavior. *Child Development,* 1972, *43,* 397-411.

Bradley, R. H., & Caldwell, B. M. The relation of infant's home environments to mental test performance at fifty-four months: A follow-up study. *Child Development,* 1976, *47,* 1172-1174.

Carew, I. V., Chan, I., & Halfar, C. *Observing intelligence in young children.*

Englewood Cliffs, New Jersey: P-H, 1976.

Carnegie Quarterly. New optimism about preschool education: Three reports from Ypsilanti, Michigan. *Carnegie Quarterly,* 1978, *summer,* 9.

Cohen, S. E. *Caregiver-child interaction and competence in pre-term children.* Paper presented at the biennial meeting of the Society for Research in Child Development, New Orleans, April 1977.

Dinkmeyer, D., & McKay, G. D. *Systematic training for effective parenting: Leader's manual.* Circle Pines, Minnesota: American Guidance Service, 1976.

Dodson, F. *How to parent.* New York: Signet, 1970.

Exploring Childhood Program. *Overview and catalog of materials.* Newton, Massachusetts: Education Development Center, 1976.

Federal Interagency Day Care Requirements. Washington, D. C.: D.H.E.W., 1968.

Finch, M. A. Odds and ends: Learning activities for preschoolers (Extension Bulletin No. 105). Newark, Delaware: Cooperative Extension Service, undated.

Forrester, B. J. *Parents as educational change agents for infants: Competencies not credentials.* Paper presented at the meeting of the Council on Exceptional Children, Washington, D. C., March 1972.

Fraiberg, S., Adelson, E., & Shapiro, V. Ghosts in the nursery: A psychoanalytic approach to the problem of impaired infant-mother relationships. *Journal of the American Academy of Child Psychiatry,* 1975.

Garcia, A. Developing questioning children: A parent program. *Teem Exchange,* 1972, 2(2), 3-7.

Ginott, H. *Between parent and child: New solutions to old problems.* New York: MacMillan, 1965.

Gordon, I. J. *Early child stimulation through parent education. Final report* (Project No. PHS-R-306). Washington, D. C.: D.H.E.W. Children's Bureau, Social and Rehabilitation Service, 1971.

Gordon, S. *Let's make sex a household word: A guide for parents and children.* New York: John Day, 1975.

Gordon, T. *P.E.T. in action.* New York: Bantam, 1976.

Gray, S. Home visiting programs for parents of young children. *DARCEE Papers and Reports,* 1971, 5(4).

Heber, R., Garber, H., Harrington, S., Hoffman, C., & Fallender, C. *Rehabilitation of families at risk for mental retardation. A progress report.* Madison: University of Wisconsin Rehabilitation Research and Training Center in Mental Retardation, 1972.

Henderson, R. W. Application of social learning principles in a field setting. *Exceptional Children,* 1976, 53-55.

Hess, R. D. Parental behavior and children's school achievement: Implications for Head Start. In E. Grotberg (Ed.), *Critical issues in research related to disadvantaged children.* Princeton, New Jersey: Educational Testing Service, 1969.

Honig, A. S. Curriculum for infants in day care. *Child Welfare*, 1974, *53*, 633-642.

Honig, A. S. *Parent involvement in early childhood education.* Washington, D. C.: Natl Assn Child Ed, 1975.

Honig, A. S. *A review of recent infancy research.* Washington, D. C.: Dingle Associates, Inc., 1978.

Honig, A. S. *Parent involvement and the development of handicapped children.* Unpublished manuscript, Columbia University Teacher's College, New York, 1979.

Honig, A. S., & Lally, J. R. How good is your infant program? Use an observation method to find out. *Child Care Quarterly*, 1975, *4*, 194-207.

Honig, A. S., Lally, J. R., & Matthieson, D. H. *Personal-social adjustment of school children after five years in a family enrichment program.* Urbana, Illinois: ERIC Clearinghouse on Early Childhood Education, 1979.

Howard, M. Improving services for young fathers. *Sharing*, 1975, *spring*, 45-53.

Jackson, R. H., & Terdal, L. Parent education within a pediatric practice. *Journal of Pediatric Psychology*, 1978, *3*, 2-5.

John Tracy Clinic. *Getting your baby ready to talk: A home study plan for infant language development.* Los Angeles: John Tracy Clinic, 1968.

Johnson, D. L., & Leler, H. L. *Progress report: Houston Parent-Child Development Center.* Houston, Texas: Parent-Child Development Center, 1975.

Johnson, V. M., & Werner, R. A. *A step-by-step learning guide for retarded infants and children.* Syracuse, New York: Syracuse University Press, 1975.

Klaus, M. H., & Kennell, J. H. *Maternal-infant bonding.* St. Louis: Mosby, 1976.

Knox, L. *Parents are people too.* Nashville: Intersect, 1978.

Lally, J. R., & Gordon, I. J. *Learning games for infants and toddlers.* Syracuse, New York: New Readers Press, 1977.

Lally, J. R., & Honig, A. S. Education of infants and toddlers from low-income and low-education backgrounds: Support for the family's role and identity. In B. Friedlander, G. Kirk, & G. Sterritt (Eds.) *Infant assessment and intervention.* New York: Brunner-Mazel, 1975.

Lally, J. R., & Honig, A. S. The family development research program. In M. C. Day & R. K. Parker (Eds.), *The preschool in action: Exploring early childhood programs* (2nd ed). Boston: Allyn, 1977. (a)

Lally, J. R., & Honig, A. S. *Final report: Family development research program.* Syracuse, New York: Children's Center, 1977. (b)

Lambie, D. Z., Bond, J. T., & Weikart, D. P. *Home teaching with mothers and infants.* Ypsilanti, Michigan: High/Scope Educational Research Foundation, 1974.

Laosa, L. M. Socialization, education and continuity: The importance of the sociocultural context. *Young Children*, 1977, *32*, 21-27.

Lasater, T. M., Briggs, J., Malone, P., Gilliom, C. F., & Weisberg, P. *The Birmingham model for parent education.* Paper presented at the biennial meeting of the Society for Research in Child Development, Denver, Colorado, April 1975.

Levenstein, P. The mother-child home program. In M. C. Day and R. K. Parker (Eds.), *The preschool in action: Exploring early childhood programs* (2nd ed.). Boston: Allyn, 1977.

Ligon, E. M., Barber, L. W., & Williams, H. J. *Let me introduce myself: The first 30 months of life: A guide for the parents of infant children.* Schenectady, New York: Character Res, 1976.

Love, J. M. et al. *National Home Start evaluation: Final report, findings and implications.* Ypsilanti, Michigan: High/Scope Educational Research Foundation: Cambridge, Massachusetts. Abt Assoc, 1976.

Milner, E. A. A study of the relationship between reading readiness and grade one school children and patterns of parent-child interaction. *Child Development*, 1951, *22*, 95-112.

Morris, A. G. Parent education for child education being carried out in a pediatric clinic playroom. *Clinical Pediatrics*, 1973, 235-239.

Morrison, G. S. *Parent involvement in the home, school, and community.* Columbus, Ohio: Merrill, 1978.

National Federation of Settlements and Neighborhood Centers. *Preparing teenagers for parenthood: A recommended "How To" program guide.* New York: NFSNC, 1976.

Nimnicht, G. P., Brown, E., Addison, B., & Johnson, S. *Parent guide: How to play learning games with a preschool child.* Morristown, New Jersey: Gen Learn Pr, 1971.

O'Keefe, R. A. *The child and family resource program: An overview.* Washington, D. C.: D.H.E.W. Administration for Children, Youth and Families, 1978.

Pannor, R., Massarik, F., & Evans, B. The unmarried father: New approaches for unmarried young parents. New York: Springer, 1971.

P.A.R. Project. *P.A.R. presents: Workshop procedures.* Winnetka, Illinois: P.A.R. Project, 1971.

Pierson, D. E. *The Brookline program for infants and their families — Progress report.* Brookline, Massachusetts: BEEP, 1973.

Pushaw, D. (Ed.). *Teach your child to talk: A parent handbook.* Cincinnati: CDBCO Standard Publishing Company, 1969.

Rabinowitz, M., Weiner, G., & Jackson, C. R. *In the beginning: A parent guide of activities and experiences for infants from birth to six months* (Book 1). New Orleans: Parent-Child Development Center, 1973.

Scheinfeld, D., Bowles, D., Tuck, S., & Gold, R. Parents' values, family networks and family development: Working with disadvantaged families. Paper presented at the annual meeting of the American Orthopsychiatric Association, New York, April 1969. *Research Report*, 1969, *6*(9).

Segner, L., & Patterson, C. *Ways to help babies grow and learn.* Denver, Colorado: World Press, 1970.

Shearer, M. S., & Shearer, D. E. The Portage Project: A model for early childhood education. *Exceptional Children,* 1972, *39,* 210-217.

Shure, M. B., & Spivack, G. *Problem solving techniques in childrearing.* San Francisco: Jossey-Bass, 1978.

Smilansky, S. *The effects of socio-dramatic play on disadvantaged preschool children.* New York: Wiley, 1968.

Smith, H. W. *Survival handbook for preschool mothers.* Chicago: Follett, 1978.

Southwest Educational Development Laboratory. *Booklets for parents of preschoolers.* Austin, Texas: Early Childhood Program, 1977.

Sprigle, H. Learning to learn program. In S. Ryan (Ed.), *A report of longitudinal evaluations of preschool programs.* Washington, D.C.: Office of Child Development. 1972.

Sroufe, L. A., & Waters, E. Attachment as an organizational construct. *Child Development.* 1977. *48,* 1184-1199.

Stevens, J. H., Jr. Current directions in the study of parental facilitation of children's cognitive development. *Educational Horizons,* 1973, *50*(2), 62-66.

Stitt, S. The parent place. *Human Behavior,* 1978, *7,* 36-37.

Strodtbeck, F. L. The hidden curriculum in the middle-class home. In J. D. Krumboltz (Ed.), *Learning and the educational process.* Skokie, Illinois: Rand, 1965.

Swan, R. W., & Stavros, H. Child-rearing practices associated with the development of cognitive skills of children in low socio-economic areas. *Early Child Development and Care,* 1973, *2,* 23-38.

Washington, K. R. SUCCESS: A parent effectiveness approach for developing urban children's self-concepts. *Young Children,* 1977, *32,* 5-10.

White, B. *Guidelines for parent education.* Paper presented at the Planning Education Conference, Flint, Michigan, September 1977.

Chapter 16

PARAPROFESSIONALS IN BEHAVIORAL PARENT TRAINING

BARBARA D. INGERSOLL AND A. MARGARET EASTMAN

THE utilization of paraprofessionals as parent educators or trainers is by no means a recent development in child mental health. Parent discussion groups, widely employed in the 1950s and 1960s, were frequently led by ministers, teachers, public health nurses, and other lay persons trained in programs such as those sponsored by the Child Study Association of America. Numerous research programs, including those conducted by the Hogg Foundation and the Child Study Association, were undertaken to explore the utility of the discussion group approach and the feasibility of utilizing paraprofessionals as group leaders.

Despite considerable research effort, however, results were inconclusive and the effectiveness of parent discussion groups as a means of altering parent and child behavior was not convincingly demonstrated (*see* reviews by Auerbach, 1968; Brim, 1959). In the mid 1960s, parent discussion groups began to wane in popularity, and the approach itself was eclipsed by the rapid rise of behavior modification approaches to parent training.

Employing behavioral methods, researchers have reported considerable success in training parents to modify a wide variety of childhood behavior disorders (*see* reviews by Cone & Sloop, 1971; Graziano, 1977; O'Dell, 1974). Behavior problems successfully treated in this fashion have run the gamut from complex "syndromes" to relatively simple isolated behaviors. Parents have functioned as effective change agents for the behavior of severely retarded and autistic children and have obtained equal success with the everyday behavior problems presented by normal children everywhere.

This approach, which has been found to be of use at the levels of secondary and tertiary prevention, also holds promise at the level of primary prevention. Direct observation of family interaction indicates that "normal" families, as well as families with identified problems, exhibit poor contingency management skills (Forehand & Wells, 1977; Wahl, Johnson, Johanson, & Martin, 1974; Taplin & Reid, 1977). Risley, Clark, and Cataldo (1976) concluded, from an analysis of birth rates and patterns of age distribution within the society, that "More children than in the past will be raised by inexperienced parents . . . who are surrounded by other inexperienced parents and are usually cut off from (traditional sources of) child rearing advice and support" (pp. 38, 40).

For these reasons, many within the field of child mental health have urged that training in parenting skills be made available to all parents from all levels of society. Horowitz (1976) has suggested that community-based "parent-child research stations" be developed to offer consultation and training to parents on a continuous basis, in much the same fashion as agricultural research stations provide information and advice to farmers. Family participation in such a service might be reinforced by social activities, free bowling, free babysitting, and even tax credits.

The public school system has also been proposed as a setting in which such primary prevention programs might be implemented. Simpson (1973) and Hawkins (1972) argue that the school must ultimately accept the responsibility for broad parent training programs; indeed, Hawkins suggests that such programs be made mandatory.

Currently, however, mental health services for those families with identified problems are exorbitant in cost and quite limited in availability (Graziano, 1977). The cost of implementing large-scale programs such as have been suggested would be staggering, even if there were sufficient personnel to meet the demands of the task. Of course, the current shortage of highly trained mental health professionals is a widely known and well-documented fact, and the situation is not expected to change in the foreseeable future (Albee, 1959).

Acutely aware of these problems, the helping professions have sought to develop new methods of service delivery to minimize costs and demands on professional time. The utilization of paraprofessional personnel to carry out some of the tasks traditionally performed by mental health professionals has been proposed as one means of achieving these ends (Guerney, 1969; Hobbs, 1964). A more recent development is the use of packaged intervention programs designed to be implemented with little or, in some cases, no professional supervision (Clark, Greene, Macrae, McNees, Davis, & Risley, 1977; Risley et al., 1976). Both approaches merit careful scrutiny as potential methods for achieving mass dissemination of parenting skills and knowledge.

PARAPROFESSIONALS AS PARENT TRAINERS

The utilization of paraprofessional manpower has increased rapidly in recent years. The movement had its origins in Albee's (1959) well-known paper describing current and projected shortages of highly trained personnel to provide mental health services. It was legitimized, in part, by the report of the Joint Commission on Mental Illness and Health (1961) and received additional impetus from federally funded training programs and the development of associate degree programs to train paraprofessional workers.

Paraprofessionals in Behavioral Parent Training

Evidence indicated that paraprofessionals can function effectively in a variety of roles and settings (Fabry & Reid, 1978; Gruver, 1971; Keeley, Shemberg, & Ferber, 1973). In the specific area of behavioral parent training, paraprofessionals have been used with reported success to train individual parents as well as groups of parents. As an example of the former, Pomerantz, Peterson, Marholin, and Stern (1977) reported the results of a study in which a paraprofessional trained and supervised a mother in the successful treatment of her child's water phobia.

Undergraduates trained as behavior analysts were used by Ferber, Keeley, and Shemberg (1974) to provide individual treatment to families of aggressive children. The authors described problems encountered in the course of this work, but these problems appeared to be unrelated to trainer status (undergraduate trainer versus doctoral-level trainer).

On a larger scale, Wahler and Erickson (1969) trained 14 community volunteers to work with parents and teachers. Training was primarily of an in-service nature, with little in the way of formal didactic instruction. In the 66 children treated in the program, significant reductions in the frequencies of all problem behavior categories were obtained. In addition, length of time from screening to termination was considerably shorter than treatment time for cases treated by more traditional methods.

Tharp and Wetzel (1969) provided a 3-week seminar and on-the-job training to paraprofessionals with no previous training in the helping professions. The paraprofessionals served as trainers and consultants to parents and teachers who, in turn, mediated child behavior change. Of 135 problem behaviors exhibited by 77 children treated in the program, 21 were reduced in rate to 0; 99 were reduced to 50% or less of baseline rate.

Evidence from studies in which paraprofessionals have functioned as group leaders for groups of parents undergoing training is somewhat meager. Rinn, Vernon, and Wise (1975) found no difference in outcome between groups conducted by a doctoral-level instructor and those conducted by a masters-level instructor. These authors tentatively concluded that paraprofessionals and masters-level personnel could be used effectively as parent training group leaders.

The use of parents to provide behavioral parent training to other parents was reported by Ora (1971) and Wagner and Ora (1970), but this potentially exciting extension of the group training approach has received surprisingly little attention in terms of controlled research. An exception is the work in progress of Marilyn Clark-Hall and her associates (1978), using the Responsive Parent Training program with a nonclinic population. The format for each of the 12 sessions consists of didactic instruction provided by a program director, followed by a small group session in which individual behavior change programs are the focus of attention. The small groups are conducted by parents and other individuals who have previously completed the program and have undergone training at the apprentice level to serve as group leaders. After serving as a group leader, the paraprofessional may complete a second course of training designed to teach him/her to serve as program director and to assume responsibility for groups conducted in the community under his/her direction. Over 675 parents have been trained in this program, and more than 50 parents have participated as staff members. A variety of outcome measures have been included in this study, which promises to shed further light on the issue of paraprofessionals as parent trainers.

Issues in the Training and Utilization of Paraprofessionals

The results of the studies cited here suggest that paraprofessionals can function effectively as parent trainers. However, these studies must be interpreted with considerable caution. Many contain serious methodological weaknesses that severely limit the conclusions that can be drawn from the results. Furthermore, for the most part, these studies fail to address a number of problems and issues surrounding the use of paraprofessionals in any capacity within an agency or program. Surveys of agencies in which paraprofessionals are employed and of the paraprofessionals themselves indicate that problems do, indeed, exist (Baker, 1972; Bartels & Tyler, 1975), and a number of vital questions confront the agency director or program administrator who contemplates the use of paraprofessional personnel.

Selection of Paraprofessionals

The first of these questions concerns appropriate criteria for the selection of paraprofessionals. This has emerged as a thorny problem; Siegel (1973) has noted that, despite research efforts in this area, no uniform selection criteria have been developed to serve as guidelines for the potential employer.

Bartels and Tyler (1975) surveyed directors of federally funded comprehensive community mental health centers concerning selection criteria and found a close correspondence between qualities sought in paraprofessionals and those considered desirable in professional mental health workers. These expectations, the authors warn, might be unrealistically high and may lead to problems and dissatisfaction with paraprofessional performance. These authors also caution against emphasis on intellectual or educational criteria, as these criteria were ranked important by a significantly greater percentage of respondents classified as indicating low satisfaction with paraprofessional performance than by respondents indicating high satisfaction. Again, they suggest that this criterion is poorly suited for choosing paraprofessional employees and results in dissatisfaction.

Role Definition

Unclear role definition has been cited as a problem by paraprofessionals (Baker, 1972) and by employers of paraprofessionals (Bartels & Tyler, 1975). As Crisler (1973) noted, "(Paraprofessionals) are often employed with nebulous titles and job descriptions and are expected to become, through some osmotic process, a fully functioning helper" (p. 44). Bartels and Tyler suggest that lack of clear demarcation between professional and paraprofessional roles contributes to difficulties the two groups encounter in attempting to work together, which may promote lack of acceptance of the paraprofessional by the professional staff. Thus, specific tasks to be performed by the paraprofessional must be clearly delineated, and a systematic task analysis undertaken to identify requisite target skills for these tasks.

With respect to behavioral parent training, it is necessary to distinguish between the tasks to be performed by the paraprofessional who serves a clinical population and tasks to be performed by the paraprofessional who provides educational and preventive services to a nonclinical population. In the former case, although s/he may provide basic instruction in contingency management skills to groups of parents in the clinic, typically the paraprofessional works individually with parents and others in the child's environment to develop interventions for specified problems. In such a role, s/he is closely supervised by a professional, under whose direction the paraprofessional performs a variety of tasks that cannot be assumed by the professional due to time and cost factors.

The paraprofessional who provides parent training to groups of parents from a nonclinical population does not, generally speaking, receive close supervision, since the provision of such supervision would be too costly and time-consuming. Rather, in this role, the paraprofessional must function with relative independence and must, therefore, master a broad range of skills and knowledge.

Training

After the skills ultimately expected of the paraprofessional have been identified, the development of an appropriate training program becomes the program administrator's next concern. Specific content of the training program must be defined and a decision made as to who will provide the training: Is the requisite expertise available "in-house," or must assistance be obtained from sources external to the agency? Of course, much depends on the depth and breadth of target skills that will ultimately be expected of the paraprofessional trainee, but there is some evidence to indicate that provision of appropriate training can pose problems. Crisler, Porter, and Jones (1972) surveyed state vocational rehabilitation agencies and found that 60% indicated a need for assistance in paraprofessional training. Similarly, Bartels and Tyler (1975) found that 12.5% of mental health centers surveyed cited educational inadequacy as a problem, with 7.1% specifically noting agency difficulty in developing training programs.

A point of special importance is the cost of training. As Baker (1972) noted, the attrition rate in many programs employing paraprofessionals is high, and the cost-conscious administrator will be wary of providing expensive training for individuals who may remain in the agency's employ for only a short period of time. Unfortunately, the administrator who wishes to utilize paraprofessional parent trainers will find new solutions to these problems in the research literature. In none of the behavioral parent training studies cited here is specific information provided concerning the content, methodology, or cost of training. Thus, it is not possible to systematically analyze and compare different training procedures on these dimensions.

With regard to training format, however, considerable evidence from the literature related to other categories of paraprofessional workers bears on this issue. This evidence suggests, for example, that the format of the training program should include a variety of instructional modes, as restriction to a single mode may limit the degree and generality of behavior change produced. As Kazdin and Moyer (1976) have pointed out, training programs that combine a number of procedures may have the potential to produce results that no one procedure could accomplish individually.

In our view, didactic presentations, including lectures and written material, should be included to provide verbal theoretical knowledge concerning behavioral principles, although there has been some debate concerning the necessity or even the desirability of including formalized classroom instruction (Colarelli & Siegel, 1966). However, unless the skills to be mastered and applied by the paraprofessional are extremely limited in scope, we believe that it is preferable to provide a conceptual framework within which the application of these skills can be understood by the trainee. Data from a study of Paul, McInnis, and Mariotto (1973) seem to support this point of view: These authors found that academic performance was significantly correlated with quality of on-the-floor work performance.

As concerns the presentation of didactic material, Houts and Hench (1976) suggest that general principles should follow, not precede, clinical examples and illustrations. This advice is based on the authors' experiences in teaching medical students who, they find, are often hostile to the social sciences and are "turned off" by the presentation of "even a sentence or two of abstractions at the beginning of the presentation." This advice seems admirably suited to the training of paraprofessionals, many of whom are limited in formal education and may be uncomfortable with abstract material.

Didactic instruction alone is not a sufficient course of training for the paraprofessional: Evidence from a variety of sources indicates that training approaches that emphasize the acquisition of verbal-theoretical knowledge do not insure the acquisition of skills necessary to implement such knowledge (Gardner, 1972; Sepler & Myers, 1978). To insure that trainees acquire requisite skills to implement behavioral principles, researchers have supplemented lectures and written material with modeling (Gladstone & Spencer, 1977), cueing (Cone & Sheldon, 1973), practice with feedback and social reinforcement (Panyan, Boozer, & Morris, 1970), and combinations of these methods (Fabry & Reid, 1978; Gardner, 1972; Gladstone & Sherman, 1975; Martin & Pear, 1970).

Integration of theoretical-academic material with skill learning is an important aspect of training that should not be overlooked. Several studies have shown that training programs in which academic material is integrated with opportunities to observe and practice skills produce results superior to programs in which a more traditional academics/skill mastery sequence is employed (Batman, 1968; Krieger, 1970).

The specific content of the training program will, of course, vary with the target behaviors expected of the trainee. An approach that seems particularly well suited to training paraprofessionals to function in a clinical setting under supervision is that of a system of *levels* with levels based on categorization of target behaviors expected of the trainee. Brink (1974) has proposed four levels ranging from technician, whose training is aimed at solving one or a few specific problems, to consultant, for whom training results in an ability to analyze a complete continuum of situations, as well as an ability to engage in research and to train others at all levels. Similar systems have been proposed by Gardner (1973) and Poser (1967).

Evaluation

Following the training program, paraprofessional performance must be evaluated. It must be demonstrated that the trainee has acquired certain skills and can effectively perform those tasks for which s/he was trained. In evaluating the outcome of training, the administrator must avoid a short-sighted focus on process goals; that is, s/he must not be content merely to demonstrate changes in trainee behavior, but must also document change in the ultimate target group — the clients served.

Studies utilizing paraprofessionals as behavioral parent trainers *have* documented changes in the target groups served (although, as noted, lack of methodological rigor limits the extent to which firm conclusions can be drawn concerning client change). They have failed altogether, however, to document that the changes in trainee behavior resulted from the training program. Such information is of considerable importance in developing effective, efficient training programs, and researchers are urged to employ a variety of evaluation measures to assess training and service delivery.

A related issue concerns the comparability of results produced by paraprofessionals with those achieved by professionals. The paraprofessional might provide service at less cost than that provided by the professional. However, unless the evidence indicates that outcome to the client is the same, or nearly the same, in both cases, the question quickly changes from "At *what* cost?" to "At *whose* cost?"

In summary, the decision to utilize paraprofessionals to provide parent training services in the clinic or community is one that cannot be made lightly. Issues of training and evaluation of service delivery are complex, and the procedures are costly and often beyond the means of the small agency with limited funds.

PACKAGED INTERVENTION PROGRAMS

At first glance, the recent trend toward packaged intervention programs appears to hold considerable promise as a means of minimizing or eliminating many of the problems associated with the training and utilization of paraprofessionals. These packages are designed to address specific client problems and to be administered without the need for lengthy and expensive training programs.

Self-Help Packages

Some packaged intervention programs are designed to be utilized directly by the consumer and require neither professional consultation nor the services of mental health workers as intermediaries. Examples of such packaged programs in the area of parenting include self-help programs for toilet training (Azrin & Foxx, 1974) and managing children's behavior on family shopping trips (Clark et al., 1977).

These self-administered intervention programs may achieve success with the highly specific problem behaviors that they are designed to address. However, the range of application of each program is quite narrow, and there is little reason to expect generalization of parent knowledge from a single behavior to other unrelated areas of child behavior. Koegel, Glahn, and Nieminen (1978), for example, demonstrated that only when parents/trainees received instructions in general principles of behavior change were they able to acquire a general set of skills effective across multiple children and target behaviors.

An additional criticism is that the use of a single instructional mode, typical of self-help programs, may restrict the degree and generality of behavior change produced. In addition, many self-help programs focus, of necessity, on the acquisition of verbal-theoretical knowledge. As has been shown with other groups of paraprofessionals, parental knowledge does not necessarily result in an ability to utilize behavior skills (Nay, 1975; O'Dell, Flynn, & Benlolo, 1977).

Many of the same methods that have been found useful in enhancing paraprofessional skill acquisition have also proved effective in insuring that parents have the requisite skills to implement behavioral principles. These methods include modeling, both live and filmed or taped (Johnson & Brown, 1969; Mash, Lazere, Terdal, & Garner, 1973; Nay, 1975; Rose, 1969; Wagner & Ora, 1970), and procedures in which modeling is combined with behavior rehearsal and feedback (Johnson, 1971; Rose, 1974). Some investigators have included the use of audiotapes or videotaped feedback to parents (Bernal, 1969; Bernal, Williams, Miller, & Reagor, 1972; Doleys, Doster, & Cartelli, 1976).

In a well-designed study, O'Dell, Mahoney, Horton, and Turner (in press) compared several parent training techniques, including live and filmed modeling. Behavior rehearsal with feedback was superior to all other methods, followed by filmed modeling alone. The authors note the following advantages of filmed or taped material: A diversity of models and settings can be provided; the material can be widely disseminated and can be used by paraprofessionals; and the procedures are completely replicable.

These advantages suggest that filmed material might be utilized in self-help packages as a means of providing opportunities for modeling. Koegel et al. (1978), for example, found that videotaped demonstrations, without the presence of a teacher, were sufficient to teach a set of behavior change skills. Anecdotally, however, these authors noted that parents trained with a teacher "seemed more confident" than parents trained with videotapes alone. This, they conjecture, might result in less willingness to employ the procedures and, thus, poor generalization over time.

This criticism of lack of generalization can be leveled at all self-help programs, regardless of the instructional mode(s) employed. In addition, although leaderless self-help packages might combine several instructional modes to teach both general principles and specific skills, such packages can make no provisions for behavior rehearsal, corrective feedback, or positive reinforcement. These weaknesses, inherent in all self-help packages, suggest that the shortcomings of self-help programs may outweigh the advantages in cost and efficiency for dealing with all but the narrowest of child behavior problems.

Leader-Mediated Packaged Programs

Packaged programs designed to be implemented by paraprofessionals appear potentially superior both to self-help packages and to current methods of utilizing paraprofessionals to provide parent training. Such programs have been developed for use in other areas of service delivery (Fawcett, Mathews, Fletcher, Morrow, & Stokes, 1976; Mathews & Fawcett, 1977), but, to date, little attention has been directed toward the application of this approach in parent training.

The implementation of a parent training package by paraprofessionals could substantially reduce the cost of paraprofessional training and supervision, as the package itself should, if properly designed, insure successful parent and child behavior change. The package should be complete, with each aspect of training specified in detail. It must also be designed for ease of use, with minimal pretraining required. A variety of instructional modes could and indeed should be incorporated, including filmed modeling and opportunities for verbal practice and behavior rehearsal and for feedback and positive reinforcement. The complete package, including built-in measures of program evaluation, could provide a simple, inexpensive, but demonstrably effective means of providing quality training to large numbers of parents. An additional advantage of such a package would be ease of replication, an important advantage for the researcher.

ESP, Exercises in Successful Parenting (Ingersoll & Eastman, 1978), was developed to meet the criteria listed above and was designed for use by professionals as well as paraprofessionals in clinic or community settings. The package incorporates a variety of instructional modes. Verbal-theoretical material for each of the 6 lessons is contained in the leader's script. This material is presented in brief segments, followed by programmed questions to which parents must respond verbally. Questions and appropriate responses are included in the lesson script.

Correct and incorrect use of each skill is modeled by means of videotaped vignettes. Verbal practice and behavior rehearsal exercises accompany the audiovisual material. Through this approach, parents are provided with the opportunity to receive immediate feedback and positive reinforcement for their efforts.

Parents gain additional practice in behavioral skills through implementing behavior change programs by way of home practice exercises assigned each week. Data from home practice assignments is used to assess child behavior change and serves as an important measure of program evaluation. Other evaluation measures include parent responses to programmed questions and behavior rehearsal exercises and responses to consumer questionnaires completed weekly.

To date, 40 parents have been trained in an outpatient clinic setting, and 14 have been trained in a public school setting. Professional group leaders have included psychologists, social workers, and psychiatry residents.

The following study is an initial attempt to explore the feasibility of using paraprofessionals to implement a programmed parent training package with normal families, i.e., families with no reported severe child behavior problems.

METHOD

Subjects

From parents in 2 public schools participating in a federally funded educational enrichment program, 2 paraprofessionals were recruited. Of these paraprofessionals, 1 had previously participated as a member of an ESP group conducted in the school. Both were college graduates and active participants in activities related to their children's schools.

Parents were recruited through mailings, telephone contact, radio and newspaper advertisements, and announcements made through the Parent Teacher Association. Through these means, 18 families were located.

Families were randomly assigned to the treatment group and the waiting list control group so that each group contained 9 members. A prior agreement with the staff of the sponsoring enrichment program made complete randomization impossible: 4 mothers whose children were not enrolled in either of the 2 participating schools were automatically assigned to the waiting list control group.

Target children of parents in the treatment group were 67% male, ranged in age from 2 to 11 years, with a mean age of 6 years, and had a mean of 1.1 siblings. Target children of parents in the control group were 29% male, ranged in age from 2 to 9 years, with a mean of 5.4 years, and had a mean of 0.86 siblings. Family income for the treatment group ranged from $10,000 to $40,000 per year (mean $13,777) and for the control group from $7,000 to $24,000 (mean $16,214). No significant differences were found between groups on any of these measures.

Treatment Procedures*

Paraprofessional Training

The paraprofessional group leaders received three training sessions

---

*Detailed information concerning all training procedures and copies of all measurement instruments employed can be obtained from the senior author.

covering the use of the ESP parent training package. The first training session included a brief review of research in parent training and a discussion of outcome data from ESP groups conducted by professional leaders. An overview of operant behavior modification principles was presented and the ESP package materials were introduced.

In the second training session, the paraprofessional leaders viewed a videotaped sequence in which 2 professional trainers used the ESP package with a parent group. This sequence served as a model of correct group leader performance. Emphasis was placed on correct use of all package materials, and trainees were instructed in effective delivery techniques.

In the third session, paraprofessionals rehearsed use of the package with a group of undergraduate assistants who role-played parent group members. Feedback and social reinforcement were provided for a variety of target behaviors described in detail in the section covering *Measures* in this paper.

Parent Training Treatment Group

The 2 paraprofessionals served as leaders of the experimental parent training group. Using the ESP package, the paraprofessionals conducted a 2-hour parent training session once a week for 6 weeks.

Waiting List Control Group

After pretreatment measures had been obtained from all parents, waiting list control parents were informed that they would have to wait for a second training group to begin in 6 weeks. From the 2 waiting list subjects who enrolled in the second group, all pretreatment data were again collected. The remaining 7 parents completed questionnaires, but only 2 completed the additional measures.

Measures of Treatment Process

Evaluation of this intervention was conducted on several levels to determine the impact of a variety of factors on successful treatment outcome (Table 16-I). Of primary importance in this study was the determination of paraprofessional leader effectiveness. If leader performance is satisfactory, this should lead to subsequent change in parental knowledge and behavior. In turn, if parent performance is satisfactory, this should yield changes in child behavior and in ex-

pressed parental satisfaction with child behavior. Thus, both leader
and parent behaviors are conceptualized as process variables relative
to the ultimate outcome variables of child behavior change and parent
satisfaction with child behavior.

Table 16-I

MEASURES EMPLOYED TO ASSESS
TREATMENT PROCESS AND OUTCOME

	Process Measures		Outcome Measures
Measures	*Leader*	*Parent*	*Child*
Direct observation of trainer behavior	X		
Correct response to programmed questions		X	
Attendance		X	
Completion of home practice assignments		X	
ESP Consumer Satisfaction Form	X	X	X
Therapy Attitude Inventory	X	X	X
*Parent Attitude Survey		X	
ESP Behavior Management Survey		X	
*Becker Bi-Polar Adjective Checklist			X
*Behavior Description Checklist			X
*Direct observation of parent/ child interaction			X
Home practice assignment/behavior change programs			X

*Indicates these measures were obtained from parents in both the treatment and control
groups.

Paraprofessional Leader Variables

Paraprofessional performance was assessed from parent ratings of leader effectiveness and by means of direct observation of leader behavior. Parent ratings were obtained from the ESP Consumer Satisfaction Form, administered at the end of each session, and from a modified version of the Therapy Attitude Inventory (Eyberg & Johnson, 1974), administered post-treatment.

Direct observation of leader behavior focused on on-task performance, as it was assumed that a leader would be effective if s/he adhered very closely to the programmed format of the ESP package. On-task performance was defined as occurring when leaders and group members were observed to follow the lesson format explicitly. Other leader behaviors directly observed were eye contact, voice level, and voice quality. On all measures, paraprofessional performance was compared with that of professional leaders using the ESP package.

Using a time sampling procedure, 2 observers rated leader behavior at each of the 6 sessions. Interobserver agreement on all of the behaviors observed ranged from 90% to 95%. Agreement on ratings for the individual behavior categories ranged from 84% to 98%, with a median of 93%.

Parent Variables

Measures of parent performance included compliance with program requirements (attendance, completion of home assignments) and gains in verbal-theoretical knowledge. The latter were assessed from parent responses to in-class programmed questions and from scores on the ESP Behavior Management Survey, a multiple choice inventory administered pre- and post-treatment.

Self-report measures of improvement as a parent consisted of the ESP Consumer Satisfaction Form, administered weekly, and the Therapy Attitude Inventory, administered post-treatment. Parents also provided self-report data on frequency of use of behavioral strategies, using a modified version of the Parent Attitude Survey (Clark, Collier, Fayman, Grinstead, Kearns, Robie, & Rooten, 1976), administered post-treatment.

Measures of Treatment Outcome

There were 3 categories of outcome measures employed: change in parent-child interaction; child behavior change; and change in parent perception of and satisfaction with child behavior.

Parent-Child Interaction

Parents completed two 15-minute audiotape observations each day in the home. One period occurred immediately following dinner ("set time"); the other occurred at a problem time selected by the mother ("picked time") and held constant across the 5-day pre- and post-treatment observation periods.

The audiotape recordings were evaluated using the direct observational coding system developed for use with audiotape recordings by Royce, Christensen, Johnson and Bolstad. Raters were trained to a final reliability criterion of 75% agreement. Reliability scores were calculated for directionality (mean agreement 74.47%; range 30% to 100%) and for content (mean agreement 70.33%; range 25.88% to 100%).

Child Behavior Change

Home practice assignments provided measures of child behavior change in three areas of child behavior: compliance, performance of a specific target behavior selected by the parent from a "menu," and frequency of a specific problem behavior selected in the same manner.

Parent Perception of Child Behavior Change

Parent perception of child behavior change was assessed from responses to the ESP Consumer Satisfaction Form, administered weekly; a modified version of the Becker Bi-Polar Adjective Checklist (Becker, 1960); and the Behavior Description Checklist (American Institutes for Research, 1969). The latter instruments were administered pre- and post-treatment. Parents also rated their satisfaction with child behavior change, using the Therapy Attitude Inventory administered post-treatment.

RESULTS

Treatment Process Variables

Paraprofessional Performance

Results of direct observation indicated that paraprofessional leaders followed the program format more closely than did the professional leaders: Paraprofessionals were on-task at 86% of the intervals, while the professionals were on-task at only 72%. Similarly, paraprofessionals maintained eye contact with group members in 90% of the intervals, professionals in 87%. Voice level and voice quality were rated as appropriate in 100% of the intervals in which the leaders, both professional and paraprofessional, were speaking.

On both questionnaires employed, the ESP Consumer Satisfaction Form and the Therapy Attitude Inventory, parents consistently rated leader performance as excellent. On the former, leaders received the highest scores possible on 91% of all measuring occasions across all parents. Similar results emerged from the Therapy Attitude Inventory. In no case was dissatisfaction with leader performance expressed.

Parent Performance

Parent compliance measures included attendance and completion of assignments. For the 6 lessons, overall attendance was 94%. Absent parents made up all lesson material missed. Completion of assignments remained high for the first 4 assignments (mean 84%) but dropped to 44% in the last lesson. Verbally, parents indicated a preference for the positive strategies employed in the first 4 assignments and a reluctance to intervene with negative contingencies as was required in the final assignment. This is especially understandable in light of the fact that these were not parents of problem children.

In response to in-class programmed questions, parents obtained a mean of 97% correct responses across all lessons. Results of an analysis of variance performed on parent scores on ESP Behavior Management Survey indicated significant main effects for treatment ($F = 12.57$, $df = 1$, $p \geq .01$), time ($F = 28.03$, $df = 1$, $p \geq .0001$), and for the treatment $\times$ time interaction ($F = 28.60$, $df = 1$, $p \geq .0001$). These results indicate excellent learning of verbal-theoretical material.

On self-report measures (ESP Consumer Satisfaction Form, Therapy Attitude Inventory), parents consistently rated their own performance as very much improved. Using the Parent Attitude Survey, parents rated the frequency with which they employed behavioral techniques. Analysis of variance did not reveal any significant differences between group mean scores as a function of time or treatment (treatment group mean scores were 43.11 pretreatment and 44.0 post-treatment). However, inspection of individual items indicated that, of treatment group parents, 89% reported an increase in rewards given to the child for work completed and a decrease in responding to child arguments and protests. Furthermore, 55% reported an increase in rewards given to the child for following parental rules and decreases in both verbal reprimands and reminders to perform a task. Thus, self-report measures indicate that the treatment group experienced improvement in several areas specifically addressed in the ESP program.

Treatment Outcome Variables

Parent-Child Interaction

From the audiotape recordings made in the home, changes in parent-child interaction were assessed for 4 summary behavior categories: child negative, parent negative, parent positive, and parent commanding. The very low rates at which these behaviors occurred in both groups across all assessment periods ("set" and "picked" times, pre- and post-treatment assessments) presented special problems in attempting to assess change, especially change of clinical significance.

Results of analyses of variance indicated no significant effects of treatment or time for any of the 4 behavior categories. However, these results should be interpreted with caution, due to the small number of subjects and the unequal number of subjects per group on this measure.

Although not statistically significant, differences were observed between pre- and post-treatment measures of child negative behavior in the 2 groups. Children in the experimental group showed a decrease from a mean of .476 negative behaviors per minute to .319; children in the control group increased from a mean of .399 per minute to .735.

Planned comparison t tests were used to determine within-group change as a function of time. Significant increase in parent negative behavior emerged for treatment group parents (t = 2.64, df = 3, $p \geq .01$).

Child Behavior Change

Data from home practice assignments provided measures of child behavior change in 3 areas of behavior: compliance, performance of a specific target behavior, and frequency of a specific problem behavior. Baseline data indicated a mean of 72.1% compliance with parental requests (range 44% to 89%).† Intervention with social reinforcement

---

†Baseline data, as reported here, probably reflect an inflated estimate of compliance typically exhibited by these children, as parents were instructed to specify a behavior, place, and time limit for each request made during baseline. This strategy was adopted merely to standardize parent requests or commands, but many parents, especially those who used a kitchen timer to clock time limits, reported considerable increase in compliance through the use of this procedure alone. Thus, this procedure can be expected to negatively bias outcome data, even indicating spurious decreases in compliance in some cases. Research on this issue is currently in progress.

for compliance produced at 12.5% mean increase (range −6.25% to 36.98%) to a mean of 81.2% compliance. Data from 2 children indicated decreases in compliance (−6.25% and −3.41%): These children complied with more than 80% of parental requests during baseline.

From the following list, parents chose a targeted goal and 5 behavioral steps necessary to achieve the goal: ready for bed or school on time, completion of chores, or completion of homework. During baseline, a mean of 79% of the steps were completed (range 50% to 100%). Intervention with point programs resulted in a mean increase of 12% (range 3% to 100%) to a group mean of 88.57% of steps completed (range 72% to 100%). The 2 children whose data indicated decreases in performance had very high initial performance rates (92% and 100%). In both cases, intervention was continued for an additional week, at which time performance reached 98% and 97%, respectively.

Using negative consequences such as fines and time-out, parents reduced a specific undesirable behavior (fighting, whining, or tantrums) from a base rate of 3.6 per day to 1.2 per day. As previously noted, only 1/3 of the group completed this assignment. However, these parents reported decreases of 47%, 53%, and 72% from base rates.

Parent Perception of Child Behavior Change

Parent perception of child behavior change was assessed from questionnaires administered pre- and post-treatment and from responses to the ESP Consumer Satisfaction Form, administered weekly to treatment group parents. Analyses of variance revealed no difference as a function of treatment or time on any of the 5 factor scores or on the total measure score obtained on the Becker Bi-Polar Adjective Checklist.

Similarly, results of an analysis of variance indicated no difference as a function of treatment or time on scores on the Behavior Description Checklist. However, at pretreatment assessment, each parent selected items from the inventory on which s/he would especially like to see change; of the 16 items selected by treatment group parents, 75% were rated as improved after treatment. The remaining 25% were rated as unchanged. Control group parents selected 8 items, only 1 of which was rated as improved at the time of final assessment. In no case was a behavior rated as worse.

In response to the ESP Consumer Satisfaction Form question dealing with improvement in child behavior, parents initially rated their children as only slightly improved. By the final week of the program, 50% rated their child as very much improved. This item was administered to treatment group parents only, none of whom failed to report improvement.

On the Therapy Attitude Inventory, parents gave high ratings for child progress in areas specifically addressed by the program. Lowest ratings were received for items dealing with areas not treated and for sibling problems.

DISCUSSION

Direct observation of leader behaviors indicated that the paraprofessional leaders adhered closely to the program format and performed as well as, or better than, professional leaders on all behaviors observed. Additional direct support for the efficacy of paraprofessional leaders is provided by consistently high parent ratings of leader performance.

Measures of parent performance and child behavior change bear indirect but essential testimony to the effectiveness of the combination of the paraprofessional leader with the programmed package. Parent compliance with program requirements was considered very satisfactory, as were gains in parent verbal-theoretical knowledge. On self-report measures, parents consistently rated their own performance as a parent as very much improved. Parents indicated improvement in several areas specifically addressed by the program, although this improvement was not reflected in statistically significant changes in total scores from pre- to post-treatment assessment.

Data from home intervention programs indicated effective parental use of contingency management skills, as reflected in a moderate degree of child behavior change for those children whose data indicated poorer base rate performance. Failure to show behavior change was associated in all cases except one with a high rate of performance prior to intervention. As these children had little room for improvement in their performance, group mean change scores may reflect this *ceiling effect.*

Parents reported improvement in a variety of child behaviors and consistently assigned global ratings of "improved" or "very much improved" to child behavior, especially in the latter weeks of the program. However, total scores on questionnaires used to assess parent perception of and satisfaction with child behavior change did not reflect change.

Failure to obtain changes on these measures and on direct observation measures of parent-child interaction may reflect problems with the instruments and techniques used to assess outcome. The questionnaires, for example, were developed for use with a deviant population: Therefore, their suitability for use with a normal population is questionable, and it is not unlikely that a ceiling effect was obtained on these measures. In addition, it may be that two 15-minute daily samples of parent-child interaction did not provide a sufficient data base for analysis of change. In future research in our laboratory, longer observation periods will be employed.

Alternately, it is possible that the outcome variables themselves were poorly suited to the purposes of this study, given the nature of the population employed. It may be naive to assume that a 6-week program is sufficient to produce across-the-board changes in parenting styles, child behavior, and parent-child interaction. Indeed, the need for such sweeping changes is questionable with a normal population.

In our sample, virtually every parent emphasized that s/he enrolled, not because his/her child presented problems, but simply to become a better parent. Anecdotally, our parents reported that they benefited from learning that other parents have similar concerns and sometimes feel uncertain and inept. Furthermore, they found the skills taught in the program reasonably easy to integrate into their parenting repertoire and reported feeling reassured concerning the adequacy of their own parenting skills.

It has recently been suggested that parent perception of and attitudes toward child behavior are, in many cases, all that must be changed to produce a satisfactory outcome that is stable over time (Johnson & Eyberg, 1975; Karoly & Rosenthal, 1977). It seems reasonable to hypothesize that an equally important dimension of parent-child relations is the parent's perception of his/her own parenting skills. Feelings of anxiety and ineptitude in the parental role can have multiple origins: e.g., unsatisfactory interaction with a temperamentally "difficult" child (Thomas, Chess, & Birch, 1968); conflicting child-rearing advice from family, friends, and "experts"; or a generalized perception of the self as inadequate. Whatever the cause, it is reasonable to assume that the parent who is unsure of his/her adequacy in the parental role is likely to vacillate in his/her behavior toward the child and to evidence considerable inconsistency in his/her approach to child management.

These findings indicate that the most important contributions of behavioral parent training with nonclinical, and perhaps even clinical, populations may include the following: reassuring parents that their skills are, for the most part, adequate; encouraging greater precision and consistency in the use of these skills; and providing, not only specific techniques to manage problem behaviors, but a conceptual framework within which the parent can function with increased assurance.

These speculations are, of course, in need of further investigation, as are many of the conceptual and methodological problems highlighted by the present pilot research. Issues of appropriate outcome goals and assessment devices remain to be resolved, as does the question of stability of effects over time. In addition, the research must be extended to include greater numbers of parents and paraprofessional trainers. Direct comparisons of paraprofessional-professional performance must be undertaken, and the effectiveness of paraprofessional trainers with a clinical population remains to be investigated.

Nevertheless, the results of this preliminary research are encouragingly optimistic and suggest that, given an appropriately designed vehicle for delivery of service, paraprofessionals can function as effective parent training group leaders after only minimal training. These results support Horowitz's (1976) contention that current knowledge and ability to train personnel are sufficient to render feasible the development of large-scale programs to help parents and to prevent developmental difficulties. If, as she claims, there is a "vast reservoir of time and service" available in every community, we must develop methods to draw upon and utilize such resources. Programmed service delivery packages present a potential means by which this might be accomplished. Such packages, designed to be implemented by paraprofessionals, need not be restricted in content to contingency management skills, but could address various aspects of parent-child interaction and child development and behavior, including affective development, self-control skills, and moral and social responsibility. Through these means, effective training and guidance could be made inexpensive and easily accessible to large numbers of parents across society.

REFERENCES

Albee, G. *Mental health manpower trends.* New York: Basic, 1959.

American Institutes for Research. *Behavior description.* Palo Alto, California: Am Inst Res, 1969.

Auerbach, A. B. *Parents learn through discussion.* New York: Wiley, 1968.

Azrin, N. H., & Foxx, R. M. *Toilet training in less than a day.* New York: S&S, 1974.

Baker, E. J. The mental health associate: A new approach in mental health. *Community Mental Health Journal,* 1972, *8,* 281-291.

Bartels, B. D., & Tyler, J. D. Paraprofessionals in the community mental health center. *Professional Psychology,* 1975, *6,* 442-452.

Batman, R. H. Consultation as an educational technique in psychiatric nursing. *Mental Hygiene,* 1968, *52,* 617-621.

Becker, W. C. The relationship of factors in parental rating of self and each other to the behavior of kindergarten children as rated by mothers, fathers, and teachers. *Journal of Consulting Psychology,* 1960, *24,* 507-527.

Bernal, M. E. Behavioral feedback in the modification of brat behaviors.

Journal of Nervous and Mental Disease, 1969, *148,* 375-385.

Bernal, M. E., Williams, D. E., Miller, W. H., & Reagor, P. A. The use of videotape feedback and operant learning principles in training parents in management of deviant children. In R. D. Rubin, H. Festerheim, J. D. Henderson, & L. P. Ullman (Eds.). *Advances in behavior therapy.* New York: Acad Pr, 1972.

Brim, O. G. *Education for child rearing.* New York: Free Pr, 1959.

Brink, R. W. *Research on training behavior therapists.* Paper presented at the Eighth Annual Convention of the Association for the Advancement of Behavior Therapy, Chicago, 1974.

Clark, H. B., Greene, B. F., Macrae, J. W., McNees, M. P., Davis, J. L., & Risley, T. R. A parent advice package for family shopping trips: Development and evaluation. *Journal of Applied Behavior Analysis,* 1977, *10,* 605-624.

Clark, M. L., Collier, H., Fayman, K., Grinstead, J., Kearns, L., Robie, D., & Rooten, M. J. *The responsive parent training manual.* Lawrence, Kansas: H & H Enterprises, 1976.

Clark-Hall, M. Personal communication, May 1978.

Colarelli, N. P., & Siegel, S. M. *Ward H: An adventure in innovation.* New York: D Van Nostrand, 1966.

Cone, J. D., & Sheldon, S. S. *Training behavior modifiers: Getting it going with remote auditory prompting.* Paper presented at American Psychological Association Convention, Montreal, 1973.

Cone, J. D., & Sloop, E. W. Parents as agents of change. In A. Jacobs & W. Spradlin (Eds.), *The group as agent of change.* New York: Behavioral Pub, 1971.

Crisler, J. R. Effective paraprofessional utilization — Myth or reality. *Journal of Applied Rehabilitation Counseling,* 1973, *4,* 41-46.

Crisler, J. R., Porter, T. L., & Jones, R. D. Rehabilitation counselor salaries and benefits. *Journal of Applied Rehabilitation Counseling,* 1972, *3,* 152-166.

Doleys, D. M., Doster, J., & Cartelli, L. M. Parent training techniques: Effects of lecture-roleplaying followed by feedback and self-recording. *Journal of Behavior Therapy and Experimental Psychiatry,* 1976, *7,* 359-362.

Eyberg, S. M., & Johnson, S. M. Multiple assessment of behavior modification with families: Effects of contingency contracting and order of treated problems. *Journal of Consulting and Clinical Psychology,* 1974, *42,* 151-156.

Fabry, P. L., & Reid, D. H. Teaching foster grandparents to train severely handicapped persons. *Journal of Applied Behavior Analysis,* 1978, *11,* 111-124.

Fawcett, S. B., Mathews, R. M., Fletcher, R. K., Morrow, R., & Stokes, T. F. Personalized instruction in the community: Teaching helping skills to low-income neighborhood residents. *Journal of Personalized Instruction,* 1976, *1,* 86-90.

Ferber, H., Keeley, S. M., & Shemberg, K. M. Training parents in behavior modification: Outcome of and problems encountered in a program after Patterson's work. *Behavior Therapy*, 1974, *5*, 415-419.

Forehand, R., & Wells, K. C. Teachers and parents: Where have all the "good" contingency managers gone? *Behavior Therapy*, 1977, *8*, 1-10.

Gardner, J. M. Teaching behavior modification to nonprofessionals. *Journal of Applied Behavior Analysis*, 1972, *5*, 517-521.

Gardner, J. M. Training the trainers: A review of research on teaching behavior modification. In R. D. Rubin, J. P. Brady, & J. D. Henderson (Eds.), *Advances in behavior therapy* (Vol. 4). New York: Acad Pr, 1973.

Gladstone, B. W., & Sherman, J. A. Developing generalized behavior modification skills in high-school students working with retarded children. *Journal of Applied Behavior Analysis*, 1975, *8*, 169-180.

Gladstone, B. W., & Spencer, C. J. The effects of modeling on the contingent praise of mental retardation counselors. *Journal of Applied Behavior Analysis*, 1977, *10*, 75-84.

Graziano, A. Parents as behavior therapists. In M. Hersen, R. Eisler, & P. Miller (Eds.), *Progress in behavior modification* (Vol. 4). New York: Acad Pr, 1977.

Gruver, G. G. College students as therapeutic agents. *Psychological Bulletin*, 1971, *76*, 111-127.

Guerney, B. G. (Ed.) *Psychotherapeutic agents: New roles for nonprofessionals, parents and teachers*. New York: HR&W, 1969.

Hawkins, R. P. It's time we taught the young how to be good parents (and don't you wish we'd started a long time ago?). *Psychology Today*, 1972, *6*, 28.

Hobbs, N. Mental health's third revolution. *American Journal of Orthopsychiatry*, 1964, *34*, 822-833.

Horowitz, F. D. Directions for parenting. In E. J. Mash, L. A. Hamerlynck, & L. C. Handy (Eds.), *Behavior modification and families*. New York: Brunner/Mazel, 1976.

Houts, P. S., & Hench, R. W., Jr. Teaching behavior modification in professional schools. In S. Yen & R. W. McIntire (Eds.), *Teaching behavior modification*. Kalamazoo, Michigan: Behaviordelia, 1976.

Ingersoll, B. D., & Eastman, A. M. Exercises in successful parenting: Child management skills for parents. Maidsville, West Virginia: CriComm, 1978.

Johnson, J. M. Using parents as contingency managers. *Psychological Reports*, 1971, *28*, 703-710.

Johnson, S. A., & Brown, R. A. Producing behavior change in parents of disturbed children. *Journal of Child Psychology and Psychiatry*, 1969, *10*, 107-121.

Johnson, S. M., & Eyberg, S. Evaluating outcome data: A reply to Gordon. *Journal of Consulting and Clinical Psychology*, 1975, *43*, 917-919.

Joint Commission on Mental Illness and Health. *Action for mental health: Final report of the Joint Commission on Mental Health*. New York: Basic, 1961.

Karoly, P., & Rosenthal, M. Training parents in behavior modification: Effects on perceptions of family interaction and deviant child behavior. *Behavior Therapy*, 1977, *8*, 406-410.

Kazdin, A. E., & Moyer, W. Training teachers to use behavior modification. In S. Yen & R. W. McIntire (Eds.), *Teaching behavior modification.* Kalamazoo, Michigan: Behaviordelia, 1976.

Keeley, S. M., Shemberg, K. M., & Ferber, H. The training and use of undergraduates as behavior analysts in the consultative process. *Professional Psychology*, 1973, *4*, 59-63.

Koegel, R. L., Glahn, T. J., & Nieminen, G. S. Generalization of parent-training results. *Journal of Applied Behavior Analysis*, 1978, *11*, 95-110.

Krieger, G. Training nursing assistants for subprofessional role. *Mental Hygiene*, 1970, *54*, 152.

Martin, G. L., & Pear, J. J. Short term participation by 130 undergraduates as operant conditioners in an ongoing project with autistic children. *Psychological Record*, 1971, *20*, 327-336.

Mash, E. J., Lazere, R., Terdal, L., & Garner, A. Modification of mother-child interactions: A modeling approach for groups. *Child Study Journal*, 1973, *3*, 131-143.

Mathews, R. M., & Fawcett, S. B. Community applications of instructional technology: Training low-income proctors. *Journal of Applied Behavior Analysis*, 1977, *10*, 747-754.

Nay, W. R. A systematic comparison of instructional techniques for parents. *Behavior Therapy*, 1975, *6*, 14-21.

O'Dell, S. Training parents in behavior modification: A review. *Psychological Bulletin*, 1974, *81*, 418-433.

O'Dell, S., Flynn, J., & Benlolo, L. A comparison of parent training techniques in child behavior modification. *Journal of Behavior Therapy and Experimental Psychiatry*, 1977, *8*, 261-268.

O'Dell, S. L., Mahoney, N. D., Horton, W. G., & Turner, P. E. Media-assisted parent training: Alternative models. *Behavior Therapy*, 1979, in press.

Ora, J. *Instruction pamphlet for parents of oppositional children* (Regional Intervention Project for Preschoolers and Parents). Nashville: George Peabody College, 1971.

Panyan, M., Boozer, H., & Morris, N. Feedback to attendants as a reinforcer for applying operant techniques. *Journal of Applied Behavior Analysis*, 1970, *3*, 1-4.

Paul, G. L., McInnis, T. L., & Mariotto, M. J. Objective performance outcomes associated with two approaches to training mental health technicians in milieu and social-learning programs. *Journal of Abnormal Psychology*, 1973, *82*, 523-532.

Pomerantz, P. B., Peterson, N. T., Marholin, D., & Stern, S. The in vivo elimination of a child's water phobia by a paraprofessional at home. *Journal of Behavior Therapy and Experimental Psychiatry*, 1977, *4*, 417-422.

Poser, E. G. Training behavior therapists. *Behavior Research and Therapy*, 1967, *5*, 37-41.

Rinn, R. C., Vernon, J. C., & Wise, J. J. Training parents of behaviorally-disordered children in groups: A three year's program evaluational. *Behavior Therapy*, 1975, *6*, 378-387.

Risley, T. R., Clark, H. B., & Cataldo, M. F. Behavior technology for the normal, middle-class family. In E. J. Mash, L. A. Hamerlynck, & L. C. Handy (Eds.), *Behavior modification and families*. New York: Brunner/Mazel, 1976.

Rose, S. D. A behavioral approach to the group treatment of parents. *Social Work*, 1969, *14*, 12-29.

Rose, S. D. Training parents in groups as behavior modifiers of their mentally retarded children. *Journal of Behavior Therapy and Experimental Psychiatry*, 1974, *5*, 135-140.

Royce, K., Christensen, A., Johnson, S., & Bolstad, O. *A manual for coding family interactions obtained from audio tape recordings*. Unpublished manuscript, University of Oregon.

Sepler, H. J., and Meyers, S. L. The effectiveness of verbal instructions on teaching behavior modification skills to nonprofessionals. *Journal of Applied Behavior Analysis*, 1978, *11*, 198.

Siegel, J. M. Mental health volunteers as change agents. *American Journal of Community Psychology*, 1973, *1*, 138-158.

Simpson, B. J. *The parent as change agent for problem behavior* (Doctoral dissertation, University of Southern California, 1973) University Microfilms No. 73-30040.

Taplin, P. S., & Reid, J. B. Changes in parent consequences as a function of family intervention. *Journal of Consulting and Clinical Psychology*, 1977, *45*, 973-981.

Tharp, R. G., & Wetzel, F. J. *Behavior modification in the natural environment*. New York: Acad Pr, 1969.

Thomas, A., Chess, S., & Birch, H. G. *Temperament and behavior disorders in children*. New York: New York U Pr, 1968.

Wagner, L., & Ora, J. *Parental control of the very young severely oppositional child*. Paper read at the Southeastern Psychological Association, Louisville, April 1970.

Wahl, G., Johnson, S. M., Johanson, S., & Martin, S. An operant analysis of parent/child interaction. *Behavior Therapy*, 1974, *5*, 64-78.

Wahler, R. G., & Erickson, M. Child behavior therapy: A community program in Appalachia. *Behavior Research and Therapy*, 1969, 7, 71-78.

Chapter 17

WORKING WITH FOSTER PARENTS

Michael R. Rosmann

WHILE education for parenthood of one's own children has been a matter of general concern down through the ages and has been a focus of attention by professional workers and researchers for over 100 years, education for rearing other people's children in foster family care has become a desired and feasible endeavor only within the past 2 decades. In their review, Stone and Hunzeker (1974) observed that before 1960 only three books referred to the child-rearing role of foster parents. Journal articles and other published reports mentioning the training of foster parents were extremely rare in the 1950s, and only five appeared in the first half of the 1960s. By 1970, however, there was a growing impulse among foster care caseworkers and foster parents for the development of curricula and techniques for training foster parents, both prior to and during placement of foster children in surrogate families. As of 1978, there were at least two dozen published curricula for educating foster parents and numerous articles and books describing model training programs.

The push toward educating foster parents has received impetus from at least four sources: foster child caseworkers and researchers in the field who have felt a need to upgrade the quality of foster care; foster parents who have wanted help in dealing with their wards and the many complex issues surrounding foster parenthood; the public, whose social consciousness of foster children and acceptance of continuing education is increasing; and the mandates of laws in many communities, states, and countries. Let us examine each of these influences further.

Over the past several decades, there has been a growing recognition among foster care caseworkers of the need for improved foster care that has paralleled the entrance of increasingly better educated professionals, chiefly social workers, into the service arena and the increased use of homes for provision of foster care. A greater proportion of foster care agency personnel than decades ago have advanced degrees in social work and related fields; because of their broadened training and outlook, they tend to upgrade the services offered by their agencies. The Child Welfare League of America, through its many sponsored conferences and publications, has been especially instrumental in encouraging foster care caseworkers to improve the standards of foster care in all facets, among which training of foster parents has been given high priority (Stone & Hunzeker, 1974).

One particularly significant change in foster care practices over the years is the increased use of foster homes rather than institutions for child rearing. Whereas the proportion of foster children in the general population of the United States under 18 years of age has decreased from 59 per 10,000 in 1933 to 45 per 10,000 in 1969, the percentage in foster homes has increased from 42.4% to 75.5% during the same span (National Center for Social Statistics, 1969). A more recent estimate (Gruber, 1978) of the proportion in foster family care is even greater. The shift from institutional to home placement is founded on the premise that foster families are more likely to provide the emotional climate necessary for normal child development (Kline & Forbush Overstreet, 1972; Wolins & Piliavin, 1964). There is considerable research support for this contention (e.g., Maas, 1963; Parker, 1966; Trasler, 1960; Yarrow, 1964), but the nurturing quality of the foster family and institutional environments varies widely and affects outcomes of placements accordingly.

With the increasing reliance on foster family care have come the needs for better selection of foster parents, improved criteria for matching foster children with foster parents, and enhanced education of the foster family units. Systematic research addressing these needs has been scanty. Taylor and Starr's (1967) review was an important contribution because it pointed out that the literature was replete with duplications, contradictions, and little hard data, and it spurred researchers to carry out more methodologically sound empirical studies. Since that paper was published, at least 6 studies (Cautley & Aldridge, 1975; Fanshel, 1971, 1976; Kraus, 1971; Murphy, 1974; Touliatos & Lindholm, 1977) were undertaken to identify variables of foster parents that correlated with placement outcome in regression analyses. At least 2 studies (Cautley & Aldridge, 1975; Hampson, 1975) sought empirically determined criteria for matching foster parents and foster children. Several experimental studies (Hampson, 1975; Hampson, Tavormina, Grieger, & Taylor, 1977; Mamula & Newman, 1973) compared foster parents who received training with those who did not. Thus, there is now a small but expanding empirical data base to which foster care caseworkers in applied settings can turn for guidance in selecting foster parents, matching them with foster children, and training the foster family units. Unfortunately, the application of this developing data base is lagging. One purpose of this chapter is to translate empirically derived information about selection, matching, and evaluation of training into suggestions for actual foster parent education.

In addition to the foster care caseworkers and researchers, foster parents themselves have been a significant force in promoting foster parent training efforts. Mrs. Ruby Kennedy, herself a foster parent, spoke for many at the first National Conference on Foster Care in 1967 when she said:

> (1) There should be workshops where foster parents meet with social workers to plan and train together rather than to be "talked" to. (2) Generally, all foster parents agree that they gain by talking with experienced skillful parents, and that this kind of training should be encouraged. (3) Single orientation programs say too much too soon; a series is more effective. (4) Special training for foster parents working with the emotionally ill or the handicapped is important. (5) There should be more planned contact with agency administration as well as with the social workers who represent it (pp. 246-247).

Chiefly in response to the calls by foster parents associations, the Child Welfare League of America initiated a Foster Parent Project in 1971, which had as its objective the stimulation, collection, and dissemination of foster parent education training programs and materials (Stone & Hunzeker, 1974). By 1974, every state had foster parent training programs in one or more of its communities (Stone & Hunzeker, 1974).

The public awareness of foster parenthood issues in general and foster parent education in particular has increased greatly in the past few years, partly as a result of an accelerating involvement of foster care caseworkers and parents with non-foster parents in local associations (e.g., Community Assistance to Homeless Youngsters, Kennedy, 1970), and partly because of expanded attention in the communication media. In addition to national television coverage and exposure through popular magazines such as *Women's Day* and *Parents' Magazine,* foster parent training efforts and ideas are disseminated to professionals and lay people alike in such publications as *Exchange,* the bulletin of the Child Welfare Resource Information Exchange of the United States Department of Health, Education and Welfare, and *Fostering Ideas,* which is published by Eastern Michigan University. Stone and Hunzeker (1974) give credit also to community colleges and the continuing education division of numerous universities that offer courses in parent education and provide training of foster parents on contract to some foster care agencies. They maintain further that attitudes toward education for parenthood are changing so that such training is not considered "different" or unusual, but is endorsed as a means of self-actualization and self-fulfillment. Such popular books on child rearing as *Between Parent and Teenager* by Ginott (1969), *Parent Effectiveness Training* by Gordon (1970), and *Families* by Patterson (1971b), while they do not deal with foster parents and children specifically, have done much to raise the public conscious-ness of parenting issues and thereby have had spin-off effects on the acceptance of foster parent training as well.

Finally, the beginnings of a trend toward legally mandated training for foster parents can be discerned and may emerge as a major move-ment in the nation and other countries in the next few years. The push for legally mandated training springs from the discontent of many foster care evaluators, foster parents, and other interested citizens with the current state of foster care in general and foster parent educa-tion in particular. The latter subject will be reviewed in greater detail in the next section of this chapter. Evaluation studies of foster care in the states of Arizona, California, and Massachusetts in the early 1970s (reviewed by Vasaly, 1976) all cited the increasing demands for foster homes, the highly variable quality of care of foster parents, and the generally poor quality of foster parent training prior to and during placement of foster children in homes. Among the numerous recom-mendations made in each study to deal with these and other related problems was the proposal for improved foster parent education. Specifically, it was recommended in Arizona that training programs be set up for the orientation and ongoing training of workers, super-visors, and foster parents. In California, it was recommended that foster parents be given orientation, training, and status as team members and that foster parent training programs be required and coupled with ongoing consultation and adequate support services from the agency. In Massachusetts, it was proposed that all foster parents should have the training and skills necessary for meeting the needs of their foster children and that professional foster parents should be trained and paid to care for handicapped and other special foster children. The National Foster Parent Association in 1973 also called for the adoption by states of three mandatory training require-ments for foster parents in the form of preservice training, agency supervision of foster home service, and ongoing parent development (Stone & Hunzeker, 1974).

Although every state has licensing procedures for foster parents, few currently require training of foster parents prior to granting licenses or regular follow-up visits by agency personnel to homes with foster children. In 1973, South Dakota issued a regulation requiring that all foster home applicants participate in a minimum number of hours of preservice training prior to receiving licenses (Stone & Hunzeker, 1974), and there may be additional states with such regulations at the time of this writing. Although some authorities and writers in this country (e.g., Gruber, 1978; Mnookin, 1973) and abroad (e.g., George, 1970) are disappointed with the lack of legislative progress toward improving the standards of training for foster parents and care of their wards, there seems to be a movement toward forcing foster care agencies to be more accountable for the quantity and quality of foster parent care that they allow. Legislatures in almost every state have bills or proposals pending that would raise the standards of foster care and in some cases stipulate that the agencies must educate prospective foster parents for a minimum number of hours prior to licensing. Relatively recent federal legislation, such as the Social Security Act (Title IV-A) and the Education of the Handicapped Act, enables states to use federal funds for training foster parents. Indeed, within the next few years, participation in training may become a routine requirement for licensure of foster parents in most states, similar to many occupational and business licensing procedures that now require proof of certain educational attainments and continuing education.

CURRENT STATE OF FOSTER PARENT EDUCATION

While the growing movement toward foster parent education might give the impression that training of foster parents is fairly customary, the opposite is true. The actual practice of preplacement and inservice training of foster parents is lagging behind the proliferation of literature in foster parent selection and education.

Vasaly (1976) reviewed the status of foster parent training and preparation prior to placement in the states of Arizona, California, and Massachusetts. She reported that 12% of a random sample of 295 foster parents in Arizona in 1975 received some preplacement training. In California, 37% of a sample of 311 foster parents of handicapped children in 1972 felt they did not receive an adequate explanation of "what they were getting into." In Massachusetts, 25% of a sample of 149 foster parents in 1972 said they had received preplacement training. Gruber's (1978) survey of the amount of preplacement training offered by 27 private foster placement agencies in Massachusetts in 1972 showed that 1/3 of the agencies provided no training, another 1/3 offered general orientation, and the remainder provided extra training that was not described further. Regarding the status of foster parent training during placement, Vasaly (1976) noted that almost no in-service training was provided to the Arizona sample of foster parents. In California, 49% of the foster mothers of 311 handicapped children received some training, but most mothers wanted more. In Massachusetts, 46% of 149 foster mothers received some training, most of whom had to seek it themselves; 40% of the foster parents desired more training.

George (1970) surveyed 135 foster parents and 28 child care officers in a large county in England and found that 28% of the foster parents and 86% of the child care officers attended evening training courses in foster care principles and methods. The parents tended to reject the training sessions because as one foster mother commented, "Such courses were necessary only for the few foster parents who looked after 'children in need of special care or treatment'" (p. 74). Other parents felt that the training courses had little practical utility, and some respondents did not wish to be identified as foster parents to others in attendance. The foster parent respondents were only slightly more favorable toward attending parent discussion groups, despite the advantages reported by some parents and writers (Dall, 1967; Goldstein, 1967) of such programs.

The reports of low participation rates of foster parents in preplacement and in-service education endeavors come on the heels of much criticism by foster parents, evaluators, and concerned citizens about the failure of many foster care agencies to provide foster parents with information and support conducive to their own good functioning as parents and the optimal development of their foster children. Kennedy (1970) expressed the concerns of many foster parents when she stated:

> (1) Too often, foster parents are not helped to understand the rights or limitations of their role. They may be told, "A child needs a home; love him like your own", and yet a dozen different agency regulations prevent this "simplification". (2) Foster parents are not always given continuing help in understanding the role of the social worker and agency. (3) Many foster parents do not feel respected; they feel "used". One hears time and again, "Are social workers really interested in the child and our home, or are they just getting a case off their desk?" There are reasons for this question: (a) Many foster parents see social workers irregularly, and workers are not always available when needed. (b) Often, foster parents are not told the truth about the child or the natural parents. (c) Foster parents sometimes feel that their knowledge and day-to-day experience are not accepted as valuable. (p. 243)

The evaluations of foster care in Arizona, California, and Massachusetts reviewed by Vasaly (1976) reveal statistics supporting some of Kennedy's charges. Only 21% of the 295 families in the Arizona sample were visited by a foster care worker after licensing in preparation for receiving a foster child. A common complaint of these same foster parents was that they received little information about the child and no training on such agency procedures as who to call for help. In both the California and Massachusetts samples, 75% of the foster parents were not aware of the child's special needs prior to placement. Of the sample of foster parents in Massachusetts, 61% were given no indication of the anticipated length of the placement; 33% expected a temporary stay, but the average actual placement exceeded 3 1/2 years. Clearly, if the evaluation findings regarding foster parent training in Arizona, California, Massachusetts, and England and Kennedy's comments are representative of the state of foster parent training as a whole, then education for foster parenthood is in great need of upgrading.

Rapid turnover of foster parents is yet another problem that might be ameliorated by stepped-up foster parent training efforts. The Arizona report cited by Vasaly (1976) indicated an attrition rate of 33.3% of foster parents in that state per year. The average length of time that foster parents remained in the program was between 1 and 2 years, during which time they received an average of 4 to 5 children. A joint legislative audit report of foster care in California reviewed by Vasaly found that 18% of all foster family homes licensed in San Francisco in 1970 were still active in April 1973. Other studies cited by Vasaly mention longer durations of homes in foster care service: Almost 50% of 311 foster homes for handicapped children in California had remained in service for over 5 years, 42% of 55 foster homes in a San Gabriel, California sample had remained in service for 2 to 5 years, while another 29% were in service 5 to 10 years. The average duration of parents in foster care service seems to be about 3 years.

Rapid turnover of foster homes is a contributing factor, although only one of many, to increasing the frequency of multiple placements for some children. Vasaly (1976) noted that complaints by foster parents of their inability to cope with the special needs or problems of the foster children was the major known reason for replacing foster children in Arizona (20.7% of 449 cases) and Massachusetts (25% of 2,442 cases). The legislative audit report on foster care in California in 1974 disclosed the inability of the foster family to deal with the misbehaviors of the foster child as the major reason for replacement of the foster children. Other reasons Vasaly found for replacement in Arizona included: closure of the foster home by the parents (14.5%), move initiated by the foster care worker (10.2%), placement of the foster child with the natural parents or other relatives (11.4%), running away of the foster child (4.9%), request of the child to move

(4.9%), adoption (4.4%), and a variety of less frequently reported reasons. George (1970) found the following reasons for removing 99 of 128 foster children from their first foster homes in England: behavior difficulties of the child (22%); behavior difficulties of the foster parents (15%); both child and foster parents responsible for the breakdown (20%); uncontrollable circumstances within the foster home such as death, illness, or major translocation (10%); and placement with the natural parents (14%). Another 16% of the 99 children were removed from foster care status because they were adopted by the surrogate parents. In sum, a variety of reasons emerges for replacement of foster children, some of which might be addressed in foster parent training efforts. In particular, foster parents should receive training in behavior management prior to and augmented by consultations during placement so as to deal with the major reported reasons for replacement, namely, inability to cope with foster child misbehaviors and lack of knowledge and skills to deal with the special needs of many foster children. Furthermore, because of such therapeutic help, parents may be more likely to continue in foster care service for longer durations. Empirical data is needed that bears on this point.

Reducing the number of foster placements of children is especially important in light of the considerable research data illustrating the negative effects of multiple foster homes. Maas and Engler (1959) and Williams (1961) found a strong positive relationship between the number of different home placements and the degree of personality maladjustment of foster children. George (1970) found that multiply placed children had the least successful outcomes, with success defined as the ability to stay in any one home for at least 5 years. Yet frequent placement of some foster children is a persistent phenomenon. Eisenberg (1962) discovered that 36% of his sample had been placed 4 or more times. Gruber (1978) noted that approximately 25% of 5,862 children in foster care in Massachusetts in 1972 had been moved at least 3 times. A vicious cycle develops whereby certain children who, because of their own behavioral disturbance and special needs or the inability of the foster parents and perhaps faults of the agency, fail in one home, are moved to another where the problems of the child are exacerbated because of the previous unstable environment. Eventually, some children become impossible to place in foster homes and are relegated to institutions, which are known to often produce even further damage (Maas, 1963; Yarrow, 1964).

Because of the high potential for harm to foster children through multiple placements, some authorities (Glickman, 1957; Kline, 1965; Pratt, 1967; Tavormina, Hampson, Grieger, & Tedesco, 1977) have argued that only long-term foster placements should be attempted with specially selected and intensively trained foster parents. Others (Maas & Engler, 1959; Mnookin, 1973; Sherman, Neuman, & Shyne, 1973) recommend that the effects of poor placements and the trauma of separation from the natural home should be minimized through temporary short-term foster placements, and the goal of the child care agency should be returning foster children to their natural homes as soon as possible. Jones, Neuman, & Shyne (1976), Kautz (1969), and Kinney, Madsen, Fleming, and Haapala (1977) have shown that intensive counseling of families in crises has been effective in preventing removal of children from some natural homes, but this is not feasible in all instances. In fact, only in a small percentage of cases is placement back in the natural home (i.e., 25% in Maas & Engler, 1959; 14% in George, 1970) or in permanent adoptive homes (i.e., 16% in George, 1970; 17% in Shyne, 1969) ever accomplished. Creditably, the states of Arizona, California, Iowa, Massachusetts, New York, Vermont and possibly others are considering education and crisis intervention programs for natural parents in an effort to reduce the overall foster placement rate. The documented harmful effects such as personality maladjustment (DeFries, Jenkins, & Williams, 1965), higher arrest rates, and poorer work histories in comparison to a control group (Ferguson, 1966; McCord, McCord, & Thurber, 1960) of foster care in general are often further intensified by multiple foster placements as reported above.

An overall summary of the current state of foster parent education warrants the conclusions that training of foster parents occurs with about 12% to 63% of foster parents prior to becoming service providers and 1% to 49% of foster parents while they are caring for foster children. Most foster parents seem to want further preservice and inservice training. Stepped-up training efforts are especially desirable in view of the high rate of turnover of foster children in foster homes and the damaging effects of such multiple placements. Problems frequently reported by foster parents in dealing with foster child behavior difficulties and special needs might be alleviated through foster family education, which might also help stem the higher turnover rate of foster parents. Foster parent education should entail, at the minimum, the following features: (1) There should be clear specifications of the foster child's needs, particularly any special concerns about behavioral difficulties, handicaps, or emotional maladjustments; (2) accurate statements should be provided about the anticipated length of stay of the foster child, insofar as possible; (3) the rights and responsibilities of the foster parents should be delineated, and the same for the foster child's role, the agency's role, and the natural parents' role; (4) all the above issues should be handled explicitly in preplacement training sessions, and prospective foster parents should have the right to make informed decisions about whether or not they wish to become foster parents in general and take specific cases in particular; (5) there should be ongoing regular consultation sessions with foster care caseworkers and other foster parents for the purpose of providing guidance and feedback about the rearing of foster children after they are placed in the home. These features represent the minimal content for foster parent education programs; additional content and issues for inclusion in training efforts will be identified from subsequent sections of this chapter dealing with the role of the foster children in foster education endeavors, foster parent selection and matching, and method of foster parent education.

THE CHILD IN EDUCATION FOR FOSTER CARE

As a child enters into foster care, he is confronted with three major elements of change that tax his adaptive resources and exaggerate his vulnerability to symptoms of distress: (1) separation from his family and extended environment, (2) introduction to the foster care agency and personnel, (3) introduction to a new family or group facility and extended environment of different persons and places (Kline & Forbush Overstreet, 1972). Each element of change contains a complicated system of persons with sets of relationships the child must leave behind or enter into. The natural family system is usually undergoing severe shock from a variety of external causes (e.g., poverty) or internal events (e.g., loss of one or both parents) for which the child often feels at least partly responsible (Bowlby & Parkes, 1970; Littner, 1956) and yet helpless to cope with (Kline & Forbush Overstreet, 1972). Although the child physically leaves his natural family system, his psychological reference to his natural family persists for some time afterward. Simultaneously, the foster child must become acquainted with an agency system that is often overburdened with case responsibilities and regulations (Gruber, 1978). Consequently, there can be some resistance from the agency system to deal with yet another custody client. Finally, the child enters a new family system with frequently foreign expectations and practices.

Each system, that is, the natural family, the agency, and the foster family, has a natural tendency to maintain equilibrium. The addition or subtraction of component members from the system disrupts the equilibrium. The foster child is the prime cause of disequilibrium in each system and, as such, is the focus of reorganization. Leaving the foster child out of the reorganization business within each system is failing to deal with the most important component. Thus, foster care education efforts should necessarily involve the foster child in at least some phases of the training program, as Wilkes (1974) also suggests.

There are no empirical studies that examine the question of whether conjoint foster family education including the foster child is more effective than education of the foster parents alone or the foster child alone. Even the literature regarding family therapy and parent education fail to clarify this issue with natural family units. What are available are two studies (Shostak & Rosmann, 1977; Wellisch, Vincent, & Ro-Trock, 1976) that compare family versus individual modes of therapy for specific presenting problems, but both studies lack comparisons with a parent therapy mode. Shostak and Rosmann found that a behavioral family focus resulted in greater improvements by family members on specified target behaviors and a lower recidivism rate of delinquents than a behavioral treatment focus on the individual referred adolescent and a no-treatment control condition. Wellisch and colleagues compared family therapy versus individual therapy for hospitalized adolescents (diagnosed chiefly as schizophrenics) and found that subjects in the family therapy condition required fewer days to return to functioning and had a lower rehospitalization rate (i.e., 0% for family therapy subjects vs. 43% for individual therapy subjects) during a 3-month follow-up. The results of these two studies, combined with the more favorable outcomes of conjoint couple therapy versus individual therapy for married persons reported in two different reviews (Beck, 1976; Cookerly, 1976) and the positive effects of training family members as behavior change agents with deviant children (Patterson, 1971a; Tavormina, 1974), suggest that inclusion of the foster child in education with his/her foster family would likely be beneficial. Working with the foster child and his/her foster family together would insure greater generalization and maintenance of the therapeutic gains than working with the foster parents or the child alone. There may even be instances when it would be advisable to include the natural parents in the training effort, such as when placement of the foster child back in the natural home is a potentially feasible goal. At least one study (Jones, Neuman, & Shyne, 1976) has demonstrated the benefits of involving the natural family in training, but further research of this issue is needed.

The research literature is more helpful in characterizing children who enter foster care than it is in addressing whether or not foster children should be included in foster training. Examination of this literature affords identification of characteristics of foster children that might be productively utilized in preparing the parents prior to receiving foster children. The literature points to areas of potential maladjustment that should be dealt with in foster family counseling.

As a group, foster children tend to be emotionally and socially maladjusted as they enter their new families. Vasaly's (1976) analysis of foster care in the states of Arizona, California, Iowa, Massachusetts, and Vermont provides the following summary descriptions of foster children and their natural parents. The average age of foster children at the time of first placement is approximately 11 years, although this varies across localities and seems to be increasing in some communities. Approximately 54% of the children entering foster care are male and 46% are female. There are greater representations of racial and ethnic minorities among children in foster care than the racial and ethnic proportions existent in the general population of the United States. Approximately 1/3 of all foster children have known physical, mental, or emotional handicaps. Most foster children have siblings in foster care, although usually not all are in the same foster family. The natural parents are most apt to be in their thirties. They tend to have histories of marital instability and frequently are divorced at the time their children are placed in foster care. Most of the children do not live with either parent. The natural parents are generally poorly educated; many are unemployed, and those who are employed work at unskilled or semi-skilled jobs. Most have incomes below the federally established poverty level, and many are receiving public assistance. Very few natural parents contribute toward the financial support of their children in foster care, although most have some interest in visiting the children at their foster placements and taking their children back at a later date. Studies by George (1970) and Parker (1966) in England and Maas and Engler (1959) and Shyne (1969) in the United States yielded findings that tend to agree with those reported by Vasaly when the same indices are compared.

The reasons children are given up or forcibly removed for foster placements are also important to understand. A comparison of Jenkins and Norman's (1972) data for a New York City sample with Gruber's (1978) Massachusetts sample, Vasaly's (1976) findings for samples in Arizona and California, and Shyne's (1969) sample from 7 cities in the United States yields the same reasons but considerable variability in their frequency. Abuse and neglect of children was the most common reason for foster placement in the Arizona (13.6%), California (46.3%), and Shyne (21%) studies, but only the third most frequently cited reason in the Massachusetts (13.6%) and New York

City (14%) studies. Incapacity of the parents was the most frequent reason reported by Gruber (25%), followed by mental illness of the parent (23%). The latter reason was the most common obtained by Jenkins and Norman (22%). Desertion, death, divorce, and physical illness of the parents are reported quite often as reasons for foster placement in all studies. All the reasons reported thus far deal in some respect with incapacity or unwillingness of the natural parent(s) in fulfilling his/her role as care giver. Reasons for foster placement that have their origins with the child are less common. Child misbehavior or disability accounted for 16% of the placement reasons in Jenkins and Norman's sample, 9.6% in Gruber's sample, 19.2% in the California report, 13% in Shyne's study, and 2.1% in the Arizona survey. In short, foster children are generally the victims of the circumstances rather than the causes of the circumstances leading to their foster placement.

Not only should foster parents be prepared in their preplacement education, but the whole foster family unit should undergo counseling to learn to cope with the effects associated with being the helpless victim of circumstances, namely anxiety, depression, withdrawal, and passivity (Miller, Rosellini, & Seligman, 1977) of the foster child. Frequently also, because of his/her poor socialization and the unstable environment of the natural home, the foster child may exhibit oppositional and aggressive behavior. These behaviors should be understood as reflections of the child's own insecurity (Littner, 1956). Because of the frequently impoverished background, the foster child may attempt hoarding behaviors, theft, and lying to defend himself/herself. Sex role identity problems are also likely because of the child's exposure in many cases, to only one parent, who may have provided a poor model at that (Maluccio, 1966).

The available research literature suggests several child-related variables that may be predictive of special foster care problems and warrant preventive measures for the foster parents and their wards. The number of previous foster placements has been shown to be highly correlated with foster placement failure (George, 1970; Eisenberg, 1962; Parker, 1966; Williams, 1961). Eisenberg (1962) and Trasler (1960) found that foster placement failures are related to the child's history in such a way that the more disruptive, unsuitable, and rejecting the natural home, the more likely the foster placement will fail. The symptoms of maladjustment that began in the natural home usually intensify as the child is shuffled from one foster home to another. This vicious cycle can be broken through placement with specially trained professional foster parents (Levin, Rubenstein, &

Streiner, 1976). Age of the foster child is positively correlated with likelihood of foster care failure (George, 1970; Parker, 1966). Older children have usually had more opportunities to experience maladaptive environments and rearing practices so may be more set in their behavior patterns. The presence and degree of physical, mental, or emotional handicaps are positively related to placement failure (Gray & Parr, 1957; Parker, 1966). Ferman and Warren (1974), Maas (1969), and Vasaly (1976) found that these children are harder to place than children who exhibit no identifiable handicaps. The number and type of behavior problems of the child are positively correlated with foster placement failure (George, 1970; Parker, 1966). Many foster parents refuse to take children who have histories of delinquency, sexual promiscuity, aggressive behaviors, or other illegal offenses. Finally, there is a variety of reasons for foster placement that have been shown to positively correlate with the probability of foster care failure such as abandonment by the parent (Eisenberg, 1962; Fanshel, 1971; Murphy, 1964; Vasaly, 1976), alcoholism combined with mental illness of the parent (Murphy, 1964), and child abuse (Eisenberg, 1962; Murphy, 1964).

In summary, if the foster child is to spend 5 years in foster care, as some statistical averages suggest (Gruber, 1978; Maas & Engler, 1959; Vasaly, 1976), it makes sense to identify before placement variables of the child that may mitigate against foster care success and to work with the foster family and child jointly to deal with these particular problems. Both the child and the foster parents should be given as thorough advance preparation as possible about what to expect in foster care, as well as continuing advice and feedback throughout the course of placement. It may be necessary to place foster children with special problems such as handicaps and behavior difficulties with foster parents who have had specific extra training. Professional foster parents, whose means of livelihood derives from being paid to care for these children, may have to be used. Foster parent reimbursement rates must be adjusted to make this option feasible in many localities. Programs such as those described by Bedford and Hybertson (1975), Boaz and Retish (1977), Cox and James (1970), Levin, Rubenstein, and Streiner (1976), and Mamula and Newman (1973) offer models.

FOSTER PARENT SELECTION AND MATCHING

A large proportion of foster parents are not good ones. Wolins (1963) found that as the need for foster parents increased, the rate of rejection of foster parent candidates decreased and was accompanied by a concomitant decrease in the quality of the applicants accepted as foster parents. This finding, combined with results of several studies documenting the deleterious effects of some foster homes (Cohagan, 1960; DeFries, Jenkins, & Williams, 1964, 1965; Maas & Engler, 1959), argues for better selection of foster parents and improved matching of these parents with foster children. Two areas of the research literature are relevant here. The first involves studies describing the characteristics of foster parents in general. The second examines foster parent variables that correlate positively with success as foster care providers. The aim of this section is to use the research literature to define the population of foster parents who should be participating in education for foster parenthood and to determine characteristics of foster parents that might be useful for matching foster parent to child because of their validity as predictors of foster care success.

Taylor and Starr's (1967) review of characteristics of foster parents who were recruited was inconclusive in its descriptions and called for additional research, especially regarding the relationship between the spouses and the relationship with the foster child. Other reviews (Dinnage & Kellmer Pringle, 1967) and recent studies (Fanshel, 1971, 1976; George, 1970; Gruber, 1978; Vasaly, 1976) yield descriptions of foster parents that allow formulation of a clearer picture when combined with some of the earlier works mentioned by Taylor and Starr. The following composite is based on consistent evidence combined from all these sources. The majority of foster parents are in their mid 30s to late 40s and have 2 to 4 children of their own, but increasingly young and often childless couples are volunteering for foster parenthood. Most foster parents have low middle incomes, although the full range of income levels is represented in some studies. Over 3/4 of all foster parents are in their first marriage, but there is a trend in recent years to place more children than formerly with single parents and couples in which the spouses have been married more than once. The education level varies from college training to less than a high school education, with the majority of foster parents having a high school education or less. All racial and ethnic groups are represented among foster parents, and it is usually possible to place most foster children with same-race foster parents, except in certain communities with a very high preponderance of low-income minorities. Most foster parents can be classified as skilled or semi-skilled blue collar workers. The motives, listed in order of importance, expressed by persons who became foster parents include the following: became interested in the program after hearing about it from another foster parent or news media report, love children or other altruistic reason, seeking companionship of a child for themselves or for a child of their own, replace a child who died or left home after reaching adulthood, have no children of their own and desire one or more, and seeking financial gain.

An important implication provided by these descriptors is that foster parent education must be fairly simple, direct, and practical so that lesser educated persons, who comprise the majority of foster parents, can understand and profit from the training. Also, recognizing the parents' experience as care givers for their own children and giving them credit for their generally benevolent motivations may be helpful in winning their participation as foster team members who share in the training efforts.

Given the general description of foster parents as fairly solid, stable community citizens, why are many foster parents unsuccessful as foster child rearers? Aside from the already established fact that most foster parents receive little or no preplacement and in-service training, there are a number of foster parent variables shown to correlate with foster care success or failure. The following summary is drawn from the review of Taylor and Starr (1967) and more recent empirical studies by Cautley and Aldridge (1975), Fanshel (1971, 1976), Hampson (1975), and Kraus (1971). Age is correlated with foster care success, such that older persons (i.e., above 46) and young parents (i.e., below 25) are less likely to retain foster care wards for long durations and are more likely to have high turnover rates of foster children. Reasons for this might be that older parents usually have less energy and tend to be more rigid in their standards of acceptable behavior, while young persons have less experience as parents. Indeed, parents who tend to be authoritarian in their disciplinary methods are also less successful foster parents, and they are more likely to be older. Successful foster parents usually have stable marital relationships and fulfilling relationships with their own children, whereas unsuccessful foster parents often have complaints in one or both of these areas of relationships and may be seeking compensation for their lack of fulfillment. Persons who become foster parents in order to help others are usually more successful in their roles than persons who become foster parents in order to satisfy personal deficits. Desire for financial gain is positively correlated with success as foster parents, perhaps because this motive characterizes many "professional" foster care providers. The presence of a foster father is conducive to success, as is having children of one's own who are older than the foster child. The presence of natural children in the home who are younger than the foster child correlates negatively with the duration of foster care. Reasons for this might be that the parents feel more obligated to care for their own younger children; fears that older foster children might negatively influence younger natural children also play a part. Foster parents who are able to accept the foster child's natural parents tend to be better foster care providers. Murphy (1964), O'Reilly (1961), and Vasaly (1976) reported that the frequency of visits by the natural parents was linked with better emotional adjustments of the foster children and often was indicative of earlier returns to the natural home. In these cases, success of foster care is defined as a short stay in the temporary home. Finally, Kline and Forbush Overstreet (1972), Murphy (1974), and Taylor and Starr (1967) revealed a number of factors associated with less than adequate foster parenthood, including residence in a suburban area, overemphasis on academic achievement of the foster child, deprivation of the foster parents themselves as children, and changes within the family system such as birth of a new family member, death of a family member, serious illness, major job change, move to a new community, or some other considerable loss or gain of social status.

It is often not possible for foster parent trainers to effect changes in many of the situations or circumstances of foster homes that have been positively correlated with lack of success. For example, foster care agencies might not be able to recruit parents who are in the ideal age group. In these cases, it is even more imperative that foster parents and foster children participate in advance preparation and ongoing education. Perhaps through intensive consultations with trained family counselors, the effects of the high-risk factors can be minimized. In other instances, it *is* possible to effect change on some of the variables positively correlated with lack of success. For example, foster parents who tend to be authoritarian might be able to develop alternative disciplinary styles flexibly suited to the foster child. Similarly, foster families who are undergoing significant changes such as moving to a new community could deal productively with the impact of these changes by analyzing them in family education sessions and receiving support from the foster care caseworker. Foster children could profit immensely from participating in a smoothly handled major change. Foster care caseworkers should sensitize themselves to the positive and negative attributes of the foster care parents and should prepare training sessions tailored to the strengths and weaknesses of each family. Individualized training with each family is probably necessary, at least for part of the course, so that the particular set of circumstances presented by each family can be addressed.

In addition to the stated preferences of the prospective foster parents, the relative assets and deficits presented by each set of parents should be taken into account in matching them with foster children. Foster parents with a high number of assets should be matched with difficult foster cases when possible, instead of with the "best" cases, as is the common practice in some agencies (Bradley, 1966; Fanshel, 1971). There is evidence (Cautley & Aldridge, 1975; Murphy, 1964) that successful placements do occur with such matching. Instruments such as Touliatos and Lindholm's (1977) scale for measuring potential for foster parenthood, Soforenko's (1974) inventory, Fanshel's (1971, 1976) interview format, and Mamula's (1970) questionnaire may prove useful in addition to the list of characteristics presented here, but further validation work is necessary to substantiate their utility.

METHODS OF FOSTER PARENT EDUCATION

There are many published curricula (e.g., Stone & Hunzeker, 1974; Ward, 1976) for the training of foster parents, but the vast majority of these curricula have not been systematically evaluated for their effects on foster parent practices, and consequently, they are not reviewed here. The only studies reviewed here are those in which some attempt was made to evaluate the outcome of the training. Even these studies lacked control groups, the combination of pretest and post-test measures, or long-term follow-up checks, so the certainty of their conclusions is tenuous. Nevertheless, let us examine this research regarding methods of foster parent education.

Two central questions emerge: (1) Does foster parent training have any beneficial effects? (2) If there are beneficial effects of training, what is the best method of achieving them? There are several reports (Dall, 1967; Goldstein, 1967; Kohn, 1961; Mills, Sandle, & Sher, 1967; Roberts, 1962; Thomas, 1961) of the use of group meetings of parents with foster children to stimulate discussion and sharing of ideas among the foster parents and agency workers. The authors indicated variously that the use of in-service groups aided in retention of foster parents and had beneficial cathartic effects on parents who discussed their mutual problems of foster parenthood. McCoy and Donahue (1961) reported that discussion groups facilitated parent interaction and attempts to use specific suggestions, but these effects did not generalize over to the parents' interaction with their foster children in most other situations. All these applications of group discussion approaches lacked comparisons with control groups of parents who did not participate in discussion, and all lacked both pretest and post-test measures. Ambinder (1969) combined parent group discussions and home case management consultations with foster parents. He found that this combined approach to training did not produce positive behavior change in the foster children. He concluded that while training might enhance the child-rearing skills of some foster parents, his particular sample of parents had deficits (e.g., low educational attainment) for which training could not compensate. Soffen (1962) conducted the only controlled study using the group discussion method of training. He found that the trained group of foster parents showed significant improvement relative to the control group in the following six areas: relationship to agency, understanding the growth needs of children, ability to respond to their growth needs, understanding the meaning of difficult behavior, ability to respond appropriately to difficult behavior, and ability to respond appropriately to children's needs. However, significant change was not noted in five other key areas: relationship to caseworker, motivation, climate in family, adequacy of home, and potential response of home in receiving foster children. The evidence reviewed thus far is inconclusive regarding the effectiveness of foster parent group discussions with trained leaders.

Levin, Rubenstein, and Streiner (1976) and Stein and Gambrill (1976) taught behavior management principles to their foster parents. Both studies obtained behavioral improvements in such areas as social skills, academic achievement, and goal setting, but both studies lacked control groups for comparison purposes. Hampson (1975) combined tactics in behavioral management with reflective group techniques in the training of foster parents for handicapped children. He had 2 experimental and 2 control groups, thus affording a replication of the experimental manipulation of training or its lack thereof. He found that the trained foster parents, in comparison to the controls, improved significantly on 4 of 5 measures before and after training including parent self-report inventories, behavioral observations, and ratings by trained data collectors. Hampson, Tavormina, Grieger, and Taylor (1977) compared the relative effectiveness of behavioral versus reflective training approaches with foster mothers of nonhandicapped children. The behavioral method consisted of teaching the mothers operant techniques, which they then applied to specific problems of their foster children. Primarily, the mothers learned to set goals, make reinforcement contingent upon appropriate behavior, and keep track of certain behaviors of interest. The reflective method entailed group discussions of Ginott's (1969) principles of reflecting feelings, setting appropriate limits, and providing alternative activities when the child's current activities are inappropriate. The group leaders also attempted to convey the importance of empathy, acceptance, and understanding in dealing with children. The results indicated that both types of parent training had beneficial effects relative to a control condition in which no training was provided, and the group trained in behavioral techniques showed greater positive change on behavioral and observational measures of child rearing than the group of mothers trained in reflective techniques.

None of the studies reviewed thus far in this section undertook to examine the long-term effects of foster parent training on the parents and, more importantly, on the foster children. There is only one study that attempted this. Mamula and Newman (1973) employed family consultants to help foster parents devise developmental plans and implement them with foster children who were being released from institutions. The investigators found that 7% of the children placed with trained foster parents required reinstitutionalization within 1 year, whereas 25% of the children placed with untrained parents required reinstitutionalization within 1 year.

Several tentative conclusions are suggested from this review of foster parent training methods. First, training resulted in improved foster parent skills in most of the studies, and the results were more favorable in the more methodologically sound studies. Second, individual consultation with foster families for the purpose of handling problems particular to each family was the key heuristic component in those studies where it was undertaken (e.g., Hampson, 1975; Mamula & Newman, 1973), but the feasibility of this approach with all families is unknown (Ambinder, 1969). Generally, though, individualized structured training resulted in more consistently favorable results than less-structured foster parent group discussions; this conclusion is consistent with the recommendation derived in the preceding section. Third, training in behavioral techniques seemed to produce more beneficial results than training in reflective communications techniques. Fourth, no single study corrected for all three major methodological deficits, namely, lack of control groups, pretest and post-test measures, and long-term follow-up checks. Consequently, all these conclusions are tentative, and further research is needed in order to be more certain about these issues. Furthermore, there is a severe paucity of empirical information concerning the effects of foster parent training on the foster child's behavior and adult outcome.

Examination of the research literature on the outcome of educational counseling with natural parents and family therapy sheds additional light on the question of which method works best in foster parent training. In his review of parent counseling techniques, Tavormina (1974) discerned two main approaches: reflective counseling, which places emphasis on the parental awareness, understanding, and acceptance of the child's feelings; and behavioral counseling, which emphasizes the teaching of parents to manage their children's behavior through the application of known behavioral principles. The first method is illustrated in the writings of Ginott (1969) and Gordon (1970), while the second is exemplified in Patterson's (1971b) work. Tavormina noted that both approaches were successful with a variety of problems and divergent child populations when compared in well-designed studies. He concluded that further comparative cost-effectiveness studies with specific problems and types of children were needed to suggest which approach was optimal in various circumstances. Tavormina (1975) conducted a study that addressed this issue when he compared reflective with behavioral group counseling for parents of mentally retarded children. Results indicated that each type of counseling had a beneficial effect relative to an untreated control condition, while the behavioral method resulted in a significantly larger improvement than the reflective method on most criteria, including direct observations, attitudinal scales, and maternal reports.

In the family therapy literature also, both the reflective communications and behavioral approaches have enjoyed popularity and considerable empirically ascertained success. The most methodologically sound comparative evaluations of these approaches have been undertaken by Alexander and his colleagues (Klein, Alexander & Parsons, 1977; Parsons & Alexander, 1973). They compared four approaches with families of delinquent youths: no treatment, a client-centered (i.e., reflective) family approach, a church-sponsored eclectic method of family counseling, and behaviorally oriented family therapy. Behaviorally oriented family therapy yielded the greatest positive impact on family interaction variables and resulted in the lowest rates of recidivism of the referred adolescents and their siblings.

Overall, the greater efficacy of behavioral techniques obtained in parent counseling and family therapy is consistent with the tentative conclusion reached earlier regarding this method of educating foster parents. Although some elements of this method have been mentioned already, elaboration is warranted for those seeking to understand and apply the approach.

A MODEL FOR FOSTER FAMILY EDUCATION

At this junction, it seems desirable to recapitulate some of the major points derived in the foregoing sections of this chapter because they furnish the base on which to build a social foundation for foster parent education. First, as was concluded in the section regarding the current state of foster parent education, prior to receiving a foster placement, foster parents should be prepared with information regarding the child's needs, the anticipated length of stay, and the rights and responsibilities of the foster parents, the child, his natural parents, and the agency. The foster parents should have the right to accept or refuse a foster child after considering this information. Second, foster children and parents should be matched by taking into account not only such usual considerations as preferences of parents for a certain age, sex, and race of foster child, but also the special needs and problems of the child (e.g., handicap or behavior maladjustment) and the characteristics of foster parents that have been shown to correlate positively with success in rearing foster children. Some children may have to be placed with "professional" foster parents who are specially trained to deal with certain child problems. Furthermore, the "best" children should not necessarily be matched to the "best" parents. Third, there should be preparation of the foster parents and child prior to placement about "what to expect"; consultations should continue with the foster family during the placement tenure. Insofar as possible, the child should be included in the preparation phase, and certainly in most parts of the in-service phase. Fourth, the foster family education should be simple, practical, and individualized for each family in order to effectively reach all foster parents and children. Training in behavioral management is the most efficacious approach because it satisfies these conditions and has proven effectiveness. Group discussion among foster parents could have facilitative effects, but the main focus on the educational effort should be individualized family consultations. Finally, the natural family of the child should be encouraged to visit him/her at the foster home and to participate in parenthood education sessions if transition back to the natural home is planned.

The method espoused as most promising for educating foster parents and children might be termed the *behavioral systems approach* because it combines a system view of the foster family with proven behavioral change techniques. According to the systems framework, behavior change of any family member is seen as having repercussions within the whole family. Successful treatment is predicated upon working with the entire system of significant persons; in most instances this is the foster family unit, but in some cases other persons (e.g., relatives, friends, and natural parents and siblings) could become productively involved in some of the deliberations. The behavioral systems procedures consist of 4 sets of operations used in helping the foster family unit make changes to accommodate the needs of the foster child and the assets and deficits of the rest of the family: (1) specifying problem areas within the family system, (2) analyzing problematic situations, (3) developing appropriate response patterns, and (4) keeping records.

SPECIFYING PROBLEM AREAS WITHIN THE FAMILY SYSTEM: While many of the special needs and problems of the foster child and his/her foster family will have been identified from the initial screening and matching, it is important to explore their perceptions of these and any additional issues in the sessions before placement and following the actual move of the child into the new home. Several assessment techniques are recommended: (1) interviewing each family member (including the foster child) separately; (2) interviewing the family together; and (3) recording observations of family processes with the permission of the family on audio or audiovisual tape for further analyses. Obviously, with very young children, little verbal input can be gained from the individual interviews, and the conjoint family interactions and recordings may provide the bulk of the useful information. During these early sessions, the major aims are to form a list of problem areas and to establish each family member's position concerning each problem. Malouf and Alexander (1972) have mentioned several benefits of this operation. First, the caseworker and family members are able to achieve clearer understandings of the relevant issues and the roles played by each member. Second, the family members often discover differences among the members' perceptions and interpretations of events and issues. Third, the family members begin to see the need for clear interpersonal communication and consistent approaches to problem solving. Fourth, the family members begin to develop rapport among themselves, which usually eases discomforts felt by the foster child and within the new family and generalizes to the caseworker.

Usually, the kinds of problems that emerge center around the feelings of the foster child about separation from his/her natural family, the foster parents' and natural childrens' feelings about the new addition and his/her previous family, and the special needs and concerns presented by the foster child. It is appropriate to organize the problems into a hierarchy in which the problems are listed according to level of difficulty. The list can be used for reference on future occasions and suggests starting points for solving the problems. Rather than attempting to resolve the most difficult problems first, it is usually best to begin work on less severe problems in the hope that these can be solved and lead to successful experiences and so lend to the family members' confidence that more difficult problems can also be handled. Generally also, the first few meetings with the caseworker are times for educating all the involved persons, and especially the foster parents, about what is expected behavior and developmental progress for the age and ability level of the foster child. This is particularly important for foster parents who have no children of their own or whose children are younger than the foster child.

ANALYZING PROBLEMATIC SITUATIONS: This operation begins as soon as a hierarchy of problems has been tentatively specified. The word *tentative* is used because the list of problems is almost always modified in the course of ongoing meetings as new problems occur and additional information becomes available. The purpose of analyzing problematic situations is to determine what behaviors control and maintain deviant response patterns. It is important to identify the contingencies within family interactions that are linked with the production and maintenance of deviant response patterns because this knowledge suggests how a maladjusted pattern can be changed. Analysis of problem situations proceeds by seeking information from family members and by reviewing recorded interactions about the events that precede and follow problem situations. Each family member is asked what his/her needs are. Having identified each person's needs concerning an issue and the contingencies that seem to maintain the faulty ways of satisfying these needs, the next step is to devise appropriate alternative ways of satisfying each individual's needs. This leads to the next set of operations.

DEVELOPING APPROPRIATE RESPONSE PATTERNS: Appropriate resolution of family problems is best achieved through interpersonal negotiation. The guiding principle for this collective bargaining effort is that the resolution should have reciprocal benefits for all the family members. The family members should agree on appropriate behavioral requirements for each person and appropriate consequences for failure to comply with the terms of the bargain. In some cases, it is desirable to formalize the terms of the interpersonal bargains by writing out contracts that each of the family members signs. However, it is the process of contract negotiation rather than the content of the agreement that critically determines the success of the approach. Family members learn a style of problem solving that they can apply in a variety of situations.

Over the course of consultations with the foster care caseworker, the foster family analyzes many problematic situations and undertakes many interpersonal negotiation sessions, from which it learns an enduring style of appropriate problem solving. After resolving less difficult issues, more serious problems are approached. At times, also, issues may need to be renegotiated when the resolution falls flat or when the issue reappears in another form. Initially, the caseworker plays the role of an active director in helping the family members analyze problematic situations and develop reciprocal bargains, but s/he should progressively fade himself/herself out of this role and into that of a commentator as the family develops skills. Whereas the caseworker may initially have to coach actively and even rehearse appropriate interchanges, eventually the family members can usually carry out complete problem analyses and contract negotiations themselves.

KEEPING RECORDS: Keeping accurate accounts of the problems addressed and the interpersonal bargains worked out is essential because it affords a measure of progress or lack thereof in the foster family education effort. After a contract has been worked out, the caseworker should begin the next meeting by asking the family members if and how the terms of the bargain were kept. While the reports of the family members are one measure of progress, review of recorded sessions provides additional clues. Measures of duration of speech (Alexander & Parsons, 1973; Shostak, 1977), response style (Alexander, 1973), and frequency of interruptions (Alexander & Parsons, 1973), which can be taken from tape recordings, have all been shown to be useful indices of the degree of family adjustment.

An overview of the behavioral systems approach to educating foster families suggests several distinguishing characteristics, some of which have been alluded to earlier, but which can bear pointing out again. First, it focuses on the present circumstances. Past events are worth reviewing in order to help explain how current conditions have been reached, but focusing on them further in the foster family context seldom leads to productive resolution of the foster child's misgivings and may even contribute to more ambivalence between the foster parents and the child. Second, the behavioral systems approach is fairly simple to learn and apply. Its practical nature appeals to children and families who have immediate real problems and needs. There is no need to learn a new vocabulary such as some reflective and dynamic counseling approaches seem to encourage. Third, the term *foster parent education* can be misleading when applied to the approach espoused here because it connotes the training of foster parents only. Instead, the term *foster family education* has been adopted because the whole foster family unit is involved in the assessment and problem-solving phases. Finally, the behavioral systems approach leads to the development of a style of handling problems that can be applied to many different issues and problems posed, not only by the foster child, but by his foster family as well. The likelihood of generalization of learning across situations is a built-in advantage.

CONCLUSION

While one major purpose of this chapter has been to examine the status of foster parent education and to translate empirically derived information regarding selection issues, matching, and method of training into prescriptions for improved education for foster families, a second purpose has been to identify gaps in the research in this area. Several critical deficiencies are apparent. There is a severe shortage of methodologically sound research evaluating the long-term effects of education on child-rearing tactics of the foster parents, the longevity of these effects in foster care service, and most importantly, on the foster children themselves. The impact on natural children of having foster children in their families is largely unknown. Likewise, little is known about the effects of having children in foster care on the foster parents and the natural parents. More research is needed to examine the components of foster family education that maximize the beneficial effects of educational programs. The roles of the natural family, extended kin and friends of both the foster child and the foster family, and community supports (e.g., churches and schools) in effecting successful foster care arrangements need clarification. Perhaps even greater scrutiny should be placed on who goes into foster care and in maintaining or reconstituting the natural family, if possible, so that long-term foster child care can be obviated in many more instances than is the current practice.

REFERENCES

Alexander, J. F. Defensive and supportive communications in normal and deviant families. *Journal of Consulting and Clinical Psychology*, 1973, *40*, 223-231.

Alexander, J. F., & Parsons, B. V. Short-term behavioral intervention with delinquent families: Impact on family process and recidivism. *Journal of Abnormal Psychology*, 1973, *81*, 219-225.

Ambinder, W. J. Teaching child management techniques to foster parents: A pessimistic report. *Journal of School Health*, 1969, *39*, 257-261.

Beck, D. F. Research findings on the outcomes of marital counseling. In D. H. L. Olson (Ed.), *Treating relationships.* Lake Mills, Iowa: Graphic

Pub, 1976.

Bedford, L., & Hybertson, L. D. Emotionally disturbed children: A program of alternatives to residential treatment. *Child Welfare*, 1975, *54*, 109-115.

Boaz, R., & Retish, P. A model for de-institutionalization. *Mental Retardation*, 1977, *15*, 26-27.

Bowlby, J., & Parkes, C. M. Separation and loss within the family. In E. J. Anthony & C. Koupernik (Eds.), *The child in his family* (Vol. 1). New York: Wiley, 1970.

Bradley, T. *Exploration of case workers' perceptions of adoptive applicants.* New York: Child Welfare, 1966.

Cautley, P. W. & Aldridge, M. J. Predicting success for new foster parents. *Social Work*, 1975, *20*, 48-53.

Cohagan, G. B. *Adoptability: A study of 100 children in foster care.* New York: State Charities Aid Association, 1960.

Cookerly, J. R. Evaluating different approaches to marriage counseling. In D. H. L. Olson (Ed.), *Treating relationships.* Lake Mills, Iowa: Graphic Pub, 1976.

Cox, R. W., & James, M. H. Rescue from limbo: Foster home placement for hospitalized physically disabled children. *Child Welfare*, 1970, *49*, 21-28.

Dall, A. G. Group learning for foster parents. II. In a public agency. *Children*, 1967, *14*, 185-187.

DeFries, Z., Jenkins, S., & Williams, E. C. Treatment of disturbed children in foster care. *American Journal of Orthopsychiatry*, 1964, *34*, 615-624.

DeFries, Z., Jenkins, S., & Williams, E. C. Foster family care — A non-sentimental view. *Child Welfare*, 1965, *44*, 73-85.

Dinnage, R., & Kellmer Pringle, M. L. *Foster home care facts and fallacies.* New York: Humanities, 1967.

Eisenberg, L. The sins of the fathers: Urban decay and social pathology. *American Journal of Orthopsychiatry*, 1962, *32*, 5-17.

Fanshel, D. The exit of the children from foster care: An interim report. *Child Welfare*, 1971, *50*, 65-81.

Fanshel, D. Status changes of children in foster care: Final results of the Columbia University longitudinal study. *Child Welfare*, 1976, *55*, 143-171.

Ferguson, T. *Children in care — And after.* London: Oxford Univ Pr, 1966.

Ferman, P. R., & Warren, B. L. *Finding families for the children.* Ypsilanti, Michigan: Eastern Michigan University, 1974.

George, V. *Foster care theory and practice.* London: Routledge & Kegan Paul, 1970.

Ginott, H. *Between parent and teenager.* New York: Macmillan, 1969.

Glickman, E. *Child placement through clinically oriented casework.* New York: Columbia U Pr, 1957.

Goldstein, H. Group learning for foster parents. I. In a voluntary agency.

Children, 1967, *14*, 180-184.

Gordon, T. *Parent effectiveness training*. New York: McKay, 1970.

Gray, P. G., & Parr, E. A. *Children in care and the recruitment of foster parents*. London: H.M.S.O., 1957.

Gruber, A. R. *Children in foster care*. New York: Human Sci Pr, 1978.

Hampson, R. B. *Selecting and training foster parents as therapists: Community care for handicapped children*. Unpublished masters thesis, University of Virginia, 1975.

Hampson, R. B., Tavormina, J. B., Grieger, R., & Taylor, J. R. *Relative effectiveness of behavioral versus reflective counseling with foster parents*. Paper presented at the meeting of the American Psychological Association, San Francisco, August 1977.

Jenkins, S., & Norman, E. *Filial deprivation and foster care*. New York: Columbia U Pr, 1972.

Jones, M. A., Neuman, R., & Shyne, A. W. *A second chance for families: Evaluation of a program to reduce foster care*. New York: Child Welfare, 1976.

Kautz, E. Family services that obviate the need for child placement. *Child Welfare*, 1969, *48*, 289-295.

Kennedy, R. A foster parent looks at foster care. In H. D. Stone (Ed.), *Foster care in question: A national reassessment by twenty-one experts*. New York: Child Welfare, 1970.

Kinney, J. M., Madsen, B., Fleming, T., & Haapala, D. A. Homebuilders: Keeping families together. *Journal of Consulting and Clinical Psychology*, 1977, *45*, 667-673.

Klein, N. C., Alexander, J. F., & Parsons, B. V. Impact of family systems intervention on recidivism and sibling delinquency: A model of primary prevention and program evaluation. *Journal of Consulting and Clinical Psychology*, 1977, *45*, 469-474.

Kline, D. The validity of long-term foster family care. *Child Welfare*, 1965, *44*, 185-195.

Kline, D., & Forbush Overstreet, H. M. *Foster care of children: Nurture and treatment*. New York: Columbia U Pr, 1972.

Kohn, E. A. A joint project for providing group meetings for foster parents. *Child Welfare*, 1961, *40*, 31-33.

Kraus, J. Predicting success of foster placements for school-age children. *Social Work*, 1971, *16*, 63-72.

Levin, S., Rubenstein, J. S., & Streiner, D. L. The parent-therapist program: An innovative approach to treating emotionally disturbed children. *Hospital and Community Psychiatry*, 1976, *27*, 407-410.

Littner, N. *Some traumatic effects of separation and placement*. New York: Child Welfare, 1956.

Maas, H. S. Long-term effects of early childhood separation and group care. *Vita Humana*, 1963, *6*, 34-56.

Maas, H. S. Children in long term foster care. *Child Welfare*, 1969, *48*, 321-332.

Maas, H. S., & Engler, R. E. *Children in need of parents.* New York: Columbia U Pr, 1959.

Malouf, R. E., & Alexander, J. F. *Family crisis intervention: A model and technique of training.* Paper presented at the National Conference on Training in Family Therapy, sponsored by the Philadelphia Child Guidance Clinic, Philadelphia, November 1972.

Maluccio, A. N. Selecting foster parents for disturbed children. *Children,* 1966, *13,* 69-74.

Mamula, R. A. Developing a training program for family caretakers. *Mental Retardation,* 1970, *8,* 30-35.

Mamula, R. A., & Newman, N. *Community placement of the mentally retarded: A handbook for community agencies and social work practitioners.* Springfield: Thomas, 1973.

McCord, J., McCord, W., & Thurber, E. The effects of foster home placement in the prevention of adult anti-social behaviour. *Social Science Review,* 1960, *34,* 415-420.

McCoy, J., & Donahue, J. M. Educating foster parents through the group process. *Child Welfare,* 1961, *40,* 29-31.

Miller, W. R., Rosellini, R. A., & Seligman, M. E. P. Learned helplessness and depression. In J. D. Maser & M. E. P. Seligman (Eds.), *Psychopathology: Experimental models.* San Francisco: W. H. Freeman, 1977.

Mills, R. B., Sandle, R. B., & Sher, M. A. Introducing foster mother training groups in a voluntary child welfare agency. *Child Welfare,* 1967, *46,* 575-580.

Mnookin, R. H. Foster care — In whose best interest? *Harvard Educational Review,* 1973, *43,* 599-638.

Murphy, H. B. M. Foster home variables and adult outcomes. *Mental Hygiene,* 1964, *48,* 587-599.

Murphy, H. B. M. Long term foster care and its influence on adjustment to adult life. In E. J. Anthony & C. Koupernik (Eds.), *The child in his family: Children at psychiatric risk.* New York: Wiley, 1974.

National Center for Social Statistics. *Child welfare statistics.* Washington, D.C.: U.S. D.H.E.W., 1969.

O'Reilly, C. T. *Foster children — Profile and problems.* Chicago: Loyola University School of Social Work, 1961. (Reviewed by R. Dinnage & M. L. Kellmer Pringle, *Foster home care facts and fallacies.* New York: Humanities, 1967.

Parker, R. *Decision in child care.* London: Allen & Unwin, 1966.

Parsons, B. V., & Alexander, J. F. Short-term family intervention: A therapy outcome study. *Journal of Consulting and Clinical Psychology,* 1973, *41,* 195-201.

Patterson, G. R. Behavioral intervention procedures in the classroom and in the home. In A. E. Bergin & S. L. Garfield (Eds.), *Handbook of psychotherapy and behavior change.* New York: Wiley, 1971. (a)

Patterson, G. R. *Families.* Champaign, Illinois: Res Press, 1971. (b)

Pratt, C. Assembled families. *Child Welfare,* 1967, *46,* 94-96.

Roberts, V. K. An experiment in group work with foster parents. *Case Conference,* 1962, *9,* 149-152.

Sherman, E. A., Neuman, R., & Shyne, A. W. *Children adrift in foster care: A study of alternative approaches.* New York: Child Welfare, 1973.

Shostak, D. A. *Family versus individual oriented behavior therapy as treatment approaches to juvenile delinquency.* Unpublished doctoral dissertation, University of Virginia, 1977.

Shostak, D. A., & Rosmann, M. R. *Family versus individual oriented behavior therapy in the treatment of delinquency.* Paper presented at the meeting of the Eastern Psychological Association, Boston, Massachusetts, April 1977.

Shyne, A. W. (Ed.). *The need for foster care: An incidence study of requests for foster care and agency response in seven metropolitan areas.* New York: Child Welfare, 1969.

Soffen, J. The impact of a group educational program for foster parents. *Child Welfare,* 1962, *41,* 195-201.

Soforenko, A. Z. Computer client-data programs. *Mental Retardation,* 1974, *12,* 40-41.

Stein, T. J., & Gambrill, E. D. Behavioral techniques in foster care, *Social Work,* 1976, *21,* 34-39.

Stone, H. D., & Hunzeker, J. M. *Education for foster family care: Models and methods for foster parents and social workers.* New York: Child Welfare, 1974.

Tavormina, J. B. Basic models of parent counseling: A critical review. *Psychological Bulletin,* 1974, *81,* 827-836.

Tavormina, J. B. Relative effectiveness of behavioral and reflective group counseling with parents of mentally retarded children. *Journal of Consulting and Clinical Psychology,* 1975, *43,* 22-31.

Tavormina, J. B., Hampson, R. B., Grieger, R. A., & Tedesco, J. Examining foster care: A viable solution for placement of handicapped children? *American Journal of Community Psychology,* 1977, *5,* 435-446.

Taylor, D. A., & Starr, P. Foster parenting: An integrative review of the literature. *Child Welfare,* 1967, *46,* 371-385.

Thomas, C. The use of group methods with foster parents. *Children,* 1961, *8,* 218-222.

Touliatos, J., & Lindholm, B. W. Development of a scale for measuring potential for foster parenthood. *Psychological Reports,* 1977, *40,* 1190.

Trasler, C. *In place of parents.* London: Routledge & Kegan Paul, 1960.

Vasaly, S. M. *Foster care in five states: A synthesis and analysis of studies from Arizona, California, Iowa, Massachusetts, and Vermont* (DHEW Publication No. 76-30097). Washington, D.C.: U.S. D.H.E.W., 1976.

Ward, K. (Ed.). *Foundations for foster parent education* (2nd ed.). Manhattan, Kansas: Kansas State University Department of Family and Child Development, 1976.

Wellisch, D. K., Vincent, J., & Ro-Trock, G. K. Family therapy versus individual therapy: A study of adolescents and their parents. In D. H. L. Olson (Ed.), *Treating relationships*. Lake Mills, Iowa: Graphic Pub, 1976.

Wilkes, J. R. The impact of fostering on the foster family. *Child Welfare,* 1974, *53,* 373-379.

Williams, J. M. Children who break down in foster homes: A psychological study of patterns of personality growth in grossly deprived children. *Journal of Child Psychology and Psychiatry,* 1961, *2,* 5-20.

Wolins, M. *Selecting foster parents.* New York: Columbia U Pr, 1963.

Wolins, M., & Piliavin, I. *Institution or foster family: A century of debate.* New York: Child Welfare, 1964.

Yarrow, L. J. Separation from parents during early childhood. In M. L. Hoffman & L. W. Hoffman (Eds.), *Review of child development research* (Vol. 1). New York: Russell Sage, 1964.

Chapter 18

WORKING WITH PARENTS
IN RURAL COMMUNITIES

SHERRY P. KRAFT

IT is ironic that the rural community, in many
ways the cornerstone of American culture, should be viewed as a
special variable in the planning and delivery of health-related services
to parents and children. In fact, rural environments increasingly have
been targeted as areas where vital health and educational needs are
sorely neglected (Coles, 1969; Economic Development Division, 1971;
Economic Research Service, 1970; Economic Research Service, 1971;
U.S. Department of Agriculture, 1970) and where special strategies
and procedures must be employed to insure that new services will be
accepted and utilized (Eisdorfer, Altrocchi & Young, 1968; Huessy,
1972; Segal, 1973; Wedel, 1969). This situation stands as a testimonial
to the tremendous impact of technological change on the distribution
of resources in our society, on the problems and needs that families
experience, and on the behaviors, attitudes, and environments that are
valued and promoted by our culture. One of the most consistent and
striking conclusions from the literature on intervention in rural settings is that the industry of modern-day mental health is itself a
product of an urbanized society and, as such, is primarily oriented
toward the needs, activities, and resources of an urban population.
The consequences of applying "urbanized" notions in a rural setting
are evidenced in the combination of faulty problem definition and
application of inappropriate intervention strategies. The opposite
side of this dilemma is the romanticization of rural America, resulting
in the belief that rural people are devoid of the social and emotional
concerns that prevail in city areas. This chapter is intended to provide
a realistic and comprehensive portrayal of rural settings that impinge
— at times brutally — on the lives and behavior of parents and
children and on the professionals who provide health care services to
these families. Characteristics and needs of various rural populations
are discussed. Existing programs geared toward intervention with
rural families are presented; finally, practical strategies for working
with rural families and suggestions for innovation in professional

489

training are presented.

The first difficulty in addressing this topic becomes apparent in light of the fact that rural America comprises approximately 25% of the population and occupies a staggering 90% of the country's land.* The differences in geography, climate, and environment are vast. In New England or the Midwest, one finds farms located a few miles apart, sophisticated machinery and other signs of agricultural technology in evidence, and a fairly high degree of interaction among neighbors. Contrast this with the stark poverty of the Appalachian mountain regions or the southern coastal plains, the isolation of ranchlands in the West and Southwest, or the complexities of poverty and culture conflict faced by communities of Native Americans, Mexican Americans, or Eskimos. Rural communities differ markedly in basic economic resources as well: A 1967 survey of Midwestern rural communities reported that 11% of these families had incomes below the poverty level (Economic Research Service, 1971) while in the Mississippi delta region of the South, 50% of the families were economically deprived (Economic Research Service, 1970). Needless to say, rural America is comprised of vastly diverse settings, people, lifestyles, and needs. Generalization of a set of strategies and techniques appropriate for rural families becomes a near impossibility. If any subset of this population warrants less attention, it is the upper-class or well-to-do family, not that their problems are less significant, but because their greater mobility largely diminishes the impact of the rural setting on their lives and access to resources. As Coles (1977b) notes, the horizons of these "privileged ones" often extend far beyond the boundaries of their family's acreage. In contrast, this chapter will focus on the families for whom the mountains, valleys, or plains paradoxically constitute both their life source and the greatest obstacle to progress and change. While recognizing the existence of vast differences in climate and geography, a few basic dimensions of rural settings stand out by the significance of their influence on the lives of families and the services available to them.

CHARACTERISTICS OF RURAL SETTINGS

Space and Distance

Whether reflected in treacherous mountain roads or seemingly endless stretches of wheat and cornfields, the lives of rural families are

---

*The United States government defines a rural community as less than 2,500 in population and not located on the fringe of a larger urban center.

defined by the actuality of greater expanses of physical space. The environment functions to enhance the autonomy of the family unit by reducing the opportunity for social interaction and greatly increasing the time and effort required to make use of medical, social, or educational resources. Compounding the difficulty in gaining access to these services is the fact that decreased proximity inhibits the development of the familiarity with outside service agencies that prevails in today's urban and suburban environments — the sense that such services play an important and respected part in maximizing the quality of life and opportunities for growth. Hence, the demand and support for services is low; symptoms of physical, behavioral, and emotional problems may not be recognized as such by families or may not be visible enough to be picked up by trained professionals. The fallacy of efforts to compare the amount of "pathology" in rural versus urban settings is highlighted by in-depth accounts of the effects of poverty and isolation (Coles, 1969), as well as by statistics that suggest that admission rates to mental hospitals are directly proportional to geographical distance from state institutions (Huessy, 1972). The high level of poverty (twice that of urban areas) coupled with geographical isolation does not tend to attract highly trained professionals; as of the mid 1960s, the proportion of medical specialists in isolated rural areas was 8/100,000 as compared to 45/100,000 in semi-rural areas and from 95 to 137/100,000 in urban areas. Only 3% of the nation's practicing psychiatrists were working in rural settings (Segal, 1973).

Although improvements in communication and travel are opening new avenues for change in rural settings, the physical isolation does not facilitate exposure to the variety of cultural and occupational alternatives available in the nation. A cycle of limited educational resources, lack of alternative role models, underdevelopment of either basic or technical skills, and subsistence level employment is perpetuated in many rural settings. For example, an OEO-sponsored study of the developmental environments of poor, rural preschool children found that the median education for fathers was 6 years, with 15% having had no schooling and only 5% having completed high school. Mothers had an average education of 8 years, and 13% had been graduated from high school.† The annual income was under $3000 for 48% of the families, which is even more disheartening given that the me-

---

†Needless to say, reports of education levels for rural adults are varied, depending upon the population sampled. One study showed 50% of the men having completed high school (Shively, 1975), while another reported that 25% of a rural adult population had completed 8 or more years of schooling. (Segal, 1973).

dian number of children in these families was 6 (Aquizap & Vargas, 1970). The lack of occupational alternatives is particularly alarming given that the proportion of rural families supported by farming has dwindled from 3:5 in 1920 to 1:5 in 1970, suggesting that people are not finding adequate alternative sources of income.

Time and Pace of Life

The isolated effect of the environment and resultant perpetuation of life-styles leads to a greater continuity of culture than that which characterizes the mobility-oriented urban settings. As one mountaineer described this relationship, "The hills were so steep where I grew up even the tarpins had to wear shoulder straps. Had to pipe in sunshine. It was the sort of place you couldn't hardly get to from any other place — you just about had to be born there" (Murray, 1974). Rural families often have a great familiarity with past generations of kin, who most likely dwelled in close proximity, perhaps in the same house. Young couples frequently settle in the vicinity of their parents, resulting in the development of rural communities that are dominated by two or three extended family networks. Strong ties to the past plus lack of familiarity with cultural innovations lead to an environment in which traditional yet outmoded practices are strongly entrenched and changes are incorporated slowly. This aspect of rural culture significantly affects the delivery of services to rural families; frequently interpreted as hostility, resistance, or indifference to basic health needs, the attitude of many rural people toward new health care services may be viewed as a reflection of an inappropriate attempt "to impose the urban pattern on the rural situation" (Huessy, 1972, p. 701). For while the new technology would certainly relieve many pressing health care needs, the old ways represent a vital link to a culture in danger of being lost. The dignity and respect rural people hold for "their ways" may be reflected in an air of indignation and contempt toward blatant attempts to "city-fy" their lives. Coles (1969) reports the following comments of a West Virginia coal miner:

> I can't bring myself to move out of here, I'll admit that. We've been here a couple hundred years more or less, and we've given everything we have to the land here. . . . In New England and New York or in the Rocky Mountains they were glad to get our coal, but then the companies got rid of us — that was just the ways things happen. Then if we don't get new jobs, we're all supposed to move over a thousand miles, over to Detroit or Cleveland and start life again. Is that fair?. . . There's a lot of bad talk from people who come here and then they go, pretty fast they're gone and talking, talking about

us "poor folks"; and how it's awful sad about us, and aren't we the funniest people, the way we live, real peculiar they say, and isn't it the limit, us here all these years, and sticking to our guns, and keeping our habits like we do. (pp. 58, 62)

While the professional may view improvements in transportation and service delivery in terms of what will be gained, rural families may be much more in touch with what will be lost in the process. In what he calls *the Appalachia Syndrome*, Louv (1977) describes the cognitive dissonance that frequently results from increased economic dependence of rural mountain people on the larger social system — a sense of despair, helplessness, and loss of integrity that Louv sees as undermining the internal solidarity with which these families have endured the hardships of survival through several generations. The circumscribed specialization of modern professionals may dim our awareness of the problems of cultural transition with which rural families and communities are confronted as a result of introducing new services. The lack of continuity of services to rural communities noted by Huessy (1972) suggests that this is too frequently the case. In discussing health care services to Appalachian families, Perrotta and English (1977) emphasize "the dilemma of balance needed between the cultural roots of Appalachia versus the critical needs of the population for progress toward a healthier way of life" (p. 2). The specialist who visits a community once a week or once a month may be frustrated, not because the family does not respect his/her ability to tell them what they need, but because the specialist cannot acknowledge what they already have to offer. Respect for the historical and cultural roots of rural families is an essential professional responsibility and involves introducing new services in a manner the community can assimilate.

Professional Issues

This discussion suggests that the professional involved in the introduction of new services to a rural area may face a host of unfamiliar pressures. Much of the discomfort may be related to the unique and paradoxical combination of isolation and visibility which confronts the newcomer. Often lacking the support and familiarity of a group of colleagues, the incoming professional may find his/her public and private life closely scrutinized; as Huessy (1972) notes, "Slight lapses of social judgment can prove disastrous" (p. 701). Methods of establishing rapport and reputation learned during formal training are frequently ineffective or outright counterproductive. As Jeffrey and

Reeve (1978) point out, "A person can be seen as a useful professional only if he can be seen as a trustworthy individual; in a rural setting, personal trust supercedes issues of competence" (p. 57). Long hours of driving, an alien pace of life and set of values, minimal reinforcement for one's efforts, and possible hostility from other service providers are all characteristics of the rural setting that contribute to burn out and depression among professionals. These issues must be anticipated and dealt with by any professional or agency entering a rural setting. However, since this topic is not the focus of this chapter, the reader is referred to Eisdorfer, Altrocchi, and Young (1968); Huessy (1972); Jeffrey and Reeve (1978); and Wedel (1969) for further discussion of professional issues and entry strategies for implementing new programs in rural settings.

CHARACTERISTICS OF RURAL FAMILIES

The previous discussion hopefully has dispelled the notion that there is a single "type" of rural family; to try to depict such a type would be as misleading as assuming that the media's offerings in this area (*The Beverly Hillbillies, The Waltons, The Real McCoys*) are viable representatives. Unfortunately, literature in this area has done little to dispel stereotypic, patronizing, and often discriminatory views of rural people. For example, one report (Matthias, 1972) depicted rural families (especially farmers) as work oriented, puritanical, prejudiced, ethnocentric, uninformed, distrustful, intolerant of deviance, opposed to civil liberties, opposed to birth control, and holding traditional religious beliefs. These "work-oriented" parents supposedly become bored and tired, which leads to problems in the home. Another study (Barton & Weber, 1975) compared a rural population with a group of health science students on the Rokeach Dogmatism Questionnaire and concluded that the high level of dogmatism in the rural setting may discourage therapists from practicing there. Such reports lack any contextual base from which to describe or interpret behaviors and attitudes and therefore are of highly questionable validity.

At the other end of the spectrum is Robert Coles' (1977a, b) lengthy, open-ended, anthropological portrayals of rural families in the mountains, the South, the plains, the Southwest, and in Alaska. While these works are invaluable as resources for professionals working with such populations, the average professional has neither the time nor the resources to duplicate these procedures in other communities. However, by maintaining an ecological perspective, some useful notions about the relationship of environmental conditions to behavior, attitudes, and values can be developed. In addition, it should be noted that much of the available literature on rural families focuses on the Appalachian regions, Alabama, Kentucky, Tennessee, Georgia, North Carolina, Virginia, and West Virginia, reflecting the funding priorities of recent years. Families from different parts of the country can be expected to show as much variety as the environments that surround them. Descriptive information is intended only to provide broad guidelines, and generalizations should be made with caution.

Family Structure

As previously indicated, rural families in general tend to have fewer years of formal schooling and lower annual incomes than the national norm. One contributing factor to the economic situation is suggested by Shively (1975), who surveyed households in Appalachian regions and found that 73.1% of the mothers did not work outside the home. Aquizap and Vargas (1970) estimated that approximately 1/3 of the families in Appalachian regions are supported by public welfare. In the same report, they discussed techniques of discipline employed by parents; spanking or some form of physical punishment and deprivation accounted for almost all the disciplinary techniques. The mother was the major disciplinarian in the family, although parents tended to agree and support each other in areas of child rearing. Psychological punishment was not approved of in general, and appropriate behavior was seldom acknowledged or rewarded.

Close proximity of an extended family network plus the tendency toward larger families frequently results in child-caring functions being assumed by a grandmother, aunt, or older sibling. As a result, many rural families lack the clear generational boundaries and role relationships that characterize more urbanized, middle-class families. Young mothers may allow care of a sickly or handicapped child to be assumed by their own mother and develop a more siblinglike relationship to the child. This arrangement may function as a perfectly adequate support system for the child and should not be judged automatically as dysfunctional. The adequacy of care-taking functions in rural families depends on the consistency of care-taking functions and the sense of responsibility for the child's well-being that exists in the family.

While information on family functioning is skewed by the lack of services to diagnose or remedy existing problems, one study (Mercer,

1967) reported that rural area marriages tend to be more stable and to last longer. This may be accounted for, in part, by the fact that the family fulfills a much broader function in rural areas, and parents tend to be more similar in beliefs, attitudes, and values than in urban areas.

Values

As indicated previously, attempts to ascertain the values and priorities of rural families have been fraught with biases introduced by inappropriate methodologies and interpretations taken out of context. The few patterns that emerge suggest, simply, that the values of rural families reflect the realities of their life. Bruce (1975) conducted open-ended interviews with low-income rural men and women and found that thrift, good health, and obligations to family and society were considered of prime importance, while status, appearances, and material possessions were of lesser value. Similarly, McMillan (1967) in a comparison of low-income rural and urban mothers found that rural women placed greater value on basic necessities and transportation; material possessions were viewed as a lower priority. Aquizap and Vargas (1970) found that parents in rural Appalachian areas tended to permit and even encourage expression of aggression by their children toward peers, though aggression was clearly not permitted toward parents. Children tended to approve of their parents' modes and values toward discipline.

Just as the integrity of the family unit is valued, the tradition of autonomy and self-sufficiency, so much a part of rural living, may be evidenced in a tendency to endure rather than alleviate hardship (Coles, 1971). This tendency may take the form of fatalism and is frequently interpreted by outsiders as stubbornness or ignorance when they offer help. Viewed in the context of scarce resources and the harsh demands of survival, one can see in this stance both an effort to maintain a semblance of integrity and a deep respect for the power of the environment. The dilemma is movingly stated by a rural Alabama midwife, following the death of an infant:

> I wonder sometimes if I shouldn't be doing more. Yes, sir, I say to myself isn't there something I could do to save a few Rachels, just a few of them. I ask my husband, but he knows that it's me who knows, and we both know that the answer is no. Then I catch myself saying that maybe if I gave some of our food to them, and reminded them to boil the water all the time, and clean up as best they can, even with all the rest they have to do. Then I'll say that it's no good, trying to contradict things around here. Either the whole business

changes and a girl like Rachel can live, or a person like me is wasting her time trying to do what she can't do. (Coles, 1969, pp. 25, 27)

The complex balance of wishing for life to be different yet needing to accept the cruelties that God or life bestows must be appreciated by anyone who would intervene in the lives of these families.

Attitudes Toward Mental Health

The wry acceptance of hardship and the expectation that life will continue to take its toll become particularly problematic in the identification of handicapped children, for whom intervention could signify a profound change in the quality of life. While parents who have little experience with the technology of intervention may approach the idea with a protective wariness, this stance is frequently misinterpreted as indicating opposition to outside help or even indifference to the welfare of their child. At the risk of redundancy, it should be emphasized that this attitude has been shaped by the historical and cultural traditions by which these families have met their needs under conditions of extremely scarce resources. For many rural families, their introduction to the larger social system has involved the loss of jobs or land, particularly evident in the big business takeover of farming and mining. For these families and others, the idea of receiving help from a stranger to whom one has no bond of kinship or shared hardships requires a total paradigm shift. In this author's opinion, the notion of the *therapeutic relationship* involving the sharing of problems and intimacies with a heretofore total stranger is an invention peculiar to a highly mobile, urban society. Lacking familiarity with the goals of the "helping professions," the sudden interest of these "strangers" in their children's and their own well-being may be quite perplexing.

However, improvements in transportation and communication, which have connected rural communities to the larger social system in many ways, have altered people's awareness of and attitudes toward health-related intervention. A North Carolina Survey of attitudes of rural people toward mental illness and help (Bentz & Edgerton, 1970) found that the average rural person had a positive, accepting attitude, contrary to stereotypic beliefs. In this study, 82% believed that something effective could be done with the mentally ill; 87% felt that psychiatric help could be beneficial. Approximately 90% said they would encourage a friend with emotional troubles to see a psychiatrist, and 86% would see a psychiatrist themselves. Of the total, 96%

felt that other professionals (physicians, nurses, teachers) could help with emotional troubles, and a majority approved of such programs as parent discussion groups focusing on child-rearing problems.

While the acceptance of hardship and suffering may be considered a liability in some ways, it is a definite resource in others. In a study of rural and urban families' attitudes toward relatives who had been hospitalized for emotional problems (Michaux), rural families rated their relatives as less helpless, more stable, and less of a nuisance to the family. Rural families had a greater expectation that the "ill" member would perform socially expected activities, though they also showed greater dissatisfaction with this member's actual performance. These results suggest that while a family member's problem or handicap may not be itself the cause of rejection or distancing by other family members, ignorance of the effects of the handicap or the need for intervention may lead to inappropriate expectations and destructive patterns of interaction among family members. While individuals and families show considerable variation in their awareness, acceptance, or rejection of handicapping conditions within their family, an understanding of the forces that generally shape their view of the world is an essential tool in the development of appropriate intervention programs.

INTERVENTION: PRINCIPLES AND EXISTING PROGRAMS

During the past 12 to 15 years, the development of the community mental health center and the increased awareness of the needs of underserved populations have greatly improved the availability of health care services to rural families. However, as Segal (1973) noted in the comprehensive National Institute of Mental Health report on rural America, as of 1973, 2/3 of the rural counties in the United States still were not within the catchment areas of community mental health centers; those counties that are predominantly nonwhite were most critically underserved. This section describes recent efforts through programs around the country to deal with the shortage of services to rural areas. While the specific focus is on services to parents and children, other programs will be mentioned as well, since any effective program in an understaffed setting will touch the needs of parents and children and stimulate new programs. These programs are described as a means of illustrating three basic principles that this author views as primary considerations in effective service delivery to rural areas: decentralization of services, a developmental-ecological focus, and an emphasis on consultation and training.

Decentralization of Services:
The Importance of Outreach

In his report on the impact of the early intervention programs of the 1960s, Bronfenbrenner (1974) noted that the environmental circumstances of many families were so oppressive that these parents lacked the time and energy necessary to engage in the follow-up activities required by their child's intervention program. In the rural environment, the combination of limited education, low income, and geographical isolation seriously dims the chance that parents will follow up on recommendations for further intervention with their handicapped child. Traditional models of service delivery that require families to identify problems and bring their child to a facility (which may be several hours away) are particularly inappropriate and prone to failure in the rural setting. As mentioned previously, rural families may be less sensitized to many of the developmental delays and handicaps that afflict their children; even if these problems are recognized, they are less likely to seek help, and the probability that they will seek help is diminished the farther away these services are located. Effective service delivery of rural families requires an active, concerted effort by professionals to make their services accessible to these families. The initial response to this need was to send specialists to various rural communities for a few days per month. While this practice still exists in many places, it is fraught with problems of inefficient use of professional time (spending half their time in transit to and from the towns) and lack of continuity or follow-up (Huessy, 1972; Perrotta & English, 1977). More recently, this effort has involved relocation of services into the communities and implementation of home-based intervention. The results of such a shift can be striking, as in the case of a program of active aftercare in rural Kentucky that was implemented to offset an alarmingly high recidivism rate at a state hospital (Gragg). After 2 years, readmissions to the hospital dropped 67%, and the caseload of the outreach program had changed such that 50% of those seeking treatment had never been hospitalized. The success of this program led to other mental health services in the community.

The change in focus of a developmental evaluation center (DEC) serving developmentally delayed children and their families in the mountainous western portion of North Carolina is described by Ray and Ponder (1977) and Perrotta and English (1977). A significant aspect of this shift involved movement from a single center serving three widely scattered regions to area teams with permanent offices in each region. The benefits of decentralization for the DEC have included savings in staff time and travel expenses, increased awareness of DEC staff as members of the community (enhancing acceptance and trust), and the ability of staff to actively solicit families, leading to earlier detection and prevention of disabilities among children.

For this DEC program, the focus on early identification of developmental delays in children entailed a shift in the target population from school-aged children to infants, toddlers, and preschoolers. To locate these high-risk youngsters meant bringing the services to where they could be found — to their homes. Home-based intervention has become, an increasingly important dimension of early intervention with high-risk populations, since follow-up data on children in Head Start and other enrichment preschool programs has showed that the gains these children made were often not maintained (Bronfenbrenner, 1974; White, 1970).

The concept of home intervention is particularly relevant in rural settings for several reasons. First, it allows for the identification of a population of high-risk children, most of whom would remain invisible until they entered school. In addition to the target child, other siblings are frequently in need of special attention.

Secondly, home-based intervention enables assessment of the child in his/her natural environment. Not only is the child's behavior more typical at home than in a clinic (the discrepancy is particularly marked for rural families), but environmental conditions affecting the child's situation may be more readily discerned.

Third, home-based intervention facilitates a focus on the parent, fostering the development of a trusting relationship between parent (usually the mother) and home visitor. Many rural mothers do not work outside the home and have few opportunities to interact with others. Such isolation frequently results in depression, which seriously impairs the mother's ability to provide a stimulating and healthy environment for her children, especially with the added burden of a handicapped child. The development of a warm, supportive relationship in which these women are helped to feel better about themselves has been shown to produce great improvement (Padfield, 1976). The home visitor who shows an interest in the mother's well-being and sense of competence can have a significant impact on the development of more positive, enduring parent-child relationships. As Ray and Ponder (1977) note, this may be the most important intervention for the handicapped child.

A fourth advantage of home intervention is the ability to connect diagnostic assessment with follow-up intervention. The lack of follow-up services to insure implementation of recommendations is one of the greatest obstacles to successful intervention with developmentally delayed or handicapped children (Perrotta & English, 1977). The home visitor is able to assist the parent in becoming the child's primary educator by utilizing resources in the home environment and guiding the parent through specific exercises and activities with the child.

The continuity and consistency provided by having one person serve as the primary contact with a family is a fifth important advantage of home-based intervention. Relationships develop in a more relaxed and "homey" way, the parent and home visitor may share common information and concerns about the community, and the home visitor can understand the environmental and geographical constraints that the family faces. In an environment where new faces are viewed warily, where common bonds and shared history are especially important to good relationships, the style and pace of home intervention are much more suited to the development of openness and trust. Through the home visitor, the family can develop an awareness of their needs and existing resources while maintaining pride and appreciation for the resources and competencies they already have. During the last decade, home-based intervention programs have developed in several rural Appalachian regions (Foster, Scanlan, D'Antonio, Horton, & Kraft, 1974; Perrotta & English, 1977; Ponder, 1977). While the long-term impact of these programs remains to be evaluated, they have opened up options and opportunities for hundreds of high-risk children and their families.

A Developmental-Ecological Perspective

Working with rural families necessitates an awareness of the conditions under which they live; as Segal (1973) notes, "In the end, concern for neither the mental nor the physical health of rural Americans can be separated from such other concerns as adequate income, decent housing, proper nutrition, good schools, and a healthful environment" (p. 166). An ecological focus assumes that physical, mental, and emotional difficulties of children are integrally related to the settings and relationships in which the child grows and develops from conception. Assessment and intervention from this perspective focus on building relationships among family members and helping the family gain access to resources that will enhance the growth of the entire family, as well as the identified child.

From the ecological perspective, problems are defined not as signs of pathology or illness to be made well by an expert, but rather as difficulties in living that can be mastered by families working together with professional consultants. This focus on active involvement of family members and specific problem-solving strategies is particularly important for rural families, who may often feel as though the events of their lives are moved by forces beyond their control; this feeling is certainly reinforced by the drastic change in recent generations from self-sufficiency with its endurance of pain to dependence on the larger economic and social system. An ecological perspective helps families to understand the changes in their lives and the relationships of each component in their system to the others. In rural North Carolina, a network of Family Counseling and Education Centers began weekly meetings in each community at which "problems" were submitted anonymously, written on a blackboard, and discussed by residents; an area resident who had received training as a mental health worker led the discussions. The success of these meetings led to the introduction of other services to the community: parent discussion groups, group meetings for unmarried mothers, high school discussion groups, a child clinic, and screening services for children (Hollister). In a related situation in rural Arkansas, discussion groups focusing on problems faced by relatives of patients who were being discharged from a state mental hospital led to marked improvement in attitudes as well as recognition of the need for new services (Payne). As a result, groups for mothers of handicapped children were initiated. In a program aimed at lowering the high school dropout rate of Native American Indian youth, the importance of coordinating academic tutoring with follow-up consultation to parents was emphasized. The success of this program was related to the ability to view these parents as primary educators and care givers, maintaining an equal, nonpatronizing relationship (Mason).

In working with parents and children, the ecological perspective is complemented by a developmental focus, which assumes that there is a developmental "next step" for each child to master. This perspective is very much oriented to the current conditions that affect the child's future opportunities. Assessment for the purpose of documenting evidence of pathology would find much among the rural poor, but to what end? As Coles (1969) states, "Hunger, pain — indeed any medical complaint or symptom — cannot be neatly and conveniently separated from the world. . . . Children not only grow physically and incur one or another disease; they also learn to live with what is *around* them" (p. 6). A developmental-ecological perspective is geared to intervention and change. As Perrotta and English (1977) note, "The interest in assessment is not in knowing how much a child departs from a norm, but rather in knowing how handicaps have influenced a child's sequence and pattern of development. There is interest in learning the specific intervention strategies that could be utilized in promoting the development of a child" (p. 4). This assessment-intervention sequence is geared toward enhancing the parent-child relationship and preventing irreversible disabilities through early detection.

Consultation and Training

The scarcity of professional resources in rural communities is not likely to be met by an influx of specialists who would abandon more lucrative positions in urban areas to settle in communities where their own families would not receive the same quality of health and educational services. Therefore, an increased emphasis must be placed on building the resources that already exist in these communities through training and consultation in assessment and intervention skills related to the well-being of rural families. This function may be realized in several ways: through training of "natural helpers" in the community, through training of parents as educators and developmental specialists for their families, and by the training of professionals and paraprofessionals in an innovative combination of interdisciplinary skills.

Programs of consultation and training with natural helpers who reside in rural areas have been successfully implemented in several communities. Programs in Kansas (Patterson), South Carolina (Parker), Michigan (Robinson), and Vermont (Marshall) have provided training to clergy, nurses, teachers, doctors, grocers, and druggists in concepts of mental health, family life education, crisis intervention, and behavior management with children. Training and consultation in psychiatric issues for rural physicians have been offered through special seminars at the Nebraska Psychiatric Institute (Eaton) and an innovative use of two-way television consultation in New Hampshire (Weiss). A consultation program sponsored by the New Mexico Department of Public Health (Libo) for local health, welfare, education, and law enforcement agencies in rural areas led to a new day school for retarded children, parents' groups, a school for emotionally disturbed children, and a new family casework agency. North Carolina has sponsored consultation and training programs on marital problems for public health nurses and on behavior management techniques for teachers and social welfare workers (Hollister). New training programs in mental health and psychiatry have been started in Wisconsin (Glover) and Colorado (Pollock). In western Texas, a training program for teachers of Mexican Americans has emphasized cultural sensitivity, self-awareness of one's impact on others, and increased interaction with these children and their parents in the community (Lewis). Programs such as these capitalize on the rapport and relationships that already exist between these natural helpers and families, thus increasing the probability that suggestions and advice will be carried out.

The role of teacher/consultant to parents, in the interest of facilitating the healthy development of their children, is one of the most important components of intervention for any helping professional in a rural community. The teacher/consultant guides parents in learning specific skills and competencies for interacting with their children; the results of this "teaching" may be quickly revealed through the child's behavior, and the parent leaves the interaction with a feeling of greater competence and self-esteem. In contrast to the "expert," who takes responsibility for helping a child as the parent waits or watches, the *consultant* allows parents to maintain their integrity as the primary care givers and educators for their children. The parent may provide input and ideas for the creative use of materials and objects in the home environment or for new activities to use with the child; in turn, a parent may "teach" a neighbor the new activities and ideas s/he has learned. Involvement of other family members in the new activities is an important offshoot of intervention.

The consultative function extends to other aspects of the family's life, since the ecological perspective advocated here includes a focus on the family's physical and emotional well-being. The consultant shows an interest in the hardships of daily living and the sufficiency of resources available to meet the family's needs. The consultant shares information and advice with the family on ways to gain access to additional resources and may accompany them to insure that their initial contacts with other agencies and professionals are successful. Teaching rural families to negotiate the more urbanized service delivery systems (particularly when a handicapped child is involved), helping them to receive the payoffs that will promote future utilization of these services, is a vital need and component of effective intervention. The support and trust that develop in this advocacy-type relationship often fulfills a crucial need for companionship and intimacy that many isolated rural people experience in the form of loneliness and depression. They are more likely to share other problems and concerns in this context than they would ever bring to a mental health center.

This discussion implies that a single individual would perform the several functions outlined above while building a trusting relationship with the family. These functions entail skills and understanding in the areas of assessment and intervention techniques related to developmental delays in children, principles and sequence of normative child development, behavior management, social work, nutrition, and counseling. Such skills have traditionally been the domains of several separate specialty areas, and traditional assessment procedures would involve contact by the family with a representative of each area. This model is particularly inappropriate with rural families, for whom contact with strangers is uncomfortable and likely to produce minimal cooperation and substantial distortion of their typical behavior. The problem of fragmentation of professional services has been expressed by parents and professionals alike (Banus, 1971; Gorham, Des Jardins, Page, Pettis, & Scheiber, 1975). Banus has articulated the need for a single person to coordinate services for families, listen to their needs, and maintain personal contact. This role is especially critical in rural settings; while urban parents are more likely to endure the professional runaround in the interest of obtaining needed services, rural parents are far more likely to withdraw.

The training of natural helpers discussed previously represents one way of consolidating services and skills. Another method has been implemented by programs designed for rural settings (Foster et al., 1974; Perrotta & English, 1977; Ponder, 1977) and involves the training of a new type of specialist. A project entitled the Training Project for Home Intervention (Foster et al., 1974) was developed at the Demonstration and Research Center for Early Education (DARCEE) in Nashville, Tennessee in conjunction with the Tennessee Department of Public Health. The project's goal was the development of a viable method of training paraprofessional home visitors in areas of child development, assessment of developmental delays, developmental intervention strategies, nutrition and health care, communication, and behavior management. These home visitors were residents of the Appalachian regions of eastern and southern Tennessee that they served. The training program has since been incorporated into the Department of Public Health.

A state-supported Developmental Evaluation Center in North Carolina, based at Western Carolina University in the mountainous area of Cullowhee, recently altered its structure and approach to provide services more compatible with both the geography and culture of this rural environment (Ponder, 1977). One aspect of this shift entailed the development of a transdisciplinary concept of service delivery. Persons were intentionally recruited from a wide range of human service disciplines. Each of these developmental disabilities specialists functions as a resource person in his/her area, teaching specific skills or information to other members of the team, allowing for services that are both integrated and specialized. The most important advantage of this approach is that it enables comprehensive services to be offered while limiting the number of people who are in direct contact with the family. The transdisciplinary concept appears to be at the core of innovative service delivery programs such as the Training Project for Home Intervention described above (Foster et al., 1974) and the Atypical Infant Development Program for disabled infants in Marin County, California (Nielson, Collins, Meisel, Lowry, Engh, & Johnson, 1975). This approach seems much more closely aligned to the developmental and ecological needs of children and families in a setting where both geography and culture provide a sound rationale for a limited number of professionals with a broad and flexible set of skills.

INTERVENTION
PRACTICAL STRATEGIES FOR
WORKING WITH PARENTS

In exploring various aspects of rural environments and populations, several suggestions for facilitating relationships with parents have been implied. Though all components of the ecological perspective are advocated by this author, these strategies are specified and discussed as follows:

Go Slowly: Allow time for the development of trust and rapport, and pace the introduction of sensitive topics according to the family's general responsiveness. Allow a substantial amount of time for chatting and discussion of nonproblem areas. Develop common areas of interest and concern, particularly where the parent's expressed skills and competencies lie. This is important, not only for assessing the family's ecological system, but also for developing a more equal relationship; the latter is crucial for facilitating mutual respect for areas of competency and greater openness on the parent's part to the suggestions of the professional.

ESTABLISH A CONSISTENT PATTERN OF CONTACT: As mentioned previously, the concept of shared history is often a highly valued aspect of relationships in a rural setting, as well as an index of trust. Rural people may show considerable wariness toward the expert who comes and goes quickly, stopping only long enough to point out the family's needs and deficiencies. A pattern of weekly contacts of an hour or two over a period of time will have far greater long-term impact than an all-day intensive evaluation session. The continual predictable presence of the intervenor in the community demonstrates a commitment to and understanding of the people and their environment.

BE A HISTORIAN: Learn about the history of the region and of the families who have lived there. Promote the telling of stories and yarns, for these are often rich in information about the values, norms, and traditions by which these families have lived. Families can be helped to appreciate and understand the impact of cultural transition brought about by rapid encroachment of urban technology. By showing respect for their values and beliefs, the professional can more effectively communicate that, while the parents have been doing the best that they could to live up to their values, there are other ways to accomplish the same goals more effectively. Most importantly, the expressed interest of the professional in rural parents as people communicates appreciation for the complexities of their lives and validation of their integrity.

USE THEIR LANGUAGE AND STYLE OF COMMUNICATION: Much of the impasse between rural families and professionals is paraphrased in the wide discrepancy in language and communication styles by which each group represents its experience of the world. The responsibility of the professional working with rural families involves not only sharing information, but insuring that this information is heard and understood. Language can serve as either a barrier or a bridge to an effective working relationship. Contrast the response of a 12-year-old boy to the words of his teachers, when they "just shouted at you and made you feel real bad" (Coles, 1969, p. 101), versus those of a minister who told the boy that "It didn't mean we were going to Heaven because we are poor. So we might as well try to get something more if we can — as well as pray" (Coles, 1969, p. 105). The intent of both, to encourage change and initiative, was similar, but the form and message produced a strikingly different response in this boy, who foreclosed on his education before he was 12. The use of metaphor and analogy can be an effective means of relating to the experience of rural parents, and the content of the metaphors can be chosen from the experiences that they relate.

UTILIZE RESOURCES IN THE ENVIRONMENT: Rural America poses an illogical contrast for many families because of the serious scarcity of resources needed for the physical and emotional well-being of parents and children amidst an idyllic physical setting. The physical surroundings offer an abundance of natural materials that can be marshalled and used creatively to stimulate growth and development. The professional who works with rural parents can intervene effectively by helping these parents utilize simple, homemade materials to enhance the ability of their children to master important developmental tasks (Foster, 1974; Foster et al., 1974). Other resources in the environment include siblings, extended family, neighbors, and key individuals in the community; the long-standing familiarity and connections that are common in rural areas can be used to meet the special needs of handicapped children, particularly when the child's parents are overburdened. Intervention may involve restructuring generational boundaries in the family, for example, by helping a mother accept and establish a parenting role with her child who has been attended to mainly by siblings. Siblings and relatives can be enlisted as supports to the mother for various functions. In other cases, the caretaking responsibility for a child may be assumed most appropriately by a grandmother or older sister when this is in the best interests of the child. While some children will require additional, specialized care outside the family, the attitude and behavior of the family are affected by their ability both to understand the nature of their child's special needs and to manage the child within the realistic limits of their environment. To insure the cooperation of parents, the professional must maintain a balance between pointing out their needs and acknowledging what they already have to offer.

WORK IN THE HOME ENVIRONMENT: As discussed previously, home-based intervention is particularly appropriate for rural families for whom transportation difficulties, unfamiliarity with office settings, and managing several children make regular clinic appointments quite difficult. While requiring more time and effort by the professional, home intervention provides an invaluable opportunity to assess the family's living environment, fosters a more equal relationship with parents, and provides the opportunity to model desired behavior and skills in the same environment in which they will be used. Other siblings frequently benefit from intervention aimed at a particular child especially when parent-child interaction is focused on. Strengths and resources in the environment can be discerned and utilized, and the genuine interest of the professional is often felt more strongly in his/her willingness to meet on the family's "territory," Home intervention decreases the chances that high-risk children will not be attended to because they are not brought into a clinic for treatment. By establishing a strong, trusting relationship with the home visitor, the parents will be more likely to seek out other needed services.

SET EXPLICIT GOALS: Be explicit and clear in explaining the role of the professional and what can be accomplished with the family — for example, to help a mother teach her child things that will help him/her be more successful in school or to make sure that a child is doing the things s/he should be doing at a certain age. Be sure to focus explicitly on what the parents can expect as a result of working together. Find out their goals and needs and, if possible, include these in the contract. Be explicit in explaining how to get access to other services; specific, step-by-step references to people, locations, and application procedures in other agencies may be required for parents to successfully master these tasks. Explain these procedures in a matter-of-fact manner, without becoming patronizing or condescending.

SET REASONABLE GOALS: Many rural families, particularly those with a handicapped child, face an overwhelming array of obstacles and difficulties in achieving a satisfying quality of life. It is important to realize that resources for intervention — both financial and man-power, are limited, and that all of a family's difficulties in living cannot be directly attended to. Setting priorities and focusing on teaching specific skills and competencies to parents are both essential. A behavioral framework is particularly useful in teaching parents the principles of behavior management and change. These skills plus skills involved in gaining access to other resources and forming a viable support system are skills that will generalize and lead to changes far beyond the scope of the intervention.

DEVELOP LASTING CONNECTIONS: For families who are isolated, long-standing depression may inhibit the development of friendships and support systems in a rural community. Group meetings for parents who are dealing with common difficulties, a handicapped child or problems of single parenthood, for example, provide an opportunity to meet social needs as well as to learn new strategies and techniques. Neighborhood meetings or discussion groups on topics of common concern can also be useful in this regard. The professional who is also a resident of the area is in a particularly good position to promote supportive interaction in the community. Teachers, physicians, nurses, clergy, and other professionals should be encouraged to develop an informal familiarity that will encourage reluctant parents to seek them out.

AVOID PROFESSIONAL ISOLATION: The isolation and depression that exists for parents can also be a reality for the professional in a rural community. This is a particular hazard for the professional who spends a great deal of time traveling on country roads. To avoid depression and burnout, the area team approach is preferable, in that it fosters regular staff meetings and more frequent interaction. Consulting with colleagues, sharing work experiences, trading ideas, and attending professional meetings and conferences are all ways of maintaining a support system to counteract the frustrations and disappointments of this work.

CONCLUSION
THE PROFESSIONAL IN THE RURAL COMMUNITY

In this chapter, the needs and problems of rural families have been related to the urbanization of our society and its resultant models of service delivery to meet the health and economic needs of families. A century ago, such a chapter would have had little meaning; because we know that many families are getting more, we can also say that many rural families are getting less. From an ecological perspective, it is apparent that the characteristics of many rural environments make the urbanized model of service delivery inappropriate and that an adequate description of intervention strategies cannot be given without first establishing a context for intervention and acknowledging the crucial social issues that affect every aspect of program development and intervention.

Throughout this chapter, the roles, responsibilities, and skills of the professional working with rural families have been discussed.—from the standpoint of program development as well as direct service to families. Clearly the mode of service delivery, whether through the community mental health center, the state department of public health, or local resources, must be reshaped to emphasize outreach, consultation, and training. The professional who works effectively with rural families must show a commitment to the area and to the environment, which suggests that the most effective intervention will be accomplished by those who live in the rural communities in which they work. A few innovative programs have demonstrated that effective intervention can be accomplished with rural families when the program and the skills of the intervenor are tailored to the needs and characteristics of the families they serve. It is this author's belief that a wealth of untapped resources exists in rural areas in terms of skilled and committed individuals who could reach many families in need of assistance. What is needed is an alteration in training priorities to more realistically reflect the needs and resources of rural areas. To accomplish this most effectively (and efficiently), both an ecological and a transdisciplinary perspective are needed. Professionals must have a clear understanding of the impact of environmental conditions and the relationships among various components of a social system. Effective intervention for rural families involves altering and improving environmental conditions and access to resources, as well as helping families to utilize more effectively what they have.

To meet the need for intervention in the areas of child development, assessment and intervention strategies for developmental delay, social work, health care, and counseling without increasing the number of specialists with whom a family has contact, professional training must be discipline–flexible. Not only must various professional schools be willing to share skill areas, but a new class of professionals must be willing to cope with the ambiguity of their role and their professional identity. Many of these now on the forefront of work with rural families contend that the rewards are well worth the frustrations; these families embody a heritage of determination, persistence, endurance, and respect for nature that can be rechanneled and preserved and can serve as reminders to all of us concerning the limits of technology and growth. Intervention that is truly effective involves not only technology, but creativity and commitment, in order to find and maintain a proper balance between meeting families' needs and respecting the values that have helped them survive and maintain a sense of integrity.

REFERENCES

Aquizap, R. B., & Vargas, E. A. Technology, power and socialization in Appalachia. *Social Casework*, 1970, *51*, 131-139.

Banus, B. A. *The developmental therapist.* Thorofare, New Jersey: C B Slack, 1971.

Barton, S. N., & Weber, R. G. Cognitive differences between health science students and a rural population. *Journal of Medical Education*, 1975, *50*, 1120-1122.

Bentz, W. K., & Edgerton, J. W. Consensus of attitudes towards mental illness. *Archives of General Psychiatry*, 1970, *22*, 468-473.

Bronfenbrenner, U. *A report on longitudinal evaluations of preschool programs* (Vol. 2). Washington, D.C.: Office of Child Development, 1974.

Bruce, R. L. *Value orientations of a low-income rural audience: Paths out of poverty* (Working Paper No. 20: Preliminary Report). Ithica, New York: State University of New York, College of Agriculture and Life Sciences, 1975.

Chapman, M. E. *Psychiatric nursing.* (NIMH Grant No 7875). Berea, Kentucky: Berea College.

Coles, R. *Still hungry in America.* New York: World Publishing Company, 1969.

Coles, R. *Children of crisis II: Migrants, sharecroppers, mountaineers.* Boston: Little, 1971.

Coles, R. *Children of crisis IV: Eskimos, Chicanos, Indians.* Boston: Little, 1977. (a)

Coles, R. *Children of crisis V: Privileged ones.* Boston: Little, 1977. (b)

Eaton, M. T. *Psychiatry — GP postgraduate education* (NIMH Grant No. 6939). Lincoln: University of Nebraska.

Economic Development Division, Economic Research Service, U.S. Department of Agriculture for the Senate Committee on Government Operations. *The economic and social conditions of rural America in the 1970's.* Washington, D.C.: U.S. Government Printing Office, 1971.

Economic Research Service, U.S. Department of Agriculture. *Rural poverty in three southern regions: Mississippi delta, Ozarks, Southeast coastal plain* (Agricultural Economic Report No. 176). Washington, D.C.: U.S. Government Printing Office, 1970.

Economic Research Service, U.S. Department of Agriculture. *Open country poverty in a relatively affluent area — The east north central states* (Agricultural Economic Report No. 208). Washington, D.C.: U.S. Government Printing Office, 1971.

Eisdorfer, C., Altrocchi, J., & Young, R. F. Mental health in a rural setting. *Community Mental Health Journal,* 1968, *4,* 211-220.

Foster, M. *Promoting infant development: A guide for working with parents.* Nashville, Tennessee: Demonstration and Research Center for Early Education, George Peabody College for Teachers, 1974.

Foster, M., Scanlan, J., D'Antonio, A., Horton, D., & Kraft, S. *Training for home intervention.* Nashville, Tennessee: Demonstration and Research Center for Early Education, George Peabody College for Teachers, 1974.

Glover, B. H. *Psychiatry — GP postgraduate education* (NIMH Grant No. 8599). Madison: University of Wisconsin.

Gorham, K. A., Des Jardins, C., Page, R., Pettis, E., & Scheiber, B. Effects on parents. In N. Hobbs (Ed.), *Issues in the classification of children* (Vol. 2). San Francisco: Jossey-Bass, 1975.

Gragg, L., Jr. *Social worker-nurse clinical team in eastern Kentucky* (NIMH Grant No. 14974). Frankfort: Kentucky Mental Health Foundation.

Hadley, J. M. *Two-year program for training mental health workers* (NIMH Grant No. 10281). Lafayette, Indiana: Purdue University.

Harris, W. J., & Mahar, C. Problems in implementing resource programs in rural schools. *Exceptional Children,* 1975, *42,* 95-101.

Henry, J. G. Child-rearing practices in Mountain County, Kentucky. *Dissertation Abstracts*, 1971, *31*(8-11), 3956.

Herjanic, B. M. A rural versus urban children's mental health clinic population. *Journal of the American Academy of Child Psychiatry*, 1972, *11*, 583-594.

Hollister, W. G. *Mental health program leaders* (NIMH Grant No. 11179). Chapel Hill: University of North Carolina.

Hollister, W. G., & Edgerton, J. W. *Feasibility study of a rural mental health service* (NIMH Grant No. 14854). Chapel Hill: University of North Carolina.

Huessy, H. R. Tactics and targets in the rural setting. In S. E. Golann & C. Eisdorfer (Eds.), *Handbook of community mental health*. New York: ACC, 1972.

Jeffrey, M. J., & Reeve, R. E. Community mental health services in rural areas: Some practical issues. *Community Mental Health Journal*, 1978, *14*, 54-62.

Lewis, J. N. *The Mexican-American through teacher exchange* (NIMH Grant No. 12342). Midland: West Texas Education Center.

Libo, L. *Mental health consultation in underdeveloped areas* (NIMH Grant No. 286). Santa Fe: New Mexico Department of Public Health.

Louv, R. The Appalachia syndrome. *Human Behavior*, May 1977.

Marshall, C. *Indigenous nurse as crisis intervenor for suicide prevention* (NIMH Grant No. 15097). Burlington: University of Vermont College of Medicine.

Mason, E. P. *Evaluation of programs to prevent high school dropouts* (NIMH Grant No. 16852). Bellingham: Western Washington State College.

Matthias, R. *Counseling the rural disadvantaged student*. Washington, D.C.: National Institute of Education, 1972.

McLaughlin, B. E. Recognition and treatment of youthful depression in a rural area. *Psychosomatics*, 1970, *11*, 420-425.

McMillan, S. R. Aspirations of low-income mothers. *Journal of Marriage and the Family*, 1967, *29*, 282-287.

Mercer, C. V. Intercorrelations among family stability, family composition, residence and race. *Journal of Marriage and the Family*, 1967, *29*, 456-460.

Michaux, M. H. *Day center and inpatient treatment: A controlled study* (NIMH Grant No. 15374). Sykesville, Maryland: Springfield State Hospital.

Murray, K. *Down to earth people of Appalachia*. Boone, North Carolina: Appalachian Consortium Press, 1974.

Nielson, G., Collins, S., Meisel, J., Lowry, M., Engh, H., & Johnson, D. An intervention program for atypical infants. In B. F. Friedlander, G. M. Sterritt, & G. E. Kirk (Eds.), *Exceptional infant* (Vol. 3). New York: Brunner/Mazel, 1975.

Niswander, D. *Project leading to intervention in high risk suicides* (NIMH

Grant No. 14697). Concord: New Hampshire Department of Health and Welfare.

Padfield, M. The comparative effects of two counseling approaches on the intensity of depression among rural women of low SES. *Journal of Counseling Psychology*, 1976, *23*, 209-214.

Parker, K. J. *Continuing education for clergy* (NIMH Grant No. 12710). Spartenburg, South Carolina: Spartenburg Area Mental Health Center.

Patterson, S. *Utilization of human resources for mental health* (NIMH Grant No. 16618). Lawrence: University of Kansas.

Payne, M. F. *Mental health education. The family and community* (NIMH Grant No. 14867). Little Rock: Arkansas State Hospital.

Perrotta, E. L. *Social issues in health service delivery to Appalachian families.* Paper presented at the annual meeting of Medical-Social Consultants, Chicago, Illinois, May 1966.

Perrotta, E., & English, R. The DEC area team: Rationale and functions of service provisions. In H. Ponder, Jr. (Ed.), *Serving young developmentally handicapped children in rural Appalachia* (Vol. 1). Cullowhee, North Carolina: Developmental Evaluation Center, Western Carolina University, 1977.

Pollock, C. B. *Psychiatric postgraduate education of practicing physicians* (NIMH Grant No. 8269). Denver: University of Colorado.

Ponder, H., Jr. (Ed.). *Serving young developmentally handicapped children in rural Appalachia* (Vol. 1). Cullowhee, North Carolina: Developmental Evaluation Center, Western Carolina University, 1977.

Ray, J. S., & Ponder, H., Jr. A changing strategy for serving handicapped children in a rural setting. In H. Ponder, Jr. (Ed.), *Serving young developmentally handicapped children in rural Appalachia* (Vol. 1). Cullowhee, North Carolina: Developmental Evaluation Center, Western Carolina University, 1977.

Robinson, P. S. *Preventive mental health through skills of community caretaker* (NIMH Grant No. 12156). Marquette: Northern Michigan University.

Segal, J. (Ed.). *The mental health of rural America.* (Publication No. (HSM) 73-9035). Washington, D.C.: Department of Health, Education, and Welfare, 1973.

Shively, J. *A demographic survey of Appalachian parents of pre-school children.* Charleston, West Virginia: Appalachia Education Lab, 1975.

Summers, G. F., Seiler, L. H., & Hough, R. L. Psychiatric symptoms: Cross-validation with a rural sample. *Rural Sociology*, 1971, *36*, 367-378.

Taylor, L. *Urban-rural problems.* Belmont, California: Dickenson, 1968.

U.S. Department of Agriculture. *Rurality, poverty, and health: Medical problems in rural areas* (Agricultural Economic Report No. 172). Washington, D.C.: U.S. Government Printing Office, 1970.

Wedel, H. L. Characteristics of community mental health center operations in small communities. *Community Mental Health Journal*, 1969, *5*, 437-444.

Weiss, R. *24-hour psychiatric consultation via television* (NIMH Grant No. 15007). Hanover, New Hampshire: Dartmouth Medical School.

White, S. H. The national impact study of Head Start. In J. Hellmuth (Ed.), *Disadvantaged child* (Vol. 3), *Compensatory education: A national debate*. New York: Brunner/Mazel, 1970.

Chapter 19

PARENTING STRESS INDEX (PSI): A FAMILY SYSTEM ASSESSMENT APPROACH

WILLIAM T. BURKE AND RICHARD R. ABIDIN

THE rapidly growing interest in preventive mea-
sures in the field of mental health reflects an increasing awareness on
the part of professionals that dealing with the outcome of disordered
development is an expensive and difficult undertaking. Developing
techniques and programs that can effectively intervene before damage
is done requires a basic understanding of the processes important in
both normal and dysfunctional development. Such an understanding
may then serve as the base upon which techniques and programs
aimed at reducing the incidence of maladaptive behavior and emotional anguish can be built.

The importance of early identification of groups at risk and subsequent preventive intervention is reflected in the United States government's attempts to provide such services by making early diagnostic
and treatment services available through Medicaid and Title XIX.
This legislative interest has resulted in a wide range of programs. The
American Orthopsychiatric Association (1978) has noted the emphasis
in these programs on the cognitive and intellectual domain and the
relative lack of emphasis in the area of social and emotional development.

The practical significance of early identification and intervention
efforts lies in the potential for reducing the frequency and intensity of
behavioral and emotional disturbance among children in our society.
A growing body of research literature exists that focuses on the early
identification of children who are at risk for later developmental
difficulty in the cognitive domain (AOA, 1978), while considerably
less attention has been paid to the area of emotional development.
Those efforts that focus on predicting the future emotional/behav-
ioral development of children have typically approached the task by
almost exclusively assessing the child's attributes (Carey, 1972, Mc-
Inerny & Chamberlain, 1978). Research on the development of behavior disorders in children (Thomas, Chess, & Birch, 1968; Cameron,

1977) has identified the existence of excessively stressful characteristics of the child as only one of the major factors contributing to the development of behavioral disturbances. Stress in the parenting system during the first 3 years of life is especially critical in relation to the child's emotional/behavioral development and to the parent/child relationship. What appears needed is an approach that assesses the many facets of the parent/child system. Child characteristics, mother characteristics, situational factors, and life stress events are but some of the demands that must be considered.

Research concerning infancy and early childhood has provided evidence of the potential for early identification and intervention with families at risk for developing serious behavioral and emotional problems. Lagercrantz & Lagercrantz (1975), in a longitudinal study of adaptation in mothers and their firstborn children, strongly suggest that it is possible to make such discriminations at a very early stage. The preliminary results reported indicate that it was possible to identify families at risk prior to the child's reaching 6 months of age through measurement of maternal attitudes and mother/child interactions.

A number of authors have emphasized the importance of being able to identify families who are at risk and under high degrees of stress. Soderling (1975) noted that children may react to stress through developing a variety of behavioral symptoms. He describes the crucial need for a means of identifying potentially high stress situations before they result in trauma-induced symptom formation. Further support for this approach is offered by Kagan and Levi (1975), Masse (1975), and Caplan (1975), all of whom emphasize the need for early identification of potentially high stress situations to make a variety of forms of preventive intervention possible.

The importance of early preventive programs is apparent when one considers that children typically come to the attention of mental health professionals around the time they begin school. This delay in identification of from 1 to 5 years often permits a negative situation to influence the child's development to such a degree as to make subsequent remediation difficult and expensive. The ability to identify such high-risk situations at the earliest possible time would allow for more efficient and effective intervention.

Understanding the stresses that affect parents of young children is an important part of efforts aimed at early identification and intervention. The task of raising children is a difficult and complicated undertaking. Parents normally experience a certain degree of stress to which they are able to adapt without dysfunctional consequences. However, the existence of stress in extreme amounts may result in adverse consequences if necessary interventions are not undertaken. These adverse consequences affect the parent as an individual and the developing parent/child relationship. This relationship, which serves as the foundation for the child's emotional social development (Mahler, Pine, & Bergman, 1975), exerts a profound influence on the course of later development.

A large body of research literature exists relevant to the topic of stresses that operate in families with young children. Studies on the influence of children's temperamental characteristics on later development (Thomas et al., 1968) and the development of maternal feelings toward children (Robson & Moss, 1970) are examples of the variety of existing research regarding the roles that social factors, child characteristics, and parent variables play in the development of children. The research literature contains numerous instances of factors found to influence the parent/child relationship.

Understanding the stress in early parent/child relationships requires that this existing information be integrated within a framework that can account for the operation of the many and varied factors relevant to stress within the family system. This integration would allow for the development of techniques for assessing the stresses parents experience in raising young children. Development of such assessment techniques is one of the ways in which this information can be made useful to practitioners.

PURPOSE OF THE PROJECT

The problem addressed in this research project was the development of a measurement device designed to assess stress in the mother/child system. Hopefully, the instrument would serve as a screening device in a pediatric medical practice and/or could be used as part of a psychological assessment battery. The instrument was designed such that it would yield a total index of stress in the parent/child system. This total score, if found to be significantly deviant from the norms, could then be analyzed into domain scores, e.g., child characteristics, and subsequently into subscale scores, e.g., child distractibility/activity. The utility of the instrument in identifying systems under stress is enhanced by the fact that the total score on the index can be broken down to focus on the various sources of stress. This feature guides the clinician in developing an intervention program by pointing out aspects of the parent/child system that seem to be involved in producing the stress.

The use of the mother as the "measuring point" in the study is based on the assumption that the mother is typically the keystone of the family system and will be most knowledgeable about and most reflective of the pressures and stresses present in the entire parent/ child system.

Procedure

The project began with a series of wide-ranging literature reviews related to child rearing in order to make maximal use of relevant research as the basis for developing the assessment technique items. Domains were identified in the research literature that suggested variables to be assessed by the items to be developed. This approach resulted in over 95% of the items being directly related to specific research findings. The initial item pool included questionnaire items and behavior rating items of varying formats. These items were field-tested and revised 3 times using pilot samples of mothers of widely varying SES and educational levels. The mothers who participated in the field tests were asked for their reactions to the items and the procedures used. These procedures were used to select the most acceptable and easily understood formats, revise instructions, and make changes in item content. The items were then rated as to the relevance of their content and the adequacy of their construction by a panel of 6 professional judges. Suggested revisions were also solicited from the judges. The ratings and suggestions made by the judges were used to make further revisions. The judges' ratings indicated a high degree of face validity for both individual items and the scale as a whole.

These procedures resulted in a questionnaire (Parenting Stress Index) containing 147 items. The items were assigned to *a priori* domain scales (Child Characteristics, Mother Characteristics, Situational/Demographic Characteristics) based on their manifest content and the research domain the item represented. The field tests indicated that most mothers were able to complete the questionnaire in 20 to 30 minutes and that it was understandable to mothers having a sixth-grade reading level.

The initial sample was comprised of 208 mothers with children younger than 3 years of age who brought their children to the well-child clinic of a private pediatric group practice in Charlottesville, Virginia. Mothers participating in the study were mostly young (mean age 28), white (95% white), and middle class (median income $15 to $20 thousand per year). They were asked to complete the questionnaire at home and return it in a self-addressed, stamped envelope.

The mothers were rated by their pediatrician as to the overall degree of stress s/he perceived the mother to be under. Ratings were made on a

5-point scale ranging from *Overwhelmed by her responsibilities* to *Extremely competent and effective.* The initial sample of mothers participating in this study consisted of the first 208 mothers who returned questionnaires for whom doctor ratings were available. A second replication sample of 262 parent/child dyads was collected from the same pediatric practice. The combined samples therefore produced a normative pool of 470 parent/child systems. The return rate on the questionnaires was more than 60%.

A subsample of 40 mothers was asked to complete the questionnaire a second time after a 3-week period in order to provide an assessment of the test-retest reliability of the instrument over a short period of time. The first 15 returned were used in the computation of the test-retest reliability results.

Results and Discussion

Factor Structure

In order to accommodate the limitations of the statistical program package used in the data analysis, it was necessary to reduce the number of variables included in the factor analysis. This was accomplished by running 3 separate initial factor analyses to screen out variables that loaded less than .40 on any factor. A 4-factor solution provided a parsimonious interpretation of the data. The 4 factors accounted for 35% of the total variance in the 80 remaining variables. Based on the items that loaded on them, the four factors were given the following labels:

Factor I — Parent Feelings About Self and Situation
Factor II — Child Characteristics, Difficult to Easy
Factor III — Reinforcement in Mother/Child Interaction
Factor IV — Degree of Bother

As an example of the items that loaded on the factors, the 3 items with highest loadings on Factor I included #78, *Things about her life bother mother,* #96, *Mother feels unhappy about her life,* and #59, *Mother feels alone.* The 3 items that loaded highest on Factor II included #6, *Child demandingness,* #34, *Child hangs on parent,* and #39, *Child is more of a problem than expected.* High-loading items on Factor III were #21, *Child doesn't smile as much as expected,* #4, *Mother doesn't feel appreciated by her child,* and #12, *Child doesn't learn as quickly as expected.* Items loading highest on Factor IV were #13, *Child bothers mother,* #27, *Child has difficulty concentrating,* and #98, *Child cooperates with mother.*

Construct Validity

The factor structure of the instrument was consistent with expectations based on knowledge of the nature of the phenomenon. Stress is a multifaceted phenomenon. It would be expected that an instrument of this type would consist of a few factors accounting for small portions of the variance combined with a number of smaller clusters of items tapping more specific areas. Some support for the construct validity of the instrument is provided by the observed congruence between the factor structure and the expectations based on knowledge of the phenomenon.

The procedures used in constructing and pilot-testing the scale provided strong evidence of a good degree of face validity and construct validity for the items included on the scale. Items were based on research that had suggested their importance and relevance to the stress experienced by parents. Ratings by professional judges provided further support for the face validity of the items, the construct validity of the scale, and the assignment of the items to the logically derived domain scales and subscales.

Further evidence to support the construct validity of the scale comes from the analysis of mean differences between primiparous and multiparous mothers. The results of the analysis of differences between mothers having only one child and mothers having more than one child revealed three statistically significant differences at the .05 level. Primiparous mothers described their children's behavior in more negative terms than did multiparous mothers (V.162, Factor II, *Child characteristics, difficult to easy*). This finding is similar to that found in the study of referrals to mental health facilities (Schaefer & Cole, 1977). Results of that study suggested that primiparous mothers were more likely to view childrens' behavior as extreme than were multiparous mothers. However, on V.163 (Factor IV, *Degree of bother*), multiparous mothers described themselves as experiencing a significantly greater degree of difficulty than primiparous mothers. It seems that mothers with more than one child tend to accept a wider range of child behaviors as being expected or normal, while at the same time reporting more stress as a result of having to deal with certain child behaviors that prove to "bother" the parent. Overall, primiparous mothers tended to describe their children's behavior in more negative terms than their counterparts with more than one child and at the same time report experiencing a lesser degree of being bothered by their children than multiparous mothers.

These results are consistent with the differences observed between experienced and nonexperienced mothers in studies of maternal reactions to infant behavior (Bell & Ainsworth, 1972; Greenberg & Lind, 1973; Lewis & Lee-Painter, 1974). This research suggests that experienced mothers are more able to make judgments about the states of their children, that is, they are more able to "read" their infants. In the case of the mothers in this study, it seems that multiparous mothers describe fewer of their childrens' behaviors as discrepant from expectation based on their greater experience with children. Primiparous mothers do not have the experiential base of the multipari to use in modifying their expectations. Primipari, as a result of their not having had the same degree of experience with children as multiparous mothers, may also be less willing to label behaviors exhibited by their children as problems.

The differences observed on the scale between primiparous and multiparous mothers, as well as the nature of these differences, provide further support for the construct validity of the scale. In order for such statistically significant and conceptually meaningful results to be found, the scale must be measuring a construct that has practical significance in the parenting situation.

Reliability Indices

The test-retest reliability coefficients for the individual subscales and the total questionnaire are statistically significant at the .01 level and of a magnitude that is generally considered to indicate a high degree of this form of reliability for an instrument of this type. The rank order correlation coefficients resulting from this analysis suggest that the individual subscale scores and the total score are relatively stable measures over a short period of time. The test-retest coefficients were as follows: Child characteristics, $p = .84$; Mother characteristics, $p = .71$; Situational/Demographic characteristics, $p = .77$; and for the total questionnaire, $p = .82$.

The alpha-reliability coefficients reported for the logically derived subscales and the total questionnaire ranged from $r = .67$ for the Situational/Demographic subscale, $r = .87$ for the Child characteristic subscale, $r = .91$ for the Mother characteristic subscale and $r = .93$ for the total questionnaire. The magnitude of these coefficients indicates that the individual subscales and the questionnaire taken as a whole show a relatively good level of internal consistency. The correlation coefficients are of a size generally considered to be of practical significance and achieve statistical significance at the .01 level.

Since the reliability of a measure has important implications for its potential validity, the information from the reliability indices suggests a significant potential for the questionnaire in terms of reliably and validly measuring the stress that parents experience. Nunally (1967) describes one of the more important implications of coefficient alpha as "The square root of coefficient alpha is the estimated correlation of a test with errorless true scores." Given this statement and the magnitude of both the test-retest reliability coefficients and the alpha-reliability coefficients, it seems that the scale is a measure with good stability over short periods of time, good internal consistency, and good potential in terms of construct and concurrent and predictive validity.

Correlational Analyses

The pattern of intercorrelations among the logically derived subscales emerged as would be expected. The largest amount of common variance was shared by the Mother characteristics and Child characteristics subscales ($r = .63$). This would be expected, as this interaction represents the relationship with the most impact on both mother and child. The second largest amount of shared variance was between the Mother characteristics and Situational/Demographic subscales ($r = .37$). It would also be expected that mothers would be more directly affected by situational factors than their children, resulting in a larger correlation (Child characteristics and Situational/Demographic characteristics correlated, $r = .18$).

Correlations of the factor scores with the overall stress ratings provided by the physicians failed to attain statistical significance. In contrast with that finding, all but one of the correlations between the logically derived scores and the physician ratings of overall stress were statistically significant at the .05 level. Correlations with physician ratings of overall stress were as follows:

Child characteristics	$r = .16$	significance = .02
Mother characteristics	$r = .15$	significance = .03
Situational/Demographic characteristics	$r = .06$	significance = .34
Total stress score	$r = .14$	significance = .04

While the absolute magnitude of the correlations is not striking, they do represent a good initial index of concurrent validity for a screening instrument of this type.

The issues involved in developing evidence that supports the validity of an instrument of this type are quite complex. Since the instrument is designed to function primarily as a screening instrument rather than a diagnostic tool, the predictive validity of the instrument should not be so great as to result in underidentification or excessive false negatives. In order to be practical in a setting such as the one used in this study, the instrument must exceed the judgment of physicians in terms of identifying parent/child systems at risk for later problems. Thus, while physician ratings may be an appropriate initial step in assessing the concurrent validity of the scale, future efforts aimed at assessing both concurrent and predictive validity must make use of other criterion variables.

Practicality

One of the goals of the research project was to develop an instrument that had good practical utility as well as adequate psychometric properties. The instrument developed during this project has proven to be quite practical. The reading level required to complete the scale (sixth grade) is such that it is understandable to a large majority of the population. It is an easy instrument to administer since it is in the form of a questionnaire; it requires no trained personnel to administer the items. Scoring is easily automated through the use of machine-readable answer forms. The total cost in the present study is estimated at $3 per subject, which would be reduced if it were used in larger numbers. This cost included the return postage for the questionnaires. The time required to complete the scale is not excessive (between 15 and 30 minutes), and the procedures fit into the routine workings of a pediatric office without causing major disruptions. The time required in the study to acquaint secretarial personnel with the procedures (2 hours) and the demands on their time were small for such an instrument.

In comparison to other projects with similar aims, the present instrument is both less expensive and more easily administered. The study conducted by Lagercrantz and Lagercrantz (1975) provided a great deal of information about the interaction between mother and child but required a good deal of time from trained observers. Metz et al. (1976) developed a screening program that was comparable in cost (estimated $3 per subject) but required hiring and training technicians to administer a battery of assessment techniques. Their procedures also required the presence of the child in order to complete the assessment battery.

Clinical and Research Implications

The results of this research project have a number of implications for the further development of this instrument, its uses in future research related to parenting and child development, and the implications of findings for the potential clinical uses of the instrument. The scores on the Index are distributed in such a fashion as to approximate a normal distribution, with distortion of the normal distribution in the direction of a platykurtic distribution.

Given that the phenomenon of parenting stress is one resulting in a distribution of scores that roughly approximates a normal curve, it is possible to identify those individuals who fall at different points along the dimension of parenting stress in a fairly reliable fashion. The ability to identify children at risk for the later development of emotional and behavioral problems presents a significant potential for the development of programs aimed at early intervention and the prevention of more serious later difficulties. Such potential exists within the current health services delivery system in the form of pediatric well-baby clinics operated through both the private and public sectors. Identification of parents and infants at risk prior to the end of the first year of life is possible on a mass basis given a technique that can reliably and validly predict the occurrence of serious difficulty.

In addition to the overall index of stress provided by the total score on the questionnaire, the subscale scores provide a valuable source of information for the clinical use of the scale. The subscale scores provide a basis for further, more focused clinical investigation by suggesting areas that seem to serve as primary sources of stress for parents. Determining the sources of stress affecting parents and children allows intervention strategies to be tailored to the needs of the family. Intervention could take many forms, including parent education, psychotherapy for child or parents, parent consultation, and a variety of supportive services.

Parenting Stress Index

(List of scores available for research and clinical purposes)

1. Total score of all items on Index (N of items = 147)
2. Child characteristics domain score (N = 46)
3. Child adaptability/Plasticity (N = 12)
4. Acceptability of child to mother (N = 7)
5. Child demandingness/Degree of bother (N = 12)

6. Child mood ($N = 6$)
7. Child distractibility/Activity ($N = 9$).
8. Interaction of mother and child: Mother is reinforced by child ($N = 7$)
9. Mother characteristics domain score ($N = 7$)
10. Mother depression, unhappiness, guilt ($N = 16$)
11. Mother attachment ($N = 10$)
12. Restrictions imposed by parental role ($N = 8$)
13. Mother's sense of competence ($n = 16$)
14. Social isolation ($N = 7$)
15. Realistic attitude toward children ($N = 5$)
16. Relationship with husband ($N = 5$)
17. Parental health ($N = 4$)
18. Situational/Demographic domain score ($N = 33$)
19. Situational stress score ($N = 13$)
20. Stressful life events ($N = 20$)
21. Conceptual duplicate items, Validity Scale ($N = 12$)

Continued exploration of the relationship of this instrument to other measures of stress, the parent/child relationship, and child behavior is necessary to explore the construct and predictive validity of the instrument. The instrument as developed through this project has been shown to possess an adequate degree of reliability and to have good potential validity. Further research, however, will be required before the instrument can be fully developed and its true potential assessed.

REFERENCES

American Orthopsychiatric Association. Developmental assessment in EPSDT. *American Journal of Orthopsychiatry*, 1978, *48*(1) 7-21.

Bell, S. M., & Ainsworth, M. D. S. Infant crying and maternal responsiveness. *Child Development*, 1972, *43*(4), 1171-1190.

Cameron, J. R. Parental treatment, children's temperament, and the risk of childhood behavioral problems: 1. Relationships between parental characteristics and changes in children's temperament over time. *American Journal of Orthopsychiatry*, 1977, *47*(4), 568-576.

Cameron, J. R. Parental treatment, children's temperament, and the risk of childhood behavioral problems: 2. Initial temperament, parental attitudes and the incidence and form of behavioral problems. *American Journal of Orthopsychiatry*, 1978, *48*(1), 140-147.

Caplan, G. A multi-model approach to primary prevention of mental disorders in children. In L. Levi (Ed.), *Society stress and disease* (Vol. 2). London: Oxford University Press, 1975.

Carey, W. B. Measuring infant temperament. *Journal of Pediatrics*, 1972, *81*, 414.

Greenberg, M., & Lind, J. First mothers rooming-in with their newborns: Its impact upon the mother. *American Journal of Orthopsychiatry*, 1973, *43*, 783-788.

Kagan, A., & Levi, L. Health and environment — psychosocial stimuli: A review. In L. Levi (Ed.), *Society stress and disease* (Vol. 2). London: Oxford University Press, 1975.

Lagercrantz, E., & Lagercrantz, R. The mother and her first born. In L. Levi (Ed.), *Society stress and disease* (Vol. 2). London: Oxford University Press, 1975.

Lewis, M., & Lee-Painter, S. An interactional approach to the mother-infant dyad. In M. Lewis & L. Rosenblum (Eds.), *The effect of the infant on its caregiver*. New York: Wiley, 1974.

Mahler, M. S., Pine, F., & Bergman, A. *The psychological birth of the human infant*. New York: Basic, 1975.

Masse, N. P. Perinatal care and mental health of the child. In L. Levi (Ed.), *Society, stress and disease* (Vol. 2). London: Oxford University Press, 1975.

McInerny, T., & Chamberlain, R. W. Is it feasible to identify infants who are at risk for later behavioral problems. *Clinical Pediatrics*, 1978, *17*(3), 233-238.

Metz, J. R., Allen, C. M., et al. A pediatric screening examination for psychosocial problems. *Pediatrics*, 1976, *58*(4), 595-606.

Nunally, J. C. *Psychometric Theory*. New York: McGraw, 1967.

Robson, K. S., & Moss, H. A. Patterns and determinants of maternal attachment. *Journal of Pediatrics*, 1970, *77*(6), 976-985.

Schaefer & Cole. Maternal reactions to problem behaviors and ordinal position of the child. Paper presented at American Psychological Association Convention, San Francisco, August 1977.

Soderling, B. Psychosomatic reactions and diseases in childhood — Some clinical viewpoints. In L. Levi (Ed.), *Society, stress and disease* (Vol. 2). London: Oxford University Press, 1975.

Thomas, A., Chess, S., & Birch, H. *Temperament and behavior disorders in children*. New York: NYU Pr, 1968.

SECTION III

REVIEWS OF PARENT
EDUCATION MATERIALS
AND PACKAGED PROGRAMS

THIS section of the *Parent Education and Intervention Handbook* consists of brief reviews of parent education and training materials, programs, projects, and texts. The intent is to provide a guide to a wide array of existing materials that may be of use to those who work with parents and children. The bulk of the published materials reviewed are appropriate for use with parent training groups.

In addition to an evaluative overview of each program, information has been provided as to the populations with which the materials may be appropriate, the level of reading difficulty of printed texts, and the cost of the material, along with information for ordering. While this listing is not exhaustive, it is hoped that it will provide a representative sample of the parent education packages currently in use and will facilitate further investigation of the usefulness of these materials in working with parents and families.

Isn't it Time He Outgrew this? or A Training Program for Parents of Retarded Children, 1973

AUTHORS: Victor L. Baldwin, H.D. Bud Fredericks, and Gerry Brodsky.

POPULATIONS WITH WHICH IT MAY BE USED: This book was written both for the parents of retarded children and for those who conduct parent training programs for this population.

SOURCE: Charles C Thomas, Publishers, 301-327 East Lawrence Avenue, Springfield, Illinois, 62717.

COST: $12.25.

This publication was designed for use with training groups of parents of retarded children but may be adapted for individual self-instruction. The objective of the program is to train parents in becoming more effective behavior managers and teachers of the mentally handicapped child through the use of principles of social learning theory.

The authors have given careful attention to the application of these principles and techniques to the development of self-help and adaptive behaviors with the retarded child. The use of response-eliciting stimulus cues, reinforcement principles, and shaping strategies is applied to a variety of practical skills such as feeding, toilet training, dressing, washing and personal care habits, language acquisition, physical education, etc. The parent is carefully guided through the

531

steps of developing a token economy system for eliciting and maintaining these adaptive skills. An additional section discusses the application of behavioral techniques to a number of behavior problems typical of this population of children, e.g., temper tantrums, socially inappropriate behavior, etc. Behavioral strategies are presented clearly with sufficient detail for the parents to model the program for their own child.

The material provided in this program may serve as an excellent introduction to behavior management techniques with parents of retarded children.

REVIEWED BY: Bryan D. Carter and Pat Sinicrope.

Parents/Children/Discipline: A Positive Approach, 1972

AUTHORS: Clifford K. Madsen and Charles H. Madsen, Jr.

POPULATIONS WITH WHICH IT MAY BE USED: This book is designed for use by parents of normal children or children with moderate behavior problems. The level of reading difficulty is moderate.

SOURCE: Allyn & Bacon, Inc., 470 Atlantic Avenue, Boston, Massachusetts, 02210.

COST: $5.00 (approximate).

This book is designed to introduce principles of behavior modification to parents for use in the day-to-day management of their child's behavior. Presented as an approach to discipline, the material in this text addresses a number of issues regarding the role of rules and structure in parent-child relationships, advocating specificity in behavior-response contingencies in child rearing.

The basic behavioral format the authors present involves pinpointing the behavior(s) to be changed, recording the behavior, consequating, and evaluating the change in the behavior. Considerable attention is given to the mechanics of observation and record keeping in maintaining a successful behavior modification program.

The second section of the book contains over 100 specific examples of behavioral programs devised to deal with problems in parent-child interactions. These examples are presented in fairly nontechnical terminology so as to meet the needs of the typical parent reader. The last section provides the parent with comprehensive lists of specific responses that they can use in positively reinforcing a wide variety of child and adult behaviors.

Throughout the book the authors stress their "positive" approach to behavior change and discipline, which attempts to minimize the use of punitive techniques. The materials appear most appropriate as an introduction to behavioral principles for parent groups.

REVIEWED BY: Bryan D. Carter and Pat Sinicrope.

Child Management: A Program for Parents and Teachers, 1976

AUTHORS: Judith M. Smith and Donald E. P. Smith.

POPULATIONS WITH WHICH IT MAY BE USED: This book is essentially designed for use by parents and teachers dealing with normal children or children with mild behavior problems, from preschool to adolescence. The text is appropriate for persons with a sixth-grade reading level. An additional Discussion Guide is available for use by the group leader.

SOURCE: Research Press, Box 31778, Champaign, Illinois, 61820.

COST: $3.95; Discussion guide, $2.50.

This book, along with the discussion guide, is designed to teach parents and other child care specialists techniques for handling certain problems of child management. In the beginning chapter, the authors present data regarding assessment of changes in trainees' attitudes and behavior after involvement in the program. The results are cited as supportive of the effectiveness of the material and techniques.

The main thrust of the material is behaviorally oriented. Using a partially programmed format, the authors cover the topics of the need for consistency in parent behavior and techniques of rule selection, rule enforcement, program monitoring, and record keeping. The authors diverge from the behavioral orientation in their discussion of the use of natural and logical consequences and the need to provide freedom for the child to discover his/her world and assume more personal responsibility.

Consistency and predictability are emphasized in special sections devoted to eating and sleeping difficulties. Issues surrounding moral training are given considerable treatment by the authors. The role of immediate and delayed consequential learning, parental modeling, parental objectivity in reconstructing behavioral sequences, and the role of the parent as seer and conscience are treated in relation to moral training.

In the discussion guide to their book, the authors have attempted to set up a format for discussion and training sessions with parent groups. The guide is extremely general and lacks organization and a structured sequence of activities. The group leader's role is portrayed as that of a modeler and discussion catalyst rather than as an information resource or child behavior expert. The *Child Management* materials would appear to be most appropriate as resource reading for other more structured parent training programs in augmenting the parents' effective use of rules and limit setting in child management.

REVIEWED BY: Bryan D. Carter.

Ice Cream, Poker Chips, and Very Goods: A Behavior Modification Manual for Parents, 1971

AUTHORS: David L. Williams & Elliot B. Jaffa.

POPULATIONS WITH WHICH IT MAY BE USED: This program was designed for use in teaching parents and teachers the basic principles of behavior modification for use with normal and "exceptional" children, e.g., mentally retarded, brain injured, emotionally disturbed, autistic, learning disabled, etc. Although the material does discuss the application of behavior management techniques to a broad variety of behaviors, it does not attempt to address the specific problems inherent in each child's type of dysfunction. It appears most appropriate as a basic overview of behavior modification principles. The level of reading difficulty and use of technical language would restrict the use of this material to those with at least a high school education.

SOURCE: The Maryland Book Exchange, 4500 College Avenue, College Park, Maryland, 20740.

COST: $5.00 (approximate).

In this manual the authors cover a basic overview of behavior management principles and techniques, including specification and measurement of the problem behavior, observation and collection of data, record keeping, identification and application of reinforcers, establishing a token economy, contingency contracting, increasing the frequency of desirable behavior and decreasing undesirable behavior, maintenance of behavior change, and troubleshooting ineffective behavior management programs. Numerous examples of the application of behavior modification principles to everyday child behavior problems are provided.

Although the scope of treatment of behavior modification techniques in this manual is fairly broad, the material is not presented in a structured format for use with parent education groups. With some modification, it could be suitable for this purpose.

The authors devote additional attention to the details of fading out the use of material and activity reinforcers, discontinuing a token economy system, and issues surrounding the care giver's change and maintenance of his/her own behavior.

REVIEWED BY: Bryan D. Carter.

Parenting Skills, 1976

AUTHOR: Richard R. Abidin.

POPULATIONS WITH WHICH IT MAY BE USED: This program is designed for use with groups of parents of normal children or children with moderate behavior problems. The materials include a Trainer's Manual and a parents' Workbook that is intended to be expendable during the course of the parent group sessions.

SOURCE: Human Sciences Press, 72 Fifth Avenue, New York, New York, 10011.

COST: Trainer's Manual, $11.95; Workbook, $3.50; Set, $13.50.

The *Parenting Skills* program provides a flexible model for conducting parent education groups in four or more different course formats. Each course, ranging from 21 sessions for the basic course to 7 sessions for the shortest program, is discussed, with the objectives being delineated according to the material covered.

The author has taken an eclectic approach in choosing a theoretical orientation for the course, which includes concepts from behavior modification, Rational Emotive Therapy, Parent Effectiveness Training, and the Adlerian model for parent-child interaction, among others. Additional optional material is provided near the end of the program to assist the parents in stimulating their childrens' intellectual and academic readiness skills during the preschool period, issues related to special education of the exceptional child, and suggestions for parental tutoring with their children's schoolwork.

Each session of the *Parenting Skills* course is composed of three major parts: (1) the review and sharing of the previous week's homework; (2) the teaching of a new lesson; and (3) the discussion of the meaning of the ideas presented to each parent. However, the content and focus of each successive session is unique and varied. The initial sessions focus on encouraging group identity and cohesiveness and ways of communicating with children that enhance self-acceptance and self-confidence.

Sample parent-child dialogues are utilized to assist the parents in identifying signs of undesirable interactions that can be used in evaluating the parent-child relationship. From here the course moves toward teaching methods of relationship building through the communication of positive affect, both verbally and nonverbally. Principles of reflective listening and parental sharing through effective communication skills are treated.

In the author's treatment of issues regarding discipline, a moderate approach is advocated that is constructive and consistent and communicates warmth. Several sessions are devoted to the application of behavioral principles to issues of child management as well as parental behavior change.

A unique element of the *Parenting Skills* program is the material dealing with the management of parental emotions in parent-child interactions. The author has employed concepts from Rational Emotive Therapy in assisting the parent in both analyzing parent-child conflict as well as controlling his/her own emotions in problem situations involving his/her children.

The Workbook provides the parent with reading material and homework forms to augment the parent education experience. The writing style is straightforward and clear.

Results of a field-testing project in training day-care providers utilizing the *Parenting Skills* materials have been reported (Martin et al., 1977). The nine participants in the workshop were female home day-care providers ranging in age from 22 to 65 years. The children they cared for ranged in age from 5 months to 12 years. This training program only involved the use of the first 8 modules in relationship building, as the day-care providers had previous training in behavior modification. Responses by the day-care providers on an evaluation questionnaire indicated: (a) group sharing as a major positive aspect of the program; (b) reported generalization of the use of the procedures to their own interaction with their children at home; (c) reported increase in subjective reports of the children's "happiness" in the day-care setting in virtually every case; and (d) a more positive attitude reported toward their children. The day-care training supervisor evaluated the program as having a positive effect on the group members, although it was felt that more practice and examples were needed in specific skill areas than were provided in the 8-session format.

Cantor (1976) investigated the effectiveness of the *Parenting Skills* program in regard to the following hypotheses: (1) teacher perception of child as better adjusted as a result of parental participation in the program; (2) increase in positive parental perception of children at home and at school; (3) improvement in parental self-image; and (4) decreased disparity between parental self-perception and their ideal parent perception. While the trends were in the direction of supporting all four hypotheses, the results failed to attain statistical significance, possibly due to small sample size (experimental group = 6, control group = 8).

BIBLIOGRAPHY:

Cantor, D. W. *Evaluation of a parenting skills training program with the parents of first grade children at-risk.* Unpublished doctoral dissertation, Rutgers University, 1976.

Martin, C. A., Dawson, M. M., Abidin, R. R., & Williams, M. M. *Parenting skills training for day care providers.* Central Virginia Child Development Association, 1976.

REVIEWED BY: Bryan D. Carter.

Since You Care: A Parenting Skills Training Manual, 1976

AUTHORS: Kathi Petersen and Gary Vermeire.

POPULATIONS WITH WHICH IT MAY BE USED: The *Since You Care* materials were developed to serve as preventive education training for parents in the area of parent-child communication. The level of the material is most appropriate for use with groups of high-school educated parents of normal rather than severely disturbed children.

SOURCE: Erie Council on Prevention of Alcoholism and Drug Abuse, Sumner Nichols Building, 155 West 8th Street, Erie, Pennsylvania, 16501.

COST: $8.00 (approximate).

This program is the outcome of a primary prevention approach to socially dysfunctional behaviors. It is based upon the philosophy that offering parents structure, perspective, alternatives, and modes of action to use in their family situations can serve to prevent those child and family difficulties that lead to substance abuse and other disturbances in child adjustment. The manual is set up to conduct parent training groups of up to 30 people in six weekly 2-hour sessions. However, the authors provide a guide for conducting the workshop in a greater or fewer number of units.

The conceptual framework of this package is based upon the assumption that giving parents an awareness of the modes of communication utilized, along with a set of communication skills, can facilitate both parental attitude change and more effective ways of interacting with and directing their children. A variety of group experiences is provided to focus on developing an awareness and personal evaluation of one's existing attitudes and feelings in regard to parent-child interactions. Rather than prescribing predetermined patterns for child rearing, the facilitator's goal is to give parents experiences that will increase their perspective taking and thus the options they have available.

Various components of the training program include learning the barriers to communication; concepts of ownership language, including "I" messages, reflective listening, nonverbal communication, and verbal/nonverbal incongruity; the decision-making process; function of feedback in communication, role-taking skills; and minimizing defensive behavior. A variety of group experiences is designed to dramatically illustrate to parents the impact that dysfunctional forms of communication have on task accomplishment and family relationships. Ordering information is provided for several films utilized in the group sessions.

An evaluation of the *Since You Care* program was conducted (Gamble and Meltzer, 1977) to measure its effectiveness in changing parents' attitudes and altering parent-child communication patterns. An experimental/control post-only design was utilized consisting of six families in each group. A variety of measures was used and provided evidence that the program successfully increased parental skills in several areas congruent with the program goals.

BIBLIOGRAPHY:

Gamble, K., and Meltzer, D. *The effects of a parenting skill program on parent-child interaction.* Erie, Pennsylvania, Erie Council on Prevention of Alcoholism and Drug Abuse, 1977.

REVIEWED BY: Bryan D. Carter.

Portage Parent Program, 1977

AUTHORS: Richard D. Boyd, Kathleen A. Stauber, and Susan M. Bluma.

POPULATIONS WITH WHICH IT MAY BE USED: The Portage Project was originally designed for use in home intervention with preschool handicapped children and their families. Additional replications of the program have been conducted with a wide variety of child populations and cultural and ethnic groups. The materials appear suitable for use with parents of normal and moderately behaviorally disturbed children. Since the implementation of parent training from the Portage model involves direct intervention by the parent educator in the home, the materials can be modified accordingly for use with parents with a wide range of reading abilities.

SOURCE: Portage Parent Program, The Portage Project, Cooperative Educational Services Agency 12, 412 East Slifer Street, Portage, Wisconsin, 53901.

COST: $11.00 set.

The Portage materials have been developed as an outgrowth of a project that began in 1969 designed to serve handicapped preschool children and their families through a home-based direct intervention program. The Parent Readings handbook consists of a structured sequence of material (humorously illustrated with cartoons from Bil Keane's *Family Circus*) in the use of behavior modification principles and techniques in both the management of child behavior and their application to child learning and preschool education. At the end of each chapter in the Readings, the parent must put his/her knowledge to the test by completing written and practical exercises. While providing an excellent review of behavior management procedures, this program goes considerably beyond most other behavior modification training packages in the application of principles of shaping, chaining, modeling, the use of aids and cues, correction, the use of timers and other devices, etc., to preschool learning experiences between parents and child.

As the Portage materials were designed for use in augmenting direct intervention by a visiting teacher, their most effective implementation is in a home-based program. The Instructors' Manual that accompanies the program provides a wealth of detailed material for the home teacher or parent educator in the application of the program materials in the home environment. Extensive coverage is given to issues surrounding the presentation of the parent program, strategies for initiating and maintaining discussions regarding the parent readings, recording parent behavior, use of the Parental Behavior Inventory in intervention and evaluation, and generalization and maintenance of the program intervention effects.

In a typical home intervention session, the teacher will obtain a post-baseline score of the previously assigned activity, present the parent and child with a new learning activity, record the baseline, have the parent model the new activity with corrective feedback, and then the parent and teacher will review the activity and the mechanics of recording the behavior. With the use of modeling, discussion, corrective feedback, and written activity charts, the parent and child are provided a structure that allows the parent to independently instruct the child during the remainder of the week before the next session. Program evaluation of the Portage Project (Portage Project Progress Report, 1975) and replication studies with other child populations (Shearer & Shearer, 1976) have shown these procedures to result in significant gains in developmental and learning progress as compared to controls. The Portage materials are highly suitable for use with a variety of groups of parents of preschoolers in teaching behavioral concepts of behavior management and the learning of educational and academic readiness skills.

BIBILIOGRAPHY:

Portage Project Progress Report. *Portage guide to home teaching.* Portage, Wisconsin: Cooperative Educational Service Agency 12, 1975.

Shearer, D., & Shearer, S. The Portage Project: A model for early childhood intervention. In T. Tjossem (Ed.), *Intervention strategies for high risk infants and young children*. Baltimore: Univ Park, 1976.
REVIEWED BY: Bryan D. Carter.

Systematic Training for Effective Parenting, 1976

AUTHORS: Don Dinkmeyer and Gary D. McKay.

POPULATIONS WITH WHICH IT MAY BE USED: The STEP program is designed for use with parent study groups. The material is most appropriate for use with parents of normal children or children with mild behavior problems rather than more severe behavioral distur-bances.

SOURCE: American Guidance Services, Inc., Circle Pines, Minnesota, 55014.

COST: $65.00.

Systematic Training for Effective Parenting (STEP) is an educa-tional program for parent groups based upon the child management principles of Alfred Adler and Rudolf Dreikurs. The program mate-rials include the leader's manual, parents' handbook, brochures, large posters illustrating program principles, and five cassette tapes of sample parent-child interactions and author narrative, all packaged in a case that doubles as a display easel.

The purpose of the STEP program is to teach parents effective "democratic" ways of relating to their children based upon develop-ment of an understanding of the purposes of children's behavior and misbehavior, encouragement of responsible behavior, effective lis-tening and communication skills, the use of logical and natural con-sequences, and constructive planning through family meetings and discussion. Each session involves group discussion of assigned read-ings and activities for the week plus practice responses to parent-child interaction sequences from the audio cassette series with corrective feedback.

This particular program is unique in that it is one of the only training packages based on the Adlerian model. Throughout the de-velopment of the program, it was editorially reviewed by the staff of the Alfred Adler Institute and numerous Adlerian practitioners, in-cluding Dr. Rudolf Dreikurs.

Although the leader's manual provides a comprehensive description of the training program and procedures, there is no inclusion of research evidence as to the validity of the theoretical orientation of the program or the effectiveness of the program with children and parents. The authors provide a list of names and addresses of group leaders who participated in the field-testing of the STEP program, but empirical data and discussion of the results obtained during the development of the course are lacking.

In conducting the program, the authors place less emphasis on data collection by parents between sessions than is found with most behaviorally oriented programs. The role of the group leader is more that of a catalyst for group discussion rather than that of a teacher or expert in parenting skills. The audio cassette tapes provide numerous practice situations for parents to test their acquisition of the principles and skills of the STEP parenting model with immediate feedback from the authors (on tape) and the group leader.

Communications training is an integral part of the parenting skills program and involves the techniques of "active listening," a reflecting of the child's feelings at the moment, and the use of "I" messages, including admitting and explaining adult feelings to the child. The child's taking responsibility for problem solving is encouraged through suggestions for helping the child discuss the problem, enumerate different possible solutions, and arriving at a mutually satisfactory resolution.

REVIEWED BY: Bryan D. Carter.

Parent Readiness Education Project (PREP) Manual, 1977

AUTHORS: Parent Readiness Education Project, Redford Union School District, Detroit, Michigan, Dr. Diane K. Bert, Project Director.

POPULATIONS WITH WHICH IT MAY BE USED: The PREP program was designed for use with preschool children with potential learning problems as identified through a standardized screening process. It is an educational program that requires extensive parent involvement in the remediation effort. The parent materials require a junior high reading level.

SOURCE: Diane K. Bert, Ph.D., Project Director, PREP, Redford Union School District No. 1, 18499 Beech Daly Road, Detroit, Michigan, 48240.

COST: $25.00 complete program manual.

The Parent Readiness Education Project is a unique and innovative approach to training parents as remedial agents with their preschool children (4-year-olds) who have been identified as being at risk for developing learning problems. Through a comprehensive screening program of 3-year-olds in the school district, those children who show evidence of delayed development of skills, that are considered precursors of abilities necessary for later academic achievement are selected for **PREP** enrollment.

The project accepts 48 children each year; these children are divided into 4 classes of 12 each. Each class meets one day per week. The mothers are required to attend the classes with their child, both observing the activities from an observation room with teacher instruction and actively participating with their preschoolers in the learning experience. Scheduled home activities are assigned to the parents and are designed to reinforce the classroom curriculum and to increase family interaction and parental involvement.

Both the classroom and home curricula involve six major skill areas: language and conceptual development; auditory perceptual development; visual perceptual development; motor coordination development; development of self-concept and self-awareness; and the development of an awareness of the child's environment, e.g., community, school, nature, etc.

In addition to the mothers' attendance with their children at school, the parents also meet with school social workers and **PREP** teachers several times through the academic year to discuss topics relating to raising children and adapting to their roles as parents. The extensive handbook of home activities stimulates family involvement through positive interaction and fosters a stimulating learning environment for the younger children in the home.

Another unique aspect of the **PREP** program is the involvement of high school students as classroom aids in one-to-one contact with the preschoolers. This phase is introduced in the second half of the school term and the students learn through assigned readings and seminar instruction concepts pertaining to early childhood development and child management. These 12 high school seniors are thus given experiences that will assist them in their preparation for future parenthood roles.

The **PREP** Manual includes samples of numerous materials and program activities, administrative and funding information, and data supporting the effectiveness of the program in remediating preschoolers' learning deficits and improving parents' effectiveness in facilitating home learning experiences and child management. While the project was designed for use with this special population, the wealth of materials employed are suitable for use with parents of normal preschoolers.

REVIEWED BY: Bryan D. Carter.

How to Talk with Children (and Other People), 1973

AUTHOR: Gabriel Della-Piana.

POPULATIONS WITH WHICH IT MAY BE USED: This book appears most appropriate for use as reading material for parents and care givers dealing with normal problems of child rearing and parent-child communication. The level of reading difficulty is moderate, it would be suitable for persons with at least an eighth-grade education. The author does not provide the group leader with a guide to the use of the material in a structured parent education group format. However, the material is readily adaptable for such use.

SOURCE: John Wiley & Sons, Inc., 605 Third Avenue, New York, New York, 10016.

COST: $2.95.

How to Talk with Children (and Other People) is an interesting parenting resource that provides the parent or care giver with information regarding the principles of communication between parent and child as well as instruction in the use of behavior management techniques. The text is programmed to facilitate the understanding and application of the concepts in everyday situations with children.

The author thoroughly covers the use of specific parent responses in talking with children, including the appropriate use of statements that are supportive, accepting, questioning, explanatory, directing, distracting, punitive, and nonreinforcing. Exercises involving sample parent-child exchanges are provided with immediate feedback designed to improve the reader's communication skills. Care has been taken by the author to provide guidance as to when each form of communicative statement is most appropriate and the ways to measure the effectiveness of the parental response.

The sections of this book that deal with child management are based on social learning theory. Alternatives to punishment encouraged include ignoring undesirable behavior, removal of eliciting stimuli, short-term and long-term time-out, and distraction. Shaping incompatible desirable behavior is covered in detail as an alternative to punitive techniques.

A self-control program, presented in an instructive flowchart format, is described with application to problems of changing the parents' behavior. This same format is also used as a communication device to help young adolescents develop their own solutions to problems of peer pressure in social situations. Application of other communication and behavioral principles is discussed in response to issues of handling bedwetting, teaching reading, and developing study habits.

The appendices offer the reader additional helpful instruction in methods of constructing enjoyable and educational stories for children and a guide to additional readings on subjects such as creative expression in children, teaching reading, ethnic groups, sex education, and child rearing. This text would be a welcome reference for parents as well as resource material for parent training groups. The author effectively employs wit and humor to make the learning experience most enjoyable.

REVIEWED BY: Bryan D. Carter.

Positive Parenting, 1977

AUTHORS: Roger C. Rinn and Allan Markle.

POPULATIONS WITH WHICH IT MAY BE USED: This parent training program is used for a wide variety of children and teenagers with a broad range of problem behaviors. However, the material is not suitable for more severe behavior problems.

SOURCE: Research Media, Inc., 96 Mount Auburn Street, Cambridge, Massachusetts, 02138.

COST: $5.00 (approximate).

This book is the result of the authors' experiences of several years in conducting behaviorally oriented parent training groups with the Huntsville-Madison County Mental Health Center in Huntsville, Alabama. The publication is designed to be used by parents as an instructional device to accompany their group experience, but it can also be used as a self-study guide in learning behavioral principles and techniques.

Principles governing child behavior from the social learning model are outlined in a set of rules and are clearly illustrated by way of anecdotes and clinical case studies. Included in the book are sections on principles and applications of behavioral measurement, methods and principles of reinforcement (social, activity, and material), techniques and programs for increasing desirable behaviors and decreasing undesirable and inappropriate behaviors, the use of token economies, and behavioral contracting with adolescents. One chapter is devoted exclusively to case examples of the application of the positive parenting approach to common problems of child management.

The authors devote additional material to troubleshooting an unsuccessful program and to self-management of undesirable parental behavior including the use of relaxation training. As this book is intended for use as a parent guide, no special instructions are included for the professional who desires to implement the positive parenting material in a program or training group format. However, it would be most appropriate as reference material for most behaviorally oriented groups.

REVIEWED BY: Bryan D. Carter.

Groups for Parents: A Guide for Teaching Child Management to Parents, 1974

AUTHORS: O. W. Sadler and T. Seyden.

POPULATIONS WITH WHICH IT MAY BE USED: Parent groups of varied educational levels with normal and exceptional children. Format can be modified to ability level of parents.

SOURCE: Clinical Psychology Publishing Co., Inc., 4 Conant Square, Brandon, Vermont, 05733.

COST: $8.00.

The authors of this monograph present a structured eight-session training program designed to teach parenting skills from a behavior modification orientation with humanistic overtones. As outlined, the program is appropriate for use with a variety of parent groups and can be employed by professionals, paraprofessionals, and intelligent laymen in the helping professions. Suggestions are made for modification from a problem-oriented focus for work with groups of parents whose children have special needs, e.g., learning disabled, mentally retarded, hyperactive, predelinquent, etc. to a more educational model to meet the needs of parents who are attempting to improve their parenting skills of children whose behavior is less pathological.

Although the major emphasis of this training program is to teach parents behavior modification techniques and skills, e.g., positive reinforcement, token economy, behavioral contracting, time-out, etc., the authors have also included group and home practice exercises in nondirective reflective listening (communications skills), group relaxation, and small group encounter experiences (as a group facilitative device).

This program's main strength lies in the effective utilization of skits and role-playing exercises, group leader modeling, token reinforcement of parents' participation and progress, *in vivo* experiences with children during the group sessions, emphasis on on-going data collection and evaluation, and small group experiences that vividly illustrate key principles and skills. However, with the exception of one or two group exercises, the program offers little in the way of innovation and relies heavily on resource materials from other parent training packages, e.g., Patterson's *Families* and Gordon's *Parent Effectiveness Training*.

REVIEWED BY: Bryan D. Carter.

Problem-Solving Techniques in Childrearing, 1978

AUTHORS: Myrna B. Shure and George Spivack.

POPULATIONS WITH WHICH IT MAY BE USED: This program was designed for use with parents of at-risk children of preschool age from socioeconomically disadvantaged families. However, it is appropriate for use in training parents and caretakers in a variety of settings with varied socioeconomic backgrounds. The target behaviors in this program are those skills involved in the interpersonal and social adjustment of young children, e.g., social withdrawal, aggressive behavior, peer relationship difficulties, etc.

SOURCE: Jossey-Bass, Inc., Publishers, 433 California Street, San Francisco, California, 94104.

COST: $15.00 (approximate).

Based upon previous research with preschool youngsters in promoting interpersonal cognitive problem solving (ICPS) skills using classroom teachers as intervention agents (Shure & Spivack, 1974), the authors have developed a program using parents as social cognition change agents with their children. Rather than training parents in methods of discipline or management of child behavior, the problem-solving approach emphasizes teaching the child to think so that s/he can deal with each new problem as it arises. The parent is instructed in how to teach the child a repertoire of thinking skills that lead to accurate problem identification, an understanding of how his/her behavior affects others, an anticipation of the consequences of his/her behavior, and a recognition of more than one alternative solution to a problem situation. A set of structured interaction exercises is provided to the parent in the form of game situations to be conducted with the child in 20-minute daily sessions over a period of 43 days.

The exercises begin by teaching the child various word-concepts utilized in the problem-solving approach that are a part of alternative-solution and consequential thinking. After these concepts are understood, the program progresses to teaching the child to identify emotions, investigating individual differences in preferences, understanding causality, means-ends concepts, consequential thinking, fairness concepts, alternative-solution thinking, and solution-consequence pairing. Parent-child interaction exercises are enlivened through the use of materials such as puppets, pictures, drawings, storybooks, etc.

The authors have provided an excellent survey of the social adjustment research literature as an introduction to the objectives of the problem-solving approach to teaching social competence to preschool children. Their program is the result of a primary prevention intervention effort to reach a high-risk population of lower-income minority preschool children through parent training (usually involving mothers in single parent families) of cognitive skills.

Of particular merit in the manual is the inclusion of the program evaluation data of their previous studies and the present study on the effects of the problem-solving parent training program. The pilot and final study were based upon samples of minority mothers and children (identified as behaviorally impulsive or inhibited) from the Philadelphia area and attempted to assess improvement in children's ICPS skills, and home and school behavior. The evaluation also assessed changes in the mothers' child-rearing styles and their own ICPS skills. The findings are highly supportive of the program's effectiveness in improving alternative-solution thinking in impulsive and inhibited children, in decreasing maladaptive behaviors and strengthening adaptive behaviors both at school and in the home, increasing alternative-solution thinking in the trained mothers, and increasing consequential thinking in children with maladaptive behaviors.

Extensive additional material is provided the trainer in the professional implementation of the program with client populations, training other professionals in the use of the program, and the content and use of the research and evaluation tools employed by the authors in their assessment.

REVIEWED BY: Bryan D. Carter.

Parenting in 1977: A Listing of Parenting Materials, 1977

AUTHOR: Parenting Materials Information Center (PMIC), Southwest Educational Development Laboratory.

POPULATIONS WITH WHICH MATERIALS MAY BE USED: This publication is intended for use by those interested in parent education as a resource for locating parenting materials.

SOURCE: Parenting Materials Information Center, Southwest Educational Development Laboratory, 211 East 7th Street, Austin, Texas,

78701.

COST: $5.00.

This booklet contains a listing of the current holdings of the Parenting Materials Information Center (PMIC), which is a project of the Division of Community and Family Education of the Southwest Education Development Laboratory (SEDL). This organization is located in Austin, Texas, and is funded by the National Institute of Education.

The PMIC has attempted to gather, store, and disseminate information concerning parenting materials that may be of interest to parent educators. Although the listings do not describe the content of the materials, a one- or two-page information sheet is available on many of the listed materials and can be obtained from PMIC on request.

REVIEWED BY: Bryan D. Carter.

How to Parent Alone: A Guide for Single Parents, 1974

AUTHOR: Joan Bel Geddes.

POPULATIONS WITH WHICH IT MAY BE USED: Rather than providing a structured parent training program, this book serves as a self-help guide to the single parent. In issues of parent care, i.e., how the single parent can increase self-confidence, manage financial difficulties, develop an active social life, etc., it appears most appropriate as a reading resource for the single woman raising children and might be used as supplemental reading in parent education groups composed of single parents.

SOURCE: The Seabury Press, 815 Second Avenue, New York, New York, 10017.

COST: $8.95.

In this book, the author has attempted to give the single parent encouragement and advice about the process of taking care of his/her own emotional needs as the sole primary caretaker of his/her children. Addressing primarily the divorced young woman raising children of preschool and elementary school age in an urban and suburban environment, the author confronts the problems facing this group and offers practical suggestions as to possible remedies and solutions. Little advice is offered regarding child-rearing practices as they pertain to the single parent.

From her own experience as a single parent adjusting to the demands of raising a family without a spouse, the author offers a plethora of advice to her fellow single parents in regard to self-acceptance, self-exploration, changing one's own behavior, dealing with depression and self-pity, conquering feelings of guilt and self-hatred, becoming more assertive and socially involved, etc. Other chapters deal with important issues surrounding seeking employment, financial management, and communicating with the children and answering the numerous questions they may have about divorce, death, step-parents, etc.

Primarily a self-help book with advice for laymen, this material appears to be useful as additional reading material for use with single parents.

REVIEWED BY: Bryan D. Carter.

Active Parent Concern: A New Home Guide to Help Your Child Do Better, 1976

AUTHOR: Terrel H. Bell.

POPULATIONS WITH WHICH IT MAY BE USED: Although this book is intended for parents in general, the material has a high reading difficulty level, restricting its range of use.

SOURCE: Prentice-Hall, Englewood Cliffs, New Jersey, 07632.

COST: $8.95.

This handbook is intended to serve as a parents' guide to the educational systems of the school, the home, the church, and the community. The author's goal is to give the parent a reference that will help to promote the greatest educational opportunities and the highest educational standards in both home and formal school systems. By enabling the parents to become more effective teachers, counselors, and advocates of quality education for all children at all levels of the educational process, the author hopes to promote the educational, social, emotional, and attitudinal development of the child.

The parent is offered guidance in creating a positive learning atmosphere both in the home and through cooperative work with the child's school. Guidelines are provided for motivating learning experiences and helping the child to build a positive self-image through parent-child educational experiences.

A home-based curriculum is presented with the author's "incidental" teaching method, which employs use of the natural sequence of everyday events. The reader is taken on a guided tour of the school system and familiarized with the different roles of school personnel, given an overview of school curriculum planning, instructed in the purposes and functions of school tests and examinations, and given concrete advice as to the measures to take when his/her child is failing in school.

This publication would appear to be most useful in working with parent groups related to children's academic performance and parental-school relations.

REVIEWED BY: Bryan D. Carter.

Helping Your Child Learn Right From Wrong: A Guide to Values Clarification, 1976

AUTHORS: Sidney B. Simon and Sally Wendkos Olds.

POPULATIONS WITH WHICH IT MAY BE USED: Parents of normal school-aged children. This material is of a moderate reading difficulty level.

SOURCE: Simon & Schuster, Rockefeller Center, 630 Fifth Avenue, New York, New York, 10020.

COST: $7.95.

This book is designed to assist parents in helping their school-aged and adolescent children discover their own identities through exploring what they believe in and value. The authors have developed a variety of games, exercises, and strategies designed to assist families in identifying the principles they employ in their daily lives. The structured activities, conducted in the context of a supportive and accepting family atmosphere, attempt to teach children methods for clarifying values, taking responsibility for one's own values, sharing through two-way communication, developing an appreciation for the values held by others, examining alternatives, and participating in the problem-solving process. This book provides excellent material for facilitating family discussion of important moral and relationship issues. However, the program basically presupposes a family structure with only a minimal level of communicational difficulties.

REVIEWED BY: Bryan D. Carter.

Tuning Into Your Child: Awareness Training for Parents, 1975

AUTHOR: Betty Rowan.

POPULATIONS WITH WHICH IT MAY BE USED: This material is designed for use with well-motivated parents of normal children from infancy to school age.

SOURCE: Humanics Press, 881 Peachtree Street, N.E., Atlanta, Georgia, 30309.

COST: $5.00.

The purpose of this book is to guide parents in ways of becoming more sensitive to and aware of their children. Basic knowledge of child developmental trends is presented, while the uniqueness of each individual child is also stressed. Various activities, e.g., observation games, listening games, role-playing empathy practice, etc., are suggested to assist the parent in developing an appreciation of their child's perspective. Creative activities involving self-expression, such as dancing, painting, or puppet play, are encouraged as methods through which the child can indirectly reveal himself or herself to the parent.

The author provides specific suggestions and exercises for the parent in observing the infant, interacting with the toddler, and building relationships with the preschooler and school beginner. Additional material is devoted to ways a parent can assist children during the school years, with particular attention to specific problems that frequently occur during the growth process. Helpful suggestions are offered as anticipatory guidance in dealing with specific developmental crises that arise, e.g., school entry.

This book offers practical helpful advice to parents in growing with and responding to their developing children.

REVIEWED BY: Bryan D. Carter.

Parenting: A Guide for Young People, 1975

AUTHORS: Sol Gordon and Mina Wollin.

POPULATIONS WITH WHICH IT MAY BE USED: This publication was designed to be used as a textbook in education-for-parenthood programs with adolescents in the school setting. The material is of moderate reading difficulty level.

SOURCE: Oxford Book Company, 11 Park Place, New York, New York, 10007.

COST: Text, $2.84: Teacher's Guide, $2.64.

This book and the accompanying Teacher's Guide are intended for use with adolescents in parenthood education classes in the high school curriculum. Major emphasis is placed on the responsibilities of parenthood in planning for a wanted child and providing the proper physical and emotional environment for fostering maximal growth and development.

The material progresses through the stages of making the decision to marry (or not), building a strong marriage as a foundation for parenthood, and the rights of the child to responsible parents. Technical information is provided as to the mechanics of human reproduction, physiological changes during pregnancy, the intrauterine development of the infant, and the actual birth process.

Practical and sound advice is given regarding the care of the newborn and the mother. The physical, mental, and emotional development of the child during the preschool years is discussed, along with specific concerns of the stages, e.g., children and sex, creative parenting, etc. The Teacher's Guide provides information regarding enrichment resources, projects, and discussions that can facilitate the learning experience.

REVIEWED BY: Bryan D. Carter.

Brushing Up on Parenthood, 1974

AUTHOR: Institute of Family Home Education.

POPULATIONS WITH WHICH IT MAY BE USED: This self-guided parent education program consists of a series of audio cassette tapes that parents from a variety of backgrounds can use, along with an accompanying manual of parent-child activities, to learn how to more effectively foster their children's social, cognitive, creative, and affective growth and development. However, the book is written at a high level of reading difficulty.

SOURCE: Institute of Family Home Education, P. O. Box 539, Provo, Utah, 84601.

COST: Kit (16 audio cassette tapes and manual in a vinyl fold-out pack) $109.00.

This program is designed to be used independently by parents in a self-guided parent education project. The user follows the procedure of listening to the tapes and then performing the activities in the accompanying manual with the child to reinforce the content of the tapes. The cassettes contain dialogue that illustrates typical parent-child difficulties and possible problem-solving responses.

The main thrust of this field-tested program is to facilitate parental fostering of cognitive and intellectual abilities. Numerous activities have been developed to teach parents to assist their child in concept development, language development, perceptual-motor functioning, reading, music, and creative expression through art, literature, writing, science, etc. Other subjects dealt with include the development of physical skills, social growth, moral and value development, and physical maturation. Parenting information and activities are also provided in relation to the topics of making learning an enjoyable process, use of direct instruction, discipline, and the emotional growth of the child.

These materials appear most suitable for use with the well-motivated and sophisticated parent who is in need of instruction in facilitating his/her child's cognitive development. The program can best be implemented if there is a solid parent-child relationship based upon affection and caring.

REVIEWED BY: Bryan D. Carter.

Your Children and You: How to Manage Growing Up Problems in the Years One to Five, 1975

AUTHOR: Eleanor Weisberger.

POPULATIONS WITH WHICH IT MAY BE USED: Parents of preschool children with a normal range of behavior problems.

SOURCE: E. P. Dutton & Company, Inc., 201 Park Avenue South, New York, New York, 10003.

COST: $7.95.

This book focuses on the role of the parents as educators of their preschool children. It attempts to assist parents in giving guidance to their children to facilitate their development and emotional maturity.

The thrust of the material in this book deals with the developmental issues of the period from 1 to 5 years, with specific reference to the psychosexual concomitants of each age group. Issues dealt with include toilet training, discipline, sex education, temporary and long-term separations (death), hospitalization, divorce, and the role of the father in the child's development. The author has also included advice on certain communications techniques, e.g., the parallel story, which can be used to facilitate the parent-child relationship. Specific behavior problems of this age group, e.g., eating difficulties, sleeping problems, studying, fighting, whining, etc., are given individual treatment.

This book appears to be most suitable for use with parents of preschool children to assist them in understanding the course of child development and in developing skills of responding to their children's developmental needs.

REVIEWED BY: Bryan D. Carter.

Managing Behavior, Parts 1, 2, and 3 (1, Behavior Modification: The Measurement of Behavior, 1974; 2, Behavior Modification: Basic Principles, 1975; 3, Behavior Modification: Applications in School and Home, 1974)

AUTHOR: R. Vance Hall.

POPULATIONS WITH WHICH IT MAY BE USED: Parents and para-professionals. This material requires a junior high school reading level.

SOURCE: H & H Enterprises, Inc., P. O. Box 1070, Lawrence, Kansas, 66044.

COST: $2.45 each.

The manuals propose to teach the application of behavior modification techniques based on principles of operant conditioning, or the "responsive teaching model." Part 1 emphasizes measuring behavior. Part 2 discusses basic principles of behavior and behavior management. Part 3 presents summaries of behavior modification projects completed in home and school settings. Three characteristics are basic to the responsive teaching model: (a) the behavior/task is defined, observed, and recorded; (b) an intervention to improve the student's performance is implemented; and (c) if a desirable change occurs, it can be determined whether the intervention caused the change; however, if no change occurs or if the behavior worsens, feedback from the attempted intervention guides teacher/parent in determining more effective procedures.

The three manuals comprise an introduction to the principles of behavior modification that is comprehensive, considering the relative brevity of the text. Using a straightforward style, the author employs short explanations with built-in organizers, including subheadings and frequent listing of major points. Charts and graphs are clear, presented in context, and thoroughly discussed in the text. Following short sections, quizzes provide the reader with opportunities to apply knowledge to programmed questions, with correct answers supplied at the end of each manual. Brief references to hypothetical cases in Parts 1 and 2 and more extensive case studies in Part 3 demonstrate applications of specific principles, measurement, design, and intervention techniques described in the text.

Although parents are part of the targeted population, it is questionable how applicable many of the more technical concepts and procedures would be to many parents. Specifically, items including reliability checks, calculation of reliability, calculation of median and means of measurements, description of automated cumulative records, and details of ratio schedules will have limited relevance to most parents. In addition, the use of the reversal design probably has minimal applicability to the reality of daily living, for parents and for many teachers. For individuals who require an introduction to terminology and concepts for purposes of their reviewing behavior-based literature and applying it to practical situations, the series gives a concise overview.

Research reporting use of the responsive teaching model as outlined in the series includes references to behavior management programs in school and home settings involving single-subject interventions using both reversal and multiple baseline designs. Parents are reported to have significantly decreased undesirable behaviors including (a) whining and shouting, (b) negative verbalizations, and (c) nail biting. Parents are reported to have significantly increased desirable behaviors including (a) wearing an orthodontic device, (b) completing routine housekeeping tasks, and (c) dressing more quickly.

BIBLIOGRAPHY:

Broden, M., Beasley, A., & Hall, R. V. Effects of parent home tutoring on in-class spelling performance. *Behavior Modification*, 1978, 2, 511-530.

Hall, R. V., Axelrod, S., Tyler, L., Grief, E., Jones, F. C., & Robertson, R. Modification of behavior problems in the home with a parent observer and experimenter. *Journal of Applied Behavior Analysis*, 1972, 5, 53-64.

Hall, R. V., & Broden, M. Helping teachers and parents to modify behavior of their retarded and behavior-disordered children. In P. Mittler, *Research to Practice in Mental Retardation*, Vol. 3. Baltimore: Univ Park, 1977.

Hall, R. V., Copeland, R., & Clark, M. Management strategies for teachers and parents: Responsive teaching. In N. G. Haring & R. L. Schiefelbusch (Eds.), *Teaching special children*. New York: McGraw, 1976.

REVIEWED BY: Kathleen G. Taylor, University of Virginia.

Families: Applications of Social Learning to Family Life, 1975

AUTHOR: Gerald R. Patterson.

POPULATIONS WITH WHICH IT MAY BE USED: Parents, paraprofessionals, teachers, and others working with children. This material requires a junior high school reading level.

SOURCE: Research Press, 2612 North Mattis Avenue, Champaign, Illinois, 61820.

COST: $4.00.

Note: Also available from Research Press are two sets of 30-minute tapes, *Family Living Series, Parts I and II*, which pinpoint key concepts in *Families* and *Living with Children*. They are billed as being especially useful for parents whose reading level makes it difficult for them to respond to the texts. Part I has 5 tapes ($34.95), and Part II has 3 tapes ($20.95).

Families provides an introduction to social learning principles and applies them within the context of family members undergoing change, both normally and with planned intervention. Procedures for applying principles of behavior change in common family problems are provided (e.g., toilet training, tantrums, marital negotiations). The last section of the book proposes applications of behavior principles to more complicated management problems, including children who steal and who are aggressive or noncompliant.

The format of *Families* makes it a functional text for use with a broad range of individuals. The text is well organized, with sections addressing various topics covering only a few basic points at a time in a concise fashion. The material is programmed in two ways: (a) blanks in the text are left, to be filled in by the reader, as a means of allowing for his/her active response; and (b) key points covered are listed briefly at the end of each section. Illustrative graphs and simple recording forms are positioned in the text to facilitate both the reader's comprehension of the content and its application.

The writing style is straightforward. Although basic social learning terminology is used, terms are omitted that would not aid the reader's understanding of the material. Brief case studies are employed to clarify content.

The author and his colleagues have published the results of various aspects of their training and intervention with families at the Oregon Research Institute and in many journals and monographs. *Living with Children* (Patterson & Gullion, 1968) presents basic techniques of behavior management and learning in the context of the parent teaching his child. *Families* is seen as an extension of this original primer, describing in more depth applications of behavior change methodology. Results of trained parent intervention using behavioral techniques with males ages 6 to 13 having high rates of aggressive behavior have been reported. The first 13 families in the study were reported by Patterson, Cobb, & Ray (1973); an additional 11 families were reported on by Patterson & Reid (1973); and a cumulative total of the first 27 families was described by Patterson in 1974. In Patterson's 1974 report, the following results were reported: (a) a mean total deviant behavior score of .75 behaviors per minute during baseline decreased significantly to .40; (b) two out of three boys decreased 30% or more in aggressive behaviors following intervention; (c) there was a noted trend toward reduction of deviant behaviors that were not the subject of intervention. In addition, a 4-month follow-up on 20 families demonstrated a mean total deviant behavior score of .34.

Furthermore, the postintervention scores were determined to be within the normal range of behavior.

The foregoing studies did not include control group comparison. However, Walter and Gilmore (1973) compared the use of the intervention procedures involving parent group training sessions, use of the test, in-home behavioral observation, and collection of parent checklist data with a group that did not have a therapist present at the training sessions and that did not read the text. The experimental group decreased targeted aggressive behaviors, but the placebo group did not. In a similar study, Wiltz and Patterson (1974) compared an experimental intervention group with a waiting list control group. After 5 weeks of intervention, the experimental group demonstrated significant decreases in deviant behavior, unlike the control.

Another study by Arnold, Levine, and Patterson (1975) reports data on 55 siblings of 27 boys referred for treatment. Initial intake data showed that the siblings' behavior scores did not differ significantly from the referred boys. Although the behavioral intervention programs and training done with the families was not directed at the siblings, there was a significant reduction in deviant behavior by the end of the intervention, which was maintained during a 6-month follow-up.

BIBLIOGRAPHY:

Arnold, J. E., Levine, A. B., & Patterson, G. R. Changes in sibling behavior following family intervention. *Journal of Consulting and Clinical Psychology*, 1975, *43*, 683-688.

Patterson, G. R. Interventions for boys with conduct problems: Multiple settings, treatments, and criteria. *Journal of Consulting and Clinical Psychology*, 1974, *42*, 471-481.

Patterson, G. R., Cobb, J. A., & Ray, R. S. A social engineering technology for retraining the families of aggressive boys. In H. E. Adams & I. P. Unikel (Eds.), *Issues and trends in behavior therapy*. Springfield: Thomas, 1973.

Patterson, G. R., & Gullion, M. E. *Living with children: New methods for parents and teachers*. Champaign, Illinois: Res Press, 1968.

Patterson, G. R., & Reid, J. B. Intervention for families of aggressive boys: A replication study. *Behavior Research and Therapy*, 1973, *11*, 383-394.

Walter, H. I., & Gilmore, S. K. Placebo versus social learning effects of parent training procedures designed to alter the behavior of aggressive boys. *Behavior Therapy*, 1973, *4*, 361-377.

Wiltz, N. A., & Patterson, G. R. An evaluation of parent training

procedures designed to alter inappropriate aggressive behavior of boys. *Behavior Therapy*, 1974, *5*, 215-221.
REVIEWED BY: Kathleen G. Taylor, University of Virginia.

Responsive Parent Training Manual, 1976

AUTHOR: Marilyn Clark-Hall and Staff (Ellen Blattenberg, Helen Collier, Karen Fayman Leiker, Joe Grinstead, Lynda Kearns, Martha Jo Rotton, and Jerry Wyckoff).

POPULATIONS WITH WHICH IT MAY BE USED: The manual contains instructional materials for program director, group leaders, and parents. Teachers, psychologists, counselors, social workers, or lay parents could fill the role of group leader. Populations to which the instruction could be presented are parents, paraprofessionals, and others providing child care services. This material requires a junior high school to high school reading level.

SOURCE: H & H Enterprises, Inc., P.O. Box 1070, Lawrence, Kansas, 66044.

COST: $14.00.

The manual provides directions and outlines for both individuals who direct and those who enroll in a responsive teaching course. Directions for the director and group leaders are detailed and sometimes mundane, but they may be of particular assistance for persons who have never initiated a parent training group prior to reading the manual. Topics covered include babysitting, fees, evaluation, staff training, and job descriptions for all trainers and directors involved. The section containing the responsive parenting program is similar, in content to the original version of the program by Hall (1971). Its stated intent is to provide new models of parenting, specifically, to teach new skills that will give parents different alternatives to solving problems with their children. The text is intended to be handed out to the parents section by section and inserted into individual loose-leaf notebooks provided by each participant in the training. It is basically a simplified format of the original Hall manuals, with added cartoons and additional opportunities to make active and written responses within the limits of the text. Frequent use of short true-to-life examples occurs throughout the text.

The organization of the manual is logical, i.e., points are made and then clarified by frequent listings of major topics. In the parent section of the manual, an "Important Points" section summarizes vital areas of understanding. In addition, an applied case study illustrates these points, and a "Think Abouts" section gives suggested activities for the reader to implement in his/her own setting. Another section common throughout the parent manual is a definition list that occurs following each chapter; definitions are generally well stated. Assignments, worksheets, and quizzes give the participant further opportunity to respond to questions and posed problems and to apply information learned in the preceding section(s). This consistent format, with built-in opportunities for programmed responses, makes the manual easy to follow for training purposes.

Unfortunately, in this revision of the original responsive teaching manual, the authors are still intent on providing the parent with a thorough knowledge of behavior modification, something that may not be necessary for a broad range of parents and professionals who may use this program. Technical aspects of calculating reliability, for example, are not especially relevant to the daily demands of most parents and teachers who are not interested in publishing their projects. In addition, the use of the reversal design probably has minimal applicability to most parents and teachers. On the whole, however, the program of instruction is sound and the exercises are excellent.

Research reporting use of the responsive teaching model as outlined in the series includes references to behavior management programs in school and home settings involving single-subject interventions using both reversal and multiple baseline designs. Parents are reported to have significantly decreased undesirable behaviors including (a) whining and shouting (Hall, Axelrod, Tyler, Grief, Jones, & Robertson, 1972), (b) nail biting and pouting (Hall, '971), and (c) getting out of bed at night (Hall, 1971). Parents are reported to have significantly increased desirable behaviors including (a) wearing an orthodontic device (Hall et al., 1972), (b) completing routine housekeeping tasks (Hall et al., 1972), (c) dressing more quickly (Hall et al., 1972), (d) spelling performance on quizzes in school (Broden, Beasley, & Hall, 1978), and (e) time spent on extracurricular activities (Hall, Cristler, Cranston, & Tucker, 1970).

BIBLIOGRAPHY:

Broden, M., Beasley, A., & Hall, R. V. Effects of parent home tutoring on in-class spelling performance. *Behavior Modification*, 1978, 2, 511-530.

Hall, R. V. Responsive teaching: Focus on measurement and research in the classroom and the home. *Focus on Exceptional Children*, 1971, 3(7), 1-7.

Hall, R. V., Axelrod, S., Tyler, L., Grief, E., Jones, F. C., & Robertson, R. Modification of behavior problems in the home with a parent observer and experimenter. *Journal of Applied Behavior Analysis*, 1972, 5, 53-64.

Hall, R. V., & Broden, M. Helping teachers and parents to modify behavior of their retarded and behavior-disordered children. In P. Mittler, *Research to Practice in Mental Retardation*, Vol. 3. Baltimore: Univ Park, 1977.

Hall, R. V., Cristler, C., Cranston, S. S., & Tucker, B. Teachers and parents as researchers using multiple baseline designs. *Journal of Applied Behavior Analysis*, 1970, *3*, 247-255.

REVIEWED BY: Kathleen G. Taylor, University of Virginia.

Parents Are Teachers, 1971

AUTHOR: Wesley C. Becker.

POPULATIONS WITH WHICH IT MAY BE USED: Parents, paraprofessionals, teachers, and others who work with normal or moderately behaviorally disordered children. These materials require a junior high school to high school reading level.

SOURCE: Research Press, Box 217702, Champaign, Illinois, 61820.

COST: $4.50; *Review Tests*, sold only in sets of 5, are available for $5.00 per set; and the *Group Leader's Guide* is available for $2.50.

The stated objective of the manual is to help parents learn to be more effective in their role as teachers of their children by employing behavioral techniques. Because the text is programmed, it can be done independently or in conjunction with group training sessions. The ten units include case study examples and general problems in child management for the reader to discuss and/or solve. The manual provides an introduction and overview of some easily applied behavioral techniques, including pinpointing behaviors, determining appropriate and effective reinforcers, issues relating to choices and use of punishment, setting up and using intervention programs, etc.

The organization of the content of the manual is logical and follows the format of (a) short explanatory sections, (b) brief programmed exercises, and (c) answers that are supplied at the end of the book. Terms that may confuse the reader are marked with an asterisk, and a definition is supplied at the bottom of the same page on which it appears. Case studies and role-play samples are liberally distributed throughout the text, serving to clarify and amplify important points in the content. Sample charts and some drawings are included to further illustrate points. The compactness of the print and sophistication of the vocabulary (even though defined) may serve to make the manual difficult for individuals who are not academically oriented. The *Group Leader's Guide* is explicit in details that would facilitate learning for groups who are using the manual as the core of their discussions and activities.

In his introduction to the book, the author notes that the manual has been used effectively with parents of children in Project Follow Through (Becker, 1971). Its use is described as part of an ongoing group treatment program for mothers of 7- to 12-year-old children referred to the Department of Medical Psychology at the University of Oregon Medical School (Tams & Eyberg, 1976). Various aspects of the interventions described in the manual have been substantiated by others elsewhere, including the following: (a) the use of contingent attention (Becker, Madsen, Arnold, & Thomas, 1967), (b) the effects of verbal attention on behavior (Madsen, Becker, Thomas, Koser, & Plager, 1968), and (c) the effects of different reinforcement on behaviors (Johnston, Kelley, Harris, & Wolf, 1966) as cited by Becker. Kroth (1972) cites the Becker manual as a helpful resource for teachers in preparing information handbooks for parents on tips, activities, and management practices.

BIBLIOGRAPHY:

Becker, W. C., Madsen, C. H., Arnold, C. R., & Thomas, D. R. The contingent use of teacher attention and praise in reducing classroom behavior problems. *Journal of Special Education*, 1967, *1*, 287-307.

Johnston, M. K., Kelley, C. S., Harris, R. F., & Wolf, M. M. An application of reinforcement principles to development of motor skills of a young child. *Child Development*, 1966, *37*, 380-387.

Kroth, R. Facilitating educational progress by improving parent conferences. *Focus on Exceptional Children*, 1972, *4*(7), 1-10.

Madsen, C. H., Becker, W. C., Thomas, D. R., Koser, L., & Plager, E. An analysis of the reinforcing function of "sit down" commands. In R. K. Parker, (Ed.), *Readings in educational psychology*. Boston: Allyn & Bacon, 1968.

Tams, V., & Eyberg, S. A group treatment program for parents. In E. J. Mash, L. C. Handy, & L. A. Hamerlynck (Eds.), *Behavior modification approaches to parenting*. New York: Brunner/Mazel, 1976.

REVIEWED BY: Kathleen G. Taylor, University of Virginia.

Steps to Independence: A Skills Training Series for Children with Special Needs, 1976.

AUTHORS: Bruce L. Baker, Alan J. Brightman, Louis J. Heifetz, and Diane M. Murphy.

POPULATIONS WITH WHICH IT MAY BE USED: (1) Parents of developmentally delayed children who lack self-help and language skills; (2)

paraprofessionals who will be teaching children with developmental delays or their parents; (3) teachers or clinicians working with delayed children or their parents. These materials require a sixth-grade reading level.

SOURCE: Research Press, 2612 North Mattis Avenue, Champaign, Illinois, 61820.

COST: $36.95 for the complete program; or $5.95 per title plus $1.95 for Training Guide.

The series consists of seven titles: *Early Self-Help Skills, Intermediate Self-Help Skills, Advanced Self-Help Skills, Toilet Training, Speech and Language Level I, Speech and Language Level II,* and *Behavior Problems*. In addition, a *Training Guide* for teacher or clinician is available. The series was conceived and piloted in a residential camp program for children with special needs and their families. The materials provide instruction in behavior modification as a means of teaching self-help and language skills and controlling behavior problems in the home. Self-help skills covered include prerequisite motor and attending skills, dressing, grooming, eating and drinking, basic daily living skills (e.g., making beds, sweeping, doing dishes).

Each skills manual uses a consistent approach to teaching new skills, specifically: (a) determining current needs and functioning; (b) targeting appropriate skills to be taught; (c) choosing powerful and appropriate rewards for learning; (d) planning a teaching program; and (e) carrying through on the program, using rewards and keeping records. The skills sequences are based on a simple task analysis procedure, with backward chaining emphasized in the outlined programs and activities for targeted skills. Because the manuals are consistent in their format and use of terms, parents can progress easily through them as their children gain skills. The *Behavior Problems* manual is the single title that departs from the consistent format. However, the presentation is well organized in its own style, emphasizing the antecedent-behavior-consequence model and appropriate intervention at each phase of the model.

The manuals are attractive and durable, each published in a spiral-bound 8 1/2 by 11 inch form. The content is highlighted with frequent case studies and cartoon drawings. The case studies are particularly effective in emphasizing and clarifying content. Included in the manuals are practical suggestions and a simple record-keeping system for denoting performance on teaching programs. Separate sections in each of the skills manuals provide task analyses and basically sound suggestions for training specific skills. Some of the dressing skill sequences, however, should offer descriptions of variations in teaching procedure and methods of shaping. One of the greatest strengths evident in the materials is the clarity of the presentation, which minimizes the use of jargon. Cartoons and highlighted side headings keep the reader on-task.

A large-scale evaluation has been made of the manuals in conjunction with three larger parent training programs (Baker, Heifetz, & Brightman, 1974; Baker, Murphy, Heifetz, & Brightman, 1975; Baker, 1976; Baker & Heifetz, 1976; Baker, 1977; Heifetz, 1977). They involved different amounts of professional assistance to parents, including telephone consultations, training groups, and training groups plus home visits. Self-selected families of 160 special needs children, ages 3 to 14, were randomly assigned to the three 20-week intervention models or to a manuals-alone group that received no additional training. Results indicated that the group training models produced more effort expended in behavior-problem management, greater gains in informational competencies by fathers, and greater self-confidence in parents as teachers of their own children. The telephone consultation was the least effective intervention. The manuals-alone format was as effective as the group training formats for this largely middle-class self-selected population.

A follow-up study, completed 14 months after the end of the training program, involved 95 families (Baker, 1977). Children basically maintained gains in self-help skills learned during the training, with only a slight improvement noted. Only 29% of the families continued programs to satisfactory completion, and only 16% began new formal instructional programs. However, 76% reported new incidental teaching of specific skills, with only 14% reporting no gradable teaching during follow-up. The highest-ranked obstacles to greater home programming were (a) limited time; (b) child variables (behavior problems, lack of skills and progress); and (c) perceived inability with need for external support.

BIBLIOGRAPHY:

Baker, B. L. Parent involvement in programming for developmentally disabled children. In L. L. Lloyd (Ed.), *Communication assessment and intervention strategies.* Baltimore: Univ Park, 1976.

Baker, B. L. Support systems for the parent as therapist. In P. Mittler (Ed.), *Research to practice in mental retardation,* Vol. 1. Baltimore: Univ Park, 1977.

Baker, B. L., & Heifetz, L. J. The Read Project: Teaching manuals for parents of retarded children. In T. D. Tjossem (Ed.), *Intervention strategies for high risk infants and young children.* Baltimore: Univ

Park, 1976.

Baker, B. L., Heifetz, L. J., & Brightman, A. J. *Parents as teachers.* Cambridge, Massachusetts: Behavioral Education Projects, Inc., Harvard University, 1974.

Baker, B. L., Murphy, D., Heifetz, L. J., & Brightman, A. J. *Parents as teachers: Follow-up study.* Cambridge, Massachusetts: Behavioral Education Projects, Inc., Harvard University, 1975.

Heifetz, L. J. Behavioral training for parents of retarded children: Alternative formats based on instructional manuals. *American Journal of Mental Deficiency*, 1977, *82*, 194-203.

REVIEWED BY: Kathleen G. Taylor, University of Virginia.

Systematic Parent Training: Procedures, Cases and Issues, 1975.

AUTHOR: William Hansford Miller.

POPULATIONS WITH WHICH IT MAY BE USED: Professionals in the fields of education and mental health with prior knowledge of behavioral principles.

SOURCE: Research Press, Box 317702, Champaign, Illinois, 61820.

COST: $8.95. In addition, the *Therapists Guidebook* (by William Hansford Miller and Nancy Brown Miller) is available for $3.95.

The stated purpose of the manual is to relate intervention procedures that can be used by professionals in working with parents of children with disturbing behaviors. As such, the author has three objectives: (a) to delineate a systematic method of parent-child assessment, intervention, and follow-up to be used as part of outpatient care for children; (b) to describe principles and procedures for parent training, and (c) to examine issues relating to the use of systematic parent training.

With wide reference to research in the areas of parent training and intervention and the application of behavioral techniques, the manual provides a sequential analysis of behavioral/therapeutic intervention with parents, as reportedly practiced at the Children's Outpatient Department of the Neuropsychiatric Institute, UCLA. Using a master flowchart as a guide, Miller organizes procedures for screening, collecting baseline information, providing intervention, and maintaining follow-up measurement of targeted behaviors in behavior disordered children. Suggestions are generally well substantiated by current behavioral research. The writing is concise, with extensive in-text listing of major points. In addition, detailed case studies, including hypothetical scripts of therapeutic sessions, are distributed advantageously throughout the text. A few charts and graphs are employed to illustrate data collection and analysis procedures.

No research other than references cited within the text was located. In particular, these included two works by the author (Guilbert & Miller, 1973; Miller & Gottlieb, 1974).

BIBLIOGRAPHY:

Guilbert, P., & Miller, W. H. The use of behavior therapy with an hyperactive child. In *Behavior Therapy: Praktische und theoretische Aspekte*. European Association for Behaviour Therapy and Modification, First Meeting, 1971, Munich. Munich: Urban and Schwarzenberg, 1973.

Miller, W. H., & Gottlieb, F. Predicting behavioral treatment outcome in disturbed children: A preliminary report on the responsivity index of parents (RIP). *Behavior Therapy*, 1974, *5*(2), 210-214.

REVIEWED BY: Kathleen G. Taylor, University of Virginia.

ABC's for Parents: An Educational Workshop in Behavior Modification, 1973, and ABC's for Teachers: An In-Service Training Program in Behavior Modification, 1975

AUTHORS: Edward B. Rettig and Terry L. Paulson.

POPULATIONS WITH WHICH IT MAY BE USED: The *ABC's for Parents* material is most suitable for use with parent training groups of normal children or those with mild behavior problems, e.g., noncompliance, moderate aggression, etc. *ABC's for Teachers* is an extension of the earlier book for parents with application to classroom and educational settings. Typical problems of classroom management and individual pupil behavior change with normal children are dealt with in this program. Both manuals are written at a level of difficulty most suitable to the high school graduate.

SOURCE: Research Press, Box 31778, Champaign, Illinois, 61820.

COST: *ABC's for Parents* (Text, $5.95; Workbook, $3.25); *ABC's for Teachers* (Text, $5.95; Workbook, $3.25).

ABC's for Parents provides the basic structure and content for a 9-week workshop in the principles and practice of behavior modification. The materials are designed to assist in guiding parents in a systematic step-by-step fashion through the process of setting up and implementing a behavior management program. While the text is reusable, the workbooks are designed to be consumed during the implementation of behavior modification programs. The authors, in covering the ABC components (antecedents, behaviors, and consequences), provide systematic training behavior analysis, observation and tracking of behavior, developing an intervention program, techniques of strengthening and maintaining behaviors, weakening and eliminating behaviors, and teaching and shaping new behaviors. An aspect unique to this program is the emphasis on returning to baseline management conditions as a training device for the effectiveness of the behavioral intervention, followed by a return to the intervention management conditions. This may be problematic with some parents.

ABC's for Teachers was derived from experiences with the parent training program and is basically a revision and extension of the materials for use with groups of teachers and educators. This program is divided into ten sessions, and its goal is to teach behavior modification principles as they can be applied in the classroom. Lessons are presented with each concept building on previously learned material. The text covers the topic of group contingencies with examples of several applications.

Both of these programs provide a thorough coverage of behavior modification principles and techniques. No material is provided the prospective group leader or professional in the methods of using the texts in conducting parent or teacher groups.

REVIEWED BY: Bryan D. Carter.

P.E.T. (Parent Effectiveness Training), 1975

AUTHOR: Dr. Thomas Gordon.

POPULATIONS WITH WHICH IT MAY BE USED: May be read independently by parents or used by certified trainers in P.E.T. workshops. Teaches communication skills useful with all ages and a problem-solving method most appropriate for parents of children aged 6 to 8 and up. These materials are most appropriate for use with parents of normal children.

SOURCE: Available at bookstores in hard-cover edition (Peter H. Wyden, Inc., 750 Third Ave., New York, 10017) or paperback (New American Library, Inc., 1301 Avenue of the Americas, New York, 10019). Manual, tapes, and instructional materials available to trainers from Effectiveness Training, 531 Stevens Avenue, Solana Beach, California, 92705.

COST: Hardcover, $9.95; paperback, $4.95.

Dr. Gordon presents an approach to parenting in which parent and child negotiate as equal partners toward the solution of problems. His approach rests on the assumption that parental use of power and authority alienates a child, produces retaliatory behavior, and denies him/her the chance to learn self-discipline and self-responsibility.

Emphasis is given to specific communications skills that help prevent parent-child conflicts. The first, "active listening," replaces passive reception of a child's verbal or nonverbal behavior with an active decoding process in which the parent seeks out and tests his/her understanding of both the child's message and the feelings behind it. The second, "I-message," is a skill taught to parents as a way of clearly expressing their own feelings about the child's behavior in a non-alienating fashion, designed to make the child more likely to listen.

Crises that do arise in spite of good communication are to be dealt with through a problem-solving method in which parent and child are equal partners in proposing, evaluating, and implementing solutions. As part of this process, parents are advised to set aside any attitudes or values that might prevent them from seeing the problem as a negotiable one and to look at all proposed solutions as potentially acceptable alternatives. Parents are to communicate their values by living them rather than by insisting that they be followed by the child.

These approaches to communication and problem solving on the part of the parents are seen as helping the child learn the same skills through his/her own active participation in the process. His/her ability to communicate clearly and listen well is expected to increase as a result of better interaction with his/her parents. His/her behavior is therefore expected to become more self-directed and responsible when s/he has been an active and equal participant in determining what the limitations should be.

The strength of this how-to book lies in its attention to the communication problems often arising between parent and child. It is a persuasive, easy-to-read presentation of more effective ways to talk and listen, and the skills taught here can be practiced beyond parent-child interaction.

Dr. Gordon takes an extreme position when he describes the use of authority, even by parents, as probably unethical. Obviously realizing this, he spends many of the book's pages trying to allay parents' fears at the prospect of replacing a more powerful role with one giving the child equal status in negotiating problems. Somewhat neglected, as a result, is a full development of the steps in his problem-solving method. The one chapter devoted to details of his negotiating technique does not deal with the problems likely to be encountered when this method is attempted by parents whose abilities, personality characteristics, or values are incompatible with this approach. A trainer using this book with parents should be aware that what is advocated is not only foreign to many traditional approaches to parenting, but also demands skills that most parents do not practice even in interaction with other adults.

The fact that parents come into a crisis or problem situation with values, knowledge, and perspectives acquired through experience argues against Dr. Gordon's parenting style as always in the best interest of the child. Especially with young children, the need to negotiate most problems and to give equal authority to the child in such negotiations seems inappropriate and inconsistent with the cognitive development of children below age 5. His discussion of the problem-solving process is an attractive one and appears useful with older children, especially when a solution is truly negotiable.

One of the most controversial aspects of this book is Dr. Gordon's treatment of anger as nothing more than an act deliberately and consciously assumed for the purpose of punishing someone else. This description seems less than helpful to parents who are trying to better understand and cope with their own or their child's anger.

Typical of the research findings on the effectiveness of P.E.T. are increased levels of acceptance and understanding of their children (Schofield, 1976) and greater facilitative self-disclosure when faced with a problem of their own (Piercy & Brush, 1971) among parents who have participated in P.E.T. workshops. A study conducted at the Youth Research Center in Minneapolis (Larson, 1972) found P.E.T. more effective than a discussion/encounter group approach or an achievement motivation program in achieving improved parent-child relations and improved school performance among children designated as underachievers. Research results are conflicting in the area of changes in children's perception of parents after P.E.T. and in areas of change in the children themselves, although there is relative agreement that children of P.E.T. graduates subsequently show an increase in self-esteem as measured on the Coopersmith Self-Esteem Inventory (Stearn, 1970).

BIBLIOGRAPHY:

Larson, R. S. Can parent classes affect family communications? *The School Counselor,* 1972, *19,* 261-270.

Piercy, F., & Brush, D. *Effects of P.E.T. on empathy and self-disclosure.* Ft. Benning, Georgia: Mental Hygiene Consultation Service, 1971.

Schofield, R. G. *A comparison of two parent education programs: Parent effectiveness training and behavior modification, and their effects on the child's self-esteem.* Unpublished doctoral dissertation, University of Northern Colorado, Greely, Colorado, 1976.

Stearn, M. *The relationship of P.E.T. to parent attitudes, parent behavior and child self-esteem.* Unpublished doctoral dissertation, United States International University, San Diego, California, 1970.

REVIEWED BY: Mary Alice Varner.

AUTHOR INDEX*

A

Aaronson, M., 25, *34*
Abernathy, S. R., 7, 16, *35*
Abeson, A., 94, *106*
Abidin, R. R., 131, *152, 535*, 536, *537*
Abikoff, H., 212, *221*
Adamowics, D., *270*
Adams, H. B., 359, *378*
Adams, H. E., *183, 557*
Adams, W., 202, *219*
Adamson, L., 18, 21, *31, 35*, 43, *58*
Adamson, W. C., 226, *249*
Addison, B., 392, *430*
Adelson, E., 401, *428*
Adkins, D. C., 400, *427*
Adler, A., 225, 247, *250*, 540
Agati, G. J., 248, *250*
Ainsworth, M. D., 41, 42, *54*, 69, *79*, 387, *427, 522, 526*
Albee, G. W., 357, *378*, 433, 434, *453*
Albiso, F. P., 185, *219*
Aldridge, M. J., 459, 473, 475, *484*
Alexander, H., 262, *270*
Alexander, J. F., 142, 143, 144, *152, 154*, 478, 480, 482, *483, 485, 486*
Alexander, R., 94, 95, 99, *103*
Alford, R. D., 405, *427*
Allen, C. M., 524, *527*
Allen, K. E., 201, *219*
Allen, R. P., 185, 201, *223*
Alloway, T., *31*
Als, H., 18, 21, *31, 35*, 43, *58*
Altemeier, W. A., 10, 25, *33*
Altrocchi, J., 489, 494, *512*
Ambinder, W. J., 476, 477, *483*
Ambrose, A., 20, *30*
American Institutes for Research, 447, *453*
American Orthopsychiatric Association,

516, *526*
American Psychiatric Association, 185, *219*
Ames, T., 375, *378*
Anderson, B. J., 15, 16, 26, 27, *30, 35*, 50, *58*
Anderson, K., 95, *102*, 140, *154*
Andres, D., 64, 65, 67, *80*
Andronico, M. P., 136, *152, 153*, 298, *319, 320*
Andrulous, P. A., 202, *220*
Anthony, E. J., *104, 484, 486*
Appell, T., 100, *102*
Aquizap, R. B., 492, 495, 496, *511*
Arnold, C. R., 561, *561*
Arnold, J. E., 162, *181*, 557, *557*
Arnstein, S. R., 329, *345*
Aronson, H., 162, *182*
Ashe, M. L., 7, 16, 27, *30, 35*
Ashem, B. A., *382*
Auerbach, A. B., 108, *128*, 131, 134, *152*, 432, *453*
Authier, J., 298, *319*
Axelrod, S. *555*, 559, *559*
Ayllon, T., 201, *219*
Ayres, A. J., 190, *219*
Azrin, N. H., 440, *453*

B

Bachrach, A. J., 364, *378*
Badger, E., 393, *427*
Baer, D. M., 6, *30*, 201, *219*
Baher, D., 269, *270*
Bahm, A., 160, *181*
Bakeman, R., 27, *30*
Baker, B. L., 355, 357, 366, 374, *378, 561*, 563, *563, 564*
Baker, E. J., 435, 436, 437, *453*

---

*Italicized citations are to References.

571

HQ755.8 .P37   CU-Main
c.1
Abidin, Richard R./Parent education and interventi

3 9371 00030 6655

HQ
755.8
P37   Parent education and
        intervention
        handbook

DATE

MAY			
MAY 15 '82			
APR 15 '84			
JUN '86			
OCT 19			

51191

CONCORDIA COLLEGE LIBRARY
2811 N. E. HOLMAN ST.
PORTLAND, OREGON 97211

© THE BAKER & TAYLOR CO.